NATIONAL GEOGRAPHIC
TRAVELER
Germany

NATIONAL GEOGRAPHIC

TRAVELER
Germany

Michael Ivory

National Geographic
Washington, D.C.

Contents

Page 1: German beer—
as good as it gets!
Pages 2–3: Spangenberg
in Hesse
Left: All the fun of the fair

How to use this guide

See back flap for keys to text and map symbols.

The National Geographic Traveler brings you the best of Germany in text, pictures, and maps. Divided into three main sections, the guide begins with an overview of history and culture. Following are 12 regional chapters with featured sites selected by the author for their particular interest and treated in depth. Each chapter opens with its own contents list for easy reference.

The regions, and sites within them, are arranged geographically, each one introduced with a map highlighting the featured sites. Walks and drives, plotted on their own maps, suggest routes for discovering an area. Features and sidebars offer intriguing detail on history, culture, or contemporary life. A More Places to Visit page generally rounds off the regional chapters.

The final section, Travelwise, lists essential information for the traveler—pretrip planning, special events, getting around, and what to do in emergencies—plus a selection of hotels and restaurants arranged by region, shops, and entertainment.

To the best of our knowledge, site information is accurate as of the press date. However, it is always advisable to call ahead when possible.

Color coding

58

Each region is color coded for easy reference. Find the region you want on the map on the front flap, and look for the color flash at the top of the pages of the relevant chapter. Information in **Travelwise** is also color coded to each region.

Pergamon Museum

- 🗺 Map p. 61
- ✉ Am Kupfergraben
- ☎ 030 20 90 50
- 🕐 Closed Mon.
- 💲 $$
- 🚇 U-Bahn/S-Bahn: Friedrichstrasse, S Hackescher Markt, Bus: 100

Visitor information

Practical information for most sites is given in the side column (see key to symbols on back flap). The map reference gives the page number of the map and usually a grid reference. Other details are address, telephone number, days closed, entrance charge in a range from $ (under $5) to $$$$$ (over $25), and nearest public transport in Berlin. Other sites have information in italics and parentheses in the text.

Hotel & restaurant prices

An explanation of the price bands used in entries is given in the Hotels & Restaurants section (beginning on p. 355).

TRAVELWISE

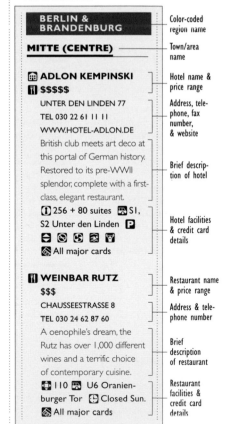

BERLIN & BRANDENBURG — Color-coded region name

MITTE (CENTRE) — Town/area name

🏨 **ADLON KEMPINSKI** — Hotel name & price range
🍴 **$$$$$**

UNTER DEN LINDEN 77 — Address, telephone, fax number, & website
TEL 030 22 61 11 11
WWW.HOTEL-ADLON.DE

British club meets art deco at this portal of German history. Restored to its pre-WWII splendor, complete with a first-class, elegant restaurant. — Brief description of hotel

ℹ 256 + 80 suites 🚇 S1, S2 Unter den Linden 🅿 ⊟ ⊘ ⊗ ⊟ ⊟ 💳 All major cards — Hotel facilities & credit card details

🍴 **WEINBAR RUTZ** — Restaurant name & price range
$$$

CHAUSSEESTRASSE 8 — Address & telephone number
TEL 030 24 62 87 60

A oenophile's dream, the Rutz has over 1,000 different wines and a terrific choice of contemporary cuisine. — Brief description of restaurant

🪑 110 🚇 U6 Oranienburger Tor 🕐 Closed Sun. 💳 All major cards — Restaurant facilities & credit card details

REGIONAL MAPS

Adjoining chapter

Map reference

Point of interest

Important featured town

Road number

Drive start point

- A locator map accompanies each regional map and shows the location of that region in the country.
- Adjacent regions are shown, each with a page reference.

WALKING TOURS

Point of interest not on walk route

Start point

Red numbered bullets link sites on map to descriptions in the text

Building outline

Direction of walk route

Featured site (in bold) on walk route

Walk route

- An information box gives the starting and finishing points, time and length of walk, and places not to be missed along the route.

DRIVING TOURS

Drive start point

Drive tour route

Road number

Important place of interest

Red numbered bullets link sites on map to descriptions in the text

- An information box gives the starting and finishing points, time and length of drive, and places not to be missed along the route.

NATIONAL GEOGRAPHIC

TRAVELER

Germany

About the author

Before studying modern languages at Oxford University, Michael Ivory perfected his German by spending the best part of a year at a Rhineland boarding school. He subsequently taught in Germany and, after qualifying as a landscape architect and urban planner, took student groups there to learn from the country's considerable achievements in these fields. He has traveled extensively in central and eastern Europe, and has watched with particular interest as the peoples and countries of the former Soviet bloc have adapted to the post-Communist world. In writing this guide to the whole of Germany, the fulfillment of a long-standing ambition, he took a thorough look at the rapidly changing face of what used to be known as the German Democratic Republic. Michael is also the author of the *National Geographic Traveler: Canada*.

Josephine Grever wrote the Travelwise section. Born in Aachen, she now works as the London correspondent for the German magazines *Architektur & Wohnen* and *Feinschmecker*.

Jeremy Gray wrote the update for the second edition. Jeremy has more than a dozen guidebooks to his credit including bestselling titles to Amsterdam, Montreal, and Munich. As a photographer he contributes travel images to publications worldwide. Jeremy now lives in the pulsing heart of Berlin's Mitte district.

The author would like to thank the following for their help in researching this book: Christian Hardt (Rostock), Karsten Klaene (Jasmund National Park, Ruegen Island), Dr. Achim Schloemer (Rodenkirchen), Maria Antoinette Ritter and Helmut Will (Cologne), Christa Konzok and Franky Bulmer (Duesseldorf), Fred de Gast (Bremen), Joerg Hoenicke and Sybille von Kummer (Hamburg), David and Henriette Roberts, Natascha Kompatzki, and Frances Calvert (Berlin), C. Taenzler and Kevin Kennedy (Potsdam), Joachim Weber (Halle), Ines Nebelung and Wolfgang Gaertner (Dresden), Sabine Muench (Meissen), Johannes Tschech-Loeffler (Colditz), Gudrun Engelhard (Weimar), Renate Klein (Erfurt), Michael Schoenemann and Sally Slenczka (Nuremberg), Vera Goluecke (Munich), Marie-Jose Suess (Stuttgart), Thomas Drubba (Breitnau), Bernhard Joachim (Meersburg), Peter Maniger (Garmisch-Partenkirchen), Hannes Hiergeist (Oberammergau), Michael and Barbara Miess (Karlsruhe).

History
& culture

Black, red, and gold—the German flag

Germany today

THIS VARIED AND BEAUTIFUL COUNTRY OF 83 MILLION INHABITANTS stretches from the Rhine to the Polish border and from the coasts of the North Sea and Baltic to the Alps. The prosperity and modernity, built up in West Germany since the end of World War II and now slowly spreading to the East, coexist almost everywhere with historic towns and villages, more castles than can be counted, and a countryside of impeccably managed farmland, deep forests, and a patchwork of jealously protected nature parks and reserves. The country's ever more cosmopolitan cities are crammed with galleries, museums, historic buildings, and entertainment of all kinds, from opera to the most outrageous nightlife.

PEOPLE

Few peoples are as fond of their homeland— their *Heimat*—as the Germans, and this exceptional heritage is both appreciated and lovingly maintained. Excellent cultural facilities abound, and it is rare to find an uncared-for building. Visitors flock here from all over the globe, but the country's most enthusiastic visitors are the Germans themselves, with all kinds of agreeable results. Expect high standards, whether in hotels, bed-and-breakfast establishments, or restaurants.

Don't believe a word of what you may have heard about Germans being glum or lacking a sense of humor. They love a good time, whether it be in a raucous beer hall, a cozy wine tavern, or an animated street café. To really see them at their most uninhibited, join them when they let their hair down at one of the country's countless festivals, the most exuberant of which are Fasching in Munich and Karneval in Cologne (see pp. 158–159), among the world's great popular folk festivals. These are the equivalent of Mardi Gras in other countries and take place in the run-up to Lent.

Local identity is expressed in all sorts of ways. Dialects have survived longer in Germany than in many European countries: The everyday language spoken along the lower Rhine has more in common with Dutch than with the German spoken by Bavarians. The media tend to be locally based, with regional newspapers concentrating on the news that affects their particular readership. Some of the country's 1,274 breweries have achieved national prominence, but most people are perfectly happy with the beer brewed locally.

With traditional ideas of nationhood debased and disgraced by the Nazis, many Germans have been inhibited about putting too much enthusiasm into anything smacking of nationalism. In 2001 President Johannes Rau questioned whether it was even possible to be proud to be German, setting off a predictable debate, with many people citing the building of democracy, a strong economy, and the bloodless achievement of reunification. Patriotism was hardly mentioned, and what the rest of the world thinks of as typical German characteristics featured hardly at all.

These characteristics still exist, however. A liking for order and security in personal and working life can perhaps be explained by the traumas of history, when the country's very shape seemed uncertain and there was an unthinkable burden of guilt. Germans study for their careers, often at great length, and plan them down to the final pension contribution. Correct procedures govern many aspects of life; timekeeping is meticulous; jobs are done properly and standards are defined and adhered to. The material world is kept under control and everything has its proper place.

In the last decades of the 20th century there was a reaction against what were seen as repressive, "traditional" values. Levels of tidiness and cleanliness slipped (but not too much), and people cultivated a deliberately casual manner, with the young defiantly flouting the strict standards of their elders. Germany has in consequence become a country of greater contrasts than before; smaller towns and their inhabitants still have that impeccably groomed look, while parts of the

Beer, pretzels, a brass band, and good company are the essential ingredients of Munich's Oktoberfest.

Football fans parade beneath the German eagle on Römer Square in central Frankfurt am Main.

bigger cities and sections of their population almost flaunt their scruffiness. The graffiti artists of great German cities are second to none in their ability to decorate vast surfaces.

LIFESTYLE

Traditionally, German women were expected to devote themselves to *Kinder, Küche, Kirche* (kids, kitchen, and church), while men … well, many men found great satisfaction in buttoning themselves up in some sort of uniform. To be a *Beamter* (any kind of public official from diplomat to railwayman) guaranteed status, as well as a good pension.

Nowadays there is a far greater variety of roles to choose from, and Germans enter the 21st century with great determination to make a go of it. Punks seem more outlandish here than elsewhere in Europe, squatters more militant, skinheads more deliberately repulsive. To describe the million-strong Love Parade in Berlin as colorful would be putting it mildly. At the other end of the scale, there are probably more would-be English gentlemen in tweeds and Burberrys than in England itself, and Germany is easily the biggest market in Europe for the expensive casual look in suede and leather. Those with nothing to hide (and plenty who do) opt for nudity when relaxing in urban parks as well as on the beach.

Nevertheless, German manners still tend to formality. It takes longer to get on first-name

ENVIRONMENTAL CONCERNS

Concern for the environment is high on the national agenda. As well as a wonderful system of parks and open spaces (see pp. 204–205), German towns and cities have extensive networks of pedestrian-only streets, most of them models of attractive urban design, beautifully paved with natural materials and

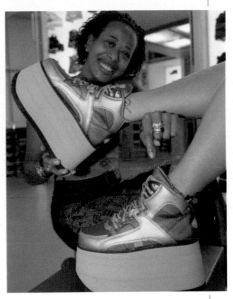

Trying on the latest style—sport platform shoes—in Frankfurt

terms in Germany than in English-speaking countries, and there is more use of titles like Herr Doktor or Herr Professor. The distinction between the informal *du* ("thou") and the polite *Sie* ("you") still exists. When you enter or leave a shop or an office it's good manners to wish people *"guten Tag"* and *"auf Wiedersehen."* By contrast, public behavior can sometimes seem crude and unfeeling. There is no concept of taking your turn in a line, or mutual apologies when people collide with one another on the side-walk. At the same time, there is a creeping tide of U.S.-style politeness, and in shops and restaurants you now hear phrases like *"Schönen Abend noch*—have a nice evening," something that only a few years ago would have earned an uncomprehending stare.

embellished with statuary and fountains. The lavish provision of bicycle paths means that cycling is a pleasure, and many town dwellers make their local trips by bike.

People here are as car-crazy as anyone, but they have made sure that virtually every destination is served by superlative public transport, so you will be able to reach wherever you want to go even without your own vehicle. There are still trams in German towns—in fact the networks have been extended, with trams going underground in congested city centers or gliding gondola-like through the shopping streets. Getting about can be great fun, too—on no account should you miss a relaxing trip aboard a gleaming white riverboat or an exhilarating ride in a chairlift to some giddy viewpoint.

The private car remains a great German icon. On the autobahn, where the recommended speed limit is 75–85 mph (110–130 kph), the car is given its head, but in town it has been tamed by severe parking restrictions.

At a national level, environmental politics are taken seriously. The Green Party has moved from the fringe to the center, entering

Cologne Cathedral acted as a backdrop for German artist HA Schult's 2006 installation, "Trash People," featuring one thousand life-sized sculptures.

government and supplying a dynamic if controversial minister for foreign affairs. A commitment has been made to phase out nuclear power, and Germany has taken a lead in environmentally friendly forms of energy generation, notably in the use of wind power. Wind farms are a prominent feature in the countryside, particularly along the coasts of the North Sea and the Baltic. The environmental impact of new developments is scrupulously evaluated; in 2001 Chancellor Gerhard Schröder expressed amazement when the construction of the new autobahn along the Baltic coast was expensively held up by the need to conserve an important frog habitat.

EAST IS EAST …

Once the euphoria of 1989 over the opening of the Berlin Wall had died down, East and West Germans settled down to digest the implications of reunification. The German Democratic Republic (GDR) had collapsed, as had its former markets in the communist world, so the West German state was in effect taking over a bankrupt economy. Despite Chancellor Kohl's promises that taxes would not be increased to pay for reunification and that the East would soon be a land of "blossoming landscapes," huge amounts of taxpayers' money are still being channeled east more than a decade later, and the eastern industrial landscape still only blossoms in places. In the East, or what are referred to as *Die neuen Länder* (the New States), Germany's

unemployment problem is particularly severe, although its true extent is masked by subsidies and job creation schemes. Some Easterners (slightingly referred to by Westerners as *Ossis,* from *Ostdeutsche* meaning East Germans) feel that their country has become a kind of colony of West Germany. Today the infrastructure almost matches that of the West, and visitors can be sure of finding most of the services and facilities they are used to. But there are still crumbling buildings (sometimes because their ownership is disputed between their Eastern occupants and Western claimants), and whole sections of some towns have been abandoned as the population has moved away westward, in search of jobs.

Some Germans feel that, although the Berlin Wall has physically disappeared, it is

Berlin's grand Hotel Adlon reopened its doors in 1997 after being demolished in 1984 and rebuilt from scratch.

more present than ever in people's minds. Certainly the *Wessi* (the Easterners' disparaging term for West Germans, or *Westdeutsche)* and *Ossi* stereotypes are well established. Easterners think of Wessis as arrogant, spoiled, self-centered, materialistic, and patronizing, while many Westerners feel that Ossis are passive, lack initiative, and grumble instead of being grateful for all the help they have received. After living under a system that, oppressive as it was, provided security and predictability, many Easterners have found it difficult to adapt to Western ways, particularly in an era when social welfare systems are in

Giant figures fill the streets during the Karneval parade in Mainz.

crisis and individual ambition and willingness to take on responsibility are crucial. It may be that true reunification will only take place once the older generation has passed away.

GOVERNMENT & POLITICS

One surprise in the period following reunification was the continued existence of a successor to the old East German SED Communist Party. Renamed the PDS (Party of Democratic Socialism), the party won the support of many Easterners who felt abandoned in the new dispensation. In more than one of the New States, the PDS (later renamed the *Linkspartei*, or Party of the Left) entered government coalitions, to the horror of some Westerners, who pointed to its failure to disassociate itself completely from the crimes of its predecessor, including construction of the Wall. However, the *Linkspartei* remains a minor player on the national stage. The Bundestag (lower house of the Federal Parliament) continues to be dominated by long-established parties, such as the SPD (Socialists) and the CDU/CSU (Conservatives). The latter returned to national office in 2005 when Angela Merkel, an Easterner and a former physicist, narrowly defeated Gerhard Schröder in a snap election

to become Germany's first female chancellor. The upper house of parliament, the Bundesrat, consists of representatives of the Lander and has limited powers over national legislation.

For many years, West Germany was regarded as an economic giant and a political pygmy, very inhibited about playing a decisive role in the international arena. Its economic muscle and political energy were directed toward an ever greater degree of European integration. The reunited country has edged toward a more assertive posture, although it underwent agonies of uncertainty about the morality of deploying its troops beyond its borders, refusing altogether in the Gulf War of 1991. But in 1999, Bundeswehr tanks were in the vanguard of the NATO formations rolling into Kosovo. Germany did not back the U.S.-led invasion of Iraq, but has deployed forces in support of counterterrorist action to Afghanistan, Kuwait, the Horn of Africa, Macedonia, and Bosnia-Herzegovina.

THE LAND

Covering a total area of 137,847 square miles (357,021 sq km), Germany is endowed with the fine natural frontiers of the North and Baltic Seas to the north and the Bavarian Alps to the south. To east and west there are few

Braving sea breezes and salty spray on the tidal mudflats of the Wattenmeer

such barriers. The North European Plain extends into Germany from Holland and continues all the way across the north of the country into Poland. The highlands around the border with the Czech Republic look formidable on the map, but they are easily penetrated and have never inhibited movement and exchange. In the west, upland massifs continue into Belgium and Luxembourg, while the valley of the Upper Rhine is shared with France.

Northern plain & coastlands

Like much of eastern Germany, the coastlands facing the almost tideless Baltic were given their basic shape in the last Ice Age, although the broad and shallow inlets known as *Bodden* were created in the postglacial period. Long sandy beaches backed by dunes have made it an important vacation area, including the island of Rügen with its pristine chalk cliffs. Inland, Germany's largest lakeland is now the Müritz National Park. Upstream from Berlin the Spree River divides into a multitude of tree-shaded streams, and people still get around the Spreewald in flat-bottomed boats.

Fjords provide natural harbors for fishing ports and seaside resorts on the east coast of Schleswig-Holstein, while the exposed west coast and the islands of Lower Saxony boast sandy beaches and dunes, a bracing climate, and sunshine. Grand rivers such as the Elbe, Weser, and Ems reach the sea in broad estuaries, and all have given rise to harbor cities, of which Hamburg is the greatest.

Inland from the North Sea, the Münsterland is famous for its array of moated castles and country houses, while the rolling Lüneburger Heide (Lüneberg Heath) is one of Europe's most extensive heathlands. To the west, Germany's greatest water highway, the Rhine, rolls majestically toward Holland, where it reaches the sea in multiple outlets.

Central uplands & valleys

A series of massifs divided by river valleys stretches right across the middle of Germany. Farming has shaped some of the landscape, but yields have rarely been high, and the main crop is trees. This is the heartland of the German forest, which has always played an important part in German life and been the setting for many tales and legends. As the land rises, oak gives way to beech, then to coniferous species such as spruce and fir. Occasionally there are glorious open summits like the Brocken (3,747 feet/1,142 m) in the Harz

Mountains, the Feldberg (4,899 feet/1,493 m) in the Black Forest, and the Arber (4,777 feet/ 1,456 m) in the Bavarian Forest. Pleasure boats provide the ideal way of exploring the river valleys, above all the Rhine gorge, where the river flows swiftly in a narrow channel beneath vineyards and a succession of crag-top castles. Farther upstream, the Rhine flows in a broad rift valley, bounded by the Odenwald and Black Forest to the east and to the west by parallel ranges, the Palatine Forest in Germany and the Vosges Mountains in France. This is Germany's warmest area, with the most extensive vineyards.

In the 19th century the presence of coal in the valley of the River Ruhr gave rise to Germany's greatest industrial area, but medieval miners had exploited minerals in the Ore Mountains (Erzgebirge) in Saxony long before. The Erzgebirge continue eastward into Saxon Switzerland (Sächsische Schweiz), a striking landscape of sandstone cliffs and

columns cut through by the Elbe upstream of Saxony's capital, Dresden. The Bavarian Forest and the Bohemian Forest between the Danube and the Czech border possess that rarity in Europe, true primeval forest, forming the basis for a national park.

Alpine lands

Germany only possesses a fraction of the Alps, but they make a formidable, north-facing wall, which reaches its highest point in the summit

In the cool green jungle of the Bavarian Forest near Waldkirchen

of the Zugspitze (9,724 feet/2,964 m), overlooking the town of Garmisch-Partenkirchen, one of many mountain resorts as popular in summer as they are in winter. From the Alps, rivers like the Lech and the Isar hurry down toward the Danube. Closer to Salzburg than to Munich, the Berchtesgadener *Land* runs deep into Austria, and the Königsee area contains

Salt-studded pretzels, onion bread, and cheese straws at the kiosk

some of the most glorious Alpine scenery anywhere, including the country's second highest peak, the Watzmann (8,898 feet/2,712 m). At their western extremity in Bavaria, the Alps descend to Germany's largest lake, the Bodensee (Lake Constance), shared with Switzerland and Austria. Here, a warm climate encourages orchards and vineyards and helps give an Italian ambience to lakeside cities like Lindau and Konstanz.

FOOD & DRINK

German food is wholesome and satisfying. The flair of French or Italian cuisine may be lacking, but food in Germany is almost always honest and made from good ingredients—if a bit on the heavy side. It's unusual to leave the table with much appetite left.

Hearty breakfasts get the day off to a good start. There's usually a choice of cheeses, cold meats, and hard-boiled eggs, as well as marmalades, jams, and honey, all of which go well with a wonderful selection of breads, ranging from crisp white rolls to tangy rye bread or gloriously rich and heavy pumpernickel. Fruit and cereals are supplemented by yogurt and creamy *Quark* (curd cheese). Lunch is often the principal meal of the day,

with soup and a main course, while the evening meal, if eaten at home, may be a modest affair more like breakfast. *Kaffee und Kuchen* (coffee and cakes) is a German institution, offered in smart patisseries-cum-coffee shops, rather like afternoon tea in the U.K.

Vegetarianism has made some progress in recent years, but this is still a nation of meat-eaters. Beef, game, and poultry all appear on the menu, but the king of the kitchen remains the pig. Pork is served in many forms, of which the most ubiquitous is the *Schnitzel*, a slice of lean meat in breadcrumbs or served with a sauce; *Eisbein* is a succulent pork knuckle. Pork is the main ingredient in many a *Wurst* (sausage); made from pork, bacon fat, and spices, frankfurters have conquered the world. *Bockwurst* is similar, but more interesting, smaller sausages come from Nuremberg (served several at a time on sauerkraut). Thuringian sausages are blood-red, and Munich's are white, made from veal. *Bratwurst* is the generic name for coarse-textured sausages, fried rather than boiled. All benefit from being dipped into German mustard.

As for vegetables, the most common are cabbage (white or red) and potatoes. The latter come in all forms, from purée to pancake, but

Bavarian beer—better by the liter in one of the breweries' tents at Munich's Oktoberfest

the best are *Bratkartoffeln*, sautéed with bacon cubes and onion. In southwestern Germany potatoes give way to *Spätzle*, chewy noodles, or dumplings. The country's favorite vegetable is asparagus, the fat, pale variety; whole regions are given over to its cultivation, and the season (in May) is keenly anticipated.

Beer & wine

Since 1516 the composition of German beer has been governed by the Reinheitsgebot (Purity Law), which forbids the use of ingredients other than hops, malt, yeast, barley, and, of course, water. Most of the country's myriad breweries turn out a lager-type product and usually a specialty or two. *Alt*, not unlike British bitter, is drunk in Düsseldorf and *Kölsch* in Cologne. Beers such as the famous Dortmunder from the Ruhr industrial area, originally intended to slake the thirst of hard-working miners, tend to be stronger than their equivalents in Bavaria. This is no doubt the reason why Munich brews can be served in such huge steins. Bavarian breweries mark the progress of the year by producing seasonal beers such as *Märzenbier*, while in Berlin a summer treat is *Berliner Weisse*, a pale Berlin brew with a shot of acidic fruit juice.

The reputation of German wine has improved in recent years as a taste for drier, subtler wines has emerged. The principal grape is the versatile Riesling, although varieties such as Müller-Thurgau, Silvaner, Grauburgunder (Pinot gris), and Weissburgunder (Pinot blanc) also feature. To help catch the sun, many German wines are grown on terraces chiseled out of the steep slopes rising from the Rhine and its tributaries (Moselle, Main, Ahr, and Nahe). But the greatest quantities come from the flat and sunny countryside of Rhine-Hessen and the Palatinate. In eastern Germany, the valley of the Elbe around Dresden has a long winemaking tradition. Most German wine is white, but there are good reds too, even if less full bodied than wines made farther south. The highest quality wine is labeled *Qualitätswein mit Prädikat*, then comes *Qualitätswein*, and finally *Tafelwein*, which is basic table wine. German sparkling wine, *Sekt*, should not be sniffed at, but quaffed! And there are excellent spirits, ranging from ginlike *Steinhäger* in the north to good grape brandy along the Rhine (Asbach) and fiery fruit brandies (*Kirschwasser, Himbeergeist*) in orchard country. ∎

History of Germany

TODAY'S UNITED GERMANY SEEMS A FIXED AND STABLE STATE, ITS FORM OF government and its frontiers unquestioned at home and abroad. In historical terms this is an unusual situation; the country's identity, its governance, and its borders have been subject to constant change, its evolution mostly a story of division rather than unity. Even today, many German speakers live outside the frontiers of Germany, in Austria, Switzerland, Alsace in France, and Silesia in Poland, echoing the fragmentation that has characterized so much of the country's history since the Romans colonized "Germania."

GERMANS & ROMANS

The area we now call Germany was settled in prehistoric times. The jawbone of *Homo heidelbergensis,* unearthed near the south German city of Heidelberg, is thought to be nearly 400,000 years old, and Neanderthal Man is named after the Neander Valley near Düsseldorf where the first remains of this early form of Homo sapiens were found in 1856. These discoveries have greatly contributed to our understanding of the early evolution of the human race. In the last millennium B.C. the area was settled by Celtic peoples. They left few traces, although remains of their lakeside stilt dwellings survive on the shores of Lake Constance.

The life of the Celts was increasingly disrupted by the incursions of restless Germanic tribes closing in on them from the east and north. With no sense of themselves as a nation, these ancestors of today's Germans eventually came up against the power of a Rome expanding its empire eastward from conquered Celtic Gaul (today's France). In 58 B.C. Julius Caesar checked an attempt by Ariovist, leader of the Swabians, to move into Alsace and flung his forces back across the Rhine. There Caesar halted his legions, believing the land across the river to be nothing more than barren forests. Later expeditions did cross the Rhine, marching as far east as the Elbe. All seemed set for the incorporation of "Germania" into the Roman Empire, when, in A.D. 9, three of Rome's crack legions were annihilated at the Battle of the Teutoburg Forest by warriors led by Arminius ("Hermann" to much later Germans looking for national heroes). The Romans gave up their attempts at subjugating the lands beyond the Rhine and settled for the romanization of the western and southern parts of the country.

The writer Tacitus described the Germans as quarrelsome and slothful, although he acknowledged their bravery in battle, and who wrote off their land as "unlovely, with a bitter climate, and generally dreary in appearance." However, within the area now protected by the "Limes," a continuous line of defenses roughly following the course of the Rhine and Danube, his compatriots made themselves thoroughly at home. Cities, lesser towns, and

military bases arose, some of which have survived until today, including Cologne ("Colonia"), Augsburg, named after Emperor Augustus, and Trier (originally Augusta Treverorum), also honoring the name of Augustus and rich in Roman remains.

In 275 Trier was sacked by Germanic invaders, but it recovered, becoming the capital of the reorganized Western Empire and, under Emperor Constantine, a great center of Christianity. But the end of the empire was approaching; great movements of people in eastern Europe put pressure on the always restless Germans, and during the fifth century various groups moved westward, overwhelming the already weakened Roman defenses.

The Romans departed and their empire collapsed, but they left a heritage that influenced much of the country's subsequent history. Christianity consolidated itself and spread the message eastward. Urban life of a sort continued in many of the towns the Romans had founded. Even today, the previously occupied lands along the Rhine have a distinct identity, with a joie de vivre not always present elsewhere—perhaps something to do with the vines brought over from Italy. In the post-1945 division of Germany, a West Germany ruled from a Rhineland capital (Bonn), and a Communist Germany ruled from Berlin far to the east seemed an echo of this ancient historical division.

IMPERIAL REVIVAL

Known in German as the *Völkerwanderung* ("Migration of the Peoples"), the period following the demise of the Roman Empire, from the fourth to the early seventh

Germany reunited: Berliners, from both East and West, storm the Wall on the night of November 9, 1989.

centuries A.D., saw a complex redistribution of the populations of Europe. The Franks, who settled in the fertile land around the lower Rhine and Moselle Rivers with Aachen as their base, became increasingly powerful. Their greatest leader, Charlemagne—Charles the Great—became king of the Franks in 768. On Christmas Day in 800, he was crowned emper-

A reliquary bust from the Treasury in Aachen Cathedral expresses the power and prestige of Emperor Charlemagne.

or in Rome, in keeping with his view of himself and his realm as successors to the now almost legendary Romans. Both ruthless and enlightened, he subjugated enemies on all sides and promoted literacy, learning, and the arts. His greatest visible monument is his cathedral at Aachen.

After Charlemagne's death, his kingdom was split into three parts, the basis for what were later to become separate French and German states. Central authority continued to diminish, and it was left to local lords to attempt to maintain order and fend off attacks from Vikings and Magyars. From their

successes, great dukedoms developed such as Saxony, Franconia, Bavaria, and Swabia. Duke Henry of Saxony, known as Henry the Fowler, succeeded in placating the other dukes and restoring a degree of unity to the realm. His son Otto, known as "The Great," arranged a glittering ceremony for his coronation as king of Germany in Aachen in 936, consciously presenting himself as heir to Charlemagne. Otto's greatest achievement was finally to eliminate the threat to European stability posed by the marauding Magyars from the east, routing them at the Lechfeld near Augsburg, one of the definitive battles in German history. In 962, Otto was crowned emperor by the pope in Rome; this union of German and imperial crowns was to persist for hundreds of years, causing endless strife, since German kings had constantly to intervene in the affairs of Italy and contend with the temporal and spiritual power of popes.

EASTWARD MOVES

In the early years of the second millennium, emperors also had to keep an eye on the growing power of the nobility and of bishops who were territorial lords as well as church leaders. In 1077 this balancing act led Emperor Henry IV into a bizarre act of humiliation. With his authority undermined by unrest among the German princes, and fearful that Pope Gregory VII would assert his power in Germany, he traveled to where the pope was staying at the castle of Canossa in Italy. Here, dressed in nothing but a hair shirt, he humbly waited in the snow until granted an audience, then prostrated himself, his arms held out in the form of a cross. Satisfied, Gregory granted him absolution and confirmed his authority, although this did little to prevent further conflicts. Imperial power and prestige was constantly challenged by ambitious rulers. Emperor Frederick I, who ruled from 1152 to 1190, was the outstanding member of an outstanding dynasty, the Hohenstaufens. His glittering court with its poets and troubadours—the eloquent *Minnesänger*—came to be seen as the high point of medieval chivalry. Despite the continuing political fragmentation of Germany and the lack of a central bureaucracy and armed forces, the empire persisted, becoming known toward the end of the Middle Ages as the Holy Roman Empire of the German Nation.

In principle, the office of German king and emperor was not hereditary. Selection was in the hands of seven Electors, rulers of some of the most important German states, among them the archbishoprics of Trier, Mainz, and Cologne. But eventually the office of emperor became a more or less hereditary possession of the Habsburg dynasty, rulers for considerable periods of time not only of Austria, but of other German provinces, the Netherlands, and Spain. Again, this meant that emperors could often only focus part of their energies on German affairs, a constant temptation for local rulers to assert themselves against imperial authority.

THE REFORMATION

The 95 Theses nailed to the door of Wittenberg church by the young monk Martin Luther in 1517 set in motion a train of events that was to split the Church and completely recast the political geography of Germany and Europe. Well before Luther's day, voices had been raised in condemnation of the worldliness of popes and prelates, and attempts made to return the Church to the people, cut through excessive ceremony, and assert the original teachings of the Bible. A particularly flagrant abuse was the sale of indulgences, fundamentally a device for extracting funds from credulous congregations in order to finance the political ambitions of high churchmen. But an ossified Church was resistant to change, preferring to send reformers like Jan Huss to the stake than take heed of his message. Huss was put to death at Konstanz in 1415. In 1521 Luther was summoned to the imperial Diet meeting at the city of Worms, where he was condemned and excommunicated, with dire threats issued against anyone coming to his aid. But more was at stake than the freedom of a monk to defy pope and emperor. Many German rulers found his teachings a convenient peg on which to hang their own political ambitions. As Luther left Worms, he was apprehended by followers of the Elector of Saxony and spirited off to Wartburg Castle high above the town of Eisenach. Here he spent the best part of a year in disguise, devoting himself to translating the Bible into a form of German that could be understood by everyone, thereby helping lay the foundations of modern German.

The years that followed were particularly turbulent. One peasant uprising followed another, although all were more or less brutally suppressed. Reformist, even revolutionary religious sects rose up and subsided.

Martin Luther spreads the Word from his pulpit in Wittenberg.

Well before the middle of the 16th century many princes as well as a majority of the free cities had adopted Lutheranism, and attempts by Emperor Charles V to crush the Reformation ended in compromise: The 1555 Peace of Augsburg was in effect an agreement to disagree, and the principle of *"cuius regio, eius religio"* was adopted, allowing the ruler of a territory to determine its religious confession without outside interference. This gave rise to a confessional pattern that still exists today, despite the population upheavals of the 20th century, with central and eastern Germany predominantly Protestant, Bavaria and the Rhineland mostly Catholic.

The destruction of the city of Magdeburg by imperial troops led by Count Tilly in 1632

THIRTY YEARS OF WAR

Between 1618 and 1648, Central Europe was the theater of a complex sequence of conflicts that came to be called the Thirty Years War, often involving external powers like France and Sweden. It was precipitated by the famous incident called the Defenestration of Prague, when Protestant noblemen, enraged by the emperor's attack on their privileges, threw two of his representatives from the windows of Prague Castle. Imperial revenge followed in 1621, when the forces of the Bohemian nobles were routed by the emperor's army at the Battle of the White Mountain outside Prague. There was fighting from one end of Germany to the other, with armies often composed of rapacious mercenaries whose prime interest was in plunder. Whole cities like Magdeburg were wiped out, peasants fled the land, harvests went uncollected, and epidemics raged. At this time the New World was being opened up and the great trade routes were shifting away from Central Europe to the wider world of the Atlantic. After the Peace of Westphalia in 1648, the German lands slowly recovered, but in economic terms had now fallen way behind countries like France and England. The Peace of Westphalia confirmed the fragmented political map of Germany, and allowed territorial rulers much more sovereignty, further limiting the powers of the emperor. Alsace was ceded to France, parts of the Baltic coast to Sweden.

ABSOLUTISM & ENLIGHTENMENT

In the late 17th century and throughout the 18th, the key political actors in Germany were the rulers of the larger states, above all the kings of Prussia. Following the example of France, and impressed by the ruling style of the Sun King Louis XIV, they reorganized their realms on absolutist lines, centralizing power, governing through bureaucracies, and creating standing armies. Rulers often abandoned their cramped medieval castles and built themselves spacious baroque palaces set in formal gardens with avenues and parterres on the French model. Some of the most ambitious and extravagant rulers were powerful churchmen, so-called prince-bishops, such as the Schönborn dynasty, who held sway from their sumptuous Residenz in Würzburg. Many princes strove to enhance their prestige by cultivating whatever intellectual, artistic, and musical talent was available. One of the greatest prizes was the presence of French writer and thinker Voltaire, whose wit and erudition graced several courts, notably the Potsdam of

Frederick the Great of Prussia. Use of the French language was de rigueur in all the best circles. Frederick was an exceptionally cultured man, his talent as a flautist celebrated in a famous 19th-century painting by Adolf von Menzel. Johann Sebastian Bach's "Musical Offering" was based on a theme given him by the king, but the great composer (see p. 44) spent most of his creative life as the director of music of one of the free cities, Leipzig, where his employer was no king but a town council.

Frederick the Great was a Hohenzollern, the family that had built up the state of Prussia, centered on Brandenburg and the then small city of Berlin. During the 18th century, the Hohenzollerns created a tightly run state with an efficient bureaucracy and a well-disciplined army. Relatively liberal at home, Prussia pursued an aggressive foreign policy, regularly expanding its territory, particularly at the expense of its great rival, Austria, from whom it took the province of Silesia after the Seven Years War (1756–1763). Still holding the increasingly nominal office of Holy Roman Emperor, the Austrian Hapsburg rulers turned their attention away from German affairs, finding enough to occupy themselves with in Hungary and the Balkans, where they were filling the vacuum left by the retreating Ottoman Empire. The other German states watched the rise of Prussia with apprehension, perhaps sensing that in the next century it would be this militaristic state that would lead the struggle for German unity and impose its style on what was still a highly fragmented country with very diverse traditions.

REVOLUTIONS & RESTORATIONS

The outburst of energy released by the French Revolution of 1789 soon led to France's confrontation with Germany, and by 1794 all of the country west of the Rhine was in French hands. Napoleon pushed French conquests farther still, eventually bringing the whole of Germany into a continental system dominated by France and run on French lines. Many much-needed reforms were introduced, including partial emancipation of the Jews. The political map of Germany was tidied up: Church states were abolished, while others such as Baden and Bavaria, which both became kingdoms, were greatly extended. In

1806 that extraordinarily long-lived but now meaningless institution, the Holy Roman Empire, was finally laid to rest.

Resentment at foreign domination fanned patriotic feelings. In the spring of 1813, anti-French rioting broke out all over Germany; in October, at the so-called Battle of the Nations outside Leipzig, the allied armies of Russia, Austria, and a revived Prussia defeated Napoleon's army. But there was to be no new order in Central Europe. The victorious powers meeting at the Congress of Vienna in 1814-15 were determined to forestall any further possibilities of revolution. Although much of the Napoleonic reorganization of Germany remained in place, Russia, Prussia, and Austria combined to reinstate authoritarian regimes. Nevertheless, disturbances and protests took place. At a great festival at Wartburg Castle in 1817, students first raised the black-red-and-gold banner, later to become the national flag. It was flown again at a rally attended by 30,000 at Hambach Castle in the Palatinate, where passionate speeches were made demanding democracy and national unity. In 1848, a year of revolution throughout Europe, it looked as if the old order might at last crumble. Fearful governments made significant concessions, and a national parliament met in St. Paul's Church in Frankfurt to decide exactly what kind of united, constitutional, democratic country Germany should be. When nothing was agreed, the conservative forces regrouped, dismissed the parliament, and ruthlessly put down further protests.

UNIFICATION PRUSSIAN STYLE

German unification was eventually achieved, not through rational discussion and with the participation of all interested parties, but through the ruthless diplomacy and judicious use of force favored by Otto von Bismarck, appointed Chancellor of Prussia in 1862. In 1864, Bismarck used Austria to help him acquire Schleswig-Holstein, then in 1866 turned on his ally. The annihilating victory of the Prussian army over the Austrians at the Battle of Königgrätz (Sadova) in Bohemia finally closed the door on potential Austrian interference in German affairs and meant that it would be Prussia alone that would lead Germany to unity. In 1870 the south German

German unity proclaimed in the sumptuous setting of the Palace of Versailles

states honored the alliances with Prussia into which they had been coerced, and joined in the Franco-Prussian war, which ended with a resounding German victory. France was forced to pay a huge indemnity, and the largely German-speaking provinces of Alsace and Lorraine, which had been part of France since the 17th century, were incorporated into what was now known as the Second Reich (the Holy Roman Empire constituting the First Reich). On January 18, 1871, the King of Prussia was proclaimed German Emperor. The new Kaiser, Wilhelm I, thought it would mean the end of the Prussian monarchy, and many of the other German rulers were fearful for their position; the consent of King Ludwig II of Bavaria had to be bought with a huge bribe.

Nevertheless, Germany as a whole was filled with nationalistic euphoria, and the next few years saw an explosion of economic activity; industry flourished, there was a building boom, and Germany soon had Europe's most extensive rail network. Germany caught up and overtook Britain in coal and steel production, and inaugurated a second industrial revolution with its innovative electrical and chemical industries. Social welfare provision included unemployment and sickness benefit and was maintained at a high level, partly to preempt the emerging Socialist movement, dominated by the Social Democratic Party, which maintained a constant presence in the Reichstag (parliament). But the Reichstag's powers were few; policy was made first by Bismarck, then after his dramatic dismissal in 1890, by Kaiser Wilhelm II and the small clique around him, which increasingly consisted of military men.

THE GREAT WAR

Germany came late to the "scramble for Africa," and its colonial aspirations irritated its rivals Britain and France, while its determination to build a naval force able to take on Britain's Royal Navy could only be interpreted as a deliberate provocation. During the first years of the 20th century, the great European powers became more and more suspicious of each other's intentions and sought security in piling up armaments. When in June 1914 the Austrian heir to the throne, Archduke Franz Ferdinand, was assassinated at Sarajevo by a Serbian student, Germany rashly encouraged Austria to settle scores with her unruly Serbian neighbor. Europe's interlocking alliances were activated, with Germany and Austria facing Russia, France, and Great Britain. When the long-prepared knockout blow against France

German troops leave the trenches in the ill-fated final offensive of World War I.

failed to work, Germany could not, in the long run, hope to survive the attrition of the trench warfare that ensued, least of all once the United States, provoked by reckless submarine attacks on its shipping, had entered the fray with its limitless material resources and reserves of manpower. By late summer 1918, the German military leadership realized the war was lost, but it cleverly managed to evade blame by shifting responsibility on to a civilian government that had requested an armistice. The army marched home with bands playing and colors flying, and the legend of the "stab in the back" was born.

WEIMAR INTERLUDE

Germany's new republican government—Kaiser Wilhelm II had abdicated and fled to Holland—met initially in Weimar because of revolutionary disturbances in Berlin. Its first task was to accept the harsh terms of the Versailles peace settlement: admission of war guilt, onerous reparations, the occupation of the Rhineland, the return of Alsace and Lorraine to France, and the loss of parts of Prussia in order to give Poland a corridor to the Baltic. Its acceptance was construed by many as treachery. The government also had to contend in 1923 with hyperinflation, which

destroyed the savings of millions of middle-class people, and with a French occupation of the Ruhr industrial area. But cultural life flourished, freed from the stifling atmosphere of the Second Reich, and Berlin's more than colorful nightlife drew in cosmopolitans from all over Europe. For a few short years in the late 1920s there was a degree of prosperity, while social reforms seemed to be laying the foundation for a more hopeful future. But the Weimar Republic was dealt a fatal blow by the Great Depression starting in 1929. By 1932 there were six million unemployed, and the German National Socialist Workers' Party (the Nazis) was the biggest party in the Reichstag. After a second, inconclusive round of elections in 1932, the aging President Hindenburg was persuaded to make Adolf Hitler chancellor to lead a coalition government. Hitler was sworn in on January 30, 1933.

THE THIRD REICH & WORLD WAR II

On the night of February 27, 1933, the Reichstag was burned down, supposedly by a Dutch communist, but possibly by Nazi stormtroopers. Hitler then had an excuse to imprison his opponents, and he consolidated his power in March elections. He had an uncanny ability to tap into the fears, frustrations, and ambitions of all sorts of Germans and a masterly understanding of how to exploit them. Apart from the excluded Jews and other "undesirables," there was something for everyone in the Nazi grab bag. Industrialists profited from a revived economy and a rearmament that also kept the military

Adolf Hitler and a grinning Joseph Goebbels, confident in the future of their Thousand-Year Reich

on side. Provided they abandoned any allegiance to communism, workers no longer feared unemployment. The middle classes had to tighten their belts but no longer feared inflation, while many small businessmen rejoiced at the elimination of Jewish competition. Bullies found plenty of opportunities to don a smart uniform and push people around. Once Hitler had started on his string of foreign policy successes, beginning with the reoccupation of the Rhineland in 1936, nearly all Germans rejoiced that the shame of defeat and the humiliation of Versailles were being overcome.

It seemed to many that the nationalist dreams of the 19th century were coming dramatically true. Opponents were crushed or fled abroad, and the army, the sole center of power that could have stopped Hitler, was reluctant to act.

In 1939 Britain and France declared war on Germany in response to the latter's invasion of Poland. Enthusiasm for war was not unbounded, but as one Blitzkrieg victory succeeded another, many Germans felt that Hitler was invincible. Doubts came with the invasion of the Soviet Union in June 1941 and with the entry of the United States into the war later that year. They were confirmed by the disaster at Stalingrad in January 1943, but by then there seemed no way out, particularly when the Allies declared their policy of unconditional surrender. Nevertheless,

resistance elements within the army went ahead with their plans to assassinate Hitler, and in July 1944 nearly succeeded. But Hitler survived, and Germany fought on for nearly another year, during which time more physical destruction took place than during all the previous years of war, with whole cities leveled by Allied air forces who had perfected the bombing techniques first practiced by the Luftwaffe (German Air Force). In the last months of the war and the early years of the peace, some 15 million Germans either fled or were expelled from lands where many of them had lived for generations—from Poland, Hungary, Yugoslavia, Czechoslovakia—and from those parts of Germany proper which now passed into other hands: East Prussia, Silesia, most of Pomerania.

On May 30, 1942, more than a thousand British bombers caused massive damage to historic Cologne.

RECOVERY & DIVISION

Physically devastated, half-starved, shivering in terrible postwar winters, full of displaced people, utterly demoralized and discredited, and ruled by foreign armies, it seemed as if Germany might never revive.

At the end of the war, the country was formally divided into separate zones of occupation. The British, American, and French zones became the Bundesrepublik Deutschland (Federal Republic of Germany), lifted out of its postwar misery by an ingenious currency reform that destroyed the black market and cleared the way for the

President John F. Kennedy visits the Berlin Wall in 1963.

Wirtschaftswunder (Economic Miracle) that made the country one of the wealthiest nations of the Western world. The Soviet zone became the Deutsche Demokratische Republik or DDR (German Democratic Republic or GDR). This was run on Soviet lines by the Socialist Unity Party, a merger forced on the Social Democratic Party by their once bitter rivals the Communists.

Germany became the principal theater of the Cold War. By 1948, the fragile alliance between the Western powers and the Soviet Union had completely collapsed. In May of that year, the Soviet Union blockaded all routes into Berlin by rail, road, and waterway. The decision was eventually made to defy the one-time ally by flying in essential supplies to the western sectors of Berlin. Over the following months British and American aircraft brought in almost 2.5 million tons of supplies, including vast quantities of coal. Nearly a year later the Soviets abandoned the blockade. The Berlin airlift marked a turning point in the Cold War, and in a short space of time had transformed Western perceptions of Berlin from Nazi capital to outpost of freedom.

Despite remarkable progress in some areas—low rents, lavish social provision, guaranteed employment—the DDR could

only ever command limited allegiance from its population. By 1961, some three million of its citizens had left for the West, passing through what was still a permeable frontier. The construction of the Berlin Wall in that year was a desperate measure, a reaction to the exodus that was crippling the country's economy.

FROM DIVISION TO REUNIFICATION

From the 1960s to the late 1980s, the division of Germany seemed a fact of the European political landscape. The Federal Republic continued to prosper, but ghosts emerged from the Nazi past to torment it. The generation that came to maturity in the 1960s put questions that their parents were often reluctant to answer. A tiny but not insignificant minority, calling themselves the Red Army Faction, turned to extreme violence and kidnapping, hoping that the state reaction to their terrorism would unmask it as fundamentally fascist. Captured and tried, their ringleaders committed suicide in prison.

The GDR liked to proclaim that it was on the way to becoming one of the world's leading industrial powers, but its triumphs were based on careful manipulation of statistics, and its industries mainly produced goods that

Macedonia 2001: German troops help keep the peace in the Balkans.

only captive consumers could be persuaded to buy, like the bone-shaking and polluting little Trabant automobile. In reality, like its patron, the Soviet Union, it was falling further and further behind the West. When Mikail Gorbachev began to relax the iron certainties of the Soviet system in the late 1980s, General Secretary Erich Honecker thought that the GDR could carry on regardless, but once Soviet support was removed, the regime started to collapse. In 1989, popular pressure built up and eventually hundreds of thousands filled the streets demanding change.

DIE WENDE

Meaning "the change" or "turning point," *die Wende* is the term Germans use to describe the momentous events of 1989–1990 that led to the reunification of their country. A united Germany was not the inevitable outcome of the collapse of the hard-line Communist regime in the GDR; many urged a lengthy transition period while the country digested the implications of its newly found freedom.

The opening of the Berlin Wall on November 9, 1989, was an event of huge symbolic significance, yet it represented only one stage in the slow-motion collapse of East Germany. Many members of the Communist leadership thought the dismissal of figures such as General Secretary Honecker and the implementation of reforms would preserve the shape of the regime. Western leaders took a lot of convincing that German reunification was either necessary or desirable. And once the hated barrier of the Wall had been breached, far from fleeing, the majority of East Germans were content to take day trips to the West, do some shopping, and return home. But as details emerged of the extent of *Stasi* (secret police) surveillance and control and of the corruption and privilege of the regime and its servants, more and more Easterners looked to the West for salvation. Chancellor Kohl of the Federal Republic quickly understood their mood, and in December responded by declaring to a huge crowd in Dresden, "My goal … is the unity of the nation!" All the government of the GDR could do was to prepare for the first free and fair elections in the country's history. The result, in March 1990, was a triumph for the Christian Democrats, backed by Kohl's sister party in the West. The task of the new administration was not to reform the GDR, but to organize its absorption into the Federal Republic. Reunification took place on October 3, 1990, but the long haul to create a country that was truly one had only just begun. ■

The arts

GERMANY HAS MADE A MAJOR CONTRIBUTION TO THE ARTS OF EUROPE throughout the continent's history. The sumptuous baroque and rococo palaces and churches of the 17th and 18th centuries mark a high point in German architecture. Writers such as Goethe and Schiller were at the forefront of the Classical and Romantic movements. In music, composers such as Bach and Beethoven put Germany on the musical map of Europe, and the early 20th century saw an explosion of artistic talent.

ARCHITECTURE IN GERMANY

Architectural influences from other countries abound throughout Germany, France's Gothic and Italy's Renaissance revival styles in particular. But Germany has contributed to the world's architectural scene too, most notably with modernism in the early 20th century.

Prevalent in Germany as well is a rich

Romanesque harmony in St. Michael's nave, Hildesheim

tradition in vernacular architecture, apparent in the unique local styles of farmsteads and town houses in old German towns. Wooden frameworks were common, since timber has historically been more available than good building stone. One recognizable trait you'll see throughout Germany's villages are the carved wooden decorations on houses.

Carolingian to Romanesque

The Romans erected town walls, baths, villas, and places of worship, but the story of German building really begins around A.D. 790 with the construction of the Palatinate chapel, Münster, at Aachen (see pp. 160–161) by Emperor Charlemagne. This 16-sided, stone-built structure with a central octagon and rounded arches was inspired by the Byzantine church of San Vitale in Ravenna, Italy, but Charlemagne's edifice is bolder and simpler. Part of a great imperial palace (Kaiserpfalz), long since destroyed, it was one of several used by Charlemagne's court as it toured around his vast domains. In a much restored state, a later, 11th-century Kaiserpfalz survives at Goslar in the Harz Mountains. The chapel at Aachen served as a model for other churches in Carolingian style, of which parts have survived in the minster at Essen (see p. 168) and the monastery church of St. Peter in Bad Wimpfen (see p. 327). A characteristic feature of early churches was the westwork, a fortress-like entrance vestibule with a chapel above; there is a fine example, in an idyllic rural setting, on Reichenau Island in Lake Constance (see pp. 340–342).

Architecture of greater ambition and complexity appeared in the revived empire after the tenth century, of which the outstanding example is St. Michael's Church at Hildesheim (see p. 144), built between 1001 and 1033, a richly satisfying composition of simple geometrical forms: semicircular apses at both ends, two square central towers, and a quarter of cylindrical staircase towers. The later flowering of the German Romanesque style produced magnificent multi-towered cathedrals in the Rhineland, at Mainz, Trier, Worms, and Speyer (see pp. 178–179,

High-gabled, many storied town houses are the glory of many an old town square.

Late Gothic exuberance in the ornate vault of St. Anne's Church, Annaberg-Buchholz

187–188, 191, and 194), their austere appearance relieved by decorative patterns based on the repeated use of rounded arches, while Cologne (see pp. 148– 159) boasts Germany's greatest heritage of Romanesque churches.

Gothic

Tentative beginnings of the Gothic style can be seen at Limburg an der Lahn (see p. 207), where the exterior of the cathedral begun in 1211 is exuberantly Romanesque, while the interior incorporates characteristically Gothic rib vaulting. The first fully fledged Gothic structures in Germany are the Liebfrauenkirche at Trier and St. Elisabeth's Church at Marburg (see p. 206), both begun in the 1230s. The latter is a hall church— with a nave and aisles of the same height—a pattern common in Germany. Work started in 1248 on the greatest German Gothic buildings, Cologne Cathedral (see pp. 151–153). After the choir was completed work proceeded slowly, and Cologne's cathedral was one of several great churches that had to wait until the 19th century for completion—sometimes because the daring vision of their Gothic designers was beyond the technology of the time. Another was Ulm; its 528-foot (161 m) spire, finally erected in 1890, is the world's tallest.

The 12th and 13th centuries were a great period of monastery building. At Maulbronn in Baden-Württemberg (see pp. 345–346) a near perfect example has survived of the whole, townlike complex that formed the setting for monastic life. (Today, Maulbronn is a UNESCO World Heritage site.)

Most Gothic structures were built in stone, but, along the Baltic coast and elsewhere in northern Germany, a variant developed called *Backsteingotik* (Brick Gothic). You can see this brick-built style in churches and city halls, where they lend great distinction to the centers of Hansa trading cities such as Lübeck and Stralsund.

Renaissance

The architectural forms of the Italian Renaissance, at first often misunderstood in Germany, were used only for decorative effect, or incongruously combined with Gothic features. For instance, the Fugger family chapel of 1512 in St. Anne's Church in Augsburg (see pp. 272–273), Germany's very first structure in Renaissance style, was still given a Gothic net vault. Munich, strongly Catholic and in closer touch with Italy than other cities, saw building in a thoroughgoing Renaissance manner. The finest examples are

The rococo church of Würzburg's Residenz was a sumptuous setting for princely worship.

the Church of St. Michael (Michaelskirche) (see p. 286), completed by the Jesuits in 1597, and the rulers' palace, the Residenz (see pp. 293–294), where the Antiquarium was built as a spectacular setting for the ducal art treasures. In northern, largely Protestant Germany, Dutch and Flemish influences found their most striking expression in the "Weser Renaissance" style, characterized by extravagant ornamentation with gables, oriel, scrolls, spikes, obelisks, and statuary.

Baroque & rococo

The baroque style originated in Italy but, in the hands of German architects and craftsmen, took on distinctive characteristics, particularly in the Catholic south. Here Counter-Reformation worship was given a theatrical setting of great sensual appeal. This reached an extreme of opulence and fantasy in the rococo pilgrimage church of Vierzehnheiligen (see pp. 256–257), begun in 1744 to designs by Johann Balthasar Neumann (1687–1753). Neumann also built or contributed to the palaces of the Schönborn dynasty of prince-bishops at Brühl, Bruchsal (see p. 346), and at Würzburg (see pp. 260–261), where the mighty staircase leads to state rooms of the utmost splendor.

On the ground floor, a grottolike space (the *sala terrena*) leads to a formal garden conceived as an integral part of the whole design. The most spectacular baroque garden in Germany was at Wilhelmshöhe outside Kassel (see p. 203), where an immensely long cascade led downhill from a temple topped by a giant statue of Hercules. First laid out at the end of the 18th century, Wilhelmshöhe was later transformed, like most German baroque gardens, into an English-style naturalistic park.

Baroque opulence and rococo fantasy were not entirely confined to southern Germany. The courtyard and pavilions of the Zwinger in Dresden are among the most ambitious settings for court festivities ever devised, while the gracious rococo interiors of Frederick the Great's Sanssouci Palace at Potsdam contradict all assumptions about Prussian austerity.

From classicism to confusion

In the 18th century the classical architecture of antiquity was reinterpreted as an appropriate style for state capitals. At Potsdam, Sanssouci was given a classical colonnade by Frederick the Great's court architect Georg Wenzeslaus von Knobelsdorff (1699–1753). In 1791 the approach to Berlin was ennobled by the colossal Brandenburg Gate (see pp. 58–59),

Wilhelm Brücke captured the classical elegance of the boulevard of Unter den Linden in Prussia's capital, Berlin, in his 1842 painting.

directly inspired by the Propylaea on the Acropolis in Athens.

The greatest Prussian architect of this period, and also director of the kingdom's Department of Public Works, was Karl Friedrich Schinkel (1781–1841). He transformed the face of Berlin and its surroundings, with museums, palaces, and country houses in a restrained, but wonderfully inventive, neoclassic style. His counterpart in Bavaria was Franz Karl Leo von Klenze (1784–1864). He gave Munich an appropriately regal air (Bavaria had recently become a kingdom) with buildings like the

Glyptothek (see p. 292), the world's first public sculpture museum. He also designed monuments intended to give the rising tide of German nationalism a noble focus—Walhalla (see p. 278) high above the Danube and the Befreiungshalle near Kelheim (see p. 271).

Further national monuments rose in many parts of Germany after unification in 1871. Effort went into looking for an architectural style appropriate for the Second Reich, but much late 19th-century building was little more than a dull rehash of historical styles.

Modernism

At the turn of the 20th century, *Jugendstil*, the German variant of art nouveau, flourished briefly—most notably in the setting of the Mathildenhöhe in Darmstadt (see p. 209). An

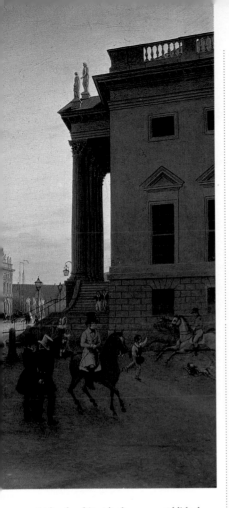

Nazi seizure of power in 1933, Gropius and most kindred spirits fled Germany, to spread the modernist message abroad.

The Nazis took up the monumental style of imposing functional buildings like the superb station at Stuttgart, built between 1914 and 1927. They also favored a "stripped classical" style exemplified by the Haus der Kunst in Munich. One lasting achievement of the 1930s, a fine synthesis of engineering, architecture, and landscape design, was the autobahn network of strategic highways.

The Bauhaus in Dessau, designed by Walter Gropius in 1926, epitomizes German modernism.

artists' and architects' colony was established here in 1899. The first decades of the century saw an extraordinary efflorescence of architectural styles and new directions. Strange, organic-looking structures, such as Erich Mendelsohn's Einstein Tower at Potsdam, were grouped under the same heading of expressionism as the shiplike offices of the Chilehaus in Hamburg or the circular Rheinhalle in Düsseldorf. In contrast, the pioneering Fagus Factory at Alfeld by Walter Gropius (1883–1969), with its flat roof, glass curtain-walling, and boxy outline, foreshadowed the things to come. In 1919 Gropius founded the Bauhaus in Weimar (see pp. 214–217) and so created a Utopian aesthetic for the modern, machine age. The Bauhaus spirit was reflected in superb public housing in cities such as Berlin and Frankfurt. After the

The epic scale of wartime destruction was matched in the 1950s and '60s by a rebuilding program of similar proportions. Much of it was carried out in a rather bland, but inoffensive mainstream modernist style. However, there are outstanding individual structures such as the crisply elegant Thyssen tower in Düsseldorf. Germany probably has more modern churches than any other country; the Kaiser Wilhelm Memorial Church in western Berlin is a poignant synthesis of a contemporary setting for worship and wartime ruins. When the Olympic Games returned to Germany in 1972, Günther Behnisch surpassed his predecessors

The sun sets over Albrecht Altdorfer's vision of the "Battle of Alexander" (1529).

of 1936 by designing a stadium of inspired originality, harmoniously integrated with the surrounding parkland and covered by a joyously swelling tentlike canopy. As ever, the country has been open to influences and ideas from abroad, and some of the most exciting recent buildings have been the work of foreign architects such as Scot James Stirling (Stuttgart State Gallery) and Brit Norman Foster (Frankfurt's Commerzbank and the restoration of the Reichstag in Berlin).

PAINTING & SCULPTURE
German paintings and sculptures have tended to stay in the country. English aristocrats on the Grand Tour would take home expensive souvenirs from Italy and France rather than Germany, and in the 19th century the devel-

opment of public collections and museums coincided with the rise of nationalism and a concern for the country's artistic heritage. Then, at the beginning of the 20th century, the prestige of the work of Paris-based artists was so great that it overshadowed the art of other countries. More recently, however, the world has discovered what Germans have long known— that their country's painting and sculpture embraces some of the finest art ever created.

Beginnings

Early examples of German sculpture include the Halle museum's relief panel of an early eighth-century Saxon horseman trotting into battle with shield and lance and, in Cologne Cathedral, the expressive tenth-century Cross of Gero. Painting at this time was largely confined to manuscript illumination, carried out by schools of skilled craftsmen at monastic centers such as Trier and Reichenau Island on Lake Constance. In St. George's Church on Reichenau, wall paintings of Christ's miracles date from about 1000.

Romanesque sculptors gave Germany symbols that still resonate today: The Brunswick Lion of around 1166 symbolized the power and determination of Duke Henry the Lion, and the sculptures created in the 1230s for Bamberg Cathedral, particularly the equestrian statue known as the "Bamberg Rider," portray the ideals of medieval chivalry.

Fifteenth & sixteenth centuries

In the Middle Ages every church needed an altarpiece, and their production reached a high point of achievement in Cologne, where Stefan Lochner (died 1451) was unsurpassed in depicting spiritual grace and sweetness, as in his "Madonna in the Rose Garden" of 1445. Late medieval piety of this kind combines with the beginnings of Renaissance humanism in the masterly linden-wood carvings of Veit Stoss (ca 1447–1533) and Tilman Riemenschneider (ca 1460–1531), both of whom worked mostly in Franconia (northern Bavaria).

The early 16th century was a golden age in German painting. No one has conveyed human suffering more intensely in the form of Christ crucified than Matthias Grünewald (ca 1470–1528). Albrecht Altdorfer (ca 1480–1538) was a pioneer of landscape

painting, subordinating conventional subjects to their setting as in his "St. George and the Dragon," set in the primeval forest of southern Germany. Lucas Cranach the Elder (1472–1553) specialized in female nudes of great sensuality, and in portraits, including a famous one of Martin Luther.

The outstanding figure of the era was Albrecht Dürer (1471–1528), who mastered drawing and engraving as well as oil painting, and virtually invented watercolor. Travels in Italy gave him a deep understanding of Renaissance ideals, to which he added a characteristically German expressiveness; his portraits, such as the one of Oswolt Krel in Munich's Alte Pinakothek (see pp. 288–289), seem to reach into the soul of his sitters. The great portraitist Hans Holbein the Younger (1497–1543), on the other hand, concentrated on the detailed physical appearance of his subjects and their typical surroundings, as in his "Portrait of Georg Gisze" in Berlin's Gemäldegalerie (see pp. 66–67).

Seventeenth & eighteenth centuries

Artistic production was affected by both the Reformation and the disturbances of the Thirty Years War (1618–1648). A short-lived but influential painter was Adam Elsheimer (1578–1610), who produced subtle effects of dark and light in pictures like "The Flight into Egypt." He worked on a small scale, but the proliferation of baroque churches and palaces required artists able to cover vast surfaces with illusionistic paintings and to work in close collaboration with craftsmen like plasterers, gilders, and stucco workers as well as with architects. The Bavarian Cosmas Damian Asam (1686–1739) and his brother Egid Quirin (1692–1750) were artists who combined more than one of these roles; the Asams' masterpieces are the church named after them in Munich (see p. 285) and Weltenburg Abbey (see p. 277) on the Danube. Another team of brothers, Dominikus (1685–1766) and Johann Baptist Zimmermann (1680–1758) collaborated in similar fashion on the pilgrimage church of the Wieskirche (see p. 316) in the Bavarian Alp foothills.

The outstanding sculptors of the German baroque were Andreas Schlüter (circa 1660–1714), whose dynamic equestrian statue

"Stages of Life," by Romantic painter Caspar David Friedrich (1774–1840)

of the Great Elector stands in front of Charlottenburg Palace (see pp. 72–73) in Berlin, and Balthasar Permoser (1651–1732), who populated Dresden's Zwinger (see pp. 230–233) with stone cupids, maidens, and other figures.

Nineteenth century

The major painter of Germany's Romantic movement was Caspar David Friedrich (1774–1840), whose canvases show dreamlike landscapes, often inhabited by a solitary figure apparently contemplating the mystery and melancholy of the universe. It is almost impossible to look at Friedrich's favorite subjects—Rügen Island, the Baltic shore, and the Elbe Valley—without seeing them through this visionary artist's eyes.

By mid-century, artists were concentrating on the detail of life, exemplified in "The Poor Poet" and "The Sunday Huntsman" by Carl Spitzweg (1808–1885), which evoke small-town Germany with humor and compassion (see p. 290). Famous for his depictions of high society and his idealized history pictures, Adolf von Menzel (1815–1905) also painted scenes of industry, such as a steel mill. The specialty of Wilhelm Leibl (1844–1900) was country folk painted in the meticulous manner of the old masters. The idea of a "good and simple life" in the countryside led to the establishment of rural artists' colonies. The best known of these, at Worpswede (see p. 139) near Bremen, numbered Paula Modersohn-Becker (1876–1907) among its members; her deceptively naïve-seeming pictures of village life are still much loved today.

At the end of the century, French Impressionism found an important echo in Germany in the work of Max Liebermann (1847–1935) and Lovis Corinth (1858–1925), but it was with the expressionism of the early 20th century that German art made its own, startlingly original contribution.

Twentieth century

Early in the century, two distinct groups of artists came together to find new ways of expressing a characteristically German preoccupation with feeling. In 1905 Die Brücke (The Bridge) was formed in Dresden. Its leading member, Ernst Ludwig Kirchner (1880–1938), used simplified forms and the boldest of colors to convey dynamic meaning in pictures like "Nude with Hat" of 1911. Glorious colors pervade the palettes of both August Macke (1887–1914) and Franz Marc (1880–1916), members of Der Blaue Reiter

Ernest Ludwig Kirchner's "Brandenburg Gate" (1915), an expressionist vision of urban dynamism

(The Blue Rider) group established in Munich in 1911. With something of the quality of medieval stained glass, Marc's sensitive pictures of animals in their habitat have remained extremely popular. The group's most influential member was the Russian-born Wassily Kandinsky (1866–1944), who pioneered abstraction, as did Paul Klee (1879–1940). After World War I, Klee became one of the leading figures in the Bauhaus founded in Weimar by Walter Gropius.

To deal with the horrors of war and the social chaos and misery of the Weimar years, Neue Sachlichkeit (New Objectivity) advocated a return to a form of realism. Its foremost exponent, Otto Dix (1891–1969), had served in the trenches in Flanders; his apocalyptic Dresden triptych "War" has an impact equal to that of Grünewald's late medieval Crucifixion. The Dada movement rejoiced in absurdity, with the Hanover artist Kurt Schwitters (1887–1948) making collages from found objects and rubbish. The surrealist Max Ernst (1891–1976) anticipated the coming catastrophe of World War II in some of his unearthly landscapes. George Grosz (1893–1959) was perhaps the most bitingly satirical chronicler of the 1920s. Like many artists, he escaped the Nazi clampdown on all but the most slavishly

conventional art by emigrating to the United States. Max Beckmann (1884–1950) left Germany after listening to Hitler's speech opening the Nazi exhibition of "Degenerate Art," held in Munich in 1937 with the intention of humiliating their artistic adversaries. Beckmann's powerful vision of the torments of modern man continues to resonate; in 2001 his "Self-Portrait with Horn" was sold in New York for $22.5 million, the highest price ever paid for a German painting.

The Nazis' favorite sculptor was Arno Breker (1900–1991), whose muscle-bound supermen adorned public places like the Berlin Olympic Stadium and Reich Chancellery. In contrast, profound feeling is simply expressed in the figures of Ernst Barlach (1870–1938), which range in scale from the modest to the monumental ("Hovering Angel" in Güstrow Cathedral).

In the second half of the 20th century German art seemed to hesitate between re-establishing connections with the vitality of the 1920s and making its own contribution to international trends. The outstanding figure in West Germany was Joseph Beuys (1921–1986), who sculpted in such unorthodox materials as fat, felt, blood, and honey, and organized happenings and performances.

MUSIC

Music continues to be important in the German-speaking world, which has produced far more than its share of great composers and performers. Germany has an exceptional number of orchestras, several of world class such as the Berlin Philharmonic and the Leipzig Gewandhaus, and opera houses can

the 12th century, when *Minnesänger,* lyric poets influenced by the troubadours of Provence, celebrated courtly love, sometimes to the accompaniment of fiddle, lute, or harp. The greatest Minnesänger was Walter von der Vogelweide (ca 1170–1230), who is supposed to have participated in the legendary "Contest of the Troubadours" at Wartburg Castle (see

Germany's greatest musical genius, Ludwig van Beethoven

Franz Schubert, unsurpassed creator of Romantic lieder

be found in the most unlikely of industrial towns. Festivals abound, the most prestigious being Bayreuth's annual celebration of the works of Richard Wagner.

Beginnings to baroque

The very first German musicians seem to have performed on the long, curved horns of bronze known as *Luren,* which date from the first half of the first millennium B.C. And we know from the Romans that the later Germanic tribesmen went into battle singing. In the early Middle Ages, music was the preserve of the church, with Gregorian chant sung in Latin. German song really begins in

p. 222). The Minnesänger also dealt with religious, social, and political themes, as did the wandering songsters known as *Vaganten;* earthier altogether, some of the latter's efforts were collected in the "Carmina Burana" of around 1280, rousingly reworked by Carl Orff in 1937. The successors to the Minnesänger were the *Meistersinger,* singers organized into guilds. The most prominent mastersinger was Hans Sachs (1494–1576), celebrated by Wagner in his opera *The Mastersingers of Nuremberg.*

Martin Luther, who wrote the words of hymns such as "Eine feste Burg" ("A Stronghold Sure"), understood the importance of music to true devotion. The chorales of his time developed into the later cantata, one of the specialties of Johann Sebastian Bach (1685–1750). The outstanding master of all the musical forms of the baroque age, he is perhaps best remembered for developing polyphony. Bach served the courts at Weimar and Köthen before becoming musical director

Operas, symphonies, and orchestral suites by Richard Strauss mark the transition from the 19th to the 20th century.

for the city of Leipzig in 1723, where he remained until his death. Bach's reputation has continued to grow, although at the time it was Georg Philipp Telemann (1681–1767) who enjoyed greater acclaim. The other towering figure of baroque music was Georg Friedrich Händel (1685–1759), many of whose greatest works, like his oratorio *The Messiah*, were composed for the Hanoverian court in England. The ducal court at Mannheim was a fruitful environment for musicians from all over the German lands, and it was here that the foundations were laid for the development of the symphony.

Classical to Romantic

The evolution of the symphony and the establishment of the string quartet owed much to the Austrian composers Joseph Haydn (1732–1809) and Wolfgang Amadeus Mozart (1756–1791), but these forms were taken to a new level by the German Ludwig van Beethoven (1770–1827). His nine sym-

Kurt Weill collaborated with Bertolt Brecht to produce *The Threepenny Opera*.

phonies gave musical expression to profound human emotions, and his ability to probe the deep recesses of individual experience pointed the way for the next generation of German composers, generally classified as Romantics.

The greatest achievement of Franz Schubert (1797–1828) was his lieder, songs in which the lyric, the voice, and the piano fuse in exquisite harmony. A virtuoso pianist, Robert Schumann (1810–1856) also wrote intensely expressive lieder, although he himself considered his C-minor symphony to be his greatest work. Opera in German had reached early glories in Mozart's *Magic Flute* and Beethoven's *Fidelio*, while Carl Maria von

Weber's *Freischütz* of 1821 created musical and dramatic harmonies anticipating the work of Richard Wagner (see p. 260). Johannes Brahms (1833–1897) successfully fused Romanticism with the Classical tradition, and he was seen by supporters as counterbalancing the trend to formlessness of Wagner's work. Richard Strauss (1864–1949) drew on all

Heinrich Heine enraged the censor with his provocative prose.

musical traditions with equal virtuosity; he is best known for his symphonic poems such as *Don Juan,* and operas, including the popular *Der Rosenkavalier.*

Twentieth century

Germans and Austrians were wholly or partly responsible for many of the musical innovations of the 20th century, including the use of atonality (Arnold Schönberg, 1874–1951) and electronic techniques (Karl-Heinz Stockhausen, 1928–). The satirical operas of Kurt Weill (1900–1950), such as *The Threepenny Opera* and *The Rise and Fall of the City of Mahagonny,* are among the most popular and accessible music of the century. An emigrant to the United States, Weill was much influenced by jazz.

LITERATURE

Germany has one of the world's great literary traditions, and writing in German spans a vast range, encompassing medieval epic and troubadours' love poetry, Luther's Bible and the heights of Weimar Classicism, right up to the novels of modernism.

The Middle Ages

The spirit of medieval Germany is epitomized by the late 12th-century anonymous epic poem *Das Nibelungenlied (Song of the Nibelungs),* a rich compound of myth, human passions, and historical reality, which furnished Richard Wagner with material for his *Ring* cycle of operas. In an epic poem of the early 13th century, Wolfram von Eschenbach told the tale of the quest for the Holy Grail in *Parzifal.* Like the love songs of the *Minnesänger* (see p. 44), these epics were written in Middle High German, the predecessor of the modern version of the language, New High German. As the 16th century began, a wave of comic and satirical writing culminated in the figure of the jester and practical joker *Till Eulenspiegel,* whose pranks were recounted by a Brunswick revenue man, Hermann Bote.

Luther & after

Martin Luther's greatest contribution to German culture was his translation of the Bible, completed in 1534. The first translation freed from the bonds of regional dialect, it could be understood by all Germans, while its simplicity and clarity made an immense contribution to the development of German as a literary language. The turbulence of the Reformation and the Thirty Years War inhibited literary production, although out of the war came the picaresque novel *Simplicissimus* of 1669 by Jakob Christoph von Grimmelshausen, whose anti-hero experiences everything the chaos of the time can offer.

From Enlightenment to "Storm & Stress"

Gotthold Ephraim Lessing (1729–1781) put drama on a new footing. He pleaded for religious and social tolerance and, in defiance of theatrical convention, drew his characters from the rising middle classes. As the old European order crumbled into the chaos of the French Revolution, a dynamic literary movement arose that took its name from a German play dealing with the American War of Independence; *Sturm und Drang (Storm*

Weimar Classicism. For some Romantics folk and fairy tales provided inspiration; they included E.T.A. Hoffmann (1776–1822) and Clemens Brentano, who in 1805 published an anthology entitled *Des Knaben Wunderhorn (The Boy's Magic Horn)*. The greatest collectors of such material were the Brothers Grimm (see p. 203). Serious scholars,

Apotheosis of the silent movie: Robert Wiene's *The Cabinet of Dr. Caligari* (1919)

and Stress) preached liberation from tyranny and the supremacy of the emotions. The greatest German literary figure, Johann Wolfgang von Goethe (1749–1832) was an adherent in the early days, but its most representative figure was his friend Friedrich Schiller (1759–1805), some of whose plays, including *Die Räuber (The Robbers)*, continued to upset dictatorial regimes well into the 20th century. Goethe used his enormous talent in many fields, but it is for his lyric poetry, his historical dramas, and above all his definitive rendering of the tale of Faust that he is most remembered. He is a universal figure, incorporating the wild Romanticism of *Storm and Stress* into the nobility and harmony of

they believed passionately in the accumulated wisdom expressed in folk songs and traditional stories.

Naturalism & realism
A wonderful writer of lyric poetry in a folk manner *(Die Loreley)*, Heinrich Heine (1797–1856) also wrote about the injustices and inequalities of his time. Heine wrote wittily about his travels in Germany, and sensitivity to place and landscape was a prominent theme in later 19th-century literature. No one has evoked the scenery of Brandenburg and the Baltic provinces so tellingly as the novelist Theodor Fontane (1819–1898), particularly in his masterpiece *Effi Briest,* which tells the story

of an ill-fated marriage. *Der Schimmelreiter (The Rider on the White Horse)* by Theodor Storm (1817–1888) is compulsory reading for visitors to the coastline of Schleswig-Holstein. A critical social realism pervades plays such as *Die Weber (The Weavers)* by Gerhart Hauptmann (1862–1946).

Twentieth century

In the novels of Thomas Mann (1875–1955), the currents of the changing times throughout his life are reflected in the fate of the individual. *Buddenbrooks* (1901) is a chronicle of decaying upper-middle-class life in Lübeck, while half a century later, his *Doktor Faustus* deals with the agonies of the Hitler era. Thomas Mann's brother, Heinrich (1871–1950), is best known for his portrait in *Der Untertan (Man of Straw)* of the spiritual emptiness of a typical citizen of the Second Reich; his *Professor Unrat* formed the basis of the film *Blue Angel*. A very different perspective on the perils of the 20th century was offered by the Prague German writer Franz Kafka (1883–1924), with his nightmarish short stories and novels such as *Der Prozess (The Trial)*. A German tendency to blindly obey authority was well satirized in *Der Hauptmann von Köpenick* by Carl Zuckmayr (1896–1977), in which a complete nobody gets everyone to do his bidding by donning Prussian uniform and issuing orders.

Works dealing with the great issues of the 20th century have come from writers such as Günther Grass, famous for his novel *Die Blechtrommel (The Tin Drum)* of 1959, and Rolf Hochhuth with his play *Der Stellvertreter (The Representative)* of 1963, which questioned the ambivalent role of the papacy in World War II. The most internationally acclaimed dramatist remains Bertolt Brecht (1898–1956), who established the prestigious Berliner Ensemble theater. Grass and writers such as the Nobel Prize winner Heinrich Böll (1917–1985) strove to keep moral issues alive in West Germany. A similar role was played in the East by writers Christa Wolf (1929–) and Stefan Heym (1913–), who at the age of 81 entered the parliament of united Germany as its oldest member.

CINEMA

German cinema enjoyed a golden age in the the 1920s and early '30s, when the Ufa Studios in Babelsberg (part of Potsdam) made films that were not only commercial successes but high points of cinematic art and technique. As early as 1919, Robert Wiene directed *The Cabinet of Dr. Caligari*, a silent film using expressionist devices (unusual camera angles, dramatic contrasts of light and shadow, stylized sets) to tell a tale of madness and murder. In his *Dr. Mabuse* films, Fritz Lang created a monstrous figure bent on world domination. His *Metropolis* of 1926, an evocation of the horrors of the future city, put the science fiction film on a sound footing, just as F. W. Murnau's *Nosferatu* of 1921 established the vampire film genre. Erich Pommer's *Blue Angel* of 1930 was shot in English as well as German and made an instant star of Marlene Dietrich.

Ufa had originally been established by the German High Command as a propaganda machine in World War I. The cinema again became a propaganda tool after 1933, when Josef Goebbels used it to excite, entertain, and misinform the masses. Leni Riefenstahl's documentaries on the Nazi Party's Nuremberg Rally of 1934 and the Berlin Olympics of 1936 turned these into enthralling spectacles. Even in the last days of the Third Reich, resources were found to make the historical epic *Kolberg*, premiered in a Wehrmacht bunker in the besieged city of La Rochelle in January 1945.

Much of the film industry's talent (Dietrich, Wilder, Zinnemann) fled to Hollywood in the 1930s, and it was many years before German cinema regained a degree of international credibility. Wolfgang Staudte's *The Murderers Are among Us* of 1946 dealt with the aftermath of Nazi rule, but the characteristic genre of West German cinema were so-called *Heimat* ("homeland") movies, romantic comedies in nostalgic rural settings. From the 1960s, inspired by the French *nouvelle vague*, young German directors saved the German cinema from banality, and films by Werner Herzog (*Young Törless*, 1966), Volker Schlöndorff (*The Lost Honor of Katharina Blum*, 1975, and *The Tin Drum*, 1979), Rainer Werner Fassbinder (*The Marriage of Maria Braun*, 1978), and Wim Wenders (*Paris, Texas*, 1984) achieved international recognition. Edgar Reitz attempted to reclaim the concept of *Heimat* with his 1984 TV epic of that title, which won millions of viewers in Germany and abroad. ∎

Nowhere is the spirit of reunited Germany more vibrant than in Berlin, rapidly reclaiming its place as one of Europe's great capital cities. In the surrounding *Land* of Brandenburg, the palaces of royal Potsdam are the jewels.

Berlin & Brandenburg

**Spike-helmeted
Berlin bandsman**

Berlin & Brandenburg

LIKE THE REST OF GERMANY, BERLIN WAS DIVIDED FROM 1949 TO 1990 INTO East and West. While East Berlin proclaimed itself capital of the German Democratic Republic, West Berlin was a kind of island state, linked by air and strictly guarded land corridors to West Germany, and kept alive by massive subsidies. Since 1990, the capital once more of a united country, Berlin has recovered a proper relationship with its natural hinterland, the towns and countryside of the region now known as the *Land* of Brandenburg. Nevertheless, fearful of domination by the metropolis, in 1996 the people of Brandenburg forcefully rejected a proposal that would unite Brandenburg with Berlin, and elected to stay a separate entity.

It was the glaciers and meltwater channels of the Ice Age that formed the landscape shared by Berlin and Brandenburg. Water is everywhere, in the form of lakes, streams, and sluggish rivers, as well as the great canals that link Berlin to the rest of the country. There are few hills, some of the most prominent being those made from the heaped-up rubble cleared in the postwar period from the devastated capital. Great forests of pine and oak grow on the

Berlin bear with his organ grinder

sandy, infertile soils that cover much of the area; one of the most extensive woodlands is the Grunewald, western Berlin's green lung. Brandenburg's countryside has its own sweet and melancholy charm; between Berlin and Potsdam, the banks of the broad River Havel were transformed by generations of gardeners and architects and their royal masters into a kind of "Prussian Arcadia," a regional landscape of such outstanding beauty that in 1990 it was awarded World Heritage status by UNESCO.

This is indeed the heartland of Prussia. Brandenburg was originally the *Mark,* the border territory seized from its Slav inhabitants as the German eastward movement began in the tenth century. From this core grew a principality, then a kingdom, ruled for 500 years by the Hohenzollern dynasty who built themselves splendid residences at both Berlin and Potsdam. As Berlin grew into a great metropolis in the late 19th and early 20th centuries, it drew in people from all over Germany and beyond, molding them into characteristic big-city dwellers, quick-witted, with their own acerbic sense of humor and a dislike of being pushed around. Brandenburgers, by contrast, are held to be loyal, rather slow moving, and essentially reliable. Their region tends to be ignored in the rush to get to the excitements of the capital, yet the superlative palaces and parks of Potsdam are only some of the region's multitude of attractions. ■

Putli

Karstädt

NATURPARK
BRANDENBURGISCHE
ELBTALAUE

Perleberg

Wittenber

Bad
Wilsna

LOWER SAXONY

p. 125

△
A

Area of map detail

Berlin

0   50 kilometers
0   30 miles

◁ 5

MECKLENBURG-WEST POMERANIA
p. 87

A24 Meyenburg
Pritzwalk
Wittstock
Schönebeck   Rheinsberg
A19
A24
E26
Kyritz   Neuruppin
Bückwitz   Herzberg
167
Ruppinersee
E55
Rhinow   Kremmen
Briesen   Oranienburg
Pessin   Hennigsdorf
Rathenow   Nauen   Falkensee
Premnitz
Plaue
Brandenburg   Potsdam
Ziesar   Golzow
A2   E30
Beelitz   Mittenwalde
Görzke   Belzig   A9   Treuenbrietzen
Wiesenburg
Marzahna   Jüterbog
SAXONY-ANHALT
p. 211   Dahme
Brandis
Schlieben
Herzberg
Falkenberg
Bad Liebenwerda
Elsterwerda

Prenzlau
A20
Unterückersee
Ravensbrück   Hassleben   Gartz
Fürstenberg   Gramzow
Oberückersee   NATIONALPARK UNTERES ODERTAL
Templin   A11
Gransee   Schwedt
Zehdenick   Joachimsthal   Angermünde
Löwenberg   Werbellinsee
Liebenwalde   Kloster Chorin   POLAND   ◁ 4
E251   Eberswalde
A11   Bad Freienwalde
E28   Wriezen
Birkenwerder   Tiefensee
Bernau
BERLIN   Prötzel
Olympiastadion   Strausberg
120m   Neuenhagen   Seelow   Manschnow
Teufelsberg   BERLIN   Müncheberg
Schloss   Jagdschloss   Rüdersdorf
Sanssouci   Grunewald   A10
Wannsee   Eichwalde   Fürstenwalde   Frankfurt an der Oder   ◁ 3
Königs   A12   E30
A10   Rangsdorf   Wusterhausen   Storkow   Müllrose
Zossen   Scharmützelsee
Trebbin   Beeskow   Eisenhüttenstadt
Baruth   Märkisch Buchholz   246
A13   Heide   Schwielochsee   Lieberose   112
Golssen   Spreewald
Lübben   Guben
BIOSPHÄRENRESERVAT   ◁ 2
Luckau   SPREEWALD   Peitz
Lübbenau   Spreewald Museum
Calau   Vetschau
Cottbus
E36   Schloss Branitz   Forst
A13   A15
Drebkau
Doberlug-   E55
Kirchhain   Finsterwalde   Grossräschen
Senftenberg   Spremberg
Lauchhammer   Schwarze Pumze
Ruhland   SAXONY   ◁ 1
p. 227

B   C   D   E

Berlin

Berlin air—*Berliner Luft*—is supposed to be especially exhilarating, possibly because 30 percent of the city is devoted to green space. These days, the refreshing aura might also come from the sense that the rapidly developing capital, having survived the trauma of Cold War division, is on its way to becoming the focal point of a 21st-century Europe—one that has absorbed reunited Germany and is welcoming the post-communist countries of the East.

Berlin is a big city, less in terms of its population—half that of London or Paris—than in its area of nearly 560 square miles (900 sq km). A good way to learn its layout, and see how various points of interest are linked, is to use the excellent transportation system.

Board the No. 100 double-decker bus at Bahnhof Zoo and you start in the center of what was West Berlin, with its fashionable shops and prestigious residential quarters. The bus heads east through the greenery of the Tiergarten, the old royal hunting park, skirting

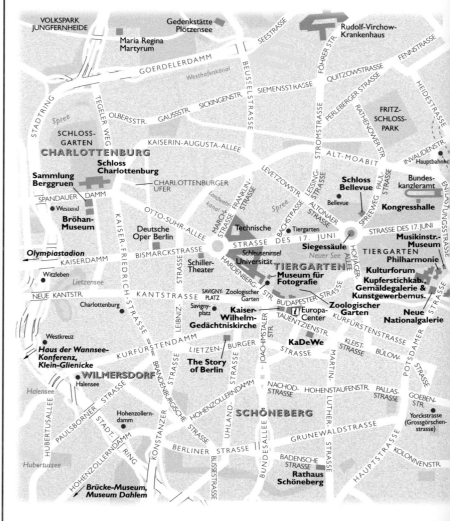

the Reichstag and the burgeoning new government quarter. To the south you get a glimpse of the sparkling modern structures around Potsdamer Platz, reviving an area that was left divided and derelict by the building of the Berlin Wall. The nearby Forum of Culture groups world-class modern museums, galleries, and concert halls.

Beyond the Brandenburg Gate, the bus enters what was East Berlin, the historic core of the city. Although a good deal of its heritage was destroyed by bombing and the advance of the Red Army in 1945, much was preserved and restored, even under communism—which left its mark in the shape of the tall TV tower, the Fernsehturm, the bleak spaces of

Alexanderplatz, and the monumental boulevard of Karl-Marx-Allee.

Beyond the city center is a ring of semi-independent boroughs. Kreuzberg has a heady mix of Turkish immigrants and alternative lifestylers, although its role as trendsetter in inner-city living seems to have been taken over by Prenzlauer Berg. Schöneberg and Tempelhof keep memories of the airlift (see p. 32) and Cold War alive, while Charlottenburg has the boulevard of the Kurfürstendamm and its own restored Schloss and museum district. To the west, the prestigious residential areas of Wilmersdorf and Zehlendorf extend into the belt of forests, lakes, and parkland linking Berlin with Potsdam. ■

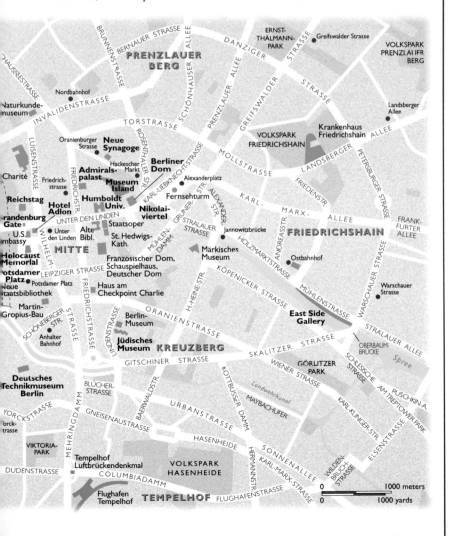

The Reichstag

SINCE IT REOPENED IN 1999, THE MASSIVE REICHSTAG
building has regained its role as the seat of the Bundestag, Germany's
parliament, and, crowned by British architect Sir Norman Foster's
glittering steel-and-glass cupola, it has become a powerful symbol of
the country's unity. Designed to express the openness of the political
process and to be welcoming to the public, it attracted more than
three million visitors in the first year of its reopening.

**Deutscher
Bundestag
(Reichstag)**
www.bundestag.de

- Map p. 53
- Platz der Republik 1
- 030 227 3 21 52
- Bus: 100

Imperial Germany had been united
for more than 20 years before its
parliament building was finally
completed in 1894, its every detail
watched over jealously by Kaiser
Wilhelm II, no great friend of
parliamentary democracy. Even so,
the great neo-Renaissance building
failed to gain his approval. He
called it "the height of tastelessness"

and characterized the activity that
went on inside as "the monkey-
house." The Reichstag had its
revenge; in November 1918 it was
from here that the end of the
Hohenzollern dynasty was
announced and the German
Republic proclaimed.

In 1933 the building was set on
fire and partially burned out; the

Members debate the issues of the day in the Bundestag's main chamber.

ostensible culprit, a feeble-minded Dutchman, was sentenced to death, but Hitler's storm troopers may well have been the real perpetrators. In any event, the Reichstag Fire was used by the Nazi regime as an excuse to terrorize and imprison its opponents, among them many parliamentary deputies.

As the Red Army fought its way into Berlin in April 1945, the Reichstag became a fortress, its formidable walls standing up to all but the heaviest artillery fire. But it was stormed on April 30, and the raising of the hammer and sickle banner over its gaping roof yielded one of the most unforgettable photographic images of World War II.

In the postwar period, the area in front of the ruined Reichstag remained a focus for mass demonstrations of all kinds. In 1948, as the Soviet blockade of Berlin began (see p. 32), it was here that a huge crowd assembled to hear the mayor, Ernst Reuter, hurl an eloquent appeal to the people of the free world to "Look on this city—*Schaut auf diese Stadt*—and know that it and its people must not be abandoned!" Berlin was not abandoned, but the construction of the Wall in 1961 immediately to the east of the Reichstag cut off the great building from the city center. In the 1970s, the interior was made usable again, although Soviet pressure meant that it could not host sessions of the West German parliament. Instead, it housed an exhibition, "Questions to German History," a compulsory stop for school parties from the West.

With reunification accomplished, not everyone wanted the seat of government moved back to Berlin, and not everyone wanted to revive the Reichstag. Its isolated, ponderous mass of darkened stone seemed too heavily symbolic of the darker aspects of German history.

But the Bulgarian environmental sculptor Christo's "Reichstag Wrapping" of 1995 (he encased the building in silver plastic sheeting) transformed people's perceptions of it. Cleaned, reconstructed, thrown open to the people, and with its workings made visible, it now seems the only possible choice.

Visits are popular, so avoid the lines by getting here early. An elevator takes you to the viewing terrace in the dome and from a spiral ramp you can gaze down on the parliamentary chamber below, and enjoy the superlative views over the city.

NEW GOVERNMENT QUARTER

Foster may have breathed new life into an old building, but Berlin

Right: The ceremonial entrance to the Bundeskanzleramt (Office of the Federal Chancellor), in the heart of Berlin's new government quarter

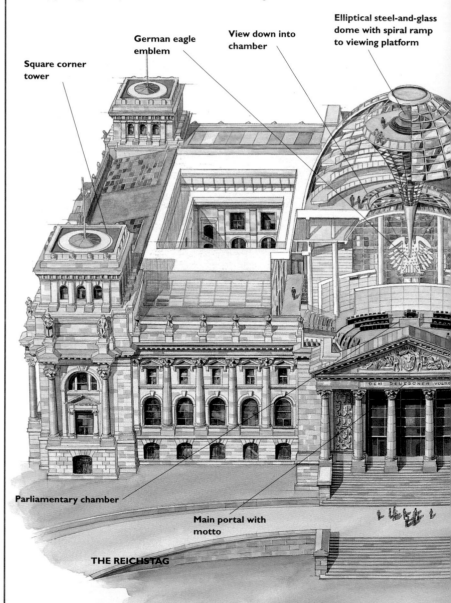

Square corner tower

German eagle emblem

View down into chamber

Elliptical steel-and-glass dome with spiral ramp to viewing platform

DEM DEUTSCHEN VOLKE

Parliamentary chamber

Main portal with motto

THE REICHSTAG

Internal courtyard

Rusticated pedestal facade

architects Charlotte Frank and Axel Schultes have remodeled an entire tract of the city around the Reichstag to make a setting for the whole business of modern government. A ribbon of new buildings cuts across the base of a meander in the River Spree, then boldly leaps the river itself into what was East Berlin, providing accommodations for deputies, their staff, and government employees. The most prominent single building is the Bundeskanzleramt, the Federal Chancellor's Office, completed in early 2001 and now occupied by Angela Merkel. Farther to the west, the Spree was redirected to create room for a splendid new central railroad station. Unveiled in 2006, this cathedral-like marvel of German engineering was constructed in a gentle bend so that each of its 9,000 glass panels had to be cut individually. Suburban, long-distance, and underground trains cross at three levels, and a north-south tunnel beginning here emerges much further south, near the shiny complexes around Potsdamer Platz. ■

Brandenburg Gate & Unter den Linden

RIGHT ON THE FAULT LINE BETWEEN EAST AND WEST
during the decades of the Cold War, the Brandenburg Gate
(Brandenburger Tor) was recognized the world over as the most
potent symbol of the division of Germany and its capital city. In
October 1990, it gained new meaning as a backdrop to scenes of joy
as countless thousands celebrated the country's newfound unity.

Brandenburg Gate
🅼 Map p. 53

**Memorial to the
Murdered Jews of
Europe**
🅼 Map p. 53
✉ Cora-Berliner-Strasse
1
☎ 030 26 39 43 36
🕐 Open daily
💲 Free

Inspired by the Propylaea on the
Acropolis in Athens, the gateway
with its sextet of Doric columns on
each side was completed in 1791. It
marks the boundary between the
historic core of the city to the east
and the old royal hunting preserve
of the Tiergarten to the west. None
but the Kaiser and his family were
allowed to pass through the central
opening. Crowning the gate is the
Quadriga, a chariot drawn by four
horses and driven by the goddess of
Victory. She survived being carried
off to Paris by Napoleon, but fell victim to the bombardments of World
War II. Luckily a plaster cast had
been made, and she was replaced

in 1958 in a rare act of cooperation between East and West.

South of the Brandenburg Gate stands the sobering **Memorial to the Murdered Jews In Europe**. This field of 2,700 granite slabs, each one unsettlingly askew, is the work of American architect Peter Eisenman, unveiled in 2005 on the former site of Hitler's chancellery. A rear ramp descends to an information center with labels in English and German.

The linden trees and carriageways of **Unter den Linden,** central Berlin's most prestigious thoroughfare, run for more than half a mile from Pariser Platz by the Brandenburg Gate in the west to Museum Island (see pp. 62–67) in the east. Over the centuries, Prussian kings converted what had been a dusty track leading to the countryside into a grand avenue lined with splendid structures. The storied **Hotel Adlon** on the south side of Pariser Platz is a remake of one of Berlin's great traditional hotels, for long a kind of neutral meeting place for foreign diplomats.

The truly monumental part of the Linden begins on the far side of Friedrichstrasse, with great institutions such as the **Humboldt University** (to the left) and the magnificent trio of buildings (Old Library/Alte Bibliothek, St. Hedwig's Cathedral, and State Opera) defining the **Forum Fredericianum** or **Bebelplatz** (to the right). In the middle of the street is a fine equestrian statue of Frederick the Great. Next to the university stands a small but perfect neoclassic temple, the **New Guardhouse** (Neue Wache), an early work by Karl Friedrich Schinkel (1781–1841), venerated as the greatest of all Prussian architects. It is now a memorial to victims of war and tyranny. The imposing building beside it is the baroque **Arsenal** (Zeughaus), which has been restored to house the German Historical Museum. ■

Floodlighting enhances the Brandenburg Gate's grandeur.

PLACE-NAMES

These German words often occur in place-names:

Berg mountain
Burg castle, fortress
Meer sea or lake
Palast palace
Platz square
Rathaus town hall
Schloss may be a castle, a palace, or a grand country house
See lake
Tor gate

A walk through Red Berlin

Taking in some of the key sites of Cold War history, this walk reveals how the old center of Berlin, from the Brandenburg Gate in the west to Alexanderplatz in the east, was marked by more than four decades of communist rule.

The walk starts a few hundred yards west of the Brandenburg Gate (Brandenburger Tor), at the **Soviet War Memorial** (Sowjetisches Ehrenmal) **①**, built from marble and granite taken from Hitler's Chancellery headquarters. A brace of T34 tanks, supposedly the first to break into the city in April 1945, flanks a colonnade dominated by the dignified figure of a Red Army soldier. More than 20,000 Soviet servicemen perished in the battle for Berlin. Until the fall of the Wall in 1989, the memorial was a kind of enclave in West Berlin, guarded for two hours at a time by Red Army soldiers.

Before passing through the Brandenburg Gate (see pp. 58–59), veer south to see the **Memorial to the Murdered Jews of Europe ②**. The undulating lines of dull granite blocks evoke the pre-communist World War II horror that is both individual and collective. Back on Unter den Linden, pause at the corner of Friedrichstrasse. To the north, the overpass carries the tracks of the S-Bahn, which was one of the few ways in which visitors could pass from East to West. **Friedrichstrasse Train Station** (Bahnhof) **③** was a dingy place of poignant arrivals and partings, its customs hall known as the Palace of Tears (Tränenpalast).

Turn right and walk south along Friedrichstrasse. The building boom of the 1990s has given back the long straight street something of its prewar bustle after the German Democratic Republic (GDR) rulers' neglect. A cornucopia of consumer goods unimaginable to communist shoppers is available in the fine arcades and in great stores such as the Berlin branch of Paris's Galeries Lafayette. **Checkpoint Charlie,** farther down Friedrichstrasse, is the world-famous crossing point where American and Soviet tank crews eyeballed each other as the Wall went up. The crowded exhibits in the museum of the **Haus am Checkpoint Charlie ④** (*Friedrichstrasse 44, tel 030 253 72 50*) tell the story of the Wall.

Go back up Friedrichstrasse and turn right along Mohrenstrasse into the

Gendarmenmarkt ⑤. With its three dominant structures of Theater (Schauspielhaus), German Cathedral (Deutscher Dom), and French Cathedral (Französischer Dom), this is perhaps the finest classical square in Berlin. Cross Französische Strasse and Behrenstrasse into **Bebelplatz,** the square flanked by St. Hedwig's Cathedral (St. Hedwigs-Kathedrale), the Old Library (Alte Bibliothek), and the Opera (Deutsche Staatsoper). A memorial recalls that this is the spot where, on May 10, 1933, the Nazis organized their book-burning ceremony, beginning with the works of Karl Marx.

Walk eastward over the bridge into Domplatz, the grassy square bordered by the enormous **Berliner Dom ⑥** (*see p. 78*). Taller than St. Paul's in London, the cathedral

holds the remains of the royal Hohenzollerns and somehow survived communist efforts to erase the monarchical past. On nearby Schlossplatz stood the Palast der Republik, the GDR's parliament-cum-social center that has been razed to make way for a replica of a Prussian palace.

Beyond the bridge over the River Spree lies the heart of what was intended to be the showpiece Socialist metropolis of "Berlin, Capital of the GDR." The immense scale of the area is hardly relieved by the presence of one or two surviving old buildings such as the Marienkirche and the **Rotes Rathaus** ❼. The "Red City Hall" got its name, not from the politics inside, but from its skin of warm red brick. In the center of this area are surprisingly modest bronze figures of Marx and Engels. The dominant structure is the 1,197-foot-high (365 m) **TV Tower** (Fernsehturm) ❽, completed in 1969 and nicknamed the "Pope's Revenge" because of the crosslike reflection that appears when the sun shines on its top.

Beyond the overhead railway tracks is

Alexanderplatz ❾, a focal point for eastern Berliners. On the square's eastern side, on a 1960s building called the House of the Teacher (Haus des Lehrers), a mural painted in Social Realist style proclaims the merits of Marxism. Beyond it, miles of Stalinist neoclassic facades stretch along the Karl-Marx-Allee, the "First Socialist Boulevard." ■

🗺 Also see map pp. 52–53
➤ Soviet War Memorial/ Sowjetisches Ehrenmal
↔ 3 miles (5 km)
🕐 Half a day
➤ Alexanderplatz

NOT TO BE MISSED
- Memorial to the Murdered Jews of Europe
- Haus am Checkpoint Charlie
- Gendarmenmarkt
- TV Tower (Fernsehturm)
- Alexanderplatz

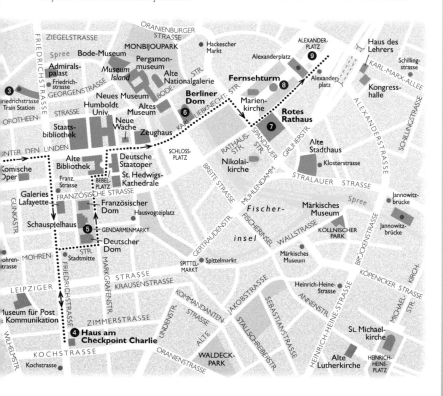

The Pergamon
Museum houses
such great ancient
monuments as
Babylon's Ishtar
Gate.

Museum Island
www.smb.museum
🅰 Maps pp. 53 & 61

Old Museum
www.smb.spk-berlin.de/
🅰 Map p. 61
✉ Lustgarten
☎ 030 20 90 55 77
🕐 Closed Mon.
💲 $$$
🚇 U-Bahn/S-Bahn:
   Friedrichstrasse or
   S Hackescher Markt,
   Bus: 100

Museum Island

SOMETIMES CALLED THE "PRUSSIAN ACROPOLIS" AND NOW a World Heritage site, Berlin's central complex of five museums on Museum Island (Museumsinsel) occupies the northern tip of the island in the River Spree. Nineteenth-century Germans were pioneer archaeologists and antiquarians who unearthed the heritage of the ancient world. The incomparable spoils they brought home include the Pergamon Altar and Babylon's Ishtar Gate.

Many of the island's buildings suffered severe damage during World War II, followed by neglect under communism. An ambitious and extremely expensive master plan is underway, aimed at restoring the built fabric and reassembling in this key location many of the city's treasures. If all goes well the project, including a fancy new visitors' center and an underground passageway connecting all the museums, will be completed in 2009.

OLD MUSEUM
Prussia's royal architect, Karl Friedrich Schinkel (see p. 38), considered the Old Museum (Altes Museum) his finest work. The long

Above right: The painted limestone bust of Nefertiti, discovered in 1912, will be housed and displayed in the Old Museum until the New Museum opens in 2009.

Old National Gallery

- Map p. 61
- Bodestrasse 1–3
- 030 20 90 55 77
- Closed Mon.
- $$$
- U-Bahn/S-Bahn: Friedrichstrasse or S Hackescher Markt, Bus: 100

colonnaded facade of his neoclassic temple, which looks south to where the royal Schloss once stood, symbolized the high cultural aspirations of the Prussian State (see p. 28). On completion in 1830, it was one of the world's first public museums. The central feature, inspired by the Pantheon in Rome, is a harmonious rotunda lined with classical statues. Even if time is short, be sure not to miss the lovely figure known as the "Praying Boy" ("Der betende Knabe"), created by an unknown sculptor on the island of Rhodes circa late 300 B.C.

Beyond the Old Museum is the **New Museum** (Neues Museum), erected in the 19th century to keep up with the Prussians' buying sprees of historic artifacts.

When the restored building is unveiled in 2009, visitors will be able to see two fabulously ornate courtyards in Greek and Egyptian style, as well as treasures going back to the dawn of civilization. But ancient Egypt remains the star turn, most notably for its array of papyrus texts and the celebrated bust of Queen Nefertiti dating from 1340 B.C. In the interim, some of the finds are displayed in the Old Museum.

OLD NATIONAL GALLERY

The Alte Nationalgalerie vies with the Altes Museum in proclaiming Germany's love of culture and determination to display its devotion in as imposing a setting as possible. Completed in 1876, it, too, is a neoclassic temple, though

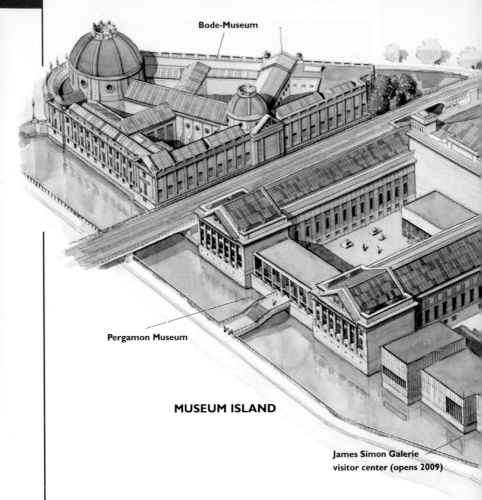

Bode-Museum

Pergamon Museum

MUSEUM ISLAND

James Simon Galerie
visitor center (opens 2009)

of a very different kind. It is raised on a substantial podium and approached via a double stairway. After a building and refurbishment program lasting three years and costing 68 million euros (67 million dollars), the Alte Nationalgalerie now forms a magnificent home for 19th-century German art.

The gallery is easily the best place to admire the country's particular contribution to Romanticism; there are no fewer than two dozen works by Caspar David Friedrich (1774–1840), including his atmospheric "Monk by the Sea" and "The Lonely Tree." Here, too, are paintings by the versatile Karl Friedrich Schinkel (1781–1841), visionary architectural depictions of an idealized classical or Gothic world.

Most of the other great German artists of the century are represented: Philipp Otto Runge's intensely realized portraits; Carl Spitzweg's humorous evocations of placid small-town life; and, in contrast, Adolph Menzel's hymn to the country's burgeoning heavy industry, "The Rolling Mill." Works by late 19th-century painters such

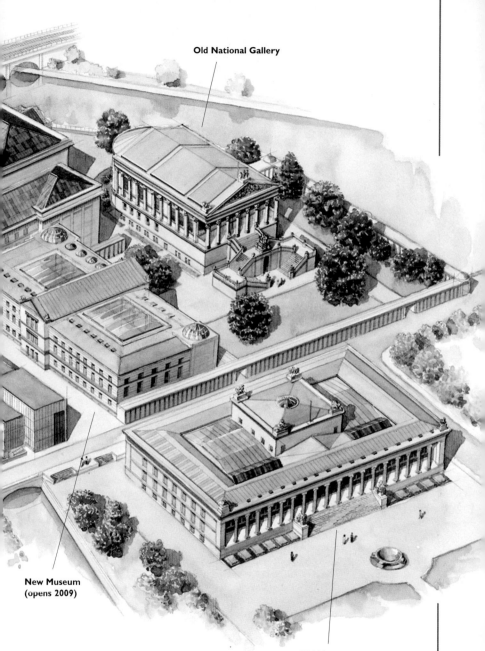

Old National Gallery

New Museum
(opens 2009)

Old Museum

as Max Liebermann and Lovis Corinth bear comparison with their French Impressionist contemporaries—Monet, Renoir, Degas, and Cézanne.

PERGAMON MUSEUM

No rival to Schinkel's masterpiece in architectural terms, the Pergamon Museum was built between 1912 and 1930 specifically to house the reconstructed second-century altar from the Greek city of Pergamon in Asia Minor, now Turkey, but its collections of antiquities from the ancient world are almost inexhaustible. The first artifacts were gathered by the Electors of Brandenburg as far back as 1698, although the displays were made accessible to the public only in the 19th century. The scale of the

Pergamon Altar is overwhelming, and the sculpture of its frieze depicting the struggle of gods and giants extraordinarily expressive. Almost equal in impact is the **market gateway,** dating from the second century A.D., from the city of Miletus. Largest of all, the mighty Ishtar Gate from Babylon, with its processional way, is adorned with glazed bricks and figures of bulls and dragons. An imposing remnant of an 8th-century desert palace, the Mshatta Facade was a gift from the Ottoman Empire to Wilhelm II, and today forms the centerpiece of a permanent exhibition of Islamic art.

BODE-MUSEUM

Separated from the Pergamon Museum by the tracks of the ele-

Pergamon Museum

- Map p. 61
- Am Kupfergraben
- 030 20 90 55 77
- Closed Mon.
- $$$
- U-Bahn/S-Bahn: Friedrichstrasse, S Hackescher Markt, Bus: 100

vated S-Bahn, the Bode-Museum is a superb neo-baroque edifice dating from 1904. Its clever design with a dome and rounded elevation enhances the promontory between the two arms of the Spree. Originally called the Kaiser-Friedrich-Museum, its present name honors Wilhelm von Bode, its founder and the great director of the Prussian State Museums in the early 20th century. A total refurbishment was completed in late 2006, providing much-needed space for several of the museum's prime collections.

The **Coin Collection** (Münzkabinett) includes coins—several thousand of them—banknotes, seals and medals, minting equipment, and an array of objects used for exchange and barter by people who did not use metal coinage.

An outstanding sculpture collection, ranging from the Middle Ages to the 18th century, contains both Italian and German masterpieces. Highlights here include works by the talented court sculptor Tilman Riemenschneider, whose works include *Noli me tangere* ('Touch me not'), a meticulously carved relief of Christ appearing before Mary Magdalene. The **Byzantine Art Museum** (Museum für Spätantike und Byzantinische Kunst) will also move here, showing sculpture, textiles, ceramics, and paintings from Italy, Greece, the Near East, and the Balkans, plus a collection of religious icons dating from the 14th to the 19th centuries. ∎

The huge Greek altar brought from Pergamon in Asia Minor (now part of Turkey) looms at the core of the Pergamon Museum.

Bode-Museum
- Map p. 61
- Am Kupfergraben
- 030 20 90 55 77
- Closed Mon.
- $$$
- U-Bahn/S-Bahn: Friedrichstrasse, S Hackescher Markt, Bus: 100

Kulturforum

WHEN, IN THE 1950s, THE CITY'S DIVISION LOOKED PER-
manent, the city fathers of West Berlin decided to implement the idea
of a major cultural center on wasteland by the southeastern corner
of the Tiergarten. It was hoped the Kulturforum could form a link in
an eventual East–West cultural axis that would help bring the city
together on reunification. This ambition has yet to be achieved: The
Kulturforum still feels like a collection of individual buildings well off
the beaten track. But for visitors with the slightest interest in the arts
it has become an essential destination.

The first structure to take shape
was a new home for the Berlin
Philharmonic Orchestra, directed
by Herbert von Karajan from 1954
to 1989. Designed by the city's
architect-in-chief, Hans Scharoun,
the asymmetrical, tentlike
Philharmonie was opened in
time for the Berlin Festival of 1963.
Book tickets for a concert as far in
advance as you can. Scharoun also
drew up the plans for the
Musikinstrumenten-Museum
next door, where the superlative
collection of about 3,000 musical
instruments dates back to the
16th century.

Opposite the Philharmonie, a
sloping plaza leads to a complex of
bunkerlike buildings with a vast
foyer shared by several museums.
There's the **Kupferstichkabinett**
with an outstanding collection of
prints and drawings, and the
Kunstgewerbemuseum,
covering the decorative arts from
the Middle Ages to art nouveau, art
deco, and beyond. However, most
visitors come here principally for
the **Gemäldegalerie,** containing
some of the world's great old master
paintings. About 1,000 are on display
in the main part of the gallery. How
to choose between Botticelli, Titian,

**Above: The
strange exterior
of Scharoun's
Philharmonie
Above left: The
Gemäldegalerie
offers perfect
conditions for
viewing old
master paintings.**

**Musikinstrumenten
-Museum**

🄰 Map p. 52

✉ Tiergartenstrasse 1

☎ 030 25 48 11 78

🕑 Closed Mon.

🅂 $

🚇 U-Bahn/S-Bahn:
Potsdamer Platz,
Bus: 129, 148, 200
248, 341, 348

Raphael, Caravaggio, Claude Lorrain, and Poussin; Rembrandt, Rubens, Breughel, and Franz Hals; Gainsborough and Reynolds? One way would be to concentrate on the galleries of German greats: Dürer ("Portrait of Hieronymous Holzschuher"), Cranach the Elder ("Fountain of Youth"), Baldung Grien ("Crucifixion"), and Holbein the Younger ("Portrait of the Merchant Georg Gisze") give an idea of the range of German painting in the 13th to 16th centuries. Or you could spend a whole day here, taking frequent breaks in the coffee shop and excellent cafeteria.

Leave time to walk the short distance past the delicately detailed 19th-century brick **Church of St. Matthew** on the way to the **New National Gallery** (Neue National-galerie). Designed by one-time Bauhaus director Ludwig Mies van der Rohe, this steel-and-glass gallery has one of the best collections anywhere of 20th-century German art.

Most of the modern German masters are well represented, including Kirchner and other expressionists. Compare his "Potsdamer Platz" (1914) with the real thing just outside the gallery. Klee and Kandinsky, both teachers of the Bauhaus school, are exhibited here, as well as surrealists including Ernst, and the searing social commentators Dix and Grosz. In addition, there are pictures by their foreign contemporaries—Magritte, de Chirico, Dalí, and Picasso—as well as by Americans such as Rauschenberg and Lichtenstein. ■

Gemäldegalerie (& other Kulturforum museums)
www.smb.museum
🅰 Map p. 52
✉ Stauffenbergstr. 40
☎ 030 266 29 51
🕐 Closed Mon.
💲 $$

New National Gallery
🅰 Map p. 52
✉ Am Kulturforum, Potsdamer Strasse 50
☎ 030 266 29 51
🕐 Closed Mon.
💲 $

Central-western Berlin

Central-western Berlin
🅰 Map p. 52

RUNNING FOR 2 MILES (3.5 KM) FROM THE HEART OF WEST Berlin toward the countrified suburbs around the Grunewald, the boulevard of the Kurfürstendamm is still the city's liveliest shopping street and the place to see and be seen. In contrast, Berlin's great central park, the Tiergarten, is somewhere to relax. This former royal hunting park is now a much-appreciated public place, where you can find seclusion, or where families set up a Sunday barbecue.

Battered by war, Berlin's great landmark, the Kaiser-Wilhelm-Gedächtniskirche, still stands.

Long ago the "Ku'damm" was the route taken by princes and kings to their hunting lodge in the "Green Wood" (see p. 74), but in its present form it dates from the 1870s, when Bismarck ordered a Parisian-style grand avenue to be laid out. At its eastern end stands the **Kaiser-**

Wilhelm-Gedächtniskirche (*Breitscheidplatz, tel 030 218 50 23*), completed in 1895 to honor the first emperor of newly united Germany. In 1943 the church was almost completely destroyed in a bombing raid; a new belfry and church were erected around the shell of the old tower, known to sardonic Berliners as the "hollow tooth."

Breitscheidplatz around the church is one of the busiest spots in Berlin, with constant traffic and a mixed population of punks, skateboarders, and all sorts of idlers. Inside the new octagonal church, however, all is tranquil; calming light filters through the honeycomb of double-glazed stained glass, its deep blue shot with intense flashes of other colors, and a golden figure of Christ hangs serenely over the scene. The square's eastern side is dominated by the 22-story tower of the **Europa-Center,** topped by the Mercedes star and built in the early 1960s as Berlin's first American-style shopping complex.

Farther east from the square along Tauentzienstrasse is a very different kind of retail experience. The **Kaufhaus des Westens** (*Wittenbergplatz*), known simply as KaDeWe, is one of the world's great department stores, opened in 1906. More shops extend westward along the Ku'damm, where the street's trademark showcases stand in the middle of the broad sidewalks, although more exclusive outlets have colonized the side streets.

West of Breitscheidplatz there are galleries and luxury shops on Fasanenstrasse, a street running south off the Kurfürstendam, while, just to the north, the area around **Savignyplatz** is particularly atmospheric, with restaurants, antique shops, and bookdealers. On Ku'damm Karree trace Berlin's convoluted history by immersing yourself in **The Story of Berlin.** Don a headset (English version available) and listen to the events of each period of the city's history as you walk through a series of historically themed rooms.

Busy **Zoo Railroad Station** (Bahnhof Zoo), just northwest of Breitscheidplatz, is the main point of arrival by train. In the 1970s it became synonymous with dinginess, drug dealing, and street crime, but subsequent face-lifts have made it more salubrious. The nearby **Zoologischer Garten** is one of the world's finest zoos, with some 15,000 animals and an aquarium.

The Zoo merges into the **Tiergarten,** which is bisected by Strasse des 17 Juni, the triumphal avenue widened in the 1930s to link the city center with the Olympic Stadium in the west. Other avenues join it at the roundabout dominated by the **Siegessäule,** the victory column originally erected in front of the Reichstag to commemorate victorious 19th-century Prussian campaigns, and moved here in 1939. One avenue leads northeastward toward the River Spree and **Schloss Bellevue,** a harmonious and relatively modest neoclassic palace, built in 1785 as a princely residence and now the official home of the German President.

Farther to the east, on the banks of the Spree, the **Kongresshalle** looms over the trees. It was built in 1955–57 by the United States, not just as a congress hall but as a symbol of progressive architecture and of the West's attachment to Berlin. In 1980 it suddenly collapsed, but reconstruction was successful. The building now serves as a multicultural meeting place, the **Haus der Kulturen der Welt** (*John-Foster-Dulles Allee 10, tel 030 39 78 70, closed Mon.*), with changing exhibitions on globally cultural themes. ■

The sculpture clock entertains shoppers in the Europa-Center.

The Story of Berlin
- Map p. 52
- Ku'damm-Karree, Kurfürstendamm 206–208
- 030 88 72 01 00
- $$$
- U-Bahn: Uhlandstrasse
  Bus: 109, 119, 129, 219, 249

Zoologischer Garten
- Map p. 52
- Hardenbergplatz 8
- 030 25 40 10
- $$$$ (zoo and aquarium)
- U-Bahn/S-Bahn: Zoologischer Garten

The Wall

During the 28 years of its existence, this most baleful symbol of the Cold War separated West Berlin from the eastern part of the city and from the GDR proper. By the time it crumbled in 1989, the 104-mile-long (155 km) Berlin Wall—called by its creators the "Anti-Fascist Protection Rampart"— had claimed the lives of at least a hundred would-be escapers. The first instinct of Berliners was to destroy the hated barrier. Few traces of it remain today.

Before 1961, there were no physical barriers to movement between the eastern and western parts of the city. West Berliners and tourists were free to move around East Berlin, where prices were low and an evening at the opera with Russian champagne in the interval could be enjoyed for the price of a cinema ticket in the West. Every day, more than 50,000 East Berliners commuted to well-paid jobs in the West. Far more serious, the economy of the GDR was slowly grinding to a halt as the country's labor force—particularly its more skilled members—voted with their feet by moving to the West.

By the summer of 1961, more than 3.4 million GDR citizens had decamped, and the regime had become desperate. On the night of August 13, all movement between East and West was halted, and, in an operation of military thoroughness, a temporary wall was thrown up, consisting in some sections of barbed wire, in others of crudely laid building blocks. Official reaction from the West was mostly verbal, although there was a standoff between

American and Soviet tanks at Checkpoint Charlie when GDR guards attempted to block Allied access to the East. The hastily laid initial barrier was succeeded by more sophisticated defenses. Eventually there was the west-facing Wall itself, a smooth-faced pale concrete structure 13 feet high (4 m), with a curved top offering no purchase for hands or grappling irons. Behind it came the "death strip" that not even the border guards were allowed to enter, an anti-vehicle ditch, a patrol track, trip-wires, a guard-dog run, tank traps, and then a further high fence. A total of 300 watchtowers with machine-gun openings and an array of bunkers provided cover for the border guards.

The Wall became a grisly attraction for Westerners. Platforms were erected so that visitors could peer over the top and catch a glimpse of East Berlin. Western graffiti artists found the smooth concrete an irresistible surface for their efforts. In 1989, when the Wall was demolished, the most prized souvenir fragments were those with the best graffiti. The longest intact section of the Wall, running for well over half a mile along the Spree in eastern Berlin, is the graffiti-covered so-called East Side Gallery, though this was decorated post-1989 by artists from around the world. Another section remains on Bernauer Strasse. The scene of last-minute escape attempts in 1961, this section is now a memorial to itself with a chapel and documentation center. ■

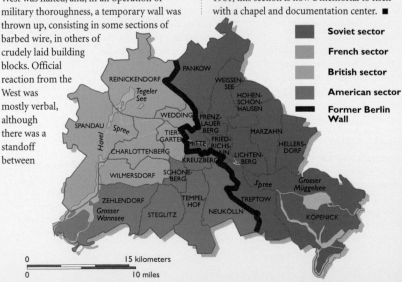

Soviet sector

French sector

British sector

American sector

Former Berlin Wall

PANKOW
REINICKENDORF
Tegeler See
WEISSEN-SEE
HOHEN-SCHÖN-HAUSEN
WEDDING
PRENZ-LAUER-BERG
SPANDAU
Spree
Havel
TIER-GARTEN
MITTE
FRIED-RICHS-HAIN
MARZAHN
HELLERS-DORF
CHARLOTTENBERG
KREUZBERG
LICHTEN-BERG
WILMERSDORF
SCHÖNE-BERG
Spree
Grosser Müggelsee
ZEHLENDORF
TEMPEL-HOF
TREPTOW
NEUKÖLLN
KÖPENICK
Grosser Wannsee
STEGLITZ

0   15 kilometers
0   10 miles

Above: Jubilant Berliners sit astride the hated symbol of Germany's division after the opening of the border in November 1989. Below: In its early days, the Wall was a rudimentary affair, as here on Stresemannstrasse in 1961.

Schloss
Charlottenburg
became a royal
residence of great
magnificence.

**Schloss
Charlottenburg**
www.spsg.de
- Map p. 52
- Spandauerdamm
  20–24
- 030 32 08 14 40
- Closed Mon.
- $ or $$$ incl.
  guided tour
- U-Bahn: Sophie-
  Charlotte-Platz,
  Richard-Wagner-
  Platz, S-Bahn:
  Westend, Bus: 109,
  145, 210, X21

**Sammlung
Berggruen**
- Schlossstrasse 1
- 030 32 69 58 15
- Closed Mon.
- $$
- See Schloss entry
  above

Charlottenburg

THE GRACEFUL TOWER OF SCHLOSS CHARLOTTENBURG IS
one of Berlin's landmarks, rising proudly over the western borough of
Charlottenburg and acting as a beacon for a group of first-rate
museums. The palace was severely damaged by bombing in World
War II, and could well have been completely demolished afterward.
However, following the 1950 destruction of the Schloss in the city
center by the East Berlin authorities (see pp. 60–61), the decision was
taken to restore Charlottenburg to its former royal glory.

The borough of Charlottenburg now
extends as far as the Tiergarten and
the Brandenburg Gate, but in the late
17th century this suburb of Berlin
was still deep in the countryside, and
a suitable site for a summer palace
for Sophie Charlotte, wife of Elector
Frederick, later Frederick I of
Prussia. She died in 1705, and
Frederick changed the palace's name
to Charlottenburg, in her memory.

The tone is set by the regal
entrance court, with its statue of
the Great Elector Frederick William
(1640–1688) on horseback. Behind
the palace's long facade, a succession of stunning interiors includes
the sumptuous **Chapel** with its

royal box, the glittering **Porcelain
Cabinet,** and the **Golden
Gallery,** with delicate rococo
decoration. Only the almost-too-
perfect state of some of the rooms
reminds you that many of them
were not simply restored but
reconstructed from scratch. Among
the paintings on display are masterworks by the French artist Antoine
Watteau, one of the favorite
painters of Frederick the Great.

The palace's west wing houses
the **Museum of Prehistory,** a
heterogenous collection of antiquities that will eventually be moved to
Museum Island in central Berlin
(see pp. 62–67).

Charlottenburg's extensive grounds are a favorite place for Berliners to stroll and relax. Like the palace itself, they show the development of taste, in this case from the formal symmetry of the baroque gardens close to the castle, to the Romantic, English-style landscape extending along the banks of the River Spree. Focal points in the park include the **Mausoleum,** the burial place of Queen Luise and her husband, Frederick William III; the **Belvedere,** with a collection of porcelain; and the **Schinkel-Pavillon,** an Italian-style villa designed by the Prussian architect Karl Friedrich Schinkel.

MUSEUMS

Opposite the Schloss and flanking the broad avenue of Schlossstrasse stands a pair of museum buildings that once served as barracks for the royal guardsmen. The one on the west side is the **Sammlung Berggruen,** a high-quality collection of early 20th-century art assembled by Heinz Berggruen, a native of Berlin. An art dealer in Paris, he befriended Picasso, and more than

80 paintings by Picasso are displayed here, including his portrait of Georges Braque, as well as works by Paul Klee and other contemporaries. The adjoining **Bröhan-Museum** concentrates on the applied arts in Europe from the late 19th century to World War II, and there are fabulous examples of art nouveau and art deco porcelain, silver, glass, metalwork, and furniture.

Located in a classical building near the Zoo railway station, the Museum für Fotografie brings together the collections of the Helmut Newton Foundation and the art library of Berlin's public museums. Newton, a Jew, fled from Germany to Australia in 1938 but nevertheless kept a soft spot for Berlin, his hometown. The noted fashion photographer and his wife donated over 1,000 works to help start the museum in 2003. In the airy upstairs gallery you'll find regular exhibits of contemporary and Newtonian works (such as his iconic and controversial Big Nudes), while the ground floor is a permanent showcase of the late photographer's personal effects. ■

The Porcelain Room at Schloss Charlottenburg has over 2,700 figurines, vases, and other pieces jammed everywhere the eye can see.

Bröhan-Museum
www.broehan-museum.de/
✉ Schlossstrasse 1a
☎ 030 32 69 06 00
🕐 Closed Mon.
💲 $$
🚇 See Schloss entry p. 74

Museum für Fotografie
www.smb.spk-berlin.de
🗺 Map p. 52
✉ Jebensstrasse 2
☎ 030 31 86 48 25
🕐 Closed Mon.
💲 $$
🚇 U-Bahn/S-Bahn: Zoologischer Garten

Berlin's far west

THE WOODS, RIVERS, AND LAKELAND OF THE WESTERN
part of the city exert a great pull on Berliners of every social class,
intent on enjoying their Sunday in the countryside. In a few minutes, the S-Bahn will sweep you into woodland where wild boar still
roam, or to a sandy beach just like the shores of the Baltic.

**Jagdschloss
Grunewald**
- 🅰 51 C3
- ✉ Hüttenweg 10 (Am
  Grunewaldsee)
- ☎ 030 8 13 35 97
- 🕐 Closed Mon.
- 💲 $

Brücke-Museum
www.bruecke-museum.de
- 🅰 Map p. 52
- ✉ Bussardsteig 9
- ☎ 030 8 31 20 29
- 🕐 Closed Tues.
- 💲 $$
- 🚌 Bus: 115

Museum Dahlem
www.smb.museum
- 🅰 Map p. 52
- ✉ Lansstrasse 8
- ☎ 030 83 01 438
- 🕐 Closed Mon.
- 💲 $$
- 🚌 Bus: 110, 183, X11

In 1542 the Hohenzollern rulers
built their hunting lodge, the
Jagdschloss Grunewald,
among the trees of the "Green
Wood." It still covers an area of
about 12 square miles (32 sq km)
between the built-up area of Berlin
and the wide River Havel. Altered,
but still with its Renaissance great
hall, the Jagdschloss is decorated
with furniture and paintings from
the royal collection. Nearby is the
modern **Brücke-Museum,** with
a collection of expressionist paintings by members of the radical
group called Die Brücke. Pictures
are shown in rotation, but look for
Ludwig Kirchner's "Berlin Street
Scene" (1913) and Emil Nolde's
"Mocking" (1919).

Visitors come to the leafy suburb
of Dahlem to study the superlative

exhibits of the **Museum
Dahlem,** one of the world's great
ethnographical collections. The
"American Archaeology" exhibition
displays items such as painted
stoneware vessels of the Maya,
Aztec idols, and gold artifacts from
Central America, Columbia, and
Peru. Among the various exhibits in
the Boat Hall you can climb aboard
a twin-hulled boat from Tonga.

The Grunewald is bisected by
the ruler-straight highway called
the **AVUS,** laid out as a test track
in 1909 and converted into the very
first autobahn in 1921. To the west,
two viewpoints give you the chance
to get above tree level and enjoy a
prospect of the forest and the city
beyond. The 377-foot-high (115 m)
Teufelsberg is an artificial hill
made up of 26 million cubic yards

(25 million cu m) of rubble carted here from the ruins of bombed-out Berlin. Not quite as tall, but with fine views over the Havel, is the riverside **Grunewald-Turm,** a brick tower in neo-Gothic style.

At Wannsee the River Havel expands to form a lovely bay; the most popular spot is the half-mile-long (0.8 km) sandy beach. The **Strandbad Wannsee,** a resort complex laid out in the late 1920s, has every imaginable facility, Opulent villas stand on grounds along the shore to the west; one of them is the infamous **Haus der Wannsee-Konferenz,** where the crucial decision was taken in 1942 to implement the "Final Solution to the Jewish Problem." It is not easy to reconcile the tale told in the exhibits here with the beauty and harmony of the surroundings.

As the road from Wannsee heads west toward Potsdam, the influence of the royal presence there begins to make itself felt. A detour through the forest leads to the ferry landing for **Peacock Island** (Pfaueninsel) and Potsdam. Less than a mile long,

Peacock Island was transformed with the construction in 1794–97 of a charming mock castle for King Frederick William II's mistress, Countess Lichtenau. In the early 19th century, royal landscape architect Peter Joseph Lenné (1789–1866) created an idyllic English-style park around the castle. Other follies were added, and a stroll around the island reveals one enchanting tree-framed view after the other. In this rural enclave it's difficult to believe that the city is only minutes away.

At **Klein-Glienicke,** Lenné and Schinkel worked from the mid-1820s with the artistically minded Prince Carl of Prussia to transform hills, woods, and waterside into a landscape of Mediterranean charm. The prince's modest Schloss Park looks out over Lenné's "Pleasure Ground" across the Havel to the domes and towers of Potsdam. Close by, the steel spans of the **Glienicke Bridge** were the spooky setting for Cold War exchanges of spies and agents. It is now just the boundary between Berlin and Potsdam. ■

The Glienicke Bridge was once the frontier between West Berlin and the German Democratic Republic.

Haus der Wannsee-Konferenz
www.ghwk.de
🅜 Map p. 52
✉ Am Grossen Wannsee 56–58
☎ 030 8 05 00 10
🚈 S-Bahn: Wannsee, then Bus 114

Klein-Glienicke
🅜 Map p. 52
✉ Königstrasse 36
☎ 030 8 05 30 41
🚈 S-Bahn: Wannsee, then Bus 93, 116

More places to visit in Berlin

Kaiser Wilhelm II built the Berliner Dom in Italian Renaissance style with the intent to overawe.

BERLIN CATHEDRAL (BERLINER DOM)

The contrast on Lustgarden between the bombast of the enormous Protestant cathedral and the calm classicism of Schinkel's Altes Museum (see pp. 62–63) neatly illustrates the development of Prussian royal taste in the 19th century. The Dom is the outstanding example of the kind of overblown architecture favored by Kaiser William II. The emperor kept an eye on every detail of the Dom's design, only accepting the architect's proposals after they had been modified again and again. The building is undeniably impressive, inside and out, even after losing some of its overload of ornament during the extensive reconstruction that took place from 1983 onward. Perhaps the most evocative part of the building is the crypt, not for its architecture but for its contents: the coffins of 89 members of the Hohenzollern royal family are preserved.

🅼 Map p. 53 ✉ Am Lustgarten ☎ 030 20 26 91 36 🚇 U-Bahn: Friedrichstrasse, S-Bahn: Hackescher Markt; Bus: 100, 157, 348

EAST SIDE GALLERY

The Wall used to run along the riverside, and in 1990 artists from all over the world exercised their talents on it, giving rise to the East Side Gallery (see also p. 72). Some of the panels bear political images ranging from the Cold War to the present day, while others are playfully surreal and light-hearted. Despite the name, it costs nothing to see the artworks, which are best viewed on a stroll along Mühlenstrasse in the borough of Friedrichshain. At the eastern end of the gallery, at an unusually broad part of the Spree, the area's distinctly industrial character is relieved somewhat by the Oberbaum Bridge, with its red-brick faux-medieval towers and pixie-like turrets.

🅼 Map p. 52 🚇 S-Bahn/U-Bahn: Warschauer Strasse; Bus: 142

KREUZBERG

The inner-city borough that, as well as having a large Turkish population, has enjoyed great fame as a stronghold of every conceivable alternative late 20th-century lifestyle. To some extent yuppies have now moved into Kreuzberg, but there's plenty of atmosphere around the **Maybachufer,** where a colorful Turkish market is held. The 'mountain' of Kreuzberg rises all of 66 m (216 ft) in the Viktoriapark, a somewhat unkempt but pretty park criss-crossed with short trails, some of them quite steep. On the peak you'll come to a memorial, designed by famed architect Schinkel, to the Wars of Liberation that ejected Napoleon from Germany in 1813. The view reaches to nearby Tempelhof Airport, where a huge three-pronged sculpture mimics the three air corridors along which supplies were ferried during the Berlin airlift.

🅼 Map p. 52 🕐 Turkish Market open Tues. and Fri. afternoons 🚇 U-Bahn: Schönleinstrasse or Platz der Luftbrücke; Bus: 140 or 141

JEWISH MUSEUM
(JÜDISCHES MUSEUM)

Reached by an underground passageway from
the neighboring 18th-century former courthouse, the Jewish Museum was built in the
1990s to house exhibits documenting the
course of Jewish history in Germany from its
beginnings in the ninth century. The plan of
this unique building, designed by the Polish-
American architect Daniel Libeskind, is a
deconstructed version of the star of David
imposed on Germany's Jewish citizens by the
Nazi regime. A central axis running through
the interior is intended to evoke the terrible
void left by the attempted destruction of
European Jewry; this, and the asymmetrical
spaces adjoining it are so striking that many
thought it best that they be left empty.
⚒ Map p. 53 ✉ Lindenstrasse 9–14 ☎ 030
25 99 33 00 💲 $$ 🚇 U-Bahn: Hallesches Tor

NEUE SYNAGOGE

With its glittering gilded cupola dominating the
busy inner city district around Oranienburger
Strasse, Berlin's New Synagogue was completed
in 1866. Probably the most magnificent build-
ing of its kind at the time, its opulent, oriental
style reflected the pride and growing status of
the city's Jewish community who had tradition-
ally settled in this area. Members of the
Prussian government, led by Bismarck, attend-
ed the opening ceremony as a mark of respect
to the city's Jewish community and as a snub to
anti-Semitic feeling. On Kristallnacht in 1938,
the Neue Synagoge was one of the many syna-
gogues in Germany attacked by Nazi thugs,
although in this case the attackers were held off
by a courageous policeman, Wilhelm Krützfeld.
A few years later, in 1943, the building was
largely destroyed by Allied bombs.
Reconstruction began in GDR times, and today
it houses displays on Berlin Jewish life.
⚒ Map p. 53 ✉ Oranienburger Strasse 28/30
☎ 030 88 02 83 00 (Zentrum Judaicum)
🕐 Closed Sat. 💲 $ 🚇 S-Bahn:
Oranienburger Strasse

NIKOLAIVIERTEL

Flattened in a 1943 air raid , the area around
St. Nicholas' Church is the oldest part of

**Science, transport, and technology are on
display at Berlin's Deutsches
Technikmuseum.**

Berlin. For the city's 750th anniversary in
1987, the GDR authorities, repenting of their
past zeal in demolishing traces of the pre-
communist past, rebuilt the district in some-
thing like its old form. Architectural purists
objected to the not always accurate re-creation
of old buildings, but Berliners love it, and so
probably will you; not only does it represent
something impossible to find anywhere else in
this modern city, it also has interesting shops,
a number of interiors are accessible, and there
are several convincingly traditional places to
eat and drink.
⚒ Map p. 53 🚌 Bus: 142, 157

OLYMPIASTADION

In 1936, 110,000 spectators watched the main
events of the Olympic Games in this immense
stadium in the western part of the city. The
Games were a propaganda coup for the Nazi
regime, which managed to cover up some of

The Sony Center is one of the bright lights of the transformed Potsdamer Platz, filled with shops, restaurants, theaters, and flats.

the more repulsive aspects of its rule for the duration. Germany won the most medals, and a stunning film of the events was made by Leni Riefenstahl. Hitler walked out rather than have to congratulate the African-American gold-medal sprinter Jesse Owens, who had conclusively disproved the Nazi's theories of Aryan superiority. The design of the stadium was begun before the Nazis came to power, and although it shows many traces of their aesthetic preferences, it is essentially a sober and functional structure, its vast size partly concealed by its being sunk into the ground. It was completely restored in time for soccer's World Cup in 2006, when Berlin hosted the prestigious final match.
🅰 51 C3 🔳 U-Bahn/S-Bahn: Olympiastadion

POTSDAMER PLATZ
The old Potsdamer Platz was the busiest intersection in Berlin, the meeting point of S- and U-Bahn lines and 26 tram routes. In 1925 the flood of motor vehicles was so great a new invention, a traffic signal, was installed. After 1945, those cafés, bars, restaurants, hotels, stores, and places of entertainment that had survived the war were pulled down. The

coup de grâce came when the Wall was built right across what had been Berlin's liveliest and most cosmopolitan square. Now life has returned in full, and the new Potsdamer Platz promises to be one of the focal points of 21st-century Berlin. Innovative building complexes by international architects extend southward from the grandiosely rebuilt S-Bahn station to the banks of the Landwehr Canal. Despite the office space, this is an area for city folks to live and enjoy themselves: There are flats, theaters, cinemas, and restaurants in abundance, as well as spacious shopping malls.
🅰 Map p. 53 🔳 S-Bahn/U-Bahn: Potsdamer Platz

SCHÖNEBERG TOWN HALL
This massive building was chosen as the seat of the West Berlin Senate once the communists had taken over the Red Rathaus in East Berlin. It was here, on July 26, 1963, that U.S. President John F. Kennedy made his passionate declaration of solidarity with beleaguered West Berliners. The fact that his much-quoted line "*Ich bin ein Berliner*" was not, strictly speaking, grammatically corrrect, and could be taken to mean, "I am a jam doughnut," added to rather than detracted from the intense gratitude and affection he evoked among his listeners. High up in the building's tower is a copy of Philadelphia's Liberty Bell, presented to the city by Gen. Lucius D. Clay, one of the architects of the Berlin airlift.
🅰 Map p. 52 ✉ Rathausstr. 15 ☎ 030 756 00 🔳 S-Bahn/U-Bahn: Alexanderplatz; Bus: 100, 142, 157, 200, 348

TECHNOLOGY & TRANSPORT MUSEUM (DEUTSCHES TECHNIKMUSEUM BERLIN)
The Technology Museum's "Spectrum" building offers plenty of interactive exhibits to keep the keenest science buff interested, but the real stars of the show are the vintage locomotives and rolling stock, appropriately housed in former roundhouses. As well as trains, there are boats and planes, and gadgetry galore.
🅰 Map p. 53 ✉ Trebbiner Strasse 9 ☎ 030 90 25 40 🕒 Closed Mon. 🅂 $$ 🔳 U-Bahn: Gleisdreieck or Möckernbrücke ∎

The best way to explore the tranquil Spreewald area is aboard a punt.

Brandenburg

A sigh of relief went up from beleaguered West Berliners as the Wall came down in 1989, and, among other things, they regained their freedom to explore the hinterland of their city, the area now covered by much of the *Land* of Brandenburg. The classic destinations are the palaces and parks of Potsdam and the shady streams of the Spreewald, but there is much else to see and do in the course of a day's excursion from the capital.

Flat or gently undulating Brandenburg, with its woods and waterways, is a delight for ramblers, cyclists, and boating enthusiasts. If it's just a quiet day in the countryside you want, take local advice on footpaths, bike rental, and river trips. The Spreewald is an area settled by the Sorbs (see pp. 240–241), a Slav minority who came to this area of Germany in the sixth century and who retain their language and many of their customs.

For a more focused outing, look beyond Potsdam, the Land capital, to the city that gave the area its name. Old Brandenburg was one of the many places that was over-enthusiastically industrialized by the communist regime. Despite this and the slow pace of restoration, it retains some of its medieval appeal, built as it is around a series of lakes along the River Havel and with many fine buildings. The Land

has more outstanding historic architecture in the shape of Frederick the Great's palace at Rheinsberg and the medieval monastery at Chorin (Kloster Chorin).

Beyond the Spreewald are the moonscapes left behind by reckless open cast brown-coal mining, slowly being converted into recreational parkland. Cottbus, with one of Germany's loveliest landscaped estates at Schloss Branitz, is the country's easternmost big city. But it is Frankfurt an der Oder, on the border with Poland and split between Germany and Poland in 1945, that has become a symbol of the complex and sometimes difficult process of reconciliation between the two nations. One place of painful memory is Oranienburg; built by the Nazis as one of their main concentration camps, it was later used by the Soviets for their own purposes. ■

The royal palace of Schloss Sanssouci crowns the vine-clad terraces of Frederick the Great's park.

Potsdam & the Royal Palaces

POTSDAM IS TO BERLIN WHAT VERSAILLES IS TO PARIS, A royal town salubriously sited to the west of the city and dominated by palaces, parks, and gardens. Just as the château at Versailles is indissolubly linked to the Sun King, Louis XIV, so Potsdam's Sanssouci Palace reflects the personality of Frederick the Great. And just as no stay in Paris is complete without a visit to Versailles, so every visitor to Berlin will feel the pull of Potsdam. The city is reached swiftly by train, or in a more leisurely way by boat from Wannsee through the lovely woods and parklands fringing the River Havel.

Potsdam

🄰 51 C3

Visitor information

✉ Friedrich-Ebert-Strasse 5

☎ 0331 27 55 80

Don't be put off by the first sight of Potsdam as you walk from the railway station. The town begins with a disappointment: the empty space where the Great Elector's Stadtschloss once stood. The royal residence was in ruins at the end of World War II, and in 1961 GDR authorities, offended by its symbolism of the "Prussian-German militarism" that the Democratic Republic claimed to have overcome, tore it down. There are now plans to rebuild at least part of it.

The palace defined the **Old Marketplace** (Alter Markt),

which overall is in a happier state, although there are still plenty of buildings awaiting repair or repainting. Two buildings of note include the 18th-century **Town Hall** (Rathaus) and the early 19th-century **Nikolaikirche,** with its massive dome.

Potsdam was essentially a residential town, with a population dominated by high-ranking officers and senior bureaucrats. The streets are lined with fine 18th- and 19th-century houses and villas, many of them now occupied by prosperous commuters from western Berlin.

To the north of Bassinplatz with the Huguenot church is the **Dutch Quarter** (Holländisches Viertel). Its grid of streets and brick-built houses date from 1742, when Frederick William I hoped to attract industrious immigrants from the Netherlands. In the end not many Dutch came, but the gabled dwellings prepared for them now attract visitors with shops, bookstores, and bars.

Farther north still is the **Alexandrowka,** the "Russian Colony," a group of timber chalets that provided accommodations for the members of a Russian soldiers' choir who had ended up here during the Napoleonic wars. One or two of the Siberian-style houses are still inhabited by descendants of the original choristers, and a delightful little Orthodox church tops the nearby hill. With its many military facilities, Potsdam attracted more recent Russians, becoming an important Red Army base after 1945. The KGB was here too in strength, with a major intelligence center, interrogation facilities, and a prison.

THE ROYAL PALACES

Fascinating though the town of Potsdam is, it inevitably lives in the shadow of its royal palaces, above all of **Sanssouci,** the supreme expression of the Prussian rococo style. Long and low, the single-story edifice with its modest dome sits atop a plateau from which a stairway and six curving terraces descend to formal gardens below. The palace was designed for

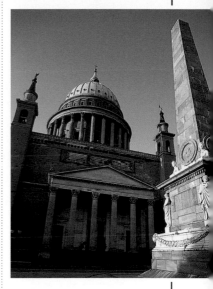

Frederick the Great by the court architect Georg Wenzeslaus von Knobelsdorff (1699–1753), based on draft plans prepared by the monarch himself. It was intended to be a place "free of care" *("sans souci"),* to which this cultured king could escape from affairs of state and devote himself to music, philosophizing, and conversation (in fashionable French).

Take time to enjoy the well-restored gardens. The south-facing terraces with their glasshouses were intended for the cultivation of fruit and vines. The Bacchanalian figures supporting the palace's cornice strike an intentionally festive note, as do the arbors to either side with their glittering sunburst decoration.

The main entrance to the palace is from the colonnaded court to the

Right: Designed by Schinkel and completed by his pupils, the Nikolaikirche dominates Potsdam's market square.

Schloss Sanssouci

🗺 51 C3

Historic Windmill Visitor Center

☎ 0331 96 94 200/201/202

🕐 Palace closed Mon.

💲 $$

🚈 S-Bahn & Regional express train to Potsdam Hauptbahnhof, then Bus 695

north. The guided tour takes in a series of rooms that are sumptuous without being overwhelming. The **Marble Hall** with its cupola formed a dignified setting for the king's famous round table discussions with eminent men of letters, among them Voltaire, whom he hoped to install as court philosopher (vainly, as it turned out). The finest interior is perhaps the gorgeously ornate **Concert Room,** where Frederick loved to play the

flute, a passion celebrated in a famous painting by the 19th-century artist Adolf von Menzel.

Two buildings in similar style flank Sanssouci. To the east is the **Picture Gallery** (Bildergalerie), its immaculately restored rococo interior almost upstaging the old master paintings assembled by Frederick the Great. To the west, and equally appealing, are the **New Chambers** (Neue Kammern), built as guest accom-

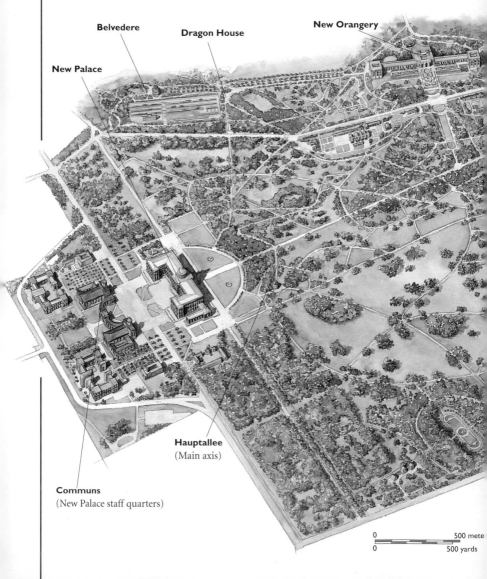

Belvedere

Dragon House

New Orangery

New Palace

Hauptallee
(Main axis)

Communs
(New Palace staff quarters)

0   500 mete

0   500 yards

modations. There is plenty more to see in the park along a nine-mile circuit of sights. Its present appearance was dreamed up by Peter Joseph Lenné, the royal landscape architect.

On the upper level, the **New Orangery** (Neue Orangerie) is an Italian-style building decorated with paintings in imitation of Raphael; beyond it are the pagoda-like **Dragon Building** (Drachenhaus) and the **Belvedere** with views over the park. Down below, the fantastical, tentlike **Chinese Teahouse** (Chinesisches Teehaus) is topped by the gilded figure of a mandarin with a parasol. A little farther on are the **Roman Baths** (Römische

Fanciful figures merge with ornate pilasters on Schloss Sanssouci's main facade.

Historic Windmill
New Chambers
Schloss Sanssouci
Picture Gallery
Vineyard terraces
Chinese Teahouse
Roman Baths
Schloss Charlottenhof

Bäder), then **Schloss Charlottenhof,** a lovely little neoclassic country house designed by Schinkel in 1826 as a summer residence for the Crown Prince.

The western end of the park is dominated by the long facade of the **New Palace** (Neues Palais), a huge, ostentatious structure that contrasts strongly with the restraint of Sanssouci. While Sanssouci represented the cultured, private life of the monarch, the New Palace expresses Prussian pride following the country's victories in the Seven Years War. Its bombast appealed to Kaiser Wilhelm II, who used it as a summer residence. The most striking interior is the Grotto Hall (Grottensaal), with an over-the-top decor of mineral fragments, shells, and semiprecious stones. ■

New Palace
🕐 Closed Fri.
🚇 S-Bahn; Wildpark

More places to visit in Brandenburg

COTTBUS

Germany's easternmost large city suffered both wartime damage and extensive industrialization in the GDR period. It is very proud of its theater, not only for its productions but because it is one of the finest examples of an art nouveau building in the country. However, the town is on the tourist trail mainly because of the obsessions of the local lord, Prince Pückler-Muskau (1785–1871). Having had to leave his family home of Muskau in 1845 through bankruptcy, the prince established himself here at **Schloss Branitz** *(Kastanienallee 11, tel 0355 751 50, closed Mon.)*. A passionate gardener, he created a fine, picturesque park, which today extends to around 250 acres (100 ha) and contains the prince's pyramid-shaped mausoleum.

🅰 51 D2   **Visitor information**
✉ Berlinerplatz 6   ☎ 0355 7 54 20   🆂 $

Frederick the Great's baroque palace of Rheinsberg replaced a late medieval moated castle on this site.

RHEINSBERG

One of the most popular destinations for day trips from Berlin is Rheinsberg, an attractive little town with a lakeside **Schloss** *(tel 033931 72 60, closed Mon.)*, where Frederick the Great spent part of his youth. The future king lent his imprimatur to the place, as did the writer Kurt Tucholsky (1890–1935), author of the 1912 bestseller, *Rheinsberg—A Picture Book for Lovers,* in which he described how he fell in love here, both with the Schloss and with his sweetheart. The tale still draws couples to Rheinsberg for romantic weekends.

🅰 51 C4   🆂 $

SPREEWALD

Upstream from Berlin, less than an hour's drive from the capital, the River Spree divides into countless slow-moving channels, a strange kind of inland delta shaded by alder, poplar, and ash trees, where the morning mists never seem quite to clear. For centuries, the watery and inaccessible Spreewald stayed off the beaten track, quite literally, for there were no roads; local people got around by flat-bottomed punt. In the early 19th century, Berliners on the lookout for a rural retreat discovered the area's charms. Today more than two million visitors a year come here, some for longer vacations, some to enjoy a sociable trip aboard a many-seated punt, poled by the German version of a gondolier. But it's easy enough to get away from the crowds and enjoy the natural beauties of what is now a UNESCO-designated biosphere reserve by renting a canoe, cycling, or walking.

The most popular gateway to the Spreewald is the pleasant town of **Lübbenau,** which has the alternative Slavonic name of Lubnjow; this is the northern edge of the homeland of Germany's Sorbs, a Slav nation whose language and way of life somehow survived centuries of envelopment by German culture (see pp. 240–241). You can find out about them at the open-air section of the **Spreewald-Museum** *(tel 03542 24 72, closed mid-Oct.–March, $),* where a number of traditional timber farmsteads and other buildings have been reassembled. The museum is at **Lehde** (Lehdy in Sorbian), a short punt trip or a walk of a little over a mile (2 km) from Lübbenau. Another museum, almost certainly the only one of its kind in the world, celebrates the gherkin, the area's most famous contribution to gastronomy *(Bauernhaus-und Gurkenmuseum Lehde, tel 03542 8 99 90).*

🅰 51 D2 ■

S plendidly preserved old cities, Germany's most attractive coastline, and a glorious lake district—with all these, the *Land* of Mecklenburg-West Pomerania seems set to become one of Germany's most popular visitor destinations.

Mecklenburg-West Pomerania

Stylish speedster

Exploring the watery landscape aboard a cruiser on the River Prerow

Mecklenburg-West Pomerania

STRETCHING FROM NEAR LÜBECK IN SCHLESWIG-HOLSTEIN TO THE Polish border along the River Oder, Mecklenburg-Vorpommern is the most northeasterly of the German *Länder*. Its landscapes were formed by ice and water: Glaciers gouged out lakes and ponds and deposited sands and gravels to form a gently undulating countryside. Along the Baltic Sea, the winds and waves modeled a shoreline of bays, spits, islands, and peninsulas, sheltering the lagoon-like inlets known as *Bodden*.

The landscapes and wildlife of the Bodden of West Pomerania are protected as a national park. Two other national parks in the region —like that of the Bodden created since reunification—are the spectacular chalk cliffs and superb beech forests of Jasmund on the island of Rügen, and the Mecklenburg Lake District (Mecklenburgische Seenplatte). The lakes, which include the Müritz, Germany's second largest body of fresh water, are a great place for wildlife as well as for yachtsmen and canoeists. But the region's biggest magnet is the Baltic coast, with its endless sandy beaches. Two centuries ago, aristocratic entrepreneurs laid out resorts and spa facilities, and German vacationers have ever since flocked to enjoy them. Since reunification, there has been no

shortage of funds to spruce up the faded glories of resorts such as Heringsdorf and Ahlbeck on the island of Usedom, Binz on Rügen, or Kühlungsborn near Rostock.

A leading member of the Hanseatic League of trading cities (see sidebar p. 121), Rostock is the region's largest town. The city and its harbor were promoted as the German Democratic Republic's Gateway to the World. It's a lively place, with a sense of history despite much modernization. History is even more evident in the other Hansa harbor towns: With their heritage of fine building, Wismar and Stralsund are candidates for UNESCO World Heritage status; Greifswald preserves the memory of Caspar David Friedrich, to many the most appealing of Germany's Romantic painters; and in Güstrow is the studio of the early 20th-century expressionist sculptor Ernst Barlach. Of other fine towns, Neubrandenburg has its intact ring of medieval walls, Ludwigslust its great ducal Schloss, and Schwerin, the Land capital, its palaces and galleries in an unequaled lakeside setting. ■

Area of map detail

Berlin ✪

Kap Arkona

Baltic Sea

Vitt
Dranske
Tromper Wiek
Königsstuhl Stubbenkammer
Kloster
Hiddensee
96
NATIONALPARK JASMUND
◁4
Darsser Ort
NATIONALPARK VORPOMMERSCHE BODDENLANDSCHAFT
Schaprode
Grosser Jasmunder Bodden
Sassnitz
Zingst
Prerow
Zingst
Ummanz
E251
Rügen
Bergen
Prora
Jagdschloss Granitz

Wustrow
Barth
Samtens
E22
Binz
Sellin
Bucht
Graal-Müritz
E22
Löbnitz
Stralsund
Garz
Putbus
Vilm
Göhren
BIOSPHÄRENRESERVAT SÜDOST-RÜGEN
Warnemünde
105
Ribnitz-Damgarten
Barthe
Steinhagen
96
194
Zudar
Greifswalder Bodden
Bad Doberan
Sanitz
Bad Sülze
Grimmen
Ryck
E251
Peenemünde
◁3
Rostock
110
Glewitz
Wieck
Greifswald
Eldena Monastery
Zinnowitz
Satow
A19 E55
Recknitz
Laage
Gnoien
Trebel
Loitz
Poggendorf
96
111
Wolgast
Achterwasser
Usedom
Ückeritz
Bansin Heringsdorf
Ahlbeck
Schwaan
Dargun
Demmin
Peene
Jarmen
109
NATURPARK USEDOM
110
Bützow
Güstrow
104
Thürkow
Kummerower See
Golchen
Anklam
Usedom
Stettiner Haff
Ueckermünde
◁2
192
Krakow am See
103
Teterow
Malchin
Malchiner See
104
Reuterstadt Stavenhagen
Altentreptow
Friedland
197
Ducherow
109
Torgelow
Randow
POLAND
Goldberg
Kölpin- see
108
194
192
Neubrandenburg
Galenbecker See
Pasewalk
Lübz
191 Plau
Plauer See
Malchow
Müritz See
Waren
Penzlin
Tollensesee
Burg Stargard
198
Woldegk
104
Löcknitz
Marnitz
A19 E55
198
Röbel
NATIONALPARK MÜRITZ
E251
Mirow
Wesenberg
NATIONALPARK MÜRITZ
96
Carwitzer See
Carwitz
Neustrelitz
A11
E28
◁1
Ueckermünder Heide
Uecker

MECKLENBURG-
WEST POMERANIA
Lake District

BRANDENBURG
p. 49

0 _____ 50 kilometers
0 _____ 30 miles

C   D   E   F

Schwerin

WHEN THE BERLIN WALL CAME DOWN IN 1989, WEST German visitors flocked to the capital of Mecklenburg-West Pomerania, drawn not only by its lakeside location but by its ease of access: It is only an hour's drive from Hamburg. One of Europe's longest reigning noble families held sway here. When the last Grand Duke of Mecklenburg departed in 1918, he left a legacy of fine building that may have tipped the scales when it came to choosing a capital for the new state in 1990.

The elaborate skyline of Schwerin's Schloss, with the spire of the city's cathedral visible in the distance

Schwerin stands on a rise among seven lakes. Complete with cathedral and market place, the city's medieval core still occupies this ancient site, chosen by Henry the Lion in the middle of the 12th century as a base for extending his rule eastward into unknown Slavic territory. You will certainly want to explore the streets and alleyways of the Altstadt, but your city tour will probably start by the lakeside, where a group of splendid public buildings make an aristocratic backdrop to summer concerts and performances.

Tear your eyes away for a moment from the extraordinary silhouette of the Schloss on its lake island to look at the **Staatstheater,** a big white neo-baroque building dating from the 1880s, and the even grander neoclassic **Staatliches Museum,** completed around the same time. Great collectors, the Grand Dukes of Mecklenburg had a particular penchant for Dutch and Flemish painting, and the museum's collection by such masters as Rubens, Franz Hals, and Jan Brueghel has few equals in Germany. In complete contrast are modern German works and those by 20th-century conceptual artists, such as Frenchman Marcel Duchamp (1887–1968).

The galleries are well worth a visit, but if time is short, cross the bridge to the castle island. Turn left and walk clockwise around the landscaped gardens surrounding the castle with their fine views across the Schweriner See, Germany's third largest lake. Three-quarters of a circuit brings you to the castle entrance or to another

bridge. This leads to the much larger Schlossgarten, a baroque park laid out on formal lines by a French landscape architect, with a canal, statues, and clipped hedges.

Schwerin's **Schloss** is a glorious confection of towers, turrets, and pinnacles, one for every day of the year according to those who have taken the trouble to count them. The first stronghold was built by the area's Slavic inhabitants in the 11th century; they burned it down rather than surrender it, but the island was soon refortified by the invading Germans. Their castle was strengthened and extended at various times, but its present appearance is mostly due to the 19th duke's desire for a palace that would look more medieval than the Middle Ages. The 19th-century architects who remodeled it were inspired by the château of Chambord in France's Loire Valley.

The interior is largely a celebration of the ducal line, its climax the sumptuous **Throne Room** with its frescoes, coats of arms, and columns of Carrara marble. On the second floor you can visit the

Dining Room and adjoining circular **Tea Room,** and in the **Ancestors' Gallery** hang the portraits of former dukes of Mecklenburg.

Back on the town side of the bridge, head toward the **Old Town** (Altstadt), using the 384-foot (117 m) cathedral tower as a landmark. The Marketplace has a more jolly and lived-in atmosphere than the area around the castle. The colonnaded structure on its northern side was intended as a market hall, while the Town Hall (Rathaus) was rebuilt in a vaguely English neo-Tudor style in the mid-19th century. Schwerin's **Cathedral** (Dom) is a grandiose example of the medieval Brick Gothic style (see p. 36), although the tower looming over the marketplace is a 19th-century addition. You could climb its 220 steps for the definitive panorama of the city in its watery setting. To the north is the **Pfaffenteich,** the Priests' Pond, created to supply power to the city's medieval water-mills. It is crossed by a little ferryboat, which provides a feel of Mecklenburg's lakeland. ■

The Ancestors' Gallery of Schwerin's Schloss depicts more than 600 years of ducal rule.

Schwerin

🅰 88 B2

Visitor information

✉ Am Markt 14

☎ 0385 5 92 52 12

Staatliches Museum

✉ Alter Garten 3

☎ 0385 5 95 80

🕐 Closed Mon. mid-October–mid-April

💲 $

Schwerin's Schloss (Schlossmuseum)

✉ Lennéstrasse 1

☎ 0385 5 25 29 20

🕐 Closed Mon.

💲 $

Rostock

ROSTOCK LOST OUT TO SCHWERIN WHEN A CAPITAL CITY was chosen for the new *Land* after reunification, a slight that continues to irritate what was a proud seafaring town with one of the first universities in northern Europe. Much of the city's medieval heritage was destroyed in World War II, but enough remains to evoke a splendid past. Together with the neighboring ferry port and resort of Warnemünde, Rostock is a lively place, with good facilities and plenty of accommodations, an ideal base for your exploration of Germany's Baltic coast.

In its early days, Rostock was not one, but three towns (Old Town to the east, Middle Town, and New Town, to the west), laid out on the south bank of the broad River Warnow in the 13th century, each with its church and market square. If you arrive in town at the main railway station (Hauptbahnhof), a tram or taxi will bring you quickly to the spacious **New Market Place** (Neuer Markt), laid out as the focal point of the **Middle Town** (Mittelstadt) in 1232. On the way, the tramlines and the broad roadway swirl around the 16th-century gateway known as the **Steintor,** part of the fortifications that once surrounded the town.

The New Market's dominant feature is the **Town Hall** (Rathaus). It may take you a minute or two to make sense of Rostock's rather strange city hall. A fairly conventional baroque facade with a ground floor arcade is topped by a row of fierce-looking brick spikes with pointed openings below. This is the roof of the original, medieval Rathaus, one of the finest of all the Brick Gothic city halls along the Baltic coast. Its baroque front was added in the 18th century.

Overlooked by the tall tower of **St. Peter's Church** (the Petrikirche), for long a familiar beacon to seafarers, the **Old Town** (Altstadt) is interesting but rather run down, so head west along Rostock's traffic-free main street, **Kröpeliner Strasse,** which bisects the New Town (Neustadt).

Spare a few moments for the massive brick-built **Marienkirche** just to the north; fortresslike outside, the church has exceptionally rich furnishings inside, including an astonishing bronze font from the late 13th century. If you are here at midday, make sure you see the parade of saintly figures set in motion as the 15th-century astronomical clock strikes noon.

Continue west along Kröpeliner Strasse into the **Universitäts-platz,** lined with stately buildings. The core of the New Town, this square is lively today with its open-air cafés, market traders shouting their wares, and children darting

Left: The strawberries-and-cream facade of Rostock's Rathaus

Rostock

🅰 89 C3

Visitor information

✉ Neuer Markt 3–8

☎ 0381 I 94 33

Participants in the Hansa Sail festival are put through their paces by a Force 6 gale.

Maritime Museum (Schiffahrtsmuseum)

✉ IGA Park

☎ 0381 12 83 13 64

🕐 Closed Mon.

💲 $

among the water jets and sculptures of the modern fountain.

Housed in an old monastery, the **Historical Museum** (Kulturhistorisches Museum; *Klosterhof, tel 0381 2 03 59 10, closed Mon.*) has historical artifacts and paintings—look for those of the Ahrenshoop artists, evoking the Baltic coast. It is worth climbing to the top of the lofty gateway of **Kröpeliner Tor** farther west along Kröpeliner Strasse (*Kröpeliner Strasse, tel 0381 121 64 15*) for the view, and there is a local history museum inside.

Head back to the Middle Town and go south to the **Maritime Museum** (Schiffahrtsmuseum). East Germany's foremost shipping museum tells the story of the area's relationship with the Baltic. Ships

portrayed in oil, watercolor, and even silk embroidery form the large collection of pictures owned or commissioned by ships' captains.

The River Warnow and Rostock's harbor lie beyond Lange Strasse, a boulevard built in the early years of the GDR. The quayside is liveliest in August, when the river fills with the sails of windjammers and other vessels taking part in the annual Hansa Sail, an event that attracts a million onlookers.

As well as a sandy beach, Rostock's old seaside suburb of **Warnemünde** has elegant villas, and fishermen's houses converted into restaurants. Make the 7-mile (11 km) trip to Warnemünde by the S-Bahn from the main station, or, in summer, by boat from the Kabutzenhof quay. ■

Wismar

Wismar
⬛ 88 B2
Visitor information
✉ Am Markt 11
☎ 03841 1 94 33

SECOND ONLY TO LÜBECK AMONG THE HISTORIC PORT cities of the Hanseatic League (see sidebar p. 121), Wismar is putting right the neglect of GDR times and sprucing itself up to welcome an ever swelling tide of visitors. Together with Stralsund, it is one of the best places to get the feel of Germany's Baltic heritage, with an intact medieval street network, an array of architecture from all periods, and an atmospheric old harbor.

Crowds gather by Wismar's quayside during the old Hansa city's Hafenfest (harbor festival).

City Hall vaults (Rathauskeller)
✉ Am Markt
☎ 03841 251 30 25
💲 $

Schabbellhaus
✉ Schweinsbrücke 8
☎ 03841 28 23 50
🕐 Closed Mon.
💲 $

Boat trips
Details at visitor information center (see above)

The gently sloping cobbled **Markt** is the city centerpiece, a square whose sides measure an almost exact 100 meters (328 feet). The big draw here is the **Wasserkunst,** the little copper-domed pavilion covering the fountain that supplied the citizenry with water right up to the end of the 19th century. Among the dignified buildings lining the east side of the marketplace is the 14th-century high-gabled, brick house known as the **Old Swede** (Alter Schwede), a reminder that the city was handed over to Sweden after the Thirty Years War and only returned to Mecklenburg in 1803.

To discover more about Wismar's history, find the side entrance to the civic museum in the vaults of the **City Hall** (Rathaus), the serene neoclassic

structure filling the northern side of the square. Or visit the town historical museum in the **Schabbellhaus,** a mansion built 1569–1571 for Wismar's mayor.

Best of all, stroll through the old streets, making sure you walk along the **Grube,** the narrow canal running past the city's great **Nikolaikirche.** One of the grandest of Germany's Baltic Brick Gothic (see p. 36) churches, its lofty interior soars to a height of 121 feet (37 m). In this superb setting admire the medieval altarpieces, mural paintings, and a beautiful bronze font. The city's other churches include the **Georgenkirche,** infamous as the GDR's biggest ruin but scheduled to be fully restored by 2010; the intimate **Church of the Holy Ghost** (Heilig-Geist-Kirche) on Lübsche Strasse; and the **Marienkirche** on St.-Marien-Kirchhof, of which only the 262-foot (80 m) tower survived wartime destruction.

Under communism, lack of care for Wismar's environment and built heritage went hand in hand with growth and development. The city became the GDR's second most important port, after Rostock. More interesting than the modern installations is the **Old Harbor** (Alter Hafen) with the one surviving **City Gate** (the Wassertor), ancient warehouses, and the chance to brave the Baltic waves aboard one of the old sailing vessels moored here. ■

Stralsund

ALMOST COMPLETELY SURROUNDED BY WATER, COMPACT
Stralsund is one of the best preserved of all the Baltic harbor towns,
its skyline still dominated by the towers of three great churches, its
streets still lined with houses dating from the town's glory days before
the Thirty Years War. Stralsund is not only attractive in itself, but its
central location along the coast also makes it an excellent base for
exploration in various directions.

Stralsund
🅰 89 D3
Visitor information
✉ Alter Markt 9
☎ 03831 246 90

Its strategic location and sheltered
harbor helped the city to prosperity
as one of the leading members of
the Hanseatic League, with trading
links to Scandinavia and Russia in
one direction, and to England and
Spain in the other. Stralsund's former power and wealth are proudly
expressed in the **Old Market**
(Alter Markt) overlooked by its
great central church and city hall,
almost welded together into a single
integrated structure incorporating
several houses. The medieval **City
Hall** (Rathaus) is one of the most
startling civic buildings in the
whole of Germany; its seven-gabled
facade is exactly that—a front with
nothing but air behind most of it.
The adjoining **Nikolaikirche** has
treasures such as the naively carved
panels of fork-bearded Russians

hunting sables and handing the
pelts over to a skeptical-looking
Stralsund merchant. Still on the
square, you can admire the Gothic
buildings of **Wulflamhaus,**
and—in contrast—the
Commandanten-Hus, a
baroque relic of the time when
the Swedes ruled Stralsund.
To the south, **New Market**
(Neue Markt) boasts the
Marienkirche rebuilt in 1416,
which has vaulting of great delicacy.
Climb the tower for a breathtaking
view of the city. Exhibits in the
**Museum of the Sea and
Fisheries** (Deutsches Museum für
Meereskunde und Fischerei) range
from a fin whale skeleton to a con-
vincingly reproduced coral reef.
The aquarium has displays on
North Sea marine life. ■

**Views from
the tower of
Stralsund's
Marienkirche look
out over the old
city across to
Rügen Island and
the Strelasund
sea inlet.**

**Oceanographic
Museum**
(Deutsches Meeresmuseum)
✉ Katherinenberg
14–20
☎ 03831 265 02 10
💲 $$

A drive along the Baltic coast

Old-fashioned resorts, tranquil landscapes, and intriguing inland towns feature in this two-day journey along the Baltic's sandy shores.

Leave the old Hanseatic port city of **Wismar** on the B105 toward Rostock. Ignore the "Autobahn Rostock" signs and continue on the old main road toward Rostock and Bad Doberan. After 20.5 miles (33 km), leave the main road, following signs to Kühlungsborn. The road runs north toward the coast through a short stretch of attractive, well-wooded hill country, the Kühlung.

Kühlungsborn ❶ is the biggest resort along this coast, with 2.5 miles (4 km) of sandy beach and many opulent hotels and villas (although finding somewhere to stay is not always easy if you haven't made an advance reservation). Kühlungsborn West and

Kühlungsborn Ost once vied for the favors of vacationers, but they were joined in shotgun matrimony in 1938. The main symbol of their present togetherness is the **Ostseeallee,** the long drive running parallel to the shore and separated from it by a fine belt of trees. Drivers need to keep their eyes off its grand villas and on the road: The traffic-calming measures here include occasional solid-looking timber posts sticking up out of the carriageway. Even if you don't swim, surf, or sunbathe in Kühlungsborn, you should stroll out on to the newly built pier for the sea air.

Continue along the coast to little **Heiligendamm ❷,** Germany's very first purpose-built seaside resort, developed with splendid neoclassic buildings in the 1790s by Grand Duke Friedrich Franz I of Mecklenburg. The main road (105) now leaves the coast and heads inland on a lovely avenue of linden trees alongside the little railroad that has run the few miles between Kühlungsborn and Bad Doberan since 1886.

- 🅼 See area map p. 88 B2
- ➤ Wismar
- 🔁 93 miles (150 km)
- 🕐 Two days
- ➤ Barth

NOT TO BE MISSED

- A walk on the pier at Kühlungsborn
- The amber museum at Ribnitz-Damgarten
- The harbor and seamen's church at Ahrenshoop
- The church at Prerow

Baltic gold: amber

Wismar quayside

The Kempinski Grand Hotel overlooks the coast in the historic resort town of Heiligendamm.

The Cistercians founded a monastery in **Bad Doberan** ❸, and their great Brick Gothic minster contains original furnishings including a gilded high altar and a tabernacle carved in oak. Outside, look for the pretty ossuary (*Beinhaus*) where the monks' bones were preserved. The town itself bears the imprint of Duke Friedrich Franz, who made it the summer capital of his court. His palace is now a hotel, and one of the charming Chinese-style pavilions in the middle of the *Kamp*, a parklike village green, is a café.

Continue on the 105, passing through the city of Rostock and on for 16 miles (26 km) to the town of **Ribnitz-Damgarten** ❹. The

Bernstein-Museum (*Im Kloster, tel 0 3821 29 31, $$*) here, housed in a monastery building, has examples of amber, many containing immaculately preserved insects of long ago.

Now backtrack a few yards and find the minor road leading northwest toward Dierhagen. You are now entering the Fischland-Darss-Zingst peninsula. Much of this area is conserved as part of the **Nationalpark Vorpommersche Boddenlandschaft** (*National Park administration, Im Forst 5, Born, tel 038234 50 20*), with woods, meadows, boglands, dunes, and saltwater lagoons (*Bodden*). It is a popular vacation area, but the old fishing villages have kept much of their character. Artists, rather than aristocrats, set the tone here, so the vacation houses are thatched cottages rather than swanky villas. The village of **Ahrenshoop** ❺ is a good place to get the feel of the Fischland. Sandy lanes lead down to the sheltered Bodden, and the harbor usually has some of the typical fishing boats known as *Zeesenboote*. Ahrenshoop's tiny timber church is built in the shape of an upturned boat.

The Darss area is dominated by woodland and by the resort of **Prerow** ❻, its cottages scattered among the trees. Just off the main road, Prerow's redbrick church reflects the sea, with suspended ship models and bold, colorful carvings reminiscent of ships' figureheads. Climb up on to the grassy dike for a look at the Baltic shore, and then continue along the sea wall for 2.5 miles (4 km), where the road turns south back toward the mainland. The final stop is at **Barth** ❼, a little place with a long history as a harbor town. In spring and fall, countless birders flock here to admire the tens of thousands of migrating cranes. ∎

Darsser Ort

N

NATIONALPARK
VORPOMMERSCHE
BODDENLANDSCHAFT

❻ **Prerow**

Darss

Zingst

Zingst

Ahrenshoop

Wustrow

❺

Fischland

Saaler Bodden

Barth

❼

Dierhagen

❹

E22

105

Ribnitz-Damgarten

110

On the beach at Prerow

Rügen

RÜGEN IS GERMANY'S LARGEST ISLAND. IN THE OPINION OF its many visitors, it is also the most beautiful, with a variety of landscapes that range from glorious beech woods to sandy shores and spectacular chalk cliffs. Tourism has a long history here, beginning with the creation of a princely spa in the early 1800s. Elegant seaside resorts then developed, and these saw a revival after German reunification. Even more of a vacation paradise than the main island is traffic-free Hiddensee Island, a favorite with artists and intellectuals for more than a hundred years.

Fishermen spread their nets at the little village of Vierow.

Rügen

🅰 89 D4–E4

Visitor information

✉ Bahnhofstrasse 15, Bergen

☎ 03838 80 77 80

A 1.5-mile (2.5 km) causeway and bridge links Rügen with the mainland at Stralsund. The main road and railroad head directly toward Bergen, the island's little capital, but you should take the side road past Gustow and Barz to **Putbus.** Centered on a ring of white villas known as the Circus, this pretty little spa town was the brainchild in 1810 of the local lord, Prince Wilhelm Malte. He hoped to attract an exclusive clientele with landscaped gardens, theatrical entertainments, and the excitements of saltwater bathing. The exotic trees he planted in his English-style park are still here, but his mansion was too redolent of feudal symbolism for the communist rulers, who demolished it in the 1960s. Other buildings survived

however, among them the church, originally built as a ballroom; the orangery, guarded by stone lions saved from the mansion; and, above all, the templelike theater.

In the early 20th century, theater guests were conveyed to Putbus from their hotels on the coast aboard the dining cars of a little railroad that still runs today. Once nicknamed the *Turnip Express,* it has been re-branded *Rasender Roland* (*Rushing Roland*), although it dawdles rather than races the 15 miles (25 km) to its terminus at Göhren. Steam locomotives still snort and shunt in the station and depot at Putbus, which is also served by a branch off Rügen's main line.

The railroad continues one stop farther to the harbor at Lauterbach. From here you can board a boat and sail around the little island of **Vilm,** although you can only land by prior arrangement (*tel 038301 6 18 96*). No timber has been felled on Vilm for hundreds of years, and visitor numbers to what is now a designated nature reserve are carefully controlled. In GDR times the island's charms were reserved for the enjoyment of the Communist Party elite.

Rushing Roland is an entertaining way of getting to Rügen's premier resort of **Binz,** which faces the bracing Baltic breezes on the

island's east coast. Binz has a promenade, a pier, and a Kurhaus (assembly rooms), and villas flaunting white-painted fancy fretwork balconies and gables line its century-old streets. Although Binz has come up in the world again, its real glory days were the period just before World War I. The entertaining little **Historisches Binz Museum,** housed in the Villa Odin *(Zeppelinstrasse 8),* brings this epoch to life.

South from Binz, the train puffs up an incline toward the little station for the **Granitz Hunting Lodge** (Jagdschloss Granitz), a massive mock-medieval hunting lodge built on the hilltop by Prince Wilhelm. Fight any feelings of vertigo, and climb the winding wrought-iron stairway

inside the castle tower for a magnificent panorama of this end of the island. With its woods, flower-rich meadows, and intricate coastline, the whole area is a UNESCO-designated biosphere reserve, coexisting with small resorts such as Sellin and Baabe, their early 1930s atmosphere immortalized by the novelist Christopher Isherwood in his semi-autobiographical *Goodbye to Berlin.*

GOING NORTH

To the north, among the sand dunes and pine forest in the other direction from Binz, is one of Germany's most outlandish sights, a massive wall of concrete stretching more than 2.5 miles (4 km) along the curving shore.

In Jasmund National Park, sheer, beech-capped cliffs rise from the Baltic shore.

Granitz Hunting Lodge (Jagdschloss Granitz)

✉ Lancken-Granitz

☎ 038393 22 63

🕐 Closed Mon. off season

💲 $

The old-fashioned resort of Binz has one of the Baltic coast's many sandy beaches.

Prora-Museum

✉ Prora bei Binz, Objektstrasse 3

☎ 038393 3 26 40

💲 $

This overwhelming presence is **Prora,** a relic of the Nazis' "Strength Through Joy" program, designed to keep the working masses happy. Families would vacation in the countless apartments slotted into the six-story structure, the centerpiece of which was to be a festival hall with seats for 20,000. But war intervened, and Prora's only guests were refugees from Germany's bombed-out cities. It was subsequently occupied by the Volkspolizei (People's Police) and then, until 1990, by the Nationale Volksarmee (People's Army).

What to do with such a monstrous white (or rather gray) elephant? For the time being, it is home to several museums, the most interesting being the **Prora-Museum,** which puts the complex

in its historical and contemporary context. You can also visit the **NVA-Museum,** with East German Army memorabilia, a **Rügen-Museum,** with models of the geological development of the island, and the **Railway and Technology Museum** (Eisenbahn- und Technik-Museum), with restored steam locomotives and an assemblage of veteran motor vehicles *(all three museums: KulturKunststatt Prora, tel 038393 3 26 96).*

Prora is built on a narrow strip of land separating the Baltic from the Kleiner Jasmunder Bodden, the lagoon that, together with the Grosser Jasmunder Bodden, brings saltwater right into the heart of the island. To the north is Jasmund, a more substantial block of land,

which was once an island in its own right. The first substantial sights here are the extensive installations of the modern ferry port of Neu Mukran. With its train ferry facilities, the harbor was built to link East Germany with Soviet ports, an alternative to the rail and road routes through Poland, which was seen as an unreliable ally in the Solidarity era in the 1980s.

Beyond the old harbor town of Sassnitz, much of Jasmund is covered by splendid beech forests of the **Stubbenkammer,** protected as part of a national park. The crowds mostly come here to gasp at the spectacular chalk cliffs dropping hundreds of feet into the Baltic. The drama of their jagged forms and pristine whiteness fascinated the Romantic painter Caspar David Friedrich (see p. 42); his 1818 picture of early tourists gazing in awe from the cliff edge is a frequently reproduced classic of German art.

The most adventurous way of experiencing the cliffs is on foot along the coastal path from Sassnitz. But this is a whole day's walk, and most visitors content themselves with taking the shuttle bus from the parking lot to the main viewpoint known as the **King's Seat** (Königsstuhl). This is spectacular enough, but those with really strong nerves should venture on to the **Viktoriasicht,** a tiny platform that projects out over the abyss. A precipitous and potentially slippery path takes you to the beach. If none of this appeals to you, why not take a mini-cruise along the coastline aboard a pleasure cruiser from Sassnitz.

After the Stubbenkammer, almost anything would be an anti-climax, but it is still worthwhile continuing to Rügen's northern-most tip, **Kap Arkona,** with its two lighthouses and remains of the

Right: Kap Arkona boasts a pair of lighthouses—old (1827) and new (1902).

**Sassnitz
visitor information**
 Bahnhofstrasse 19a
☎ 038392 64 90

Slavic fortress of Jaromarsburg. Nearby is the idyllic fishing village of **Vitt,** with thatched cottages and a church containing a striking modern mural. Or take the ferry from Schaprode on Rügen's western coast to the long, narrow island of **Hiddensee,** 10 miles (17 km) offshore. Hiddensee preserves its tranquility by banning cars, and it is even more peaceful once the day visitors have departed. There is a bus service, but renting a bike is the best way to explore the island, with its old thatched houses and sandy beaches. Figures as famous as Sigmund Freud have fallen under Hiddensee's spell, but the most famous resident was the playwright and Nobel Prize winner, Gerhart Hauptmann (1862–1946), who is buried in the village of Kloster. ∎

A cabin cruiser passes through Wieck's drawbridge over the River Ryck.

Greifswald

GREIFSWALD'S MOST FAMOUS SON IS THE ROMANTIC artist, Caspar David Friedrich (1774–1840), and the silhouette of the ancient university town remains much as it was when he painted it in the early 19th century. Still dominating the skyline are the towers of the city's three main churches. But the town's best-known monument is the ruined monastery of Eldena, one of Friedrich's favorite subjects.

Greifswald
🗺 89 E3
Visitor information
✉ Am Markt 1
☎ 03834 52 13 80

Pommersche Landesmuseum
✉ Mühlenstrasse 15
☎ 03834 83 12 10
🕐 Closed Mon.
💲 $$

Eldena was founded at the mouth of the little River Ryck in 1199. The market established by the monks a short distance upstream grew into an oval-shaped town with a regular checkerboard of streets. Greifswald became a member of the Hanseatic League, and in 1456 the university was founded, one of the earliest in northern Europe.

The city suffered badly in the Thirty Years War, but its surrender to the Red Army in April 1945 saved it from more destruction. Bronze relief panels commemorate these events at the entrance to the **Town Hall** (Rathaus) in the main square, Marktplatz. Here, open-air cafés mingle with a variety of fine

buildings, among them the early 15th-century **Giebelhaus,** a rare example of a Baltic Brick Gothic (see p. 36) town house.

Caspar David Friedrich's paintings are scattered, but Greifswald makes the most of what it has in the **Pommersche Landesmuseum,** installed in sensitively adapted turn-of-the-18th-century buildings. The Friedrich paintings on display include a much-loved depiction of Eldena. Don't miss **Eldena monastery;** the sandstone ruins stand among fine old trees. Nearby is the fishing village of **Wieck,** reached by a Dutch-style drawbridge that could be out of a van Gogh painting. ■

Usedom

SECOND ONLY TO RÜGEN IN SIZE, GERMANY'S EASTERN-most island owes its fame to the magnificent sandy beaches that stretch almost its entire length. When bathing in the sea became fashionable in the 19th century, Usedom enjoyed royal patronage, and its three most prestigious resorts style themselves imperial bathing places (*Kaiserbäder*). However, its good rail connections with the capital earned the island the jollier nickname of Berlin's Bathtub.

There are two approaches to Usedom from the mainland. The road and rail bridge to the northern part of the island goes from the old port of **Wolgast,** with its big brick medieval church in the upper town, and a timber-framed warehouse by the quayside. Farther south, the road from **Anklam** crosses the channel on a modern drawbridge. From it can be seen the massive remains of the railroad bridge that carried express trains from Berlin, blown up in the last days of World War II. Local Greens have campaigned for its restoration as part of a package of measures to deal with the flood of private cars engulfing the island every summer.

Usedom is all about the pleasures of the sea, but the island has a sinister side as well. A left turn off the main road from Wolgast will bring you to **Peenemünde** at the island's northern tip. It was here in the 1930s that Werner von Braun, the man later responsible for America's Apollo missions, toiled with teams of thousands of technicians to perfect a practical long-range missile. The fruit of his efforts was the V2, thousands of which were launched in the later stages of World War II, devastating towns and cities in southern England. The vast complex is mostly in ruins, but the **Historisch-Technische**

Beach "baskets" by the pier at Ahlbeck protect sunbathers from Baltic breezes.

Usedom
🅰 89 E3–F3
Visitor information
✉ Bäderstrasse 5, Ückeritz
☎ 038375 234 10

Historisch-Technische Informations-zentrum
✉ Im Kraftwerk
☎ 038371 50 50
💲 $$

Villa Irmgard
✉ Maxim-Gorki-Strasse 13, Heringsdorf
☎ 038378 2 23 61

Informations-zentrum has displays and shows films on the place. Outside the center there are Soviet-era aircraft and a full-size model of a V2. In GDR days, the harbor at Peenemünde was enlarged as a base for the Volksmarine. One of the rocket-launching vessels of the People's Navy is still here and is open to visitors.

Seaside resorts along the 23.5-mile (38 km) beach facing the Baltic include **Zinnowitz,** with the usual amenities of pier and promenade. It was a favorite vacation destination of trade unionists and their families in communist times. The big Red October hotel built in the 1970s has been privatized, modernized, renamed the Baltic, and restyled to harmonize with the traditional architecture of the place. Beyond Zinnowitz, the island narrows to a thin strip of sand separating the Baltic from the great embayment of the Achterwasser, a kind of inland sea. Road and railroad lead southeastward to Usedom's formerly fashionable *Kaiserbäder,* Bansin, Heringsdorf, and Ahlbeck.

The three resorts have kept their individual

A copy of the Nazis' death-dealing V2 rocket bomb dominates the museum grounds at Peenemünde.

identities, despite being linked by a promenade promoted as the longest in Europe. They are all attractive, with ravishing white villas and hotels that today attract prosperous visitors from all over German-speaking Europe and beyond.

Despite its workaday name (Herring Village), **Heringsdorf** thinks of itself as the most gracious of the three, with a tradition going back to a visit by the King of Prussia in 1836. Within a few decades it had become, in the words of Baedeker's guidebook, the "most fashionable of the Baltic sea-bathing places." Stroll along the promenade and enjoy the parade of prestigious residences on their landscaped grounds. Kaiser Wilhelm vacationed here several times, as did the German-American painter Lyonel Feininger (1871–1956). Russian writer Maxim Gorki (1868–1936) stayed in the **Villa Irmgard,** hoping the fresh sea breeze would clear his congested lungs. The villa is now the local museum. Heringsdorf's **pier,** a replacement for one burned down in 1958, is particularly elaborate, with a shopping mall, cinema, and apartments at the landward end, and a restaurant and landing stage 550 yards (500 m) out to sea.

The jaunty, red-roofed pier at **Ahlbeck,** a more middle-class resort than Heringsdorf, can claim the special distinction of being the only one of the prewar piers to have survived. Ahlbeck's eastern limit is also Germany's boundary with Poland. For the moment, only pedestrians and cyclists can cross the frontier here, but the Polish harbor town of **Swinoujscie** (formerly German Swinemünde) can also be reached on a day trip by pleasure cruiser from many of the resorts along the coast. ■

Mecklenburg Lake District

AT THE END OF THE LAST ICE AGE, THE GLACIERS RETREATED eastward across Mecklenburg, carving out lakebeds and meltwater channels and dumping sand and gravel. The landscape created consists of moorland, marsh, woodland, and innumerable bodies of water. The Mecklenburg Lake District (Mecklenburgische Seenplatte) extends from Schleswig-Holstein across southern Mecklenburg. At its heart is the glorious Müritz, Germany's second largest lake, 18 miles (29 km) long and covering an area of 45 square miles (117 sq km).

Mecklenburg Lake District

🅜 88–89 B2–D1

Visitor information

✉ Nationalpark-
Information Waren,
(Forest parking on
Specker Strasse)

☎ 03991 66 27 86

The lakes, connected by rivers and canals, are heaven for lovers of every kind of boating. Sailboats, motor cruisers, kayaks, and canoes crowd into the marinas and mooring places, and some of the lakes can be noisy with the activities of watersports enthusiasts. However, the eastern shore of the Müritz is protected as part of **Müritz National Park,** and pleasure boats must keep well away from its banks. Most of the national park is ancient woodland broken by heathland and flower-rich meadows grazed by rare breeds of sheep and cattle. Plentiful bird life includes a number of endangered species; there are buzzards, cranes, and storks, as well as ospreys and mighty sea eagles, Germany's national emblem.

Your best way of getting to know the lake district is, of course, by taking to the water. There are cruises aboard pleasure boats from places such as **Waren,** the attractive old town at the northern end of the Müritzsee. For a more challenging experience, rent a canoe or a raft and set out for a longer trip. With a map and no sense of urgency, you could get as far as Berlin, a minimum of four days' paddling away! Landlubbers should consider renting a bicycle and circling the lake along the **Müritz-Rundweg,** a well signed cycle route. Because of the irregular outline of the lake, it's farther than you might think—a total of 51 miles (82 km)—but well worthwhile, with ever changing landscapes and plenty of places to overnight. ∎

Boathouses at Röbel stud the shore of the vast Müritzsee.

Pleasure cruises

✉ Warener Schiffahrts-
gesellschaft, Waren,
Strandstrasse 3

☎ 03991 66 30 34

Boat rental

✉ Jörg Marlow, Waren,
Müritzstrasse 14

☎ 03991 66 23 94

More places to visit in Mecklenburg-West Pomerania

GÜSTROW

This old ducal town in the middle of the Mecklenburg Lake District has an exceptionally well-preserved townscape and fine civic buildings. The **parish church** dominating the main square and the **cathedral,** tucked away in a secluded corner of the Old Town (Altstadt), have good altarpieces and other treasures, while the massive Renaissance **Schloss** *(Franz-Parr-Platz, tel 03843 75 20, closed Mon.)* has a richly decorated interior and a restored baroque garden. In addition, Güstrow was the home of Ernst Barlach (1870–1938), one of Germany's greatest 20th-century sculptors, and some of his most heartfelt and appealing work is on show here. Don't miss his "Hovering Angel" floating serenely in an aisle of the cathedral. Then move on to the **Gertrudenkapelle** *(Gertrudenplatz 1, closed Mon., combined ticket with Atelierhaus $$),*

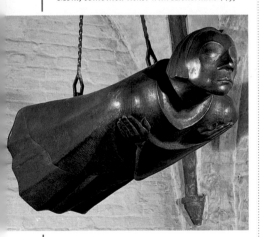

Barlach's "Hovering Angel," one of the great religious sculptures of the 20th century

a converted 15th-century chapel in a little park just outside the Altstadt, where archetypal figures such as "The Singer" and "Woman in the Wind" convey the humane vision that caused the Nazis to condemn Barlach as a "degenerate artist." Finally, visit his studio, the **Atelierhaus,** in its lovely lakeside setting

2 miles (3 km) south of the Altstadt *(Heidberg 15, tel 03843 84 40 00, closed Mon.).*

🅼 89 C2 **Visitor information**
✉ Domstrasse 9 ☎ 03843 01805 68 10 68

NEUBRANDENBURG

Disaster befell Neubrandenburg in the very last days of World War II, when fierce rearguard fighting almost completely destroyed the historic part of the town. By some miracle, the city walls and their four handsome gateways survived; together they make up one of the finest examples of a medieval fortification system anywhere in Germany. The 23-foot-high (7 m) walls were studded with *Wieckhäuser,* fortlets permanently manned by the sturdiest of burghers. A few of these quaint, mostly timber-framed dwellings survive and have been restored. The four brick gateways, complex structures, with an inner and outer gate and with soaring gables proclaiming Neubrandenburg's importance, defy any enemy to attack. You can walk all around the walls, but be warned—they stretch for well over a mile (2.3 km).

🅼 89 D2 **Visitor information**
✉ Marktplatz 1 ☎ 0395 1 94 33

SCHLOSS LUDWIGSLUST

This monumental palace 22 miles (35 km) south of Schwerin grew out of a far more modest hunting lodge built in the early 18th century by Duke Christian Ludwig II of Mecklenburg-Schwerin, from whom it got its name "Ludwig's Pleasure." The next duke, Friedrich, was more ambitious. He set out to make a North German Versailles with a vast English-style park. With its 17 bays and massive central section, the palace makes an almost overwhelming impression, and you would certainly not guess that its construction was constantly held up by lack of funds. The solid-looking stonework clads walls of common brick, and much of the interior decor is made of a patent papier-mâché (which has stood the test of time better than other more permanent-seeming materials).

🅼 88 B1 ☎ 03874 5 71 90
🕐 Closed Mon. ∎

G entle hills, shining lakes,
pastoral landscapes, and
the contrasting coastlines of the
North and Baltic Seas epito-
mize northernmost Germany,
while the great port of Hamburg,
Germany's second city, has its
own big-city sophistication.

Hamburg & Schleswig-Holstein

Traditional trades of Lübeck

Hamburg & Schleswig-Holstein

RUNNING FROM THE MIGHTY RIVER ELBE TO THE DANISH BORDER, THESE northern *Bundesländer* have a particularly intimate relationship with the sea—or rather seas. Forming a kind of causeway linking Central Europe with Scandinavia, Schleswig-Holstein is bounded on one side by the North Sea and on the other by the Baltic (the Ostsee, or Eastern Sea, in German). Sixty miles (100 km) inland from the mouth of the Elbe, Hamburg is the country's second biggest city, after Berlin, and its greatest seaport, looking not just to the North Sea, but also to the oceans of the world. Its equivalent on the Baltic is Lübeck, still an important harbor town, although the days when it dominated the Hanseatic League of trading cities have long since gone.

The North Sea and Baltic coasts are quite different in character. To the west, the sea battles with the low-lying land, whose outline is continually being reshaped by the action of wind and waves, strong tides and currents. The North Frisian Islands (Nordfriesische Inseln), the area's greatest attraction, were once part of the mainland. There has been gain as well as loss, however, with much land reclaimed from the sea between the mainland and the outer islands. Hundreds of miles of dikes have been constructed to resist further encroachment.

Most of the islands' splendid beaches face west; to the east stretches the strange landscape of the Wattenmeer, a vast expanse of mud and sand exposed twice daily by the receding tide. It harbors a rich and intriguing wildlife, nourishment for millions of seabirds, but it is a fragile ecosystem, vulnerable to pollution and other human impact. A vast, 1,100 square miles (2,850 sq km) of it, stretching from the mouth of the Elbe to the northern tip of the island of Sylt, is now designated as the Nationalpark Schleswig–Holsteinisches Wattenmeer.

To the east, the almost tideless Baltic is fronted for much of its length by low cliffs, interrupted by fjord-like inlets of the sea, which make good natural harbors and

Container ship in dry dock in Hamburg's busy harbor

sites for towns and cities, such as Kiel, Schleswig, and Flensburg. Right on the border with Denmark, Flensburg is Germany's northernmost city. The town's substantial Danish minority is a reminder that this is a border region, with a convoluted history, much of it spent under Danish rule. A German-speaking minority lives north of today's frontier, the line of which was only determined as a result of a plebiscite in 1920.

Most foreign visitors spend their time only in ancient Lübeck and mighty Hamburg—a pity, since the rest of the region offers unique landscapes and a host of minor delights. ■

Hamburg

Proud to call itself a "Free and Hansa City," Hamburg is a *Land* in its own right, and it has always felt itself to be at least the equal of any of its nominal rulers, whether Danish king or German kaiser. Its long-standing trading links with the rest of the world have given it a readiness to innovate not always characteristic of German cities.

While it still relies on its great port, second only in Europe to Rotterdam, Hamburg is also a manufacturing center (the European super jumbo airliner is assembled here) and a service center of the first importance. Banks, insurance companies, and media interests are based here, including the publishers of the internationally read *Stern* magazine and the influential weekly *Die Zeit*. The city's identity is strong enough to encompass striking contrasts: There are more wealthy people

The line of the long since demolished city walls forms a semicircular boundary to the north, followed by the broad ring road, while St. Pauli stands on slightly higher ground to the west. The high ground extends farther west along the Elbe through Altona, once under Danish rule and quite independent of Hamburg, then on to the retired sea captains' houses and millionaires' villas of the desirable suburb of Blankenese. ■

Hamburg's skyline is best appreciated from a pleasure boat plying the waters of the harbor or the Alster lakes.

here than anywhere else in Germany, but modernization of the harbor has left a high rate of unemployment. Hamburg has traditionally worn a stern and sober face, but nothing could be more outrageous than what goes on along the notorious Reeperbahn in the red-light district of St. Pauli.

The city's general layout is easy to grasp. From the great natural boundary of the Elbe in the south the channels (*Fleete*) of the River Alster divide the old city center roughly into half and link through to the magnificent lakelike stretches of water known as the Binnen- (Inner) and Aussen- (Outer) Alster.

City center

A GREAT FIRE IN 1842 DESTROYED MOST OF OLD HAMBURG, which until then must have looked like a larger version of its Hansa partner and rival Lübeck. The 19th- and early 20th-century city was then devastated by bombing, particularly during the week-long Allied air raids of July 1943, which unleashed a firestorm, killing 55,000 people. The Hamburg that rose from the rubble would not claim to be Germany's most beautiful city, but plenty of reminders of its long past are preserved among the matrix of modern building.

Hamburg has kept its distinctive silhouette, dominated by the five towers of its great civic churches. You could start your exploration of the city at **St. Michaelis-Kirche,** built in 1762 and one of the great-est of North German baroque churches. "Der Michel" is a much-loved city symbol, and its 433-foot (132 m) tower a landmark for sailors. Climb the tower for an unsurpassable view of river, harbor,

Hamburg
🗺 108 DI
Visitor information
✉ Hauptbahnhof,
  Kirchenallee exit
☎ 040 30 05 12 00

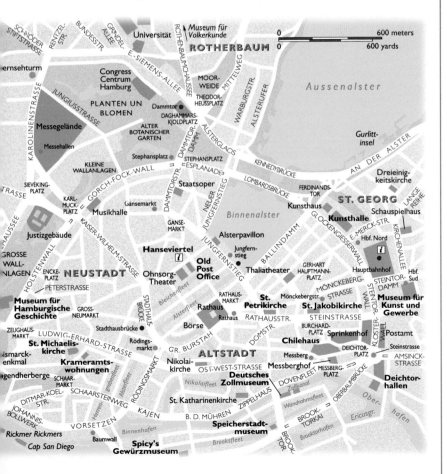

St. Michaelis-Kirche
- Map p. 111
- Krayenkamp 4C
- 040 37 67 81 00
- $ (tower & Multivision)

Almshouses
- Map p. 111
- Krayenkamp 10
- 040 37 50 19 88
- Closed Mon.
- $

and the town as a whole, then enjoy the exciting "Multivision" slide show, which gives a fascinating overview of Hamburg history. Just down from the church, the **Almshouses** (Krameramts-wohnungen), reached through doorway at No. 10 & 11 Krayenkamp, have somehow survived to give an idea of living conditions for poor widows in the 17th century. More upscale 18th-century merchants' residences, heavily restored, line **Peterstrasse.** Johannes Brahms was born nearby in 1833, and No. 39, with its sign showing the bearded composer enjoying a cigar, is devoted to his memory. A short distance to the west is the superb **Hamburg History Museum** (see p. 115).

Hamburg's epicenter is the **Rathausmarkt,** the spacious square in front of the monumental Northern Renaissance (Nordische Renaissance) **City Hall** completed in 1897, when Hamburg was prospering as imperial Germany's foremost port. Governed for centuries by patrician merchants rather than princes or nobles, Hamburg is still

very careful to remind its visitors that it is a "Free and Hansa City." The mayor does not descend the steps to greet heads of state, but waits regally for them at the top (an exception being made for Queen Elizabeth II).

One side of the Rathausmarkt is bounded by the channel through which the River Alster finds its way to the Elbe from the Binnenalster to the north. On the far side, Venetian-style arcades announce the city's prestige retail district, with exclusive stores serving the needs of, among others, the city's thousands of millionaires. You'll find few bargains here, but some great window shopping in the streets and passageways that Hamburgers claim make their city a far more chic place to shop than anywhere else in Germany, Munich not excepted. The area is an attractive combination of old and new; the Italianate **Old Post Office** on Poststrasse now houses one of the very first shopping arcades, which contrasts with the airy shopping galleries of the **Hanseviertel,** the largest development of its kind.

There's more shopping farther east, where department stores line **Mönckebergstrasse,** laid out early in the 20th century with the U-Bahn line running underneath. **St. Petrikirche,** in Mönckeberg-strasse, is the city center's oldest place of worship, first mentioned in 1195, although the present church is a reconstruction following the great fire of 1842. Next to it, No. 9 is a charming building, to all appearances a historic Hanseatic town house but built in 1911.

Farther along, to the south of Gerhart-Hauptmann-Platz, **St. Jacobikirche** dates from 1350, but the church had to be almost completely rebuilt after 1945. Many original fittings, such as the great organ of 1693, were preserved. ■

Hamburg's port—once the centerpiece of its infamous red-light district—is now a popular meeting place for young Hamburgers and tourist crowds.

St. Pauli & the harbor

THE NOTORIOUS RED-LIGHT DISTRICT OF ST. PAULI HAS cleaned up its act since the sleazy days of the 1960s and '70s. The full range of sexual preferences is still catered for, but today's St. Pauli attracts a mixed crowd of visitors, many millions a year, who fill pubs, bars, restaurants, discos, cabarets, clubs, and theaters and keep the action going into the small hours and beyond. If you decide to join them and spend an evening here, be sure to keep your hand on your wallet. There's more than one way to lose money!

St. Pauli owes its existence to the distaste felt by Hamburg's Protestant city fathers for the sort of leisure pursuits enjoyed by sailors with money in their pockets and time to spend it while their ships unloaded. Those catering to their needs were forced to set up shop outside the walls, along the **Reeperbahn,** the old ropewalk that stretched from the city's western gateway to the separate borough of Altona. The rope-

makers have long since gone, as have the sailors, and ships now load and unload in a matter of hours rather than weeks. St. Pauli is a mixed community today, with one-third of its residents non-Germans. Bad behavior is kept within bounds by the district's famous police station on the corner of Davidstrasse, one of the streets that is otherwise patrolled by ladies of the night. Aspiring rock musicians still make their way to St. Pauli, as did a

Visitor information

✉ St. Pauli Landungs-brücken (between Brücke 4 & 5)

☎ 040 30 05 12 03

Speicherstadt-museum

- 🅼 Map p. 111
- ✉ St. Annenufer 2
- ☎ 040 32 11 91
- 🕐 Closed Mon.
- 💲 $

Spicy's Gewürzmuseum

- 🅼 Map p. 111
- ✉ Am Sandtorkai 32
- ☎ 040 36 79 89
- 🕐 Closed Mon. in winter
- 💲 $

Deutsches Zollmuseum

- 🅼 Map p. 111
- ✉ Alter Wandrahm 16
- ☎ 040 30 08 76 11
- 🕐 Closed Mon.

certain John, Paul, George, Stuart, and Pete in 1960, but there is no Beatles-Platz. Instead, there is a statue and a square named after Hamburg heartthrob of the early 20th century, Hans Albers, film star and singer of, among many other hits, "La Paloma."

St. Pauli extends down to the Elbe. Along the waterfront stands the stately **Landungsbrücken,** where ocean liners used to dock. The old **Fischmarkt** still sells fish here early on Sunday mornings, along with fruit and vegetables and much else. The colorful and noisy scene attracts crowds of bleary-eyed Saturday-night survivors as well as bargain hunters. Hafenstrasse, linking the market building with the ocean terminal, was the stronghold of "alternatives" in the 1980s, but its tatty, graffiti-covered buildings are now more squalid than utopian.

As its activity expanded, Hamburg's **harbor** moved from the channels of the Alster in the city center to the Elbe waterfront, and then migrated to the far side of the river. Big ships can still be seen moving majestically up and down the river. To grasp the full magnitude of the harbor, take one of the many trips offered. As well as giving you a view of dry docks, seemingly endless quaysides, and great stacks of containers, most cruises take you around the **Speicherstadt.** This complex of beautifully decorated late 19th-century redbrick warehouses was part of the Free Port.

Among the splendid warehouses are several museums (take a taxi if you want to visit). The **Speicherstadtmuseum/Museum der Arbeit** deals with the history of the district, the highly aromatic **Spicy's Gewürzmuseum** is devoted to spices, and the **Deutsches Zollmuseum** is about customs and revenue. A section covers Hamburg's role as an emigration port for many Europeans leaving their homelands forever. ∎

Hamburg museums & art galleries

Left: St. Pauli's brightly lit Grosse Freiheit (Liberty) Street

Right: One of Caspar David Friedrich's best-known paintings, the "Wanderer above the Sea of Fog" (ca 1818), hangs in the Kunsthalle.

Erotic Art Museum
- Map p. 110
- Bernhard-Nocht-Strasse 69
- 040 3 17 84 10
- $$

Hamburg History Museum
www.hamburgmuseum.de
- Map p. 111
- Holstenwall 24
- 040 42 81 32 23 80
- Closed Mon.
- $$

Art & Craft Museum
- Map p. 111
- Steintorplatz 1
- 040 4 28 54 2 630
- Closed Mon.
- $$

Kunsthalle
- Map p. 111
- Glockengiesserwall 1
- 040 4 28 13 12 00
- Closed Mon.
- $$

HAMBURG HAS A RANGE OF MUSEUMS MANY CAPITAL cities might envy. St. Pauli is, to no one's surprise, home to an Erotic Art Museum, which is as tasteful as its subject permits, while the splendid 19th-century warehouse complex of Speicherstadt has three museums evoking Hamburg's commercial past (see p. 114).

The general history of the city is covered in the excellent **Hamburg History Museum** (Museum für Hamburgische Geschichte), which stands on parkland on the western edge of the city center. The comprehensive displays deal with every possible aspect of the city's past. The huge model railway, a meticulous re-creation of one of the city's principal stations, amazes most people, not just rail enthusiasts.

The city's art collections are spread along an "Art Mile" that extends from the Binnenalster to the Upper Harbor (Oberhafen), where the old wholesale flower market, the **Deichtorhallen** *(Deichtorstrasse, closed Mon.)*, has been converted into a spectacular setting for exhibitions of contemporary art.

South of the main station, the **Art & Craft Museum** (Museum für Kunst und Gewerbe) contains an exceptional array of decorative arts, among which the beautifully presented collection of historic musical instruments is outstanding. There are also whole rooms furnished in art nouveau or art deco style by masters such as Henry van de Velde (1863–1957), whose Weimar school of design became the Bauhaus.

North of the station, the **Kunsthalle** is one of Germany's great art galleries, housed in a dignified 19th-century building. A recent, highly controversial extension was specifically designed

for contemporary art. The main collection is huge, covering works from the Middle Ages to the mid-20th century. It would take many visits to the gallery to take in the important pieces.

If time is short, concentrate perhaps on the German art of the 19th and early 20th centuries. Among the Romantics, watch for "The Sea of Ice" and "Wanderer above the Sea of Fog" by Caspar David Friedrich (1774–1840), and "Morning" by Philipp Otto Runge (1777–1810). Impressionists such as Max Liebermann (1847–1935) are represented with "The Netmenders" and "Ulysses and Calypso," and there are works by such modern masters as Otto Dix (1891–1969) and Max Beckmann (1884–1950). ∎

The houses lining the Nikolaifleet once served as warehouses and shops as well as residences.

Walk: Dryshod from Alster to Elbe

This walk starts on the Jungfernstieg, the esplanade overlooking the calm waters of the Binnenalster, and then zigzags through the city center to the busy harbor overlooking the River Elbe.

The **Jungfernstieg** ❶ is a fashionable shopping boulevard as well as a good place to sit and admire the Binnenalster from a waterside café. Pleasure boats depart from here for trips around both inner and outer Alsters and farther up the river itself. The sober gray buildings along the lakeside include the prestigious Vier Jahreszeiten Hotel and the 1901 headquarters of the world's then biggest shipping line, Hapag.

The area "inland" from the Jungfernstieg is home to Hamburg's most exclusive shopping streets and arcades (see p. 112). The **Alster Arcades** (Alsterarkaden) frame the view over the channel of the Alsterfleet to the **City Hall** (Rathaus) ❷ (see p. 112). Pass through the main portal and the imposing vaulted foyer of the City Hall into the courtyard beyond. The elaborate Hygeia fountain commemorates the terrible cholera epidemic of 1892. Go out to the left, turn right, then left onto the street called Börsenbrücke. Look up the long narrow space to the left where there is a rare trace of the medieval trading city, the back of a timber-framed building with the upper floors jettied out. Cross the bridge over the Alster, with its statues of city founders Archbishop Ansgar and Graf (Count)

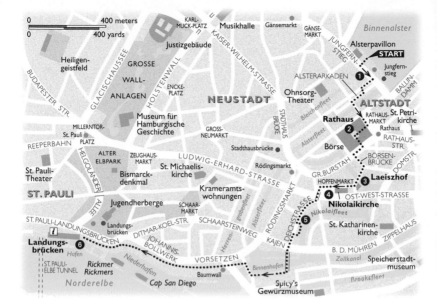

Adolf III. von Schaumburg. Take a look at the **Laeiszhof ❸,** a typical Hamburg shipping line headquarters building, put up by one of the founders of Hapag. The poodle crowning it is a reminder of the magnate's pet name for his wife: "Poodle."

The dominant feature in this part of town is the tall spire of the bombed-out **Nikolaikirche ❹,** left as a memorial and warning. From the far end of the Hopfen-markt square, a footbridge spans the multiple lanes of the busy east–west arterial road. Steps lead you down into **Deichstrasse** (Dike Street), where the grand facades of the mer-chants' houses, dating from the 17th through 19th centuries, give a good idea of what the old Hansa town must have been like before the Great Fire of 1842. You can squeeze down a narrow passageway and walk along the pon-toon on the **Nikolaifleet ❺** to get a view of the brick-built backs of the tall buildings, which combined access to the water with storerooms, offices, and living quarters. Most surviving buildings are now pubs and restaurants.

Cross the waterside road, and climb up on to the **embankment** that runs all the way west to **St. Pauli,** the city's red-light district (see pp. 113–114), giving views of the activity on the Elbe. Don't head west straight away, but

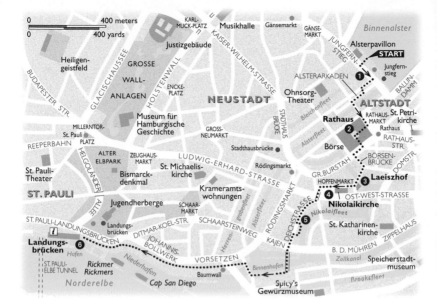
Also see map pp. 110–111
Jungfernstieg
1.75 miles (3 km)
1.5 hours
St. Pauli Landungsbrücken

NOT TO BE MISSED
- Jungfernstieg
- City Hall
- Deichstrasse and Nikolaifleet
- *Rickmer Rickmers*
- St. Pauli Landungsbrücken

cross the water of the Binnenhafen by the footbridge, and walk along the quayside for views back to the "mainland."

The **museum vessels** moored along the embankment include the classic mid-20th-century freighter *Cap San Diego,* and the *Rickmer Rickmers,* a splendid East India windjammer of 1896, both of which are open to visitors daily. The towers and copper domes at the end of the embankment belong to the **St. Pauli Landungsbrücken ❻,** where ocean liners formerly tied up. Now it's just used by ferries and harbor cruisers, but there are plenty of places to eat, drink, and rest your legs after the walk. ■

The Westerheversand lighthouse and its keeper's cottages

Schleswig-Holstein

The two great visitor destinations of Schleswig-Holstein could hardly be more different in character. In the southeast, on the border with Mecklenburg, lovely Lübeck is a near-perfect example of a medieval Hansa trading city, and in the far northwest, the North Frisian Islands have been attracting crowds of vacationers in search of sun, sand, and sea for more than a century and a half.

Between these two poles, there is much more to see and do. The Baltic coast has its share of fine beaches and seaside resorts, rivaling the similar old bathing places farther east; Travemünde is associated with Lübeck and Laboe with Kiel, the state capital. Kiel is a workaday place at the end of the famous canal named for it, but its fjord is a yachtsman's paradise, host to one of the world's great annual sailing events, the Kiel Week (Kieler Woche) in June. Farther north, an even longer fjord than Kiel's leads far inland to Schleswig, the former capital, with an outstanding cathedral and castle. The harbor town of Flensburg is as far north as you can go in Germany, and it is worth the journey for its bustling harbor and Danish flavor. The more exposed western coast facing the North Sea has hardly any substantial towns, the exception being the old fishing port of Husum, a good base for exploring the smaller islands studding the Wattenmeer.

Inland Schleswig-Holstein has hardly been disturbed by international tourism. There are few trees, but this is partly compensated for by the 30,000 or so miles (50,000 km) of hedges, planted as windbreaks and stock barriers in the 18th and 19th centuries. There's little to break the force of the wind on the North Frisian mainland, where the dominant structures are the huge modern wind turbines. The great skies and bright light of the area inspired expressionist painter Emil Nolde, and a gallery near Niebüll housing a superb selection of his work provides a good reason for exploring this unique part of Germany. Eastward to the Baltic are the gentler landscapes of the Holsteinische Schweiz (Holstein Switzerland), low wooded hills enfolding a constellation of lakes. ∎

Kiel

THE CAPITAL OF SCHLESWIG-HOLSTEIN STANDS AT THE head of its wonderful natural harbor, the Kiel Fjord (Kieler Förde) running inland from the Baltic. Every June the fjord is the scene of the world's greatest sailing event, Kiel Week (Kieler Woche), when up to three million spectators watch thousands of competitors participate in a range of thrilling events.

In the 19th century when imperial Germany began to build itself a great navy, Kiel rose to prominence. Shipyards and naval bases spread along the banks of the fjord, whose strategic value was immensely enhanced by the building of the **Kiel Canal** (1887-1895). Called the Nord-Ostsee-Kanal (North Sea-Baltic Canal), the 61.5-mile-long (99 km) waterway enabled warships to pass quickly between the two seas, avoiding the detour around Denmark. Today the traffic consists of freighters rather than battleships, 37,000 of them a year, making the canal one of the world's busiest artificial waterways.

From the tower of the **City Hall** (Rathaus), view the Old Town (Altstadt) and the winding fjord with its shipyards. A visit to the waterside **Maritime Museum** (Schiffahrtsmuseum) informs you about the city's relationship with the sea, and three historic craft are moored alongside *(no access to boats mid-Oct.–mid-April)*.

Take a trip aboard one of the ferries that call at various points along the fjord. At the beach resort of **Laboe,** the towering **Marine-Ehrenmal,** a 280-foot-high (85 m) monument in the form of a ship's prow, was built in 1936 as Germany's principal naval war memorial. It is now dedicated to the memory of sailors of all nations who have died at sea. The top of the tower is accessible by 341 steps or elevator. At its foot is a U-995, a World War II submarine. ∎

Sailing ships of many nations fill Kiel's fjord in June for the famous Kieler Woche festival.

Kiel
🅜 108 D3
Visitor information
✉ Andreas-Gayk-Strasse 31
☎ 0431 67 91 00

City Hall
✉ Rathausplatz
☎ 0431 90 10
🕐 Closed weekends
💲 $

Maritime Museum
✉ Wall 65
☎ 0431 901 34 28
💲 $

Marine-Ehrenmal
✉ Laboe, Strandstrasse 92
☎ 04343 42 700
💲 $

Lübeck

STILL SURROUNDED BY ELABORATE WATER DEFENSES, THIS ancient port and trading city has preserved much of the atmosphere of its heyday when, as leader of the medieval Hanseatic League of trading cities, its influence extended all around the Baltic Sea and beyond. Lübeck remains an important harbor, with the focus of activity nowadays farther downstream toward the mouth of the River Trave. But most people come to enjoy the town's old streets and squares lined with brick buildings in styles reflected all along the north European coasts from the Netherlands to Estonia.

Lübeck
⚛ 109 E2
Visitor information
✉ Holstentorplatz 1
☎ 01805 88 22 33 or
0451 409 19 57

Petrikirche
✉ Schmiedstrasse
🕐 Lift closed Nov.–Feb.
💲 $

Buddenbrookhaus
✉ Mengstrasse 4
☎ 0451 1 22 42 42
💲 $$

Heiligen-Geist-Hospital
✉ Koberg
☎ 0451 790 78 41
🕐 Closed Mon.
💲 $

Museum for Art and Cultural History
✉ Kunsthalle St. Annen, St. Annen-Strasse 15
☎ 0451 122 41 34
🕐 Closed Mon.
💲 $

Seven church towers and spires dominate Lübeck's skyline. To get to them, you must pass the city's great emblem, the massive 15th-century gateway called the **Holstentor** *(tel 0451 122 41 29, closed Mon.)*. Built of brick, like nearly every structure in the city, it consists of two sturdy cylinders topped by conical slate roofs and linked by a gabled section above the original archway. The local history museum inside displays a superb model of the town in the 17th century.

The city proper begins on the far side of the bridge beyond the gateway. You could get an overall view of its oval shape and intricate street pattern by taking the elevator up the tower of the **Petrikirche,** but first take in the unsurpassed group of buildings dominating the city center. The **Town Hall** (Rathaus) and the twin-towered **Marienkirche,** both begun in the mid-13th century, express the pride of the citizens in the independent status of their city, free from domination by prince or bishop. The bold circular openings in the upper wall of the city hall are not there for effect, but to lessen wind resistance. The church is full of artworks of the highest quality. The most poignant items, however, are probably the shattered bells beneath the south tower, left as they fell during

the terrible night of March 28, 1942, when British bombs destroyed 25 percent of the city.

Just to the north of the church, the splendid white mansion of the **Buddenbrookhaus** is named after *Die Buddenbrooks*, the family saga set in Lübeck and one of the best-loved novels by Thomas Mann (1875–1955), a native of the city. The building is now devoted to his memory and that of his brother and fellow-writer, Heinrich Mann.

Farther north along Breite Strasse, past the Jakobikirche, the seamen's church, you will find the **Haus der Schiffergesellschaft** *(Breite Strasse 2),* once the head-quarters of the sea captains' guild. Today it's one of the best places to eat in town, with a carefully re-created maritime atmosphere and, of course, good fish dishes. Breite Strasse leads eventually to another formidable gateway, the medieval Burgtor.

On Königstrasse, running parallel to Breite Strasse, the **Heiligen-Geist-Hospital** was founded about 1280 by charitably minded merchants to house those citizens less fortunate than themselves. Its elaborate facade is matched by the interior with its medieval wall paintings and great hall. A few paces away, a pair of fine old dwellings have been converted to house the **Museum for Art and**

Cultural History (Museum für Kunst und Kulturgeschichte), with paintings and furniture evoking the lifestyle of prosperous 19th-century Lübeckers. Farther south, off Glockengiesserstrasse, are some little 17th-century almshouses laid out around charming courtyards.

TRAVEMÜNDE

Lübeck's location a few miles up the River Trave from the Baltic meant that in medieval times the city fathers had to pay tolls to the Holsteiners, who controlled the river mouth at Travemünde. So in 1320 the Lübeckers bought the place. Travemünde still has some old timber-framed houses where fisherfolk lived, as well as the church in which they worshiped. For some years now, however, the tone of the place has been set by its spruce casino and Kurhaus, its villas, and the long promenade. The town was one of the very first of Germany's seaside resorts, and it is still one of the most elegant. ∎

Lübeck's Rathaus encloses the city's brick marketplace.

The sturdy *Kogge* (flat-bottomed ship) secured the seaways of the Hansa.

The Hanseatic League

An association of trading cities, the Hansa was formed for protection against pirates and to control the lucrative trade around the Baltic Sea. Raw materials—furs, wax, amber, salt, timber, and honey—were traded for products from the west, such as textiles, wine, and metalwork. Lübeck led the way, but many other German ports, and even inland cities such as Cologne, were members with trading privileges in towns and cities as far away as England. Goods were transported by *Koggen,* broad sailing ships, some of which could carry a cargo of 600 tons. Although the League last assembled in 1669, its name lives on. The national airline is called Lufthansa (Hansa of the air), and car license plates in Hamburg and Bremen carry the letter "H." ∎

North Frisian Islands

IN THE DAYS BEFORE 1989, WHEN THE EAST GERMAN BALTIC coast was closed to West Germans, West Germany's favorite seaside destination was the archipelago of the Nord-friesische Inseln off Schleswig-Holstein's North Sea coast. Of these windswept isles, Sylt was its swankiest island, dubbed the St. Tropez of the North.

Typical thatched houses shelter amid the sand-dunes of Sylt island.

North Frisian Islands

🗺 108 B4

Visitor information

www.westerland.de

✉ Strandstrasse 25

☎ 04651 99 88

The islands were once part of the mainland, but the restless sea broke in on more than one occasion, and today saltwater covers the vast area designated as the **Schleswig-Holstein Wattenmeer National Park.** The largest island, **Sylt,** is only 24 miles long (38.5 km), and in places it is only a few hundred yards wide, with sand dunes rising as high as 172 feet (52.5 m). By contrast, parts of the "Halligen," the islands in the area's southern part, are actually below sea level, with farmsteads built on artificial mounds as refuges from frequent flooding.

The *Watten* of the Wattenmeer are the extensive slicks of sand and mud exposed by the twice-daily retreat of the sea, temporarily joining certain islands to each other or to the mainland. Watten-walking (Wattwandern) has become popular, preferably with an experienced guide who can explain the strange but teeming life that flourishes here and alert to the dangers posed as the tide sweeps in. Colonies of seals are another attraction.

People have been coming to the islands since the 19th century—for the bracing air (the sea breeze never falters), the sunshine (more of it than on the mainland), the sandy beaches, the sea (beautiful breakers), and society. The social whirl began in a modest way in 1842, when the king of Denmark decided to spend his summer vacation at **Wyk** on the second largest island, **Föhr.** Wyk is a charming old harbor town, with a tree-lined promenade above its long sandy beach, and Föhr in general is a fine spot for family vacations.

However, the center of the action shifted long ago to **Sylt.** Thomas Mann praised it, Marlene Dietrich loved it, and in the 1960s every swinger and jetsetter had to be seen here. The hub of the island is the substantial town of **Westerland,** the terminus of the railroad connecting Sylt with the mainland via the 7-mile (11 km) causeway of the Hindenburgdamm (there is no road access to Sylt; cars must be put aboard the train at Niebüll). Westerland likes to think of itself as terribly sophisticated. There's a classy casino and plenty of bistros, bars, and discos, but you are unlikely to meet many stars on the very ordinary shopping street linking the station to the seafront

and the splendid sandy beach. (All visitors have to pay a small tax, which gets you a *Kurkarte*, resort card. Hotels will add this to the bill; for day visits, you can get a day card from kiosks near the beach.) Westerland is the victim of its popularity, with too many day-trippers and high-rise apartments destroying what character the place once possessed.

The super-rich Germans have retreated elsewhere on the island, to relax in the privacy of their expensive vacation houses. **Kampen** is popular, with its 2.8-mile-long (4.5 km) Rote Kliff, a copper-colored, 82-foot-high (30 m) cliff. Strict building regulations enforce a thatched roof on every new building, whether it be vacation home,

gourmet restaurant, antique shop, or exclusive boutique.

Get off the train a couple of train stops before Westerland and you are in **Keitum**, a leafy village of charming old Frisian houses. From the church there is a vast panorama over the infinite expanse of the Wattenmeer.

Beyond Kampen, near the northern end of the island, is Germany's northernmost community, **List,** the harbor for ferries making the 50-minute crossing to Rømø in Denmark. This part of Sylt, just north of List, is famous for the shifting sand dunes that creep eastward at the rate of 13 feet (4 m) a year; they make up the largest area of this kind in Europe and have been a designated nature reserve since the 1920s. ∎

Barefoot walkers follow their guide across the mudflats of the Wattenmeer.

More places to visit in Schleswig-Holstein

FLENSBURG

Germany's northernmost city belonged to Denmark until 1920, and for many years its harbor was a more important port than Copenhagen's. Danes still make up some 20 percent of the population and help give Flensburg its unique atmosphere. It is an attractive place, partly built on the higher land rising steeply from both sides of the busy harbor. If you walk up the long main street leading north to the brick gateway of the Nordertor, take time to explore the intimate **Höfe,** the old merchants' courtyards running down toward the quayside. A number of historic vessels are moored near the **Maritime Museum** (Schiffahrtsmuseum), which has a fine array of ship models, maritime paintings, and navigational instruments. A special exhibition in the basement is devoted to rum, once Flensburg's most famous product *(Schiffbrücke 39, tel 0461 85 29 70, closed Mon.).*

Pretty housefronts in the heart of Husum

⚏ 108 C4 **Visitor information**
✉ Rathausstrasse 1 ☎ 0461 9 09 09 20

HUSUM

"The old gray town by the sea" was how Schleswig-Holstein's greatest writer, Theodor Storm (1817–1888), described this charming harbor town on the province's western coast.

Storm's home, the **Theodor-Storm-Haus** *(Wasserreihe 31, tel 04841 66 62 70, closed Mon., Wed., Sun. Nov.–March),* was where he wrote the novella *Der Schimmelreiter (Rider on a White Horse),* a wonderful evocation of one man's struggle to keep the restless sea from reclaiming these hard-won coastlands. Husum is really rather more colorful than Storm implied. There may be no great monuments, but you could spend a very pleasant half-day here, wandering the old streets and watching the activity in the tidal inner harbor. There are plenty of bars and fish restaurants, and the town is a good base for exploring the North Frisian coast and islands. To the south is the tiny town of **Friedrichstadt,** founded by Dutch settlers in 1621, a little bit of Holland with canals and high-gabled houses.

⚏ 108 B4 **Visitor information**
✉ Grossstrasse 27 ☎ 04841 8 98 70

SCHLESWIG

Schleswig stands on the Schlei, a fjord running 27 miles (43 km) inland from the Baltic. The finest view of the old capital of the province is across the water from the south. It was on this bank of the Schlei that the Vikings settled at the beginning of the ninth century. Among the most interesting relics of that time housed in the modern **Wikinger Museum Haithabu** *(Haddeby bei Schleswig, tel 04621 81 32 22, closed Mon. Nov.–March)* is a reconstructed longship.

Even more impressive is the fourth-century Nydam Boat, one of the star exhibits in **Schloss Gottorf.** The boat is 75 feet long (23 m) and a unique relic from the time of the great migrations of the Germanic tribes. Formerly the mighty ducal residence, the Schloss is the province's finest Renaissance building and now the regional museum *(Schloss Gottorf, tel 04621 81 32 22, closed Mon. Nov.–March).* It stands apart from Schleswig's charming Old Town (Altstadt). Above the old streets rises the 19th-century tower of the **cathedral,** containing a beautiful masterpiece of late medieval carving, the Bordesholm (Bordesholmer) Altar.

⚏ 108 C4 **Visitor information**
✉ Plessenstrasse 7 ☎ 04621 98 16 16 ∎

From the Dutch border to the River Elbe and south to the Harz Mountains, Lower Saxony, Germany's second largest *Land,* has varied landscapes and intriguing cities. The adjacent state of Bremen has a proud history as a free city.

Lower Saxony & Bremen

Hamelin's Pied Piper

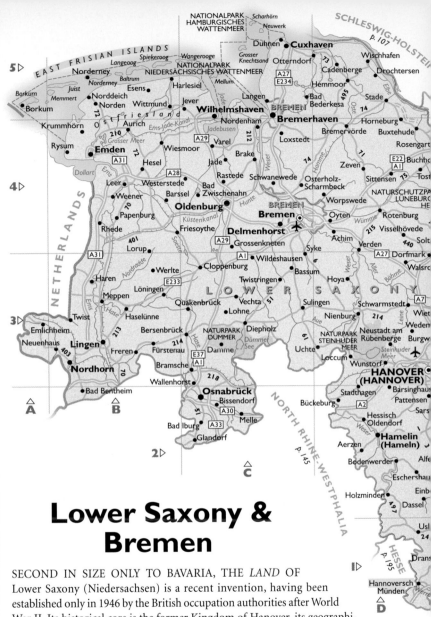

SCHLESWIG-HOLSTEIN *p. 107*

HESSE *p. 195*

NORTH RHINE-WESTPHALIA *p. 145*

Lower Saxony & Bremen

SECOND IN SIZE ONLY TO BAVARIA, THE *LAND* OF
Lower Saxony (Niedersachsen) is a recent invention, having been
established only in 1946 by the British occupation authorities after World
War II. Its historical core is the former Kingdom of Hanover, its geographical core a substantial slice of the Northern European Plain. Its northern boundary
extends to the North Sea, where the dunes and sandy beaches of the East Frisian Islands
form one of Germany's favorite vacation areas. At the eastern end of the plain is the
Lüneburg Heath (Lüneburger Heide), a vast tract of rolling heathland. To the south the
land gradually rises to form fine hill country, and in the Harz, shared with neighboring
Saxony-Anhalt, the nearest thing to high mountains that north Germany possesses. In the
center is the fine old river port of Bremen, not part of Lower Saxony but a separate political entity in its own right, a recognition of its past as an independent city.

0 _____ 60 kilometers
0 _____ 40 miles

SCHLESWIG-HOLSTEIN *p.107*

MECKLENBURG-WEST POMERANIA *p.87*

HAMBURG *p.107*

eevetal • Winsen
A250
Bleckede •

A7
E45
• Lüneburg

Elbe

• Undeloh
9m
ilseder Berg

216

Dahlenburg •

• Bad
Bevensen

Dannenberg •

BRANDENBURG *p.51*

191

Gartow •

Lüneburg
• Munster

493

Lüchow •

Uelzen

71

Heath
NATURPARK
SÜDHEIDE

Bodenteich •

Bergen • Hankensbüttel •

edenkstätte
ergen-Belsen

Wittingen •

• Celle
• Wienhausen

244

• Uetze

214

Gifhorn •

Ehra-Lessien •

Burgdorf

188

• Velpke

E30
Edemissen • Wolfsburg

hnde
A2
• Peine

Brunswick
(Braunschweig)

Mittellandkanal

494

• Harsum

A39

Helmstedt •

• Wolfenbüttel

ildesheim • Salzgitter

244

A395

• Bad
zdetfurth

Vienenburg •

Bad
ndersheim

Goslar •

NATURPARK
HARZ

• Bad Harzburg

Harz Mts.

Torfhaus •

Clausthal-•
Zellerfeld
A7

NATIONALPARK HARZ

• Osterode

• Braunlage

Northeim •

243

• St. Andreasberg

Herzberg •

NATURPARK
HARZ

27

• Bad Lauterberg

öttingen •

• Duderstadt

THURINGIA *p.211*

SAXONY-ANHALT *p.211*

△
E

△
F

Area of map detail

Berlin ✪

Lower Saxony's capital is Hanover, its greatest attraction not so much its rebuilt city center as the great baroque gardens at Herrenhausen. Larger than Hanover by a whisker is the city of Bremen. Bremerhaven, its modern, workaday satellite at the mouth of the River Weser, attracts hundreds of thousands of visitors to Germany's national museum of shipping.

There are more working towns to the east of Hanover: Brunswick (Braunschweig) looks back on a glorious past as the home base of the medieval duke of Saxony, Henry the Lion, while the Volkswagen town of Wolfsburg is entirely a creation of the automobile age.

The famous town of Hamelin is as picturesque today as when the Pied Piper led its children away to an unknown fate. Just as lovely are Lüneburg and Celle at opposite extremities of Lüneburg Heath. Hildesheim and its glorious heritage of Romanesque churches is protected by its UNESCO designation, as is Goslar, a medieval mining town with an unparalleled legacy of timber-framed dwellings. And in Göttingen, Lower Saxony has one of Germany's most prestigious old university cities. ■

Driving a four-in-hand at the Lower Saxon State Stud Farm, Celle

Hanover

THE STATE CAPITAL OF LOWER SAXONY IS SOMETHING OF
an upstart, certainly compared with other, far older places in the area
such as Brunswick and Goslar. Hanover's importance goes back only
to the mid-17th century, when it became a ducal residence of the
family who were later to supply England with a ruler in the shape of
George I. They also created the city's main glory, the complex of
gardens laid out from the mid-17th century onward at Herrenhausen
in the northwest part of the town.

Above left: The
world shows off
its wares in the
vast halls of
Hanover's
Messegelände.

Since then, Hanover (Hannover
in German) has evolved into northern Germany's second largest city
(after Hamburg), an industrial,
administrative, and cultural
center of first rank. On the whole,
Hanover is not a place to contemplate the remains of the past;
wartime bombing effectively razed
the city center, and the rapid
rebuilding that took place lacks
any particular distinction.
However, the city hosts some of
Europe's most important trade
fairs. In 2000, Germany's first
international expo was held here,
helping to put the city firmly on
the international map.

Many business visitors go
straight to the extensive
Messegelände, the trade fair
grounds with their own main-line
railroad station and parking for
45,000 cars. The great annual trade
fair was instituted by the British
occupation authorities in 1947.
Nowadays it is supplemented by a
whole series of specialist fairs,
including the world's biggest
computer bonanza, the CeBit.
    If you are not on business, you
are likely to arrive at the stately
19th-century **Hauptbahnhof,** the
city-center station, from which you
emerge on to spacious **Ernst-
August-Platz,** with its equestrian

Hanover
⚑ 126 D3
Visitor information
✉ Ernst-August-Platz 8
☎ 0511 12 34 51 11

New City Hall
✉ Trammplatz 2
☎ 0511 16 84 53 33
$ $

Opened in 1913, the grand neo-Gothic appearance of Hanover's New City Hall belies its relatively recent construction date.

Regional Museum of Lower Saxony
- ✉ Willy-Brandt-Allee 5
- ☎ 0511 98 07-5
- 🕐 Closed Mon.
- 💲 $

Sprengel-Museum
www.sprengel-museum.de
- ✉ Kurt-Schwitters-Platz
- ☎ 0511 16 84 38 75
- 🕐 Closed Mon.
- 💲 $$

statue of Elector Ernst August. Locals often arrange to meet *"unterm Schwanz"* ("under the tail") of this prominent landmark. Beyond the area of pedestrian-only shopping streets stretching southward from the station are the scant remains of Hanover's Old Town (Altstadt). They include the **Marktkirche,** with its distinctive gabled tower, together with a number of rebuilt timber-framed houses that give an idea of what the pre-industrial city must have looked like.

Farther south still, the huge and flamboyant early 20th-century **New City Hall** (Neues Rathaus) marks the transition from the densely built-up city center to an extensive area of lakes and parkland. Its neo-baroque exterior

conceals what at the time was an up-to-the-minute art nouveau interior. A unique inclined elevator takes you up into the dome for a fine panorama over the city and its surroundings. The nearby **Regional Museum of Lower Saxony** (Niedersächsiches Landesmuseum) has a worthy collection of old master paintings, but if you are pressed for time, the one gallery to see in Hanover is the **Sprengel-Museum.** This striking modern building functions perfectly as a treasure house of 20th-century art. The star here is local artist Kurt Schwitters (1887–1948), a subversive polymath of a man who drew, painted, sculpted, wrote, published, and organized happenings long before happenings were heard of.

Herrenhausen Gardens

www.herrenhaeuser-gaerten.de

✉ 2 miles (4 km) northwest of Hanover

$ \$ $, free in winter

🚇 U-Bahn: 4, 5

Wilhelm-Busch-Museum

✉ Georgengarten 1

☎ 0511 16 99 99 16

🕐 Closed Mon.

$ \$\$ $

HERRENHAUSEN GARDENS

These four gardens all differ but are linked by an avenue of lime trees. Walk north from the town on Nienberger Strasse, past the least interesting of the four, the **Welfengarten,** now part of the university. To the left is the Georgengarten and next to it the pride of them all, the Great Garden. Across Herrenhäuser Strasse to the north is the Berggarten.

Begun in 1655 and continuing until 1714, the **Great Garden** (Grosser Garten) was transformed into one of Europe's most ambitious baroque gardens, largely under the direction of the wife of Elector Ernst August, Sophie von der Pfalz. Even without its Schloss, destroyed in World War II, it is a regal sight, a triumph of geometry and rationality over nature. On entering you see the outdoor theater, which is still used for performances in summer. To the east is a great parterre, with geometric plantings of flowers and shrubs, and in front a Great Fountain spurts an imposing jet 262 feet (80 m) into the air. The 1930s model gardens show historic styles of garden design; one reconstructs the fabled Renaissance garden of Heidelberg Castle.

The **Georgengarten** was laid out on naturalistic lines in the early 19th century. The Georgenpalais houses the **Wilhelm-Busch-Museum** of caricature. The fine **Berggarten,** begun in the mid-17th century, is now the botanical garden of the university. ∎

House of Hanover

One man, two titles: Elector Georg Ludwig of Hanover, aka King George I of England

The Electress Sophie, grand-daughter of James I of England, not only inspired one of Europe's finest gardens, she also provided England with a king. In 1714 her son, Georg Ludwig, was invited to take the English throne as George I. He did so with little enthusiasm, being very attached to the sedate court at Hanover. Neither were the English very enthusiastic about him, mocking his rustic manners and his faltering attempts to speak their language.

George I and his successors ruled over both England and Hanover, gradually becoming more English in the process. On the death of William IV in 1837 a problem arose; his niece Victoria was next in succession, but Hanover's laws would not allow a woman to rule. The kingdoms had to go their separate ways, with Victoria crowned in London while an uncle became King Ernst August of Hanover. When Victoria's son Edward VII became king, the House of Hanover became the House of Saxe-Coburg-Gotha (Prince Albert's family). In the feverish atmosphere of World War I, this was far too Germanic, and George V changed the name of his dynasty to the House of Windsor. ∎

Hamelin

"A PLEASANTER SPOT YOU NEVER SPIED," WROTE BRITISH poet Robert Browning of 19th-century Hamelin (Hameln in German), and it is still the handsomest town on the River Weser, with its dignified buildings in the style known as Weser Renaissance (see p. 37).

Browning's memorable verses, written in 1842, have immortalized for English-speakers the legend of the Pied Piper of Hamelin originally written down by the Brothers Grimm. A stranger to the town and dressed in multicolored garb, the piper spirited the city's children away with a few notes on his flute after the citizens refused to pay him for clearing the city of rats in the same manner. Vermin were a constant problem in medieval towns, but the tale of the Pied Piper probably has more to do with the forced emigration of young people from poverty-stricken areas than rat infestation.

Hamelin's great glory is its ornamented town mansions with high gables and oriel windows, the epitome of the style that developed along the Weser in the 16th and early 17th centuries. Among the most striking houses along the main street, Osterstrasse, are the **Ratcatcher's House** of 1603 (Rattenfängerhaus), named for the Pied Piper, and the **Leisthaus** at No. 9. Together with the adjacent timber-framed **Stiftsherrenhaus** at No. 8, the Leisthaus is home to the local museum, the **Museum Hameln,** with material on the Pied Piper legend. The story of the stingy citizens and the colorfully clad trickster is reenacted every Sunday at noon (mid-May–mid-Sept.) on the marketplace outside the town's massive stone-built **Marriage Building** (Hochzeitshaus). If you miss the show, the Hochzeithaus carillon displays the story daily at 1:05, 3:35, and 5:35 p.m. ∎

Hamelin
- 126 D2

Visitor information
- ✉ Deisterallee 1
- ☎ 05151 20 26 17

Museum Hameln
- ✉ Osterstrasse 8–9
- ☎ 05151 20 22 15
- 🕐 Closed Mon.
- 💲 $

Harz Mountains

THE HILLS AND MOUNTAINS OF THE HARZ ARE GERMANY'S northernmost uplands, stretching across from Lower Saxony into Saxony-Anhalt and Thuringia. They include the country's highest summit outside the Alps, the Brocken (see pp. 218–219). Hikers can explore trails leading through ravines and woodlands to windswept summits.

Harz Mountains

🅜 127 E2

Mining Museum of the Upper Harz

✉ Bornhardtstrasse 16, Clausthal-Zellerfeld

☎ 05323 9 89 50

💲 $

Samson Silver Mine

✉ St Andreasberg

☎ 05582 12 49

💲 $

The fine scenery belies the fact that the Harz was once Germany's foremost industrial area. More than a thousand years ago, silver was being mined here, followed by copper, iron, and lead, sources of wealth that gave the mining town of Goslar (see p. 133) the status of a Free Imperial City. The metals have nearly all been worked out, leaving a legacy of tree-covered spoil heaps.

The geographical unity of the Harz was shattered when the frontline of the Cold War ran between Lower Saxony and Saxony-Anhalt. Apart from the Berlin Wall, it was here, in a popular vacation area, that Germany's division was most poignantly expressed. On the East German side, powerful surveillance equipment on the summit of the Brocken monitored all electronic communication between West Berlin and the outside world.

Torfhaus, in the western Harz, is the starting point for many walks, including a 7.5-mile (12 km) hike up the Brocken. **Clausthal-Zellerfeld** is a double town, once the area's most important mining center. Clausthal has a huge timber church, one of the largest in Europe. Zellerfeld, rebuilt in baroque style in the 18th century, has the absorbing **Mining Museum of the Upper Harz** (Oberharzer Bergwerkmuseum). **St. Andreasberg,** at about 2,050 feet (630 m), is the highest town in the Harz. Here you can visit the old **Samson Silver Mine** (Silberbergwerk Samson), where once miners had to climb ladders down a 2,658-foot-deep (810 m) shaft. ■

Goslar

IDYLLICALLY LOCATED AMONG THE WOODED OUTLIERS OF the Harz Mountains, Goslar has ancient churches, medieval fortifications, and a great imperial palace. Its greatest treasure, however, and the reason for its inclusion on UNESCO's World Heritage List, is its unsurpassed array of timber-framed houses.

The cobbled streets and alleyways of the old town center are lined with something like a thousand dwellings, most timber-framed and many built before the middle of the 16th century. A stroll in any direction from the central Marktplatz reveals a wealth of carved detail and innumerable picturesque compositions around little squares, on street corners, and along the town's stream. Be sure not to miss highlights such as the late 17th-century **Siemens-haus,** with its charming internal courtyard, or the **Brusttuch** (*Hoher Weg 1, tel 05321 3 46 00*), a superb building in stone and timber, now a hotel. The magistrate who erected it in the early 16th century employed a master carver to adorn it with a variety of figures, including the "Butter-maid," nonchalantly scratching her bare behind. The splendid arcaded **Kaiserworth,** built in 1494 as a guild hall, shares the Marktplatz with the Gothic **Town Hall** (Rathaus).

The great stone **Imperial Palace** (Kaiserpfalz) rises majestically over grassy slopes at the edge of the town center. Originally built in the 11th century, it was restored in the 1870s as a symbol of the newly united German Empire.

The **Rammelsberg mine,** just over a mile (2 km) south, is an essential visit in Goslar. Worked continuously for at least a thousand years, the Rammelsberg closed only in 1988. You can explore the site up top or, clad in miner's gear, descend underground. ∎

Goslar
- 🅼 127 E2

Visitor information
- ✉ Markt 7
- ☎ 05321 7 80 60

Siemenshaus
- ✉ Schreiberstrasse 12
- ☎ 05321 2 38 37
- ⏰ Closed Wed., Fri.–Mon. & Tues. & Thurs. p.m.

Imperial Palace
- ✉ Kaiserbleek 6
- ☎ 05321 311 96 93
- 💲 $

Rammelsberg mine
- ✉ Bergtal 19
- ☎ 05321 75 00
- 💲 $$

Celle

Immaculately
uniformed
horsemen and
their steeds
perform at the
Lower Saxon
State Stud Farm.

THE GATEWAY TO THE SOUTHERN PART OF LÜNEBURG
Heath, Celle—like Lüneburg in the north—is an old city that has
survived unscathed by war. Here, however, it is the half-timbering
typical of southern Lower Saxony that prevails rather than brick.
And Celle was no commercial center; it remained a ducal seat up
to the mid-19th century, with its Schloss the most prominent building in town. Set apart from the main part of town, it neatly reflects
the hierarchical social order of the old regime.

Celle

■ 127 E3

Visitor information

✉ Markt 14–16

☎ 05141 12 12

**Stadtkirche
(tower)**

✉ Markt

☎ 05141 77 35

🕘 Closed Mon.

💲 $

Bomann-Museum

✉ Schlossplatz 7

☎ 05141 1 23 72

🕘 Closed Mon.

💲 $

Surrounded by its moat and lush
parkland, the **Schloss** (tel 05141 1
23 73, closed Mon.) stands at the
western end of town, its high walls
and massive corner towers giving it
a supremely confident air. The
Schlossmuseum tells the story of
the Kingdom of Hanover.

Closer to the town than the
Schloss comes the **Stadtkirche**,
the parish church, full of ducal
tombs. A trumpeter sounds the
reveille from its tall tower every
morning and evening. There's a
great view of the town from the
top. Behind the Stadtkirche is the
Town Hall (Rathaus), a big building mostly in the Weser Renaissance
style (see p. 37), with elaborate
dormers and gables. The town itself
has street after street of fine old
houses, mostly from the 16th to the

18th centuries. Watch for a number
of highlights such as the **Old
Latin School** (Alte Lateinschule)
on Kalandgasse, with its richly
carved timbers, or the equally elaborate decoration of the **Hoppener
Haus** of 1532 on the corner of
Poststrasse and Rundestrasse.

Once you've strolled around
town, visit the **Bomann-
Museum.** It's good on the history
of the region and Celle itself, and has
reconstructions of town and country
interiors, including a complete
farmhouse. Finally, visit the **Lower
Saxon State Stud Farm**
(Niedersächsisches Landgestüt),
founded as a royal stud in 1735
(Spörckenstrasse 10, tel 05141 9 29 40,
closed Sun.). The great annual parade
of the stallions takes place in late
September or early October. ■

Lüneburg & Lüneburg Heath

FOR A THOUSAND YEARS, RIGHT UP TO 1980, SALT WAS extracted from the ground below Lüneburg, one of northern Germany's most perfectly preserved medium-size cities. The salt trade linked Lüneburg with the Hansa towns of the coast, and their elaborate brick architecture was copied here with wonderfully picturesque results.

A shepherd and his dog guard their flock on Lüneburg Heath's open expanses.

Overlooking the **Markt,** the main square, is the imperious baroque facade of the **Town Hall** (Rathaus), one of the largest and finest town halls in the country. Parts of the building date from the 13th century, and the Renaissance council chamber is elaborately paneled and carved. You can strike off in two directions from here. To the east is the **Wasserviertel,** the atmospheric "water town" around the River Ilmenau, with the quayside from which the salt was dispatched to far-off destinations. An ancient crane still stands guard by the waterside.

South of the marketplace, traffic-calmed streets lead to **Am Sande,** an elongated square with some of the prettiest facades in town and the 354-foot (108 m) spire of the city's oldest church, the St. Johanniskirche. West of Am Sande, on the edge of the Old Town (Altstadt), is the **German Salt Museum** (Deutsches Salzmuseum), in the the old salt works. There are interactive displays on all aspects of salt—its history, production, even a tasting.

LÜNEBURG HEATH

Lüneburg has given its name to the Lüneburger Heide, a vast tract of heathland stretching southward to Celle. Its mosaic of landscapes comprises gently undulating stretches of heather (glorious when in flower in late summer) and juniper; marsh-lands, ponds and clear streams; and forests and farmland, some of it grazed by a unique breed of sheep. The heath is now much in favor with walkers, riders, and wildlife enthusiasts; parts are designated nature parks or reserves. To sample this unusual landscape, leave your transport at the pretty village of **Undeloh** and climb the 554-foot (169 m) Wilseder Berg, the highest point of the heath.

On the southern edge of the heath is the location of the Nazi concentration camp at **Bergen-Belsen,** now a memorial site. Lüneburg Heath was also where British Field Marshal Montgomery took the unconditional surrender of the German armed forces on May 4, 1945, which marked the final hours of World War II. ∎

Lüneburg
🗺 127 E4
Visitor information
✉ Rathaus, Am Markt 1
☎ 04131 2 07 66 22

Town Hall
✉ Am Ochsenmarkt
☎ 04131 30 92 30
§ $

German Salt Museum
✉ Sülfmeisterstrasse 1
☎ 04131 4 50 65
§ $$

Lüneburg Heath
🗺 127 E3–E4

Bergen-Belsen
🗺 127 E3

Bremen

BREMEN IS PROUD TO BE A *LAND* OF THE FEDERAL
Republic, a reminder of its independent past as Germany's first
seaport and one of the country's Free Cities. Far inland up the estuary
of the River Weser, it kept its status as a port of the first rank in the
19th century by founding a completely new daughter town and
harbor at Bremerhaven, close to the mouth of the river. Bremerhaven
is unashamedly a working town, but it attracts large numbers of
visitors to its world-class Navigation Museum. Bremen, in contrast,
has an Old Town (Altstadt) full of charm, and its wonderfully ornate
town hall alone would make your visit worthwhile.

Bremen
- ▲ 126 C4

Visitor information
- ✉ Am Bahnhofsplatz
- ☎ 01805 10 10 30

City Hall
- ✉ Am Markt
- ☎ 0421 36 10
- 💲 $

**Museum im
Roselius-Haus**
- ✉ Böttcherstrasse
  6–10
- ☎ 0421 3 36 50 77
- 🕐 Closed Mon.
- 💲 $$ (combined ticket
  with Paula
  Modersohn-Becker
  Museum, below)

**Paula Modersohn-
Becker Museum**
- ✉ Böttcherstrasse 6-10
- ☎ 0421 3 36 50 77
- 🕐 Closed Mon.
- 💲 $$ (combined ticket
  with Museum im
  Roselius-Haus, above)

Brauerei Beck & Co.
- ✉ Am Deich 18/19
- ☎ 0421 50 94 55 55
- 🕐 Closed Sun.–Wed.
- 💲 $$

Bremen's central square, the
irregularly shaped Markt, is a great
place for sitting at an outdoor café,
with fine examples of old town
houses as background.

The square is dominated by the
City Hall (Rathaus), a grand
civic structure where patrician
merchants met to take political and
commercial decisions about how
best to ensure their trading city's
prosperity. The Rathaus is medieval
in origin, but the facade you see
is the most elaborate example of
the Weser Renaissance style,
with arcade, huge windows, and
elaborate gables all added in the
early 17th century.

Before taking a guided tour
through the interior, take a look at
the two very different types of
public sculpture that adorn the
square. The 33-foot-tall (10 m)
figure of the knight Roland
beneath his Gothic canopy dates
from 1404. As elsewhere in Central
Europe, Roland symbolizes civic
rights and freedoms. More modest
in size are the famous **figures of
the Bremen Town Musicians,**
cockerel, cat, dog, and donkey from
a folktale of the same name retold
by the Brothers Grimm.

Inside the Rathaus, one elabo-
rately decorated room follows the
other, although none is quite as
grand as the spacious, 130-foot-
long (40 m) Upper Hall, with

splendid ship models hanging
from the ceiling. Downstairs, the
cheerful **Wine Cellar** (Ratskeller)
serves wine from a list featuring no
fewer than 600 wines (they don't
serve beer). This is no accident:
Bremen has long specialized in the
export of German wines.

The tall twin towers of the near-
by **Cathedral** contrast with the
horizontal lines of the Rathaus. The
towers were added in the 19th cen-
tury, but the history of the building
goes back to the late eighth century,
when Emperor Charlemagne sent
the Anglo-Saxon Bishop Willehad
here to build a church and convert
the heathen. Nothing remains of
Willehad's timber building, but the
crypt evokes the past with carved
capitals from the 11th century as
well as a quite superb 13th-century
bronze **font** carried by figures of
men riding lions.

An opening on the southern side
of the marketplace leads to
Böttcherstrasse, a narrow street
marked by a stunning relief in gold,
the "Bringer of Light," depicting the
Archangel Michael fighting a dragon.
The street is one of Bremen's most
intriguing sights, a joint enterprise in
the 1920s and early 1930s between
the wealthy coffee merchant Ludwig
Roselius and the sculptor/architect
Bernhard Hoetger. The street has a
cozy, old-world feel about it, but a
closer look reveals its brick buildings

The "Bringer of Light" relief sculpture by Bernhard Hoetger (1874–1949) adorns the entrance to the Böttcherstrasse.

Übersee Museum
- ✉ Bahnhofsplatz 13
- ☎ 0421 16 03 81 01
- 🕐 Closed Mon.
- 💲 $$

Focke-Museum
- ✉ Schwachhauser Heerstrasse 240
- ☎ 0421 3 61 35 75
- 🕐 Closed Mon.
- 💲 $

and their decoration to be of startling originality and modernity. Try to be here when Hoetger's Glockenspiel is playing (at noon, 3 p.m., and 6 p.m.). The intimate **Museum im Roselius-Haus** is a charming assemblage of the furnishings and paintings collected by Roselius, while the adjoining **Paula Modersohn-Becker Museum** *(covered by the same ticket)* is devoted to the work of this short-lived artist who worked mainly in nearby Worpswede (see sidebar p. 139). The hotel at the end of the street, the **Haus Atlantis**, is Hoetger's masterpiece. It has been much altered, but peer inside for a glimpse of his futuristic stairway.

Beyond Böttcherstrasse is the **River Weser,** quiet since docks and quays moved downstream but

the place to come in summer. There are bars, restaurants, and old ships (you can dine aboard). On the far bank is **Brauerei Becks & Co.,** one of Germany's biggest breweries, where you can take a guided tour.

The most perfectly preserved part of the Altstadt is the old fishermen's quarter known as the **Schnoorviertel,** a tiny area consisting mainly of the narrow and winding Schnoor itself, with a few alleyways and courtyards opening off it. Threatened with demolition as a slum in the early 20th century, the Schnoor is very trim nowadays, with many of its charming old houses occupied by gift shops and places to eat, yet with a lived-in feel.

The Weser forms a natural boundary to one side of the Altstadt, which is neatly defined to the north by the **Wallanlagen,** the pretty parkland laid out along the star-shaped baroque fortifications and moat. The windmill crowning a rise is the last of many that once stood here. Beyond the main railroad station is the **Bürgerpark,** a fine public park, with lakes, trees, woodland, waterways, and miles of footpaths, laid out in the mid-19th century. Its designer, Franz Wilhelm Benque, spent time in America, where he collaborated with Frederick Law Olmsted on the plans for New York's Central Park.

Several days could be spent exploring Bremen's many museums and galleries. The **Übersee Museum** has one of the country's best ethnographical collections, while the **Focke-Museum** is a treasure house of Bremen history. The **Kunsthalle** has paintings and sculpture from the 15th century onward, and the **Neues Museum Weserburg** displays work by international contemporary artists in old warehouses.

BREMERHAVEN

The port installations at Bremerhaven stretch for more than 4 miles (7 km) along the shore of the Weser estuary, a good 37 miles (60 km) downstream from Bremen. This is one of Germany's great outlets to the seas of the world, second only to Hamburg in extent and volume handled, specializing in the import of foodstuffs and the export of vehicles. The fishing harbor is the biggest in Europe, and there are important shipyards, too.

The construction of this harbor at the mouth of the Weser in the early 19th century proved to be an excellent move. Bremerhaven can handle the largest vessels without trouble. Passenger traffic has almost disappeared, the Columbus Terminal through which thousands of emigrants to the New World passed now only sees the occasional cruise ship. For many years after 1945, Bremerhaven functioned as the port for the U.S. forces in Germany. One of the last to come down the gangway off his troopship was GI Elvis Presley.

The dock completed in 1830 is now the **Old Harbor** (Alter Hafen). In it are moored several historic ships, including the three-master *Seute Deern,* now a restaurant. You can squeeze through the innards of the **U-boat *Wilhelm Bauer,*** which was launched in January 1945, too late to see action. She was scuttled, but later salvaged and used as a training vessel by the German navy.

Bremerhaven's great visitor attraction is the **German Maritime Museum** (Deutsches Schiffahrtsmuseum), housed in a building designed by Berlin architect Hans Scharoun. Displays illustrate every aspect of German ships and shipping. There are more than 500 models, and a few real vessels, but the star is a *Kogge,* emblem of the medieval Hansa trading league. This chunky timber sailing ship of about 1380 was discovered in the mud of the Weser estuary and painstakingly reconstructed. ■

Kunsthalle
- ✉ Am Wall 207
- ☎ 0421 32 90 80
- 🕐 Closed Mon.
- 💲 $$

Neues Museum Weserburg
- ✉ Teerhof 20
- ☎ 0421 59 83 90
- 🕐 Closed Mon.
- 💲 $$

Wilhelm Bauer
- ✉ Hans-Scharoun-Platz 1, Bremerhaven
- ☎ 0471 48 20 70
- 🕐 Closed Nov.–March
- 💲 $

German Maritime Museum
- www.dsm.de
- ✉ Hans-Scharoun-Platz 1, Bremerhaven
- ☎ 0471 48 20 70
- 💲 $$
- 🕐 Closed Mon Nov.–March

Worpswede

The name of Worpswede became synonymous with the desire of many late 19th-century German artists to escape the city and the straitjacket of academic painting in unspoiled rustic surroundings. On the edge of a great tract of marshland, 15 miles (24 km) north of Bremen, the village of Worpswede was home for many years to a community of artists. Among them was one of Germany's most popular women painters, Paula Modersohn-Becker, who called it "a wonderland, a land of the gods!" Her simple but touching portraits and landscapes can be seen in the village as well as in the Kunsthalle and the museum named after her in Bremen. With its charming mixture of thatched farmhouses and architectural oddities from the early 20th century, Worpswede has continued to be a congenial place to live and work for artists and craftspeople, and there's an abundance of galleries and studios. On a fine day, the waterways, reed beds, and meadows of the flat countryside do indeed become a wonderland, best explored by bicycle or aboard a turf-cutter's sailboat. ■

"Self-portrait" by Paula Modersohn-Becker (1876–1907)

Wolfsburg & the Volkswagen

"This vehicle is quite unattractive to the average buyer; it's too ugly and too noisy," declared Lord Rootes, the British motor magnate, on inspecting the Volkswagen works at Wolfsburg just after the end of World War II. He had been asked to think about taking over the factory by the British occupation authorities. In the end, the decision on what to do with it was left to Major Ivan Hirst of the British Royal Engineers. He set refugees and German prisoners of war to work at patching up the factory, and by the end of 1945 had succeeded in turning out a few dozen vehicles. In the following year the number rose to just over 10,000. By 1972, the "Beetle" had become the world's biggest-selling automobile, as popular in the United States as elsewhere. Production of the Beetle in Wolfsburg continued until 1974, although it was still produced elsewhere in Germany and abroad. In 1998 VW revived the Beetle, but in a modernized version.

In the 1930s, Hitler's Third Reich was busy building a network of the world's most advanced roads, the *Autobahnen,* but there was hardly any traffic to run on them. The Führer favored motoring, and ordered Ferdinand Porsche to develop a car that would mobilize the masses at a price they could afford (the Volkswagen or People's Car), fixed at no more than the relatively modest sum of 999 marks (about $500). Drawing on the technically advanced rear-engined and streamlined vehicles designed by Hans Ledwinka for the Tatra works in Czechoslovakia, Porsche came up with a first prototype in 1935.

Hitler was enthused. A site for a factory to make the car was chosen in what is now Lower Saxony, and in 1938 the foundation stone was laid by the Führer himself. The new town, called Kraft durch Freude Stadt (Strength through Joy Town), was planned in the Nazis'

An improbably oversized VW speeds along the Autobahn in this 1939 ad.

favorite style, with triumphal boulevards and public buildings.

War intervened before more than a few classic Volkswagens could be turned out. The design was adapted to make a jeeplike vehicle, the *Kübelwagen* (Bucket-wagon), of which some 50,000 had been produced by 1945, along with an amphibious version, the *Schwimmwagen.* When the British arrived in 1945, the town was a dismal place consisting of barrack blocks inhabited by forced

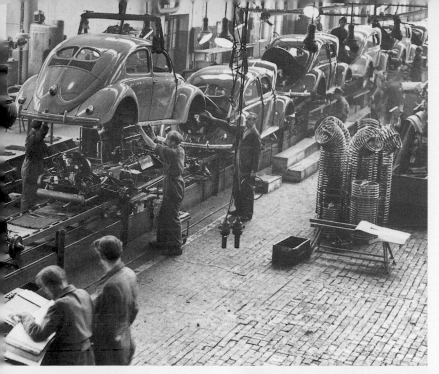

Kombi (van) and *Käfer* (Beetle), symbols of the postwar Economic Miracle

Above: Customized Beetle, California-style
Top: VWs roll off the production line at Wolfsburg in the 1950s.

laborers from all over Europe. A new name for the town was obviously needed, and the British settled on Wolfsburg, the name of the nearby castle in Weser Renaissance style, which nowadays houses the municipal museum. The barrack blocks have been replaced with mostly bland modern developments, with just a few highlights, such as the town theater, a striking design by the architect Hans Scharoun. And there's an Automuseum on the appropriately named Dieselstrasse.

Having once symbolized the Nazi ideal of mass mobility, the Volkswagen came to stand for the virtues of the postwar Federal Republic—solidity, reliability, economy, endurance, lack of ostentation. Wolfsburg itself, close to the East German border, its factory chimneys and production halls visible from the far side of the Cold War frontier, became a symbol for the achievements of capitalism and the consumer society. ■

A *Strandkorb* (beach basket) is an essential accessory on the breezy East Frisian Islands.

East Frisian Islands

STRUNG ALONG LOWER SAXONY'S COAST, THESE ISLANDS, called the OstFriesische Inseln in German, have been attracting vacationers from the mainland for nearly 200 years, ever since the Hanoverian court decided to spend its summer vacations on Norderney.

East Frisian Islands
www.ostfriesische-inseln.de
[map] 126 B5

Borkum
visitor information
[mail] Am Georg-Schütte-
Platz 5
[phone] 04932 89 10

Norderney
visitor information
[mail] Am Kurplatz 3
[phone] 04932 9 18 50

Bracing breezes characterize the islands. The sun does shine on the vast sandy beaches, but to make the most of it you absolutely have to have a *Strandkorb*, one of those solid wickerwork structures that can be turned to face the warming rays and protect you from the wind blowing off the North Sea. Vacationers come here to breathe pure air, stroll, or cycle among the sand dunes, watch birds, take trips to the various islands,

ride one of the islands' little old railroads, or simply relax in an environment largely free of cars and traffic.

The islands are in a continuous state of evolution. Tides and currents gnaw away at their western extremities and deposit sand to the east, and the wind tries constantly to reshape the dunes. A north-facing outer rampart of the mainland, they are separated from the rest of Lower

Saxony by the Wattenmeer, an area of shining mudflats that is uncovered twice daily by the receding tide and is now protected as a national park (Nationalpark Niedersächsisches Wattenmeer).

The largest and most westerly island is **Borkum,** closer to the Dutch mainland than to Germany. It rivals **Norderney,** the next in size, in its range of recreational facilities, but Norderney has the edge when it comes to character, with a Kurhaus, Kurpark, and casino as reminders of its days as an aristocratic retreat. Both islands have splendid covered swimming pools with wavemaking facilities.

Between Norderney and Borkum is **Juist,** 10.5 miles long (17 km) and only a few hundred yards across. **Baltrum** is the smallest island, like

Juist completely car-free and quiet. Impressive sand dunes, carved by the wind, mark its eastern end.

Popular **Langeoog** has its tranquil spots, and seals can sometimes be spotted hauled out on the nature reserve at the island's eastern end. Among its modern facilities, **Spiekeroog** has preserved much of its traditional character; there's even a horse tramway! The church—Alte Inselkirche—has carvings allegedly made from the timbers of one of the ships of the Spanish Armada sent against England, wrecked here in 1588.

The easternmost island, **Wangerooge,** has a little railroad that brings vacationers from the ferry landing to the village, with its museum of island life installed in the old lighthouse. ■

Juist
visitor information
✉ Kurverwaltung
☎ 04935 80 90

Langeoog
visitor information
✉ Hauptstrasse 28
☎ 04972 69 30

Spiekeroog
visitor information
✉ Noorderpad 25
☎ 04976 9 19 31 01

Wangerooge
visitor information
✉ Bahnhof
☎ 04469 9 48 80

More places to visit in Lower Saxony

GÖTTINGEN

Göttingen is one of Germany's most character-ful university cities, buzzing with student life yet not overwhelmed by the presence of one of the country's foremost seats of learning. It was founded by George II of England and Hanover in 1734 to provide his Hanoverian possessions with a reliable supply of state servants. The city's favorite statue stands in front of the medieval Rathaus; Gänseliesel ("little goose girl") is the most-kissed girl in Göttingen, traditionally honored by an obligatory salute from every successful doctoral student. Not so successful as a student was the future Chancellor Bismarck, whose youthful roistering caused him to be banned from the town center; you can visit his undergraduate lodgings, the Bismarckhäuschen.

⚠ 127 E1 **Visitor information** ✉ Altes Rathaus, Markt 9 ☎ 0551 49 98 00

HILDESHEIM

The story goes that in 815 Ludwig the Pious, a son of Charlemagne, left a reliquary hanging on a rosebush in the northwestern foothills of the Harz Mountains while he went hunting. On his return, the reliquary refused to be detached, which Ludwig took as a sign that a chapel should be built on the spot. This evolved into a bishop's seat, the town of Hildesheim. Its importance today has been recognized by UNESCO, which has put Hildesheim on the World Heritage List because of its exceptional heritage of early Romanesque art and architecture. The town has made a supreme effort to re-create its historic ambience after severe wartime destruction, and its huge main square, the **Marktplatz,** now gives a good impression of what Hildesheim was like in its heyday. The most striking building is the late medieval Knochenhaueramtshaus—literally the Bone-Basher Building—which, with its huge gable and five projecting upper stories, was the seat of the butchers' guild. But it is the town's churches that make it of international significance. The **Dom's** outstanding works of art include 11th-century bronze doors (Bernward-Tür) with graphic scenes from the Old and New Testaments, while **St. Michael**

is one of the supreme expressions of Romanesque architecture in Germany.

⚠ 127 E2 **Visitor information** ✉ Rathausstrasse 18–20 ☎ 05121 1 79 80

STADE

Close to the River Elbe downstream from Hamburg, the port of Stade was once a rival to its mighty neighbor. Today Stade seeks its fortune in its heritage of fine old buildings, many of them dating from the reconstruction that took place after a terrible fire during the Swedish occupation in the mid-17th century. After a thoroughgoing restoration program, much of the town now looks as it did then. The scene by the canal-like old harbor is particularly enchanting, with gabled houses overlooking the quayside with its antique crane. Stade is the capital of the Old Land (Altes Land), the area along the Elbe reclaimed long ago from the water by settlers brought in from Holland. Hamburgers come to get away from it all among the old farmsteads and the fruit trees: This is one of the country's biggest fruit growing areas, glorious in spring with apple and cherry blossoms.

⚠ 126 D5 **Visitor information** ✉ Hansestrasse 16 ☎ 04141 40 91 70

WOLFENBÜTTEL

For centuries, the Dukes of Brunswick chose to live in Wolfenbüttel and it is easy to see why. The town is a lovely example of a tiny capital city, its huge Renaissance Schloss (originally founded by Henry the Lion) coun-terbalanced by other fine public buildings and a wealth of timber-framed houses. Dwelling types were carefully graded, with high court officials living in stately homes, middle-rankers in smaller houses that were nevertheless profusely decorated, and the humblest in simpler but still pleasing two-storied structures. In the 17th century the ducal library was the most richly endowed in Europe; its most famous librarian was the dramatist Gotthold Ephraim Lessing. A selection of its precious books, manuscripts, maps, and globes is usually on display.

⚠ 127 E2 **Visitor information** ✉ Stadtmarkt 7 ☎ 05331 862 80 ∎

The cities along the Rhine and its tributary the Ruhr provide an extraordinary range of urban experiences. In contrast, flanking the river valleys are wooded uplands and the tranquil landscapes and moated castles of the Münsterland.

North Rhine-Westphalia

Icon of industry—
Ruhr pithead

North Rhine-Westphalia

BOUNDED ON THE WEST BY BELGIUM AND HOLLAND, THIS IS ONE OF THE most densely urbanized areas in Europe. One German in five lives in North Rhine-Westphalia, mainly in the vast industrial conurbation of the Ruhr and in the towns and cities along the River Rhine. Many people come here on business, but there is plenty to detain the more casual visitor, particularly in the cities.

LOWER SAXONY *p. 125*

0 50 kilometers
0 30 miles

NETHERLANDS

Recke
Ibbenbüren
Rheine A30
Gronau Ochtrup Emsdetten Lengerich
Ahaus Steinfurt 70 Greven
Stadtlohn Haus A1 E37 Telgte Sassenberg
Billerbeck Rüschhaus
Gescher Coesfeld Burg Münster Warendorf
Hülshoff Ems

Bocholt Borken Münsterland
Kleve Emmerich Dülmen Oelde
NATURPARK A43 Burg Vischering Ahlen Beckum
Raesfeld HOHE MARK Lüdinghausen 58 Schloss
A3 70 Haltern Nordkirchen Nordkirchen
E35 Schermbeck NORTH RHINE
Goch Lippe Reckling- Hamm
Xanten Wesel Dorsten hausen Lünen A2
Kevelaer Marl Castrop- E34 Soest
Dinslaken Gladbeck Rauxal Unna A44
Geldern Kamp- Bottrop Gelsenkirchen Herne Möhnesee
Lintfort Oberhausen ESSEN DORTMUND
Kerken Moers Villa Bochum A1 Menden Neheim
A40 DUISBURG Hügel Witten Schwerte Hüsten
Kempen E31 A3 Mülheim WESTPHALIA Arnsberg
Krefeld Kettwig Hattingen Hagen Iserlohn Sorpe
DEUTSCH- Ratingen Velbert Staubecken
NIEDERLÄNDISCHER
NATURPARK Meerbusch Wuppertal A45 Werdohl Eslohe
Viersen Halver Lüdenscheid
Mönchengladbach Neuss Hilden Remscheid E41 Sauerland Finnentrop
A61 Schloss Solingen Meinerzhagen Biggesee
Grevenbroich Benrath A59 Langenfeld Wipperfürth Kirchunde
Heinsberg A46 Erkelenz Dormagen A1 Bergisch Olpe
Geilenkirchen Leverkusen Gladbach Engelskirchen Gummersbach
Bergheim A4 Kreuzt
Jülich COLOGNE E40 Siege
A44 (KÖLN) Overath NATURPARK Siege
Eschweiler A4 Kerpen Brühl A3 BERGISCHES Waldbröl
E40 Düren Troisdorf LAND Windeck A45
AACHEN Schloss A555 Siegburg
Stolberg Augustusburg Bonn St. Augustin Burbach
A61 Königswinter
DEUTSCH- Euskirchen Godesburg 321m RHINELAND-PALATINATE
BELGISCHER A1 Drachenfels *p. 175*
E29 Bad
Monschau Schleiden Münstereifel Bad Neuenahr,
NATURPARK Maria Laach
E 258 Blankenheim Altenahr, C D
Losheim Ahrweiler
A B

Cologne (Köln), with its magnificent Gothic cathedral, is one of Germany's great historic cities. As a cultural center of the first importance, it is almost (but not quite) matched by the state capital, Düsseldorf. Then there is Bonn, Beethoven's birthplace. An old provincial town suddenly elevated to the

At a pre-Lenten Karneval celebration

role of national capital after World War II, it is trying to regain its equilibrium as government moves back to Berlin. Aachen was Emperor Charlemagne's capital, while Münster, the leading city of Westphalia, has equally venerable roots.

For the cities of the Ruhr, history means the story of the industrial revolution, when the region's coal and steel powered Germany's rise to industrial might. As the traditional industries declined toward the end of the 20th century, the Ruhr reinvented itself, greening over its devastated landscape and promoting the industrial past as a visitor attraction. Yet the Ruhr probably also has more conventional museums and galleries per head of population than anywhere else in the country.

It is easy to get around, especially by public transport, with a dense rail network and excellent rapid transit systems in all the cities. The autobahn seems to reach everywhere, but be warned—it attracts huge volumes of traffic and is frequently clogged. The most relaxing way of traveling is by boat; pleasure steamers share the Rhine with the great barges, or you can cruise the canals and smaller rivers. The Ruhr is proud of its extensive network of footpaths and cycle tracks, and you can walk or ride all along the banks of the Rhine.

There's plenty of fine countryside. On the far bank of the river from Bonn, the mini mountains of the Siebengebirge mark the start of the most romantic section of the Rhine. The wooded uplands and attractive villages and small towns of the Eifel are especially popular with the Dutch and Belgians. To the east of the Rhine there are similar landscapes in the Sauerland, Siegerland, and the Teutoburger Wald. And the moated castles of the Münsterland are a delight. ■

Cologne

Cologne

 146 C2

Visitor information

✉ Unter Fettenhennen 19 (opposite the cathedral)

☎ 0221 22 13 04 00

Municipal Museum

 Map p. 150

www.museenkoeln.de

✉ Zeughausstrasse 1–3

☎ 0221 22 12 57 89

🕐 Closed Mon.

💲 $$

Eau de Cologne (Kölnisch Wasser), once medicinal, is now a favorite toilet water.

Opposite: Relaxing beneath Cologne cathedral's soaring spires

COLOGNE (KÖLN), BESTRIDING THE RHINE, IS GERMANY'S media capital, and a center of arts and learning as well as of industry and commerce. Visitors come from all parts of the world, not only to admire its many sights, but also to participate in a continuous program of trade fairs and major cultural events. The city's emblem is its twin-towered cathedral, but, although strongly Catholic, Cologne is far from being a pious place; its people are known for their caustic humor and their love of a good time. To be here at Karneval time, just before Lent, is an experience never to be forgotten. The city swarms with people visiting pubs and beer halls, where waiters famed for their wisecracks and put-downs serve Kölsch, the hoppy local beer.

Cologne was founded by the Romans as a frontier settlement called Colonia Claudia Ara Agrippinensium, which became the capital of their province of Lower Germania. In the Middle Ages it prospered from river-borne trade, becoming Germany's largest city. The vast area forming today's Old Town (Altstadt) was enclosed by the medieval walls, whose alignment is marked by the modern Ring boulevard. Long before the Gothic cathedral was begun, the faithful had more than 150 places of worship at their disposal, of which a dozen have survived, the finest grouping of Romanesque architecture in Germany.

In the 19th century industrialization set in, but Cologne, unlike the cities of the Ruhr, was never overwhelmed by industry, not least because of the efforts of its early 20th-century Lord Mayor, Konrad Adenauer. He guided Cologne's fortunes in difficult times before becoming first Chancellor of the postwar Federal Republic. The city suffered terrible bomb damage during World War II; contemporary photographs show the battered cathedral rising over a scene of almost complete destruction. Postwar reconstruction respected the original street layout, and although most buildings are new, the city has managed to keep much of its ancient feel.

Many visitors arrive at Cologne's **Hauptbahnhof,** one of the country's busiest rail stations, sited right at the foot of the cathedral. More than 1,200 trains a day pass beneath the station's arching roof and rumble over the Hohenzollern Bridge spanning the Rhine. The teeming life of the city begins right here, visitors and citizens mingling on the great expanse of paving surrounding the cathedral. Streets first traced in Roman or medieval times head off in various directions; a fragment of Roman gateway rises from the paving, and beneath it, in the underground parking lot, is the massive masonry of the Romans' defensive wall. The line of the wall can be traced westward along Komödienstrasse and Zeughausstrasse. On the way it passes the **Municipal Museum** (Kölnisches Stadtmuseum), with historical memorabilia as well as a superb model giving an overview of the city in medieval times.

From the cathedral area, the main flow of people is southward along **Hohe Strasse,** Cologne's main shopping street. To the east, toward the Rhine, is the oldest part, the **Altstadt,** a warren of streets,

squares, and passageways with more pubs and restaurants than can be easily counted. Here, too, are the distinctive towers of the Gothic **City Hall** (Rathaus; see pp. 154–155) and the square one of the Romanesque church of **Gross St. Martin,** once part of a monastery.

You will find plenty of bargains along **Hohe Strasse,** but for more exclusive wares, turn right onto **Breite Strasse** or follow popular Schildergasse to the **Neumarkt** and the streets around, where boutiques, art galleries, and antique shops abound. ■

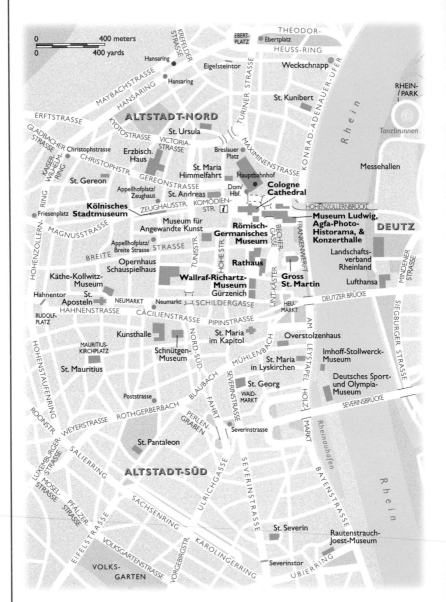

Cologne Cathedral

ITS TWIN TOWERS VISIBLE FROM FAR AWAY OVER THE Rhine plain and its lacelike stonework looming over travelers emerging from the Hauptbahnhof (main railroad station), Cologne's Gothic Dom dominates the city skyline. Near at hand, the huge edifice seems like a work of nature, a vast and intricately textured cliff rearing 515 feet (157 m) over the heads of the awestruck spectators standing on the square before it. Inspired by the cathedrals of northern France, on completion it was the tallest building in the world.

Cathedral
www.koelnerdom.de
🅰 Map p. 150
✉ Am Dom
☎ 0221 17 94 01 00

Treasury
✉ Am Dom
☎ 0221 17 94 05 55
$ $

But this dominance was only achieved relatively recently. Although building began in the mid-13th century, funds for the massive structure eventually ran out. By the 16th century, work on the nave had hardly begun, and the south tower had only been completed to the second level. Nineteenth-century enthusiasm for the Middle Ages inspired a new start. Work began again in 1842, and in 1880, when the finished cathedral could be seen as a symbol of a newly united Germany, a triumphant reopening took place in the presence of Kaiser Wilhelm II.

After gazing at the stupendous west front, it's a good idea to savor the exterior slowly. Walk around to the right, past the south facade, regarded as one of the finest achievements of the 19th-century revival of Gothic architecture, and look down into the masons' yard; restoration work continues without pause. Facing the Rhine, the flying buttresses, soaring turrets, and pinnacles of the apse, completed about 1300, are as spectacular as the west front. On the north side of the building is the entrance to the **Treasury** (Schatzkammer). Housed in its vaults deep underground are precious liturgical items. However, the finest of the cathedral's treasures are on display in the main interior.

Once inside, allow yourself a moment again to take in the breathtaking scale of the building. From entrance to choir it stretches an astonishing 472 feet (144 m), while the vaults hang 142 feet (43 m) above the floor. Once you have recovered your equilibrium, set off to the left. The bold colors

Medieval builders began Cologne's cathedral, but it wasn't completed until 1880.

Statues of saints grace the exterior of the cathedral.

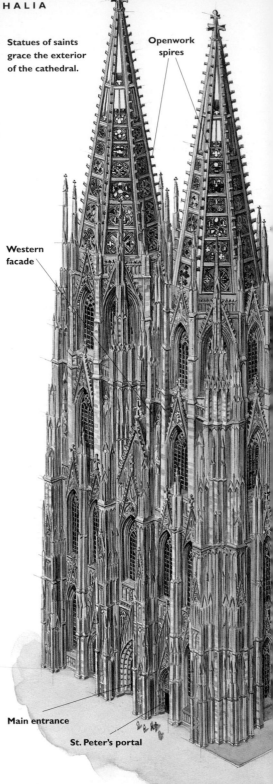

Openwork spires

Western facade

Main entrance

St. Peter's portal

and strong designs of the windows in the north aisle are the work of master craftsmen of the early 16th century. In the side chapel just beyond the north transept is a very different masterpiece, from an earlier, more somber age. Carved in oak toward the end of the tenth century, the **Cross of Gero** (Gerokreuz) shows the crucified Christ at the moment of death. It is the largest early medieval sculpture to have survived.

Continue around the ambulatory with its radiating chapels; this was the very first part of the cathedral to be completed, in use as early as 1265. Much of its stained glass is of medieval date, but all eyes here are drawn toward the cathedral's greatest single treasure and the real reason for its existence. The **Shrine of the Three Magi** (Dreikönigenschrein) behind the high altar was more than 30 years in the making. It was commissioned in the 13th century to house the relics of the Three Wise Men presented to Cologne's archbishop by Emperor Frederick Barbarossa. The number of pilgrims drawn to the city by these relics in their gloriously ornate reliquary was so great that the decision was taken to replace the Romanesque cathedral by a larger Gothic one. The Three Wise Men appear again in the exquisitely painted altarpiece in the last chapel of the ambulatory.

The work of Stefan Lochner (ca 1400–1451), Cologne's greatest medieval artist, the **Cathedral Altarpiece** (Dombild) shows the infant Christ on his mother's knee as well as the city's patron saints, St. Ursula (to the left) and St. Gereon (right).

If you leave the cathedral by the south entrance, notice the bronze doors. They may not be in the same league as the building's medieval treasures, but they are proof of the cathedral's continuing inspiration for artists. Local sculptor Ewald Mataré cast them to mark the cathedral's 700th year in 1948. ■

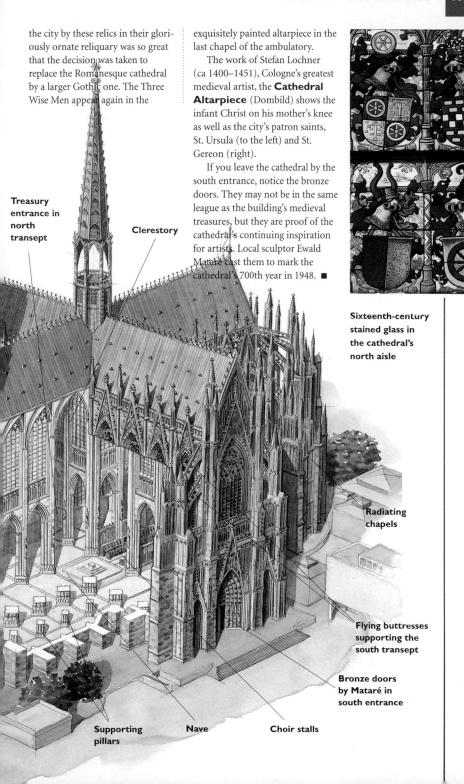

Sixteenth-century stained glass in the cathedral's north aisle

Treasury entrance in north transept

Clerestory

Radiating chapels

Flying buttresses supporting the south transept

Bronze doors by Mataré in south entrance

Supporting pillars

Nave

Choir stalls

Walk: The fountains of Cologne

Cologne abounds with fountains: ornate fountains, fountains with sparkling water jets, fairy-tale fountains, fountains carved with symbolism. Meandering from one fountain (Brunnen) to another, this short stroll takes you through the oldest streets and squares Cologne's Old Town (Altstadt).

The walk begins a few steps from the visitor information center on Domplatz, in the shadow of the great cathedral, at the delicate spiral of the **Taubenbrunnen ❶**. The Pigeon Fountain's designer, the sculptor Ewald Mataré, was much involved in the postwar rebuilding and beautification of the city.

Walk diagonally across the square toward the low-slung slab of the **Römisch-Germanisches Museum** (Roman-Germanic Museum; see pp. 156–157) on Roncalliplatz. Marking the boundary between the two squares is the 1970s concrete **Domfontäne ❷** (Cathedral Fountain), at its best when its water jets sparkle in the sun. Even if you don't have time to visit the museum, peep down through the glass wall at its spectacular **Dionysus Mosaic.**

At the far southwestern end of Roncalliplatz, on the street called Am Hof, is the charming **Heinzelmännchen-Brunnen ❸,** a fountain depicting the fairy-tale of the Heinzelmännchen. Every German child knows the verses telling how the Heinzelmännchen, Pucklike beings, came out at night to finish work left incomplete by the lazy citizens of Cologne—until they were surprised by the tailor's pretty wife and fled, never to return.

Carry on southward along Unter Goldschmied; after the next crossing, turn left across the paved area in front of the modern part of the Rathaus. The concrete **Rathausbrunnen ❹,** the City Hall Fountain, on the left, symbolizes the rebuilding of the city after wartime destruction. Pass beneath the building into Rathausplatz. With

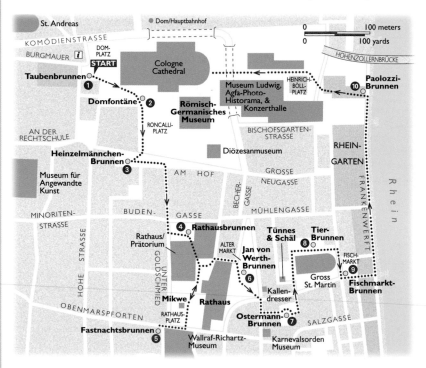

The Domfontäne (Cathedral Fountain) in front of the Roman-Germanic Museum

its tall, late medieval tower and its lovely Renaissance loggia, the **Rathaus** is emblematic of the Cologne citizens' determination not to bow and scrape to any prince or archbishop. Beneath it are substantial remains of the Prätorium, the palace of the city's Roman governor. Until the expulsion of the Jews in the 15th century, Rathausplatz was the center of Jewish life; the outline of the synagogue is traced in the paving. The 12th-century ritual bath, the **Mikwe,** is visible deep below the surface, covered by a glass pyramid.

Just off the southwestern corner of the square, in front of the brick-built Haus Neuerburg, is the copper basin of the **Fastnachtsbrunnen ❺,** the Carnival

---

Fountain, dating from 1913.

Go back across the square and down the steps to the north of the Rathaus into the Alter Markt. In the center is **Jan von Werth-Brunnen ❻,** a statue and fountain named for a stable lad who in the 17th century rose to the rank of general. Look to roof level if you want to see the bare behind of Ewald Mataré's **"Kallendresser,"** expressing his opinion of the grandees assembled in City Hall opposite.

Just beyond the Karnevalsorden Museum on the east side of the square, a narrow passageway leads left into a courtyard graced by the hilarious figures of the **Ostermann-Brunnen ❼,** a parade of Karneval characters. Turn left out of the courtyard, cross the street and into the area to the west of the Gross St. Martin church. Here stand Mataré's figures of **Tünnes and Schäl,** the Laurel and Hardy of Cologne. Take a look at the **Tier-Brunnen ❽,** the Animal Fountain, to the north, then go down the steps toward the Rhine and the **Fischmarkt ❾,** with its own distinctive cloverleaf-shaped fountain.

To get back to your starting point, go north along the riverside promenade, past the water playground called the **Paolozzi-Brunnen ❿** after its Scottish-Italian designer, and up the broad stairway toward the cathedral. ∎

🗺 Also see map p. 150

▶ Domplatz

↔ Just over a mile (1.8 km)

🕐 2 hours

▶ Domplatz

NOT TO BE MISSED
- Dionysus Mosaic
- City Hall (Rathaus)
- "Kallendresser"
- The figures of Tünnes and Schäl

Museums of Cologne

**All Cologne
museums**
www.museenkoeln.de

To publicize the
museum's pop
art collection, the
billygoat mascot
of the FC Cologne
soccer team is
paraded before
portraits by
Gerhard Richter
(1932–) at the
Museum Ludwig.

**Wallraf-Richartz-
Museum**
🄼 Map p. 150
✉ Martinstrasse 39
☎ 0221 22 12 11 19
🕐 Closed Mon.
💲 $$

Museum Ludwig
🄼 Map p. 150
✉ Bischofsgarten-
strasse 1
☎ 0221 22 12 61 65
🕐 Closed Mon.
💲 $$

IF ART IS YOUR THING, COLOGNE WILL KEEP YOU HAPPY
for days. There are collections of church art, the applied arts, and
Asiatic art, and that's in addition to the internationally renowned
Wallraf-Richartz-Museum and Museum Ludwig. There's even a
museum, the Käthe-Kollwitz Museum, devoted entirely to the work
of the expressionist artist Käthe Kollwitz (1867–1945).

WALLRAF-RICHARTZ-MUSEUM

Classical European art is well
represented here, with a range of
paintings by old masters including
Rubens, Rembrandt, and Claude
Lorrain, as well as works by the
French Impressionists and their
German equivalents. But if you
are paying only a brief visit to
the city, you should perhaps
concentrate on the museum's
outstanding collection of German
medieval art, particularly the
works of Stefan Lochner (died
1451). This master of religious
painting spent much of his life in
Cologne, where he became an
alderman of the city.

The medieval works on the first
floor of the Wallraf-Richartz
Museum's building in the heart of
the Old Town (Altstadt) give a pretty comprehensive idea of life in the
Middle Ages, with depictions of
landscapes, urban scenes, interiors,
and the fashions of the time. The
German liking for the grim and the
grotesque is given full rein, with
plenty of torments, tortures, and
beheadings. But with Lochner, an
altogether more elevated plane is
reached. The devils and monsters
dragging sinners to Hell in his large
and magnificent "Last Judgement"
(probably begun ca 1440) are horri-
ble enough, but a more typical
work is his "Madonna in the Rose
Garden" (ca 1440), an exquisite
scene of repose and harmony.
Lochner is the undoubted star
here, but don't miss the works by

his successors, notably Dürer and
Cranach, or the fine collection of
19th-century German pictures,
including many by the Cologne-
born Wilhelm Leibl (1844–1900).

MUSEUM LUDWIG

This gallery once shared its big red-
brick building with the collections
of the Wallraf-Richartz-Museum. It
now has its vast interiors to itself,
ideal spaces in which to display the
huge array of modern art, most of
it assembled by collectors Peter and
Irene Ludwig. The museum is a
good place to get acquainted with
German art of the 20th century; the
big names—Kirchner, Beckmann,
Dix, Grosz, Kandinsky, Klee, and
Beuys—are all here, as are other key
European artists including Picasso
and representatives of the Russian
avant-garde. But the Ludwigs' particular enthusiasm was apparently
for American art, with abstracts by
Rothko and de Kooning. The collection of pop art—Rauschenberg,
Warhol, and Segal—is one of the
largest and most comprehensive
outside the United States.

In the same building is the
Agfa-Photo-Historama, which
presents a superb collection of
historic photographs. Other
exhibits bring to life the cultural
history of the camera's art.

ROMAN-GERMANIC MUSEUM

Located on the fault line separating
the Roman and Germanic worlds of
two millennia ago, Cologne is espe-

cially well placed to tell the story of the encounter between these two very different cultures. In the Römisch-Germanisches Museum, it seizes the opportunity to do so. The museum's pride is the great **Dionysus Mosaic,** made up of more than a million pieces. Discovered during the construction of an air-raid bunker early in World War II, the mosaic has scenes of a drunken Dionysus attended by dancing satyrs and maidens. The building-sized tomb of the legionary soldier Poblicius stands nearby. The museum's stunning exhibits give an idea of Roman Cologne's size and wealth. The exquisite examples of Frankish jewelry and other items are reminders that the "barbarians" who eventually overcame the might of Rome were far from being without skills and fine taste.

OTHER MUSEUMS

For those with other interests there are an ethnographical museum *(Ubierring 45),* a German Sport and Olympic Museum *(Rheinauhafen),* and, nearby, the Schokoladen-museum, where a fountain flows with chocolate and exhibits trace the history of the cocoa bean. ■

Lochner's vision of "The Madonna in the Rose Garden," serenaded by angels, reveals his gentle genius.

Roman-Germanic Museum
- ⛰ Map p. 150
- ✉ Roncalliplatz 4
- ☎ 0221 22 12 44 38
- 🕐 Closed Mon.
- 💲 $$

Karneval in the Rhineland

Every year as Lent approaches and the good Catholics of the Rhineland prepare for 40 days of abstemious living in the run-up to Easter, there occurs an outbreak of merrymaking rivaling that of Mardi Gras in more southern countries. All along the Rhine, Germans cast aside their serious, hardworking image and prepare for days—and nights—of unbridled (but often highly organized) fun.

Karneval (elsewhere in Germany called Fasching or Fastnacht) goes back to pagan rites designed to drive away the evil spirits

Clowning is compulsory at Karneval time, and it's not just the children who dress up.

of winter. The Christian Church was able to take over these old festivities and harness them to its own purposes, allowing the populace to indulge itself before getting down to the serious business of Lenten fasting. Each city and town has its own slant on Karneval, but there are many common elements.

Celebrations begin well in advance. All through the winter there are dances and festivities and humorous entertainment, much of it based on folk legend and often provided in the broadest dialect. Each year produces its crop of new Karneval songs, which often become bestsellers. Costumes are elaborately stitched together and people get together in pubs, neighborhood associations, offices, schools—in fact in every conceivable sort of grouping—to make plans for the big days to come.

The real fun starts on the Thursday before Ash Wednesday. Known as Weiberfastnacht, the Women's Carnival is the ladies' chance to have their fling before the main events, which are traditionally dominated by men. Although it is a normal working day, festive costumes are worn and men are mercilessly teased and

harassed. The action intensifies in the evening, with revelry in the pubs and more extravagant jollification in ballrooms.

Things quiet down on Friday as people nurse their hangovers, then there are more dances and entertainments on Saturday. In Cologne, the city that makes more of Karneval than anywhere else, there's a folksy preview on Saturday of the big day to follow, when schools, pubs, and neighborhood associations stage their parade through the streets.

On Monday—Rosenmontag (Rose Monday)—the climax of Karneval is reached, with parades and pageants. The biggest of them all is the huge procession through Cologne's Old Town (Altstadt). A million spectators line the streets and squares to watch the dozens of elaborate floats satirizing current events or prominent people in politics, sport, and the media. Marching bands provide a stirring accompaniment, while costumed revelers throw flowers, miniature bottles of eau-de-Cologne (the city's own perfume), and a total of 40 tons of candies to the spectators. Soldiers in 18th-century uniforms make fun of the military, and there's glamour in the form of long-legged *Tanzmariechen* (like 18th-century drum majorettes). Cologne's parade—indeed the whole of Karneval—is presided over by the triumvirate of Prince, referred to graciously as *Seine Tollität* (His Craziness), Peasant *(Bauer Knut)*, and Virgin *(Jungfrau)*. All three are men, the Virgin often flagrantly so.

Celebrations wind down on Tuesday, with smaller parades in city neighborhoods, and by Wednesday, after several sleepless nights, most people are ready to face the start of Lent, perhaps with a modest fish supper. ∎

The many faces of Karneval in Cologne: a clown among the crowds watching the big parade (above), a splendidly uniformed standard-bearer riding past the cathedral (below left), and a devilish bandsman (below right)

Aachen

IN THE NINTH CENTURY, GERMANY'S WESTERNMOST CITY
rose to European prominence as the capital of the first Holy Roman
Emperor, Charlemagne (Karl der Grosse in German). Few places are
more redolent of the distant Germanic past than his great octagonal
palace chapel (now part of Aachen's cathedral), which has miraculously survived in all its glory.

Aachen
🔼 146 B2
Visitor information
✉ Elisenbrunnen,
   Friedrich-Wilhelm-
   Platz
☎ 0241 1 80 29 60

Cathedral
www.aachendom.de
✉ Münsterplatz
☎ 0241 47 70 91 27
🕐 No guided tours
   during services
💲 $ (guided tour)

City Hall
✉ Marktplatz
☎ 0241 432 73 10
🕐 Occasionally closed
   for special events
💲 $

Aachen looks not only east to
the Rhineland, but west to its
immediate neighbors, Belgium
and the Netherlands. It is very
much a gateway town, and in 1944
it was the first German city to fall
to the Allies.

Surrounded by later building,
the ancient core of the city stands
on a low hilltop, reached by
charming cobbled streets and lanes.
At the foot of the slope are the
colonnades and rotunda of
the early 19th-century **Elisa
Fountain** (Elisenbrunnen),
harnessing the thermal springs in
which Charlemagne loved to splash
and on which Aachen's reputation
as a spa is founded. Fountains are
a feature of the city; the **Money
Fountain** (Geldbrunnen), with its

satirical figures representing the
circulation of money, stands in the
top left-hand corner of the gardens
above the Elisenbrunnen.

Rising over the Münsterplatz
just beyond is the **Cathedral**
(Dom). It is not the most harmonious of structures when seen from
outside. Charlemagne's chapel is
topped by an awkwardly elongated
dome, and it appears crushed by
the great Gothic choir to the east
and dwarfed by the 19th-century
tower to the west. A baroque chapel
seems added as an afterthought.
But within all is glorious.

Charlemagne spared no effort
and expense to construct a church
that would proclaim his status as
successor to the Roman emperors
of the past. A master architect, Odo

of Metz, was employed, and Roman remains were plundered for bronze, stone, and marble with which to enhance a structure modeled on the Byzantine buildings Charlemagne had seen on his travels in Italy. Even today, the space enclosed by the great octagon is breathtaking, its effect enhanced by the huge 12th-century circular chandelier. In the arcaded gallery stands the starkly simple throne on which more than 30 Holy Roman Emperors sat after the coronation ceremony. *(Join a tour from the Treasury if you want to see the throne.)*

Later German emperors promoted the cult of Charlemagne, and the pilgrims who swarmed here after he had been canonized were so numerous that a Gothic chancel, modeled on the Sainte-Chapelle in Paris, had to be added. Here are some of the cathedral's greatest treasures, notably the 13th-century **Shrine of Charlemagne** (Karlsschrein). The **Treasury** (Schatzkammer; *Klostergasse, closed Mon. p.m.*) also has a stunning assemblage of precious objects, without equal in northern Europe, including Charlemagne's jeweled reliquary bust.

Aachen's other great building, the massive **City Hall** (Rathaus) overlooking the marketplace, incorporates stonework from Charlemagne's palace. The great emperor is difficult to escape; atop a fountain, his bronze presence even watches over your coffee break in the square. But the city has other facets to explore. Much of medieval Aachen was burned down at the end of the 17th century and rebuilt in a sober baroque style, exemplified by the **Couven-Museum.** Its interiors evoke the comfortable life led by the merchant classes of the time. It incorporates an apothecary's shop in which chocolate was first made in Aachen in 1857.

A fortune made from chocolate enabled Peter Ludwig and his wife to establish the **Ludwig Forum for International Art** (Ludwig Forum für Internationale Kunst). Much of their huge modern art collection is in Cologne (see p. 156), but there are plenty of stimulating, shocking, and entertaining works here. As well as works by German Joseph Beuys, there are examples of the New York school, such as Roy Lichtenstein's "I Know How You Must Feel, Brad!" (1963).

Aachen's nearby spa district has a lavish new spa complex, **Carolus Thermen** *(tel 0241 182 74-0),* with something of the character of decadent ancient Rome. ∎

Couven-Museum
- ✉ Hühnermarkt 17
- ☎ 0241 4 32 44 21
- 🕓 Closed Mon.
- 💲 $

Ludwig Forum for International Art
www.ludwigforum.de
- ✉ Jülicher Strasse 97–109
- ☎ 0241 180 71 04
- 🕓 Closed Mon.
- 💲 $$

Sculpture fountain on an Aachen street

Bonn's strawberry-pink Rathaus overlooks the little city's market square.

Bonn

THERE IS MORE TO BONN, GERMANY'S ONE-TIME SEAT OF government, than vacated ministries and a sense of loss. This pleasant old town is a busy city, yet on a human scale, with a cathedral, a university, several important museums, and an enviable location at the downstream end of the most romantic stretch of the Rhine.

Bonn

- 🅰 146 C2

Visitor information

- ✉ Münsterplatz
- ☎ 0228 77 50 00

Rhineland Regional Museum

- ✉ Colmantstrasse 14–16
- ☎ 0228 207 00
- 🕐 Closed Mon.
- 💲 $$

Art Museum

- ✉ Friedrich-Ebert-Allee 2
- ☎ 0228 77 62 60
- 🕐 Closed Mon.
- 💲 $$

In the western part of the country, far from the Iron Curtain and conveniently close to the home of Konrad Adenauer, the postwar Federal Republic's first chancellor, Bonn seemed as good a place as any to set up what all Germans hoped would be a temporary seat of government. But reunification was a long time coming, and over the decades the city fitted itself out with many of the trappings of a national capital.

The modern government quarter to the south of the old center is not particularly alluring, apart from the "Museum-Mile," a series of institutions stretching along the U-Bahn line and Adenauer-Allee. The pride of the completely refurbished **Rhineland Regional Museum**

(Rheinisches Landesmuseum) is the 50,000-year-old skull of Neanderthal Man, found near Düsseldorf. The **Art Museum** (Kunstmuseum) and the adjacent national **Exhibition Hall** (Ausstellungshalle) are as remarkable for their innovative architecture as for their contents. The museum displays many fine works by 20th-century German artists, particularly August Macke, a Bonn resident, and the Ausstellungshalle stages temporary exhibitions.

But the museum that cries out to be visited is the **Museum of Contemporary History** (Haus der Geschichte der Bundesrepublik Deutschland). This spacious building has a comprehensive display of well-chosen exhibits evoking the life and times

of the two Germanys. Come here by U-Bahn; the museum begins in the station's underground concourse.

Bonn makes much of its most famous son, Ludwig van Beethoven (1770–1827), and you can pay your respects to him at the **Beethoven-Haus,** the lovely old town house that was his birthplace. It contains much fascinating Beethoven memorabilia, including his piano and some stringed instruments. The museum shop has a good range of souvenirs, including reproductions of original scores and the great composer's death mask.

Before paying homage to Beethoven, wander around the city center and enjoy the fine buildings such as the baroque **Town Hall** (Rathaus), painted in gorgeous pastel colors, or the late Romanesque **Münster,** completed in the late 13th century just as the Gothic style was emerging. Walk through the city center to the riverside and take in the view of the Rhine and the enticing **Seven Mountains** (Siebengebirge) to the southeast.

The riverside promenade continues to the pleasant residential area of Bad Godesberg. There are even better views of the Seven Mountains from the hilltop ruins of the **Godesburg,** the first of many dramatically sited castles overlooking the Rhine. Actually well over seven hills in number, the wooded heights are the stumps of volcanoes that erupted 20 million years ago. Extraction of their excellent building stone began in Roman times. They are the repository of many a myth and legend. One tells of a dragon that lurked on the flank of the **Drachenfels,** terrorizing virgins and sailors until dispatched by the hero Siegfried.

One of the country's most popular visitor attractions, the "Dragon's Rock," makes a great excursion from Bonn. The U-Bahn runs conveniently to the foot of the hill, to the pretty riverside resort of **Königswinter.** From here you can walk to the top of the mountain—at 1,053 feet (321 m) not really very high—past the 19th-century neo-Gothic fantasy of Schloss Drachenburg. Or, like most of the three million annual visitors, you can take the 1883 rack railroad. ■

Beyond Bonn's leafy suburbs, the broad Rhine is dominated by the wooded heights of the Seven Mountains (Siebengebirge).

Museum of Contemporary History
www.hdg.de
✉ Willy-Brandt-Allee 14
☎ 0228 9 16 50
🕐 Closed Mon.
💲 Free

Beethoven-Haus
www.beethoven-haus-bonn.de
✉ Bonngasse 18–26
☎ 0228 9 81 75 25
💲 $

Düsseldorf

ON THE RIGHT BANK OF THE RHINE, 18 MILES (30 KM) downstream from Cologne, is Düsseldorf, little more than half the size of its great rival, but nevertheless the capital of North Rhine-Westphalia. The city carries this status easily: For centuries it was the residence of the local Dukes of Berg, whose glittering court attracted painters, musicians, and writers.

Düsseldorf

🗺 146 C3

Visitor information

✉ Immermannstrasse 65b (opposite main station)

☎ 0211 17 20 20

Castle Tower

✉ Burgplatz 30

☎ 0211 8 99 41 95

🕐 Closed Mon.

💲 $

Opposite: Glamorous arcades in Düsseldorf evoke a little Paris.

Industry plays an important role, too, although there are more head offices than manufacturing plants here. Much of what goes on in the Ruhr (see pp. 167–170) is administered from Düsseldorf, and much of the money made in Duisburg, Essen, and Dortmund seems to be spent in the fashionable shops lining the famous Königsallee. At the same time, Düsseldorf is very much an old Rhineland town, with a Karneval second only to Cologne's in scale and exuberance, and a raucous, pub-filled Altstadt proudly summed up as the "longest bar in the world."

Many visitors arrive here by Rhine cruiser, and a good spot to absorb something of the city's spirit is on the split-level riverside promenade. From here you can enjoy a breezy view of the broad river, as it sweeps past the city in a great bend, crossed by a trio of elegant modern bridges. Beyond the new state parliament building at the southern end of the embankment rises the **Rhine Tower** (Rheinturm), offering spectacular views from its observation platform and café some 565 feet (172 m) above the river. Nearby you'll find the old commercial harbor, which has been remolded by star architects like Frank Gehry into the **Mediahafen,** an entertainment quarter filled with beautiful people in chic pubs and restaurants.

The **Castle Tower** (Schlossturm) overlooking the Burgplatz is all that is left of the old fortifications. It houses a moderately interesting little navigation museum. Just beyond it to the north is the strangely crooked spire of the Lambertuskirche *(Stiftsplatz),* a 14th-century church once the emblem of the city.

Inland from the riverside are the cobbled streets and alleyways of the **Old Town** (Altstadt), where entertainment is provided, not only by bars, restaurants, nightclubs, and discotheques, but also by cartwheeling urchins who traditionally receive a small coin per trick. Uncountable gallons of the local beer are consumed here daily; called *Altbier* or simply *Alt,* it is a very distinctive brew, in taste and hue more like British bitter than Germany's more usual light-colored lagers.

The Altstadt is not a place to come for peace and quiet at any time of the day, although it becomes progressively less busy the farther south you go. Its eastern boundary is marked by **Heinrich-Heine-Allee,** named after the German-Jewish writer born here in 1797 and best known for his haunting poem "Die Lorelei" (see sidebar p. 183). The scene is dominated by large buildings including the art nouveau Kaufhaus department store and the Wilhelm-Marx-Haus, a brick-built early skyscraper.

One block farther east is elegant **Königsallee,** known to all simply as the "Kö." Fine trees, a central canal, balustraded bridges,

North-Rhine Westphalia Art Collection
www.kunstsammlung.de
- ✉ Grabbeplatz 5
- ☎ 0211 838 11 30
- 🕐 Closed Mon.
- 💲 $$

and a giant Triton fountain make a dignified setting for one of Germany's most prestigious shopping experiences.

THE ART AXIS

Many of Düsseldorf's cultural attractions are organized into an "art axis" that runs north from the Altstadt. The **North-Rhine Westphalia Art Collection** (Kunstsammlung Nordrhein

includes the domed **Tonhalle,** a splendid example of expressionist brick architecture, conceived as a planetarium but converted into a concert hall. To the north is the **Museum Kunst Palast,** a combination of the old Kunstmuseum and the Kunstpalast that opened in 2001. When Napoleon's armies came this way in 1806, many of the city's art treasures were removed for safekeeping to Munich and never have been returned. But the museum still has plenty of medieval sculpture, old masters, Romantic, Impressionist, and 20th-century German painting. And the collection of glass, particularly of art nouveau and art deco work, is outstanding.

OUTSIDE THE CITY

With its fine shops and fashion shows, Düsseldorf likes to think of itself as a little Paris; it even has its own Versailles 6 miles (10 km) outside town, in the shape of **Schloss Benrath** (*Benrather Schlossallee 104, tel 0211 899 71 40, closed Mon., $*). Built among the forests to the city's south between 1756 and 1771, Benrath is a perfect example of the late baroque fusion of architecture and landscape into a harmonious whole. No single structure dominates the scene; instead, the palace is split into a central section with detached wings and gatehouses. Space flows between the buildings, uniting lake, canal, and radiating avenues. It has been repainted in its original delicious pastel colors, and period furniture graces the interiors.

River traffic sweeps past Düsseldorf's waterfront.

Museum Kunst Palast
- ✉ Ehrenhof 5
- ☎ 0211 8 99 24 60
- 🕐 Closed Mon.
- 💲 $$$

Neanderthal-museum
- ✉ Talstrasse 300, Mettmann
- ☎ 02104 97 97 97
- 🕐 Closed Mon.
- 💲 $$

Westfalen), in an ultra-modern building with a crisply curving facade, has a fine collection of 20th-century German and European art. Its centerpiece is a stunning body of work by Paul Klee (1879–1940), who taught at the city's art academy.

The art axis continues northward into the **Hofgarten,** the city center park first laid out in the 18th century to grace the ducal **Schloss Jägerhof** at its eastern end *Jacobistrasse 2, tel 0211 8 99 62 62, closed Mon., $).* The Schloss houses a museum of Goethe memorabilia, but looming over the trees is a structure more emblematic of present-day Düsseldorf: the three slim slabs of the **Thyssen Building.**

The Hofgarten runs northwest toward the Rhine, where a concentration of cultural buildings

The art axis continues northward into the **Hofgarten,** the city center park first laid out in the 18th century to grace the ducal **Schloss Jägerhof** at its eastern end *Jacobistrasse 2, tel 0211 8 99 62 62, closed Mon., $).* The Schloss houses a museum of Goethe memorabilia, but looming over the trees is a structure more emblematic of present-day Düsseldorf: the three slim slabs of the **Thyssen Building.**

In the Düssel valley lies the village of **Neandertal.** The area has been roughly treated by limestone extraction, but it was here in 1856 that the first skeleton was unearthed of that distant relative of Homo sapiens, Neanderthal Man. A small museum presents reconstructions of what he may have looked like. ■

Ruhr region

ONE OF THE WORLD'S FOREMOST INDUSTRIAL REGIONS, named for the river running along its southern edge, the Ruhrgebiet covers an area of some 1,800 square miles (5,000 sq km) and has a population of about 5.5 million. After the demise of its coal and steel industries, alternative employment has been found for many of those affected by the closure of pits and rolling mills, while much of the industrial heritage has been turned to advantage. Dereliction has metamorphosed into parkland, old railroad lines into cycleways, and mines, coking plants, and gasholders into visitor attractions.

A floodlit blast furnace at Duisberg epitomizes the industrial importance of the Ruhr region.

For two centuries, the Ruhr was Germany's powerhouse, its days gray with a constant pall of smoke emitted by countless factories, its nights lit by the glare of blast furnaces. Deep underground lay the shafts and galleries producing the high-grade coal shipped to all parts of the country via river, canal, and railroad. But in the second half of the 20th century, decline set in; King Coal was dethroned and steel production slackened. Vigorous efforts were made to offset unemployment by promoting the service sector and attracting new industries.

Ruhr region
146 C3–C4
Visitor information
www.ruhrgebiettouristik.de
✉ Gutenbergstrasse 47, Essen
☎ 0201 176 70

From as early as the 1920s, careful control of new development protected farmland and forest. Even today much of the area is "green" along the valley of the winding River Ruhr and in the belts of countryside that penetrate throughout the conurbation, helping the individual towns and cities to maintain their identity.

Relaxing along the River Ruhr

On the cultural side, the Ruhr has countless museums, and excellent galleries and institutions, for example, Bochum's famous Schauspielhaus. But its unique asset is the "Route Industriekultur." This 250-mile (400 km) route threading through the region has its own distinctive signing, linking dozens of industrial heritage sites, most of which can easily be reached by public transportation or even along cycleways. You can descend into the depths of a coal mine, ride an old steam train, and study the lifestyle of industrial barons. Visitor centers will have details.

ESSEN

Essen is the largest city in the Ruhr and the best place to get an overall feeling for the area's often-paradoxical character. It is an old town, although the monuments of the distant past are firmly embedded in more recent developments. In the otherwise architecturally undistinguished city center, try to see Essen's **Cathedral** (Münster). The 10th- to 14th-century building and its **Treasury** (Schatzkammer) contain magnificent objects of early medieval craftsmanship, including a famous Golden Madonna made in 980. A short distance to the east is the **Alte Synagoge,** built in 1913 by Essen's prosperous Jewish community. Although its interior was devastated on Kristallnacht in 1938, its massive walls resisted destruction, and today it houses a documentation center with displays on Jewish life and on Essen during the Nazi period.

South of the city center, a single U-Bahn stop and a short walk bring you to the finest museum complex in the Ruhr. The **Ruhrland-museum** concentrates on local social and industrial history, and the **Museum Folkwang** has one of the most important collections in Germany of 19th- and 20th-century art. Works by French and German painters are hung in close proximity, making interesting comparisons possible. For instance, expressionist Emil Nolde's (1867–1956) passionate love of color is seen to outdo that of van Gogh. Max Beckmann's (1884–1950) horrific images, evoked by his experiences in World War I, are more shocking.

A longer trip by tram to the north brings you to the gates of the **Zeche Zollverein,** a giant head-frame dominating the pithead of this former colliery. When opened in 1932, the mine was the most advanced in the world, its buildings fine examples of functional architecture designed on Bauhaus

Essen

⚑ 146 C3

Visitor information

✉ Am Hauptbahnhof 2

☎ 0201 887 20 41

Cathedral Treasury

✉ Burgplatz 2, Essen

☎ 0201 220 42 06

🕐 Closed Mon.

💲 $

Alte Synagoge

✉ Steeler Strasse 29, Essen

☎ 0201 8 84 52 18

🕐 Closed Mon.

💲 Free

principles. The colliery is one of the "anchor points" along the Route Industriekultur, with a visitor center, changing exhibitions of contemporary design, guided tours around the pithead installations, a steam railroad in summer, and links to footpaths and bike paths.

A ride south by the suburban S-Bahn reveals one of the surprises of the Ruhr—the juxtaposition of densely built-up areas with thick forests and working farmland. The branch line to Kettwig and Düsseldorf soon leaves the city streets behind to run through beautiful beech woodland. Then, suddenly, you see the gleam of water as the train emerges high above the **Baldeneysee,** a reservoir formed by damming the River Ruhr and a popular leisure spot. But the real reason for getting off the train here is to visit the great villa completed in 1873 by imperial Germany's foremost industrialist, Alfred Krupp (see sidebar p. 170).

The **Villa Hügel** stands high above the valley of the River Ruhr on what was a bare hillside until Krupp transformed it into parkland. He used the profits from his hugely successful works to build an enormous modern residence to accommodate not only his family, but also visiting dignitaries from all parts of the world. Prominent guests included Kaiser Wilhelm II, who became a personal friend of the family. Before inspecting the villa with its vast halls and monumental staircase, pay a visit to the "Little House" alongside, where an exhibition emphasizes the achievements and public spirit of the family, through displays on their charitable activities, for example, rather than their role in producing the armaments that made killing possible on an industrial scale.

OTHER RUHR TOWNS

The westernmost of the Ruhr's big cities is **Duisburg.** Its favorable trading location, at the point where the River Ruhr joins the Rhine, helped it to flourish at an early date, and today it is the world's largest inland port. The **Wilhelm-Lehmbruck-Museum**

Alfred Krupp controlled a vast industrial empire from his solidly furnished study in the Villa Hügel.

(*Friedrich-Wilhelm-Strasse 40, tel 0203 283-2630, closed Mon.*) is a major museum of modern sculpture named for local artist Lehmbruck (1881–1919), one of the foremost German sculptors of the 20th century. His deeply spiritual figures inspired some of the work of Joseph Beuys (1921–1986), who is also represented here.

Bochum, in the heart of the Ruhr, was synonymous with coal, steel, and heavy engineering. Nowadays it is known more for its Opel automobile factory and its modern university. The story of coal is comprehensively told in the **German Mining Museum** (Deutsches Bergbaumuseum; *Am Bergbaumuseum 28, tel 0234 5 87 70, closed Mon., www.bergbaumuseum.de, $$*), the biggest of its kind in the world. The Mining Museum's buildings are

Ruhrlandmuseum & Museum Folkwang
www.ruhrlandmuseum.de
✉ Goethestr. 41, Essen
☎ 0201 8 84 52 00 (Ruhrlandmuseum)
0201 884 53 14 (Museum Folkwang)
🕐 Closed Mon.
💲 $$

Zeche Zollverein
www.stiftung-zollverein.de
✉ Gelsenkirchner Strasse 181, Essen
☎ 0201 8 30 36 36

Villa Hügel
✉ Hügel 15, Essen
☎ 0201 61 62 90
🕐 Closed Mon.
💲 $

You can get beneath the surface of the Ruhr at Bochum's Mining Museum.

dominated by a huge tower, which you can climb for a vista of the city. Below the surface, a demonstration mine vividly re-creates life and work underground. Down by the river at Bochum-Dahlhausen, the **Eisenbahnmuseum** (*Dr.-C-Otto-Strasse 191, tel 0234 49 25 16,*

"Dortmunder" beer) is the smaller city of **Hagen,** where the built-up area meets the wooded, hilly country of the Sauerland. The abundant water supply in the Sauerland was harnessed to power the very beginnings of the industrial revolution. These early stirrings of industrial

Duisburg
⚒ 146 C3
Visitor information
✉ Koenigstrasse 86
☎ 0234 28 54 40

Bochum
⚒ 146 C3
Visitor information
✉ Hue Strasse 9
☎ 0234 96 30 20

Hagen
⚒ 146 D3
Visitor information
✉ Rathausstrasse 13
☎ 02331 207 58 94

closed Sat.–Mon.) has a collection of old steam locomotives, diesel railcars, coaches, and wagons, and every kind of railroad memorabilia.

On the far bank of the River Ruhr to the south of Dortmund (whose main claim to fame is its

activity are traced in the open-air **Westfälisches Freilichtmuseum** (*Mäckingerbach, tel 02331 7 80 70, closed Mon. & Nov.–March*). You can watch skilled smiths at work in water-driven mills or see the sails of the windmill turn. ■

The "cannon king"

Alfred Krupp (1812–1887) embodied many virtues and some of the failings of his time and place; inventive, hardworking, and dedicated to the welfare of his workforce, he was also uncompromising and seemingly unaware of the wider consequences of his success.

Krupp guns helped Prussia defeat France in 1871, and well

after Alfred's death, the monster howitzer nicknamed "Big Bertha" played a deadly role in World War I. Later the Krupp family helped Hitler to power, and their use of slave labor to produce weapons for his regime was one of the reasons for the imprisonment of Alfried Krupp, the last head of the firm, at the end of World War II. ■

Münster

CAPITAL OF THE FLAT AND WATERY MÜNSTERLAND, THIS predominantly middle-class, 1,200-year-old cathedral city may seem a sober sort of place, but as the site of Germany's third largest university it has its forward-looking aspect, too. The 13th-century Gothic cathedral sits well amid the burghers' elegant houses.

High gables and arcades in Münster's Altstadt

The number of bicycles in Münster might make you think you have crossed into the neighboring Netherlands, an impression reinforced by the Dutch-looking high-gabled patrician houses lining **Prinzipalmarkt,** the main street. It was in Münster's **Town Hall** (Bürgerhalle) that the Peace of Westphalia was signed on October 24, 1648. This treaty finally ended the Thirty Years War and gave independence to the Netherlands. The 12th-century woodcarving in the superb **Hall of Peace** (Friedensaal; *tel 0251 4 92 27 24*), named after the treaty, is a match for the delicate stonework of the Town Hall's soaring Gothic facade. Study the scenes on the panels behind the mayor's table, an appealing mixture of piety and drollery.

A short stroll northward beneath the busy arcades of the Prinzipalmarkt will bring you to the **Lambertikirche.** The three iron cages hanging from the church's 295-foot (90 m) tower are reminders of an earlier conflict. In the early part of the 16th century Münster was a stronghold of the Anabaptists, the radical religious sect who took over the town and instituted a reign of anarchy. On their defeat, the sect's leaders were executed and their corpses displayed in the cages.

Münster is a staunchly Catholic city, and at its heart, a block from the Lambertikirche, stands its formidable-looking, twin-towered and copper-roofed **Cathedral** (Dom). Built in the 13th century when the

Romanesque style was giving way to Gothic, the cathedral has a spacious nave and, in the ambulatory, an astronomical clock of 1540 where, every day at noon, the Three Wise Men parade. The **Cathedral Treasury** (the Domkammer) contains many marvels of medieval craftsmanship, as does the nearby **Westphalian Regional Museum** (Westfälisches Landesmuseum), where there are good examples of Gothic sculpture.

The River Aa meanders through the city to the Aasee, Münster's popular recreation area. Here you can take a boat trip around the lake, visit the modern all-weather zoo, or stroll around the traditional buildings at the **Open-Air Museum** (Mühlenhof-Freilichtmuseum; *tel 0251 98 12 00).* ■

Münster
- 146 D4

Visitor information
- Klemensstrasse 9
- 0251 4 92 27 10

Cathedral Treasury
- St. Paulus-Dom
- 0251 49 53 33
- Closed Mon.
- $

Westphalian Regional Museum
- Domplatz 10
- 0251 59 07 01
- Closed Mon.
- $

Moated castles of the Münsterland

IN THIS FLAT LAND, A LOCAL LORD NEEDING A STRONG-
hold from which to defy his rivals had no rocky crags on which to
build a conventional castle. Instead, the typical fortress of the area
is a *Wasserburg,* erected on an artificial mound or an island, with water
as its main defense.

The old province of Westphalia once had more than 3,000 such moated castles, but only a fraction of this number survive, a hundred of them in the Münsterland. **Haus Rüschhaus** is on the outskirts of Münster. More like an elegant farmhouse than a castle, it was the playful creation in the mid-18th century of Johann Conrad Schlaun, who designed many of Münster's baroque buildings. Its main claim to fame is as the home of Annette von Droste-Hülshoff (1797–1848), Germany's greatest woman poet. Not far away, the brick-and-stone walls of her aristocratic family's ancestral home, **Burg Hülshoff,** rise sheer from the surrounding moat. Some of the interiors have been refurnished in early 19th-century style, and a small museum is devoted to the writer's memory.

About 18 miles (30 km) south of Münster at Lüdinghausen, one of the most accessible but most formidable of the Wasserburgen is **Burg Vischering.** It has an outer fortress, the Vorburg, on one island, and the main residence, a Renaissance castle on medieval foundations, on another. A museum in the main building deals with the history of the Wasserburgen in general, and another, in the Vorburg, with rural life.

The Wasserburg reached the peak of its development in **Schloss Nordkirchen,** 5 miles (8 km) southeast of Lüdinghausen. Schlaun built this great baroque palace in the early 18th century for Münster's ruler, Prince-Bishop Friedrich Christian von Plettenberg. The vast brick-built complex occupies a rectangular island with pepperpot towers at each corner. ∎

Haus Rüschhaus
- 🅰 146 D4
- ✉ Münster-Nienberge
- ☎ 025 33 13 17
- 🕐 Closed Mon.
- 💲 $

Burg Hülshoff
- 🅰 146 D4
- ✉ Schonebeck 6
- ☎ 025 34 10 52
- 🕐 Closed mid-Dec.– Feb.
- 💲 $

Burg Vischering
- 🅰 146 C4
- ✉ Berenbrock 1, Lüdinghausen
- ☎ 025 91 79 90-0
- 🕐 Closed Mon.
- 💲 $

Schloss Nordkirchen
- 🅰 146 D4
- ✉ Nordkirchen
- ☎ 02596 933 24 02
- 💲 $

Left: The Renaissance residence of Burg Vischering is reflected in its protective moat.

Falconry at Hellenthal in the green hills of the Eifel

More places to visit in North Rhine-Westphalia

BAD MÜNSTEREIFEL
Still surrounded by its medieval walls and
gateways, Bad Münstereifel is built along the
crooked course of the River Erft, which
trickles cheerfully along beside the main
street, crossed by numerous flower bedecked
bridges. Cobbled streets lined with attractive
old houses make leisurely exploration a sheer
delight. Focal points in the townscape are
created by the severe lines of the **parish
church,** founded in the ninth century as the
"Minster in the Eifel," by the 12th-century
Romanische Haus, now the local museum,
and by the red-painted Gothic **Town Hall**
(Rathaus) with its arcades. Among the
surrounding wooded hills, at Effelsberg, is the
unexpected sight of the huge white dish of
the world's largest radio telescope.
🅰 146 C1 **Visitor information** ✉ Kölner
Strasse 13 ☎ 0225 3 54 22 44

THE EIFEL
These cool, airy uplands stretching eastward
from the Belgian border to the Rhine and
Moselle offer deep green woodlands and
sweeping vistas rising to peaks formed by the
action of ancient volcanoes. In the past this
was one of Germany's poorest and most
isolated areas, and even today it is thinly
populated. Visitors come here for quiet days
away from the crowds, although the area is not
lacking in honeypots such as wonderfully
preserved old Monschau (see p. 174), the
man-made lakeland of the Rur reservoirs, or
the dramatic scenery of the Ahr Valley, famous
for its red wines.
🅰 146 B1–C1

HERMANNSDENKMAL
The gigantic Germanic figure of the Hermann
Monument (Hermannsdenkmal) rises from a
hilltop in the Teutoburger Wald. For nationalistic 19th-century Germany, Hermann was a
great hero, the warrior who utterly crushed
the Roman legions as they attempted to
expand their empire east of the Rhine. It now
seems that the Battle of the Teutoburger Wald
in A.D. 9 took place elsewhere, but no matter,
Hermann still looks fiercely westward,
brandishing his 23-foot-long (7 m) sword of
Krupp steel. From the plinth on which he
stands there is a fine panorama over the
wooded countryside of the Lippe area.
🅰 147 E4

LEMGO

Spared wartime destruction, this old town has a wonderfully picturesque late medieval and Renaissance townscape, and these historic houses are not museum pieces: People still live in them. Beauty went hand-in-hand with cruelty; one of the finest buildings is the **Hexenbürgermeisterhaus** (*Breite Strasse 19, tel 05261 21 32 76, closed Mon.*), the 16th-century residence of a burgomaster who was particularly zealous in his pursuit of witches; appropriately enough it houses a museum specializing in instruments of torture.

🄰 147 E4 **Visitor information** ✉ Am Historischen Marktplatz ☎ 0526 19 88 70

MARIA LAACH

Among the characteristic sights of the Eifel are the circular lakes set in the craters of extinct volcanoes. The largest of these, the Laacher See, makes a glorious setting (despite an intrusive autobahn) for one of the greatest Romanesque buildings of the Rhineland, the abbey church of Maria Laach. The austere six-towered structure is enhanced by the use of local volcanic stone in contrasting textures and colors. In the vestibule known as the Paradies, look for the intricate and often amusing carving, and, at the high altar at the eastern end of the building, for the jewel-like Gothic baldachin.

🄰 146 C1 & 177 B4 ☎ 0265 2 5 90

MONSCHAU

With its timber-framed and slate-roofed buildings crowding together along the deeply incised valley of the River Rur, Monschau seems almost too perfect. Many of the houses were little factories, using the water to clean and dye the cloth on which the town prospered in the 18th century. Occupation by the French during the Napoleonic Wars left the town in a kind of time warp, and a stroll along the traffic-free main street, over bridges, and across little squares is pure pleasure, although you are unlikely to have the place to yourself. High above the town are two ruined castles, once needed to command views down the twisting valley. You can study the lifestyle of the richest clothier and his family in the lavishly furnished **Rotes Haus** (*Laufenstrasse 10, 0247 2 50 71, closed Mon.*). The Red House

has a lovely spiral staircase and what looks like a picture gallery, but is in fact cleverly painted wallpaper.

🄰 146 B1 **Visitor information** ✉ Stadtstrasse 16 ☎ 02472 804 80

SCHLOSS AUGUSTUSBURG

Archbishop Clemens August of Cologne, a generous patron of the arts and keen falconer, began in 1725 to build a summer residence and hunting lodge on the edge of the town of Brühl, roughly halfway between Bonn and Cologne. In its formal baroque park, the gorgeous palace demonstrates the wealth, power, and refined taste of its princely owner, a member of the Bavarian royal family. The Schloss has for many years been used as a glamorous setting for state receptions, and more than a hundred heads of state have climbed the theatrically magnificent stairway designed by the archbishop's fellow Bavarian Johann Fischer von Erlach. At the far end of the park stands the more modest **Schloss Falkenlust** (Delight of Falconry), with charming rococo decor. It's said that it was in this secluded spot that Casanova seduced the wife of the Lord Mayor of Cologne.

🄰 146 C2 ✉ Schlossstrasse 6, Brühl ☎ 0223 24 40 00 🕒 Closed Mon. & Dec.–Jan. 💲 $

SOEST

This walled town about 37 miles (60 km) east of Dortmund shows what the Ruhr cities might have been like had the industrial revolution of the 19th century passed them by. People from the Ruhr come here on weekends to escape the pressures of urban living and stroll the medieval streets with their timber-framed houses and buildings constructed from the attractive local greenish sandstone. Over the rooftops arise the towers and spires of churches, foremost among them the cathedral, the massive **Patroklidom.** The church called **Our Lady of the Meadows** (Wiesenkirche) is cathedral-like in size and beauty, and it has exceptionally fine stained glass, including some showing those essential ingredients of a traditional Westphalian supper—ham, beer, and pumpernickel.

🄰 146 D3 **Visitor information** ✉ Teichsmühlengasse 3 ☎ 02921 66 35 00 50 ∎

This is the region for wine lovers. Along with historic wine towns, it includes the most romantic section of the Rhine, the vine-clad Moselle Valley, and the classic route of the Deutsche Weinstrasse.

Rhineland-Palatinate & Saarland

Sign of a wine capital

The Rivers Rhine and Moselle meet at the Deutsches Eck at Koblenz.

Rhineland-Palatinate & Saarland

THE LANDSCAPE OF THE RHINELAND-PALATINATE EMBODIES MUCH THAT IS essentially German, even though the state shares borders with France, Luxembourg, and Belgium. A lot of its territory consists of uplands—the lonely Hunsrück, the Eifel with its remains of ancient volcanoes, and the Pfälzer Wald, one of the country's most extensive forests. But dividing the uplands are the welcoming valleys, created by the Rivers Ahr, Nahe, Moselle, and, above all, the Rhine. In contrast, the Saarland is industrial, built on its huge coal deposits, but even here there are quiet forested corners.

In the southern part of the Rhineland-Palatinate, the Rhine flows smoothly past cities steeped in history: Speyer, Worms, and the Land capital, Mainz. Blessed by the sun, the area is warm enough to grow figs and tobacco, but it is the vine that gives the landscape its special character. Covering the plain that stretches along the left bank of the great river, the vast vineyards of the Pfalz (the old name for the Palatinate, still used in wine circles) and Rhein-Hessen produce a large proportion of all Germany's wine, best sampled in the cool cellars of the charming villages strung out along the German Wine Route (Deutsche Weinstrasse). West of Mainz, the Rhine turns north and enters its gorge, a very different sort of wine country, with vineyards climbing impossibly steep slopes to countless crag-top castles, once the aeries of robber barons preying on the river traffic far below.

As a political entity, Rhineland-Palatinate is a recent creation, formed from several old provinces by the French occupation authorities in 1946. Successive French kings, revolutionaries, and emperors have taken great interest in the territory west of the Rhine, and the area might well have been absorbed into France. The Romans liked it here too, and the attractive city of Trier has the greatest concentration of Roman remains in Europe north of the Alps. This is also one of the heartlands of specifically German history. The rulers of Trier, Mainz, and the Palatinate were among the seven Electors who chose the Holy Roman Emperor.

After Bremen, the Saarland is the smallest of the German *Länder*, or states. Its character has been largely determined by a heritage of heavy industry, which has furnished it with its most outstanding attraction, the great steelworks at Völklingen, the first industrial monument to feature on UNESCO's World Heritage List. ■

Area of map detail

Berlin ✹

50 kilometers
0
30 miles
0

5▷ 62
Wissen · Betzdorf
Sieg

Altenkirchen 414
NORTH RHINE-WESTPHALIA
Wied 256 Hachenburg
p.145 Rennerod
Remagen 8
Ahrweiler · Linz Dierdorf
Bad Sinzig A3 E35 Westerwald
Altenahr Neuenahr
A61 255 Montabaur
Ahr Rhein
Laacher NATURPARK
See Neuwied NASSAU Diez
4▷ 412 Burg NASSAU HESSE
Maria Laach Lahneck Koblenz p.195
Nürburg 257 Winningen Lahn Bad Ems
DEUTSCH- 421 Kobern-Gondorf Nassau
BELGISCHER 410 Schloss Stolzenfels Braubach
NATURPARK Gerolstein Eifel Vierseenblick▲ Marksburg
Prüm Daun A48 Thurant Burg Liebenstein
A60 E44 Boppard Burg Maus
Burg Eltz Burg St. Goarshausen
RHEINLAND- Cochem Rheinfels Burg Katz
Treis- St. Goar Lorelei
Karden Oberwesel Kaub
Dasburg Wittlich Alf Bacharach Pfalz
Bitburg A1 49 317 Burg Sooneck Rhein Mainz ⊙
Our Zell Burg Reichenstein
3▷ Prüm 50 Traben- Burg Rheinstein A60 Ingelheim
DEUTSCH- Trarbach A61 Bingen
LUXEMBURGISCHER 257 Kyll Bernkastel- Gemünden Bad Nierstein
NATURPARK Schweich Kues Kreuznach
257 Neumagen Hunsrück Bad 41 Bad Selz
Morbach Sobernheim Münster 6
Trier Kirn Nahe Alzey
NATURPARK PALATINATE
2▷ Konz SAAR-HUNSRÜCK 41 A63
419 Hermeskeil Idar- 420 Meisenheim E31
Mosel Oberstein Lauterecken Rockenhausen Worms
Saarburg Zerf Birkenfeld Grünstadt
407 Nohfelden 48 A6 Frankenthal
Wadern A62 NATURPARK Ludwigshafen
Orscholz Mettlach Kusel Altenglan PFÄLZER WALD
Grosse 407 Prims Glan 270 Ramstein Bad Dürkheim
Saarschleife Merzig SAARLAND St. Wendel E50 Pfälzer 39 Deidesheim
Saar 268 Lebach A1 Kaiserslautern Wald A61
Dillingen A6 270 Neustadt an der Speyer
Saarlouis St. Ingbert Neunkirchen A62 Weinstrasse A65 272
Völklingen A8 Homburg Wald Germersheim Rhein
A620 Saarbrücken Zweibrücken 10 Annweiler Haardt Landau
1▷ ✈ Blieskastel Pirmasens Rheinzabern
FRANCE Bad Bergzabern 427 Kandel
Schweigen-
Rechtenbach
Lauter BADEN-WÜRTTEMBERG p.317

△ △ △ △
A B C D

LUXEMBOURG
BELGIUM

Mainz

Print pioneer Johannes Gutenberg's press is re-created in the Gutenberg-Museum.

MAINZ WAS THE ONLY POSSIBLE CHOICE OF CAPITAL WHEN the new state of Rhineland-Palatinate was created in 1946. It had been a great city in Roman times, when all of Germania superior was ruled from there. In the Middle Ages it was the seat of the prince-bishop of Mainz, one of the seven electors who had the power to vote on who should be emperor. And Johannes Gutenberg, who began a late medieval media revolution by developing printing with movable type, was born in Mainz around the end of the 14th century.

Mainz
- 177 D3
- **Visitor information**
- ✉ Brückenturm 28
- ☎ 06131 28 62 10

Cathedral & Diocese Museum
- ✉ Domstrasse 3
- ☎ 06131 25 33 44
- 🕐 Closed Mon.
- 💲 $

Gutenberg-Museum
www.gutenberg-museum.de
- ✉ Liebfrauenplatz 5
- ☎ 06131 12 26 40
- 🕐 Closed Mon.
- 💲 $$

Mainz's grandest landmark is the **Cathedral** (Dom). City buildings crowd up against the great red sandstone edifice just as they did in medieval times, emphasizing its vast proportions. Six towers give it an unmistakable silhouette, and though it is essentially a Roman-esque structure of the 12th century, construction of the cathedral was begun as early as the end of the tenth century.

The high opinion that prince-bishops held of themselves is expressed in the superb series of funerary monuments attached to the columns of the nave. But the cathedral's finest sculpture is in the **Cathedral & Diocese Museum** (Dom- und Diözesan-museum) off the cloisters. Here fragments from a demolished

12th-century screen include scenes from the Last Judgment, while finest of all is the masterly head of a man, known as the **"Kopf mit Binde"** ("Head with Bandeau"), a medieval portrait of unique sensitivity.

Wander through the narrow streets and irregularly shaped squares around the cathedral to take in its magnificent outline from all angles. The **Markt,** with a charming Renaissance fountain at its center, is filled with traders' stalls on Tuesdays, Fridays, and Saturdays. In Liebfrauenplatz, the stately mansion called the Haus zum Römischen Kaiser is the home of the **Gutenberg-Museum.** Here you can see priceless copies of Johannes Gutenberg's 42-line Bible, as well as a reconstruction of his workshop, where there are live demonstrations of the workings of a 15th-century printing press.

The city honors its most famous son in a square named after him, and Gutenbergplatz is also home to a statue of the printer by the 19th-century Danish sculptor Bertel Thorwaldsen. More public sculpture enlivens Schillerplatz at the end of Ludwigstrasse leading from the cathedral. The **Carnival Fountain** (Fastnachtbrunnen) is a riotous tribute to what Mainzers call the Fifth Season of the Year.

Make a detour southward from here to **St. Stephen's Church** (St. Stephanskirche), a restored 13th-century building. In the early

Kissing clowns at Mainz's Karneval

1980s, Russian-born artist Marc Chagall designed some stained-glass windows for the church. Their intense blue radiates an unearthly tranquility, while their theme is the divine spirit uniting all humanity.

Many of the city's Roman antiquities are in museums.

They include finds in the **Roman-Germanic Museum** (Römisch-Germanisches Museum), river warships in the **Ancient Navigation Museum** (Museum für Antike Schiffahrt), and a column dedicated to Jupiter in the **Regional Museum** (Landesmuseum). ∎

A page of St. Luke's Gospel from Gutenberg's 1455 Bible

Gutenberg & the book

Because of disturbances in his hometown of Mainz, Gutenberg migrated to Strasbourg, where he worked in secret on a range of inventions. It was his creation of movable type that was to make possible the mass printing of books without any loss of the quality and beauty of the typical medieval manuscript. Finance was always a problem: Gutenberg was continually forced to borrow considerable sums, and just as his famous Bible with 42 lines to the page was coming off the press in 1455, a creditor obtained possession of nearly all his equipment. Gutenberg was ruined. Old and nearly blind, he survived on charity until his death in 1468. ∎

Strongholds such as Burg Katz (Cat Castle) stand guard at bends along the winding Rhine.

Rhine Gorge

FROM ITS SOURCE IN THE ALPS TO ITS OUTLET IN THE North Sea, the Rhine flows for 820 miles (1,320 km) through four countries. For more than 2,000 years it has been a commercial and cultural highway of the first importance. In the relatively short section between Bingen and Koblenz, the great river narrows and deepens, cutting its way through the rocks of the Rhineland massif in a winding defile whose steep, often precipitous slopes carry vineyards, woodlands, and precariously perched castles.

Bingen

🅰 177 C3

Visitor information

✉ Rheinkai 21

☎ 06721 18 42 05

Historical Museum by the River

✉ Museumstrasse 3, Bingen

☎ 06721 99 06 54

🕐 Closed Mon.

💲 $

This is one of Europe's great tourist landscapes, and it has been so for more than 200 years, when it was a compulsory stop for English aristocrats on their Grand Tour southward to Italy. Poets including Byron sang its praises, and artists such as Turner attempted to catch its changing moods.

Busy roads and railroads now run along both banks, and the river itself sees a constant procession, not just of white pleasure cruisers, but of great trains of barges. You should take a trip aboard a boat, preferably heading slowly upstream so that you have time to absorb the constantly changing scene. But spend

time too in some of the delightful wine towns and villages along the way, stroll among the vineyards, and climb up to a castle or two.

BINGEN TO OBERWESEL

Fed by its great tributary the Main, the Rhine flows west past Mainz (see pp. 178–179) and Wiesbaden (see p. 208). The lovely vineyards of the Rheingau overlook this stretch of the river. For a while the river runs gently on, nearly half a mile wide. At the town of **Bingen,** where it is joined by another tributary, the Nahe, it turns north and plunges between the Taunus to the right and the 1,800-foot-high (550 m) Hunsrück uplands to the left. The hills are made of hard rocks, forming treacherous reefs in the riverbed. For centuries cargoes had to be unloaded from boats and taken around these rapids. In the 19th century explosives were used to blast out a relatively safe channel for navigation. However, what is known as the "Binger Loch" (Bingen Hole) still needs to be negotiated with care.

Bingen is famous as the home of the mystic St. Hildegard (1098–1179), one of the most remarkable women of the Middle Ages. A polymath, she wrote, preached, healed, and composed music with equal facility. The 900th anniversary of her birth was marked by the opening of the **Historical Museum by the River** (Historisches Museum am Strom), which documents her life. The museum has a section on how 19th-century artists created an image of the Romantic Rhine that still persists.

A less sympathetic figure than Hildegard was Bishop Hatto of Mainz, who hoarded grain in the **Mäuseturm** (Mice Tower) standing in the stream. For this sin in a time of famine he was, legend

has it, gnawed to death by swarms of merciless mice.

The Mice Tower really was associated with the Bishops of Mainz, who built it in the 13th century as a toll station. The river was a rich source of revenue for those who could control it in such a way. This

explains the extraordinary number of castles along the Rhine.

Immediately downstream from Bingen on the left bank are **Burg Rheinstein** (Trechtingshausen, tel 06721 63 77), perched on a rocky spur; **Burg Reichenstein** (Trechtingshausen, tel 06721 63 48), a neo-medieval edifice; and the tiered **Burg Sooneck** (Niederheimbach, tel 06743 60 64). Another castle, Burg Stahleck, overlooks the vineyards around **Bacharach,** a delightful little fortified town of slate roofs and cobbled streets and squares. Farther downstream, on the right bank, is Kaub with its fortress Burg Gutenfels, as well as the extraordinary **Pfalz,** a midstream toll castle breasting the river like a ship of stone. **Oberwesel**

Right: Bacchanalia at Bacharach

RHINE RIVERBOATS
Several companies run boat trips on the Rhine. These two have websites.

Bingen-Rüdesheimer Fahrgastschiffahrt
www.bingen-ruedesheimer.com
✉ Rheinkai 10, Bingen
☎ 06721 1 41 40

Roessler-Line
www.roesslerlinie.de
✉ Lorcherstrasse 34, Assmannshausen
☎ 06722 23 53

Burg Rheinfels
- ▲ 177 C3
- ✉ St. Goar
- ☎ 06741 383
- 💲 $

Burg Maus
www.burg-maus.de
- ▲ 177 C3
- ✉ St. Goarshausen
- ☎ 06771 7669
- 🕐 Closed Mon.
- 💲 $$

Marksburg
- ▲ 177 C4
- ✉ Braubach
- ☎ 02627 2 06
- 💲 $$ (tour)

Boppard
- ▲ 177 C4
Visitor information
- ✉ Altes Rathaus,
  Marktplatz
- ☎ 06742 38 88

opposite is dominated by the towers of its fortifications.

LORELEI ROCK TO KOBLENZ

Downstream of Oberwesel, the river is hemmed in ever more tightly between its rocky banks in order to squeeze past the legendary **Lorelei rock,** a massive spur some 425 feet (130 m) above the water. The flaxen-haired siren on the rock seducing sailors through the power of song may be a myth (see sidebar p. 183), but this stretch of the river is indeed treacherous, only a third of its normal width, fast flowing, and 65 feet (20 m) deep.

Farther downstream, also on the right bank, is **St. Goarshausen,** with St. Goar across the river. A trio of castles compete with one another here. The greatest fortress along the Rhine, the ruined **Burg Rheinfels** above St. Goar, was originally built by the Counts of Katzenelnbogen about 1245. Strong enough to resist repeated French assaults until 1797, it epitomized patriotic German sentiments about the Watch on the Rhine (Wacht am Rhein).

To challenge the Katzenelnbogens' monopoly of river tolls, the Archbishop of Trier built a castle downstream from St. Goarshausen. His rivals promptly built a bigger fortress, calling it Burg Katz and referring condescendingly to the archbishop's edifice as **Burg Maus.** More rivalries are expressed downstream in the adjacent castles of Liebenstein, now in ruins, and Sterrenberg, attributed to the "Warring Brothers," whose evil intentions toward each other were kept in check by a high wall built between their two castles.

The valley now opens out as the river approaches one of the stateliest bends along its entire course, making room for orchards and the huge vineyard called the Bopparder Hamm on the sunnier left bank. The Romans chose this inviting spot to build their fortified town of Bodobrica, the nucleus of today's **Boppard,** the most substantial and elegant of all the towns along this stretch of the Rhine. In the 19th century, a 2-mile-long (3 km) promenade was laid out, and wealthy pensioners

were encouraged to build their retirement villas here.

Boppard is a pleasant place to break your river journey, with plenty of visitor facilities in a setting summing up all the attractions of the Rhineland—Roman walls, a castle, medieval gateways, venerable churches, fine old town mansions, timber-framed houses, and the ever changing spectacle of river traffic. You can walk up among the vines, or ride over them in a chairlift to the high point known as the **Four Lakes View** (Vierseenblick), from which the Rhine comes into sight as a series of separate lakes. A little railroad, one of the steepest and most cleverly engineered in the country, climbs up through glorious woodland to the high Hunsrück plateau in the west. Back in the town, there are plenty of taverns in which to try wine from the Bopparder Hamm.

Beyond the great bend in the river is **Braubach,** a smaller but equally pretty version of Boppard, and high above is the **Marksburg.** Inside the castle are displays of arms and armor and instruments of torture, while outside there is a medieval herb garden. Just downstream, the confluence of the Lahn with the Rhine is guarded by the restored **Burg Lahneck,** while on the far bank, within the city limits of Koblenz, stands **Schloss Stolzenfels.** "Proud Rock" is yet another 19th-century restoration. A Prussian royal summer residence, its lavish furnishings and artworks were designed to re-create the spirit of the Middle Ages. ■

Marksburg shelters within its protective walls.

Schloss Stolzenfels
- 177 C4
- 0261 5 16 56
- $

Stony siren: the Lorelei

Lorelei: legend & reality

The implacable-looking cliff rising over the swirling waters downstream of Oberwesel was a source of legend long before Clemens von Brentano decided in 1802 to put into ballad form the story of a blond enchantress luring boatmen to their death. In the past, the rock was thought to be the abode of gnomes, guardians of the treasure of the Nibelungs. The Lorelei was immortalized by Heinrich Heine in his ballad, published in 1827, beginning *"Ich weiss nicht was soll es bedeuten …"* ("I cannot divine what it meaneth …" in Mark Twain's translation). The rock became too popular for its own good. The Nazis bulldozed the summit to make a *Thingplatz,* one of their open-air meeting places, and it became infested with kiosks and souvenir stands after the war. A kitsch statue of the Lorelei stands at the foot of the cliff. Efforts have been made to tidy up the summit, which offers a superb view of the winding river in its gorge. You can walk there from St. Goarshausen, but most people get a view of it from a riverboat. ■

Moselle Valley

Vineyards as far
as the eye can
see along the
meandering
Moselle at
Trittenheim

THE MOSELLE RISES HIGH UP IN THE VOSGES MOUNTAINS in France and has long been used as a northeastward route from France and Luxembourg into the Rhineland. The Romans came, bringing vines with them, and wine is what the Moselle is all about: Some of the winding valley between Koblenz and Trier is like one big vineyard. The area is a vacation destination for Germans, and popular places can get very crowded at the height of the season. Stretches of the Moselle are best experienced from a riverboat, but there is also good walking among the vineyards and in the woodlands cladding the shadier slopes.

Some of the world's most enjoyable wines, such as Bernkastler Doctor and Piesporter Goldtropfchen, are produced in the Moselle Valley—as well as some of pretty average quality. The best way to try them is to make your stay coincide with one of the many wine festivals held in the pretty villages and small towns along the river, and also experience Rhineland *Gemütlichkeit* (friendliness) at its jolliest. To explore the area, you can make various roundtrips, combining river transport, roads, and railroads that follow the Moselle along its course.

Koblenz

🅰 177 C4

Visitor information

✉ Pavilion opposite Hauptbahnhof (Main Station)

☎ 0261 1 94 33

Regional Museum

✉ Ehrenbreitstein

☎ 0261 667 50

💲 $

besieging French forces, who proceeded to blow it up. When the fortress passed into the hands of the Prussians it was extensively rebuilt. It now contains the **Regional Museum** (Landesmuseum), but the main reason for making the climb (or taking the chairlift, $$) has to be the breathtaking panorama.

Just upstream from Koblenz is the little wine town of **Winningen,** followed by **Kobern-Gondorf** with two castles and **Thurant** with another.

Now comes a real highlight of a Moselle tour: **Burg Eltz** is one of the few old Rhineland castles still in its original state, including much of its furniture and fittings. Its sheer stone walls rise high above the trees on the north bank of the river. It was the long-term residence of several branches of the Eltz family, each with its own quarters in the rambling edifice. The 13th- to 16th-century interiors give you an intriguing picture of lordly life, and the family treasury has pieces of which any museum would be proud.

On the slopes above stand the ruins of **Burg Trutzeltz,** a specially built fortress from which the Archbishop of Trier, the great enemy of the Eltz dynasty, was able to bombard them into submission.

COCHEM TO NEUMAGEN

Beyond Treis-Karden comes **Cochem,** one of the most popular destinations along the Moselle for day-visitors. The town has the right ingredients, including an attractive riverside promenade, but it is the setting that lifts it far out of the ordinary. A conical, vine-clad hill rises from the river, crowned with a romantic castle, the **Reichsburg.** It is a fantasy, a mock-medieval stronghold erected in the 1870s to feed the over-active imagination of a millionaire Berlin ironmaster.

Burg Eltz sports a fantastical array of towers, turrets, spires, and spiky roofs.

Burg Eltz
www.burg-eltz.de
🅰 177 C3
✉ Münstermaifeld
☎ 02671 95 05 00
$ $$

Cochem
🅰 177 B3
Visitor information
✉ Endertplatz 1
☎ 02671 6 00 40

Reichsburg
☎ 02671 2 55
$ $$

Bernkastel-Kues
🅰 177 B3
Visitor information
✉ Gestade 6
☎ 06531 40 23

KOBLENZ TO BURG ELTZ

The promontory where the Moselle meets the Rhine at **Koblenz** is named **German Corner** (Deutsches Eck). It is dominated by a huge statue of Kaiser Wilhelm I. This is a 1990s replacement for the original, which was blown up by U.S. forces in 1945. The Romans founded a settlement here and called it Confluentes (confluence), later germanized as Koblenz.

This pleasant town has attractive promenades along both rivers, but its most striking feature is on the far side of the Rhine. Here, atop the 410-foot (125 m) cliff, is the great citadel of **Ehrenbreitstein.** Originally built by the local rulers, the Archbishops of Trier, it withstood many sieges until 1799, when its defenders were starved out by

Tools of the vintner's trade bedeck the walls of Senheim's wine museum.

Nikolaushospital/ Cusanusstift

✉ Cusanusstrasse 2

☎ 06531 22 60

Mosel- Weinmuseum

✉ Cusanusstrasse 2

☎ 06531 41 41

💲 $

Neumagen

🅰 177 B3

Visitor information

✉ Hinterburg 8a

☎ 06507 65 55

You can admire his taste in the course of a guided tour.

At Cochem, the railroad, which so far has followed the river, takes a shortcut into a 2.5-mile (4 km) tunnel, the longest in Germany. This cuts out a whole series of bends and wine villages, but the same kind of scenery continues all the way to the next place of any size, **Traben-Trarbach,** a double town straddling the river. Both halves are attractive, and Trarbach has an assortment of hundred-year-old art nouveau buildings, among them the imposing bridge gateway.

Half-timbered mansions lining the Marktplatz on the Bernkastel side of **Bernkastel-Kues** are upstaged by the tiny Pointy House (Spitzhäuschen). Now a wine bar, it is one room thick and only just squeezes into its absurdly narrow site. Kues's more sober institution, the **Nikolaushospital** or **Cusanusstift,** almshouses founded in 1458, still fulfill their intended function, with chapel, library, and dining hall. Next door, the **Mosel-Weinmuseum** has displays on the wine culture of the region, plus

a Vinothek, where you can sample more than a hundred local varieties of wine and Sekt, the German sparkling wine. Bernkastel has one of the most famous of the Moselle vineyards, called "Doctor" ever since a medieval archbishop of Trier recovered his health after drinking its wine. One of the best viewpoints over the river is from the ruined castle above the town, **Burg Landshut.**

Between Bernkastel and Trier, the wine town of **Neumagen-Dhron** is proud of the role it played in uncovering the valley's Roman past. Here, in 1884, workmen unearthed relief panels including the **Neumagen Wine Ship,** an extraordinary depiction of a barge loaded with wine barrels being rowed vigorously toward its destination by its oarsmen. Originally grave markers, the panels seem to have been hurriedly taken down and used to build a fort against the attacks of Germanic tribesmen. They are now in the Rheinisches Landesmuseum in Trier (see p. 188), but reproductions of the wine ship and a classroom scene have been put up in the town. ■

Trier

CLOSE TO THE BORDER WITH LUXEMBOURG, TRIER LOOKS back on the 2,000 years of continuous history that have left it with an exceptional architectural heritage. This, together with its fortunate location among the vineyards of the Moselle and a relaxed, mature atmosphere, make it the most appealing city in the Rhineland-Palatinate.

The greatest monument of Roman Germania is the Porta Nigra at Trier.

"*Ante Romam Treveris stetit annis mille trecentis*—Trier stood for 1,300 years before Rome" states the proud inscription in Latin on the Red House (Rotes Haus) in the marketplace. Trier is indeed one of the oldest towns in Germany, although not quite as old as the claim. It was about 16 B.C. that the Romans marched in, and over the next four centuries they made the place they called Augusta Treverorum into one of the finest cities north of the Alps. In its Roman heyday, Trier had 80,000 inhabitants, a figure not reached again until recently. Emperor Constantine and his mother, St. Helena, made Trier a center of Christianity; much later the city was ruled by powerful prince-bishops.

Trier's most famous son was Karl Marx (1818–1883), whose birthplace, now called the **Karl-Marx-Haus,** preserves his memory in documents, photographs, and first editions.

Trier's symbol is the colossal Roman gateway known as the **Porta Nigra,** guarding what was the northern entrance to the town. Built of massive blocks of blackened sandstone bound together by iron clamps, it is the best-preserved structure of its kind anywhere in Europe. In the 11th century, a Greek hermit by the name of Simcon lived in the eastern tower. After his death, the gateway was converted into a church, and a monastery, the Simeonsstift, was built next door. The monastery's two-story galleried courtyard now houses a café, the

Trier
🅰 177 B2
Visitor information
✉ An der Porta Nigra
☎ 0651 97 80 80

Karl-Marx-Haus
✉ Brückenstrasse 10
☎ 0651 97 06 80
💲 $

Porta Nigra
✉ Porta-Nigra-Platz
☎ 0651 7 54 24
💲 $

Relax over coffee in Trier's market square.

Municipal Museum
- ⊠ An der Porta Nigra
- ☎ 0651 7 18 14 50
- 💲 $

Imperial Baths
- ⊠ Kaiserstrasse/Ostallee
- ☎ 0651 97 80 80
- 💲 $

Regional Museum
- ⊠ Weimarallee 1
- ☎ 0651 9 77 40
- 🕐 Closed Mon. in winter
- 💲 $

Amphitheater
- ⊠ Olewigerstrasse
- ☎ 0651 97 80 80
- 💲 $

visitor information center, and the **Municipal Museum** (Städtisches Museum). Here you can see a large model of Trier as it was in 1800 and watch a video on post-Roman developments in the city.

From the Porta Nigra, the traffic-free Simeonstrasse runs southward more or less along the line of the Roman street to modern Trier's focal point, the **Hauptmarkt,** with cafés, market stalls, a market cross, and a Renaissance fountain. It's one of the most attractive squares in Germany, with a wonderful variety of buildings. The corner building with arcades and chisel roof is the much-restored **Steipe,** the 15th-century banqueting hall of the city notables; beside it is the Red House with its famous inscription.

From the marketplace it's only a short step to the cathedral quarter. Pause for a few minutes in the **Domfreihof,** the calm square in front of the **Cathedral** (Dom) and contemplate the austerely beautiful forms of the building, a marvel of early Romanesque architecture built on masonry dating

from the time of Constantine. Only the taller, right-hand tower breaks the symmetry of the facade facing you. The story has it that the archbishop ordered that it be given its extra inches so that the tower of the recently built citizens' church of St. Gangolf would not overlook his cathedral. The great treasure of the Dom is the Seamless Robe worn by Christ on the Cross, one of several relics purchased by St. Helena on a visit to Jerusalem and distributed by her around the important churches of Christendom. The Robe is only shown on very special occasions, when it attracts up to two million pilgrims to the city.

A charming old street winds past the adjacent **Church of Our Lady** (Liebfrauenkirche), a Gothic structure of great purity, one of the first to be built in Germany. Beyond is the **Konstantinbasilika,** a brick edifice of awe-inspiring size built as the Emperor's throne room and now a Protestant church. It is the second largest roofed structure, after the Pantheon in Rome, remaining from Roman times.

Less complete, but equally striking, are the **Imperial Baths** (Kaiserthermen) on the edge of the old city center. The site consists mainly of the foundations and basements of the Roman spa town, but the remaining walls are as imposing as the Porta Nigra. More baths, covered by a stunning modern glass structure, can be seen in the Cattle Market (Viehmarkt), while close to the Kaiserthermen is the **Regional Museum** (Rheinisches Landesmuseum), whose great pride is the original Roman **Wine Ship** from nearby Neumagen (see p. 186). A five-minute walk away is the **Amphitheater,** where 20,000 spectators once watched gladiatorial combats and other entertainments. It is now the venue for a summer drama festival. ■

Saarbrücken & Saarland

INDUSTRIAL SAARBRÜCKEN IS CAPITAL OF GERMANY'S second smallest *Land*, named after the River Saar, which rises in the Vosges Mountains in France then runs northwest to join the Moselle just above Trier. After World War I, the Saarland with its coalfields and heavy industries was ceded to France, although a 1935 plebiscite returned it to Germany. Much the same happened after 1945. The Saarland only formally became part of the Federal Republic of Germany in 1957, and there's a French flavor about the place.

Saarland
A 177 B1
Visitor information
✉ Franz-Josef-Röder
Strasse 9
☎ 0681 92 72 00

Together with a string of smaller rust-belt towns along the River Saar, **Saarbrücken** has suffered in recent years from the demise of the traditional industries of coal and steel. However, it retains a lively regional focus; bistros abound, French words find their way into everyday speech, and there are innumerable cross-border contacts.

While the city center on the right bank of the river is largely modern, there is a fine heritage of building on the left bank from the time when the Prince of Nassau beautified his capital in baroque mode. On an elevated site above the river, the 18th-century **Schloss** was neglected for many years, but a 15-year restoration program has given it a role in city life as local government offices. Its central block is now a dramatic modern steel-and-glass structure by architect Gottfried Böhm. Adjacent to the Schloss and equally striking is the **Regional History Museum** (Historisches Museum Saar; *Schlossplatz 15, tel 0681 5 06 45 02, closed Mon., $*), also designed by Böhm, which relates the Saarland's convoluted recent history.

The jewel of the baroque city is the **Ludwigskirche** (*Ludwigsplatz, tel 0681 5 25 24, closed Mon.*), built between 1762 and 1775. The church is the focal point of a masterly piece of 18th-century urban design, an ensemble of mansions whose pale coloring contrasts with the rugged external

stonework of the church. Enter the church to experience a further contrast, for inside, all is grace, light, and delicacy.

THE SAARLAND

For much of its course through the

The organ in Saarbrücken's 18th-century Ludwigskirche— lovely both to look at and to hear

The great hairpin bend formed by the River Saar near Mettlach

Saarland, the Saar is an industrial river, but the factories, old collieries, and waste tips are seen against a backdrop of wooded hills.

Downstream from the town of Merzig the river has a much more rural character, winding through a deep valley clad at first in forest, then in vines. The late 18th-century abbey at **Mettlach** is the headquarters of the long-established ceramics firm of Villeroy & Boch. Its visitor center stages an entertaining and instructive "Keravision" show about the firm's history and products *(tel 06864 81 10 20)*. From here, cross the Saar and drive toward the spa town of Orscholz, following the signs to Cloef. After a 15-minute walk from the parking lot to a viewpoint high above the **Saar Bend** (Grosse Saarschleife), you can see the most spectacular natural sight in the Saarland, a dramatic hairpin bend described by the river around a densely wooded peninsula. ■

A cathedral of industry

The first industrial monument to be put on UNESCO's World Heritage List, the **Völklinger Hütte** is a century-old iron-and-steel works at Völklingen on the River Saar, 6 miles (10 km) downstream from Saarbrücken. Since it closed in 1986, it has been turned into a compelling tourist attraction. Its description as a cathedral of industry is well founded, with the awesome impact of the towering blast furnaces and the gas blower hall of more than cathedral-like proportions. A powerful symbol of the industry that made the Saarland one of Europe's key manufacturing regions, it is unusually complete, a perfect example of all the processes that went into the manufacture of steel. You can walk around the vast plant on your own, but it's much better to join a guided tour. The true scale of the installations only becomes apparent when you see the minuscule figures of your fellow visitors climbing ladders and negotiating catwalks among the monstrous coking plants and blast furnaces. ■

Völklinger Hütte
www.voelklinger-huette.org
 Völklingen
☎ 06898 9 10 00

Worms

VISIBLE FROM FAR ACROSS THE RHINE PLAIN, CATHEDRAL towers hint at this city's importance—particularly in connection with Martin Luther and the rise of Protestantism. But Worms is more than history. It is a wine town; among the vineyards to the north stands the Gothic Church of Our Lady (Liebfrauenkirche), after which a famous German blended wine, Liebfraumilch, is named.

In the fifth century the Germanic Burgundians established a short-lived kingdom at Worms before their annihilation at the hands of Attila the Hun. Their story provides some of the basis of the anonymous 12th-century epic, *The Nibelungenlied* (*The Song of the Nibelungs*), itself the inspiration for Wagner's *Ring*. To get to Worms from the far side of the Rhine, you must cross the **Nibelungenbrücke,** passing beneath a splendidly medieval-looking (but 19th-century) gateway. By the bridge stands a statue of Hagen, the villain of the epic tale.

Dominating the center of the Old Town (Altstadt) is the huge Romanesque **St. Peter's Cathedral** (Dom St. Peter). Here at the Imperial Assembly, or Diet,

of 1521, Martin Luther, ordered to recant his heretical beliefs, spoke the defiant words: "Here stand I, I can do no other, God help me."

Inside, the west end, traditionally reserved for the emperor, has elaborate features. An 18th-century altar by Balthsar Neumann enhances the east end. A five minutes' walk north, the **Luther Monument** (Lutherdenkmal) shows the reformer with like-minded figures.

A Jewish community was established in Worms as early as the 11th century and became one of Germany's largest. Beyond the Altstadt, on the Lutherring, is the **Judenfriedhof Heiliger Sand,** the Jewish cemetery, thought to be the oldest in Europe; some of its tombstones date back 900 years. ■

St. Peter's Cathedral in Worms exudes the fine points of German Romanesque architecture.

Worms
🄰 177 D2
Visitor information
✉ Neumarkt 14
☎ 06241 2 50 45

St. Peter's Cathedral
✉ Domplatz
☎ 06241 61 15
💲 Free (donation appreciated)

Drive: The German Wine Route

The route leads through rolling countryside at the foot of the Haardt, the eastern edge of the vast Palatinate Forest (Pfälzer Wald), giving ever changing views of the vineyards running down to the plain and passing through a succession of wine villages or small towns, each more inviting than the last.

Vintners' dwellings line the streets of the old wine village of Rhodt.

A monumental gateway marks the southern starting point of the Weinstrasse at **Schweigen-Rechtenbach ❶**, on the border with Alsace. It was erected in the 1930s when the route was established. The Haardt escarpment offered fine sites for medieval castles, and there are several on the way, and also the occasional later Schloss built mainly for the wonderful views over the vineyards.

Just before reaching Eschbach, leave the Weinstrasse by turning left on route 48 to Annweiler. The turrets and ramparts of Burg Madenburg soar on the hillside to the right. Follow signs to **Burg Trifels ❷** for superlative views over forest and plain. Trifels was an imperial castle, the legendary repository of the Holy Grail and the prison of Richard Lionheart of England, captured by Emperor Henry IV in 1193 on his way home from the Third Crusade.

Return to the Weinstrasse through Albersweiler and continue northward for about 6 miles (10 km). **Rhodt ❸** is a particularly enchanting village, with plenty of half-timbered or red sandstone vintners' homes. Beautifully located above the village where the vines give way to the forest towers **Schloss Villa Ludwigshöhe,** a tasteful Italianate summer palace built by King Ludwig I of Bavaria in the early 19th century. A scenic side road leads from the pretty village of **St. Martin** to the **Kalmit ❹**, at 2,208 feet (673 m) the highest point in the Palatinate, with superb views all around.

Back on the Weinstrasse, as you approach Neustadt an der Weinstrasse you will see on the left the **Hambacher Schloss.** At this ancient stronghold 30,000 patriots demonstrated for German unity and democracy in 1832 and for the first time raised the black-red-gold tricolor, since adopted as the national flag. **Neustadt ❺** is the miniature metropolis of the Weinstrasse, a larger version of the wine villages on the route, with a well-preserved Old Town (Altstadt) and plenty of wine taverns.

See area map p. 177 C1
► Schweigen-Rechtenbach
↔ 53 miles (85 km)
⏱ Allow at least a whole day
► Bockenheim

NOT TO BE MISSED
- Burg Trifels
- A walk through the vineyards to Schloss Villa Ludwigshöhe
- A stroll around the old town center of Neustadt
- A substantial meal in Deidesheim
- Wine tasting anywhere along the route

Deidesheim 6 is smaller, but its marketplace has a stately air, lined with the mansions of the region's wealthy winegrowers; the Town Hall (Rathaus) has a splendid external staircase. It's also a center of gastronomy, with several outstanding restaurants including ex-Chancellor Helmut Kohl's favorite, Deidesheimer Hof. He used to invite visiting statesmen—and stateswomen—here (although even his powers of persuasion failed to convince British Prime Minister Margaret Thatcher that she should eat the Palatinate specialty *Saumagen* sow's belly).

About 3.5 miles (6 km) beyond Deidesheim, **Bad Dürkheim 7** is as steeped in wine culture as anywhere along the Weinstrasse. It is the venue for the September Wurstmarkt und Weinfest, claimed to be the world's biggest wine festival. Bad Dürkheim is also a spa, with saline springs and a neoclassic Kurhaus set in the lovely Kurpark. The ruins of Kloster Limburg to the west of the town are the spectacular setting for open-air performances in summer. Just east of the Weinstrasse, **Freinsheim 8** is a substantial place with a well-preserved town wall and gateways. The route ends at **Bockenheim,** with a counterpart to the gateway at the southern end of the route. ∎

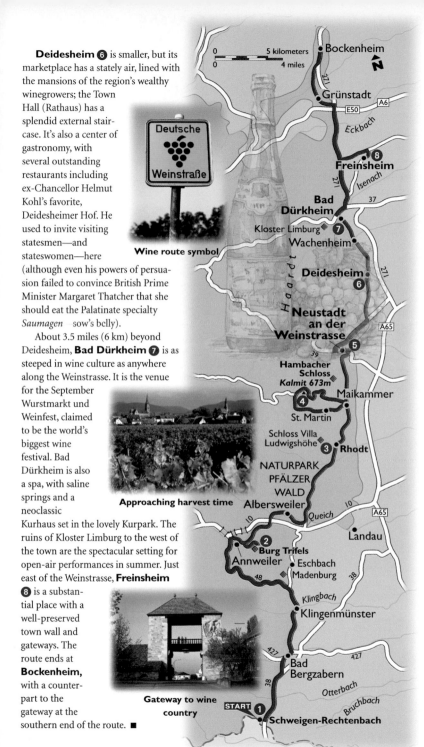

Wine route symbol

Approaching harvest time

Gateway to wine country

Speyer

SPEYER, ON THE WEST BANK OF THE RHINE, HAS ONE OF
Germany's great Romanesque cathedrals, the four towers and two
domes visible from far away. The town was destroyed by the French
in 1689, then slowly rebuilt and spared further destruction in recent
times. A cheerful place, happy with its location among the
sun-soaked vineyards of the Palatinate, it claims to be where that
essential accompaniment to a drink, the pretzel, was invented, and it
is a famous center of good eating.

The best way to approach the old
town center is through its great
medieval gateway, the 180-foot-
high (55 m) **Altpörtel.** Climb to
the top for a good overall view. In
front of you, the main street,
Maximilianstrasse, forms a gently
curving ceremonial way leading to
the cathedral. Usually known as the
Kaiserdom because of its imperial associations, the cathedral was

begun in 1030. Later in the century
its nave was given a stone vault, a
considerable technical achievement
for the time. Now on UNESCO's
World Heritage List, it is Germany's
biggest Romanesque cathedral, and
a remarkably pure example of that
style. You can appreciate its majes-
tic proportions and its fine detail-
ing by walking around it through
the surrounding parkland. The
interior is equally imposing. In the
great vaulted crypt are the tombs of
kings and emperors, including the
cathedral's founder, Kaiser
Konrad II.

Konrad's burial crown and
other precious objects from the
cathedral's treasury are on show in
the **Historical Museum of the
Palatinate** (Historisches Museum
der Pfalz). It also includes a wine
museum whose prize possession is
a bottle of Roman wine discovered
in a third-century sarcophagus.
Speyer's other main museum is
the **Technology Museum**
(Technik-Museum), a light and airy
industrial building expertly converted to house vintage
locomotives, motor vehicles, flying
machines, and even a submarine.

Like Worms, Speyer was an
important center of Jewish life,
and although little is left of the
synagogue, the underground
ritual bath, the **Mikwe**—the
oldest in Germany—is perfectly
preserved (*Judenbadgasse, tel 06232
29 19 71*). ■

Speyer
🗺 177 D2
Visitor information
✉ Maximilianstrasse 13
☎ 06232 14 23 92

Kaiserdom
✉ Domplatz
☎ 06232 10 21 18
💲 Free (donation
   appreciated)

**Historical Museum
of the Palatinate**
✉ Domplatz
☎ 06232 1 32 50
🕐 Closed Mon.
💲 $$

**Technology
Museum**
✉ Am Technik Museum
   1
☎ 06232 6 70 80
💲 $$

Designed in
classic
Romanesque
style, the
Kaiserdom
celebrates the
apex of medieval
architecture.

Linking the Rhine vineyards to cool uplands shared with Bavaria and Thuringia, the *Land* of Hesse is in the heart of Germany. Its woods, hilltop castles, and atmospheric old towns inspired the tales of the Brothers Grimm.

Hesse

"Germania" guards the Rheingau wine region.

Everything's apples at Mr. Possmann's cider barrel.

Hesse

THE *LAND* OF HESSE (HESSEN) MAY BE WHERE THE BROTHERS GRIMM (see p. 203) lived and worked for the better part of their lives, but it is not all fairy tales. The large urban sprawl along the confluence of the Rivers Rhine and Main, centered on Frankfurt, has a severely practical outlook.

Frankfurt is the focal point of international routes and the site of continental Europe's busiest airport. Its skyscrapers proclaim its prosperity and modernity. As Germany's financial capital and seat of the European Bank it seems set to play an increasingly important role as the members of the EU edge cautiously toward greater integration.

Cosmopolitan and sophisticated, Frankfurt has first-rate museums and all the attractions of a wealthy metropolis. It's a surprise to find that Frankfurters' favorite tipple is not some exotic cocktail but *Äppelwoi*, the apple wine traditionally produced from local orchards. Fruit trees grow in profusion in southwestern Hesse and make a springtime spectacle along the Bergstrasse, the tourist route running south from Frankfurt along the edge of the wooded Odenwald upland. The region's toe-hold in the wine-growing area along the Rhine is the Rheingau, whose south-facing slopes have some of the prettiest vineyards and most popular wine villages in the country.

Like many German states, Hesse has had a highly fragmented history. Unified in the late Middle Ages, it subsequently split into separate units, each with its own little capital ruled over, with luck, by enlightened rulers such as Grand Duke Ernst Ludwig, who made Darmstadt a center of European art nouveau, or Margrave Karl of Kassel, who created one of Europe's greatest landscape parks. The aristocratic imprint was also felt in Wiesbaden and in other spa towns such as Bad Homburg, while in Fulda it was prince-bishops who transformed this ancient center of German Christianity into a model baroque town.

Close to the border with Thuringia, Fulda stands in a funnel of relatively open country known as the Fulda Gap, through which the armor of the Warsaw Pact was expected to pour toward the Rhine should the Cold War ever have turned hot. They would soon have come up against American forces, concentrated in the Rhine–Main area ever since the end of World War II, when American military government carved out a new Hesse from the ruins of the Third Reich and decided state capital would be Wiesbaden. ∎

0 ————————— 50 kilometers
0 ————————— 30 miles

5▷

LOWER SAXONY
P. 125

Diemel-
Stausee
Reinhardshagen
83
80
Hofgeismar
7
Grebenstein
Witzenhausen
Bad
Arolsen
A44
Vellmar
Zierenberg
Bad Sooden-
Allendorf
Wolfhagen
450
Kassel
NATURPARK
DIEMELSEE
Korbach
Diemel
Werra
NATURPARK
MEISSNER
KAUFUNGER
WALD
Wilhelmshöhe
251
Baunatal
Kaufungen
Eschwege
Gudensberg
A49
Hessisch-
Lichtenau
7

NORTH RHINE-WESTPHALIA
P. 145

Eder-Stausee
Fritzlar
A7
E45
Melsungen
Bad
Wildungen
253
Borken
Homberg
83
27
Sontra
Frankenberg
254
Rotenburg
an der Fulda
Bebra
Battenberg
Germünden
Schwalmstadt
Bad
Hersfeld
A4

4▷

Eder
Münchhausen
3
62
Dautphetal
Biedenkopf
Stadt
Allendorf
454
Kirchhain
Lahn
Eschwege
454
Kirchheim
Niederaula
62
Marburg
Kirchhain
62
A5
E40
H E S S E
21
84
Dillenberg
Homberg
Alsfeld
Fulda
Hünfeld
A7
E45
Herborn
Lollar
49
254
255
A45
Giessen
Grünberg
275
Lauterbach
Hilders
Wetzlar
Schotten
774m
278
49
Lich
Vogelsberg
Fulda ● Petersberg
54
Weilburg
456
Braunfels
A5
457
Nidda
Neuhof
40
21
Schloss
Fasanerie
Gersfeld
Hadamar
Butzbach
A45
Gedern
THURINGIA
P. 211

3▷

Lahn
Wetter
Nidda
Runkel
Usingen
Bad Nauheim
Nidder
Schlüchtern
Limburg
A3
Bad
Camberg
Friedberg
Büdingen
Bad Soden-
Salmünster
A66
Steinau
276
Idstein
417
45
Nidderau
Bad Orb
Bad
Homburg
3
Karben
Gelnhausen
NATURPARK
HESSISCHER
SPESSART
NATURPARK
RHEIN-TAUNUS
Taunusstein
245m
Neroberg
FRANKFURT
AM MAIN
Hanau
54
Bad Schwalbach
A5
Offenbach
Main
Kinzig
BAVARIA
P. 247
Lorch
42
Kloster
Eberbach
●**Wiesbaden**
A3
Seligenstadt
Rheingau
Rhein
Rheingau
Schloss
Biebrich
Rüsselsheim
Rodgau
Rüdesheim
Gross-Gerau
26
Dieburg

RHINELAND-PALATINATE
P. 175

Rhein
44
Reinheim
Darmstadt
426
Pfungstadt
Höchst
Gernsheim
A5
45
Bensheim
Lindenfels
Michelstadt
Bürstadt
47
A67
E451
Heppenheim
3
Odenwald
NATURPARK
BERGSTRASSE-
ODENWALD
Beerfelden

BADEN-
WÜRTTEMBERG
P. 317

Neckarsteinach

△
D

Area of map detail

Berlin ✳

△   **△**   **△**   **△**
A   **B**   **C**

Above: Apple-wine festival on Frankfurt's Römerberg

Frankfurt am Main

Frankfurt am Main
🅰 197 B2
Visitor information
✉ Am Römerberg 27
☎ 069 21 23 88 00

Römer (Kaisersaal)
🅰 Map p. 201
✉ Römer, Römerberg
☎ 069 21 23 48 14
💲 $

Historical Museum
🅰 Map p. 201
✉ Saalgasse 19
☎ 069 21 23 55 99
🕐 Closed Mon.
💲 $

THE CHARACTER OF FRANKFURT, GERMANY'S FIFTH largest city, is hard to pin down. Its nickname "Mainhattan" seems particularly appropriate when you first glimpse its cluster of glittering office towers, while the epithet "Bankfurt" sums up its key role in Germany's (and continental Europe's) financial affairs. Frankfurt is the most multicultural city in Germany, one in four of its citizens being immigrants or their offspring. It retains a strong sense of local patriotism, half-jokingly expressed by its addiction to apple wine.

Some 400 financial institutions are established here, including the Börse (Stock Exchange) and the Bundesbank (German Federal Bank). But there's much more to Frankfurt than making and spending money. Its central location in western Germany, at the intersection of important routes, has long made it significant. In the Middle Ages, kings and emperors came here to be crowned, knowing that news of their glory would soon be spread around the country. Today's advertisers and publishers have built on this, and Frankfurt handles almost half of Germany's business in publishing and communications.

Frankfurt's stylish
skyline sparkles at
night.

The city exudes modernity, especially if you come here on business, arrive at its international airport—Germany's biggest and busiest—and head straight for one of the its office towers, such as the 840-foot (256 m) pencil-shaped Messeturm, now overshadowed by Norman Foster's 850-foot (259 m) Commerzbank.

NORTH OF THE RIVER

Start your visit at the **Römerberg** to get the feel of old Frankfurt. This irregularly shaped square is the historical core of the city, where citizens gathered for special occasions. A coronation feast would be held in the **Römer,** Frankfurt's old city hall, a conglomerate of several houses unified by being given high Gothic gables. In its

Kaisersaal are 19th-century portraits of several dozen emperors.

While World War II bombing left the Römer's facade standing, the tall timber-framed buildings on the opposite side of the square have been rebuilt from scratch, using traditional materials and methods. The southern part of the square is occupied by the red sandstone 13th-century **St. Nicholas' Church** (Nikolaikirche). From its roof platform the city fathers used to greet the crowds, and a trumpeter still salutes shoppers and stallholders from it during the big Christmas market on the square.

Explore the city's past further in the **Historical Museum** (Historisches Museum) just to the south. A model shows medieval Frankfurt in its prime, and another

Rebuilt timber-
framed houses on
the Römerberg re-
create the look of
prewar Frankfurt.

Schirn Art Gallery
www.schirn-kunsthalle.de
- 🅐 Map p. 201
- ✉ Am Römerberg 6a
- ☎ 069 2 99 88 20
- ⊕ Closed Mon.
- 💲 $$

**Struwwelpeter-
Museum**
- 🅐 Map p. 201
- ✉ Bendergasse 1
- ☎ 069 28 13 33
- ⊕ Closed Mon.

Cathedral
- 🅐 Map p. 201
- ✉ Domplatz
- ☎ 069 13 37 61 86
- ⊕ Closed Mon.
  (Dommuseum)
- 💲 $ (Dommuseum)

demonstrates the almost unbeliev-
able extent of the devastation in
1945. The museum incorporates
the city's oldest surviving building,
a 12th-century chapel that was part
of the imperial palace. And there's
an authentic apple wine tavern
attached to the museum.

Off the Römerberg to the north
is the 18th-century **St. Paul's
Church** (Paulskirche), In the revo-
lutionary year of 1848 delegates
came from Central Europe and
hoped, in vain, that their delibera-
tions would help to establish a
democratic and united Germany.
It's a symbol of great importance
in the country's tortured progress
toward unity and democracy.
Public donations from all over
Germany contributed toward its
postwar reconstruction in time for
the centenary in 1948.

The Römerberg and the Church
of St. Bartholmäus were controver-
sially linked by the construction
of the elongated postmodern
Schirn Art Gallery (Kunsthalle
Schirn). This gallery houses
changing exhibitions, mostly of
contemporary art, along with the

Struwwelpeter-Museum,
with exhibits on the nightmarish
children's story character ("Straw
Peter" in English) and his creator,
the 19th-century Frankfurt
psychiatrist Heinrich Hoffman.

Strictly speaking, the red sand-
stone **Cathedral** (Dom) is "only" a
parish church, the Church of St.
Bartholomäus, but few parish
churches have been the setting for
coronation ceremonies of emperors.
Ten were crowned here, beginning
with Maximilian II in 1562. Long
before the coronation the Holy
Roman Empire's seven electors
would meet in the church's Election
Chapel (Wahlkapelle) to decide on
whom should be given the title of
emperor. The cathedral was refur-
nished after a fire in 1867, but an
altarpiece of 1434 survived, showing
Mary on her deathbed attended by
the Twelve Apostles. The cathedral's
finest feature is its tower, completed
according to the plans of a 15th-cen-
tury architect in 1877, and until
recently the city's tallest structure.

On an awkwardly constricted
triangular site one block to the
north stands another postmodern

masterpiece, the **Modern Art Museum** (Museum für Moderne Kunst; *Domstrasse 10, tel 069 21 23 04 47, closed Mon., $),* designed by Austrian Hans Hollein. Nicknamed the "slice of cake," it's an architectural tour de force, almost upstaging the collection of modern works by artists such as Andy Warhol and Josef Beuys.

Farther north still is Frankfurt's main shopping street, the **Zeil.** Watching over the busy scene is the baroque **Hauptwache,** the city guardhouse and now a café. Still on the Zeil is **Les Facettes,** an ultramodern shopping complex, worth a look even if you're not buying.

Before returning to the river, you may want to make the

pilgrimage to the lovingly restored **Goethe-Haus,** the birthplace in 1749 of Germany's most revered writer. There are plenty of mementoes bringing to life the great man's early days before he left his native town; the **Goethe-Museum** sets his career in the artistic and literary context of the time.

Also on this side of the Main, close to the river, is the **Jewish Museum** (Jüdisches Museum), giving a fascinating account of Jewish life in Germany generally and of the Frankfurt Jewish community in particular, one of the largest in the country before 1939–1945. Among its 30,000 members was the Frank family, whose years of hiding in

Goethe-Haus & Goethe-Museum
- Map p. 201
- Grosser Hirschgraben 23–25
- 069 13 88 00
- $$

Jewish Museum
- Map p. 201
- Untermainkai 14–15
- 069 21 23 50 00
- Closed Mon.
- $

Städel Art Institute
www.staedelmuseum.de
🅰 Map p. 201
✉ Dürerstrasse 2
☎ 069 6 05 09 80
🕐 Closed Mon.
💲 $$

**Liebieg Museum of
Antique Sculpture**
🅰 Map p. 201
✉ Schaumainkai 71
☎ 069 21 23 86 15
🕐 Closed Mon.
💲 $

**Johann Tischbein's
"Goethe in the
Roman Campagna"**

Applied Arts Museum
🅰 Map p. 201
✉ Schaumainkai 17
☎ 069 21 23 40 37
🕐 Closed Mon.
💲 $$

Ethnological Museum
🅰 Map p. 201
✉ Schaumainkai 29–37
☎ 069 21 23 53 91
🕐 Closed Mon.
💲 $

Holland were so poignantly described in the diary kept by their daughter Anne. A model of Jew Alley (Judengasse) shows the cramped conditions the community endured before emancipation in the early 19th century.

SOUTH OF THE RIVER

On the River Main's far bank, seven major museums comprise "Museum Mile." The undoubted star is the **Städel Art Institute** (Städelsches Kunstinstitut), not just for committed art lovers. This is one of Germany's great picture galleries, covering German painting from its beginnings to the 20th century. There are also fine works by Dutch, Flemish, and Italian old masters, and French Impressionists.

Among the early German pictures on the top floor, look for the "Paradise Garden" by an anonymous artist from the Rhineland, with a dragon no bigger or more dangerous-looking than a dachshund lying vanquished in the herb-rich grass. The other picture you should try to see is the most famous of all portraits of Goethe (on the second floor). Painted by Johann Heinrich

Tischbein about 1787 and entitled "Goethe in the Roman Campagna," it shows him among ancient ruins in the Italian countryside, where he found much inspiration.

The **Liebieg Museum of Antique Sculpture** (Liebieghaus) and the **Applied Arts Museum** (Museum für Angewandte Kunst) are both broad in their coverage, the former featuring sculpture from ancient times to the 19th century, the latter with a superb collection of European, Islamic, and Asian arts and crafts. The **Ethnological Museum** (Museum für Völkerkunde) puts on changing exhibitions relating to world folk cultures. The **German Architecture Museum** (Deutsches Architekturmuseum, *Schaumainkai 43, tel 069 21 23 88 44, closed Mon., $$*)) is an imaginative amalgamation of a typical 19th-century villa with a modern structure of great purity. Its intriguing dioramas chart the history of world architecture. The **Museum für Post und Kommunikation** (*Schaumainkai 53, tel 069 6 06 00, closed Mon., $*) treats its subject imaginatively. Finally, the **German Film Museum** (Deutsches Filmmuseum; *Schaumainkai 41, tel 069 21 23 88 30, closed Mon., $*) will enchant film buffs with its cinematic memorabilia.

Where the "Museum Mile" ends, old **Sachsenhausen** begins. If you are coming from the city center to this once despised working-class suburb, the best approach is across the **Eiserner Steg,** an iron footbridge dating from 1869. The area is now quite trendy, although there are still cobbled alleyways, slate-roofed and timber-framed houses, and, above all, dozens of *Äppelwoi* taverns. Sachsenhausen is still the place to come in the evening to sample the delicious local specialty. Whatever you do, don't ask for a beer! ■

Kassel

INDUSTRIAL KASSEL IS THE STATE CAPITAL OF NORTH-ern Hessen. The rapid rebuilding of the old city center, which was almost completely destroyed in World War II, has not worn particu-larly well. But for many years it was the seat of the art-collecting Landgraves (local princes), who bequeathed the city its greatest asset, the Wilhelmshöhe park. Kassel is established on today's international art circuit with the *documenta*, a five-yearly aesthetic Olympics where the world's contemporary artists showcase their achievements.

Kassel
🏛 197 C5
Visitor information
✉ Obere Königstrasse 15
☎ 0561 70 77 07

The **Wilhelmshöhe** (William's Heights), west of the center, was created by Landgrave Karl, inspired by his travels in Italy in 1699–1700. On top of the hillside terrace garden stands a huge copper statue of Hercules that has become the symbol of Kassel. It stands 233 feet (71 m) above the ground on a pyramid set in a structure intended to be a "castle of the winds." Climb the steps for a great view over much of central Germany. On summer Sundays and Wednesdays, provided enough water is available, the cascade beneath the "castle" is acti-vated: Water rushes in a torrent downhill, eventually feeding the Great Fountain of **Schloss Wilhelmshöhe** (*tel 0561 31 68 00, closed Mon., $*) and spurting 170 feet (52 m) into the air.

The neoclassic Schloss Wilhelmshöhe was the residence of the Landgraves. It now houses the Landgraves' superlative collection of old master paintings, notably Dutch and Flemish works by the likes of Franz Hals, Rembrandt, Rubens, and Van Dyke.

Down in the town, the **Brüder-Grimm-Museum** is devoted to the compilers of *Grimm's Fairy Tales*. In the early 19th century Jakob and Wilhelm Grimm spent many years here as court librarians. They also produced grammars, language histories, and dictionaries. Because of them, characters such as Snow White and Little Red Riding Hood live on today.

Close by, the **Neue Galerie** (*Schöne Aussicht 1, tel 0561 31 68 04 00, closed Mon.*) has a fine collection of German art from the mid-18th century onward, plus items from past documenta shows. The nearby regional museum, incorporates the **Wallpaper Museum** (Deutsches Tapetenmuseum; *Brüder-Grimm-Platz 5, tel 0561 31 68 00, closed Mon.*), guaranteed to make you rethink your interior decor. ∎

Vertiginous view over the Wilhelmshöhe cascade

Brüder-Grimm-Museum
✉ Palais Bellevue, Schöne Aussicht 2
☎ 0561 787 20 33
💲 $

Green Germany—the Bundesgartenschau

German enthusiasm for everything connected with plants guarantees the success of the country's national garden festival, the Bundesgartenschau (BUGA)—literally, the Federal Garden Show—held every two years in a different location. During the months it is open (usually late April through September), the BUGA attracts millions of visitors, who come to marvel at the latest horticultural ideas and products. If the show is on anywhere near you during your stay, you should certainly see it and enjoy superlative floral displays in an expertly landscaped setting, with a full program of entertainment.

Germans are avid gardeners; even flat-dwellers fill their rooms with house plants, bedeck their balconies with flowers, and spend summer evenings and weekends tending their *Kleingärten*—garden "colonies" grouped around parks or on the edge of town.

The greenness of much of the German urban scene is impressive; trees shade the street, shrubs shelter pedestrians from traffic, and everywhere there are well-planted parks and open spaces.

Since its inception in 1951, the Bundesgartenschau has been used in a positive way to give the environment of the host city a significant boost. In the years following World War II, staging the show helped cities to repair the devastation that had affected parks and open spaces through bombing, cutting of trees for fuel, and clearing of flower beds and shrubberies to make way for vegetable plots. So the first postwar festivals (Hannover 1951, Hamburg 1953) were mostly about restoration. Trees were replanted, lawns resown, land reshaped, lakes cleared and refilled.

As the country prospered, emphasis was laid on adapting the urban environment to the changing conditions of modern life. There were traffic problems to be solved, new recreational needs to be satisfied, and a growing awareness of ecology. In 1955, Kassel used the festival to bring the run-down Karlsaue gardens by the River Fulda up to standard. By 1981, it was the

city's turn again; the historic garden was further upgraded, but this time work concentrated on the far side of the river, a neglected area of gravel pits and water meadows. This was turned into a recreational lakeland, with lavish facilities for sailboats and windsurfers, as well as open areas with sunbathing lawns and children's playgrounds. Anglers were provided for, and areas were set aside for wildlife.

Other cities have exploited the show in different ways. Munich (1983) and Berlin (1985) laid out superb new parks in the suburbs. In 1979 the old capital of Bonn

decided to give itself a new "green heart" joining the old center to outlying communities newly included within the city limits. Its 250-acre (100 ha) "Rhine Meadows Park" links both banks of the river in a completely new landscape of hills, woods, and lakes. Stuttgart has hosted the festival several times, using it to create a continuous network of green, traffic-free spaces throughout the town. Since reunification, the BUGA has migrated east, helping cities such as Magdeburg (1999) and Cottbus (1995) to overcome the environmental degradation of the GDR years. Watch for Gera (2007), Schwerin (2009) and Koblenz (2011)! ■

Above: Springtime crowds at the Potsdam garden festival (2001).
Below: A creative and colorful garden arrangement at BUGA 2005 in Munich

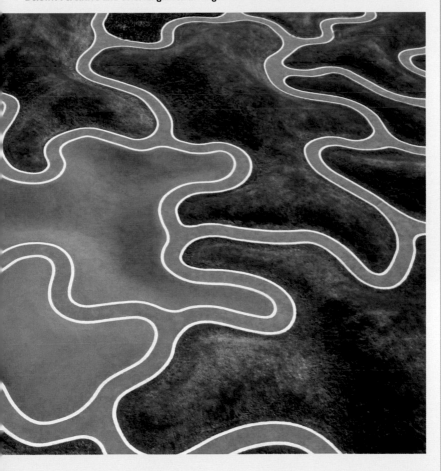

Marburg

Marburg

📍 197 B4

Visitor information

✉ Pilgrimstein 26

☎ 06421 9 91 20

Elisabethkirche

✉ Elisabethstrasse 3

☎ 06421 6 55 73

💲 $ (shrine)

Schloss

☎ 06421 282 58 71

🕐 Closed Mon.

💲 $

MARBURG IS ONE OF HESSE'S MOST ATMOSPHERIC historic settlements, with steep streets and stepped alleyways linking the upper and lower parts of the town, a hilltop Schloss, a university, and a great Gothic church dedicated to the most poignant of German saints, St. Elisabeth.

Elisabeth (1207–1231) was a Hungarian princess, betrothed aged four to the ruler of the *Land* of Thuringia. Still only 20 when her husband died, Elisabeth came to Marburg and devoted herself to helping the sick and needy. Three years later she died of exhaustion, and became the subject of a cult. She was canonized in 1235.

The golden shrine of 13th-century St. Elisabeth rests in the church named after her, the Elisabethkirche.

Around her tomb in the lower town, the Teutonic Knights built one of the first major Gothic buildings in Germany, the **Elisabethkirche.** A lovely building in its own right, the church is a treasure house of artworks, most of which commemorate the saint. Make sure you see her mausoleum with its relief panels and the superb golden shrine made to contain her remains. Three centuries after her death, determined as a good Protestant to put an end to her cult, her descendant Philip the Magnanimous (1504–1567), Landgrave of Hessen, had the shrine opened and buried the bones elsewhere with his own hands.

Around the church stand fine old buildings originally erected by the Teutonic Knights. Today they house parts of the university, founded by Philip the Magnanimous in 1527 as the first Protestant institution of its kind in Germany. Marburg is a lively place when the students are in residence, particularly around the **Marktplatz** in the upper town, reached by attractive but steep streets (or by elevator if you can't face the climb). The marketplace has all the right ingredients: a Gothic **Town Hall** (Rathaus), stately timber-framed houses, and a fountain featuring St. George and the dragon.

Walk west to **St. Mary's Church** (Marienkirche) with its Gothic charnel house and a terrace with a view over the rooftops of the old town. There are even more extensive views from the **Schloss,** reached via steps beginning just beyond the church. Originally a ninth-century fortress, the castle was the residence of the rulers of Hessen between the 13th and 17th centuries. It has a splendid Gothic Knights' Hall and displays on the history of the university and on Marburg's important role in the Reformation. ■

Limburg & the Lahn Valley

Limburg
⊠ 197 A3
Visitor information
✉ Hospitalstrasse 2
☎ 06431 61 66

Wetzlar
⊠ 197 B3
Visitor information
✉ Domplatz 8
☎ 06441 99 77 51

LIMBURG, LIKE MARBURG, IS ONE OF A NUMBER OF attractive towns along the Lahn Valley. Rising in the wooded uplands of the Rothaargebirge, the river winds its way below many a crag-top castle before meeting the Rhine near Koblenz.

Limburg is sited at a point where the river could be easily forded or bridged and where there was high ground from which a stronghold could defend the crossing. The most prominent building on Limburg's rock spur is the great seven-towered **Cathedral** (Dom; *Domstrasse, tel 06431 29 53 32*). You climb up to it through narrow streets and squares lined with carefully restored timber-framed houses. The cathedral was built in the first half of the 13th century just as masons were beginning to abandon the massive round-arched Romanesque style in favor of more elegant Gothic forms, and it combines elements of both styles. The building's massive presence is enhanced by the restoration of its original colors, the bright orange bringing out the bold lines of its construction and contrasting wonderfully with white walls and gray roofs. The sober interior has kept some original wall paintings, including a striking depiction of Samson. Outside, take a moment to enjoy the idyllic scene of river, wooded islands, and ancient bridge.

Farther upstream is another appealing combination of river, bridge, and venerable architecture at **Runkel,** where the walls and towers of the ruined medieval castle rise majestically over the little town. Almost enclosed by a loop in the river, the baroque township of **Weilburg** is dominated by its Renaissance Schloss, complete with terraced garden *(tel 06471 9 12 70, closed Mon.).* The 740-foot (225 m) boat tunnel cut through the neck of

the promontory allows river traffic to take a short cut.

From the river at **Wetzlar,** old slate-roofed houses step up the slope topped by the collegiate church known as the Dom. Wetzlar is famed for its Goethe associations— he fell in love with local girl Lotte Buff—and for its industries, notably the Leitz factory. Oskar Barnack invented the 35mm camera here. ■

Limburg's great cathedral rises over the River Lahn and its ancient stone bridge.

Wiesbaden's casino, part of the Kurhaus, retains its 1907 elegance.

Wiesbaden

THIS STATELY SPA TOWN JUST NORTH OF THE RHINE WAS chosen as the capital of Hesse in 1946. In the late 19th and early 20th centuries, Wiesbaden was perhaps the most fashionable of German spas, when Kaiser Wilhelm II was a regular summer visitor, and some 200 millionaires lived in the sumptuous villa districts laid out between the old center and the Taunus foothills.

Wiesbaden

🅰 197 B2

Visitor information

✉ Marktstrasse 6

☎ 0611 1 72 90

Kaiser-Friedrich-Bad

✉ Langgasse 38-40

☎ 0611 1 72 96 60

💲 $$$

Museum Wiesbaden

✉ Friedrich-Ebert-Allee 2

☎ 0611 3 35 22 50

🕐 Closed Mon.

💲 $

A stroll around the center reveals most of the features of the typical upscale spa. The focal point is the porticoed and domed **Assembly Rooms** (Kurhaus), completed in 1907. To the north a colonnade houses part of the casino, while the colonnade to the south forms the approach to the neo-baroque **Staatstheater.** Casino losers can seek solace in the soothing surroundings of the Kurpark to the east, while the glitzy shops of the broad Wilhelmstrassse stand ready to relieve winners of their spoils.

West of the Kurhaus, older buildings include the 19th-century Stadtschloss, where the Dukes of Nassau once lived, and now the seat of the local parliament. To the north is the **Kochbrunnen,** where some of the springs are tapped and you can sample their hot salty water. For the full experience, try the Roman-Irish steam bath in the luxuriously appointed art nouveau **Kaiser-Friedrich-Bad.**

Wiesbaden was popular with the elite of Tsarist Russia; it has an Orthodox church. The **Museum Wiesbaden** has a gallery full of colorful paintings by Alexej Jawlensky (1864–1941), a Russian member of the Blaue Reiter group of artists (see pp. 42–43).

Popular short trips out of town are to the Rhine-side summer castle of the Nassau rulers, **Schloss Biebrich,** and up the local hill, the **Neroberg,** using the water-powered funicular that has been doing the trip since 1888. ■

Darmstadt

A SINGLE AIR RAID IN 1944 SAW THE VIRTUAL DESTRUCTION of Darmstadt, yet a visit here is well worthwhile. The town has a particular distinction in the world of architecture and arts and crafts as one of the great centers of art nouveau.

Until 1918, Darmstadt was the seat of the Grand Dukes of Hessen-Darmstadt, a line of enlightened rulers who supported literature and the arts, and instituted traditions that have lived on long after them. The last and greatest of the Grand Dukes was the energetic modernizer Ernst Ludwig, who ruled from 1892 to 1918. His initials (EL) are carved into many monuments.

In the town center's **Markt-platz** is the ducal **Schloss.** Given a baroque appearance in the early 18th century, it is basically much older. The Schlossmuseum's great treasure is the "Darmstadt Madonna" by Hans Holbein the Younger. There's much more to see just to the north in the **Hessisches Landesmuseum** *(Friedensplatz 1, tel 06151 16 57 03, closed Mon., $).* This above-average regional museum contains superb works by Lochner, Cranach, Rembrandt, and Rubens; modern art, including the biggest collection anywhere of works by Joseph Beuys; and—above all—art nouveau items, such as glass, ceramics, and furniture.

In 1901, Grand Duke Ernst Ludwig assembled some exponents of *Jugendstil,* the German version of art nouveau, gave them space to work and live, and organized a great exhibition, "A Document of German Art." To appreciate this take the tram to the eastern part of town and the **Mathildenhöhe.** "Mathilda's Heights" was the site of the artists' colony and is a kind of architectural shrine to art nouveau. Some of the idiosyncratic villas still stand, the **Exhibition Building**

(Ausstellungsgebäude; *Sabaisplatz 1, tel 06151 13 33 50, closed Mon., $$)* is still used as such, and the center where artists had their studios is now the Darmstadt Artists' Colony Museum *(Olbrichweg/Bauhausweg, tel 06151 13 33 85, closed Mon.).* The most extraordinary sight is the 157-foot-high (48 m) **Wedding Tower** (Hochzeitsturm), looking like a hand. ∎

Darmstadt
🅰 197 B2
Visitor information
✉ Luisenplatz 5
☎ 06151 951 50 13

Schloss
✉ Marktplatz 15
☎ 06151 2 40 35
🕐 Closed Fri.
💲 $

Darmstadt's handlike Wedding Tower (left), topped with five "fingers," stands near the Russian Chapel (right).

More places to visit in Hesse

BAD HOMBURG

The Kurpark and the surroundings of this spa town on the edge of the Taunus uplands still have much of the allure of the glory days before World War I, when European society, led by Kaiser Wilhelm II, came for the cure. The Homburg, a soft felt hat with a dented crown and a narrow upturned brim, was invented here and made popular by Britain's King Edward VII, a frequent visitor. No surprise then that the town has a **Hat Museum** *(Tannenwaldweg 102, tel 06172 3 76 18)*. 🅐 197 B2 **Visitor information** ✉ Kurhaus ☎ 06172 17 81 10

FULDA

The principal town of eastern Hesse has long been one of the great strongholds of Christianity in Germany. Its origins go back to the foundation of a monastery in the eighth

Inn sign in Rüdesheim's Drosselgasse

century by the Englishman St. Boniface. Boniface's relics—he was murdered in the course of his mission to convert the heathen Germans—are kept in the cathedral museum. Part of **St. Michael's Church** (Michaelskirche) dates from the ninth century, but the overall character of the town was created by powerful and prosperous prince-bishops of the 18th century, who built

superlative baroque edifices, such as the cathedral, the palace, and their summer castle, Schloss Fasanerie, in the nearby countryside. 🅐 197 C3 **Visitor information** ✉ Bonifatiusplatz 1, Palais Buttlar ☎ 0661 102 1812

KLOSTER EBERBACH

The Cistercian monks who founded this wonderfully preserved monastery in 1136 chose a remote spot in a beautiful setting, where the wooded hills of the Taunus drop to the vineyards of the Rhinegau. By contrast, the church where they worshiped is simple and austere. Among the other buildings is a 236-foot-long (72 m) vaulted dormitory that provides a vivid picture of monastic life. The wine-growing tradition established by the monks continued after the monastery was secularized in 1803, and products can be sampled on site. 🅐 197 A2 ☎ 06723 917 81 15

MICHELSTADT

The little town of Michelstadt in the heart of the Odenwald uplands has one of the most photographed street scenes in Germany. The almost too-perfect composition focuses on the **Town Hall** (Rathaus); this timber-framed structure on stilts with corner towers and spiky roofs seems about to stalk across the cobbles toward the flower-bedecked fountain at the other end of the marketplace. 🅐 197 C1 **Visitor information** ✉ Hulster Strasse 2 ☎ 06061 97 99 88

RÜDESHEIM

Crowds gather in this higgledy-piggledy wine village at the southern end of the Rhine Gorge, the most popular place in the Rheingau. The narrow main street is called Drosselgasse, meaning Thrush Lane or alternatively Throttle Alley—and the press of people can indeed be choking. But no one comes to Rüdesheim for peace and quiet, so join in the fun, check out the souvenirs, drink some Riesling, then perhaps take a cable-car ride up through the vineyards to the **Niederwalddenkmal,** a monster statue of "Germania," commemorating German unification in 1871. 🅐 197 A2 **Visitor information** ✉ Geisenheimerstrasse 22 ☎ 06722 1 94 33 ∎

More overseas visitors are discovering the uplands of the Harz and the Thuringian Forest, eastern Germany's long-time favorite vacation area. Here you will find such historic sites as Weimar, Wittenberg, and Wartburg Castle.

Thuringia & Saxony-Anhalt

**Decorated column
in the Wartburg**

Thuringia & Saxony-Anhalt

LYING ON THE FORMER BORDER OF EAST AND WEST GERMANY, ONCE PART of the German Democratic Republic (GDR), Thüringen and Sachsen-Anhalt are at the geographical heart of the country. A diverse range of scenery includes the forested uplands of the Harz and the Thuringian Forest, fertile lowlands, and industrial landscapes based on the varied mineral resources beneath the ground.

The Wartburg commands the wooded heights of the Thuringian Forest.

Thuringia, with Bavaria to the south, is one of the original provinces of Germany, whereas Saxony-Anhalt, north of Thuringia, is a much more recent creation. Set up as a temporary measure in the immediate aftermath of World War II, it was abolished in GDR times, then given new life after reunification. Much of the Harz Mountains, including the Brocken, the highest summit in the northern half of Germany, lies within Saxony-Anhalt. The Thuringian Forest to the south offers equally fine walking and winter sports.

In the rain shadow of the hills stretches low-lying countryside blessed with fertile soils, some of Germany's most productive agricultural land. The favorable climate even allows vines to be cultivated along the valley of the Saale, the river running northward from the Thuringian Forest to the Elbe. The old city of Halle profited from the extraction and merchandising of that most precious medieval commodity, salt, while lignite mining helped the area's chemical industry rise to world importance. Nowadays, however, the industrial dinosaurs promoted by communist planners are on the verge of extinction, and a clean-up of derelict land is under way.

In the early Middle Ages, the area lay on the frontier between the Germanic and Slavic worlds, and consequently has many castles, churches, and monasteries, all built in the course of the German eastward movement. Magdeburg, the newly designated capital of Saxony-Anhalt, has the finest cathedral in eastern Germany, while Eisenach in Thuringia is overlooked by what many would claim to be the country's most romantic and history-laden stronghold, the Wartburg. In the 16th century the fortress provided a refuge from persecution for Martin Luther, born in Eisleben on the fringes of the Harz but most closely associated with the town of Lutherstadt Wittenberg. Eisenach, like Erfurt (Thuringia's capital) and Gotha—other old towns whose heritage of fine building is largely intact—grew up along the Via Regia, the great trading route linking Western and Eastern Europe.

Political fragmentation characterized much of the region's later history as petty principalities vied with one another from their little capital cities, some of which, most notably Weimar, became cultural centers of European importance. Other ancient places—Quedlinburg, Tangermünde—are just as picturesque, and far less visited, than many Bavarian small towns. ∎

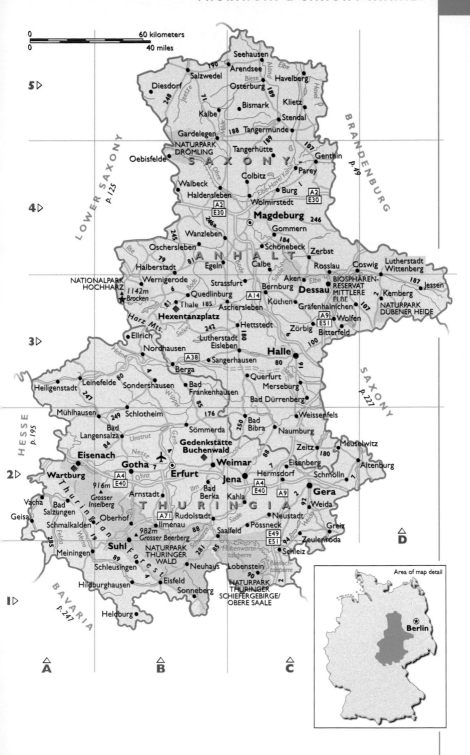

0 — 60 kilometers
0 — 40 miles

Seehausen
Arendsee
Salzwedel
Diesdorf   Havelberg
Osterburg
248   Klietz
Bismark
Kalbe   Stendal
Gardelegen   188 Tangermünde
NATURPARK   Tangerhütte
DRÖMLING   189
Oebisfelde   107 Genthin
S A X O N Y -
Colbitz   Parey
Walbeck   Burg   A2
Haldensleben   E30
A2   Wolmirstedt
E30
Magdeburg 246
Gommern
Wanzleben   184
Oschersleben   Schönebeck   Zerbst
A N H A L T
Halberstadt Egeln Calbe Rosslau Coswig Lutherstadt
Wittenberg
Wernigerode Strassfurt Aken BIOSPHÄREN- 187 Jessen
NATIONALPARK   Bernburg Dessau RESERVAT
HOCHHARZ 1142m Quedlinburg A14 MITTLERE Kemberg
Brocken Köthen ELBE
Thale 185 Aschersleben Gräfenhainichen NATURPARK
Hexentanzplatz Hettstedt A9 Wolfen DÜBENER HEIDE
Zörbig E51
242 Lutherstadt 100 Bitterfeld
Ellrich Eisleben 180 Halle 80
Nordhausen Sangerhausen
A38 Berga
Querfurt Merseburg
Heiligenstadt Leinefelde 80 Sondershausen Bad Bad Dürrenberg
247 Frankenhausen
Mühlhausen 249 Schlotheim 176 Weissenfels
Bad Sömmerda 230 Bad Naumburg Meuselwitz
Langensalza Bibra
84 Gedenkstätte Zeitz 180
Eisenach Buchenwald 88 Eisenberg Altenburg
Gotha Weimar Hermsdorf Schmölln
Wartburg A4 Erfurt Jena A4 Gera
E40 Bad E40 A9 Weida
916m Arnstadt Berka Kahla
Vacha Grosser Ilm
Bad Inselberg T H U R I N G I A Neustadt Greiz
Geisa Salzungen Oberhof A71 Rudolstadt Pössneck Zeulenroda
Schmalkalden Ilmenau 88 E49
982m Saalfeld E51 Schleiz
Meiningen Grosser Beerberg 281 Hohenwarte-
89 NATURPARK talsperre
Schleusingen THÜRINGER Neuhaus Lobenstein
WALD 90 Bleiloch-
Hildburghausen Eisfeld NATURPARK talsperre
Sonneberg THÜRINGER
SCHIEFERGEBIRGE/
Heldburg OBERE SAALE

LOWER SAXONY
p. 125

BRANDENBURG
p. 49

SAXONY
p. 227

HESSE
p. 195

BAVARIA
p. 247

Area of map detail
Berlin

Weimar

SMALL AND PROVINCIAL IT MAY BE, BUT WEIMAR OCCUPIES a unique place in German hearts, standing as it does for a golden age in the country's cultural history known as Weimar Classicism. This was a late 18th-century literary movement that sought inspiration from the Greeks. Its exponents took an essentially optimistic view of the individual's place in the world and believed that man could shape his own nature and identity as well as culture and society. They strove for a balance between restraint and humanity. A harmonious atmosphere still pervades the mansions, streets, and squares of the town.

Goethe (left) and Schiller (right), leading lights of Weimar's golden age, stand in the Theaterplatz.

Weimar

🗺 213 B2

Visitor information

✉ Markt 10

☎ 03643 74 50

Gedenkstätte Buchenwald

☎ 03643 43 00

🕐 Closed Mon.

Schlossmuseum

✉ Burgplatz 4

☎ 03643 54 59 60

🕐 Closed Sun.

💲 $$

It was in the late 18th and early 19th centuries that Weimar's ducal court attracted some of the finest minds of the time. The greatest of them was that universal genius Johann Wolfgang von Goethe (1749–1832), but his fellow poet and dramatist Friedrich von Schiller (1759–1805), the influential philosopher Johann Gottfried Herder (1744–1803), and poet Christoph-Martin Wieland (1733–1813) all flourished in the enlightened atmosphere promoted by Goethe and his patron, Grand Duke Carl August.

Weimar's artistic life did not begin or end with Goethe and Classicism. Painter Lucas Cranach the Elder (died 1553) worked here, Johann Sebastian Bach was court organist and choirmaster from

1708 to 1717, and Franz Liszt was appointed to Bach's position in 1848. Philosopher Friedrich Nietzsche (1844–1900) spent his last years in Weimar.

New ideas came to Weimar early in the 20th century when the great Belgian art nouveau designer Henri van de Velde founded a school of applied art here. Then in 1919 Walter Gropius became the first director of a state school of architecture, the Bauhaus, the famous pioneering institution of modernist design that taught the integration of all the arts and crafts.

In the aftermath of World War I, Germany's parliament met in Weimar's theater in 1919 and drew up the constitution for a republic. Until its demise in 1933 the regime was known as the Weimar Republic. However, the innovative, left-wing ideas of the Bauhaus were disliked in Weimar, and in 1926 the institution was forced to move to Dessau.

In 1932, Thuringia became the first German state to have a Nazi government, and in 1937, among the beech-clad hills 5 miles (8 km) northwest of Weimar, one of the most notorious of all concentration camps was established—Buchenwald. By 1945, more than 50,000 people from 18 nations had perished there, followed by a further 10,000 during the camp's subsequent Stalinist reincarnation. The mass graves and

buildings are now a memorial site, **Gedenkstätte Buchenwald,** and a museum charts the history of the camp.

VISITING WEIMAR

Begin your exploration of the town at **Marktplatz,** with its neo-Gothic Rathaus, and the gabled Renaissance Cranach-Haus, where the painter had his studio *(not open to the public)*. The historic, although much rebuilt, **Hotel Elefant** is one of Germany's most famous and luxurious establishments. Walk east to **Platz der Demokratie,** where an equestrian statue celebrates Grand Duke Carl August. The stately buildings around the square include the **Green Palace** (Grünes Schloss), containing a superb rococo library,

the construction of which was supervised by Goethe. Many of its 850,000 volumes relate to the literature of Weimar Classicism, but it also contains the largest collection of works by and about Shakespeare on the continent of Europe. The library is named for Grand Duchess Anna Amalia (Carl August's mother) who, with her literary gatherings, laid the foundation for the Golden Age.

The Platz der Demokratie looks north to the highly variegated group of buildings that make up the ducal **Schloss.** The medieval origins of the palace can be seen in the solid stone base of the tower, although most of the building dates from the 18th and 19th centuries. The Schloss's art collections include paintings by Dürer and Cranach.

The market trades briskly beneath the neo-Gothic Rathaus of 1842.

Goethe, evidence of the extraordinary range of his interests. But the main attraction is the house itself, much as Goethe and his family left it after 50 years of residence. Particularly evocative are his private quarters, including his library with its makeshift shelving, his collections of mineral specimens, and his small bedroom.

Schiller, too, lived for a while on Frauenplan, and the pedestrian-only street named after him leads westward from there toward Theaterplatz. Goethe's residence was granted to him by ducal favor, but the perennially hard-up Schiller was plunged into debt by his purchase in 1802 of what is now known as the **Schillerhaus.** Like Goethe's house, it has a modern annex where the poet's life and times are evoked.

Schiller chose to live here in order to be near Goethe, his friend and idol. Their relationship is celebrated in **Theaterplatz** by what is one of Germany's best-known statues. The two poets, equal in height (although Goethe was several inches shorter in real life) stand side by side. Goethe seems to be introducing his younger friend to the public, while Schiller has a faraway look in his eyes. Behind them, the much rebuilt **Deutsches Nationaltheater** was the scene of many a premiere, including Goethe's *Faust,* Schiller's *Wilhelm Tell,* and Wagner's *Lohengrin.* A plaque recalls the building's political role in 1919 (see p. 214).

Other buildings on the square include the **Wittumspalais** (*tel 03643 54 53 77, closed Mon., $*), with lovely interiors in late baroque and neoclassic style, and the **Bauhaus-Museum** (*Theaterplatz, tel 03643 54 53 77, open daily, $*). In the latter you'll find exhibits not only from the Bauhaus years of the 1920s but also from the earlier School of Applied Arts run

Poet and dramatist Friedrich von Schiller spent three fruitful years in this house, now the Schillerhaus museum.

Goethes Gartenhaus
✉ Park an der Ilm
☎ 03643 54 53 75
💲 $

Goethes Wohnhaus
✉ Frauenplan 1
☎ 03643 54 54 01
🕐 Closed Mon.
💲 $$

Schillerhaus
✉ Schillerstrasse
☎ 03643 54 51 02
🕐 Closed Tues.
💲 $

The latter's finest picture in Weimar, however, is the altarpiece completed by his son that is the pride of the nearby **Herderkirche** *(Herderplatz).* The palace overlooks the English-style **Park an der Ilm.** The kernel of this park laid out along the valley of the River Ilm was a plot of land on the far bank given by Carl August to Goethe, together with a retreat subsequently known as **Goethes Gartenhaus.** The poet spent much of his time while at Weimar in this rustic dwelling. A stroll through the greenery is enlivened by encounters with mock ruins, a fanciful house made of tree bark, and the duke's own retreat, the neoclassic **Römisches Haus.**

No tour of Weimar would be complete without a visit to Goethe's main residence, **Goethes Wohnhaus,** on the little square known as Frauenplan. Linked to it is a lavish, modern museum chronicling the events of his life in Weimar. Much will be of interest only to those with a scholarly bent, but there are intriguing items such as a model of the pioneering steam locomotive *Rocket* acquired by

by Henri van de Velde. Architecture enthusiasts will want to look at the building named for van de Velde where the revolutionary ideas of the Bauhaus were taught. Now part of the university, it is in the southern part of town, not far from the **Liszthaus** *(Marienstrasse 17, tel* *03643 54 53 85, closed Tues., $),* the composer's home from 1869 to 1886. Close by is the **Historic Cemetery** (Historischer Friedhof), where Grand Duke Carl August, Goethe, and Schiller are buried in the classical mausoleum called the **Fürstengruft. ■**

The sparsely furnished study in Goethe's Gartenhaus

Goethe's women

When the 26-year-old Goethe was first summoned to Weimar in 1775 by his friend and admirer, the teenage Grand Duke Carl August, he was something of a rough diamond, quite unschooled in the refined ways of a provincial court. His coarse manners offended Charlotte von Stein, wife of a minor aristocrat and court official, but she was to become his friend, mentor, and platonic lover. They expressed their passion for each other in innumerable letters, although only those written by Goethe have survived. Charlotte made the uncouth young man *"salonfähig"* (presentable in polite society), and

helped him lay the foundations of his career as a high-ranking court official, the essential counterpoint to his prolific poetic and scientific activity. But Goethe eventually tired of this cerebral relationship, and in 1788 he fell for the more robust charms of Christiane Vulpius, a cheerful and hearty town girl. Weimar society was shocked that the great man should consort with such a vulgar creature, and while Goethe adored his "bedroom treasure," he kept her in the background, and only married her 18 years after their first meeting. ■

Charlotte (top) and Christiane (below)

The Witches' Altar is the name given to this granite tor crowning the summit of the Brocken, northern Germany's highest mountain.

Walk: To the summit of the Brocken

The rounded summit of the Brocken, the highest point in the Harz Mountains in northern Germany at 3,747 feet (1,142 m), is visible from far away with its array of towers and masts. It enjoys great prominence in the minds of Germans because of its legendary associations with the supernatural dating back to medieval times and earlier, and also because of its place in literature from Goethe onward.

On the eve of May 1, witches are supposed to gather on the crags that stud the bleak and windswept top of the Brocken to consort with the devil and celebrate the festival of Walpurgisnacht, events immortalized by Goethe in his *Faust*. Goethe himself came here several times. The best way of experiencing the special appeal of this distinctive mountain is to do as he did, and make the climb on foot. Or you can take the easy way up by horse and carriage or aboard the *Brockenbahn*, the steam train that first chugged up the steep grade to the summit in 1899. It's tempting to take the train up and walk down, but the ascent, although hard work and slow, allows you to savor the glorious scenery to the full. On the way down,

meantime, the ruggedness of the path jars the joints and requires your full attention. Bear in mind that the Brocken is a real mountain, with a harsh and variable climate. Wear tough shoes or boots and get local advice about weather conditions, perhaps from the visitor information bureau at the little mountain resort of Schierke *(Brockenstrasse 10, tel 039455 55 86 80)*.

Begin the walk at the parking lot by the church in **Schierke.** The houses and hotels along the main street eventually give way to woodland. Turn right off the road at a waterworks where a sign announces "Brocken über Eckerloch 5 km," and follow the path that climbs alongside a stream, crosses the road, and meets it again at a bridge named after Goethe. Keep to the path, which crosses the

Brockenbahn and then traverses a stream on a bridge. The going gets more difficult beyond **Eckerloch shelter;** the path is steep, rocky, and wet in places, although sections of boardwalk help out. Eventually, as the trees begin to thin out, you emerge onto the road again, turning left and crossing the railroad once more before arriving at the summit.

Beer, sausages, and other refreshments await the crowds here, most of whom will have made their way up by train. You may well feel inclined to join them before visiting the **Brockenhaus** (tel 039455 5 0 005), opened in 2000 with exhibits explaining the history and ecology of the mountain. Find out how the Brocken, on the border between East and West Germany, was a restricted military area under the GDR and had its own version of the Berlin Wall to protect the assortment of installations that allowed the Stasi to listen in to phone conversations as far away as the English Channel. If you follow the 1.2-mile (2 km) circuit around the top of the mountain, you can enjoy the stupendous views over the wooded

ridges of the Harz and the plain beyond, and admire the fantastically weathered and eroded granite tors known as **Teufelskanzel** (Devil's Pulpit) and **Hexenaltar** (Witches' Altar). If you feel by this point that you have walked enough, take the train down to Schierke station, then walk 550 yards (502 m) down a wooded path back to your starting point. ■

See area map p. 213 B3
Church parking, Schierke
8 miles (14 km)
A whole day
Church parking, Schierke

NOT TO BE MISSED
- Views from the summit
- Brockenhaus
- Devil's Pulpit and Witches' Altar
- The sight and sound of the *Brockenbahn* steam train pounding up the grade

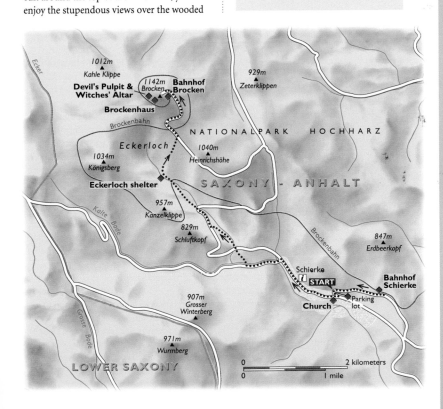

Halle

🅰 213 C3

Visitor information

✉ Leipziger Strasse 105
(Markt)

☎ 0345 122 99 84

Händel-Haus

✉ Grosse Nikolai-
strasse 5

☎ 0345 50 09 00

💲 Free

Saltworks Museum

✉ Mansfelderstrasse 52

☎ 0345 209 32 30

🕐 Closed Mon.

💲 $

Halle

SAXONY-ANHALT'S BIGGEST CITY HAS NOT HAD GOOD press. It was, after all, home to 40 percent of the GDR's environmentally unfriendly chemical industry. Yet Halle is also an ancient place, proud of its past and well worth a day or two of your time. Its university was one of the centers of the Enlightenment, and its vibrant tradition of music culminated in the great Georg Friedrich Handel (1685–1759).

Halle has recovered from the blow it suffered when Magdeburg was made the state capital, and is coping with the demise of its heavy industry. This has led to severe unemployment, but the air is now much cleaner and far fewer pollutants pour into the River Saale.

The buildings of Halle's Saltworks Museum symbolize the city's long industrial tradition.

Wartime damage was minimal, so something of the atmosphere of historic Halle remains, despite neglect of the physical fabric of the Old Town (Altstadt) and the inner suburbs during the communist period. City life revolves around **Marktplatz,** reached from the main railroad station via the **Leipziger Turm,** the only surviving town gate, and bustling, traffic-free Leipziger Strasse. The large, irregularly shaped

market square is dominated by towers, four belonging to the **Marktkirche,** which was curiously cobbled together in the 16th century from what were two separate churches. The tallest structure is the 15th-century **Red Tower** (Roter Turm), which you can climb for an overall view of Halle and its surroundings.

A figure of Roland—traditional guardian of civic rights—stands at the foot of the Red Tower, but the square's most prominent statue is that of Handel, erected in 1859 on the centenary of the composer's death. The **Händel-Haus,** the baroque mansion that was Handel's birthplace in 1685, is now a museum evoking his life and work, with exhibits of period musical instruments. Occasional performances of his music using contemporary instruments take place in the small concert hall or the inner courtyard.

Art lovers will want to scan the collections assembled in the **Moritzburg,** the fortified palace built by the archbishops in the late Middle Ages to keep the turbulent townsfolk in check *(Friedemann-Bach-Platz 5, tel 0345 21 25 90, closed Mon.).*

More unusual is the **Saltworks Museum** (Technisches Halloren-und Salinenmuseum), set up in the old saltworks on which Halle's medieval prosperity was built and which eventually led to the establishment of its vast chemical industries. ■

Magdeburg

HISTORY HAS NOT ALWAYS BEEN KIND TO MAGDEBURG, one of Germany's great historic cities. The baroque town that arose from the ashes of the Thirty Years War was bombed to bits in early 1945, and the rebuilding that took place under communism was typically insensitive. But in 1990 the city emerged victorious over Halle in the contest to become the capital of the newly created *Land* of Saxony-Anhalt.

Magdeburg
🅰 213 C4
Visitor information
✉ Ernst-Reuter-Allee 12
☎ 0391 5 40 49 03

Kloster Unser Lieben Frauen
✉ Regierungsstrasse 4–6
☎ 0391 54 50 25
🕐 Closed Mon.

Germany's 1999 National Garden Festival (see pp. 204–205) held in Magdeburg transformed land once occupied by the Soviet garrison into a new 250-acre (100 ha) park to add to the city's other open spaces. These include the **Elbe promenade** and the **Stadtpark Rotehorn,** laid out on an island in the river. City life centers on the **Alter Markt,** with its baroque Town Hall (Rathaus) and bronze reproduction statue of the 13th-century **Magdeburg Rider,** thought to be Emperor Otto I. The original is in the town's Kulturhistorisches Museum.

Magdeburg's greatest jewel is the lovely Gothic **Cathedral** (Dom), begun in the early 13th century. It stands on the left bank of the River Elbe, where German merchants had settled early in the ninth century to trade with their Slav neighbors on the far shore. Inside is the modest tomb of Emperor Otto I, together with a striking 13th-century statue of a seated couple. This almost certainly represents the emperor and his Anglo-Saxon wife, Edith. The facade of the porch known as the Paradise Portal is graced with ten expressive figures representing the Wise and Foolish Virgins.

The cathedral interior has superbly carved capitals and representations of the Apostles, as well as the masterpiece of the Nuremberg sculptor Peter Vischer the Elder, the bronze tomb of Archbishop Ernst (1495). Dating from about 1245, the damaged statue of St. Maurice is an unusual European representation of a black African. For more fine sculpture—both medieval and modern—visit the nearby **Kloster Unser Lieben Frauen,** a monastery founded about 1017, but now a museum. ■

Magdeburg's 13th-century cathedral led the way in German Gothic.

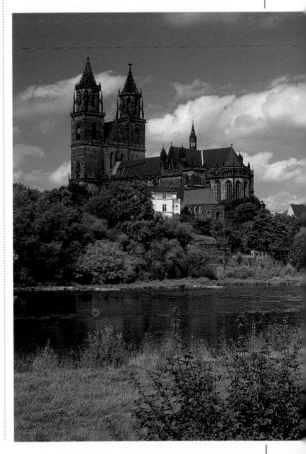

Eisenach
ⓜ 213 A2
Visitor information
✉ Markt 2
☎ 03691 7 92 30

Lutherhaus
✉ Lutherplatz 8
☎ 03691 2 98 30
💲 $

Half-timbered
buildings enclose
a homey
courtyard inside
the Wartburg.

**Automobilbau-
museum**
✉ Friedrich-Naumann-
  Strasse 10
☎ 03691 7 72 12
🕐 Closed Mon.
💲 $

Wartburg
✉ Auf der Wartburg
☎ 03691 25 00
💲 $$

Eisenach

MOST OF THE VISITORS TO EISENACH COME TO CLIMB UP
to the Wartburg, a castle so steeped in history that it was given glob-
al recognition by its inclusion on UNESCO's World Heritage List.
The steep ascent to the castle can be made on foot from the town in
about half an hour; alternatively, you can drive most of the way and
complete the climb by donkey. But first give the town itself its due,
perhaps entering through the severe Stadttor gateway.

The **Bachhaus** (Bach's Birthplace;
Frauenplan 21, tel 03691 7 93 40, $),
a few minutes' walk south of the
Markt, celebrates a famous son of
Eisenach, Johann Sebastian Bach
(1685–1750). Furnishings evoke the
period around 1700. In the Music
Room museum staff regularly give

a short performance on original
keyboard instruments.

The timber-framed, late Gothic
Lutherhaus, northwest of the
Bachhaus, is where the young
Luther is thought to have lodged
between 1498 and 1501. Twenty
years later Luther preached in the
Georgenkirche, the church
where the infant Bach was baptized
in 1685. It stands on the **Markt,**
along with the boldly painted 16th-
century **Town Hall** (Rathaus) and

the **Stadtschloss,** once the resi-
dence of the Dukes of Saxe-Weimar
and now the regional museum.

Automobiles have been manu-
factured in Eisenach for a hundred
years, and in GDR times the town
was famous for another kind of
Wartburg, the country's prestige
car. The last model came off the
assembly line in 1991. Look for it,
along with other historic vehicles
including the Dixi and older, pre-
World War II BMWs, at the
Automobilbaumuseum.

THE WARTBURG
The famous stronghold, perched on
a crag above the town, is everything
a German castle should be, with
sentry walks, timber-framed upper
stories rising from massive stone
foundations, and vaulted interiors.
Go through the outer courtyard,
with half-timbered buildings, to the
inner courtyard and the 12th-
century **Palais,** a rare surviving
example of a Romanesque palace
(guided tour). Beside the authenti-
cally medieval structures are parts
that were romantically restyled in
the 19th century. Medieval bal-
ladeers assembled in the Wartburg
for a famous singing competition,
an episode re-created by Richard
Wagner in *Tannhäuser.* In 1817 the
castle was the natural focus for
students rebelling against the denial
of German unity. Martin Luther
lived here in the **Lutherstube**
from 1521 to 1522 while he trans-
lated the Bible into German. ■

Erfurt

THE THURINGIAN CAPITAL WAS ONE OF THE GREAT CITIES of medieval Germany, and Erfurt's Old Town (Altstadt), with its buildings of all periods, survived World War II relatively intact. A walk along any street in the center will reveal delights, and few sights compare with the city's two great churches rising high above the vast main square, scene of one of Germany's largest Christmas markets.

Erfurt

🅜 213 B2

Visitor information

✉ Benediktsplatz 1

☎ 0361 6 64 00

West of the town center, **Peters Hill** (Petersberg), crowned by one of the biggest baroque strongholds in this part of Europe, provides fine views over the town. At the foot of the hill is **Domplatz.** The spacious square sets off to perfection the town buildings along two of its sides, the breathtaking architecture of the great Gothic **Cathedral** (Dom), and the **Church of St. Severus** (Severi-Kirche) on the rising ground to the west. The change in level is accentuated by a truly monumental flight of steps and by the massive buttresses of the so-called *Cavaten,* structures that support the soaring stonework of the cathedral choir.

Treasures inside the cathedral include superb stained-glass windows, a baroque altar, and the strange Romanesque sculpture known as "Wolfram," adapted for use as a candleholder. The unusual triangular porch is adorned with figures of the Wise and Foolish Virgins, and the central tower houses one of the largest church bells in Europe, the "Gloriosa." The plainness of St. Severus is offset by its trio of spiky spires. The saint's sarcophagus inside has carvings telling the tale of how the humble weaver Severus was raised to the rank of bishop.

The **Merchants' Bridge** (Krämerbrücke) over the River Gera is unique in Central Europe for its rows of shops (good for souvenirs). On your way, make sure

you see the central square called **Fischmarkt,** where the neo-Gothic Town Hall (Rathaus) competes with equally elaborate Renaissance mansions. Complete your tour with a stroll along **Anger,** a broad, curving street that is a virtual museum of 19th-century city architecture. ∎

St. Martin, Erfurt's patron saint, watches over the city's Fish Market.

Great little steam railroads

One of the pleasures of visiting eastern Germany is to travel on its steam railroads. More than just visitor attractions, they are working railroads, providing an everyday passenger (and sometimes freight) service, and manned not by amateur enthusiasts but by career railroad workers.

Once Germany's trunk rail network had been completed toward the end of the 19th century, innumerable connecting local lines were built. To save money, these lines went up hill and down dale, even through village streets, on narrow-gauge (usually 3 feet/1 m) track. For decades they took farmers and their produce to market, children to school, and tourists to the seaside; they also hauled all kinds of freight. The last to be built, these local lines were the first to be closed down, at least in West Germany where competition from cars and trucks from the 1950s onward made them uneconomical. In the GDR, however, motorization was slow to develop, and steam power flourished on the main lines well into the 1970s. The nationalized Deutsche Reichsbahn was not concerned about the profitability of its small lines, and so they survived. In the post-reunification period, their importance to the local economy, especially in tourist areas, was recognized, and with ingenious methods of privatization most have survived.

The most extensive narrow-gauge system, the **Harzquerbahn,** winds its way for 70 miles (113 km) through the Harz Mountains. Its principal lines link towns such as Wernigerode and Gernrode on the northern flank of the massif to Nordhausen in the south, and there are several branches. One is the **Brockenbahn** (see pp. 218–219), which leaves the main line at Drei Annen Hohne

A massive locomotive steams through the snow to the top of the Brocken.

and climbs up a 1:25 gradient through the forest and on to the open summit of the Brocken at 3,747 feet (1,142 m).

Brocken, the highest station in Germany, is reached by a normal railway without the help of rack or cogwheel traction. From the open coaches you can hear the throaty roar of the locomotive as it pounds up the grade. The locomotives, formidable-looking 2-10-2 machines, were especially built for the job in the 1950s and seem well set to carry it out competently for another half-century. For 30 years, the Brockenbahn was closed to the public because of the secret installations on the summit (see p. 219). Its reopening in 1991 aroused great controversy, with environmentalists arguing that the line should remain closed. The needs of tourism prevailed, but the company is limited to operating no more than five trains a day.

Another mountain line is the **Fichtelbergbahn** (Fichtel Mountain Railway), which climbs to the country's topmost town, Oberwiesenthal, through some of Saxony's most glorious countryside. Saxony is home to several other railroads, including the little **Lössnitzgrundbahn,** nicknamed the "Lössnitz Dachshund," which threads its way for 10 miles (16.5 km) through the pretty Lössnitz Valley near Dresden to the country castle of Augustus the Strong at Moritzburg.

On the Baltic coast, **Molli** steams through the streets of Bad Doberan before delivering its hordes of vacationers to the seashore at Kühlungsborn, while on the island of Rügen this duty is performed by the **Bäderbahn Lauterbach-Putbus-Göhren.** (*Check timetables and ticket information at any of the stations shown in bold.*) ∎

Above: Cars share the street with the narrow-gauge **Molli** in Bad Doberan.
Below: Veteran 91 134, Germany's oldest standard **gauge** steam locomotive, is still in service after a century.

More places to visit in Thuringia & Saxony-Anhalt

EASTERN HARZ MOUNTAINS

The moisture-laden clouds driving across the North German Plain drop their rain on the wooded Harz Mountains. The resulting rivers have carved out valleys, gorges, and caves. Within **Hochharz National Park,** the Brocken is the highest summit (see pp. 218–219). Elsewhere, the mantle of dark spruce forest gives way to glorious woods of beech and other deciduous trees, best seen in the **Bodetal,** the dramatic valley of the River Bode. From the little spa of **Thale** you can take a cable car up to the Hexentanzplatz (Witches' Dance Floor) or a chairlift up to the **Rosstrappe** for vertiginous views down into the rocky cleft. A good way to get around the eastern Harz is by the wonderful **Harzquerbahn,** the 70-mile (113 km) railroad system linking many of the towns and visitor sights (see p. 224). One of the railway's main stations is at **Wernigerode.** Ideally located at a point where the valleys running down from the mountains emerge onto the plain, this is a beautifully preserved town of neat, timber-framed burghers' houses and an impossibly picturesque Town Hall (Rathaus). 🅰 213 B3 **Visitor information** ✉ Nicolaiplatz 1, Wernigerode ☎ 03943 63 30 35

NAUMBURG

Set in the attractive countryside of the Saale valley, Naumburg is an exquisite little town whose greatest asset is the **medieval sculpture in its cathedral.** The western rood screen and the figures of Benefactors, all by the late 13th-century sculptor known as the Master of Naumburg, are works of an extraordinary emotional realism and humanity, unparalleled in medieval times. 🅰 213 C2 **Visitor information** ✉ Markt 12 ☎ 03445 27 31 12

QUEDLINBURG

Quedlinburg's appeal resides in its legacy of more than 1,600 timber-framed buildings of all periods, which have put the town on UNESCO's World Heritage List. First visit the **Burgberg** (literally "castle-mountain") with its castle, an imperial stronghold dating from as early as the tenth century. Its Romanesque church contains exquisite carvings and a fine treasury, some of whose most precious items were only recovered in the 1990s after being looted by an art-loving American lieutenant in 1945. Then stroll through the cobbled streets, squares, and alleyways. 🅰 213 B3 **Visitor information** ✉ Markt 2 ☎ 03946 9 05 62 45

THURINGIAN FOREST

These cool green uplands stretch southeastward from Eisenach for more than 60 miles (100 km). The **Rennweg** long-distance footpath follows their ridgeline. Spruce and beech woods dominate, but highland pastures and orchards around the towns and villages in the valleys create a varied, attractive landscape. This is one of eastern Germany's most important year-round vacation areas, with summer hiking giving way to winter sports centered on the 2,600-foothigh (800 m) resort of **Oberhof.** At 3,222 feet (982 m) the range's highest point is the Grosser Beerberg. The most popular peak, however, is the **Grosser Inselberg** (3,005 feet/916 m), with its fabulous views and easy accessibility by road. 🅰 213 A2–B1 **Visitor information** ✉ Crawinklerstrasse 2, Oberhof ☎ 036842 2 21 44

WITTENBERG

An otherwise unremarkable, if attractive, medium-sized town, Wittenberg (now also known as Lutherstadt Wittenberg) was the powerhouse of Protestantism, and its very name celebrates its intimate association with the architect of the Reformation, Martin Luther (see p. 25). It was to the door of the **Schlosskirche** that he nailed his 95 Theses in 1517, and his tomb is inside. An oak tree marks the spot where he publicly burned the Papal Bull, threatening him with excommunication. The **Lutherhalle** has a rich selection of documents, pictures, and other items evoking Luther's life and the rise of Protestantism. 🅰 213 D4 **Visitor information** ✉ Schlossplatz 2 ☎ 03491 49 86 10 ∎

Erased from the map in GDR times, reborn as the Free State of Saxony, this eastern German *Land* has the same kind of proud profile and strong identity as Bavaria, with castles galore, spectacular scenery, and a resplendent royal past.

Saxony

The royal crown of Saxony tops a Dresden roof.

Saxony

SACHSEN WAS A KINGDOM UNTIL 1918, AS PROUD A STATE AS PRUSSIA. ITS rulers were renowned for their munificence, which left its most imposing imprint on Dresden, one of Europe's great centers of art and culture. The name Leipzig also resounds in European culture, although Saxony's second city was heir to very different traditions, in which music, trading skills, and technical achievement were paramount. Its reputation was made by the musical genius of Bach and Mendelssohn, by printers and publishers, by traders, merchants, and inventors. And Leipzig is justly proud of the role it played in the events leading up to the fall of communism, when tens of thousands of its citizens went courageously onto the streets to defy their government.

Good cheer reigns in the depths of Leipzig's Auerbachs Keller, where Faust and Mephistopheles once caroused.

Area of map detail

Industry came early to this part of Germany. The cities built many of their monuments on the profits from the medieval mines of the Ore Mountains (Erzgebirge). In the early 18th century, it was in the little city of Meissen that a European first discovered how to use china clay to make porcelain, which was until then only produced in China. In the next century Germany's first long-distance rail line linked Leipzig and Dresden, and smoke rose from Chemnitz's many chimneys as industry grew.

Remains of early industrialization abound, none grander than the Göltzschtalbrücke, the world's highest railroad viaduct, built in brick and rivaling the aqueducts of ancient Rome. The town of Zwickau looks back on a century of automobile manufacture, its most famous, or rather notorious, product being the East German people's car, the Trabant.

The most exciting scenery in Saxony is that of Saxon Switzerland in the upper valley of the Elbe, where 1,000-foot-high (300 m) sandstone cliffs have been eroded into fantastic shapes. The woods and valleys of the Erzgebirge, crossing the south of the state to form the border with Bohemia in the Czech Republic, make fine walking country, and in the far southeast is the wooded Zittau range.

Saxony is the heartland of Germany's Slav minority, the Sorbs, whose capital, Bautzen, is a charming little city in its own right. ∎

Dresden

HAILED AS "FLORENCE ON THE ELBE," THE SAXON CAPITAL has doggedly rebuilt much of its glorious heritage since February 1945, when its historic center was destroyed by Allied bombing. Today visitors flock to Dresden to explore its museums and galleries—among the most richly stocked in Germany—and to enjoy some of Saxony's loveliest scenery nearby in the valley of the Elbe.

Dresden

⚐ 228 D3

Visitor information

✉ Prager Strasse 2a
& Theaterplatz

☎ 0351 49 19 21 00

Zwinger collections

www.skd-dresden.de

⚐ Map p. 232

☎ 0351 491 46 78

§ $$$ (comb. ticket for all collections)

Dresden's rebuilt **Old Town** (Altstadt) lies on the river's left bank, but the silhouette of its famous skyline is best viewed from the New Town (Neustadt) on the far side of the river. Before 1945, the skyline was dominated by the monumental dome of the baroque **Frauenkirche,** completed in 1743 as the city's central place of Protestant worship. Amazingly, the dome survived the 1945 firestorm (see sidebar p. 235), but collapsed after a few days as the stonework cooled. The heap of blackened rubble stood for decades, a monument to the folly of war. Then, in 1994, the decision was taken to rebuild. The surviving stonework, each piece carefully numbered, was

stored in an on-site depot ready for reuse. Fragments were turned into souvenirs—they appeared in watch faces, for example—all helping to finance the mammoth operation. The reconstructed church was unveiled in 2005, in time for the city's 800th anniversary the following year.

The rebuilding of the Frauenkirche and the restoration of the Schloss (see p. 233) are part of the process begun in the early postwar years aimed at re-creating at least some of the Altstadt's historic character (although some thought the ruined city should be abandoned).

ZWINGER

Most visitors begin their exploration

of the city at the Zwinger in the city center. Intended as an impressive setting for courtly ceremonies and festivals, this fabulous architectural creation is now a museum complex. It was built by architect Matthäus Daniel Pöppelmann (1662–1736) to the orders of the most colorful of Saxony's kings, Augustus the Strong, who came to the throne in 1694. Consisting of a series of buildings arranged around a spacious grassy courtyard with pools and fountains, the Zwinger is considered by many to be the supreme expression of German baroque architecture. It is also the repository of Dresden's outstanding collection of old master paintings.

The best way to approach the Zwinger is through the gateway of the **Glockenspielpavillon,** with its carillon of bells made from Meissen porcelain. In the center of the wing to the left is the **Crown Gate** (Kronentor), topped by sculptures of eagles guarding the crown of Poland (Augustus also ruled Saxony's neighbor to the east for a time). To the right, the massive **Semper Gallery**

designed by Gottfried Semper was added to the complex in 1847, but the structure that commands most attention is the **Wallpavillon,** on the far side of the courtyard. This is Pöppelmann's masterpiece, its bravura beauty enhanced by the lively and expressive sculptures carved by his collaborator, Balthasar Permoser (1651–1732). Even greater exuberance is on view in the adjoining **Nymphenbad,** a sunken grotto in which stone nymphs disport themselves.

Inside the Zwinger are varied treasures that rival the building's architectural and sculptural delights. With so much to see, don't try and get around everything; it's best to choose what interests you and follow the signs. The **Armory** (Rüstkammer) is one of the world's great collections of arms and armor, and the **Mathematical-Physical Salon** (Mathematisch-Physikalischer Salon) displays an extraordinary array of scientific instruments dating from the 16th to the 19th centuries. Then there is the extensive **Porcelain Collection**

Baroque architecture at its most extravagant: the Zwinger, pleasure palace of Augustus the Strong

Armory
🕐 Closed Mon.
💲 $

Mathematical-Physical Salon
🕐 Closed Mon.
💲 $

Porcelain Collection
🕐 Closed Mon.
💲 $$

Gallery of Old Masters
🕐 Closed Mon.
💲 $$

(Porzellansammlung), with superb examples of porcelain from the royal collections. Augustus the Strong was fascinated by porcelain. By experimenting in the vitrification of clays with heat, his alchemist, Johann Friedrich Böttger, discovered how to make fine china, thereby laying the foundation of an industry that is still inseparable from the names of Dresden and Meissen.

The **Gallery of Old Masters** (Gemäldegalerie Alter Meister) is also based largely on the enthusiasms of Augustus the Strong and of his successor, Friedrich Augustus II. The gallery's most celebrated painting is Raphael's "Sistine Madonna" (1512–1513), loved not only for its exquisite representation of Mother and Child, but also for the delightful pair of bored cherubs at the base of the picture. Another renowned painting from the Italian Renaissance is Giorgione's "Sleeping Venus," which remained unfinished at his death in 1510. There are also important works by many of the great names of Western European art—Rembrandt and

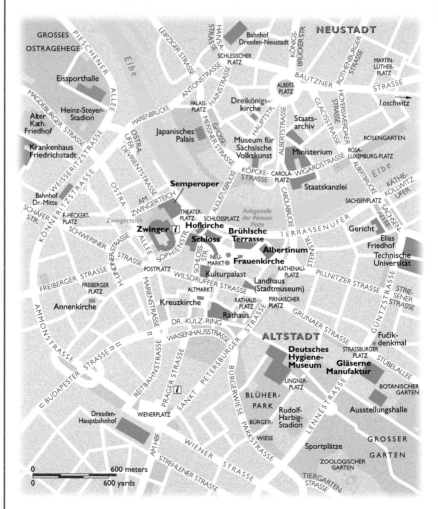

Vermeer, Claude Lorrain and Poussin, El Greco and Velazquez, Cranach and Dürer. Canaletto's townscapes are uncannily exact depictions of Dresden and Pirna as they were in the 18th century.

OLD TOWN (ALTSTADT)

The northeastern facade of the Gallery of Old Masters looks out over **Theaterplatz,** an imposing square bounded by some of Dresden's outstanding historic landmarks: Even the visitor information center is a neoclassic temple, originally a guardhouse built by the Berlin architect Karl Friedrich Schinkel in 1830–1832.

Home both of the Saxon State Opera and the State Orchestra, the grandiose **Semperoper** is named for architects Gottfried Semper and his son, Manfred. Gottfried Semper's first opera house burned down in 1869. Banned from the city because of his involvement in the abortive 1848 revolution, he entrusted its rebuilding to his son. Its sumptuous interior saw the premieres of several operas by Wagner and Richard Strauss. Left a shell in 1945, the opera house was saved from demolition by its world reputation—and its architect's revolutionary credentials. The complex task of rebuilding it, and providing it with modern facilities was completed on the 40th anniversary of its destruction, in 1985.

With its 33m-high (100 ft) tower, the nearby great **Schloss** is where the rulers of Saxony resided for centuries until 1918. Located on the outer wall facing Schlossstrasse, an extraordinary frieze made of Meissen tiles depicts a succession of princely figures glorifying the dynasty's 800-year rule. The palace, now restored to its former splendor, houses a number of museums including the so-called **Green Vaults** (Grünes Gewölbe),

a dazzling treasury of some of the most spectacular creations of the jeweler's and goldsmith's art. Don't miss the wildly extravagant piece known as the "Court of Delhi on the Birthday of the Great Moghul." Augustus the Strong's court jeweler, Johann Melchior Dinglinger, worked with his brothers for seven years to make what is a thinly-veiled exaltation of the Saxon king's own ostentatious court. They created 137 gilded and enameled figures and used countless precious stones. The eventual cost outstripped that of Augustus' grand palace at Moritzburg (see p. 246).

Linked to the palace by a bridge enabling the royal family to attend Mass without crossing the street, the Roman Catholic **Hofkirche** caused a great stir in this ultra-

Paddleboats line Dresden's waterfront with the restored Altstadt in the background.

Semperoper
- Map p. 232
- Theaterplatz 2
- 0351 49 11 496
- Guided tours $$

Schloss
- Map p. 232
- Taschenberg 2
- 0351 491 45 91
- Closed Tues.
- $$

A glittering array of treasures is displayed in the Albertinum.

Gallery of New Masters

🅰 Map p. 232

✉ Theaterplatz 2 (Semperoper) or Lennéstrasse 1 (Gläserne Manufaktur)

☎ 03 51 4 91 42 000

🕐 Closed Mon. (Semperoper only)

💲 $$

Protestant city when the Catholic convert Augustus the Strong ordered it built in 1739. The king's architect was Italian Gaetano Chiaveri, who imported many of his fellow countrymen to carry out the work, housing them on the Elbe embankment in what is still called the Italienisches Dörfchen. (The "Italian Village" is now a restaurant with a fine riverside terrace.) Sandstone statues of saints parade on the balustrade of Chiaveri's lovely church, and the interior has fine baroque furnishings. The remains of Saxon rulers lie buried in the crypt.

The classic view of the mighty River Elbe is from the **Brühlsche Terrasse,** the promenade laid out in the 18th century over the redundant riverside fortifications by Count Brühl as part of his private garden. It's a wonderful place to sit or stroll and watch the pleasure craft and paddleboats coming and going from the quayside below. On the far bank of the river, reached via the Augustusbrücke of 1910, is the **New Town** (Neustadt), laid out on planned lines in the 18th century. It was less affected than the Altstadt by the 1945 bombing and, with its shops and cafés, has a genuinely lived-in feeling about it.

The 1,600-foot (500 m) terrace is reached from near the Hofkirche by a magnificent flight of steps decorated with sculptures representing the seasons. It leads to the **Albertinum,** the building that once served as the royal arsenal. Normally home to several museums, the complex will remain closed until 2009 during installation of a watertight depot, a defensive reaction to a devastating flood a few years ago. In the interim, the Albertinum's sculpture collection is on display at the Zwinger (see pp. 230–231), while the Green Vaults are housed in the grand Schloss (p. 233). Selected works of its other main attraction, the **Gallery of New Masters** (Gemäldegalerie Neuer Meister), are being shown in rotating exhibits at the Semperoper building (p. 233) and the **Gläserne Manufaktur,** about a mile southeast of the old town. The collection is a fine place to get a grip on German 19th- and 20th-century painting. Two of the most important figures in Romantic painting, Caspar David Friedrich (1774-1840) and Ludwig Richter (1803-1884), thrived in Dresden and found inspiration in the landscapes of Saxony and nearby Bohemia. Both are represented by several fine atmospheric works. Few visitors are unmoved by Richter's "Crossing by the Schreckenstein," a metaphor for the river of life as passengers are ferried across the Elbe.

A century later, expressionism took root in Dresden with the founding in 1905 of a branch of the movement known as Die Brücke (The Bridge; see p. 76). Between 1929 and 1932 one of its members, Otto Dix (1891–1969), painted perhaps the most searing evocation of the horrors of the trench warfare of 1914–18, a triptych simply entitled "Der Krieg" ("War"), based deliberately on the great altarpieces of the Middle Ages. Similar shock value is offered by another triptych, "Das tausendjährige Reich" ("The thousand-year Reich"), completed in 1938 by Hans Grundig (1901–1958). It accurately foretells the even greater horrors about to be perpetrated by the Hitler regime.

OTHER SIGHTS

History may have been a priority in the north of the Altstadt after World War II, but to the south a new, socialist city arose over the rubble. The devastated inner suburbs were cleared and the 19th-century streets were replaced by monotonous, Soviet-style housing blocks. The "New" Dresden created by the architects and planners of GDR times is seen at its best around the **Altmarkt,** where establishments such as McDonald's occupy mock-baroque buildings of the 1950s. Once reviled as Stalinist, they are now listed as worthy of protection. Their careful proportions and their decoration with statuary and relief panels certainly make them worth a glance. An authentically "Old" Dresden remains in the outer districts with their elegant villas.

One of Dresden's most unusual museums is the **German Hygiene Museum** (Deutsches Hygiene-Museum), installed in a hygienic-looking building of the 1920s. Exhibits, many interactive, develop the theme of the body and its relationship to the environment. The "Glass Woman" reveals all the workings of the human body. ∎

Dresden's Pragerstrasse is a showpiece of communist-era urban planning.

German Hygiene Museum
- 🅜 Map p. 232
- ✉ Lingnerplatz 1
- ☎ 0351 4 84 60
- 🕐 Closed Mon.
- 💲 $$

Below: Stone-mason at work

February 1945

The last weeks of World War II saw Dresden packed with refugees from the advancing Red Army. Its population clung to the mistaken belief that their city of art and culture with its long-standing connections with Britain and America would be spared from bombing. Sharing this misconception, the German High Command had stripped its air defenses and deployed them elsewhere. At the peak of their deadly efficiency on the night of February 13–14, the Allied bomber fleets thus met little opposition, and the firestorm they unleashed destroyed 75 percent of the city and killed an unknown number of people, perhaps as many as perished at Hiroshima. ∎

Drive: The valley of the Elbe & Saxon Switzerland

This relatively short journey along the banks of the Elbe takes in palaces and castles, fine old towns, and the dramatic sandstone scenery of the National Park of Sächsische Schweiz (Saxon Switzerland).

Bastei bridge, in Nationalpark Sächsische Schweiz, was built in 1851.

Leave Dresden on the busy B172 to **Pirna ❶**. The historic center of this ancient riverside town focuses on the central marketplace. Peek inside the town church and marvel at its intricate vaulting. Continue along the B172, turning right to **Festung Königstein ❷** *(tel 035021 6 46 07, $$)*. This mighty fortress rising sheer from the crags is all the more impressive if you climb up to it on foot, but the shuttle from the parking lot is the easy way to the top. There are vertiginous views down to the winding river and over the strange landscape of Sächsische Schweiz. Back in your car, continue along the main road and over the river into the charming little spa town of **Bad Schandau ❸**, where the **National-parkhaus Sächsische Schweiz** *(An der Elbe 4, tel 035022 502 40)* has innovative exhibits on the national park.

From Bad Schandau a funny little tramway runs up the valley known as the Kirnitzschtal, the heart of the eastern section of the national park, but unless you have plenty of time to spare, turn back toward Dresden. Don't go back across the bridge over the Elbe, but keep straight on along the minor road through the village of Rathmannsdorf, then straight on at a road junction. The narrow road up through the woods brings you to the picturesque hilltop town and castle of **Hohnstein.** Beyond Hohnstein, follow signs to "Bastei," eventually turning off the main road to the left and leaving your vehicle in one of the parking lots.

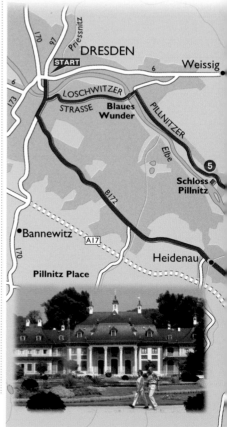

Walk up to the **Bastei ❹,** a great natural curiosity. Its weather-sculpted sandstone cliffs, crags, and pillars tower over 1,000 feet (300 m) above the curve of the Elbe far below. Best visited after the midday crowds have departed, the Bastei (bastion) has long been a visitor attraction, and paths, viewpoints, and catwalks enable you to wander around it, protected by railings from the abysses suddenly opening up beneath your feet.

Return to the main road and drive toward Pirna. Avoid the town and continue toward Dresden, stopping at **Schloss Pillnitz ❺** *(tel 0351 261 32 60).* This riverside palace in mock-Chinese style was begun on the orders of Augustus the Strong in 1720 as a summer residence. Guests were borne up the Elbe from Dresden to disembark at the splendid waterside stairway. The palace's exquisite decoration includes some of Europe's earliest examples of chinoiserie. The park, a fusion of French formality and English naturalism, is dotted with delightful structures such as the Palmenhaus, the Orangerie, and the Kamelienhaus, built especially to protect a 200-year-old camellia.

The palace houses one of Dresden's major collections, the **Kunstgewerbemuseum** *(closed Mon., $),* with fine examples of furniture, silverware, wood carving, and other crafts from medieval to modern times. Pillnitz sits among vineyards that rise up the slopes to wooded hilltops. Among the vines stands a lovely little church, the **Weinbergkirche,** which, like the palace, was the work of Augustus's court architect, Daniel Pöppelmann.

Continue along the main road toward Dresden, crossing the Elbe via the **Blaues Wunder;** the "Blue Miracle" is a steel suspension bridge dating from 1893, a considerable technical achievement for its time. ∎

See area map p. 228 D3
► Dresden city center
↔ 56 miles (90 km)
⏱ 1 day
► Dresden city center

NOT TO BE MISSED
- Pirna's town church interior
- Festung Königstein and the views from the ramparts
- The views from the Bastei
- A stroll in the grounds of Schloss Pillnitz

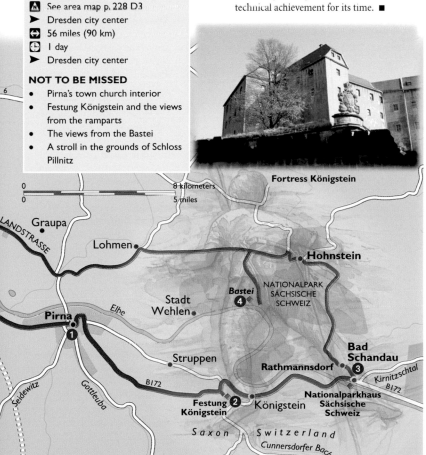

Fortress Königstein

0 _____ 8 kilometers
0 _____ 5 miles

LANDSTRASSE
Graupa
Lohmen
Hohnstein
NATIONALPARK SÄCHSISCHE SCHWEIZ
Bastei ❹
Stadt Wehlen
Elbe
Pirna ❶
Struppen
Bad Schandau ❸
Rathmannsdorf
Kirnitzschtal
B172
Festung ❷ Königstein
Königstein
Nationalparkhaus Sächsische Schweiz
Seidewitz
Gottleuba
B172
Saxon Switzerland
Cunnersdorfer Bach

Bautzen

Bautzen
229 E3
Visitor information
Hauptmarkt 1
03591 4 20 16 or
03591 1 94 33

Alte Wasserkunst
Wendischer
Kirchhof 7
03591 4 15 88
$

Bautzen's water tower is a technical wonder from the Middle Ages.

OCCUPYING A FINE AND EASILY FORTIFIED SITE HIGH above a bend in the River Spree, Bautzen owes its striking silhouette to its many towers. It is a stately old place, largely rebuilt in baroque style after being burned down more than once during the Thirty Years War.

Bautzen's towers include, in addition to those of its well-preserved medieval fortifications, church spires, the tall, slender tower of the Town Hall (Rathaus), and two curiosities: Saxony's own leaning tower, the 184-foot (56 m) **Reichenturm** (Reichenstrasse, tel 03591 46 04 31), which tilts 4.75 feet (1.44 m) out of the vertical; and the **Alte Wasserkunst,** a water tower that supplied the city with fresh water for more than 400 years before being taken out of commission in 1965. If you can face its 135 steps, the late 15th-century Reichenturm provides a splendid panorama over the town from its lookout platform. The wheel of the Alte Wasserkunst was used to pump water from the Spree up into a cistern, from where it was distributed in wooden pipes. The workings are explained in the museum inside. You can admire the tower (and enjoy the best view of the Bautzen) from the **Bridge of Peace** (Friedensbrücke), which leads into town from the west.

Buildings on the central square, the **Hauptmarkt,** include the 18th-century Rathaus, a Gothic apothecary, and the House of the Year (Jahreshaus), so-called because it has four staircases, 12 chimneys, 52 rooms, and 365 windows. The square known as Fleischmarkt, to the north, is dominated by **St. Peter's Cathedral** (Petridom), where both Roman Catholics and Protestants worship—Catholics in the choir, Protestants in the nave.

Old streets lead west to the **Ortenburg,** Bautzen's castle, dating from about 1000. It was rebuilt in Gothic style by King Matthias of Hungary, who ruled here in the late 16th century; there is a relief portrait of him on a tower. Colorful traditional costumes are among the highlights of the recently renovated **Serbski Musej** (Ortenburg 3, tel 03591 4 24 03), the museum of the Sorbian people (see pp. 240–241). ∎

Meissen

MEISSEN'S INTERNATIONAL FAME RESTS ON THE PRESTIGE of its porcelain, but there is more to it than that. With the closely packed red-roofed dwellings of its Old Town (Altstadt) overlooked by the Burgberg—the rock spur crowned by castle and cathedral— Meissen is arguably the best preserved of Saxony's smaller towns.

On arrival, pause for a moment in the riverside parking lot on the right bank of the Elbe. From here you can see the harmonious grouping of town and citadel. Cross the bridge into the Altstadt, centered on the sloping **Markt** with stately burgher houses, town apothecary, and late 15th-century Town Hall (Rathaus). The tower of the **Frauenkirche** dominates one side of the square, and close by is a famous wine tavern, the half-timbered Gasthaus Vincenz Richter.

Narrow streets, steps, and alleyways climb up the castle hill. At the center of an enclosure of buildings is the glorious Gothic **Cathedral** (Dom). Its twin spires were added in the early 20th century, but its interior is almost entirely medieval, with sculptures and furnishings of the best quality. The castle itself, the **Albrechtsburg,** was mostly built between 1471 and 1525, with striking features such as a cleverly engineered spiral staircase.

In 1709 Augustus the Strong's court alchemist Johann Friedrich Böttger discovered the technique of making perfect porcelain (see pp. 231–232). Commercial production began within the walls of Meissen's fortress. The factory moved to its present site in the Triebisch valley in the 1860s. Today the **Staatliche Porzellan-Manufaktur** welcomes guests with guided tours and demonstrations of the techniques that keep "Meissen" at the forefront of competition. Pieces from the factory's past are displayed in the exhibition halls, and there is a well-stocked shop. ■

Meissen's citadel, the Burgberg, on its rock outcrop above the River Elbe

Meissen
- 228 D3

Visitor information
- ✉ Markt 3
- ☎ 03521 4 19 40

Cathedral
- ✉ Domplatz 7
- ☎ 03521 45 24 90

Albrechtsburg
- ✉ Domplatz 1
- ☎ 03521 4 70 70
- $ $

Staatliche Porzellan-Manufaktur
www.meissen.de
- ✉ Talstrasse 9
- ☎ 03521 46 82 08
- $ $$

Germany's Slav minority

Of modern Germany's many ethnic minorities, no group has been around longer than the Sorbs of Saxony and Brandenburg. The Sorbs were one of a number of Slavic peoples who moved westward around the sixth century A.D. and occupied what is now eastern Germany.

Lacking any central political organization, the Sorbs put up little resistance when the Germans began to colonize the lands to the east of the Elbe. In the face of this advance, most of their fellow Slavs retreated, were slaughtered, or became assimilated into the German population.

Somehow the Sorbs survived, preserving their language and culture, although today their numbers have been much reduced. Some 50,000 members of this historical minority live in Oberlausitz (Upper Lusatia), the area centered on the town of Bautzen (see p. 238) in eastern Saxony, and in Niederlausitz (Lower Lusatia), around Cottbus in southeastern Brandenburg. They have their own press and schools.

The Sorb presence is most obvious in the town of Bautzen, where their central cultural and political organization, the Domowina, has its headquarters, and where many aspects of their distinctive culture are presented in the Serbski Musej (Sorbian Museum). Watch for bilingual road signs; Bautzen becomes Budysin in Sorbian, Cottbus changes to Chosebuz, Weisswasser to Bela Woda. You may come across a village where the older women wear traditional costume on an everyday basis. The dresses are usually red, green, blue, white, and black, with a red-and-white bonnet.

The Sorbs continue to celebrate their special feast days, mostly to do with life and work on the land. For the Vogelhochzeit (Marriage of the Birds) on Jan. 25, empty plates are set out to be filled with candy by thankful birds. On Easter there are horseback processions as well as intricately painted eggs; and harvest time is celebrated too. The biggest festival is probably the one held in alternate odd years in the village of Crostwitz near Bautzen.

Today's Sorbs have claimed and been granted the rights that every civilized country accords its minorities. This does not guarantee the survival of their culture, which in any case is not a homogeneous one—the Sorbian spoken in Lower Lusatia is akin to Polish and quite distinct from the Upper Lusatian dialect, which is closer to Czech. However, the prospect for Sorbian culture is more hopeful than it has often been in the past. When medieval German rulers tried to stamp out the language and force the Sorbs to assimilate into the German majority, Sorbian became confined to the villages where, paradoxically, it flourished. The community was threatened again when industrialization began in the 19th century, when Sorbian speakers became bilingual for the sake of their jobs, and many villages lost their Slav identity altogether. The worst time was under the Slav-hating Nazi regime, which not only forbade the use of the language, but plotted to expel the Sorbs to some remote corner of Europe. Many leading members of the community were imprisoned or exiled to other parts of Germany. In GDR times, the Sorbs had many privileges on paper, but all cultural life was strictly controlled and the regime's enthusiasm for large-scale open-cast brown coal mining destroyed dozens of Sorb villages in Lower Lusatia. The biggest threat today is assimilation and emigration because of lack of local employment. Nevertheless, the Sorbs remain a lively—and welcoming—presence in eastern Germany. ■

Elaborately painted eggs are an integral part of the Easter celebrations among Germany's Sorbs.

Above: Sorbian girls in their flower-embroidered traditional dress and headscarves lead a procession during the Feast of Corpus Christi. Below left: A Sorbian Easter ride at Ralbitz, near Bautzen. Below right: An expert egg painter

Leipzig

Leipzig

🅜 228 B3

Visitor information

✉ Richard-Wagner-
Strasse 1

☎ 0341 7 10 40

Nikolaikirche

🅜 Map p. 244

✉ Nikolaikirchhof 3

☎ 0341 9 60 52 70

SAXONY'S SECOND CITY IS KNOWN ABOVE ALL FOR ITS musical and intellectual traditions and for its trade fairs. Since the overthrow of the GDR regime in 1989, in which Leipzig's citizens played a leading role, the city has moved swiftly to recover its former place as one of the country's star cities. Leipzig's go-ahead spirit is expressed in a wealth of new buildings and in what is arguably the liveliest "scene" in eastern Germany, with an unequaled choice of restaurants, bars, and cabarets.

A statue of Bach graces the square in front of his famous Thomaskirche.

JOHANN
SEBASTIAN
BACH

Municipal History Museum

🅜 Map p. 244

✉ Im Altes Rathaus,
Markt 1

☎ 0341 96 51 30

🕐 Closed Mon.

💲 $

On the far side of Willy-Brandt-Platz and the ring road, Leipzig's historic core, the **Innenstadt,** is quite small and easily explored on foot. The covered shopping arcades called **Passagen** add to the pleasure of a city stroll with their boutiques, places of refreshment, and refined decor. **Steibs Hof** is a contemporary example of one of these arcades, while the early 20th-century **Specks Hof** has been brilliantly modernized.

Opposite the entrance to Specks Hof is the **Nikolaikirche.** Beginning in 1982 the regular Monday prayer meetings for peace held here became an institution, and in 1989 they were a rallying point for the demonstrators against the government. The church was originally built in Romanesque times. Its somber exterior belies the interior, renewed at the end of the 18th century, all joyfulness and light, with soaring white columns terminating in pale green palm leaves reaching high into the elaborate vaulting.

Mädlerpassage, the most splendid of the Passagen, is three stories high, but its most famous establishment is below ground. **Auerbachs Keller** (tel 0341 21 61 00) owes its world reputation to Goethe's *Faust,* in which Faust and Mephistopheles descend into the cellar tavern to carouse with students. Most visitors to Leipzig follow in their footsteps, to enjoy a glass of Saxon wine from the barrel or a substantial meal among the Faustian memorabilia. In nearby **Naschmarkt** is a statue of Goethe himself. The freshly restored small baroque building in Naschmarkt was built as a produce exchange and now serves as a concert hall.

At the center of the Innenstadt stands the **Old Town Hall** (Altes Rathaus), built in 1557, one of the first typical German Renaissance town halls, with high roof, tall tower, stepped gables, and arcaded ground floor facing the marketplace. It is now the **Municipal History Museum** (Stadtgeschichtliches Museum), with an imposing reception hall hung with portraits of princes and city fathers. One room is devoted to composer Felix Mendelssohn-Bartholdy, who spent the last 12 years of his life in the city.

Just along the Thomasgasse is Leipzig's second great civic church, the **Thomaskirche** (*Thomaskirchhof 18, tel 0341 9 60 28 55*). Founded in 1212, the church was rebuilt in Gothic style at the end of the 15th century. It is best known as the home of the Thomaner, a celebrated boys' choir. The choir is as old as the church; its members attend a boarding school where they receive an academic education and rigorous musical training. Not all stand the pace: Sebastian Krumbiegel, now lead singer in one of eastern Germany's favorite pop groups, was expelled because of "lack of discipline."

From 1723 until his death in 1750, Johann Sebastian Bach was Cantor (choirmaster) of St. Thomas's and also Leipzig's director of music. He is now buried in the church, and a statue of him stands outside. Opposite, the **Bachmuseum** *(Thomaskirchhof 16, tel 0341 9 13 72 00)* has documents and musical instruments.

The best way to honor the great musician and the choir he led, however, is to attend one of the regular services at which the Thomaner perform. *(Call the Thomaskirche, see p. 242, for details.)*

If the Thomaskirche represents one pole of Leipzig's musical life, the other is the vast **Augustusplatz,** on the far side of the

The Nikolaikirche provides a somber venue for the Thomaner choirboys.

Grassi-Museum

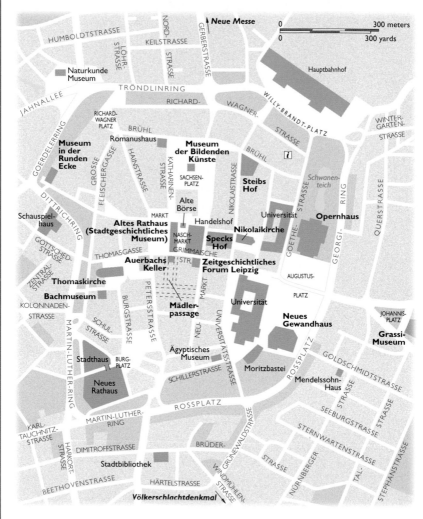

🅼 Map p. 244

✉ Johannisplatz 5–11

🕐 Closed Mon.

💲 $

Innenstadt. On one side of the square is the **Opera House** (Opernhaus) of 1960, and on the other is the **New Concert Hall** (Neues Gewandhaus), home base of the city's great orchestra, whose origins go back to the mid-18th century. Felix Mendelssohn was appointed director of the orchestra at the age of 26 in 1835. The present building is a far cry from the upper floor of the clothmakers' guildhall (Gewandhaus) where a concert hall was improvised in 1781. One of the prestige projects of GDR times, the concert hall was built in 1981. Both opera house and concert hall have excellent acoustics and a wealth of ornament and decoration. Another example of the communist regime's architectural aspirations is the 31-story university tower close by.

TRADE FAIRS

Many business people flying in to Leipzig head straight for the **Neue Messe,** the bright new trade fair center on the northern outskirts by

Neue Messe

HUMBOLDTSTRASSE

NORD-STRASSE

KEILSTRASSE

LÖHR-STRASSE

GERBERSTRASSE

Hauptbahnhof

0   300 meters

0   300 yards

Naturkunde Museum

TRÖNDLINRING

RICHARD-

RICHARD-WAGNER-PLATZ

WAGNER.

WILLY-BRANDT-PLATZ

JAHNALLEE

GOERDELERRING

BRÜHL

Romanushaus

STRASSE

WINTER-GARTEN-STRASSE

Museum in der Runden Ecke

GROSSE FLEISCHERGASSE

HAINSTRASSE

KATHARINEN-STRASSE

Museum der Bildenden Künste

SACHSEN-PLATZ

NIKOLAISTRASSE

BRÜHL

i

Schwanen-teich

RING

QUERSTRASSE

Steibs Hof

DITTRICHRING

Alte Börse

MARKT

Handelshof

Universität

Opernhaus

GOETHE-STRASSE

GEORGI-

Schauspiel-haus

Altes Rathaus (Stadtgeschichtliches Museum)

NASCH-MARKT

Specks Hof

Nikolaikirche

GOTTSCHED-STRASSE

THOMASGASSE

GRIMMAISCHE

ZENTRAL-STRASSE

Auerbachs Keller

STR.

Zeitgeschichtliches Forum Leipzig

Thomaskirche

PETERSSTRASSE

MARKT

AUGUSTUS-

PLATZ

JOHANNIS-PLATZ

Bachmuseum

KOLONNADEN-STRASSE

BURGSTRASSE

Mädler-passage

Universität

Neues Gewandhaus

Grassi-Museum

MARTIN-LUTHER-RING

SCHUL-STRASSE

BURG-PLATZ

NEU

UNIVERSITÄTSSTRASSE

ROSSPLATZ

GOLDSCHMIDTSTRASSE

Stadthaus

Ägyptisches Museum

SCHILLERSTRASSE

Moritzbastei

Mendelssohn-Haus

STRASSE

Neues Rathaus

ROSSPLATZ

SEEBURGSTRASSE

TAL-STRASSE

STEPHANSTRASSE

KARL-TAUCHNITZ-STRASSE

MARTIN-LUTHER-RING

STERNWARTENSTRASSE

HARKORT-STRASSE

DIMITROFFSTRASSE

BRÜDER-

GRÜNEWALDSTRASSE

NÜRNBERGER

Stadtbibliothek

STRASSE

WINDMÜHLEN-STRASSE

BEETHOVENSTRASSE

HÄRTELSTRASSE

Völkerschlachtdenkmal

the airport. Linked to the city by a rapid transit line, the complex of five light and airy exhibition halls centered on the 985-foot-long (300 m) Glashalle is the latest example of a tradition of markets and trade fairs that has lasted for more than 800 years. The rapid transit line whisks travelers to Leipzig's main station, the **Hauptbahnhof.** Completed in 1915, this is Europe's largest rail terminus, its vast scale tempered by well-chosen ornament and sculpture.

MUSEUMS & MORE

Built in Bauhaus style in the late 1920s, the **Grassi-Museum,** east of the city center on Johannisplatz, contains three separate museums: Ethnology (Völkerkunde, *tel 0341 973 19 00*), Musical Instruments (Musik-instrumenten, *tel 0341 973 07 50*), and Decorative Arts (Angewandte Kunst, *tel 0341 213 37 19*), the last based on a huge collection dating back to medieval times (closed until fall 2007). In its new gallery on Sachsenplatz, the **Fine Arts Museum** (Museum der Bildenden Künste) has an impressive selection

of works by early German masters and German Romantics.

Two of the most fascinating of the city's museums deal with the upheavals of recent history. The **Zeitgeschichtliches Forum Leipzig,** near the Nicholaikirche, evokes the challenges of daily life in the GDR. The **Museum in der Runden Ecke,** installed in the secret police's headquarters, west of the city center, is even more evocative. Under the title "Stasi—Power and Banality," the displays document the extraordinary lengths to which the rulers of the GDR went in order to control their subjects.

In October 1813, on the city's outskirts, Napoleon suffered one of his worst defeats at the hands of the allied armies of Prussia, Austria, and Russia. The conflict, known as the Völkerschlacht (Battle of the Nations), is commemorated by the **Völkerschlachtdenkmal** (*Prager Strasse, tel 0341 8 78 04 71*). Climb the steps of this colossal pyramidlike structure to the viewing platform 300 feet (91 m) above the crypt for the definitive view over Leipzig and its setting. ∎

Space enough to station an airship in Leipzig's trade fair entrance hall

Fine Arts Museum
www.mdbk.de
Map p. 244
Katharinenstrasse 10
0341 21 69 90
Closed Mon.
$$

Zeitgeschichtliches Forum Leipzig
Map p. 244
Grimmaische-Strasse 6
0341 2 22 00
Closed Mon.

Museum in der Runden Ecke
Map p. 244
Dittrichring 24
0341 9 61 24 43
Donation requested

More places to visit in Saxony

COLDITZ

An impregnable-looking stronghold rising high above the River Mulde dwarfs the pleasant little town of Colditz. Between 1940 and 1945 the Schloss was an "escape-proof" prisoner-of-war camp, holding Allied officers identified as incorrigible would-be escapers. It is well worth taking part in a guided tour to learn how the pool of escaping expertise thus assembled was put to good use. Of the more than 300 attempts made to break out, about 10 percent were successful. The most ambitious, a glider laboriously assembled beneath the castle roof, was never put to the test as the war ended before it could be launched. Guided tours take place when a large enough group has gathered.

🅰 228 C3 **Schloss** ✉ Schlossgasse 1
☎ 034381 437 77 🛃 $$

The figure of a miner takes shape in the skilled hands of an Erzgebirge woodcarver.

ERZGEBIRGE (ORE MOUNTAINS)

Southern Saxony consists largely of these forested uplands, which rise gently from north to south then culminate in an almost clifflike drop at the Czech frontier. In the Middle Ages this was the heartland of German industry, the place where mining techniques were invented and refined to release the treasures hidden beneath the surface: silver, tin, and iron. When the mineral resources were exhausted, the inhabitants turned to crafts to make a living. Erzgebirge woodcarvers are famous for their skill, and the area has a long tradition of toy-making. Nowadays tourism is important, not least because of the relatively reliable snowfall that makes winter sports possible.

There are plenty of signs of past prosperity in towns such as **Annaberg-Buchholz,** with a sumptuously furnished and exquisitely vaulted church, and **Freiberg,** where the cathedral has one pulpit in the form of a giant tulip and another held aloft by the figure of a silver miner. Old mines in both towns have been turned into visitor attractions. The resort of **Oberwiesenthal,** 15 miles (24 km) from Annaberg-Buchholz, lies at the foot of the highest point in the Erzgebirge, the Fichtelberg (3,983 feet/1,214 m). Climb to the top on foot, or take the easy way up by chair-lift. The most enjoyable way of making the trip to Oberwiesenthal is aboard one of the steam-hauled trains of the Fichtelbergbahn, which chugs its way up the scenic valley from its terminus at Cranzahl (see p. 224).

🅰 228 C2–D2 **Visitor information**
✉ Markt 1, Annaberg-Buchholz ☎ 03733 1 94 33

SCHLOSS MORITZBURG

Augustus the Strong had his country home to the north of Dresden, where his predecessor, Duke Moritz, had built a modest hunting lodge in Renaissance style in 1546. Modesty was not one of Augustus's most noticeable character traits, and his alterations to Schloss Moritzburg turned it into an imposing baroque palace, its corner towers reflected in the huge artificial lake on which extravagant naval pageants were held. The palace is now the **Baroque Museum,** containing porcelain, furniture, paintings, wall hangings, and hunting trophies—Augustus was known for collecting particularly spectacular trophies. Outside the palace there are great fishponds, the rococo Pheasantry Pavilion rising over a miniature harbor, and the Saxon State Stud Farm.

🅰 228 D3 ☎ 035207 87 30 🛃 $$ ∎

Nature has blessed northern Bavaria with tranquil river valleys and gloriously forested uplands, while the region's wealth of historic towns and cities richly stocked with art and culture is unmatched in Germany.

Northern Bavaria

St. Christopher, one of the Fourteen Saints depicted in the centerpiece of the Vierzehnheiligen basilica

Northern Bavaria

FROM THE TOWN OF ASCHAFFENBURG IN THE FAR NORTHWEST TO PASSAU on the Austrian border, and the Czech Republic frontier to the northeast, this region is one of the most rewarding for vacationers. Much of the area—the old provinces of Franconia in the north and part of Swabia in the southwest—was incorporated into the former kingdom of Bavaria (Bayern) in the early 19th century, and it is far removed from the typical Bavarian stereotypes of Lederhosen, beer halls, and cow-filled Alpine meadows.

Cities such as Franconian Nuremberg and Swabian Augsburg are state capitals in their own right, with a stubbornly defended identity all their own. Nuremberg combines modernity and big city dynamism with medieval charm. But for an almost hallucinatory trip back in time, Rothenburg ob der Tauber reigns supreme. Perfectly preserved, Rothenburg is the jewel of the Romantic Road (Romantische Strasse), Germany's foremost tourist road. Starting in the north at Würzburg, with its outstanding heritage of baroque buildings, the

route runs south past many lovely old towns such as Dinkelsbühl and Nördlingen to Augsburg and beyond to the Alps.

Every city in the region has something: Regensburg has an almost Italian character, as does Passau in its

Skiers revel in the fine snow conditions brought on by Bavaria's hard winters.

incomparable setting at the confluence of the Inn and Danube (Donau) Rivers; Bamberg's matchless architecture of all epochs has survived untouched by war; Wagner's Bayreuth hosts one of the world's great music festivals; and Coburg has a unique past, linking it with many of Europe's royal families.

Northern Bavaria has been home to some of Germany's finest artists and craftsmen. Albrecht Dürer was from Nuremberg, and the city has a wealth of work by his contemporaries, notably the master carver Veit Stoss. Superlative works of art are to be found throughout the region, not least in the baroque monasteries, abbeys, and pilgrimage churches. Vierzehnheiligen, overlooking the broad valley of the upper Main, is the loveliest. Weltenburg monastery stands guard over a very different river landscape, the narrow limestone gorge formed by the Danube before it joins the Altmühl. One of the country's largest protected nature parks, the valley of the Altmühl is a favorite destination for German vacationers looking for peace and quiet in a lovely setting. There is more peace and quiet in the countryside running up to the dark and mysterious wooded ridges of the Bavarian Forest along the border with the Czech Republic. ■

Nuremberg

Nuremberg
* 249 C3
Visitor information
* Hauptmarkt 18 & Königstrasse 93
* 0911 233 60

Lorenzkirche
* Map p. 252
* Lorenzer Platz 10
* 0911 2 44 69 90

Frauenkirche
* Map p. 252
* Hauptmarkt 14
* 0911 20 65 60

LOVINGLY REBUILT AFTER WARTIME DEVASTATION, Nuremberg (Nürnberg) remains the archetypal German medieval city, encircled by mighty defensive walls, its red-roofed buildings with their row on row of dormer windows overlooked by the Kaiserburg, the imperial castle on its sandstone outcrop. The undisputed capital of northern Bavaria is a city for all seasons: As well as museums of national significance, it has a colorful street life from spring to fall, and Germany's oldest and biggest Christmas market.

The stones speak strongly of German history, with the ghosts of emperors stalking the castle heights and churches filled with medieval treasures. But it was also through these streets that the brownshirts strutted on their way to the Nazi Party Rallies. The shameful race laws enacted by the Third Reich bore the name of Nuremberg, and in the aftermath of the World War unleashed by its leaders, it was here they were tried for their crimes.

Although it covers a considerable area—almost 1.5 square miles (4 sq km)—Nuremberg's **Old Town** (Altstadt) is a delight to explore on foot, with its ancient, irregular street pattern surviving intact on both banks of the River Pegnitz. Heavy traffic is kept outside the walls, where the ring road along the line of the old moat is graced by grand buildings such as the opera house and the imposing main railroad station (Hauptbahnhof).

A good starting point is **Lorenzerplatz,** the square named after one of the city's great churches, the **Lorenzkirche.** Inside the church works of art show the city at its late medieval zenith of prestige, prosperity, and creative excellence. The two outstanding works are by artists closely associated with Nuremberg: Adam Krafft created the great 66-foot-high (20 m) tabernacle in the 1490s, and the great wood-carver Veit Stoss (died 1533) painted the

limewood depiction of the Annunciation hanging in the choir.

The church's 266-foot (81 m) twin towers may dominate the scene, but as impressive in its own way is the **Nassauer Haus** opposite. This fortified town house with its corner turrets and typical oriel window dates back to the 13th century, and it nicely symbolizes the wealth of a leading Nuremberg citizen and his determination to defend it. Also on the square is the **Tugendbrunnen,** a Renaissance fountain spouting water from the figures of the Seven Virtues.

The bridges crossing the Pegnitz offer many enticing views. From the Museum Bridge (Museumsbrücke), you can get a good view of the **Hospital of the Holy Ghost** (Heilig-Geist-Spital), which spans a branch of the river farther upstream. An almshouse and hospital in medieval times, the building was faithfully reconstructed in the 1950s after its destruction in World War II. Built on low arches, it reaches across to a little island and now houses a restaurant. On the far bank is **Hauptmarkt,** the site of a daily market since the Middle Ages and the hub of city life. It is here that the Christmas market takes place against the incomparable backdrop of the **Frauenkirche,** one of the most exquisite churches in Germany. Below its steep and spiky gable covered in sculptures is an oriel with a clock; automata,

Thinkers, prelates, and princes adorn Nuremberg's Schöner Brunnen.

the so-called Männleinlaufen, perform daily at noon. The church, built in the 14th century for Emperor Charles IV as an imperial chapel, for many years housed the crown jewels. Among its proudest possessions today are the high altar with carvings by assistants of Veit Stoss, and the triptych known as the Tucher Altar. Even more spectacular than these is the fountain in the northwest corner of the martketplace; the Gothic **Schöner Brunnen** resembles a medieval space probe, 62 feet high (19 m), manned by 40 figures representing allegorical and biblical characters and the seven Imperial Electors.

From the square, Burgstrasse leads enticingly northward toward the castle height. Before beginning the climb, however, glance at the splendid Renaissance **Town Hall** (Rathaus) and perhaps spend some time exploring the 30 or so rooms of the **Fembohaus** *(Burgstrasse 15, tel 0911 2 31 25 95, closed Mon., $),* a stately 16th-century town mansion and now the municipal museum. The best plan is to take the elevator to the top floor with its superb city model, then work your way down.

The complex silhouette of the **Kaiserburg** on the city's northern rim is the result of demolitions and rebuildings spread over many centuries. The most striking internal feature is the Imperial Chapel built on two levels. A climb up the 113 steps in the tower, the Sinwellturm, affords a view over the whole city, while a penny tossed into the Deep Well takes six seconds to splash down. Just down from the castle is the **Albrecht-Dürer-Haus.** Furnished in late medieval style, it gives a good idea of the life and domestic circumstances of the great artist, although none of his best-known paintings are here.

The last of Nuremberg's trio

of great churches is **St. Sebald's** (Sebalduskirche). Its austere Romanesque west front dates from its foundation in the early 13th century, while the soaring east end of the church was completed in High Gothic style toward the end of the 14th century. The sumptuous furnishings include a Christ carrying the Cross by Adam Krafft, relief panels by Veit Stoss, and St. Sebald's

The railing surrounding Nuremberg's Schöner Brunnen dates from the 16th century.

Kaiserburg
- ✉ Kaiserburg
- ☎ 0911 2 44 65 90
- 💲 $$

Albrecht-Dürer-Haus
- ▲ Map p. 252
- ✉ Albrecht-Dürer-Strasse 39
- ☎ 0911 2 31 25 68
- 🕐 Closed Mon.
- 💲 $

The Heilig-Geist-Spital has spanned the River Regnitz since 1488.

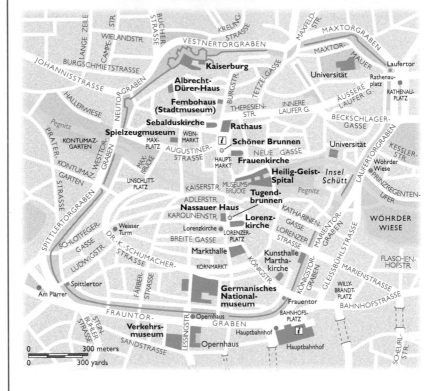

tomb, an extraordinarily elaborate work in bronze by the master craftsman Peter Vischer the Elder (1455–1529), who incorporated a self-portrait of himself at work. This level of skill was exceptional, but Nuremberg was always famous for inventiveness and meticulous workmanship—Europe's expansion in the Age of Exploration was largely carried out using instruments made or pioneered in the city.

MUSEUMS

Toymaking was another skill that flourished here, making Nuremberg a natural choice for the country's annual toy manufacturers' trade fair. In the **Toy Museum** (Spielzeugmuseum) the exhibits will appeal to adults as much as to children. Toy trains are one feature here, but it is the real thing that stars in the **Transport Museum** (Verkehrsmuseum). Germany's national museum of public transport is located here not least because the country's very first steam railroad was opened between Nuremberg and the nearby town of Fürth in 1835. A resplendent reproduction of the original locomotive, the *Adler* (Eagle), occupies pride of place, but there is much more, including the luxurious state carriage of Bavaria's Mad King Ludwig and what must be one of the world's largest and most realistic model railway layouts.

The **Germanisches Nationalmuseum,** just to the north, dates back to 1852 and has expanded remorselessly ever since to include craft objects of every kind, paintings, sculptures, house interiors, arms and armor, costumes, and folklore. Its original home, an old Carthusian monastery, is now embedded in later extensions, of which the most recent (1993) is the most striking, providing the institution with a splendid new entrance foyer as well as much needed display

space. The one section you should not miss is the painting galleries on the second floor, where Dürer's genius becomes fully apparent. Germany's greatest Renaissance artist, Dürer had a masterly ability to depict anatomical detail; look for his "Hercules Slaying the Stymphalian

Birds." His portraits reveal character with equal skill. The painting of "Michael Wolgemut," his former teacher, is an affectionate but clear-sighted tribute to an old man.

Israeli artist Dani Karavan has transformed the street separating the museum's two main parts into a sculpture by placing columns inscribed in many of the languages of the Nazis' victims. The work is a reference to the monumental structures built on the city's southeastern outskirts as a setting for Nazi rallies. The remains of the podium from which Hitler reviewed his acolytes still stands there, together with the monstrous and never completed congress building modeled on Rome's Colosseum. The extent of its megalomania is brought into focus by the innovative design of the **Dokumentationszentrum** (Documentation Center, *Bayernstrasse 110, tel 0911 231 56 66*), intended to bring home the key role of Nuremberg in the Nazi state. ■

You can always find scrumptious *Lebkuchen,* a city specialty, for sale at Nuremberg's Christmas market.

St. Sebald's Church
- Map p. 252
- Albrecht Dürer Platz 1
- 0911 2 14 25 00

Toy Museum
- Map p. 252
- Karlstrasse 13–15
- 0911 2 31 31 64
- Closed Mon.
- $

Transport Museum
- Map p. 252
- Lessingstrasse 6
- 0180 444 22 33
- Closed Mon.
- $

Germanisches Nationalmuseum
- Map p. 252
- Kartäusergasse 1
- 0911 1 33 10
- Closed Mon.
- $$

Bamberg

A WONDERFUL SYNTHESIS OF NATURE AND ARCHITECTURE, Bamberg sits at the point where low hills converge on the valley of the River Regnitz. The city's unique charm (as well as its UNESCO World Heritage status) is due not so much to individual buildings as to its completeness. Old residential districts and market gardens have survived in the city center, and streets and squares have suffered neither wartime destruction nor insensitive redevelopment. You can sense the past as a living presence. Yet Bamberg is very much a city of today, the commercial and cultural center for the surrounding rural area, with an important harbor on the Main-Danube Canal and a recently refounded university.

Bamberg's heritage is marked by the polarity of church and city, bishops and burghers. The outstanding buildings are those on the land rising steeply from the river's left bank—the great cathedral and the bishop's palace, the Residenz. But start your exploration in the **lower town,** modeled by citizens rather than clergy. The **Old Town Hall** (Altes Rathaus) is built on an islet in the river. An odd but endearing structure, it consists of three incongruously unrelated parts: a fairly conventional 18th-century section adorned with colorful frescoes; an elaborate baroque tower penetrated by the carriageway of the bridge; and what looks like a timber-framed house perched precariously above the rushing stream. Inside is an exceptional porcelain collection, the **Sammlung Ludwig.**

Linger by the river, crossing and recrossing the bridges, admiring their statuary, and absorbing the general atmosphere of the riverside scene, with its old weirs, ancient cranes, and the pleasingly irregular fishermen's houses all making up Bamberg's "Little Venice."

The lower town has many more treasures. Two of Bavaria's finest baroque architects, Georg Dientzenhofer (one of the great Dientzenhofer brothers) and Balthasar Neumann (1687–1753), worked here, designing the great Jesuit **Church of St. Martin** and the **New Town Hall** (Neues Rathaus) respectively. There are also whole streets of lovely 18th-century houses. Some of *The Tales of Hoffmann,* the basis for the opera by Offenbach, were written in the little **E.T.A.-Hoffmann-Haus,** which between 1808 and 1813 was the home of this much-loved musician and storyteller. The house contains documents and items relating to Hoffmann's time here.

Steep streets and stairways climb to the **upper town,** bringing you up on the sloping, cobbled **Domplatz,** a space of breathtaking impact. The square is lined by the glorious four-towered **Cathedral** (Dom), the late medieval palace known as the Alte Hofhaltung, and the imperious 18th-century Neue Residenz. The Dom, the third cathedral to occupy the site after the previous two burned down, took most of the 13th century to build. During that time the prevailing style changed from Romanesque to Gothic, but this shift does not affect the overall harmony of the great building.

Inside are masterpieces of medieval sculpture. The best known

Built in Gothic, baroque, and rococo styles, the Altes Rathaus crowds its little island in the River Regnitz.

Bamberg

🗺 249 C3

Visitor information

✉ Geyerswörthstrasse 3

☎ 0951 297 62 00

Sammlung Ludwig

✉ Im Alten Rathaus, Obere Brücke

☎ 0951 87 18 71

🕐 Closed Mon.

💲 $

is the **"Bamberger Reiter,"** a noble figure on horseback who seems to incorporate all the virtues of medieval Germanic chivalry. He may, in fact, be a representation of a foreign ruler, King Stephen of Hungary. Stephen was the brother-in-law of Emperor Henry II, buried here with his empress, Kunigunde. Their tomb is the work of Tilman Riemenschneider (ca 1460–1531), one of the greatest of late medieval sculptors. With its elaborate scenes from the saintly couple's lives, it took 14 years to complete. Other outstanding sculpture includes female figures representing the triumphant Church ("Ecclesia") and misguided Judaism (the blindfolded "Synagogue"), while the wonderful linden wood Nativity Altar is the last major work by Veit Stoss.

Opposite the cathedral on Domplatz, the **Alte Hofhaltung** was originally built as an imperial palace, and later converted into the bishop's residence. Beyond the Renaissance gateway is an irregular courtyard overlooked by charming high-roofed, timber-framed buildings. In 1693, Prince-Bishop Schönborn commissioned Leonhard Dientzenhofer (ca 1655–1707) to design the **Neue Residenz.** However, money ran out, and only two wings of his grandiose new baroque palace were completed. Inside are magnificent state rooms, and the **Staatsgalerie** with a collection of paintings by German masters such as Grien and Cranach. From the terrace of the Rosengarten you can look out over the whole town. ■

E.T.A.-Hoffmann-Haus
✉ Schillerplatz 26
☎ 0951 297 62 00
🕐 Closed Mon.
💲 $

Cathedral
✉ Domplatz 5
☎ 0951 50 23 30

Alte Hofhaltung
✉ Domplatz 7
☎ 0951 5 19 07 46
🕐 Closed Mon.
💲 $

Neue Residenz
✉ Domplatz 8
☎ 0951 51 93 90
💲 $

Vierzehnheiligen

CROWNING A HILLSIDE IN THE LOVELY UPPER VALLEY OF the River Main, the great pilgrimage church dedicated to the Fourteen Saints (Vierzehnheiligen) is one of the architectural wonders of Germany.

For centuries the church has attracted crowds of pilgrims, and you will not be disappointed if you follow their footsteps up the gentle slope to this rococo masterpiece. It was designed by Balthasar Neumann, one of the most creative architects of the 18th century.

The Fourteen Saints, among them St. Barbara, St. Catherine, St. Christopher, and St. Vitus, had

long been the subject of a popular cult in southern Germany, where they are called Nothelfer (Helpers in Time of Need). In 1519 they appeared in a vision, along with a figure of the Infant Jesus, to Hermann, a simple Franconian shepherd. Miracles were soon reported, and a pilgrimage chapel was erected on the spot.

Rebuilt more than once to accommodate growing crowds of pilgrims, it received the ultimate in architectural expression on the orders of Prince-Bishop Friedrich

Carl von Schönborn, already engaged in transforming the face of his episcopal city, nearby Bamberg (see pp. 254–255). Neumann, who had won fame as court architect at Würzburg (see pp. 261–262), was the natural choice to design the kind of building Schönborn had in mind. The foundation stone was laid in 1741, and the building was completed in 1772, well after Neumann's death, but in faithful compliance with his plans.

The twin towers of the church act as a beacon, signaling across the floor of the Main valley to the baroque abbey of Kloster Banz, its counterpart on the opposite slope. From the outside, Vierzehnheiligen looks like a conventional church, with walls of coarse golden sandstone apparently enclosing the conventional layout of nave, aisles, transepts, and choir. Only the undulating west front gives some hint of the pleasures to come.

The radiant glory inside is revealed as soon as you walk through the doors into a space that seems less like a logical work of architecture than the inside of some fantastical coral reef. Light streams through the many windows to illuminate exuberant, writhing, curvilinear forms in pink, white, and gold. Structure seems to have disappeared entirely beneath joyful ornamentation, the culmination of which is reached in the oval-shaped marble and stucco Altar of Mercy (Gnadenaltar) dedicated to the Fourteen Saints, placed at the very center of the church. Surrounded by a balustrade, it reproduces the

Vierzehnheiligen

🏛 249 C4

✉ Wallfahrtskirche Vierzehnheiligen

☎ 09571 9 50 80

💲 Donation requested

North transept

Left: Centerpiece of the pilgrim church is the Gnadenaltar with its statues of the Fourteen Saints.

shepherd's vision in the most extravagant way, almost like an over-life-size tableau made of Meissen porcelain. No other artifact expresses quite so vivaciously the playful and sensual spirit of the rococo. ■

Twin towers with cupolas

Centrally placed *Gnadenaltar* by Johann Michael Feichtmayer

South transept

Conventional exterior in coarse sandstone

High altar

Coburg

FOR CENTURIES, THIS TOWN BORDERING THURINGIA WAS the capital of a ducal dynasty whose mastery at marriage arrangements influenced half the royal families of Europe. The dignified buildings lining its streets and squares and its fine heritage of parks and gardens reflect Coburg's aristocratic past.

Coburg
🅰 249 C4
Visitor information
✉ Herrngasse 4
☎ 09561 7 41 80

Ehrenburg
✉ Schlossplatz
☎ 09561 80 88 10
🕐 Closed Mon.
💲 $

Veste Coburg
✉ Veste Coburg
☎ 09561 8 79 79
🕐 Open daily
💲 $

Life in Coburg centers on the bustling **Marktplatz,** where the late 16th-century Town Hall (Rathaus) faces the grand three-gabled Stadthaus, the government building erected by Duke Johann Casimir von Sachsen-Coburg-Eisenach (1564–1633). The statue in the marketplace is of his distant descendant, Albert von Sachsen-Coburg-Gotha, who in 1840 married his cousin Victoria, Queen of England. The statue was paid for by Victoria, who came here several times after his early death in 1861.

She stayed in the **Ehrenburg;** the early 19th-century ducal palace's mock-Tudor facade may have helped her to feel at home. The interior highlight is the Riesensaal, a gorgeously stuccoed ballroom, its ceiling held up by a bevy of giants *(Riesen).* The palace looks out over **Schlossplatz,** a landscaped space with arcades and the neoclassic Staatstheater.

You can climb up to the old castle, **Veste Coburg,** by road or walk through the parkland of the Hofgarten to the baroque portal. Because of its dominant position, its triple ring of walls, and its towers, the stronghold is known as the "Crown of Franconia." In the Steinerne Kemenate building are two rooms where Luther stayed for six months in 1530; works of medieval and early modern art are now displayed here. Decorative arts and glassware are on show in the Carl Eduard building. Look for the ducal family's sleighs and coaches in the Duchess's Wing. ■

Bayreuth

THIS OLD TOWN DATES BACK TO THE 12TH CENTURY, BUT it remained essentially unnoticed until the 19th century, at the time of the rising fame of composer Richard Wagner (1813–1883), who lived and worked here. His reputation is still celebrated every July and August, when visitors from all over the globe come to enjoy the famous Festspiele—the Wagner opera festival.

Elegantly attired operagoers gather outside Bayreuth's famous Festspielhaus.

The foundations for the city's fame were laid in the 17th century, when Bayreuth became the seat of the margraves of Kulmbach, who began to rebuild it in a style befitting a small princely city. The life of the court was given a great boost a century later, when Margrave Friedrich, a dull man, succeeded in winning the hand of Princess Wilhelmine, favorite sister of Frederick the Great of Prussia.

Energetic and talented, with a passion for music, theater, architecture, and landscape gardening, Wilhelmine attracted leading artists, designers, and musicians to the town, and spent her husband's money on projects such as the luxurious **Margraves' Opera House.** One of five theaters built during her reign, the Markgräfliches Opernhaus is the most splendid, with one of Germany's great baroque interiors. It is said that it was this theater that first attracted Wagner to Bayreuth, and it was here that he conducted a triumphal performance of Beethoven's Ninth Symphony on taking up residence in the town.

The Markgräfliches Opernhaus hosts Bayreuth's "other" music festival, the Fränkische Festwoche in May, which showcases the works of 18th-century composers. Also in the old town center, the rococo **Schlosskirche** holds the tombs of Wilhelmine and her husband. Close by is the **Old Palace** (Altes Schloss) rebuilt in baroque style at the end of the 17th century,

Bayreuth
◭ 249 C3
Visitor information
✉ Luitpoldplatz 9
☎ 0921 8 85 88

Margraves' Opera House
✉ Opernstrasse 14
☎ 0921 7 59 69 22
💲 $$

A performance of Das Rheingold at the 2006 Bayreuth Wagner opera festival

New Palace
- Ludwigstrasse 21
- 0921 759 69 21
- Closed Mon.
- $

Haus Wahnfried (Richard-Wagner-Museum)
- Richard-Wagner-Strasse 48
- 0921 75 72 80
- $

Festival Theater
- Festspielhügel
- 0921 7 87 80
- Closed Mon.
- $

although its core is older. Its most striking feature is the octagonal Renaissance tower, with a spiral staircase big enough for the margraves to ascend on horseback.

Not happy about living in an old castle, Wilhelmine ordered a new palace to be built, supervising much of the work herself. The delicious interiors of the **New Palace** (Neues Schloss) show her taste at its most inventive, with a Japanese room, a palm room, an extraordinary mirror room, and the splendid Cedar Room, a fine setting for the official opening of the Festspiele. Guided tours are available. Beyond is the **Hofgarten,** a park landscaped in the informal English style at the end of the 18th century.

Wagner's residence, the **Haus Wahnfried,** stands on the edge of the Hofgarten, an essential visit not only for opera fans but for anyone interested in this controversial genius. A short distance from the center of town, the **Festival Theater** (Festspielhaus) where his "musical dramas" are staged, was inaugurated with a performance of his colossal Ring cycle in 1876. ∎

Birth of a cult

At an early age, Richard Wagner stated his intention to create a truly national, Germanic opera that would be as great a cultural achievement as the symphonies of Beethoven. Deliberately turning his back on Germany's infatuation with Italy and the world of classical antiquity, he found inspiration in the country's medieval past and the deeds of the gods of Norse mythology. He also revolutionized and enriched musical language to create a web of sound of astonishing intensity and emotional power. He was saved from an erratic personal life by the generosity of one of his admirers, King Ludwig II of Bavaria. It seemed that the theater needed for Wagner's epic productions would be built in the Bavarian capital, Munich, but the composer preferred a site in Bayreuth.

Wagner's style of opera, called "musical drama," attracts near fanatical enthusiasm. But not all are entranced; it has been called "an avalanche of sound." Wagner's anti-Semitism and overblown nationalism endeared him to the Nazis (Hitler was a regular guest at the Festspiele), but has detracted from his personal stature. ∎

Stern genius in stone

Würzburg

THE HISTORY OF THIS ANCIENT UNIVERSITY CITY BEGAN in the eighth century, when a church was erected over the bones of the Irish missionary St. Kilian, martyred here when he fell foul of the local ruler. Later, the city was a center of the Counter-Reformation, and later still, in 1895, physicist Wilhelm Konrad Röntgen discovered the secrets of X-rays here. Although badly bombed in World War II, many fine individual buildings survived or have been restored, and the baroque Residenz alone is enough to justify a visit.

A stone bridge has spanned the River Main at Würzburg since the early 12th century.

After living for some 500 years in the Marienberg fortress high up on the west bank of the Main, the prince-bishops aspired to more spacious quarters. The man chosen to design their new, prestigious palace was the virtuoso architect Balthasar Neumann (see p. 37). Built between 1720 and 1744, his magnificent **Residenz** is one of Germany's great baroque buildings.

As you enter the central wing, you can't miss the spectacular grand staircase, adorned with the world's largest ceiling painting, the work of Venetian artist Giovanni Battista Tiepolo (1696–1770). After the restraint of the stucco-decorated White Room (Weisser Saal) comes the opulent, oval Imperial Chamber (Kaisersaal) with trompe l'oeil scenes from Würzburg's history on the ceiling also painted by Tiepolo. The sumptuous Sala Terrena connects the palace with the terraced garden, a perfect setting for the early summer Mozart festival.

The Romanesque **Cathedral** (Dom) west of the Residenz, badly damaged in 1945 but since rebuilt, contains tombs of the Schönborns, the most prominent and extravagant of the prince-bishops. The adjacent **Neumünster** is a Romanesque basilica lavishly rebuilt in baroque style, the resting

Würzburg
- 248 B3

Visitor information
- Marktplatz
- 0931 37 23 35

Residenz
- Residenzplatz 2
- 0931 35 51 70
- $ (Garden free)

Tiepolo's fresco above the huge baroque staircase in Würzburg's Residenz shows the four known continents paying homage to the prince-bishop.

Marienberg & Mainfränkisches Museum

✉ Festung Marienberg

☎ 0931 20 59 40

🕓 Closed Mon.

💲 $

place of the saintly Kilian. To the rear, in the tiny green space of the **Lusamgärtchen,** is a memorial to another Würzburg character, the much-loved troubadour Walther von der Vogelweide. The nearby Marktplatz is graced by the gorgeous frilly forms of the rebuilt rococo mansion known as the **Haus zum Falken** and by the graceful Gothic **Marienkapelle,** with its depiction of the Annunciation above the northern entrance. This chapel in honor of the Virgin Mary was built on the site of the ghetto, burned down in 1349 when its Jewish residents were held responsible for bringing bubonic plague to the city.

The northern part of the city center is an appropriate place to sample the products of the Franconian vineyards. The two

medieval hospices here have always gained much of their income from the vines planted by their medieval founders. The Bürgerspital was established in 1319, the Juliusspital in 1576; both have wine cellars. The **Juliusspital** *(Juliuspromenade, tel 0931 3 93 14 00, visit by guided tour only, Fri. & Sat. p.m.)* has a fine courtyard and an 18th-century pharmacy with its original furnishings.

The **Alte Mainbrücke,** the stone bridge over the Main, dates from 1133, although floods, ice, and other misfortunes have necessitated much rebuilding. It was embellished in the 18th century with baroque statuary, dramatically posturing figures of bishops and saints. As you cross the bridge, watch for the locks that allow very large barges on the Rhine-Main-Danube waterway to pass the weir.

You can climb up to the **Marienberg Fortress** (Festung Marienberg) on foot or take one of the infrequent buses. The medieval castle, the first residence of the prince-bishops, was enlarged into a Renaissance palace before they moved to the Residenz in the city below. The superb view of river and city is best appreciated from the terrace below the castle. Inside are the unusual eighth-century circular church, the **Marienkirche,** and the **Mainfränkisches Museum,** the regional museum. Do not miss the collection of very delicate linden wood carvings by Tilman Riemenschneider, whose career took off in Würzburg about 1478.

On roughly the same level as the Marienberg, although reached separately via a stepped passageway with Stations of the Cross, is the **Käppele.** This exotic-looking, onion-domed pilgrimage church was the final work in Würzburg of Balthasar Neumann. From the terrace admire the splendid view of the town and the Marienberg. ■

Rothenburg ob der Tauber

THE COUNTRYSIDE SWEEPS UNIMPEDED RIGHT UP TO Rothenburg's ring of medieval ramparts, inside which the happy accidents of history have preserved a medieval townscape of great perfection. Outstanding monuments are few, but the narrow streets and charming squares seem not to have changed since Burgomaster Nusch saved his city from destruction in the Thirty Years War by winning a famous wager, the *Meistertrunk* (see sidebar p. 265). Rothenburg is on every foreign visitor's itinerary so, if you can, come out of season or get up early before the streets fill with fellow visitors.

One of Rothenburg's medieval gateways guards the approach to the cobbled Plönlein.

The first fortification built on this headland overlooking the River Tauber a thousand years ago was on the spot where the Burggarten now stands. A small town spread out on the plateau to the east, protected by a long-since demolished line of walls. By 1300, growing prosperity brought expansion and a second line of walls and towers, over 1.5 miles long (2.5 km) with a sentry walk that can still be followed today.

After the Thirty Years War, the tide of trade ebbed, and the town—fortunately for visitors today—became a backwater, well away from all main routes. Many of its inhabitants still lived as peasants,

Rothenburg ob der Tauber
🅐 248 B3
Visitor information
✉ Marktplatz 2
☎ 09861 40 48 00

Perfectly preserved, the old walls of Rothenburg still hold the modern world at bay.

St.-Jakobs-Kirche
- ✉ Klostergasse 15
- ☎ 09861 70 06 20

Reichsstadt-museum
- ✉ Klosterhof 5
- ☎ 09861 93 90 43
- 💲 $

Town Hall
- ✉ Marktplatz 1
- ☎ 09861 40 40
- 💲 $

driving their animals into the fields during the day and herding them back in the evening.

In the mid-19th century, Rothenburg was "discovered" by sentimental painters such as Carl Spitzweg and Ludwig Richter, who saw in it the epitome of the Romantic German past. It became a stopping point for British travelers heading south to Switzerland and Italy, and the townsfolk realized where their future lay—in tourism.

For many years, Rothenburg has operated one of the most stringent preservation policies of any town in Germany, banning modern intrusions such as shop signs that might detract from its medieval image. After an air raid in the last days of World War II, J. J. McCloy, a civilian with the advancing U.S. forces, successfully argued against further raids on Rothenburg, and thereafter the town was restored and preserved.

At the very center of town is the **Marktplatz,** dominated by the stately Renaissance wing of the **Town Hall** (Rathaus), its steps a favorite sitting place for weary sightseers. On the north side of the square is the crinkly baroque gable of the **Ratsherrentrinkstube,** the tavern where the city councillors once met. Adorned with three clocks, it features the figures of Tilly and Nusch (see p. 265), who appear on the hour several times a day to reenact their historic encounter.

Just north of Marktplatz in **St.-Jakobs-Kirche** is Rothenburg's finest church treasure. The Altar of the Holy Blood is a masterpiece of delicacy and expressiveness carved in linden wood by Tilman Riemenschneider (1504). Housed in an old convent behind the church, the **Reichs-stadtmuseum's** most famous exhibit is the original *Humpen* of the *Meistertrunk* legend.

The best view of Rothenburg is from the **Town Hall** (Rathaus). You pass through the spacious Imperial Hall (Kaisersaal) and climb the steep stairway in the oldest, Gothic part of the building, to emerge on to a narrow platform at the top of the tower. Two hundred feet (60 m) below are the patterned cobblestones of the marketplace, while beyond

the crowded, red-tiled roofs and the ramparts stretch the beautiful woods and fields of Franconia.

Some of the finest old houses are on **Herrngasse,** the street leading west to the Burgtor. This was the gateway to the castle, now a park, the **Burggarten,** with idyllic views over the valley of the Tauber. South of the marketplace, **Schmiedgasse** is lined with more splendid houses, including the step-gabled **Baumeisterhaus.** Statues on the second floor represent figures of the Seven Virtues, and those above depict the Seven Deadly Sins. Just off Schmiedgasse, the **Puppet & Toy Museum** (Puppen- und Spielzeug-Museum) has one of the country's largest collections of old toys and dolls. The **Mittelalterliches Kriminalmuseum** will make you shudder with its array of torture instruments, including an example of the cruel Iron Maiden. Schmiedgasse ends in the tiny triangular square known as the **Plönlein,** a much photographed spot. ■

Puppet & Toy Museum
✉ Hofbronnengasse 13
☎ 09861 73 30
💲 $

Mittelalterliches Kriminalmuseum
✉ Burggasse
☎ 09861 53 59
💲 $

The seven-pint Humpen

The *Meistertrunk*

Rothenburg fell to the imperial army of General Tilly on October 30, 1631. The merciless warlord had decided to level the town to the ground because of its impertinent resistance, but nevertheless accepted the offer of a drink from a *Humpen,* a capacious vessel holding some seven pints (3.25 L) of the good local wine. Mellowing slightly, he proposed sparing the town if someone could empty the vessel in one draft—an almost unheard-of *Meistertrunk* (masterly drinking feat). Ex-Mayor Nusch accepted the challenge, and he succeeded in downing the wine without pausing, although it took him ten minutes. Tilly was as good as his word, and, after three days of blissful oblivion, Nusch revived to live to the ripe old age of 80. A colorful re-creation of this event is staged several times a year in the Kaisersaal of the Rathaus. ■

Drive: The Romantic Road

Tranquil countryside, the memory of great battles, natural curiosities, and, above all, an incomparable succession of historic towns make the Romantische Strasse, stretching 220 miles (350 km) from Würzburg in the Main Valley to Füssen in the Alps, Germany's most popular vacation route.

Start in the north on the first section of the specially signposted route leading from Würzburg (see pp. 261–262) along the B27 to **Tauberbischofsheim ❶**, a lovely medieval wine village located in the valley of the River Tauber. Follow the river upstream on the B290 to the spa town of **Bad Mergentheim ❷**, where the modern spa district contrasts with the old town and the Renaissance residence of the Grand Master of the Order of Teutonic Knights. From here, the route brings you to **Weikersheim,** with the moated castle of the Hohenlohe family, and on to **Creglingen.** In the Herrgottskirche here is the superb

Taking a rest along the Romantic Road in Dinkelsbühl, a taste of the Middle Ages.

Altarpiece of the Virgin Mary in linden wood, by master carver Tilman Riemenschneider in 1510. The church in **Detwang** also has an altarpiece by Riemenschneider. Stop for a stroll in peerless **Rothenburg ob der Tauber ❸** (see pp. 263–265).

To the south of Rothenburg, medieval **Feuchtwangen ❹** has a fine old marketplace and Romanesque cloisters used for open-air performances in summer. Next, perfectly preserved within its tightly drawn ring of walls and towers, **Dinkelsbühl ❺** can still only be entered through one of its four gates. Within are grand old merchant houses such as the **Deutsches Haus** (Am Weinmarkt), with seven projecting stories reaching into its immense gable. The 15th-century St. George's, one of the finest town churches in southern Germany, has a wonderfully calm and lofty interior. A horse-drawn carriage tour is a fun alternative to strolling through the streets, followed perhaps by an evening promenade around the ramparts in the footsteps of the nightwatchman. Dinkelsbühl's deliverance from destruction in the Thirty Years War is commemorated every year in July by a pageant, the Kinderzeche,

---

- 🅰   See area map p. 248 B3
- ▶   Würzburg
- ⟷   220 miles (350 km)
- 🕒   Minimum 3 days
- ▶   Füssen

NOT TO BE MISSED

- Riemenschneider altarpiece at Creglingen
- A stroll in Rothenburg ob der Tauber
- Deutsches Haus in Dinkelsbühl
- View from the church tower in Nördlingen
- Neuschwanstein Castle

celebrating the successful appeal made to the besieging commander by the town's children.

As the route nears Nördlingen, it passes through an open landscape almost devoid of woodland. This is the **Ries,** a circular crater 15.5 miles (25 km) across, formed by a giant meteorite some 15 million years ago. You can survey the area from the top of the 300-foot-high (90 m) tower of St. George's church in **Nördlingen ⑥,** and find out more about the cosmic event that created it in the town's **Rieskrater-Museum** (*Eugene-Schoemaker-Platz 1, tel 09081 2 73 82 20, closed Mon.*). The tower also gives the best view over the oval-shaped town, whose glory days were between the 14th and 16th centuries, when its huge Whitsun fair attracted traders from all over Germany. Subsequent stagnation meant that its picturesque townscape was never marred by later developments. A mighty ring of ramparts, with 16 towers and five gateways, still protects the streets radiating out from the central Marktplatz with its 13th-century Town Hall (Rathaus). In the **Municipal Museum** (*Vordere Gerbergasse 1, tel 09081 2 73 82 30, closed Mon.*), 6,000 tin soldiers still fight one of the great battles of the Thirty Years War, which took place outside the town in 1634.

From Nördlingen, the route reaches the Danube at **Donauwörth ⑦,** then beyond Augsburg crosses the **Lechfeld.** In 955 this was the site of one of Europe's most decisive battles, when Otto the Great ended the pagan Hungarians' incursions and drove them back east. Beyond Landsberg, the foothills of the Alps begin, but before the Austrian border is reached at Füssen is one of Germany's greatest romantic sights: King Ludwig II's dreamlike castle of **Neuschwanstein ⑧,** perched on its crag amid forests and waterfalls (see p. 307). ∎

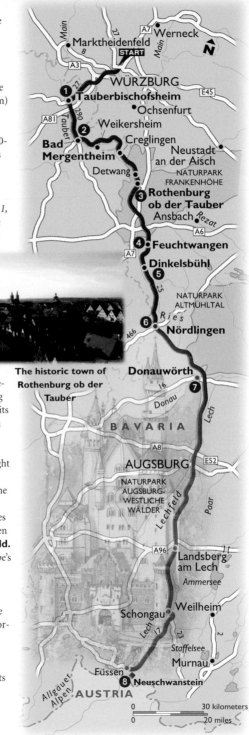

The historic town of Rothenburg ob der Tauber

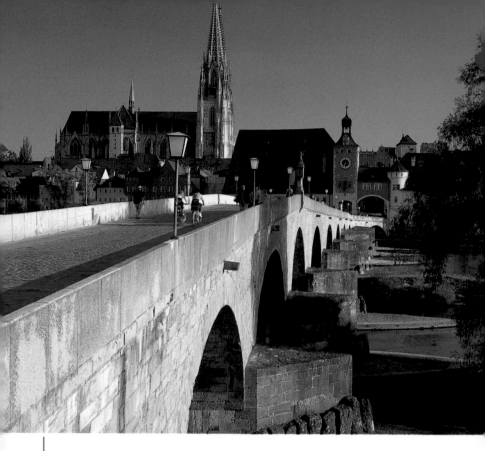

Regensburg

REGENSBURGERS LIKE TO CLAIM THAT THEIR HANDSOME old cathedral city at the confluence of the Danube and Regen Rivers enjoys the atmosphere of a mellow provincial capital long lost by cosmopolitan Munich. The pace of life is leisurely, despite the presence of a university with more than 20,000 students. The city center suffered little wartime damage and—a further plus—Regensburg was one of the first German cities to banish through-traffic, create pedestrian districts and rehabilitate old buildings. In 2006 the old town was declared a world heritage site by UNESCO.

Regensburg

🅰 249 D2

Visitor information

✉ Rathausplatz 4

☎ 0941 5 07 44 10

Cathedral

✉ Domplatz

☎ 0941 5 97 10 02

💲 $ (guided tour)

As Castra Regina, Regensburg was a Roman town, guarding the Empire's northern frontier on the Danube. The Roman walls stood for a thousand years, and the labyrinthine pattern of narrow streets still reflects the grid traced by the Roman military surveyors.

In the Middle Ages, the city's heyday, it was the most important town in southern Germany. The wealthiest families followed the Italian fashion and built fortified tower houses in competition with one another. Some 30 of these unusual structures survive today among the sea of red-roofed old houses.

The most striking view of the city is from its medieval bridge. Spanning the two arms of the Danube and 1,014 feet (309 m) long, the **Stone Bridge** (Steinerne Brücke) must have been one of the wonders of the world when completed in the middle of the 12th century. It preceded by a whole two centuries its even more spectacular counterpart, Prague's Charles Bridge. It was said that only the help of the Devil made such a structure possible, and that his fee was to claim the first soul to venture across. The citizens ensured that the sacrificial victim was an unfortunate donkey.

The bridgehead on the city side is a fine sight: A gateway and clock tower flanked by solid-looking, high-roofed buildings, both of them storehouses for the salt on which much of the city's prosperity depended in the Middle Ages. The mouth-watering aroma in the area emanates from the **Historische Wurstküche** (*Thundorferstrasse 3, tel 0941 46 62 10*), the sausage kitchen whose tasty products are supposed to have fed the masons working on the bridge. You can still get sausages and sauerkraut there today.

Beyond the bridgehead soar the twin spires of Regensburg's Gothic **Cathedral** (Dom). Work began on the great cathedral in the 13th century, but the lacelike stonework of the towers is a 19th-century addition. Art lovers come to admire the stained glass, the "laughing angel," and the other figures in the group of lovely late 13th-century statues depicting the Annunciation.

To the west of the Dom is one of the grandest of the city's merchant houses, the **Heuporthaus,** now a restaurant, and farther west still are fine examples of tower houses such

as the **Goldener Turm** in the Wahlenstrasse, the city's oldest named street. The Gothic and very picturesque **Old Town Hall** (Altes Rathaus) is where the more or less powerless German Reichstag met until it was contemptuously dissolved by Napoleon in 1806.

To the east of the city center, the **Historical Museum** (Historisches Museum) occupies an old monastery. Its extensive collections relate to local history, but of greater interest are the paintings by Albrecht Altdorfer, (ca 1480–1538), a city councillor and one of the first artists to treat landscape as a subject in itself.

The southern part of the Old Town (Altstadt) is dominated by the **Schloss Thurn und Taxis,** the residence of the princely family who amassed a fortune in the 16th century by pioneering Europewide postal services. The palace has medieval cloisters, part of the Bavarian National Museum with fine examples of the decorative arts, and a collection of coaches, carriages, sleighs, and sedan chairs. ∎

Old Town Hall
✉ Rathausplatz
☎ 0941 50 74 411
$ $

Regensburg's Haidplatz, overlooked by one of the city's several tower houses

Historical Museum
✉ Dachauplatz 2–4
☎ 0941 5 07 24 48
🕓 Closed Mon.
$ $

Schloss Thurn und Taxis
✉ Emmeramsplatz 5
☎ 0941 504 81 33
$ $$

A DRIVE ALONG THE ALTMÜHL VALLEY

A drive along the Altmühl Valley

This full-day drive takes you along one of Germany's most unspoiled river valleys. The winding Altmühl has cut deeply into a limestone plateau, creating an ecologically rich and varied landscape of sheep-grazed pastures overlooked by limestone cliffs and interspersed with lovely villages, small towns, and crag-top castles.

The drive begins at **Ellingen ❶**, 33.5 miles (54 km) south of Nuremberg just off the B2. The tiny town was largely rebuilt in the 18th century. Dominating the town is the great baroque Schloss, the former residence of the former commander of the Teutonic Knights. Continue along the old main road south to medieval **Weissenburg ❷**, which is bigger but even more picturesque, with a moat, a nearly complete set of ramparts and gateways, and Roman remains (it guarded the northern frontier of the Empire's province of *Rhaetia*).

Continue south on the B2 for 7 miles (11 km) and turn left after a railway bridge on to the road through the Altmühl valley. From here to Kelheim the road follows the course of the river and forms part of the designated Alps-to-Baltic Vacation Route (Ferienstrasse Alpen-Ostsee). Almost completely surrounded by a bend in the river, **Pappenheim ❸** is a well-preserved little place, overlooked by its castle. Near Esslingen, the river curves past a series of natural bastions, the rocks known as the Twelve Apostles, once part of a great reef on the edge of an ancient sea.

On your approach to the elegant Episcopal town of **Eichstätt ❹**, you will see the shining white Willibaldsburg standing four-square on its wooded hill above the town. The castle houses the **Jura-Museum** (*Burgstrasse 19, tel 08421 29 56*), chronicling the unusually interesting geological history of the limestone from which the landscapes of the Altmühl are formed. You should also visit the **Informationszentrum Naturpark Altmühltal** (*Notre Dame 1, tel 08421 9 87 60*), located in a former monastery.

Continue along the valley road toward the village of Pfünz, past more limestone cliffs around Arnsberg and beneath the A9 autobahn near Kinding. Beyond the town of **Beilngries ❺** and its hilltop palace of Hirschberg, the Altmühl becomes part of the Main-Danube waterway (Main-Donau-

Kanal), the latest attempt to connect the river systems flowing to the North Sea with those feeding southeastern Europe and the Black Sea. This follows efforts by Charlemagne, who failed in the eighth century, and Ludwig I of Bavaria who was only partly successful in the 19th. Today the waterway carries 360-foot-long (110 m) barges doing the work of dozens of 42-ton trucks. Environmentalists feared the canal would irreparably damage landscapes and townscapes, but ultra-conscientious restoration works have minimized its impact.

- ⛰ See area map p. 249 C2
- ► Ellingen
- ⬌ 84 miles (135 km)
- 🕐 1 day
- ► Kelheim

NOT TO BE MISSED

- Jura-Museum in the Willibaldsburg
- Sight of Prunn castle perched on its cliff
- Essing's riverside
- Befreiungshalle at Kelheim

The picturesque town of Pappenheim has been guarded by its castle for nearly a millennium.

The valley's spectacularly sited castle at **Prunn ❻** *(tel 09442 33 23, closed Mon. winter),* is on a sheer cliff above the river. Just downstream, at **Essing ❼,** the idyllic riverside scene of village, watchtower, and ancient timber bridge has been perfectly preserved. But it is a stage set: The canalized Altmühl bypasses the village, and the "river" is an artificially fed lake.

The drive ends at **Kelheim ❽,** where the Altmühl joins the Danube. Prominent on the hilltop overlooking the meeting point of the two rivers stands the **Hall of Liberation,** or Befreiungshalle *(Auf dem Michelsberg, tel 09441 68 20 70),* a neoclassic rotunda built by Ludwig I to mark the German victory over Napoleon in 1813. Outside, statues represent the German provinces. Inside, figures of the goddesses of Victory are flanked by shields made from melted-down French cannon. ∎

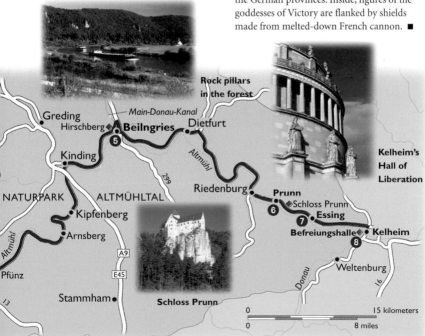

Augsburg

FOUNDED IN 15 B.C., THIS STATELY CITY WAS NAMED AFTER
Roman Emperor Augustus. Between the 15th and 17th centuries, its
banking dynasties dominated the finances of Central Europe, and the
city was rebuilt, importing design ideas from Renaissance Italy.
Martin Luther was active here, and it was also home to artists Hans
Holbein the Elder and Younger, musician Leopold Mozart, and writer
Bertolt Brecht. At the end of the 19th century, a revolutionary motor
was perfected in the factory owned by one Rudolf Diesel.

Augsburg
🅰 249 C1
Visitor information
✉ Bahnhofstrasse 7
☎ 0821 50 20 70

Fuggerei
✉ Mittlere Gasse 13
☎ 0821 319 88 10
🕐 Closed winter
💲 $ (incl. museum)

Town Hall
✉ Rathausplatz 2
☎ 0821 32 40
💲 $

The city's greatest son was
undoubtedly the financier Jakob
Fugger (1459–1529), known as
"The Rich." His **Fuggerei,** the
old people's housing scheme he
founded, was the first establishment
of its kind in the world. A town
within a town consisting of several
dozen steep-roofed buildings, it still
accommodates deserving old folk
for the annual rental of one guilder
(about 88 cents), plus the obligation to say a daily prayer for the
soul of the founder. The Fuggers
made their first fortune from linen
before diversifying into banking
and mining. Their interests extended all over Central Europe as far

away as Slovakia. They financed the imperial ambitions of the profligate Hapsburgs, enabling Charles I of Spain to bribe his way into the office of Holy Roman Emperor in 1519. Remember that the Fuggerei is home to its residents and not a theme park; the only interiors open to the public are those of the little church and the **Fuggerei-Museum.**

Much fine architecture is in evidence around the central square, **Rathausplatz,** including the Renaissance **Augustusbrunnen,** one of the elaborate fountains around the city. In 1602, Elias Holl became city architect, and the Renaissance **Town Hall** (Rathaus) is his most ambitious creation, its pediment topped by a pinecone (part of the city arms) and flanked by onion-domed towers. Inside, the Golden Hall (Goldener Saal) is also redolent of municipal pomp. Holl gave a Renaissance gloss to the tall **Perlachturm** overlooking the square, disguising its Romanesque origins. Climb the 230-foot (70 m) tower for the 360-degree panorama over the city and, if you're lucky, a view south all the way to the Alps.

Walk north from the square to Augsburg's **Cathedral** (Dom). Its rich furnishings and fittings include Romanesque bronze doors and stained glass. The same distance westward is **St. Anne's Church,** a former convent where Luther stayed and where the Fuggers chose to be buried. Their chapel is one of the first examples of Italian Renaissance design in Germany.

The Fuggers lived on the broad Maximilianstrasse running north–south through the city center. The **Fuggerhäuser** are laid out around a series of courtyards; they include the private bank still owned by the family, and a luxury hotel. Farther along the street, by one of the city's finest fountains, the **Herkulesbrunnen,** is the

Schaezlerpalais. Step inside this rococo palace to admire the gilded and painted plasterwork in the Banqueting Hall (Festsaal). In the palace are paintings of the 16th to 18th centuries, and earlier masterworks in the **Staatsgalerie** beyond *(same ticket),* among them a portrait of Jakob Fugger the Rich by Albrecht Dürer. The **Church of St. Ulrich & St. Afra,** with its Swabian onion-domed tower, closes off Maximilianstrasse to the south. Inside, the Gothic nave leads to the the tombs of the two local saints to whom the church is dedicated.

Augsburg's glorious art nouveau **Synagogue** complex dating from 1914–17 survived the Nazi era. The museum deals with the history of what was a large and progressive Jewish community. ∎

The gilded Festsaal of the Schaezlerpalais

Perlachturm
✉ Rathausplatz
🕐 Closed mid-Oct.–mid-May
💲 $

Staatsgalerie im Schaezlerpalais
✉ Maximilianstrasse 46
☎ 0821 51 03 50
🕐 Closed Mon.
💲 $

Synagogue
✉ Halderstrasse 8
☎ 0821 51 36 11
🕐 Closed Mon. & Sat.
💲 $ (museum)

A stream meanders through the thick Bavarian Forest near the Czech border.

Bavarian Forest

BETWEEN THE VALLEY OF THE DANUBE AND GERMANY'S border with the Czech Republic, the land rises gradually through lovely rolling farming countryside to the densely wooded ridges of the Bavarian Forest on the German side, and the Bohemian Forest on the Czech side. This is "Europe's Green Roof," reaching 4,777 feet (1,456 m) at the bare summit of the Grosser Arber, and covering a total area of some 2,300 square miles (6,000 sq km).

Bavarian Forest
🅰 249 E2

Schnupftabak-Museum
✉ Spitalstrasse, Grafenau,
☎ 08552 96 23 43
$ $

Hans-Eisenmann-Haus
✉ Böhmstrasse 35, Neuschönau
☎ 08558 9 61 50

Glasmuseum
✉ Am Museumspark 1, Frauenau
☎ 09926 94 10 20
$ $$

The heart of the forest is a national park, where commercial woodland management has been halted and nature has been allowed to take its course. The harsh climate and poor soils forced the people of this peripheral region to supplement the traditional activities of timber-growing and upland farming with mining, metalworking, and—above all—glassmaking. Today tourism plays a vital role. Most visitors are Germans looking for quiet and inexpensive vacations with fresh air and many opportunities to enjoy healthy pursuits such as walking, cycling, or, in winter, skiing. You could follow their example. Drive to the region, then rent accommodations in one of the villages with

an onion-domed church and convenient swimming pool, rent a bike, and take your time to explore the local trails and towns. Most of the towns have a museum, though few are as quirky as Grafenau's **Schnupftabak-Museum:** It's devoted to the pleasures of snuff taking! If possible, make your stay in the Bavarian Forest coincide with one of the folk festivals; the most spectacular is the Drachenstich (see sidebar p. 275)—sticking the dragon—at Furth im Wald during the second week in August.

If time is short, the national park interpretive center known as the **Hans-Eisenmann-Haus** in Neuschönau is a good first call. Then be sure to visit the

Glasmuseum at Frauenau, a wonderful collection of glass from three millennia and a celebration of what is still a living local craft. With the surrounding conifer-clad slopes reflected in its dark waters, the **Grosser Arbersee** seems to sum up the mystery and majesty of the region. Near the lake, a cable car whisks you up through the trees to the top of the Grosser Arber. The short walk to the summit is rewarded with fabulous views over the forested ridges. ■

Skilled glassblowers practice their traditional craft in many parts of the Bavarian Forest.

The Drachenstich festival

Every August the streets of Furth im Wald fill with smoke and fiery breath as the town's dragon attempts to devour the gallant figure of Udo the knight. Despite his great size (62 feet/19 m) and realistic writhings, the dragon always loses. The "Dragon-Sticking" festival is one of Germany's most popular pageants, based on folk memories of a 15th-century battle just across the border in Bohemia (now part of the Czech Republic). ■

Into the jaws of the fire-breathing dragon

Passau

FEW GERMAN CITIES HAVE SUCH A DISTINCTIVE SETTING as Passau's. Right on the border with Austria and overlooked by wooded heights, the old town stretches out on a narrow spit of land at the point where the Danube, the Inn, and the Ilz converge. The effect looks like some fantastical ocean liner, its prow breasting the waters of the triple rivers, its portholes the windows of the brightly painted houses, its superstructure formed by the great cathedral. Visitors are invited aboard across a series of bridge-gangways.

A Danube riverboat makes its way upstream from the landing stage at Passau.

Passau

⚑ 249 E1

Visitor information

✉ Rathausplatz 3

☎ 0851 95 59 80

Veste Oberhaus

✉ Oberhaus 125

☎ 0851 493 35 12

💲 $$ (museum)

Glasmuseum

✉ Am Rathausplatz

☎ 0851 3 50 71

💲 $$

Perhaps the best way to get the feel of the place is to drive (or steel yourself for a steep walk) up to the **Veste Oberhaus.** Perched high above the north bank of the Danube, this is the fortress-cum-palace built by Passau's powerful prince-bishops in the 13th century to keep an eye on the often unruly citizenry in the town below. The fortress contains an excellent regional museum, but the view is the thing here. Note how the three rivers betray their origin: The Inn still has a greenish, Alpine look; the Danube, which has serviced towns and farmland, is murkier; and the much smaller and shorter Ilz, tumbling down from the Bavarian Forest, has a peaty hue.

There will probably be some activity on the water. Passau lost its importance as a freight port, trading salt, cereals, and wine, long ago, but it is a starting point for riverboats going downstream to Vienna and on to Budapest, Belgrade, and the Black Sea.

The riverboats tie up by the **Town Hall** (Rathaus), with its tall tower and elaborately painted facade. Next door, in the Wilder Mann building, is the superlative **Glasmuseum,** celebrating the traditional craft of the Bavarian Forest; it has an unsurpassed collection of Bohemian glass. Walk east to the point where the rivers meet, then west past the bishops' neoclassic **Residenz** to the **Cathedral** (Dom), rebuilt in baroque style in the late 17th century; it reputedly contains the world's biggest organ. ∎

More places to visit in Northern Bavaria

ASCHAFFENBURG

The most northwesterly town in Bavaria, Aschaffenburg became part of the kingdom only in the early 19th century. Its previous rulers, the Archbishops of Mainz, left a massive mark in the shape of their local residence. The red sandstone **Schloss Johannesburg** *(Schlossplatz 4, tel 06021 38 65 70, closed Mon.),* with four uncompromising-looking

INGOLSTADT

Modern outskirts with an oil refinery and Audi factory give little hint of a distinguished old walled city with fine churches and civic buildings. Its ancient university—the setting for Mary Shelley's *Frankenstein*—was moved to Munich, but Ingolstadt upholds proud Bavarian traditions with its fascinating **Bayerisches Armeemuseum** *(Neues*

Princess Jadwiga and other authentically costumed participants gather at Landshut's great spectacle, the *Fürstenhochzeit* (Royal Wedding), held every four years.

corner towers, was one of the most ambitious Renaissance buildings in Germany. The archbishops were also enthusiastic landscapers, and their more modest summer residence of **Schönbusch** stands in an English-style park just outside town. King Ludwig I of Bavaria liked his new acquisition and came here often, calling it a "northern Nice." His particular contribution, reflecting his classical enthusiasms, was the **Pompejanum,** a re-creation of a Roman villa from Pompeii.

On the square known as **Stiftskirche** is an oddly appealing mish-mash of Romanesque, Gothic and baroque styles. The attached museum *(tel 06021 33 04 63, closed Mon., $),* is home to a 13th-century cloister and intriguing relics such as Germany's oldest chessboard.
🅰 248 A4 **Visitor information**
✉ Schlossplatz 1 ☎ 06021 39 58 00

Schloss, tel 0841 9 37 70, closed Mon.). The emphasis in this military museum, housed in the city's ducal palace, is on the glory and pageantry of long-forgotten battles. Prominently displayed is booty from the many wars against the Turks, as well as the uniforms worn by every Bavarian king. A more somber note prevails in the annex dealing with World War I, reached by a footbridge across the Danube.
🅰 249 C2 **Visitor information** ✉ Rathaus, Rathausplatz ☎ 0841 305 30 30

LANDSHUT

Little seems to have changed in this old provincial capital on the River Isar, once the seat of a branch of the powerful Bavarian Wittelsbach family (see p. 281), since its peak of fame in 1475. In that year the wedding took place here between the ruler's son and Jadwiga, daughter of the King of Poland. Few nuptials have ever been celebrated on such a scale; with banquets, pageants, processions, feasts, and tournaments, the revelries lasted for days. In the early 20th century, the celebrations were revived, and since then, the Landshuter Hochzeit, one of Germany's biggest and most lavish popular festivals, has been held here every four years. The next one will take place in late June to mid-July 2009. The town provides a perfect backdrop; high gabled and arcaded houses line its gently curving main street, Altstadt. The scene is presided over by the 436-foot (133 m) brick-built tower (the tallest of its kind in the world) of the cathedral and by the ducal castle, Burg Trausnitz, on its crag above the town. But you don't need to come at festival time to fall under the spell of one of southern Germany's best-preserved medieval towns.

🅼 249 D1   **Visitor information** ✉ Altstadt 315 ☎ 0871 92 20 50

SCHLOSS WEISSENSTEIN

This extravagant baroque palace, built between 1711 and 1718, dominates the village of Pommersfelden. Hardly a place for quiet contemplation, it continues to proclaim the wealth, power, and taste of Prince-Bishop Lothar Franz von Schönborn, ecclesiastical ruler of nearby Bamberg. A gifted amateur architect himself, he employed the very best designers of the day, Johann Dientzenhofer and Johann Lukas von Hildebrandt, court architect to the Hapsburgs. He, himself, may have been responsible for the palace's most original feature, the grandiose, courtyard-sized staircase. This gives access to a series of splendid state rooms, but the other most intriguing interior is the grottolike garden room, a fantasy of seashells and stucco figures.

🅼 249 C3 ✉ Pommersfelden ☎ 09548 981 80 🕒 Closed Mon.

WALHALLA

A gleaming white marble copy of the Parthenon in Athens, Greece, this temple high above the Danube is a monument to the great and good of German history, busts of whom adorn the sober interior. Like the Hermannsdenkmal in the Teutoburger Wald (see p. 173) and Germania

above the Rhine at Rüdesheim (see p. 210), it is a key monument to the growth of German national feeling in the 19th century. However, Walhalla is less bombastic than these other creations, perhaps because it dates from an earlier phase. The brainchild of King Ludwig I of Bavaria (*R.* 1825–1848), it was conceived when he was a young man, begun in 1830 and completed in 1842. The name Walhalla is taken from Nordic mythology and refers to the resting place for the souls of battle heroes. Every German who visits here is able to find fault with the selection of "heroes"; some dubious characters are honored, and there are inexplicable omissions. In all, about 120 busts of famous soldiers, artists, scientists, and statesmen are here, along with 64 plaques of lesser-known figures. Far from being a historical curiosity, Walhalla's pantheon is still being added to: The late Chancellor Konrad Adenauer (died 1967) has recently found a place of honor here.

🅼 249 D2 ✉ Donaustauf bei Regensburg ☎ 09403 96 16 80

WELTENBURG

Unspoiled nature and sophisticated architecture join in supreme harmony at Kloster Weltenburg, Bavaria's oldest monastery, founded in the seventh century at the entrance to the Danube gorge above Kelheim. Here, limestone cliffs squeeze the broad river into a channel one quarter of the river's normal width and correspondingly deep; glorious beech woods complete the primeval-seeming scene. The Asam brothers, architect and painter Cosmas Damian (1686–1739), and sculptor Egid Quirin (1692–1750), rebuilt the monastery, outbuildings and all, in the early 18th century. The church is an unrivaled example of baroque theatricality. A mounted figure of St. George combating the dragon presides over the interior, the action enhanced by virtuoso use of natural lighting effects. The ideal way of visiting the monastery is to walk the 3 miles (5 km) through the woods from Kelheim and return by riverboat. But even if you arrive by car, get the boatman to ferry you to the far bank, climb the wooded slope to the ramparts of the Celtic stronghold high above, and absorb the wonderful view.

🅼 249 D2 ✉ Asamstrasse 32, Kelheim/ Donau ☎ 09441 20 40 ■

Here is Germany at its most irresistible—the country's most glamorous city set against the glorious rampart of the Bavarian Alps, with their crags, fairy-tale castles, and cozy mountain resorts.

Munich & the Alps

Porcelain beer steins from Bavaria

Munich & the Alps

GERMANS FROM OTHER REGIONS SOMETIMES HAVE TO ADMIT THAT THE Bavarian heartland of Munich and its Alpine background are the most beguiling part of the country. The Alps and their foothills are Germany's foremost vacation area, while the popularity of Munich as a place to live has pushed house prices there to an impossible height. The clichés about Bavaria really do exist: Alphorns and brass bands play in beer gardens, and you'll see bewhiskered men in lederhosen and buxom girls in dirndls. The landscape offers rocky peaks, rushing torrents, upland lakes, and pastures grazed by contented cows; the village churches have onion domes, and people live in timber chalets.

Area of map detail

Berlin ✪

The chalets, of course, are triple-glazed and very well equipped, for Bavaria is far from being backward. BMW—Bavarian Motor Works—is not alone in standing for the advanced products and services characteristic of the region, and people migrate to Munich, not just because of its beauty and its ideal location, but also for hard-nosed career reasons. To convince yourself that Bavaria represents progress just as much as picturesqueness, arrange to arrive at Munich's Franz-Josef Strauss Flughafen,

the most spectacularly modern airport in the country.

Bavaria now calls itself Freistaat Bayern, a Free State rather than a kingdom, but its strong and distinctive identity can in part be attributed to the Wittelsbach dynasty who reigned here for centuries, a far longer rule than any other German royal or noble family enjoyed. Their influence still pervades this core area of their domain; Munich is very obviously a royal capital, its Residenz crammed with treasures, its townscape shaped by kingly command. Palaces and castles stud the landscape elsewhere, a good proportion of them the fantasies set in stone of the "Mad" Ludwig II (1845–1886). He may have bankrupted the royal finances at the time, but he left Bavaria with some of its most lucrative visitor attractions: the castles of Hohenschwangau, Linderhof, Herrenchiemsee, and above all Neuschwanstein, the very essence of a romantic crag-top stronghold. ■

Girls from the Alpine town of Garmisch-Partenkirchen in traditional dress

Munich

München, as the city is known in German, is situated within sight of the Alps. It is a handsome city, happily combining metropolitan facilities and sophisticated lifestyle with a small-town, homey atmosphere, symbolized to perfection by its smoky beer halls and cheerful beer gardens. It may not have quite as many millionaires as Hamburg, but some of its most stylish residents, male and female, are not ashamed to show themselves in city-slicker versions of *Tracht,* the characteristic Bavarian folk costume.

"Eins, zwei, suffe!"—a seasoned drinker makes a toast at the Oktoberfest.

Munich benefited enormously from the presence here of the Wittelsbach family (see p. 281). In addition to the spreading courtyards of their urban stronghold, the Residenz, the Wittelsbachs built out-of-town palaces at Nymphenburg and Schleissheim, decorating and furnishing them regardless of cost. In the 19th century, they turned Munich into one of Europe's great cities, endowing it with stately new suburbs, grandiose public buildings, and galleries of world-class painting and sculpture.

The superlative collections of the Old and New Picture Galleries (Alte and Neue Pinakotheken) continue to draw the crowds, and these have recently been supplemented by the Gallery of Modernism (Pinakothek der Moderne), Germany's largest gallery of 20th century and contemporary art. Art lovers will need more than one stay to see the treasures of

these and the host of other public and private collections and commercial galleries.

There are museums and institutions to suit every taste and interest. With its incomparable technical and scientific exhibits, the Deutsches Museum alone is enough to justify a visit, while other establishments cover the range from A (Anthropology Museum) to Z (the Zoo, one of the finest in Europe).

Visitors come here in huge numbers for the gargantuan Oktoberfest (see pp. 300–301), but festivals and events fill the calendar year-round. The city is maybe at its best in very early summer, when the sun shines brightly (but not too hotly) as you enjoy your half-liter of foaming beer in the shade of the chestnut trees and work up an appetite for a plateful of tasty Munich veal sausages, *Weisswurst*. ■

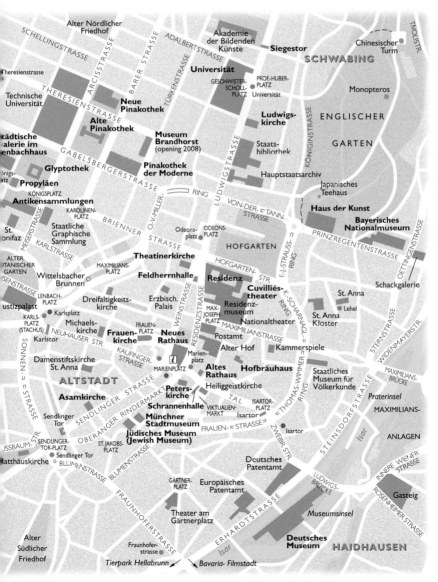

The Old Town

City Hall's barrel-makers strut their stuff as the Glockenspiel comes into action.

WITHIN ITS THREE REMAINING GATEWAYS, ISARTOR, Karlstor, and Sendlinger Tor, Munich's Altstadt is easily explored on foot; in the late 1960s and early 1970s the city led the way in excluding unnecessary traffic and creating an attractive environment for pedestrians. Strolling through the tastefully repaved streets with their fountains, statuary, and immaculately restored buildings is an experience you cannot fail to enjoy.

Munich

🅰 281 E3

Visitor information

www.muenchen-tourist.de

✉ Hauptbahnhof (Main railway station, south side of main entrance), and

✉ Marienplatz

☎ 089 23 39 65 00

Old City Hall (Toy Museum)

🅰 Map p. 283

✉ Marienplatz 15

☎ 089 29 40 01

💲 $

St. Peter's Church

🅰 Map p. 283

✉ Rindermarkt 1

Start in busy **Marienplatz,** named for the Virgin Mary whose lovely gilded statue stands atop the column erected in 1638 in the middle of the square. Throngs of tourists gather here *(at 11 a.m., noon, and, in summer, 5 p.m.)* to admire the **Glockenspiel.** It is set into the main facade of the **New City Hall** (Neues Rathaus), built in mock-Gothic style in the late 19th to early 20th centuries. After the bells of the carillon have played, mechanical figures appear and reenact two events: the traditional coopers' dance originally performed to ward off the plague, and a famous wedding celebrated in the square in 1568. The Rathaus has an elevator that will whisk you most of the way up its 262-foot-high (80 m) tower for a great view of the city.

The **Old City Hall** (Altes Rathaus) on the eastern side of the square is a genuine if much rebuilt Gothic structure; its tower has several floors of toys from times past. A taller tower looms over the square from the south; this is the belfry of Alter Peter ("Old Peter"), more properly known as **St. Peter's Church** (Peterskirche), Munich's oldest place of worship, with a wonderful baroque altar. The catwalk around the top of the tower gives a rooftop panorama, but note there are 306 steps to climb.

Hidden away in the lanes and little streets to the northeast of Marienplatz is the **Hofbräuhaus** (Court Brewery). It was established by Duke Wilhelm V in 1589 with orders to produce a beer to suit his personal palate. Only in the early 19th century were members of the public permitted to share his taste in ale. The cavernous beer hall, with its oompah band and dirndl-clad waitresses bearing an impossible number of giant mugs in both hands, still has its complement of local boozers, but most of the clientele of this famous drinking den now seem to come from other quarters of the globe.

To the west of the square is another obligatory sight: the brick-built **Church of Our Lady** (Frauenkirche), whose twin towers with their domes symbolize the city. From nearby, the scale of the building is almost overwhelming, with improbably tall, slim Gothic

windows soaring skyward. Signs warn you not to stand too close in winter, or you could be caught in minor avalanches of snow and ice cascading from the roof. An elevator takes you up one of the church towers for another view of the city.

To descend from these lofty heights into the belly of the city, walk south from Marienplatz to the **Viktualienmarkt.** This is probably Germany's most lively and colorful food market, its stalls peopled by square-jawed harpies with a great line in Bavarian banter. Don't even think of squeezing the goods or questioning the prices. The produce may not be cheap, but nearly all of it is of excellent quality and a feast for the eye as well as the stomach. There are plenty of places to snack or snatch a drink.

Not far away is the superlative **City Historical Museum** (Münchner Stadtmuseum), where the imaginatively presented exhibits tell the story of the city in fascinating detail. The stars here are the *Moriskentänzer*, wonderfully contorted and expressive figures of dancers carved in the late 15th century, but you also have one of the world's largest collections of musical instruments, a film museum, a marionette museum, a photographic department, and a brewery museum. Nearby on the Sendlinger Strasse stands the baroque **Asamkirche,** a glorious confection of a church named not after a saint, but after the Asam brothers who built it, Egid Quirin (1692–1750) and Cosmas Damian (1686–1739). ■

Munich's
Marienplatz,
center of city life

Church of Our Lady
- ▲ Map p. 283
- ✉ Frauenplatz 1
- ☎ 089 2 90 08 20
- 🕐 Elevator not operating Nov.–March

City Historical Museum
- ▲ Map p. 283
- ✉ St-Jakobs-Platz 1
- ☎ 089 23 32 23 70
- 🕐 Closed Mon.
- 💲 $

A spectacular modern sculpture strides out along Schwabing's Leopoldstrasse.

A walk from the Altstadt to Schwabing

This introduction to the historic core of Munich and its finest open space can be anything from a brisk stroll to a full day's exploration, with plenty of refreshment stops and time to take in some major attractions more fully.

The 14th-century **Charles' Gate** (Karlstor) ❶ and the crescent around it are almost like a piece of stage scenery, encouraging you to enter the old city center with a theatrical spring in your step. Before you stretches **Neuhauser Strasse,** traffic free since the 1970s and so full of activity that you wonder how it ever accommodated trams and cars. Among the delightful and unusual items you pass are the **Brunnenbuberl** (a fountain featuring a satyr and a naked boy) and the **Richard Strauss fountain** (with scenes from the Munich-born composer's opera *Salome).* Commercial buildings mix with noble edifices such as the Civic Hall (Bürgersaal), **St. Michael's Church** (Michaelskirche) ❷, the first Renaissance church of this size north of the Alps, and the Augustinerkirche, now home of the German Museum of Hunting and Fishing (Deutsches Jagd- und Fischereimuseum). Just to the north rise the towers of the great symbol of Munich, the **Frauenkirche** ❸ (see pp. 284–285).

Continue along the pedestrian-only precinct, now named Kaufingerstrasse, into the epicenter of the city, **Marienplatz** ❹.

There's standing room only when the **Glockenspiel** in the City Hall (Rathaus) tower puts on its regular performances (see p. 284). Push through the crowd and turn left onto Dienerstrasse, which runs along the side of the City Hall past, on the right, Dallmayers, one of the country's finest delicatessens. Beyond Max-Joseph-Platz with the Nationaltheater (state opera) and the **Residenz** (see pp. 293–294), Residenzstrasse leads to **Odeonsplatz** ❺,

---

🄰 Also see map pp. 282–283
▶ Karlsplatz
🔁 3 miles (4.5 km)
🕐 Minimum half a day
▶ Leopoldstrasse

NOT TO BE MISSED
- Interior of Michaelskirche
- Rathaus Glockenspiel
- View from the Monopteros
- A beer and pretzel at the Chinesischer Turm
- Watching the action on the Leopoldstrasse

dominated by the graceful three-arched **Commanders' Hall** (Feldherrnhalle; see p. 298) and the swelling, ocher-colored forms of the baroque **Theatinerkirche** (see p. 298).

The café just ahead of you is one of the oldest in Munich. Just by it, a neoclassic archway leads into the arcaded **Hofgarten 6,** the formally laid out Renaissance garden of the Residenz. Cross it diagonally, past the black granite cube commemorating members of the anti-Nazi resistance, and go through the broad underpass to the **Englischer Garten** (see p. 299). Here you could explore the Japanese garden with its teahouse (Japanisches Teehaus), find a cool place by the river channel, or even strip off and enjoy some nude

sunbathing on the meadow! Otherwise keep to the main path and walk up the spiral path to the top of the mound where the temple of the **Monopteros 7** offers a classic panorama of the city skyline rising over the trees.

Back at meadow level, continue a short distance northward to one of the city's liveliest beer gardens, laid out around the pagoda-like **Chinese Tower** (Chinesischer Turm) **8**. From the upper floor a brass band blares out on occasion. A little cheating is now allowed; take the No. 154 bus (every few minutes) two stops to **Leopoldstrasse,** the main artery of the **Schwabing** student district. There are many places here to sit and watch the scene, including the famous Roxy café, before taking the Metro home from Giselastrasse station. ■

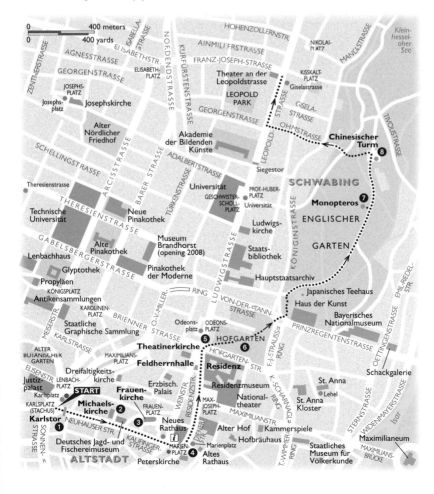

Alte Pinakothek

Alte Pinakothek
www.pinakothek.de
⬛ Map p. 283
✉ Kunstareal München,
Barer Strasse 27
☎ 089 23 80 52 16
🕐 Closed Mon.
💲 $$

MANY OF MUNICH'S FINEST MUSEUMS AND GALLERIES LIE northwest of the Old Town (Altstadt), in the area now called Art Area Munich (Kunstareal München). In the first half of the 19th century, a district of spacious streets and squares was laid out here as a dignified setting for the royal institutions that were to transform Munich into a world-class city of art. The royal collection of old master paintings was given a new home in the purpose-built palace of the Old Picture Gallery, the Alte Pinakothek.

On the upper floor, you can trace the development of **Italian Renaissance art** in Rooms IV–V from its beginnings to the achievements of Botticelli, Raphael, and Titian. Rooms XI and XIIa hold **French works** by Poussin, Claude Lorrain, and a lovely "Nude" by Boucher, and the **Spanish masters** El Greco, Murillo, and Goya hang in Room XIII. There are outstanding paintings by **Flemish and Dutch masters,** particularly Rubens, in Rooms VI–IX, 7–12, and 14–23.

If time is limited, concentrate on the great **German artists** (Rooms II–III), often less well represented in galleries outside Germany. Of several pictures by Dürer, the most striking is the "Self-portrait in a Fur Coat," while an ideal of feminine beauty seems to obsess Lucas Cranach the Elder (1472–1553) in "The Death of Lucretia." No one has depicted the dynamics of human suffering and cruelty with more feeling than Matthias Grünewald in his "Mocking of Christ" (1503), and there are few more evocative depictions of the German forest than Albrecht Altdorfer's tiny picture of "St. George and the Dragon" deep in the beech woods. Altdorfer worked on a grander scale in the "Battle of Alexander" (1529), where countless perfectly painted combatants fight in an apocalyptic landscape. Napoleon liked the picture so much that he confiscated it and hung it in his bathroom! ∎

Among the marvels in the Alte Pinakothek is "Hippopotamus and Crocodile Hunt" (1615–16) by Rubens.

Opposite: Dürer's "Self-portrait in a Fur Coat" (1500) presents the artist in a Christlike guise.

Here is one of the world's great collections of European art from the Middle Ages to the 18th century. Acquired over the centuries by the Wittelsbachs, the paintings are now on show in this Italian Renaissance-style palazzo. Commissioned by Ludwig I in 1822, the palazzo was built by architect Leo von Klenze and restored in the 1990s.

Rooms I–III on the lower floor hold **early German painting,** such as the "Nativity" by Hans Baldung Grien (1484–1545), with its cherubs and farm animals. Works of the Bruegel family occupy Rooms 16–23. Pieter Bruegel the Elder's "Land of Cockayne" fascinates visitors, with its sated guzzlers sleeping off their gluttony in a landscape of roast pigs and boiled eggs on legs.

Albertus Durerus Noricus ipsum me proprijs sic effigebam coloribus ætatis anno XXVIII.

Neue Pinakothek

Neue Pinakothek
www.pinakothek.de

🅰 Map p. 283

✉ Kunstareal München,
Barer Strasse 29

☎ 089 23 80 51 95

🕐 Closed Tues.

💲 $$

THIS 1981 MONUMENTAL CONCRETE, GRANITE, AND sandstone structure, sometimes called the "Palazzo Branca" after its architect Alexander von Branca, more than matches the older buildings in the museum district as a setting for the New Picture Gallery and its fine art. It's worthwhile spending a few minutes strolling around the outside of this outstanding building, set off by fine trees, the modern equivalent of a moat, and some choice sculpture.

Lovis Corinth's (1858–1925) many self-portraits served as self-analyses. This one in the Neue Pinakothek dates from 1914.

The suggested route around the collection takes you in more or less chronological order from late 18th paintings to the work of the French Impressionists. But the emphasis is on German art of the 19th and early 20th centuries. This is the place to admire Romantic works by artists

such as **Caspar David Friedrich** (Room 9), best represented by his picture of the mysteriously fogbound Giant Mountains on the borders of Silesia and Bohemia.

More soberly factual, yet equally compelling, are the carefully composed pictures by **Wilhelm von Kobell** (1766–1853), such as his "Siege of Kosel" of 1808. **Ludwig Richter's** (1803–1884) "Watzmann" (Room 5) contains all the essential ingredients of Alpine scenery, including crashing waterfalls, upland pastures, and rustic peasants. In Room 10a you'll find evocations of small-town life and human eccentricity by **Carl Spitzweg** (1808–1885), among them the "Poor Poet" and the "Nightly Round," in which a pot-bellied officer leads the members of his platoon through the dusk of an obviously law-abiding little place.

In contrast are large history and landscape paintings (Rooms 12, 13, 14/14a) by, for example, **Karl von Piloty** (1826–1886). There are interesting works by German contemporaries of the French Impressionists in Rooms 17–20: Take time to look at pictures such as realist **Wilhelm Leibl's** (1844–1900) "Interior with Peasants," and the cheerful "Munich Beer Garden" by leader of the German Impressionists **Max Liebermann** (1847–1935). But don't let yourself be seduced by **Franz von Stuck's** snake-entwined, extremely sexy "Sin." ∎

Pinakothek der Moderne

OPENED IN 2002, THE GALLERY OF MODERNISM IS THE country's largest gallery of modern and contemporary art, a conscious rival to the Centre Pompidou in Paris and London's Tate Modern. A superb new home for several previously separate collections, it has been designed to act as an architectural link between the city center and the buildings and squares of the museum district.

This latest of the Pinakotheken may have a bland exterior, but few visitors quibble with its cool, elegant display spaces, all wonderfully lit by natural light. The core of the building is a 46-ft (14 m) rotunda, celebrating the unity in diversity of the arts.

The main collection is that of the **Bavarian State Gallery of Modern Art** (Staatsgalerie Moderner Kunst), a world-class array of 20th- and 21st-century painting, sculpture, photography, new media, and installations. It is rich in paintings by German artists of the early 20th century, such as Max Beckmann, Wassily Kandinsky, and Paul Klee. There are also works by surrealists, such as Magritte, examples of American abstract expressionism, minimal and concept art, an Andy Warhol collection, video works, and a huge installation by Joseph Beuys entitled "The End of the Twentieth Century."

The vast number of items assembled in the gallery's **New Collection** (Neue Sammlung) is claimed to be the most comprehensive collection of design and craft objects in the world. Among the treasures of the **Architecture Museum** (Architekturmuseum) are original drawings by Frank Lloyd Wright, as well as countless photographs and 500 models tracing the development of recent and contemporary architecture.

Finally, the **Bavarian State Graphic Collection** (Staatliche Graphische Sammlung) comprises an outstanding array of more than 400,000 drawings and prints from the 15th century to the present day.

In a sleek new gallery being built next door, the **Museum Brandhorst** will focus on ultramodern and abstract artworks. Completion is scheduled for 2008. ■

Pinakothek der Moderne
www.pinakothek.de

🅰 Map p. 283
✉ Kunstareal München, Barer Strasse 40
☎ 089 23 80 53 60
🕐 Closed Mon.
$ $$$

Colorful lights illuminate the exterior of the Pinakothek der Moderne, the work of Munich architect Stephan Braunfels.

Königsplatz

SURROUNDED BY THE NEOCLASSIC BUILDINGS THAT proclaim Munich as an "Athens on the Isar," this square was laid out in the mid-19th century as the focal point of the museum district.

While still Crown Prince, Ludwig I had set about collecting Greek and Roman sculpture, which was housed in Leo von Klenze's porticoed **Glyptothek** (1830), open to the public from the outset. One of the most moving pieces in the museum is the "Barberini Faun" (ca 220 B.C.), a study of a youngster overcome by drowsiness. Others range from figures controversially acquired from the Aphaia Temple

"Tiger" by Franz Marc (1880–1916), killed in World War I

of Aegina (fifth century B.C.) to busts of Roman notables.

Opposite the Glyptothek is the building that now houses the **State Collections of Greek & Roman Antiquities** (Antikensammlungen). Its displays of Greek vases are hardly equaled elsewhere, and there are also fine Roman and Etruscan ceramics and jewelry.

The most striking structure on the square is Klenze's **Propyläen**

gateway, modeled on one guarding the approach to the Acropolis at Athens and completed in 1862. The relief sculptures evoke the Greek wars of independence and commemorate the accession to the Greek throne of Otto, Ludwig's son.

Under the Nazis the square was turned into a parade ground and location for mass ceremonies. A building at the eastern end of the square, now the College of Music, was the scene in 1938 of the signing of the Munich Agreement, which delivered up the Sudetenland to Hitler and sealed the fate of independent Czechoslovakia.

To the northwest of the Propyläen is the **City Gallery in the Lenbach House** (Städtische Galerie im Lenbachhaus). Built in 1889 as residence and studio by the successful society portraitist Franz von Lenbach, the Florentine villa is set in an authentic-looking Italian garden. The gallery presents the story of painting in Munich from the 18th century onward. Among the most appealing pictures are droll scenes of small-town life by Carl Spitzweg, together with landscapes with figures by the relatively little-known Wilhelm von Kobell; and there are, of course, portraits by Lenbach. But the gallery's great draw are works by members of the Blauer Reiter group, like-minded artists who, before World War I, burst through convention and laid the foundations of expressionism. There are many colorful canvases by their leader, Wassily Kandinsky (1866–1944), here, and works by Paul Klee, Franz Marc, August Macke, and Alexei Jawlensky. ■

The Residenz

MUNICH'S RESIDENZ, SET AROUND SEVEN COURTYARDS IN the northeastern part of the Old Town (Altstadt), demonstrates the power, wealth, and taste of Bavaria's Wittelsbach rulers. Employing the best architects, designers, and decorators, they built and rebuilt their palace over the centuries, lavishly decorating it and filling it with the results of their collecting mania. Successful restoration after World War II bomb damage conceals the fact that much of the Residenz is a re-creation. Fortunately, most of the contents, including the interior of the Cuvilliéstheater, had been taken to safety.

The Elector's box is the focal point of the ornate auditorium in the Cuvilliéstheater, named after its architect, a former court jester.

In 1385 the Wittelsbachs moved from their old home, the Alter Hof, to the Residenz, then a moated fortress on the edge of town. Two hundred years later, under Duke Albrecht V, it was a setting for courtly life rather than a fortress. In 1568 Albrecht ordered the construction of the **Antiquarium,** one of the largest, most extravagant Renaissance interiors north of the Alps. Its tunnel vault pierced by window openings allows natural light to illuminate the collection of antique sculpture. It is decorated with fantastical frescoes and views of Bavarian scenes to remind the

rulers of their realm. Outside, the **Grotto Courtyard** (Grottenhof), presided over by a bronze Perseus fountain, was completed in 1581.

By the early 17th century, the Wittelsbachs were electors of the Holy Roman Empire, and Elector Maximilian I celebrated by creating a series of magnificent interiors around the Imperial Courtyard (Kaiserhof); these include the splendid **Imperial Chamber** (Kaisersaal), a great hall designed for the most prestigious state occasions. There were further extensions and much remodeling in the 18th century.

Residenz
www.residenz-muenchen.de
- Map p. 283
- Residenzstrasse 1
- 089 29 06 71
- $$ (single tour), $$$ (combined tour)

Chapel, Reliquary Room, Silver Room, Stone Room, and Imperial Chamber.

TREASURY

Many of the treasures assembled by the Wittelsbachs over the centuries can be seen in the Treasury (Schatzkammer), one of the finest such collections of precious objects in the world. Among the most venerable items is an *altar ciborium*, made a thousand years before the Bavarian crown jewels and commissioned from Napoleon's Parisian goldsmith in 1806.

CUVILLIÉSTHEATER

Cuvilliés' greatest achievement was the court theater, which now immortalizes his name. Closed for a refurbishment until the spring of 2008, the Cuvilliéstheater is a jewel casket in red, white, and ivory, encapsulating in architectural form the rigors of court etiquette, with seating according to the exact rank and social status of the audience. The centerpiece is not really the stage, but the electors' box facing it from the far end of the auditorium. In this sublime space Mozart's opera *Idomeneo* was given its first performance in 1781. The building could be used for more than performances, since its floor could be raised to create a magnificent ballroom.

The final large-scale extensions to the Residenz were made after Ludwig I acceded to the throne in 1825. Ludwig's architect, Leo von Klenze, added wings to north (the Festsaalbau facing the Hofgarten) and south (the Königsbau facing Max-Joseph-Platz). Klenze was also responsible for the apartments reserved for Ludwig and his queen, some of which are decorated with dramatic murals based on the Nibelung legends. ■

Stone guardian of Bavaria's royal Residenz, ancestral seat of the Wittelsbach family

To reinforce the status of his line, Elector Karl Albrecht commissioned 121 family portraits, even including such "ancestors" as the great Charlemagne. The pictures are displayed in the **Ancestors' Gallery** (Ahnengalerie), a rococo version of the Antiquarium with much stuccowork and elaborate carving. The equally sumptuous **Rich Rooms** (Reiche Zimmer) and **Green Gallery** (Grüne Galerie) are also in rococo style. These were largely the work of François Cuvilliés, Elector Maximilian III Joseph's court dwarf, who doubled as architect and interior designer.

Following the demise of the monarchy in 1918, the complex passed to the Bavarian state and much is now open to the public. The Residenzmuseum entrance is on Max-Joseph-Platz, and you need to join two tours to take everything in. On the morning tour you may see the Ancestors' Gallery, Antiquarium, State Rooms, and the Royal Apartments, while the afternoon tour may visit the Porcelain Rooms, Court

Deutsches Museum

ON ITS ISLAND SITE BETWEEN TWO ARMS OF THE RIVER Isar, this enormous and interactive museum of science and technology is one of the most popular visitor attractions in the country and the most visited museum in Munich.

At every turn there are chances to press a button, set a model in motion, watch a film, or take part in a demonstration.

Children will not want to tear themselves away, and even when closing time comes, the well stocked gift shop stays open another hour.

The floor plan on p. 296 may help you decide priorities. Details of daily demonstrations and film showings are given in the foyer, and you could use these as a starting point to structure your visit.

The museum was the brainchild of visionary engineer Oskar von Miller. In 1903 he founded an association to showcase the "masterpieces of science and technology" to enlighten and stimulate the public. Kaiser Wilhelm II laid the foundation stone of the museum in 1904, but the great institution opened only in 1925. Since then its buildings have become one of Munich's landmarks, not least the distinctive tower overlooking the Isar, complete with barometer.

There are a number of highlights you should not miss. The **Aeronautics Halls** on the first and second floors are filled with flying machines, such as Otto Lilienthal's revolutionary gliders, and the monoplanes and biplanes (even triplanes!) that fought above the trenches from 1914 to 1918. There are fighters from World War II as well, among them the first jet aircraft to go into combat, the Messerschmitt 262.

Everybody thrills to the 800,000-volt flash of lightning produced in the **Electrical Power** department in Hall 9, first floor, even if it lasts for only two microseconds. In the

A 1932 Junkers Ju-52 is just one of more than 50 original airplanes on display in the Aeronautics Halls of the Deutsches Museum.

Deutsches Museum
www.deutsches-museum.de
🅰 Map p. 283
✉ Museumsinsel 1
☎ 089 2 17 91
💲 $$

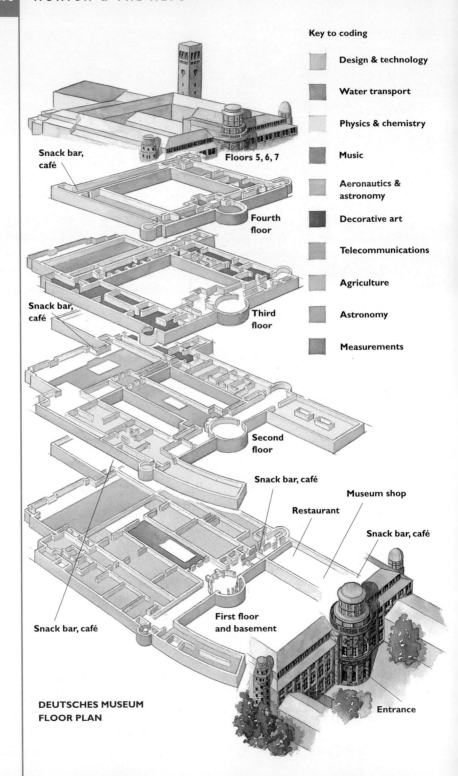

Key to coding

Design & technology

Water transport

Physics & chemistry

Music

Aeronautics & astronomy

Decorative art

Telecommunications

Agriculture

Astronomy

Measurements

Snack bar, café

Floors 5, 6, 7

Fourth floor

Snack bar, café

Third floor

Second floor

Snack bar, café

Restaurant

Museum shop

Snack bar, café

Snack bar, café

First floor and basement

Entrance

DEUTSCHES MUSEUM FLOOR PLAN

Power Machinery room you can see a working reproduction of Diesel's first engine (1897) and some early motors by Gottlieb Daimler. The basement holds a popular **reconstruction of a mine,** calling up gritty images of Germany's industrial revolution. You can see Germany's very first submarine, the U1, in the **Navigation Department** or peer into the crowded interior of a late 19th-century emigrant boat, lit by kerosene lamps.

On the second level, the **Musical Instruments** section has a "Phonolizt," a player piano contraption with violins, and some of the first synthesizers. The sound booths allow you to listen to simulations of famous concerts and analyze your own voice. Then it's up through the remaining floors to **Astronautics** and **Technical Toys** on the third, **Telecommunications** on the fourth, the **Planetarium** on the seventh and much, much more.

The museum's rolling stock has been shifted to the **German Transport Museum** (Deutsches Verkehrszentrum), an airy, ever-expanding gallery in a historic former trade fair hall overlooking the Theresienwiese. Among the **railway vehicles** on display, the pioneering *Puffing Billy* of 1814 contrasts with the resplendent green locomotives of the Royal Bavarian Railways built a century later, which hauled the Rhinegold Express. Germany was in the forefront of electric traction, although the first electric locomotive of 1879 looks more like a mobile park bench. The **motor vehicles** section is stuffed with gems including the Benz Motorwagen of 1886, the first motor vehicle powered by a gasoline engine and the forerunner of today's automobiles. Only a hundred or so models were made of the gorgeous 1929 Mercedes-Benz Tourenwagen Super-Sport, and for sheer oddity you can't beat the weird Krupp three-wheeled street-cleaner of around the same time. The small fry will enjoy the pint-sized **indoor racetrack** where the roadsters are made from toy kits cobbled together by the intrepid racers themselves. ∎

A large fishing boat is one of the seafaring vessels on display at the popular and eclectic Deutsches Museum.

German Transport Center

- 🅰 Map p. 296
- ✉ Theresienhöhe 14a
- ☎ 089 217 95 29
- 💲 $
- 🚇 U-Bahn: Schwanthaler Höhe

North of the Altstadt

The Feldherrnhalle and the Theatinerkirche frame the twin towers of the Frauenkirche.

MUCH OF THE VIBRANT LIFE OF MUNICH'S CITY CENTER IS in the area beyond the Residenz, where elegant Ludwigstrasse heads north toward the old suburb of Schwabing. A variety of establishments serves this fashionable area's highly variegated population, from antiquarian bookshops to experimental galleries, and there are cafés, "alternative" eating places, and every possible kind of bar. To the east of Ludwigstrasse stretches one of Europe's great urban parks.

House of Art

📍 Map p. 283

✉ Prinzregentenstrasse 1

☎ 089 21 12 70 or 089 21 12 71 13

💲 $

Bayerisches Nationalmuseum

📍 Map p. 283

✉ Prinzregentenstrasse 3

☎ 089 2 11 24 01

🕐 Closed Mon.

💲 $

From Odeonsplatz, beside the Residenz, **Ludwigstrasse** runs north. Named after that indefatigable city improver King Ludwig I, whose statue stands on the western side of Odeonsplatz, Ludwigstrasse is the grandest thoroughfare in Munich. At its southern end stand the three great arches of the **Commanders' Hall** (Feldherrnhalle). Modeled on the famous Loggia dei Lanzi in Florence, it was built on Ludwig's orders to honor the Bavarian army and its generals. History remembers it more as the focus of Hitler's failed Putsch in 1923, when the march he was leading was dispersed by rifle-fire from the police. After the Nazis' rise to power it became a place of sacred memory. Anti-Nazis would avoid giving the obligatory

raised-arm salute by detouring through little Viscardigasse, henceforth known as Shirkers' Alley.

West of the Feldherrnhalle rises the resplendent baroque **Theatinerkirche,** one of Munich's best-loved places of worship. The church is named after the order of Theatine monks founded in the 16th century to oppose Lutheranism. A landmark with its bold ocher facade, dome, and twin towers, it was built to celebrate the birth of a son and heir in 1662 to the Bavarian Elector, and the gorgeously decorated interior surely reflects the parents' joy.

Farther north on Ludwigstrassse, the Theatinerkirche's towers are echoed by the twin towers of the **Ludwigskirche,** a sober church of 1844. Inside, the mural painting of the "Last Judgement" by Peter Cornelius (1783–1867) is only exceeded in size by Michelangelo's treatment of the same subject in the Vatican's Sistine Chapel. The church's neighbor to the south is the immensely long Bavarian State Library (Staatsbibliothek). To the north, where Ludwigstrasse opens out into a kind of forum with fountains, is the **University,** one of the biggest in Germany, transferred from Landshut (see pp. 277–278) by Ludwig I in 1826. Among those who have taught within its walls have been physicist Wilhelm Konrad Röntgen, discoverer of X-rays, the groundbreaking 19th-century chemist Justus von Liebig,

humanist philosopher Ludwig Andreas Feuerbach, and sociologist and political economist Max Weber. Its most famous students were the members of the White Rose, a brave little group of anti-Nazi activists executed in 1943. The **Siegestor** arch, topped by four lions, makes a fitting climax to Ludwigstrasse.

A busy road cuts across Ludwigstrasse just north of the Residenz, becoming to the east **Prinzregentenstrasse.** The last royal boulevard to be built in Munich, it was laid out in the 1890s on the orders of Luitpold, the Prince Regent. Its once pleasing relationship with the Englischer Garten was spoiled when the **House of Art** (Haus der Kunst) was built in typical Third Reich style in the 1930s. Once the home

of the State Gallery of Modern Art (now in the Pinakothek der Moderne), it is used for major temporary exhibitions. Its much jollier neighbor, in an exuberant variety of styles, is the **Bayerisches Nationalmuseum,** Bavaria's state museum of arts and crafts from the Middle Ages to the 19th century. The lovingly carved Nativity scenes are a highlight.

East of Ludwigstrasse and north of Prinzregentenstrasse, the beautiful **Englischer Garten,** 3 miles (5 km) long and covering just over 1,000 acres (417 ha), was laid out in the 18th century. Today people come here from all over the city, to breathe fresh air, to row a boat, ride a bike or horse, to enjoy a drink in the huge beer garden, or to strip off for an all-over tan. ∎

Englischer Garten sunbathers cool off in the Iser.

Oktoberfest

"*Eins, zwei, suffe*"—roughly, "One, two, swallow"—is the joyous refrain of the best-known Bavarian drinking song. You're likely to hear it more than once if you attend what is claimed to be the biggest folk festival in the world. The Oktoberfest in fact begins on the last Saturday in September and lasts for 16 beery days into October. Over six million drinkers pour into the city, cramming into the tents set up on the great meadow known as the Theresienwiese and consuming vast quantities of beer and nearly half a million roast chickens, 200,000 pairs of sausages, 105,000 pounds (47,700 kg) of fish, a hundred oxen, over half a million pork knuckles and an incalculable number of pretzels. And it's all accompanied by the blare and thump of the raucous brass bands called *Blaskapellen*.

Like so much else that is characteristic of Munich, all this can be blamed on King Ludwig I. In 1810, while still Crown Prince, he marked his marriage to Princess Therese von Sachsen-Hildburghausen by inviting the citizenry to celebrations. These culminated in a horse race in what was then open country-side, but was subsequently named "Theresa's Meadow" in the bride's honor. The festivities became an annual event, expanding to include fairground attractions … and an ever growing consumption of beer.

Nowadays things begin on the opening Saturday with a parade of splendidly bedecked horse-drawn wagons carrying brewery land-lords, brass bands, and dirndl-clad waitresses. On the stroke of noon, the Lord Mayor of Munich broaches the first barrel with a cry of "*O'zapft is!*" (Bavarian for "It's tapped!"). In the evening there is a folklore concert that serves as a warm-up for another, much bigger procession the following day. This is the International Costume and Riflemen's Parade, which winds through the city center to the Theresienwiese in a seemingly never ending succession of spectacularly costumed bands,

mountain marksmen, jesters, folklore groups, and carriages drawn by horses, oxen, and goats. Once the parade has reached its destination, the fortnight's drinking can really get under way, presided over by the statue of "Bavaria," a 100-foot-high (30 m) bronze figure of a female clad in a bearskin.

The Oktoberfest is still a quin-tessentially Bavarian celebration, and the majority of your fellow drinkers will be shouting in a dialect that even other Germans find incomprehensible. The beer tents are no place for the fainthearted:

The benches are packed, the noise level is high, and the exuberance increases as the evening advances. If you consider venturing on to any of the fairground's white-knuckle rides, you are strongly advised to consider the state of your stomach—even though Bavarian beer is not particularly strong.

The city fills up for the Oktoberfest. If you intend to come, book accommodations well in advance, and think seriously about reserving a seat for the Saturday evening folklore concert, or a grandstand place for the opening ceremony and the great Sunday parade *(München Ticket GmbH, Postfach 201413, 80014 München, tel 089 54 81 81 81).* ■

Below: The Bavarian national colors, blue and white, bedeck one of the Oktoberfest's huge beer tents. Right: Brass band

The modest
baroque exterior
of Schloss
Nymphenburg
fronts formal
gardens and a
picturesque lake.

Schloss Nymphenburg

THIS PALACE ON THE WESTERN OUTSKIRTS OF MUNICH
was originally conceived as a hunting lodge and later expanded on a
grand scale to become an embodiment of the Bavarian rulers' status
and style. While its exterior is fashioned in a subdued baroque style,
the interior features rococo colors and flamboyant frescoes that are a
delight to the eye. And don't miss a tour of the 500-acre (200 ha)
park, a virtual history of landscape gardening.

**Schloss
Nymphenburg**

🅰 281 E3

✉ Schloss- und
Gartenverwaltung
Nymphenburg

☎ 089 17 90 80

💲 $$ (combined ticket
for all buildings)

The Schloss is easily accessible from
Munich's center by U-Bahn and
tram. As you arrive from the east,
Nymphenburg is a long line of har-
moniously related buildings facing
a formal lake and a semicircular
road bordered with what were once
the residences of court officials. The
central palace building grew out of
a much smaller structure of 1664, a

cubelike summer residence erected,
like the Theatinerkirche in town, to
celebrate the birth to Electress
Henriette Adelaide of a son, Max
Emanuel. On his accession to
power, Max enlarged the building,
endowing it with the **Steinerner
Saal,** one of Germany's most
opulent rococo interiors.

The most popular interior

feature was added later, by Ludwig I; his **Schönheitengalerie,** with its portraits of three dozen lovely ladies, was intended to present a definitive view of ideal femininity. It was no coincidence that it included a picture of Lola Montez, the "Spanish dancer" whose affair with the king forced his abdication.

THE PARK

From the double stairway on the palace's far side you can enjoy a view of Nymphenburg's park. A French-style parterre occupies the foreground while a rectilinear canal leads the eye into the far distance. These are remnants of the original geometrical garden. In the early 19th century it was re-landscaped in the informal English style, with winding pathways, serpentine lakes, and "naturalistic" planting.

The **Amalienburg,** a perfectly proportioned miniature rococo palace by Cuvilliés, is to the left. The interior, especially the Hall of Mirrors, is a masterpiece of rococo fantasy, with writhing silver stuccowork running riot everywhere. Beyond is the **Badenburg,** built to house a lavishly decorated heated indoor swimming pool. North of the canal is the **Pagodenburg,** containing exquisite interiors reflecting European courtly interest in chinoiserie. Max Emanuel built the Pagodenburg with parties in mind, but the later **Magdalenenklause** reflects the aging ruler's preoccupation with more serious matters. It is an artificial ruin, designed for the contemplation of mortality and eternal verities. Alas, poor Max died before it was completed.

The central palace buildings are flanked by two quadrangles. The one to the south, the **Marstall,** was built as the stables. It now houses the gorgeous vehicles used by the Wittelsbachs to transport themselves around their domains

Right: Ludwig II's gilded carriage on show in the Marstall

Museum Mensch und Natur

✉ Schloss Nymphenburg

☎ 089 179 58 90

🕐 Closed Mon.

$ $

and bedazzle their subjects. In winter sleighs were used; one of the most spectacular examples here is a fabulous rococo creation of 1740, although it is rivaled by those made for "Mad" King Ludwig more than a century later. The state coaches are even more stylish, notably the

one made in Paris for Elector Karl Albrecht when he was promoted to Holy Roman Emperor in 1742.

Nymphenburg's delicate porcelain is deservedly famous. The Marstall's upper rooms contain more than a thousand examples made between the 1740s and the 1920s. Some of the most appealing are the winsome, witty figures from the Italian Commedia dell'Arte created in the mid-18th century. A very different museum occupies the buildings of the northern quadrangle; the **Museum Mensch und Natur** uses multimedia and hands-on techniques to tell the tale of Earth history and mankind's evolution.

If you still have time and energy, visit the adjacent **Botanischer Garten,** one of Europe's finest botanical collections. ∎

More places to visit in Munich

BMW MUSEUM
The gleaming metallic BMW headquarters building in the shape of a four-cylinder engine has been a Munich landmark since the 1970s. At its foot, the famous automobile manufacturer has installed its museum in an equally

An artist's rendering of Munich's new BMW Museum, opening in 2007.

distinctive structure, a great silver chalice. No expense has been spared to create an exhibit with the same standard of technical excellence as the vehicles themselves, with all kinds of presentational wizardry to repeat the message of mobility as progress. While the museum is closed for improvements (until mid-2007), there's a modest display in the Olympiapark. ⚑ Map p. 282 ✉ Petuelring 130 ☎ 089 38 22 33 07

DACHAU
In Renaissance times, the Wittelsbachs built a summer castle in this pretty town 12 miles (19 km) northwest of Munich. In the 19th century an artists' colony thrived here, attracted by the picturesque streets and the special light effects of the countryside around. Later, ordinary Munich residents would take the

suburban train and escape the city's stuffy air in these peaceful surroundings. In March 1933 the rural idyll was grotesquely interrupted when the Nazis built their first concentration camp just outside the town. It is now a memorial to the tens of thousands that suffered and died here, and a tour of the site with its execution ground, crematoria, rebuilt barracks, and museum is an experience not easily forgotten. ⚑ 281 E4 ✉ Alter Römerstrasse 75, Dachau ☎ 08131 66 99 70 🚃 S-Bahn 2

OLYMPIAPARK
The Oberwiesenfeld on the northern edge of town was originally a parade ground for the Bavarian army, then the site of Munich's first airport. In 1972, after being relandscaped and linked to the Metro, it hosted the 20th Summer Olympics, leaving the city with a new park and superb sporting and recreational facilities. The 69,250-seat stadium, the Olympic Hall, and the swimming pool sit beneath a tentlike transparent roof tethered by cables (tel 089 30 67 27 07, tours). For an incomparable panorama that on a good day takes in a 250-mile (400 km) sweep of the Alps, ride the elevator to the viewing platform of the 950-foot (290 m) Olympic Tower. ⚑ 281 E3 🚃 U-Bahn 3

SCHLEISSHEIM
Nine miles (15 km) north of Munich await the village of Schleissheim and the palace and park complex of Schloss Schleissheim. Behind the long facade of the **Neues Schloss** (Max-Emanuel-Platz, Oberschleissheim, tel 089 3 15 87 20) are sumptuous interiors and dozens of first-rate baroque paintings. The smaller **Altes Schloss** houses a collection of religious folk art, while at the far end of the gardens **Schloss Lustheim** is now the setting for a collection of mostly 18th-century Meissen porcelain.

Nearby **Flugwerft Schleissheim** is an airfield dating back to the days when Bavaria had its own air force (Effnerstrasse 18, Oberschleissheim, tel 089 3 15 71 40), where 50 or so historic aircraft are on display. ⚑ 281 E4 $ $ 🚃 S-Bahn 1 to Oberschleissheim ■

The Alps

Germany possesses only a small section of the Alps, a relatively narrow strip running the 200 miles or so (300 km) from the Berchtesgadener *Land* in the east through the Allgäuer Alpen in Bavarian Swabia to the Bodensee (Lake Constance) in the west. But, rising from the Bavarian lowlands, this band of mountains has a dramatic impact out of proportion to its height, which nowhere quite breaks the 9,840-foot (3,000 m) barrier.

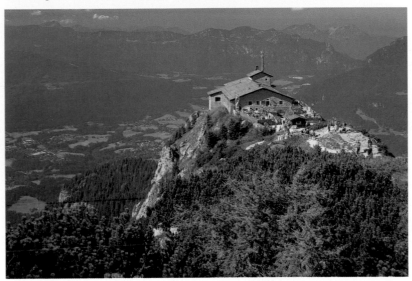

The "Eagle's Nest" perches on the summit of the Kehlstein, high above Berchtesgaden.

When the weather is clear, the mountains form a continuous rocky ridge, a marvelous backdrop to the swelling hills of the Pre-Alps, with their forests, pastures, and glittering lakes. A trip by rack railway or cable car to the top of Germany's highest mountain, the Zugspitze (9,718 feet/2,962 m), is as exciting an experience as any in the Alps.

Not every mountain is as accessible as the Zugspitze. A cable railway was proposed for the country's second highest peak, the mighty Watzmann (8,901 feet/2,713 m) above Berchtesgaden. The outrage this caused among environmentalists and others led to the creation of the Berchtesgaden National Park (Nationalpark Berchtesgaden), which protects much of the finest landscape in this far southeastern corner of Bavaria, including the Königssee, the lake with the least polluted water in Germany.

The best way to taste the pleasures of the Bavarian Alps to the full is to hike some of the hundreds of miles of waymarked footpaths. There are walks for the after-lunch stroller as well as the experienced hill walker wanting a high-level hike of several days. A number of recognized routes cater to the latter, some of them requiring familiarity with ropes, although the Heilbronner Weg in the Allgäu is an exception. Local visitor information centers will have good maps of their areas.

The Bavarian Alps are not a remote or isolated region. Attractive towns, villages, and mountain resorts crowd around the foot of the mountains. From ancient times, busy trade routes penetrated the Alps, linking central Europe with the Mediterranean and the cities of Italy. Their equivalents today are the electrified railroads and autobahns that have made the Alps more accessible than ever. ■

Royal castles

THE OBSESSIVELY ROMANTIC VISION OF THE MIDDLE AGES held by Ludwig II, the "Dream King," still captures the imagination today. More than a million visitors a year make the pilgrimage to his spectacularly sited Schloss Neuschwanstein, prototype of all theme park castles, together with neighboring Schloss Hohenschwangau.

Schloss Hohenschwangau & Schloss Neuschwanstein
www.ticket-center-hohenschwangau.de
▲ 280 C2
✉ Ticketcenter Hohenschwangau, Alpseestrasse 12
☎ 08362 93 08 30
💲 $$$$. Both castles: guided tours only. Available in English

Intense and eccentric, King Ludwig II was also called the "Dream King."

Visit Hohenschwangau first: Its impact is less dramatic than that of Neuschwanstein, and it makes sense to save the best for last. The great popularity of Neuschwanstein causes congestion, and you may have quite a long wait between finding a space for your car in one of the parking areas, buying your timed ticket in the pavilion in the village, and beginning your visit. Schloss Hohenschwangau is a 15-minute walk west from the pavilion, Neuschwanstein a stiff 25-minute hike up the hill opposite. You can take a bus or horse-drawn carriage.

HOHENSCHWANGAU

Near the old town of Füssen just over 60 miles (100 km) southwest of Munich, the Ammergebirge mountains separate Bavaria from Austrian Tyrol. The approach to this Alpine frontier was guarded by a string of medieval castles, among them Schwanstein, the stronghold of the Schwangau knights, on a wooded knoll. A ruin by the 1830s, it was rebuilt between 1832 and 1836 by Crown Prince Maximilian in a style influenced by an idealized view of Gothic and Tudor England, and renamed Hohenschwangau (High Schwangau).

For all the medievalism of Hohenschwangau, with its wall paintings of troubadours and chivalrous deeds and repeated swan motifs, it has a lived-in feeling about it. It was, indeed, often in use as a Wittelsbach family residence. Young Ludwig spent much of his childhood here, and it was at Hohenschwangau that a meeting with Richard Wagner led to friendship. You can see the piano on

"Mad" King Ludwig (1845–1886)

The handsome Ludwig came to the throne at the early age of 18. His propensity to prefer dreams to reality was reinforced by disastrous misjudgments in the complex events leading to German unification, with Bavaria giving way to Prussia on all counts. Thereafter Ludwig turned away from affairs of state and concentrated on realizing his fantasies. At Neuschwanstein these were inspired by Wagner's operas and his own idealized view of the Middle Ages. His castles at Linderhof and Herrenchiemsee (see p. 316) drew on his fascination for the extravagant age of Louis XIV in France. In 1886, increasingly concerned by Ludwig's neglect of his duties, his squandering of the royal resources, and his ever more eccentric personal behavior, the Bavarian government finally acted; Ludwig was declared insane, arrested, and taken from Neuschwanstein to Schloss Berg on Lake Starnberg south of Munich. Two days later he was dead, drowned together with his psychiatrist in the waters of the lake. To this day the manner of his death remains a mystery. ∎

which they played together in the Hohenstaufensaal, along with items of their correspondence. Ludwig's bedroom ceiling reproduced the night sky, and from here he could watch the progress of work on his dream castle on the crag far above.

NEUSCHWANSTEIN

In a wildly romantic location, Neuschwanstein crowns a rock spur above the deep Pöllat gorge, with its plunging waterfall, eroding cliffs, and primeval forest. You can immerse yourself in this wilderness by walking to the **Marienbrücke,** a footbridge spanning the torrent nearly 300 feet (100 m) below. Ludwig would come here at night to gaze at his castle, having previously ordered its lights to be illuminated, and it is the point from which the building and its setting can best be appreciated. The castle appears to grow out of the rock, its solid mass broken by fantastical crenelated towers, turrets, oriel windows, and various projections.

Work began on the castle in 1869, and Ludwig found inspiration for its creation, notably the **Minstrels' Hall,** in the Wartburg (see p. 222), supposedly the setting for the singers' contest in Wagner's opera *Tannhäuser.* The *Lohengrin* story is alluded to in the swan motifs in the sitting room. The Byzantine **Throne Room** is modeled on the Court Chapel in the Munich Residenz. In the end, however, it is a rather melancholic place; having more or less emptied the royal coffers to build it, Ludwig spent less than six months here. ■

Schloss Neuschwanstein, in all its faux-medieval glory, perches on an Alpine crag.

Berchtesgaden

RINGED BY MOUNTAIN PEAKS, THE LITTLE TOWN OF Berchtesgaden sits on a natural balcony overlooking an idyllic valley. In the surrounding area you'll find some of the most glorious sights in the Bavarian Alps, foremost among them the fjordlike Königssee in the shadow of towering Watzmann, Germany's second highest summit.

Coming to this mountain fastness from the north is almost like entering another country—not surprising, when you remember that for centuries the Berchtesgadener region was an independent state. Augustinian priors first settled the valley in the 12th century and later grew rich on the proceeds of the local salt mines. Their successors ruled the little state.

After 1810, when their domain joined Bavaria, Berchtesgaden became a favorite summer retreat for the Bavarian royal family. Others followed them, especially when a rail line was opened in 1888, and today it is one of Germany's most popular vacation spots, attracting crowds in summer and winter.

A good place to take in the panorama from Berchtesgaden is the garden of the **Nationalpark-Haus,** the interpretive center of Berchtesgaden National Park. Much of the sublime landscape visible from here is protected. An outer area of farmland and forest continues to be managed under strict environmental regulations, while in the inner, core area, natural processes are being allowed to take their course. Visit the National Park House for information about the area's heritage, its extraordinarily rich and varied wildlife, and its almost endless possibilities for walks or more challenging hikes.

A stroll through the attractive streets of old painted houses will bring you to the town's showpiece, the **Schlossplatz.** Facing the

sturdy arcaded building on the left are the church and priors' residence from the old monastery, parts of which are from the 12th century. The residence is now the **Königliches Schloss,** from 1923 until 1933 the home of Crown Prince Ruprecht, head of the deposed Bavarian royal family. Items from the Wittelsbach collections—paintings, sculptures, carvings, furniture, hunting trophies, and weapons—are attractively displayed here.

The town's other great attraction is the **Salzbergwerk,** the underground salt works on which Berchtesgaden's early prosperity was founded and which is still in operation. Clad in traditional miner's garb, you whiz underground on a heart-stopping but perfectly safe slide, explore galleries and grottoes, and are rafted across a sparkling salt lake.

The classic Berchtesgaden experience is a trip on the **Königssee** into the heart of the mountains. A silently gliding, electrically powered launch slips through the clear water to the endearing and much-photographed little church of **St. Bartholomä.** You can disembark here and stroll by the lakeside or take a two-hour walk up to the **Ice Chapel** at the foot of the east face of the Watzmann. A farther ride on the boat brings you close to the southern tip of the lake, from where a short walk leads up to the tiny lake of Obersee and the 1,542-foot

Berchtesgaden

⛰ 281 G2

Visitor information

✉ Königsseer Strasse 2

☎ 08652 96 70

Nationalpark-Haus

✉ Franziskanerplatz 7

☎ 08652 6 43 43

(470 m) Röthbach waterfall.

The name of Berchtesgaden is associated with the Berghof, Hitler's mountain chalet on the **Obersalzberg,** one of the foothills of the 6,017-foot (1,834 m) **Kehlstein.** The future Führer first came here in 1923, and it was later an alternative headquarters to Berlin. Here the carefully stage-managed fiction of a genial, friendly Hitler, a man of the people, was evolved. However, as the security zone around the chalet was steadily extended, many locals were forced to leave their property at ludicrously low prices. Allied bombers destroyed the malignant complex in the last days of the war, and most of the remains were blown up in the 1950s. In 1999 an excellent information center, the **Dokumentation**

Obersalzberg *(Salzbergstrasse 41, tel 08652 94 79 60, closed Mon. Nov.–Feb.),* was opened here; it relates events in and around Berchtesgaden to the wider history of the Third Reich. In summer, once the snow has cleared, you can take a bus *(mid-May–Oct.)* from the parking at Obersalzberg-Hintereck up the 4-mile (6.5 km) **Kehlsteinstrasse,** Germany's most spectacular mountain road, to Hitler's other chalet, the **"Eagle's Nest,"** atop the Kehlstein. The final stage of the trip from the bus terminus to this example of National Socialist architecture (now a restaurant) is via a tunnel and a brass-lined elevator (included in the bus fare). The Alpine panorama is unsurpassed. ∎

The church of St. Bartholomä sits at the edge of Königssee, at the foot of the might Watzmann.

Königliches Schloss
- ✉ Schlossplatz 2
- ☎ 08652 94 79 80
- 🕐 Closed Sat.
- 💲 $$

Salzbergwerk
- ✉ Bergwerkstrasse 83
- ☎ 08652 60 02 20
- 💲 $$$

Drive: The German Alpine Road

The Deutsche Alpenstrasse was begun in the 1930s as a kind of super-parkway opening up the German Alps for pleasure motoring. Like the autobahn, it was also a prestige project for the Nazi regime and sections of it were designed with military considerations in mind. With a few interruptions, the road runs for nearly 200 miles (300 km) between Berchtesgaden and Lindau on Lake Constance. Few travelers set out nowadays to drive its whole length; the section described is a less frantic alternative to the final section of the autobahn, between Berchtesgaden and Munich, introducing you gently to the delights of the foothills and to the Alps themselves.

When coming from Munich, leave the autobahn E52/E60 at exit 106 and follow 305 southward past Bernau to **Grassau** ❶. This old place is now a vacation and health resort, overlooked by the 5,204-foot (1,586 m) peak, the Hochplatte, and with a classic example of an onion-domed church.

Continue south to **Marquartstein** ❷, with its 11th-century castle and a ski lift up to the Hochplatte. Composer Richard Strauss lived in the town, and it was here that he composed his opera *Salome.* Carry on along the winding 305 to the resort of **Reit im Winkl** ❸, with its Tyrolean-style houses. In a sunny valley right on the border with Austria and almost surrounded by forest-mantled mountains rising to 6,500 feet (2,000 m), its reliable snowfall makes it as popular in winter as in summer. The 305 now turns east, then north through the protected landscape of the Chiemgau Mountains (Chiemgauer Alpen) with their chain of little lakes. After 15 miles (24 km) you arrive in **Ruhpolding** ❹. This busy little town has grown in popularity with visitors since Duke Wilhelm V built his Renaissance-style hunting lodge here in 1597. However, it maintains many of its traditions and still has much of the atmosphere of an Alpine village. Its fine baroque parish church houses a great treasure, the **"Ruhpolding Madonna."** A wood carving dating from about 1230, it is an exquisite example of Upper Bavarian craftsmanship.

Drive east, still on the 305, dropping in on the village of **Inzell** ❺, with its onion-domed church. The road, which now also becomes part of another named tourist route, the Alps-to-Baltic Vacation Route (Deutsche Ferienstrasse Alpen-Ostsee), runs southeast along the well-wooded Schwarzbach Valley.

It crosses the watershed at the pass known as Schwarzbachwacht-Sattel, and goes downhill through forest and pastureland with wonderful mountain views. Turn right off the main road into the village of **Ramsau** ❻. Although now almost a suburb of Berchtesgaden, the village has kept plenty of its original charm, and it has one incomparable asset: The parish church of 1512 standing on a rise above road and rushing torrent against a dramatic background of snow-capped Alps. It is an irresistible photo opportunity, and you should get out of the car

Ruhpolding wedding

and follow the sign that will lead you across the stream to the spot providing the perfect shot. Ramsau has another church, a baroque pilgrimage church known as Maria Kunterweg, dating from 1733 and with a lovingly decorated interior.

It's tempting to keep going west along the road toward the heights. Don't resist! The road leads in 2.5 miles (4 km) to the little lake called the **Hintersee** ❼, above which the clifflike slopes rise to the peaks and a glinting glacier, the northernmost one in the Alps. Now go back the way you came and rejoin 305, which brings you to your destination, **Berchtesgaden** ❽ (see pp. 308–309). ■

Christmas scene at Ramsau

🗺 See area map p. 281 F3
➤ Autobahn exit 106 (Prien-Bernau)
↔ 63 miles (102 km)
🕐 Half a day
➤ Berchtesgaden

NOT TO BE MISSED
- A short stroll in Ruhpolding
- The "Ruhpolding Madonna" in Ruhpolding
- Ramsau's church
- Hintersee

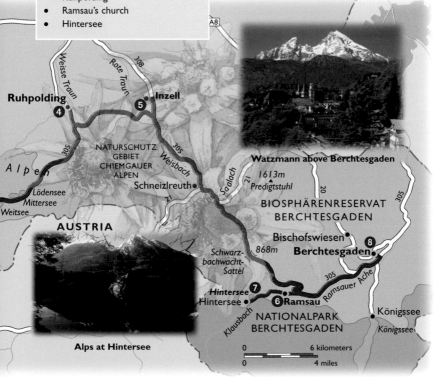

Watzmann above Berchtesgaden

Alps at Hintersee

Garmisch-Partenkirchen

THE RESORT OF GARMISCH-PARTENKIRCHEN STANDS IN A broad valley among mountains. Beautiful forest covers the lower slopes all around, but to the south arise the rocky ramparts of the Wetterstein Mountains, reaching their peak (9,718 feet/ 2,962 m) at the Zugspitze. Not much more than an hour by road and rail from Munich, it is both a winter sports mecca and Bavaria's prime summer resort with all the facilities to be expected. Yet it is still on an intimate scale, with a friendly atmosphere and local traditions. The cultural program ranges from the summer music festival named for long-term resident Richard Strauss, to zither sessions in smoky bars and folklore performances in a pair of "peasant theaters."

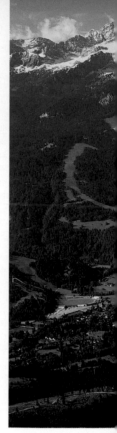

The two communities of Garmisch and Partenkirchen joined forces in 1935 to host the Winter Olympics the following year. The first-rate winter sports facilities built for the occasion consolidated the town's reputation internationally, and Garmisch-Partenkirchen was selected again for the never-to-be-held 1940 Games. Immediately after the war, the American forces of occupation were responsible for reviving winter sports here. The town continues to attract those in search of challenging skiing as well as the more gentle pursuits of *Langlauf* (cross-country skiing), skating, curling, and exploring the wild countryside on skis or snowshoes. In summer, chairlifts and cableways help hikers enjoy hundreds of miles of waymarked trails.

Partenkirchen is the more venerable of the partners with a history going back to the Romans. Little trace remains of their presence, but the stately main street, Ludwigstrasse, is lined with fine old houses, some of them with exuberant *Lüftlmalerei*, the folksy murals that are a specialty of the region. Even the mid-20th-century Town Hall (Rathaus) has been given this colorful treatment. Partenkirchen's principal inheritance from the 1936 Olympics is the **Olympische Skistadion,** with ski jump, slalom course, and space for 80,000 spectators.

To the northeast stands **St. Anton,** an early 18th-century pilgrimage church idyllically located on the lower slopes of the Wank (5,840 feet/1,780 m). It's the starting point of an easily graded 7-mile (11 km) walk called the **Philosophenweg** (Philosophers' Trail), giving superb views of the Wettersteins and the Zugspitze. You can climb a zigzag path to the summit of the Wank, or take the Wankbahn cable car.

Compared with Partenkirchen, **Garmisch** is an upstart, having first made its appearance in the records in A.D. 802. Garmisch's modern main street may not have the ancient allure of Partenkirchen's Ludwigstrasse, but its shops are full of sophisticated merchandise and souvenirs. Activity centers on the **Richard-Strauss-Platz,** with casino, Kurhaus (spa rooms), and attractive Kurpark (spa gardens).

The old core of the place is to the west around **St. Martin's Church,** where there are plenty of attractive old painted buildings. There are even more of them on the far side of the river, close to the other church (also dedicated, confusingly, to St. Martin): Look

Garmisch-Partenkirchen
🗺 280 D2
Visitor information
✉ Richard-Strauss-Platz 1A
☎ 08821 18 07 00

Richard-Strauss-Institut
✉ Schnitzschulstrasse 19
☎ 08821 91 09 50
🕓 Closed Mon.
💲 $

particularly for the **Restaurant Husar** inn, with its bold decoration in the Bavarian colors of blue and white and trompe l'oeil figures leaning from the window.

Richard Strauss lived in the town for many years until his death in 1949, and the newly founded **Richard-Strauss-Institut** is in Partenkirchen. It has a changing program of exhibitions and a "sound museum" where you can listen to extracts from the composer's work.

Not the least of Garmisch-Partenkirchen's advantages is its proximity to many other attractions. A cable car ride to the top of the **Zugspitze** (see pp. 314–315) is almost an obligatory part of a stay here, as is the spectacular walk through the narrow gorge known as the **Partnachklamm.** A two-hour walking trail leads around what is one of the loveliest lakes in the Alps, the **Eibsee** at the foot of the Zugspitze. A 12-mile (20 km) drive to the east of Garmisch is **Mittenwald,** "a living picture book" of a village as Goethe described it, famous for its tradition of violinmaking, which is still very much alive today. A similar drive north brings you past the great baroque abbey at **Ettal** to world-famous **Oberammergau,** home to countless woodcarvers of variable ability and scene of the world-renowned Passion Play (next performance 2010). An excursion here can be combined with a visit to one of Ludwig II's castles, his own favorite, **Linderhof** (see p. 316). ■

Ride a cable car up the Zupspitze for a bird's-eye view of Garmisch-Partenkirchen and the Wetterstein Mountains beyond.

To the top of the Zugspitze

HALF A MILLION PEOPLE A YEAR MAKE IT TO THE 9,718-FOOT (2,962 m) summit of Germany's highest mountain, the hardy on foot, the vast majority by cable car and rack and pinion railway. They are rewarded by a magnificent 360-degree panorama over dozens of peaks in Germany, Austria, Switzerland, and Italy, and to the north into the Bavarian lowlands. Before you set out, check the weather report; the summit is atmospheric, even when shrouded in mist, but you will never forget the views if you take the trip on a clear day.

Zugspitze
▲ 280 D1

The Zugspitze was long thought to be the abode of witches, a place to be avoided at all costs. In 1820 Lt. Josef Naus of the Royal Bavarian Army struggled to the top. He was carrying out an order from King Maximilian I of the newly created Kingdom of Bavaria to survey this part of his realm. In 1851 a golden cross was erected on the summit, and an Alpine hut was built in 1897. A weather station followed three years later, its first warden spending over a year alone there. The demand

means that you can ski here from October to May. To reach the very top take the Gletscherbahn cableway, opened in 1992.

The rocky wilderness found by Lieutenant Naus has long since disappeared under the steel and concrete of the extended weather station, the observatory, and the visitor facilities (including an art gallery, an Internet café, and a conference center). But the view is the thing, and it's worth a good stay up here to

for easier access grew, and in 1928 2,000 men started work on the construction of the rack railroad to the Zugspitzplatt, the plateau just below the peak.

The railroad was completed in two years, and it is very popular. You can board it at its station in Garmisch-Partenkirchen or drive up to the station at Eibsee and leave your vehicle in the parking lot there. Make sure you buy a round-trip ticket (*Zugspitzbahn, Garmisch-Partenkirchen, Olympiastrasse 27, tel 08821 79 70*) and allow half a day or longer to make the most of the experience.

From Eibsee, the real climb begins, with the train grinding its way up, first in forest, then in tunnels, to its 8,530-foot (2,600 m) terminus. Reliable snow cover

absorb it, particularly in changing weather conditions. The films on show include fascinating footage of the railroad under construction.

A passageway at the end of the observation deck leads from German territory to the upper station of the Austrian Zugspitzbahn. However, your recommended way down is via the Eibsee cable car, preferably with a window view. This is one of the most impressive rides in the Alps; the gondola swings out from the sheer rock face into the abyss, swaying slightly as it passes over the pylons holding up the cables, giving ever closer views of the Eibsee in its glorious setting. From the base station of the cable car, you can pick up your automobile to return to Garmisch-Partenkirchen, or rejoin the train at Eibsee station. ∎

A golden cross on the summit of the Zugspitze marks the highest point in Germany.

More places to visit in the Alps

LANDSBERG AM LECH

A handsome medieval town and an important stop on the Romantic Road linking Northern Bavaria with the Alps, Landsberg owes part of its fame to the political prison where Adolf Hitler, an inmate after the failed Putsch in 1923 (see p. 298), dictated *Mein Kampf* to his acolyte Rudolf Hess. The great 18th-century church architect Dominikus Zimmermann, who was Burgomaster here, gave the Town Hall (Rathaus) its richly decorated facade.

🄼 280 D3 **Visitor information**
✉ Hauptplatz 152 ☎ 08191 12 82 46

OBERSTDORF

Like Berchtesgaden, this mountain resort in the Allgäu Alps lies at the center of a territory protruding southward into Austria. Despite its wealth of sports and recreation facilities (ski jump, several cable cars), Oberstdorf has kept much of its village character. The most popular excursion is to the top of the 7,297-foot (2,224 m) **Nebelhorn,** the highest peak in the Allgäu, from where the panorama takes in more than 400 Alpine peaks.

🄼 280 B1 **Visitor information**
✉ Marktplatz 7 ☎ 08322 70 00

OTTOBEUREN

The little town of Ottobeuren in Bavarian Swabia is dominated, if not overwhelmed, by its **monastery church.** Founded in the eighth century, the abbey was rebuilt a millennium later by one of the greatest architects of the 18th century, Johann Michael Fischer. The vast space of the interior, richly decorated with stuccowork and frescoes, is one of the finest creations of the baroque style in Germany.

🄼 280 C3 **Visitor information**
✉ Marktplatz 14 ☎ 08332 92 19 50

SCHLOSS HERRENCHIEMSEE

Bavaria's biggest lake, the Chiemsee, is a favorite spot for weekenders from Munich as well as for admirers of Ludwig II, who built his last and most expensive palace on one of its islands, Herreninsel. Schloss Herrenchiemsee was intended to be a facsimile of Louis XIV's great château at Versailles, but it was far from finished at Ludwig's death in 1886. It is

nevertheless well worth seeing, with a 320-foot (100 m) Hall of Mirrors and a French-style formal park. The royal apartments of what is known as the **New Palace** (Neues Schloss) can be visited by guided tour only, but you can spend as long as you like in the south wing, which houses the **König Ludwig II-Museum** with much fascinating material about the life of this strange but appealing figure. The baroque **Old Palace** (Altes Schloss), a former Augustinian monastery, contains a museum celebrating the foundation of the Federal Republic of Germany. It was here in 1948 that its constitution was drawn up.

🄼 281 F3 ☎ 08051 6 88 70

SCHLOSS LINDERHOF

Lost in a quiet side valley in the heart of the Ammergebirge mountains, Schloss Linderhof is perhaps the most appealing of King Ludwig II's castles. More villa than palace, although furnished with the utmost sumptuousness, it is set on grounds that combine Italian terrace gardens, French parterres, and English-style parkland. The park's fine specimen trees merge imperceptibly with the conifer forest rising to the Alpine crags high above. Intriguing garden buildings include a Moroccan House, a Moorish Kiosk with a peacock throne, and an artfully contrived Venus Grotto, simulating a scene from Wagner's *Tannhäuser.*

🄼 280 D2 ☎ 08822 9 20 30

WIESKIRCHE

Harmonizing perfectly with its setting of swelling Alpine foothills, the Wieskirche ("Church in the Meadow") is a supreme synthesis of religious fervor and architectural virtuosity. It marks the place where an abandoned carving of Christ miraculously shed real tears. A great many pilgrims subsequently flocked to the site, and in 1746 the rococo designer Dominikus Zimmermann was commissioned to erect a church on the spot. So devoted to his task was Zimmermann that he built himself a modest dwelling next door, in which he spent the last years of his life. The church interior is a blissful confection of luxuriant stuccowork and lively ceiling frescoes.

🄼 280 D2 ☎ 08862 93 29 30 ∎

With a climate favoring vineyards and fruit growing, successful industries, and scenery ranging from the Black Forest to Germany's biggest lake, Constance, Baden-Württemberg is a tough act to follow.

Baden-Württemberg

Black Forest couple

Enjoying the cure at Baden-Baden's Friedrichsbad spa

Baden-Württemberg

THIS *LAND*, BORDERING FRANCE AND SWITZERLAND IN GERMANY'S SOUTH-western corner, has a dual character. The climate in the Rhine Valley and around the Bodensee has a touch of the south about it, perhaps explaining the area's easygoing lifestyle. On the other hand, the Swabians, as Württembergers prefer to be called, are a bit more determined in their daily endeavors—their contributions to the German economic miracle, for instance, helped make the region one of the country's most prosperous.

Baden-Württemberg has wonderful landscapes to explore or relax in. Of these, the Schwarzwald (Black Forest) is supreme, with its cloak of dark and mysterious conifers, green meadows, huge farmsteads, and living folk traditions. The region's other main upland range, the Schwäbische Alb (Swabian Jura), is more austere. Rivers such as the upper Danube cut into its series of limestone plateaus, leaving dramatic rock spurs crowned by picturebook castles.

Castles abound in Baden-Württemberg, ranging from re-created medieval strongholds such as Burg Hohenzollern to resplendent baroque palaces such as Schloss Bruchsal. There are castles almost beyond counting along the lower River Neckar, including that of the ancient university town of Heidelberg, most visited of all Baden-Württemberg's cities. The state capital, Stuttgart, is one of Germany's most progressive cities, proud of both the technical excellence of its products and of its cultural attractions. The city was the royal seat of the rulers of Württemberg, whose kingdom extended to the shores of Lake Constance.

After World War II, there was a good chance that the old kingdom would form the basis of a federal state, but a plebiscite in 1950 favored the link with Baden. Until 1918 Baden had been a Grand Duchy with its capital at Karlsruhe, and Badeners see themselves as quite distinct from Swabians. Perhaps influenced by the long line of vineyards cladding the sunny western slopes of the Black Forest, they are not quite so dedicated to work as their compatriots just to the east. And nowhere is a place more dedicated to pleasure and relaxation than that archetypal spa town, Baden-Baden. ■

Area of map detail

Berlin

50 kilometers

30 miles

HESSE
p. 195

Main

Wertheim

BAVARIA
p. 247

NATURPARK NECKARTAL-ODENWALD
Walldürn
Buchen
A81 E41

Tauberbischofsheim
Königshofen

Eberbach

Hirschhorn
Neckarsteinach
Burg Zwingenberg
Neckargerach

Bad Mergentheim

Blaufelden

MANNHEIM
Heidelberg
Schloss Schwetzingen
Walldorf
Neudorf
Schloss Bruchsal

Burg Dilsberg
Minneburg
A6 E50 Neckarzimmern
Burg Guttenberg
Bad Schönborn

Burg Hornberg
Dörzbach
Künzelsau

A5 E35
293

Bad Wimpfen
Eppingen

Öhringen
Kocher
A6 E50

BADEN
Bretten
Maulbronn

Heilbronn
NATURPARK SCHWÄBISCH-FRÄNKISCHERWALD
Sulzbach
Murrhardt

Schwäbisch Hall
Obersontheim
Gaildorf

Crailsheim

Karlsruhe
Pfinztal
Lauffen
Vaihingen

Ellwangen
19

A7 E43

Ettlingen A8 E52
Rastatt

Enz
Pforzheim
Leonberg
10

Ludwigsburg
STUTTGART 29

Aalen
Schwäbisch Gmünd

Bopfingen

Baden-Baden
Bühl

Gernsbach
Bad Wildbad
Calw

Sindelfingen
Böblingen

Esslingen
Rems
Göppingen

Neresheim
466

Heidenheim

FRANCE
Kehl
Achern
Oberkirch
Offenburg
Gengenbach
Lahr
Haslach

Herrenberg
Tübingen
Freudenstadt
Horb
Schiltach
Burg Hohenzollern
Balingen

Nürtingen
Geislingen
Bad Urach

Herbrechtingen
A8 E52
Langenau

A5 E35

Reutlingen
Haigerloch
Mössingen

Blaubeuren
Ehingen

Ulm
Laupheim

Donau
BAVARIA
p. 247

Schwarzwälder Freilichtmuseum

WÜRTTEMBERG
Triberg
Rottweil NATURPARK OBERE DONAU

Gammertingen
Riedlingen

Dietenheim

557m
Kaiserstuhl
Emmendingen
Freiburg im Breisgau
1284m
Schauinsland
1493m
Feldberg

Furtwangen E531
Villingen
Schwenningen
Donaueschingen
Titisee
Schluchsee Wutach
Blumberg

Sigmaringen
Donau

Mengen
313
Saulgau

Biberach an der Riss
312

Bad Wurzach

Tuttlingen 311
Pfullendorf

Bad Waldsee

Leutkirch

Bad Krozingen
St. Blasien

A81 E41
Stockach
A98 Ludwigshafen
Singen
Überlingen

Weingarten
Ravensburg

Schopfheim
Tiengen
Bad Säckingen
Müllheim

Jestetten
Radolfzell
Reichenau Mainau
Konstanz
L. Constance (Bodensee)

Birnau
Pfahlbaumuseum
Meersburg

Friedrichshafen
Schloss Montfort

Wangen Isny
A96

A98
Lörrach
Rhein

A   B   SWITZERLAND   C   D

Stuttgart

🗺 319 C3

Visitor information

✉ Königstrasse 1A

☎ 0711 2 22 80

The finer points
of art explained in
Stuttgart's
Staatsgalerie

Stuttgart

THE SYMBOLS OF SWABIAN STUTTGART ARE NOT VENERABLE churches or civic buildings, but the Mercedes star and the Fernsehturm, Germany's first TV tower. The city has plenty of other firsts to its credit, not least the internal combustion engine patented by Gottlieb Daimler in 1883. Daimler amalgamated with Mercedes in 1926, forming just one of Stuttgart's world-class enterprises and institutes based on scientific and technological excellence. On the arts scene, the Staatsgalerie has become an icon of postmodern design.

Fernsehturm

🗺 Map p. 323

✉ Jahnstrasse,
Stuttgart-Degerloch

☎ 0711 23 25 97

💲 $

Regional Museum

🗺 Map p. 323

✉ Altes Schloss,
Schillerplatz 6

☎ 0711 2 79 34 00

🕐 Closed Mon.

💲 $

**Stuttgart Museum
of Art**

🗺 Map p. 323

✉ Kleiner Schlossplatz 1

☎ 0711 2 16 21 88

🕐 Closed Mon.

💲 $

The city center spreads out along a valley surrounded by wooded hills. Some of the slopes are covered with vineyards, while from the summit of one of the hills rises the **Fernsehturm.** Its observation platform gives the best all-round view of the city and surrounds. The lavish provision of parks and pedestrian spaces means that you can walk unhindered by traffic from chic city center shopping arcades to the riverside several kilometers away.

Stuttgart's name comes from the stud farm ("Stuten-garten") established by the local dukes in the tenth century (a black horse still features on the city's coat of arms). When Napoleon redrew the map of Germany in 1802, the dukes were promoted to royal status, and Stuttgart became the capital of the

kingdom of Württemberg. The origins of the **Old Castle** (Altes Schloss) go back to the days of the stud farm, although the present building, with its courtyard and towers, is mostly Renaissance in date. It houses the **Regional Museum** (Landesmuseum), with wonderful examples of religious works by local master carvers and also the Württemberg crown jewels.

The Altes Schloss plays a subordinate role in the townscape compared with the baroque **New Castle** (Neues Schloss), a much more expansive structure, big enough to dominate the huge Schlossplatz that, with its formal lawns and Jubilee column, is the city's main meeting place. Built by the dukes in the second half of the 18th century, the Neues Schloss now houses some departments of state of the state government. Off the southwest corner of the square, an illuminated glass cube makes a modernist statement for the renowned **Stuttgart Museum of Art** (Kunstmuseum Stuttgart), the cutting edge among local galleries. Works by Neue Sachlichkeit (New Objectivity) artist Otto Dix (1891–1969) are prominent here, above all the tremendous "Metropolis" triptych. With its parade of crippled war veterans and strutting creatures of the night, it sums up the splendors and miseries of the Weimar years. To the west, Schlossplatz is bounded by broad

Königstrasse, Stuttgart's principal shopping street, running ruler-straight down to the main station.

For a hint of old Stuttgart, return to the Altes Schloss, which shares **Schillerplatz** with other old buildings. Beyond is a web of old streets around the **Market Hall** (Markthalle), a stylish art nouveau establishment with fruit, vegetables, and spices galore, as well as great places to eat and drink.

To see how Stuttgart has won a reputation as an immaculately landscaped city, walk north to the **Schlossgarten.** In this fine green setting you'll find the modern Baden-Württemberg Parliament Building (Landtag) and the cultural complex of the State Opera and State Theater (Staatsoper and Staatstheater).

The Calwer Passage, one of Stuttgart's fashionable shopping arcades

A Latin American *colectivo* (minibus) is one of the more colorful exhibits at at the Mercedes-Benz Museum.

STAATSGALERIE

Opposite the Staatstheater is the Staatsgalerie. Part of the collection is housed in a neoclassic building of 1843, the rest in the world-renowned extension designed by the British architect James Stirling and completed in 1984. Stonework

Feuerbach's "Iphigenie" of 1872 may intrigue you with her enigmatic thoughts. The gallery also has many first-rate canvases by **French Impressionists,** including Monet's "Fields in Spring" (1887).

In the new extension, Stirling's highly varied interior spaces make a

Staatsgalerie
- Map p. 323
- Konrad-Adenauer-Strasse 30–32
- 0711 47 04 00
- Closed Mon.
- $$

Schloss Rosenstein (Natural History Museum)
- Map p. 323
- Rosenstein 1
- 0711 8 93 60
- Closed Mon.
- $

contrasts with gaudy green, blue, and pink piping and metalwork. It's a puzzle trying to work out where external spaces end and the gallery begins; in fact, you can follow a public walkway right through the building.

Appropriately, the older building houses artworks from medieval times to the 19th century. Paintings by **Dutch and Italian old masters** are here, and there is a good selection of **early German** works. Look for the Herrenberg altarpiece by the visionary Jörg Ratgeb, a Swabian painter from Gmünd who died fighting in the Peasant Wars in 1526. Good examples of the work of 19th-century **German Romantic** painters include Caspar David Friedrich's particularly evocative "Bohemian Landscape." Anselm

superb setting for Stuttgart's outstanding collection of **early 20th-century German art.** Among works by Otto Dix, look for his grotesquely disabled yet moving "Matchseller." Apocalyptic scenes by George Grosz and Ludwig Meider foretell the horrors of war and the chaos of the Weimar years. Don't miss the beautifully lit costumes designed by Bauhaus teacher Oskar Schlemmer for his "Triadic Ballet." Here, too, is the Picasso collection, the largest in Germany.

If you have time, return to the Schlossgarten and take the footpaths north to its far end to reach the Rosensteinpark. Here, **Schloss Rosenstein,** the summer palace of Württemberg royalty, is home to the city's museum of natural history, and the old royal grounds of the **Wilhelma** have been adapted as a first-rate zoo and botanical gardens.

FARTHER AFIELD

Cross the river and you find yourself in **Bad Cannstatt,** once an independent town and famous spa, now a suburb of Stuttgart. The place is best known for its September Volksfest, a worthy rival to Munich's Oktoberfest (see pp. 300–301).

Gottlieb Daimler lived and carried out his early experiments with internal combustion engines here. Some of the fruits of his inventiveness are on display at Stuttgart's two outstanding motor museums. In the suburb of Untertürkheim south of Cannstatt, the lavish new **Mercedes-Benz Museum**

celebrates more than a century of automobile manufacture by this great company and its predecessors. The Japanese limousine used by Emperor Hirohito is here, as is Chancellor Adenauer's official car and the first of the "Popemobiles."

In the interwar years, Ferdinand Porsche was technical director of Stuttgart's Daimler works, but his fame rests on his association with the early development of the Volkswagen and then on his conquest of the upper end of the automobile market with his roadsters. These superlative machines are turned out by the factory in the suburb of Zuffenhausen, where the **Porsche-Museum** has about 80 historic examples on display. ■

Wilhelma (Zoo & Botanical Gardens)
- 🅰 Map p. 323
- ✉ Neckartalstrasse
- ☎ 0711 5 40 20
- 💲 $

Mercedes-Benz Museum
- 🅰 Map p. 323
- ✉ Mercedesstrasse 100
- ☎ 0711 173 00 00
- 🕐 Closed Mon.
- 💲 $$

Porsche-Museum
- 🅰 Map p. 323
- ✉ Porscheplatz 1, Stuttgart-Zuffenhausen
- ☎ 0711 9 11 56 85

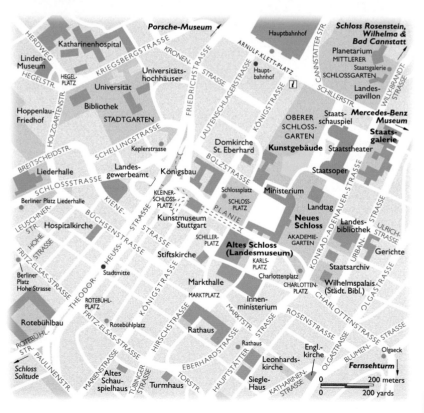

Heidelberg

Heidelberg's intellectual elite once cleared their thoughts along the Philosophers' Footpath, with its classic view of the city.

ENTICINGLY LOCATED AMONG STEEP WOODED HILLS JUST upstream from where the River Neckar flows out into the Rhine plain, this famous university city has been immortalized by writers, musicians, and artists. Mark Twain wrote about it with affection in *A Tramp Abroad*; the image of student life created by Sigmund Romberg in his musical *The Student Prince* lives on; and generations of military personnel have lived here ever since it was chosen as the headquarters of the U.S. forces in Germany.

Heidelberg
🅰 319 B4
Visitor information
✉ Hauptbahnhof (Main station), Willy-Brandt-Platz 1
☎ 06221 1 94 33

Heidelberg's story could be said to begin half a million years ago. The jawbone of Europe's oldest known inhabitant, *Homo heidelbergensis*, was found nearby. However, the town itself only developed in the Middle Ages under the rulers of the Rhineland-Palatinate, a territory extending on both sides of the Rhine. In 1386 the first university on purely German soil was founded here, and in later years Heidelberg flourished, becoming a center of Humanism and Protestantism.

Its greatest benefactor was also its nemesis: Elector Frederick V (1596–1632) beautified the castle for his bride, Elizabeth Stuart,

ruined state than it ever was before. You can take the funicular up, but the climb on foot, albeit steep, isn't all that far. If you arrive by funicular, turn left on reaching the castle grounds and enjoy a classic view over the city from the promontory where cannon once stood. The way to the courtyard is via the Elisabethentor, a gateway Frederick V had built in a single night to surprise his bride. Beyond a fortified bridge, the courtyard gateway is decorated with the formidable figure of a knight in armor. While buildings from all periods of the castle's construction line the courtyard, the most striking are the elaborately decorated Renaissance facades of the eastern and northern wings, the Ottheinrichsbau and the Friedrichsbau. The Ottheinrichsbau is home to the **German Museum of Pharmacy** (Deutsches Apotheken-Museum), with reconstructed historical pharmacies as well as an alchemist's laboratory deep underground.

What attracts the crowds into another of the courtyards is the monster wine barrel known as the **Grosses Fass,** as big as a two-story building. Built to hold the portion of the wine harvest traditionally surrendered to the Electors, it has an unbelievable capacity of about 57,720 gallons (222,000 liters).

Make sure you walk around the Schloss' perimeter to get an idea of the strength of its fortifications. The most spectacular feature is the **Gesprengter Turm** ("blown-up tower"); most of its masonry lies in the moat, leaving much of its interior exposed. Of Frederick V's great garden, with its fountains, grottoes, mazes, conservatories, and pavilions, the only remains are the high retaining walls and terraces. But it's worth exploring, for its lovely shade trees and fine views.

Schloss
☎ 06221 53 84 31
$ $

A uniformed undergraduate carries the flag for his student fraternity.

daughter of James I of England, and laid out magnificent gardens. But he also helped provoke the disasters of the Thirty Years War, when the city was sacked and plundered. In 1693 the French invaded, laying waste to town and castle. Heidelberg only emerged from obscurity when it was "discovered" by the poets of the Romantic Movement at the end of the 18th century, when ruins came into fashion.

The city has never looked back, but despite its immense popularity, Heidelberg has not sold its soul to tourism. Most visitors come on business; the city is a focus of the new economy based on brainpower, with many research and scientific institutions and a thriving university.

Start your exploration at the **Schloss,** perhaps more lovely in its

Regional Museum of the Palatinate

✉ Hauptstrasse 97
☎ 06221 583 40 20
🕐 Closed Mon.
💲 $

Studentenkarzer

✉ Augustinergasse 2
☎ 06221 54 35 54
🕐 Closed Mon April–Oct. & Sun.-Mon. Nov–March
💲 $

"Pedestrians only" on Hauptstrasse, Heidelberg's main shopping street

Heidelberg's **Old Town** (Altstadt) squeezes in between the River Neckar and the wooded slope to the south. The long main street, Hauptstrasse, runs parallel to the river from cobbled **Marktplatz.** The square, lined by fine town houses and the baroque Town Hall (Rathaus), is dominated by the **Heiliggeistkirche,** a church built from the same red sandstone as the castle. Market stalls surround the church's outer walls, just as in medieval times. Don't leave the square without peeking at the ornate facade of the **Haus zum Ritter** in the far southwestern corner, the only building to survive the disasters of the 17th century.

Leave Marktplatz by Steingasse, which leads to the **Old Bridge** (Alte Brücke). It is approached through an archway flanked by medieval towers topped by jaunty little caps added in the 18th century. There's a fine view of castle and city from the bridge, but for the very best panorama, at its most alluring in late afternoon light, you must cross to the far bank and steel yourself for a steep climb up to the **Philosophenweg.** The Philosophers' Footpath commemorates those brainy Heidelbergers who walked these slopes to clarify their thoughts or ponder the mysteries of time and decay in contemplation of the castle ruins.

Back in town, you might now explore the smaller streets leading off busy Hauptstrasse, along with **Untere Strasse,** an attractive street that runs parallel to the main one. On Hauptstrasse you'll find the city's most important museum, the **Regional Museum of the Palatinate** (Kurpfälzisches Museum). Exhibits here show what Heidelberg was like before the disasters of the 17th century; there is also a cast of the jawbone of *Homo heidelbergensis.*

Many of the university institutions are grouped around Universitätsplatz, among them the **Studentenkarzer,** Heidelberg's student prison. Until 1914, students were under the jurisdiction of the university, and misbehavior was punished by incarceration here—although prisoners were allowed to attend lectures and sit exams! Read the grafitti to see how they spent their time here. Get a taste of student life today by looking in at the **Marstall,** the former arsenal, which is now the university refectory and gathering place. You might also lift a stein in one of the old taverns such as the Sepp'l or the Roter Ochs just off Karlsplatz. ■

Neckar Valley

FORCING ITS WAY THROUGH THE UPLAND MASSIF OF THE Odenwald upstream from Heidelberg, the Neckar forms an attractive, steep-sided valley. Winding among woods, orchards, and vineyards, it offers a rapid succession of hilltop castles, small towns, and villages.

Neckarsteinach, 7 miles (12 km) east of Heidelberg, has four castles, mostly in ruins, while the remains of another fortress, **Burg Dilsberg,** crown the heights opposite, giving a superb view over the river and the Odenwald forest. Another panorama awaits a few miles farther upstream from the terrace or tower of **Burg Hirschhorn,** now a hotel and restaurant.

Eberbach, 6 miles (10 km) farther east, where the river turns west, was once an imperial town. It has a reconstructed castle, remains of its town walls, timber-framed houses, and a rare medieval bathhouse, now a restaurant, the Altes Badehaus. Once the seat of nobles who made a living extracting tolls from traffic on the river, the **Burg Zwingenberg** is the next castle upstream. Careful restoration has preserved it as perhaps the most picture-perfect medieval stronghold along the Neckar. Beyond the **Minneburg,** opposite the village of Neckargerach, the valley widens, giving more space for agriculture.

Rising through the vines above Neckarzimmern is **Burg Hornberg,** home of the Knight of the Iron Hand, Götz von Berlichingen, the subject of a play by Goethe, who attributed a certain earthy expression to him. To this day, polite Germans unwilling to say "Kiss my …!" will offer the person they wish to offend a "Götz" instead. Farther on, the castle of **Burg Guttenberg** *(tel 06266 9 10 20)* is a well-established birds of prey center *(tel 06266 3 88).*

The highlight of the valley is the old imperial town of **Bad Wimpfen.** The lower town, Bad Wimpfen im Tal, is dominated by a Gothic monastery church. In the upper town, Bad Wimpfen am Berg, streets of timber-framed houses wind up the slopes, and the turreted **Blauer Turm,** a watchtower of bluish limestone, overlooks all. On Sunday at noon a trumpeter plays from the top of the tower. ∎

Bad Wimpfen
🅰 319 C4
Visitor information
✉ Carl-Ulrich-Strasse 1, Bad Wimpfen
☎ 07063 972 00

Burg Hornberg
☎ 06261 50 01
💲 $

A typical timber-framed building in Bad Wimpfen, with the turreted Blauer Turm in the background

Karlsruhe's baroque Schloss comes to historic life during the city's international folklore festival.

Karlsruhe

🅐 319 B3

Visitor information

✉ Bahnhofplatz 6

☎ 0721 37 20 53 81

Karlsruhe

THE CITY OF KARLSRUHE IS LAID OUT IN THE SHAPE OF A fan, its principal streets radiating out from the main facade of its baroque Schloss. This feat of urban design was conceived by Karl Wilhelm, Margrave of Baden, in 1715, to reflect the absolutist ideas of the age. At the epicenter of the plan he placed his palace, the focal point of nine city streets and a further 23 avenues cut through the forest. No building was permitted to upstage the three-story Schloss by being more than two stories high. The town was given the name of "Carols Ruhe" (Charles' Rest).

Modern Karlsruhe has developed into an important university city with science-based industries and a rich cultural life. No longer a state capital, it consoles itself with being the home of two national institutions, the Federal Supreme Court and the Federal Constitutional Court. Many buildings taller than two stories have gone up since Karl Wilhelm's time, but his plan is still intact. Its bold design is best seen from the air; the next best view is from the Schloss's central tower.

Rebuilt after wartime damage, the Margraves' palace now houses the **Badisches Landesmuseum.** As the regional museum of the Grand Duchy of Baden, once a middle-ranking European power, it contains the Baden crown jewels, prehistoric objects, archaeological finds from the Mediterranean, and medieval and Renaissance art. Take a look at the **Türkenbeute,** the booty assembled by Margrave Ludwig Wilhelm during his campaigns against the Turks. Its weapons, armor, textiles, jewelry, and other items make it one of the most important collections of Islamic arts and crafts in the world.

The area around the palace has a botanical garden with exceptionally fine 19th-century glasshouses. The vast **Schlosspark,** beautified in 1967 in the course of the National Garden Festival (see pp. 204–205), merges gradually with the forest. Housed in the **Orangerie** is part of the city's outstanding art gallery, with fine examples of German and European 20th-century painting. In the main gallery, the **Staatliche Kunsthalle,** are superb French, Dutch, and German old masters, including works by Dürer, Cranach, and Holbein the Younger. The "Crucifixion" by Grünewald is unequaled in the intensity of its depiction of pain and horror. You can find relief from this searing vision in the appealing portraits and landscapes of Hans Thoma (1839–1924), who was director of the gallery for many years.

A century or so after Karl Wilhelm's reign, his successor, Archduke Karl Friedrich, employed a local architect, Friedrich Weinbrenner, to transform the face of the city. You can see the results of his work by walking from the Schloss along the axial route that leads due south. Weinbrenner laid out a new **Marktplatz,** gracing it with fine neoclassic public buildings: City Church (Stadtkirche) to the east, Town Hall (Rathaus) to the west. The red sandstone **Pyramid,** one of the city's symbols, stands over the grave of Karl Wilhelm.

Farther south is another square, Rondellplatz, flanked by another monumental neoclassic edifice, the **Markgräfliches Palais.** The central obelisk commemorates the constitution granted by the Grand

Baden's Grand Duke Karl Wilhelm chose to be interred beneath a pyramid.

Duke to his realm in 1818. Baden was always the most progressive German state, abolishing serfdom and torture early, and introducing compulsory schooling. This 1818 constitution served as a model for the liberal revolutionaries of 1848 when they assembled in Frankfurt.

Karlsruhe has a surprise for its visitors in its southwestern suburbs. Here, in an old munitions factory, is a vast complex of museums, the **Center for Art & Media Technology** (Zentrum für Kunst- und Medientechnologie). The museum shows the potential of contemporary art and new media in an entertaining and instructive way. You can admire works by the likes of Andy Warhol and Roy Lichtenstein, and also create your own art in an interactive gallery. ■

Badisches Landesmuseum
- ✉ Schloss
- ☎ 0721 9 26 65 14
- 🕐 Closed Mon.
- 💲 $

Staatliche Kunsthalle
- ✉ Hans-Thoma-Strasse 2–6
- ☎ 0721 9 26 33 55
- 🕐 Closed Mon.
- 💲 $$

Center for Art & Media Technology
- ✉ Lorenzstrasse 19
- ☎ 0721 8 10 00
- 🕐 Closed Mon. & Tues.
- 💲 $$

Mannheim

MANNHEIM WAS PLANNED IN THE 18TH CENTURY AS A grid of intersecting streets. Uniquely in Germany, the streets were not given names, but were defined with letters and numbers, making it easy to find one's way around. The town's location at the confluence of the Rhine and Neckar guaranteed its prosperity; its port is now one of the biggest inland harbors in Europe. The city, which in the 18th century was a byword for courtly culture, is now a stronghold of industry and the commercial center for much of the region.

Mannheim's great landmark is still the huge baroque **Schloss,** the palace built by Elector Carl Philipp when he moved his court here from Heidelberg in 1720. The biggest building of its kind in Germany, the Schloss was the scene of the city's

golden age as a center of the arts, theater, literature, and especially music. The musicians of the Mannheim school laid the foundations on which the great classical composers were later to build. It now houses the university, but you can visit the Knights' Hall (Rittersaal) after a revamp ending in mid-2007.

Little remains of the glories of the 18th century; the city has rebuilt itself several times over. However, **Marktplatz,** best visited when the thrice-weekly market *(Tues., Thurs., Sat.)* is in full swing, is graced by the harmonious architecture of the Town Hall (Rathaus) and the City Church (Stadtkirche). **Paradeplatz** is dominated by a pyramid glorifying Elector Johann Wilhelm.

The most interesting square is **Friedrichsplatz,** lined with exceptionally fine art nouveau buildings and centered on the city's other landmark, the 200-foot (60 m) **Wasserturm.** Built in 1886, this is probably the most splendid and elaborate of all German water towers, fully deserving of its parkland setting, and appropriately presided over by a figure of the goddess Amphitrite, wife of the sea-god Poseidon.

Mannheim's exceptional range of museums includes the **Reiss-Engelhorn-Museum,** with displays bringing to life the history of this unusual city; the **Städtische Kunsthalle,** very strong in European art of the 19th and 20th centuries; the outstanding **Regional Museum for Technology & Work** (Landesmuseum für Technik und Arbeit); and the paddle steamer *Mainz,* now the home of a museum of navigation on the Rhine and Neckar *(Am Museumsufer (Neckar), tel 0621 429 89, closed Mon.).* ∎

Mannheim
🗺 319 B4
Visitor information
✉ Willy-Brandt-Platz 3
☎ 0621 10 10 12

Schloss
☎ 0621 2 92 28 90
🕐 Closed Mon.
💲 $

Reiss-Engelhorn-Museum
✉ C5 Zeughaus
☎ 0621 2 93 31 51
🕐 Closed Mon.
💲 $

Städtische Kunsthalle
✉ Moltkestrasse 9
☎ 0621 293 64 11
🕐 Closed Mon.
💲 $

Regional Museum for Technology & Work
✉ Museumsstrasse 1
☎ 0621 4 29 87 50
🕐 Closed Mon.
💲 $

Elector Carl Philipp endowed his city with the Jesuitenkirche, one of the finest baroque churches in southwest Germany.

Tübingen

Tübingen

🗺 319 C2

Visitor information

✉ An der Neckarbrücke

☎ 07071 9 13 60

Hölderlinturm

✉ Bursagasse 6

☎ 07071 2 20 40

🕐 Closed Mon.

💲 $

Schlossmuseum

✉ Schloss
  Hohentübingen

☎ 07071 2 97 73 84

🕐 Closed Mon. & Tues.

💲 $

City Museum

✉ Kornhausstrasse 10

☎ 07071 204 17 11

🕐 Open Tues.–Sun.
  11a.m.–5 p.m.,
  Closed Mon.

💲 $

DOMINATED BY ITS ANCIENT UNIVERSITY, TÜBINGEN IS a near perfect example of a southern German medieval town, with a hilltop castle, a wealth of timber-framed houses, and an idyllic location on the banks of the River Neckar.

The river, where students can be seen punting in fine weather, is divided into two channels by a long, narrow artificial island. Here, magnificent plane trees form a splendid avenue, the **Platanenallee.** Among the old houses and weeping willows on the north bank stands a gazebo-like little yellow tower. The **Hölderlinturm** is where poet Friedrich Hölderlin (1770–1843), one of the university's illustrious alumni, spent the last 36 years of his life after being declared insane.

Just behind this tower is the oldest part of the town, centered on two squares. In **Holzmarkt** stands the Gothic **Stiftskirche,** with the elaborate tombs of many of the rulers of Württemberg, among them Duke Eberhard the Bearded, who founded the university in 1477. You can climb the church tower (tel 07071 4 20 46) for a fine view over the rooftops of the town. The charmingly irregular cobbled **Marktplatz** has a Neptune fountain and a picturesque 15th-century **Town Hall** (Rathaus) with an astronomical clock in its gable.

Schloss Hohentübingen proclaims its importance with a portal in the form of a Roman triumphal arch. Laid out around a courtyard, the present castle is a Renaissance structure built on 11th-century foundations. It houses various university departments, a museum, and a Heidelberg-style giant barrel. Unfortunately it is no longer possible to visit the cellars where the barrel is situated as they also contain south Germany's biggest bat colony! The **museum**

contains the university's eclectic collections of antiquities and prehistoric items, such as the tiny figure of a horse carved from bone in Paleolithic times.

Don't leave the castle area without enjoying the fine views over the Neckar and the town. The lower part of the old town toward the River Ammer has interesting old buildings, among them the Corn

Dating from 1435, Tübingen's Rathaus presides over the city's marketplace.

Store (Kornhaus), now home to the **City Museum** (Stadt-museum), with its model of the old town. Tübingen also has its prison for unruly students, the **Studentenkarzer,** which you can visit by guided tour only (Münzgasse 20, tel 07071 9 13 60, by appt. only). ∎

Spa guests luxuriate in the sumptuous surroundings of the 19th-century Friedrichsbad.

Baden-Baden

SYNONYMOUS WITH THE FASHIONABLE PASTIME OF "taking the cure," Baden-Baden remains the quintessential spa town. Here, quasi-medical pampering is only one element in the pleasurable round of strolling, eating, seeing and being seen, concerts, casino visits, and entertainment of all kinds.

Baden-Baden
319 B3
Visitor information
✉ Schwarzwaldstrasse 52 (off main road into town)
☎ 07221 27 52 00

Casino
✉ Kurhaus, Kaiserallee 1
☎ 07221 302 40
$ $

Friedrichsbad
✉ Römerplatz 1
☎ 07221 27 59 20
$ $$$$ (treatment)

The virtues of the waters that well up from deep underground at a temperature of 156°F were recognized by the Romans, particularly by Emperor Caracalla. Nearly two thousand years later the ultra-modern spa facilities now bear his name. People came here to be cured throughout the Middle Ages and later, but it was the 19th century that made Baden-Baden into a legend. The town has very consciously and very cleverly maintained the allure it had then, when kings and emperors, composers, artists, and writers flocked to what was deservedly called the "summer capital of Europe."

The town benefits from a mild climate as well as from an attractive setting in the wooded valley of the little River Oos running down from the Black Forest. But it benefits even more from the vision of the early 19th-century French entrepreneur Jacques Bénazet, the uncrowned "king of Baden-Baden." Together with his son Edouard, he invested huge sums in the town, turning the ailing casino into a glittering gaming palace, helped by stage designers from the Paris Opéra. Even if you prefer not to risk your hard-earned dollars at roulette, poker, or baccarat, it's well worth looking inside the casino of the **Kurhaus,** where fortunes are lost and won in surroundings worthy of the finest French châteaux. An earlier, more austere taste is evident outside, where the stately neoclassic colonnade is the work of the architect Friedrich Weinbrenner, who rebuilt much of nearby Karlsruhe.

An elegant parade of little single-story shops leads from the Kurhaus toward the town center. To the south is the **Lichtentaler Allee,** which was Baden-Baden's most fashionable promenade. Originally an avenue of oaks, it is now the jewel of the town's immaculately maintained heritage of parks and gardens. Here is the **Theater** (*Solmsstrasse 1, tel 07221 93 27 51*), built in 1860. Recently restored and staging performances again, it's an exuberant example of French neo-baroque theater design, a fitting setting for the 1862 premiere of Berlioz's Shakespearean opera *Béatrice et Bénédict.* To the north is more parkland, with the **Trinkhalle,** a colonnaded pump room decorated with frescoes of local legends.

The town center is attractive without being particularly remarkable. Stairways and narrow streets climb north to the Marktplatz and the Gothic **Stiftskirche.** The church's many treasures include a superb sandstone late medieval crucifix and an over-the-top monument to "Türkenlouis"— the "Terror of the Turk," Margrave Ludwig Wilhelm.

Farther up the hill looms the **New Castle** (Neues Schloss), until 1918 the summer residence of the Grand Dukes of Baden, with fine views from its terrace over the town. It's now a luxury hotel, but you can visit the lobby.

On the same level as the Stiftskirche you'll find the spa quarter. It begins with the most opulent of all Baden-Baden's spa establishments, the **Friedrichsbad.** Intended to replicate the luxury of ancient Rome, it opened in 1877 and created a sensation with its up-to-the-minute facilities in palatial surroundings. It has been unobtrusively modernized to accommodate a "Roman-Irish spa,"

which offers a three-hour treatment that is highly recommended if you don't mind appearing in company with no clothes on. The remains of the real Roman spa installations are beyond, upstaged by the **Caracalla-Therme,** a state-of-the-art complex of indoor and outdoor pools completed in 1985.

Among the reminders of Baden-Baden's heyday are the churches built for its cosmopolitan community. Romanian Prince Michael Stourdza commissioned the great Munich architect Leo von Klenze (1784–1864) to design the domed **Stourdza-Kapelle** in the parkland high above the Trinkhalle in memory of his son. In the 19th century and the years immediately before World War I, members of the Russian aristocracy were among the most enthusiastic visitors to Baden-Baden. The connection was strengthened when Prince Wilhelm of Baden married the sister of Tsar Alexander II. The **Russian Orthodox Church,** with its onion domes, strikes an exotic note in the southern part of town. ■

Baden-Baden's spa facilities are brought up to date in the Caracalla-Therme.

Caracalla-Therme
- ✉ Römerplatz 11
- ☎ 07221 27 59 40
- 💲 $$

Russian Orthodox Church
- ✉ Lichtentaler Strasse
- ☎ 07221 39 06 34
- 💲 $

Above: A Gothic doorway and oriel window enliven the street scene. Below: Flowers stay fresh in one of the city's water channels.

Freiburg im Breisgau

FREIBURG HAS AN ENVIABLE SUNNY LOCATION WHERE one of the main valleys running down from the Black Forest meets the Rhine plain. The city has a sunny temperament too; its citizens, and the students at its venerable university, seem more cheerful and relaxed than many of their fellow countrymen. It's a good center for exploring the surrounding region: The Black Forest, the Rhine Valley, France, and Switzerland are not far distant. Within sight of Freiburg is the Emperor's Seat (Kaiserstuhl), an ancient, vine-clad volcano.

The city's greatest treasure is its red sandstone cathedral, the **Minster of Our Lady** (Münster Unserer Lieben Frau) on Münsterplatz. It's hard to believe that this magnificent Gothic structure with its 377-foot (115 m) tower was built simply as a parish church, being elevated to the rank of cathedral only in the 19th century. It was begun in Romanesque style about 1200, but from this first period only the transepts remain, flanked by towers with openwork caps added later. These imitate the lacelike structure of the spire that crowns the western end of the cathedral. This was a pioneering effort, a great technical achievement when it was completed around 1350. You can climb to the tower's viewing platform for a vista of the city.

To appreciate the richness and complexity of the cathedral's exterior, with its flying buttresses and droll gargoyles, walk around the square; the color and bustle of the market stalls add an authentically medieval note. Pause for a look at the north door, where the sculpture includes a figure of God resting on the seventh day of the Creation. On the west portal Satan is shown as a smooth seducer leading on a lady clad only in a goatskin. You can take a guided tour of the cathedral, but the highlights are the 13th-century stained glass and a superb altarpiece by Hans Baldung Grien depicting the Coronation of the Virgin.

A word of warning: The streets and squares are seamed with channels, originally built to water animals and flush away filth, a hazard for the unwary. With this in mind, don't miss the other buildings around Münsterplatz. Note especially the arcaded, steep-roofed and oxblood-red **Historisches Kaufhaus,** the early 16th-century Merchants' Hall. The statues and coats of arms adorning its facade represent the city's Austrian rulers.

To the west of Münsterplatz, the commercial heart of Freiburg is a pleasing mixture of old and new. During World War II, accidental German bombing destroyed a good portion of the city, and further destruction occurred during an Allied air raid in 1944; much rebuilding has occurred since.

Beyond Kaiser-Joseph-Strasse is **Rathausplatz,** with its two town halls converted from once separate buildings. The New Town Hall (Neues Rathaus) has a carillon, which plays at noon. Behind St. Martin's Church in the middle of the square is one of the city's finest

old houses, the **Haus zum Walfisch,** with an exuberant Gothic doorway.

Kaiser-Joseph-Strasse leads south to the restored 13th-century city gateway called the **Martinstor.** To the left, alongside a broad water channel, is **Fischerau,** once the

district of fishermen, tanners, and others who needed water for their work. In the old Augustinian monastery, the **Augustinermuseum** has excellent examples of medieval religious art, including original gargoyles from the cathedral. The **Schwabentor,** the medieval gateway guarding the southeastern approach to the city, still stands. Close by is the 14th-century **Zum Roten Bären** (tel 0761 38 78 70, closed Sun.), said to be Germany's oldest inn. Leading north is a pretty old street, **Konviktstrasse.**

Freiburg has its own mountain within the city limits. The **Schauinsland** (4,213 feet/1,284 m) gives fantastic views over the city, Black Forest, and Rhine plain. It is accessible by cable car from Stüble, a short bus ride from the city center. ■

Freiburg im Breisgau

🅰 319 AI

Visitor information

✉ Rotteckring 14

☎ 0761 3 88 18 80

Ride the Schauinsland cable car for views over the Rhine valley to France.

Minster of Our Lady

✉ Münsterplatz

☎ 0761 20 27 90

💲 $

Augustinermuseum

✉ Am Augustinerplatz 1–3

☎ 0761 2 01 25 31

🕐 Closed Mon.

💲 $

Beautifully located Titisee makes a good base for exploring the Black Forest.

Black Forest

RUNNING NORTH FOR ABOUT 100 MILES (160 KM) FROM the Swiss border and extending some 37 miles (60 km) from east to west, the mountainous Black Forest region boasts dark masses of spruce and fir, clear streams and waterfalls, great timber farmhouses, and extravagant folk costumes. A superb network of footpaths has long attracted walkers. Today, visitors can stay in a wide range of accommodations, ranging from farmstead self-catering apartments to luxury lakeside hotels.

Black Forest
🗺 319 A1 & B1–B2

Titisee
🗺 319 B1
Visitor information
✉ Kurhaus
☎ 07651 9 80 40 or
   07651 93 55 60

German Clock Museum
www.deutsches-uhrenmuseum.de
🗺 319 B1
✉ Robert-Gerwig-Platz, Furtwangen
☎ 07723 92 28 00
💲 $

Th Black Forest reaches its highest point in the southwest, where the **Feldberg** tops out at 4,898 feet (1,493 m). The Feldberg, like other summits in this area, is bare, but coniferous forest covers the higher ground almost everywhere else. This dark cover gives way to more varied deciduous woodland and meadows on the lower slopes and in the valleys. The uplands drop gently in most directions, but in the west they fall steeply to the Rhine Valley. Along the crest, the viewpoints include the Feldberg itself and the **Schauinsland** (see p. 335), reached by cable car from **Freiburg im Breisgau**. Views

extend over the valley, where the forest cover gives way to a line of wine villages and orchards, toward the great river, and beyond to the Vosges Mountains in Alsace. On clear days, the distant line of the Alps comes into sight.

One good base for exploration in this very large area is **Titisee,** a resort on the lake of the same name, centrally located in the southern Black Forest and within reach of many of the region's highlights. Titisee can be very crowded, but there are many places to stay in the surrounding area.

The deep cleft of **Hell Valley** (Höllental) to the west is

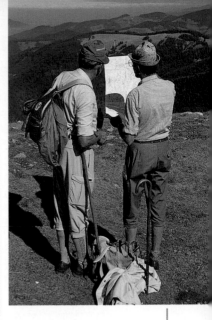

Right: Hikers
adore the
Belchen, one
of the Black
Forest's highest
summits.

spectacular. You can follow it along a main road or an ingeniously engineered railroad that links the interior of the Black Forest to Freiburg. To the north, the clockmaking town of **Furtwangen** is home to the wonderful **German Clock Museum** (Deutsches Uhrenmuseum), featuring timepieces of all kinds—including cuckoo clocks.

Triberg, farther north still, is also famous for clockmaking. Its **Schwarzwaldmuseum** has displays of local costumes and crafts. A half-hour's walk away is the country's highest waterfall (535 feet/163 m).

For more traditional Black Forest culture, continue up the road to the **Black Forest Open-Air Museum** (Schwarzwälder Freilichtmuseum). Here you'll find a collection of farm buildings and learn how all farming activities took place beneath their massive hipped roofs.

Further exploration could include a drive along one of Germany's finest scenic roads, the **Schwarzwald-Hochstrasse,** which joins Freudenstadt with Baden-Baden. However, it is on foot that you are likely to have the most memorable experiences.

Schwarzwald-museum
- 319 B2
- Wallfahrtsstrasse 4, Triberg
- 07722 44 34
- $$

Black Forest Open-Air Museum
www.vogtsbauernhof.org
- 319 B2
- Gutach
- 07831 9 35 60
- Open April–early Nov.
- $$

Visitor centers have information about local paths, but make sure you climb up to at least one of the classic high-level viewpoints (see p. 338). In the Titisee area, a rewarding walk takes you from the village of Hinterzarten into the Höllental and the Ravenna Gorge. Or you could tramp along one of the long-distance trails that crisscross the Black Forest. (Arrange to have your luggage transported on from one hotel to the next at a visitor center or travel agent.) ∎

Black Forest clocks

In the 1949 film *The Third Man,* Orson Welles may have scornfully attributed them to the Swiss, but cuckoo clocks are a quintessential Black Forest product. Clockmaking began in the region in the 17th century, as impoverished farmers looked for alternative ways of making a living. In this well-forested region, their familiarity with wood proved invaluable, and clock mechanisms were expertly carved from wood until well into the 19th century. Millions of clocks were exported, to America and the rest of Europe, until the industry drastically declined in the 1970s. A modest revival has since taken place. Souvenir shops are stocked with clocks to suit all pockets, while individual timepieces can be ordered to personal specifications from highly skilled specialists. ∎

Black Forest clock center in Titisee

The Feldberg: A walk to the Black Forest's highest summit

The Black Forest rises grandly in its southwestern corner to its highest elevation, culminating in the 4,898-foot (1,493 m) Feldberg. Virtually all visitors to this magical place feel an obligation to climb the great block of granite and gneiss, scraped into its final shape by the glaciers of the last ice age. Extensive and spectacular views reaching as far as the Swiss Alps are the reward.

This is not a difficult walk. A road leads most of the way up the Feldberg, terminating at a huge parking lot, hotels, kiosks, and souvenir shops to one side, an interpretive center, the **Haus der Natur ❶**—the Nature House— on the other. The Haus der Natur is an excellent place to find out more about local history and ecology before striking out on your walk. You will learn, for instance, that bands of chalky soil occur in places on the mountain, enriching its flora by allowing lime-loving plants to coexist with acid-tolerant species. Trees rise from its lower slopes, but the top is clear, the grasses and bog vegetation the result not only of the exceptionally harsh climate, but also of centuries of grazing by cattle.

The summit receives nearly 80 inches (2,000 mm) of precipitation a year, much of it falling as snow. The first flakes can descend as early as September, and snow covers sheltered spots on the northern slopes until well into summer. The relative reliability of snowfall led to the early popularity of the Feldberg as a place for winter sports, the first ski enthusiasts appearing in 1890. Walkers come year-round; the most favorable conditions can occur in fall or early winter, when temperature inversions fill the valleys with fog and leave the upper air wonderfully clear.

Even if you dislike walking uphill, resist the temptation to take the Feldbergbahn cable car. It saves a climb of only 575 feet (175 m) and will diminish your sense of achievement! Set off along the surfaced road to the left of the Haus der Natur and, after about 330 yards (300 m), turn right onto a path. This is the only mildly strenuous part of the walk, climbing up to the granite obelisk of the **Bismarckdenkmal ❷**, erected in 1896. There are stupendous views in all directions, including downward to the **Feldsee,** a small lake formed by a glacier. Panels help identify more distant features such as the Schwäbische Alb to the northeast and the ridge of the Vosges Mountains beyond the Rhine to the west. If conditions are exceptionally clear, you may be able to identify peaks such as the Eiger, Mönch, and Jungfrau, and even Mont Blanc, 150 miles (250 km) away.

From the Bismarckdenkmal strike off across the airy, gently undulating top of the mountain toward the high point at its western end, keeping to the path. The Feldberg has suffered serious erosion in the past from the pressure of countless pairs of feet and its mantle of vegetation is still vulnerable. The towers rising from the peak include a weather station and modern radio and television installations. From here you can return to the starting point by the service road.

If you have time, descend the mountain's southwestern flank to the welcoming chalet called the **St. Wilhelmer Hütte ❸**. A road runs down to the mountain hut, **Todtnauer Hütte ❹**, after which it continues on an almost level alignment to rejoin the service road. ∎

🅜 See area map p. 319 A1
▶ Feldberghof parking lot
🔄 4.7 miles (7.5 km), or 5.6 miles (9 km) via the chalets
🕐 2 hours (2.5 hours via the chalets)
▶ Feldberghof parking lot

NOT TO BE MISSED
- Haus der Natur
- View down to the Feldsee
- Panoramic views from the summit

Footpaths meander across the Feldberg's summit, the Black Forest's highest point.

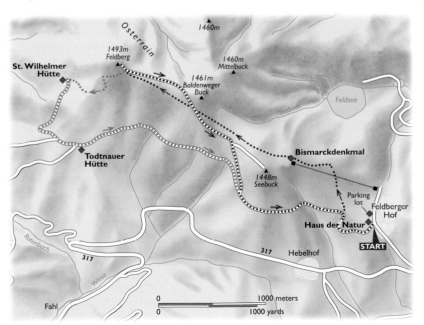

Lake Constance

Plane trees provide a touch of Old Europe charm to a lakeside café.

GERMANS LOVE LAKE CONSTANCE, A SERENE NATURAL vacation destination sharing borders with Switzerland and Austria that, in all practicality, is not a lake but a great swelling of the Rhine as it leaves the Alps. Gouged by an ice age glacier, the body of water is divided into the upper lake, between Bregenz in Austria and German Konstanz, and smaller sections to the northwest, cut by the Bodanrück peninsula. The lake tempers what would otherwise be severe winter weather and encourages the growth of vines, fruit, and other crops.

Lindau

🅜 280 A2

Visitor information

✉ Am Hauptbahnhof

☎ 08382 26 00 30

Haus zum Cavazzen

✉ Marktplatz 6, Lindau

☎ 08382 94 40 73

🕐 Closed Mon.

💲 $

Malhaus

🅜 319 D1

✉ Wasserburg

☎ 08382 895 16

🕐 Closed Mon. & winter

💲 $

The best way to explore the lake's northeastern German shore is aboard one of the pleasure boats that link its main attractions. If you are staying three days or more, buy the Lake Constance Experience ticket *(BodenseeErlebniskarte),* which gives free use of lake cruisers and entry to most attractions in the area (including those in Switzerland and Austria).

LINDAU

At the lake's northeast end, the island city of Lindau is actually in Bavaria, but it forms such an integral part of the Lake Constance region that it is included here. Linked to the mainland by a road bridge and a causeway carrying the railroad, it's a magical place, with a harbor looking south to the mountains of Appenzell in Switzerland and the Vorarlberg range rising

over the lakeside town of Bregenz in Austria. The peaks are half-hidden in haze in summer, seemingly suspended above the lake's waters. It's tempting just to sit on the café terrace of one of the quayside hotels and watch the boats coming in and out between the lighthouse at the end of one pier, and the stone lion of Bavaria at the end of the other.

Next, walk east along the quayside, past the 13th-century **Mangturm,** a relic of the medieval fortifications, and then turn inland. The old town center is full of charm, its unspoiled streets and squares lined with timber-framed and gabled houses. The Gothic **Old Town Hall** (Altes Rathaus) on Kanzleistrasse was modernized in Renaissance times with an external staircase and (much retouched) murals.

Go east along the main street, Maximilianstrasse, and you will come to **Marktplatz,** Lindau's loveliest square. The town's history began here, with the founding in the ninth century of a convent. Its church stands here, but the most striking building in the square is the **Haus zum Cavazzen,** an imposing baroque mansion that now serves as the municipal museum.

OTHER NORTH SHORE TOWNS

Still just in Bavaria, **Wasserburg** is an island settlement reached by

causeway. Packed together are its castle, onion-domed church, and the gabled courthouse, the **Malhaus,** where witches were tried in the 17th century. On view is the "Wasserburg Pear," a steel bridle used to torture them. **Schloss Montfort,** in the next settlement along the lake, **Langenargen,** is a Moorish-style summer residence of the Württemberg royal family.

The second largest lake town after Konstanz, **Friedrichshafen** is a businesslike place with modern industries carrying on the traditions established by Ferdinand Graf von Zeppelin (1838–1917). In 1900 Zeppelin oversaw the maiden flight of the first of the great airships that immortalized his name. The story is told in the splendid **Zeppelin-Museum,** housed in a gleaming white 1930s building. The highlight is a full-scale reconstruction of a section of the ill-fated *Hindenburg,* whose demise at Lakehurst Field, New Jersey, in 1937 brought their era to a tragic end. For anyone used to the cramped conditions of today's air travel, it's an uncanny experience to stroll through the spacious lounge and observation deck provided aboard the giant airship.

Perched high above the lake in the heart of the lakeside vineyards,

the little town of **Meersburg** has not one castle, but two. The lower town by the harbor is linked by the steep Steigstrasse to the upper town, full of sloping streets and squares lined by flower-bedecked houses. The **Weinbaumuseum's** historic exhibits include a monster barrel with a capacity of about 13,000 gallons (50,000 L).

Farther along the shore, the life of earlier inhabitants of the Bodensee is on show in the open-air **Stilt House Museum** (Pfahlbaumuseum) at Unteruhldingen (*Strandpromenade, tel 07556 85 43*). The museum has convincing reconstructions of a number of ancient dwellings perched over the waters of the lake.

High up among the vineyards between here and Überlingen is the pilgrimage church of **Birnau** (*normally open in daytime*), a little masterpiece of rococo architecture and interior decoration. The most famous feature is the "Honig-schlecker," a cherub sucking honey from his finger, a reference to the "honeyed eloquence" of Bernard of Clairvaux, founder of the Cistercian Order to which the church belongs.

Overlooking the Bodanrück peninsula is the lovely old imperial town of **Überlingen.** In the 19th

A pleasure boat leaves Lindau harbor and its resident Bavarian lion.

Zeppelin-Museum
- 319 C1
- Ehemaliger Hafenbahnhof, Seestrasse 22
- 07541 38 01 33
- Closed Mon.
- $$

Meersburg
- 319 C1
Visitor information
- Marktplatz 1
- 07532 44 00

Weinbaumuseum
- Vorburggasse, Meersburg
- 07532 44 00
- Closed Mon., Wed., Sat.
- $

Überlingen
- 319 C1
Visitor information
- Landungsplatz 14
- 07551 99 11 22

Mainau Island, the garden isle

Reichlin-Meldegg-Haus

✉ Krummebergstrasse 30, Überlingen

☎ 07551 99 10 79

🕐 Closed Mon.

💲 $

Konstanz

🅰 319 C1

Visitor information

✉ Bahnhofplatz 13

☎ 07531 13 30 30

Mainau

🅰 319 C1

✉ Insel Mainau

☎ 07531 30 30

💲 $$$

century it succeeded in reinventing itself as a health resort. Unlike many similar places, its people realized that the town walls and their towers were a visual asset, and preserved them.

Walk up from the lakefront to **Münsterplatz,** with its Town Hall (Rathaus) and Gothic minster church, and continue to the local museum. Housed in the 15th-century **Reichlin-Meldegg-Haus,** it has the country's biggest collection of dollhouses, and a fine view of town from its garden .

KONSTANZ

The busiest ferry service on the lake crosses the mouth of the Überlinger See, linking Meersburg to the Bodanrück peninsula and the city of Konstanz. The region's largest town, **Konstanz** stands astride the narrows through which the Rhine flows from the upper lake to the Untersee, the smaller downstream lake. On the south bank, the Old Town (Altstadt) has kept much of its medieval charm. (Allied aircraft left the city alone for fear of bombing neutral Switzerland, which begins almost at the end of the main street.) Konstanz was founded by the Romans, but the city's moment of glory came in 1414–18, when the Council of Konstanz met here to heal the great crisis of medieval Christendom, the rift between rival Popes called the Great Schism. The delegates are popularly said to have met in the massive **Konzilgebäude** by the harbor and lakeside promenade. They actually assembled in the city's cathedral, the **Münster,** with its mixture of architectural styles and magnificent 13th-century Holy Sepulchre.

ISLANDS IN THE LAKE

From Konstanz it is only a short distance to the Bodensee's two islands, both reached by causeways.

Quiet **Reichenau** is almost entirely given over to market produce, much of it under glass. You'll find two ancient monastery churches here: **St. Georg** in Oberzell has thousand-year-old wall paintings, while the **Münster St. Maria und Markus** (*tel 07534 9 20 70*) in Mittelzell is a marvel of deeply spiritual architectural simplicity.

The garden island of **Mainau** is Lake Constance's most popular single destination. The most dramatic way to reach the island is by lake boat. You then climb from the quayside through terraced Italianate gardens. This subtropical paradise, with its dazzling floral displays and superb specimen trees, is laid out around the 18th-century Schloss, originally founded by the Teutonic Knights, now owned by a branch of the Swedish royal family. Mainau's other attractions include a lovely little baroque church, a medieval watchtower, and a butterfly garden. ∎

"Burn him!"

The historical figure most closely associated with the Protestant city of Konstanz is the radical Czech preacher and church reformer—a Protestant before his time—Jan Hus (ca 1372–1415). A farmer's son with a gift for words, Hus established himself in Prague as a compelling orator, denouncing the contemporary corruption of the Church. A thorn in the flesh of his superiors, in 1414 he was summoned to Konstanz where he was tried, condemned, and burned at the stake. His ashes were cast into the Rhine but his teachings lived on, leading to destructive religious and political conflicts which came to be known as the Hussite Wars. Admirers still make their way to Konstanz to visit the **Hus-Museum** (*Hussenstrasse 64, Konstanz, closed Mon.*). ∎

Ulm

WITH ITS ANCIENT FORTIFICATIONS AND HOUSES, ALL lorded over by the minster's great spire, Ulm creates a picturesque scene on the Danube. Before exploring its narrow lanes, take a stroll along the riverbank's south (Bavarian) side to take it all in.

Stepped gables, elaborate Gothic windows, and murals adorn Ulm's Rathaus.

As you walk, spare a thought for Albrecht Ludwig Berblinger—the "Tailor of Ulm." In 1811 his homemade glider failed to fly and gave him a very public ducking in the Danube. A better known local was Nobel Prize winner Albert Einstein, born here in 1879.

Back in town, first explore the well-preserved **Fischer-Viertel** (Fishermen's Quarter). There's a good view of the one-time houses of riverside residents—tanners, dyers, ferrymen—from the promenade atop the fortifications. The **Metzgerturm** (Butchers' Tower) leans at an angle some 6 feet (2m) off center, while the 15th-century **Schiefes Haus** (Crooked House) lives up to its name, cast askew by piles sagging into the soft riverbed underneath. The picturesque **Fischerplätzle** (Fishermen's

Square) affords a great view of the 15-century Zunfthaus (the fishermen's guildhall) and the **Schönes Haus** (Pretty House), adorned with a proud scene of shipping on the Danube. A key trading post as early as the 12th century, the town would dispatch *Ulmer Schachteln*, or flat boats, laden with fabrics and goods down the waterway as far as the Black Sea.

On the first Monday in June, the mayor addresses the burghers from the balcony of the 18th-century **Schwörhaus** (Oath House), swearing on the 1397 constitution that rich and poor should be treated equally, without discrimination or reservation—a bold statement in a society run by wealthy patricians. However, the power transferred not to the people but the guilds, who maintained a vice grip on the city

Ulm
⛰ 319 D2
Visitor information
✉ Münsterplatz
☎ 0731 1 61 28 30

Ulmer Museum
✉ Markt 6
☎ 0731 161 43 00
💲 $

Although work began on Ulm's massive Münster in the 14th century, it was not completed until 1890.

council. From here, you can wander down **Kussgasse** (Kissing Alley), where the opposing eaves nearly touch each other overhead and cross over the **Lügner-Brücke** (Liar's Bridge), where shady dealers were thought to make their getaway.

Ulm's utterly photogenic **Town Hall** (Rathaus) is a Gothic-cum-Renaissance building adorned with figures of Charlemagne and the kings of Hungary and Bohemia, not to mention a dazzling astrological clock. In the foyer, Berblinger's attempt at manned flight is commemorated by a full-size copy of his machine, now considered more a visionary than foolhardy venture. On Marktplatz, the brightly-colored **Fischkastenbrunnen** (Fish Crate Fountain) is where fishmongers kept their catch alive on market days.

The giant **Münster** is not a cathedral but a parish church. Its nave (minus the pews) can hold 20,000 people—nearly twice the town's population when work was begun in 1377. The spire rises 525 feet (161 m), making it the world's tallest church tower. Climb the 768 steps to the top on a clear day, and you will see not only a close-up of the spire's openwork construction, but also the Alps more than 60 miles (100 km) away to the south.

Medieval builders conceived the tower's idea, but its completion had to await late 19th-century technology. While superb statuary graces the church's portals, the finest work of art is inside: Carved by two 15th-century locals, the choir stalls are ornamented with busts of figures from the ancient world and the Bible.

The **Ulmer Museum** has carvings by star artists like Daniel Mauch, the last of the city's great disciples of Italianate sculpture. Upstairs is a fascinating section on the four centuries of thought and toil that went into erecting the Münster, a testimony to determination if there ever was one. The treasures include the renowned Kurt Fried collection of works from the 1950s to '80s, by artists including Kandinsky, Klee, Liechtenstein, and Picasso. ■

Strange figures stroll the streets during Rottweil's *Fastnet* celebrations.

More places to visit in Baden-Württemberg

BURG HOHENZOLLERN

The harsh landscape of the Swabian Jura was the first home of the Hohenzollerns, the dynasty that built Prussia into Germany's most militarily successful state after unification in 1871, then led to its defeat in World War I. In the early 19th century, Prussian Crown Prince Friedrich Wilhelm inspected the ruins of the ancestral castle and decided to rebuild it. Between 1850 and 1867, a new building arose from the old foundations, more spectacularly medieval than the old castle ever was. Its dramatic outline visible from far and wide, Burg Hohenzollern is one of the great monuments of the rising German nationalism of the 19th century, with fascinating interiors and many reminders of the ill-fated local family.

🅰 319 C2 ✉ Hechingen ☎ 07471 24 28 💲 $$ (guided tour)

HAIGERLOCH

The point where the little River Eyach is forced into tightly constricted bends by a pair of rock spurs makes a picturesque but not very practical urban site. Of several churches here, not one could be built to face exactly east because of the limited amount of available land. Haigerloch has a castle and the **Atomkeller-Museum** (*Pfluggasse 5, tel 07474 6 97 27*), a real curiosity. In the spring of 1945, scientists evacuated from Berlin worked feverishly in underground chambers on the development of a nuclear reactor, and the museum tells the story of their vain efforts.

🅰 319 B2 **Visitor information** ✉ Rathaus ☎ 07474 69 70

MAULBRONN

The 12th-century Cistercian monastery at Maulbronn has been granted UNESCO World Heritage status as a perfectly preserved example of the architectural setting for medieval monastic life. The austere Cisterican order chose locations for their monasteries in remote, often beautiful places, where they could live a self-sufficient life apart from the temptations of the world. Inside Maulbronn's walls and towers is a complete little world, not just of buildings to worship in, but also of the structures necessary to sustain a considerable community—smithies, stables, storehouses, a bakery, a guesthouse—all grouped picturesquely around a courtyard. At the far end is the church, which originally reflected in its plain lines the Cistercian love of simplicity, but later was enhanced with artworks and decorative features such as elaborate vaulting. The monastic quarters around the cloister include a lovely washing fountain used by the monks before and after meals in the great refectory. Maulbronn was also a school, its pupils including the astronomer Johannes Kepler, the poet Friedrich Hölderlin, and the writer Hermann Hesse.

⚠ 319 B3 ✉ Ehemaliges Zisterzienserkloster Maulbronn ☎ 07043 92 66 10

ROTTWEIL

There is much more to this medieval town than the sturdy dog that has made its name familiar worldwide. In Germany, Rottweil is synonymous with particularly spectacular pre-Lenten Fastnet celebrations, whose high point is the Narrensprung, a parade of colorfully costumed and masked fools. This takes place in the setting of Rottweil's unspoiled townscape, with its elaborately decorated old houses, Renaissance fountains, and intact fortifications.

⚠ 319 B2 **Visitor information** ✉ Rathaus, Marktplatz ☎ 0741 49 42 80

SCHLOSS BRUCHSAL

The great baroque Schloss at Bruchsal is one of the most ambitious of its kind, virtually a town within a town with some 50 individual buildings and a French-style formal garden whose main avenue once led to the Rhine 10 miles (16 km) away. The grand palace was built for one of the most extravagant of Germany's 18th-century prince-bishops, Cardinal Damian Hugo von Schönborn, whose old residence in his Episcopal city of Speyer had suffered war damage. Moreover, the cardinal was at odds with the tiresomely Protestant citizens of Speyer, and he had little hesitation in laying out an up-to-the-minute architectural complex on a fresh site, free of previous associations. He is flatteringly portrayed in one of the frescoes on the upper floor, benevolently approving the plan of his palace. Behind him stands the figure of Balthasar Neumann, perhaps the greatest architect of the German baroque, responsible here at Bruchsal for the spectacular staircase. The Schloss houses the **Mechanical**

Musical Instruments Museum (Museum Mechanischer Musikinstrumente), with musicmaking apparatus from pianolas to jukeboxes *(separate ticket)*.

⚠ 319 B3 ☎ 07251 74 26 61 🕒 Closed Mon. 💲 $

SCHLOSS SCHWETZINGEN

His town palace at Mannheim gave Elector Palatine Carl Theodor (1724–1799) little scope for his passion for landscape. He turned his attention to his summer residence at nearby Schwetzingen, and over a 30-year period laid out one of the most fabulous 18th-century gardens in Europe. This mixture of French formality and English naturalism is peppered with an extraordinary array of fantastical buildings. These include Roman temples, artificial ruins, a bathhouse, and a mosque with twin minarets and a "Turkish" garden. The gardens cover an area of 180 acres (73 ha) and rather upstage the palace itself, although this is well worth visiting for its rococo theater and authentically furnished interiors. Schwetzingen's second claim to fame is as a center for growing Germany's favorite vegetable, asparagus. An asparagus seller (in bronze) greets you as you near the palace.

⚠ 319 B4 ☎ 06202 12 88 28 🕒 Closed Mon. 💲 $$ (guided tour, separate charge for gardens and theater)

SCHWÄBISCH HALL

One of the most attractive towns in southwestern Germany, Schwäbisch Hall made its first fortune from the saline springs originally exploited in prehistoric times. A second period of prosperity came when it was granted the right to mint silver coins. Called *Häller* (or *Heller)* after the town, these coins, like today's euro, were valid through out Europe, and even today *hellers* are part of the currency in the Czech Republic and Slovakia. Schwäbisch Hall's timber-framed houses rise over the River Kocher, crossed by covered bridges. The townscape is dominated by **St. Michael's Church,** reached by an enormous stairway leading up from the sloping marketplace, one of the finest urban spaces in Germany.

⚠ 319 C3 **Visitor information** ✉ Am Markt 9 ☎ 0791 75 12 46 ■

Travelwise

Intercity express train

TRAVELWISE INFORMATION

PLANNING YOUR TRIP

WHEN TO GO

Germany has its charms any time of year, so choosing when to go depends on your priorities. Spring and fall are the best for exploring the historic monuments, medieval walled towns, and fairy-tale castles. High summer, in July and August, tends to be overrun but brings fine weather to the sea and mountain areas.

The (in)famous Oktoberfest, held in Munich in late September/early October, is the largest beer festival on the planet. The Christmas markets in December have a delightful conviviality that you won't find anyplace else. Winter is perfect for skiing in the Alps, Black Forest, and Harz Mountains.

Helpful websites include: www.germany-tourism.de (German National Tourist Office) www.hhog.de (Historic Highlights of Germany) www.deutschland.de (German Government Website) Regional tourist offices (Verkehrsamt) provide information on attractions and accommodations, and sell guidebooks and maps.

CLIMATE

Germany's climate is temperate with continental extremes. Marine influences from the north and west make for cool summers and mild, damp winters. Eastern and southern parts of the country experience hotter summers and harsher winters. The region along the Alpine rim gets the most precipitation. Plan your wardrobe to allow for fickle weather—sunglasses and suntan lotion, but also a light raincoat and clothes that you can wear in layers.
Average daytime temperature: Berlin 35°F (2°C) in winter; 65°F (18°C) in summer
Hamburg 32°F (0°C) in winter; 61°F (17°C) in summer

Munich 30°F (−1°C) in winter; 63°F (17°C) in summer

MAIN EVENTS

Easter and Christmas both offer fascinating glimpses of traditional local events. The Catholic regions are alive with religious festivals, especially in the springtime.

JANUARY Grüne Woche in Berlin, mid-Jan., a consumer fair for agriculture, www.gruene woche. de. **Six-day cycle race** in Berlin, Jan. 1, www.sechsta gerennen-berlin.de.
FEBRUARY International Film Festival in Berlin, 2nd and 3rd week, www.berlinale.de. **Carnival** celebrations in Cologne, Düsseldorf, and Mainz, from the Thurs. of the week before Ash Wednesday, www.karneval.de.
MARCH Book Fair in Leipzig, mid March, www.leipziger-buchmesse.de.
APRIL Easter celebrations in Catholic villages. **Hanover International Industrial Trade Fair**, early/mid-April, www.hannovermesse.de.
Walpurgisnacht (a witches' sabbath in the Harz mountains), April 30–May 1, www.harzlife.de.
MAY Hamburger Hafenge-burtstag, sailing regattas and street entertainment, mid-May, www.hafengeburtstag.de. Ruhrfestspiele in **Reckling-hausen**, exhibitions, concerts, and theater, May 1–end June, www.ruhrfestspiele.de.
JUNE Festival of Classical Music in Mecklenburg, June–Sept., www.musiksommer-mv.de. **Kieler Woche** yachting regatta, 3rd week in June, www.kieler woche.de. **Festival of Classical Music** in Bad Kissingen, www .kissingersommer.de. **Open Air Opera Festival** in Potsdam, 2 weeks in early June, www .musikfestspiele-potsdam.de. **Karl-May Festival** in Bad Segeberg, reenactment of Apache

tales from the American West, July–end Aug., www.karl-may-spiele.de. **Burgfestspiele Jagst-hausen**, theater and classical music festival in a romantic castle, www.jagsthausen.de.
JULY Love Parade in Berlin, 2nd Sat. www.loveparade.net.
Richard Wagner Festival in Bayreuth, late July–late Aug., www.bayreuther-festspiele.de.
Festival of Classical Music in Schleswig-Holstein, early July–early Sept., www.shmf.de.
AUGUST Mainfest (celebrations of the River Main in Frankfurt) early Aug., www .frankfurt-tourismus.de. **Rhein in Flammen** in Koblenz (fireworks from boats and river banks), early Aug., www.rhein .feuerwerk-info.de
SEPTEMBER Berliner Festwochen, a month-long series of cultural events, www.festwochen.de.
Beethoven Festival in Bonn, early Sept.–early Oct., www.beethovenfest.de.
Oktoberfest in Munich, 16 days from last Sat. in Sept., www.oktoberfest.de.
Cannstatter Volksfest in Stuttgart, the world's second-largest beer festival, last week Sept., www.cannstatter-volksfest .de. **Ruhr-Triennale Arts Festival**, www.ruhrtriennale.de.
Wine Festival in Bensheim an der Bergstrasse, nine days from 1st week Sept., www.bensheim.de.
OCTOBER Frankfurt Book Fair, mid-Oct., www.frankfurt-book-fair.com. **Zwiebelmarkt** in Weimar, a colorful street market, early/mid-Oct., www.zwiebelmarkt.info. **Kassel Music Days**, classical concerts, late Oct–early Nov., www .kasseler-musiktage.de.
NOVEMBER St. Martin's Day, Nov. 11, children's procession with lanterns and singing in Catholic areas.
DECEMBER Christmas Markets until Christmas Eve; the prettiest are held in Baden-Württemberg and Bavaria, the most renowned being in Nuremberg, www.weihnachts markt-deutschland.de.

WHAT TO TAKE

Whether you're coming to admire Germany's historic monuments or its natural wonders, be sure to pack comfortable footwear. The weather can change quickly so even in summer bring along a waterproof jacket and layers of clothing. A hat and sunscreen are good ideas if you're going to be outdoors for long periods.

Don't forget any prescription drugs you might need, and a second pair of glasses if you wear them. Everything else is readily available. Pharmacies (*Apotheke*, recognizable by the patent red "A" sign) are open during normal business hours, and, in large towns, at least one is open evenings and Sundays for emergencies. Drugstores (*Drogerien*) sell a limited range of non-prescription medicines, but for anything stronger than toothpaste, you'll have to hit the pharmacy.
Lastly, don't forget the essentials: passport, driver's license, ATM cards (or traveler's checks), and insurance documents.

INSURANCE

It pays to take out a travel insurance policy. Make sure you have adequate coverage for medical treatment and expenses including repatriation, and also for baggage and money loss. It's also a good idea to take photocopies of important documents and keep them separate from the originals, in case the latter are stolen.

HOW TO GET TO GERMANY

ENTRY FORMALITIES

Visitors from the U.S., Canada, Australia, New Zealand, Israel, Hong Kong, Japan, South Korea, and most European countries may visit Germany for three months without a visa. People visiting from other countries need to apply for a visa in advance from the German

embassy in their own countries. To stay more than three months, you should apply to the German Embassy in your own country for a residence permit.

AIRLINES

All the major airlines have flights to Germany and many arrange package tours and budget-price flights. Continental and American Airlines offer direct schedule flights from North America to Frankfurt am Main; Continental and Delta fly to Berlin; Air Canada fly to Frankfurt and Munich. Connecting flights can be made to other cities. Lufthansa offers frequent flights from the U.S., together with its partners in the Star Alliance, and has booking offices abroad.

From the U.K. and Ireland, British Airways operates hundreds of flights a week to German destinations. The no-frills airlines EasyJet and Ryanair fly to several German cities from the U.K. Be aware that some of their destination airports may be some distance from the named city.

Useful numbers in Germany:
American Airlines tel 01803 24 23 24
British Airways tel 01805 26 65 22
Continental tel 01803 21 26 10
Delta tel 01803 33 78 80
EasyJet tel 01803 65 43 21
Germanwings tel 0900 19 19 100
Lufthansa tel 01803 80 38 03
Ryanair tel 0900 116 0500

In the U.S. & Canada:
Air Canada tel 1-888 247 2262
American Airlines tel 1-800 433 7300
Continental tel 1-800 231 0856
Delta tel 1-800 241 4141
Lufthansa tel 1-800 399 5838

AIRPORTS

The largest German airport is Frankfurt Rhein-Main, the busiest in Europe after London's Heathrow. The country's other

main airports are at Munich, Düsseldorf, Hamburg, and Berlin, which in fact has three airports: Tegel and Schönefeld (both for international traffic) and tiny Tempelhof. The opening of Berlin's new Brandenburg International Airport is scheduled for 2010.

Frankfurt Rhein-Main Airport
Tel 01805 372 46 36,
www.frankfurt-airport.de
This gigantic airport comprises two terminals and two railroad stations. Passengers arrive at Terminal 2 and are taken via a Skyline transfer to Terminal 1 (20 minutes). Terminal 1 has a long-distance railroad station (the AIRail Terminal, from where you can reach all major cities in Germany) as well as a local station for the S-Bahn. A journey by taxi to Frankfurt center (7 miles/12 km), takes 20 minutes.
Munich Franz-Joseph Strauss Airport
Tel 089 975 00,
www.munich-airport.de
The S-Bahn (lines S-1 and S-8; every 20 minutes) goes directly from the airport to Munich central railroad station (Hauptbahnhof) and takes 39 minutes. The bus or taxi journey to the center (22 miles, 35 km) takes 45 minutes.
Hamburg Fuhlsbüttel Airport
Tel 040 507 50,
www.ham.airport.de
S-Bahn and subway links to Hamburg city center (8 miles, 13 km) are expected to open in 2008. There are good bus services at 20-minute intervals. Journeys by bus or taxi take 30 minutes.
Düsseldorf Rhein-Ruhr Airport
Tel 0211 42 10,
www.duesseldorf-international.de
A sky train or bus takes passengers from the terminal to the airport's railroad station in five minutes. From there an efficient S-Bahn system (line 7), which leaves every 20–30 minutes, gets you to the main station in 13 minutes. A taxi

journey to Düsseldorf center (6 miles, 10 km) takes 20 minutes.

Berlin-Tegel Airport
Tel 0180 500 01 86,
www.berlin-airport.de
There is a frequent bus service (lines 109, 9, and TXL Express) about every 10 minutes from the airport to strategic points in the center of Berlin (5 miles, 8 km). From there you can connect by bus, U-Bahn, or S-Bahn to anywhere in the city. A journey by bus or taxi takes 25 minutes.

FROM THE U.K.

Frequent Eurostar rail services through the Channel Tunnel depart from London Waterloo International to Lille (France), Paris, and Brussels (Belgium) from which you can travel onward into Germany. The Eurostar central reservation office is in London (tel 08705 186 186, www.eurostar.com). Eurotunnel trains (tel 08705 35 35 35, www.eurotunnel.com) carry private cars through the Channel Tunnel. The service operates 24 hours a day and takes about half an hour. Trains go from Folkestone in England to the French terminal near Calais. Car and passenger ferries operate from Harwich or Dover (U.K.), crossing the Channel to ports in Ostend (Belgium) and Calais (France). From these ports it takes about three to four hours to drive to Germany. For details of ferry services in the U.K., contact P&O North Sea Ferries (tel 01482 37 71 77, www.ponsf.com), SeaFrance (tel 08705 711 711, www.seafrance .com) or Norfolk Line (tel 0870 870 10 20, www.norfolkline-ferries.co.uk). Ferry services from England's east coast include Stenaline (tel 08705 70 70 70, www.stenaline.com), who operate from Harwich to the Hook of Holland, and DFDS Scandinavian Seaways (tel 08705 33 30 00, www.dfdsseaways.co.uk), who make the run from Newcastle-upon-Tyne to IJmuiden near Amsterdam.

GETTING AROUND

TRAVELING IN GERMANY

BY AIR

There are domestic flights to most major cities in Germany. Some of the main routes are operated by:
Air Berlin, tel 01805 73 78 00
Cirrus, tel 06893 800 40
DBA, tel 0900 110 03 22
Eurowings, tel 0180 58 38 42 67
Hapag-Lloyd (HLX), tel 01805 09 35 09
Lufthansa, tel 01803 803 803

BY TRAIN

Germany's excellent national railway network is run by Deutsche Bahn (DB, www.db .de). The InterCityExpress (ICE), InterCity (IC) and EuroCity (EC) services link major towns and cities, usually on an hourly basis. InterRegio lines have good connections to regional centers. Flagship of DB is the super high-speed ICE3 between Cologne and Frankfurt, with its own dedicated track and tickets nearly a third more expensive. All these trains have restaurant or buffet cars. Some services require a seat reservation as well as a ticket.

The DB Nightline (Nachtzug, tel 01805 14 15 14) has routes within Germany and farther afield. The CityNightLine (tel 01805 21 34 21) is an international sleeper train connecting Germany with Denmark and the Netherlands to the north and Austria and Switzerland to the south. The DB AutoZug (Motorail, tel 01805 24 12 24) offers a wide selection of day and night services within Germany and to Austria, France, and Italy.

Timetables and service information are available at all stations; every large station has a service center (Reisezentrum). You can buy train tickets in

advance either online from the service center, or from a travel agency (Reisebüro) in Germany. Deutsche Bahn offers a variety of reduced rates that are constantly changing. Foreign visitors to Germany can buy a special vacation passes before traveling. The DB information line (tel 0800 150 70 90) is a free service with recorded information in German. For details in English, call 11861 from anywhere in Germany.

BY BUS OR TRAM

Throughout Germany, tightly-woven networks of buses, trams, subway (U-Bahn), and commuter rail (S-Bahn) will get you where you want to go fast. Buses go to villages and small towns that are not plugged into the rail network. Within a city, a local transport ticket is valid simultaneously on buses, trams, and the U-Bahn. If there is no conductor, get your ticket from one of the vending machines at stops, or in some cases from on-board machines. Before you travel you must validate your ticket in one of the time-stamping devices installed at the entrance of every bus, U-Bahn, and S-Bahn.

BY CAR

Germany has a huge network of toll-free expressways (Autobahn-en). If you are not in a hurry, secondary roads (Landstrassen or Bundesstrassen) are usually more picturesque. Since reunification, the network in the east is being speedily modernized.

Renting a car
Renting a car in Germany is expensive by U.S. standards but close to a western European average. Arranging a car rental before leaving home can be cheaper, and there are fly-drive options with most flights. Otherwise, seek out the on-site desks in airports and major railroad stations in Germany.

Central offices:
Hertz: tel 01805 33 35 35

Avis: tel 01805 21 77 02
Sixt: tel 01805 25 25 25

To rent a car in Germany you must b at least 18 years old and have a current driver's license.

Motoring information & licenses U.S. and Canadian driving licenses are valid in Germany. Although an international driving license is not legally required, it can be quite useful—obtain one before you leave home. Visitors bringing cars from non-European countries should carry an international driving license and vehicle registration document. Non-German vehicles require a nationality sticker on the back of the vehicle.

Breakdown assistance In the event of a breakdown on the autobahn, Road Patrol Assistance can be called from emergency telephones on the shoulder. They can also be contacted direct via the motoring organizations:

ACE   tel 01802 33 66 77
ADAC   tel 01802 22 22 22
AvD   tel 0800 990 9909

Children Children under the age of 8 or under 5 feet (1.5 m) in height must sit in the back seat of a vehicle. Child seats are required for children under 4, and children under 12 must use a booster cushion.

Distances All distances on signposts in Germany are shown in kilometers (1 km = 0.62 mile).

Drunk-driving The legal blood alcohol limit is 0.05 percent.

Fines Heavy fines can be imposed on the spot, e.g. for driving without a seat belt or while using a cell phone. For serious incidents, the police can confiscate the driving license and vehicle of foreign motorists even if the vehicle is a German rental.

First aid Every vehicle is required to carry a first-aid kit

on board. Rental cars always have a first-aid kit on board.

Fuel All gasoline in Germany is unleaded. At the pumps you will find Normal (regular) and Super, as well as diesel and *Flüssiggas* (LPG). Gas and service stations are open 24 hours on autobahns and in bigger cities. Most gas stations accept credit cards.

Highway code Driving is on the right-hand side. At crossings, priority is given to traffic approaching from the right unless a sign (a yellow diamond) indicates you have right of way. Buses leaving stops have priority. At traffic lights, a green arrow to the right indicates you may turn right on red. Pedestrians always have the right of way.

Parking Parking is not allowed up to 16 feet (5 m) in front of or behind a pedestrian crossing, up to 32 feet (10 m) in front of traffic lights, or up to 48 feet (15 m) in front of or behind stop signs and exits.

Most towns have on-street parking meters (*Parkuhren*) from which you can buy a ticket to display in your car. Multistory parking lots are common but check the closing times—some close overnight and many are shut by 8 p.m.

Road conditions For details of current road conditions, tune into the local radio frequency (often indicated on signs beside the road), or call 224 99 for a recording in German.

Road signs
• *Halt*: stop
• *Keine Einfahrt*: no entry
• *Licht anmachen*: switch on lights
• *Parkverbot*: no parking
• *Fussgängerübergang*: pedestrian crossing
• *Einbahnstrasse*: one-way traffic
• *Stau*: traffic jam
• *Baustelle*: roadworks

Seat belts Seat belts must be worn by all passengers in the

car. The penalty for not wearing one is €30.

Speed limits Different speed limits apply for different weather conditions and times of poor visibility (heavy rain and fog). Autobahns have a recommended limit of 75–85 mph (110–130 kph). In cities, towns, and villages the limit is 30 mph (50 kph). The limit on all other roads is 70 mph (100 kph).

Studded tires & snow chains Studded tires are generally not allowed. In the winter you are strongly advised to buy or rent snow chains before traveling to regions with medium or higher altitudes.

Tolls All autobahns and main roads are toll-free for passenger vehicles. However, a charge is levied upon some sightseeing roads in Bavaria.

TRANSPORTATION IN BERLIN

Taxi stands are located at airports, train and underground stations, and throughout the city. Taxis can also be hailed in the street. There are two rates: one for short journeys from taxi stands, and another for journeys ordered by telephone. The rate remains the same at night.

Public transportation Berlin's buses, trams, and local rail network is run by the Berlin Transport Authority (BVG). The U-Bahn (underground trains) and S-Bahn (commuter network) operate from 4:30 a.m. until at least 12:30 a.m., with some lines running until 1:30 a.m., when a nighttime bus network takes over.

The city is divided into three travel zones: Zones A and B include the urban area, and zone Zone C (including Potsdam) is further away from the center of Berlin. Most destinations can be reached with a single A + B ticket.

GETTING AROUND/PRACTICAL ADVICE

The WelcomeCard (available at ticket offices and many Berlin hotels) is a public transportation ticket valid for 72 hours on all buses, trams, and trains within the A, B, and C fare zones. In addition, WelcomeCard holders are entitled to free admission, or up to 50 percent reduction, on guided tours or walks, boat trips, museums, theaters, and leisure facilities in Berlin and Potsdam. For a good rolling tour of the city, bus lines 100 and 200 take you past all the main sights.

PRACTICAL ADVICE

COMMUNICATIONS

POST OFFICES
In large towns, post offices (Postamt) are usually open from 8 a.m. until 6 p.m. weekdays, and from 8 a.m. until noon on Saturdays. There are branches with longer opening hours and Sunday services at most airports and large railroad stations. You can buy stamps from the post office counter and at automatic vending machines.

TELEPHONES
Public telephones run by Deutsche Telecom are located in U- and S-Bahn stations, post offices, restaurants and cafés, and on street corners. The rate from telephone booths is about 15 cents a minute. Most public telephones are now card operated. Phone cards (Telefonkarten) can be bought at any post office or newspaper shop for €5, €10 and €20. Note that numbers prefixed with 0900, 0180 or 0190 are toll numbers.

Telephone rates are generally lower between 6 p.m. and 7 a.m. and on weekends. To call a German number from abroad, dial the international code (011 from the United States and Canada, 00 from the U.K.), then the code for Germany (49), followed by the number, omitting the first 0.

To make an international call from Germany, dial 00 followed by the country code and the rest of the telephone number, deleting the initial 0' if there is one. Useful country codes are: Australia 61; Canada 1; United Kingdom 44; United States 1.

USEFUL TELEPHONE NUMBERS
International inquiries 11834
National inquiries 11837 (in English)

CONVERSIONS

1 kilo = 2.2 lbs
1 liter = 0.2642 U.S gallons
1 kilometer = 0.62 mile

Women's clothing
| U.S. | 8 | 10 | 12 | 14 | 16 | 18 |
| European | 36 | 38 | 40 | 42 | 44 | 46 |

Men's clothing
| U.S. | 36 | 38 | 40 | 42 | 44 | 46 |
| European | 46 | 48 | 50 | 52 | 54 | 56 |

Women's shoes
| U.S. | 6/6.5 | 7/7.5 | 8/8.5 | 9/9.5 |
| European | 37 | 38 | 39 | 40 |

Men's shoes
| U.S. | 8 | 8.5 | 9.5 | 10.5 | 11.5 | 12 |
| European | 41 | 42 | 43 | 44 | 45 | 46 |

ELECTRICITY

German sockets are of the round, Continental two-pin variety, so you'll need a converter to use equipment with U.S. or U.K. plugs. The voltage (220, 50 Hz) is fine for British gear but you'll still need a plug adapter. Airport shops routinely carry this sort of thing.

ETIQUETTE & LOCAL CUSTOMS

Visitors from North America will find that Germans tend to be more formal in everyday situations. Dress for the occasion—shorts and halter tops are frowned upon in churches and cathedrals.

Shaking hands is common among both men and women, at least at first meeting. Friends and acquaintances, and especially the younger set will exchange a hug

and peck on both cheeks. Do not use first names or the informal Du unless invited to do so, although younger people tend to dispense with the formal Sie more or less immediately. In formal settings, people might introduce themselves as Herr or Frau (perhaps even Frau Doktor), and if they do that's how they want to be addressed.

If invited to someone's home, take along a little something like flowers or a bottle of wine. A polite thank-you card or call the next day is much appreciated.

HOLIDAYS

All banks and post offices and many museums, galleries, and stores close on public holidays. Many stores and businesses are also shut on Carnival Rose Monday (Cologne and Rhine region), Christmas Eve and New Year's Eve.

January 1 New Year's Day
January 6 Epiphany (in Bavaria, Baden-Württemberg, Saxony-Anhalt)
March/April Good Friday
March/April Easter Monday
May 1 Labor Day
May/June Ascension Day
May/June Pentecost Monday
June Corpus Christi (in Baden-Württemberg, Bavaria, Hesse, North Rhine-Westphalia, Rhineland-Palatinate)
August 15 Ascension of the Virgin Mary (Saarland, Catholic areas of Bavaria)
October 3 Day of Unity
October 31 Day of Reformation (Brandenburg, Mecklenburg-Western Pomerania, Saxony, Saxony-Anhalt, Thuringia)
November 1 All Saints' Day (Baden-Württemberg, Bavaria, North Rhine-Westphalia, Rhineland-Palatinate, Saarland, Catholic areas of Thuringia)
November 20 Repentance Day (only in Saxony)
December 25 & 26 Christmas

MEDIA

NEWSPAPERS

Serious daily newspapers are the liberal *Sueddeutsche Zeitung* (SZ), the conservative *Frankfurter Allgemeine Zeitung* (FAZ), the left-of-center *Frankfurter Rundschau* and the conservative *Die Welt*. Popular tabloids are *Bildzeitung*— Germany's best-selling paper— and *Express*. Weekly magazines also play an important role. On Mondays the hard-hitting news magazines *Der Spiegel* and *Focus* are published, on Thursdays the sophisticated *Die Zeit* as well as entertainment-oriented titles *Stern* and *Bunte*. Regional newspapers cover national and international as well as local news, and are as widely read as the national press.

American & British

newspapers American (*International Herald Tribune, USA Today, Washington Post*) and British (*The Times, Telegraph, Independent, Guardian*) are available in airports, major railroad stations, the more important vacation resorts, and most large hotels. On Mondays, the *Sueddeutsche Zeitung* carries an English-language summary of the *New York Times*.

TV CHANNELS

German television relies heavily on the two national networks ARD and ZDF, which form the parent networks for a host of regional public channels. Stiff competition comes from the private channels, above all RTL and SAT 1. The most authoritative news broadcasts are the ZDF evening news *Heute* at 7 p.m. and the ARD *Tagesschau* at 8 p.m. Channels available in English include CNN, NBC, MTV Europe, and BBC World.

MONEY MATTERS

In 2002 the euro (€) replaced the beloved deutsche mark as Germany's official currency. There are 100 cents to 1 euro. Banknotes comes in denominations of 5, 10, 20, 50 and 100, as well as the rarer 200

and 500 bills. Coins consist of €1 and €2 as well as 1, 2, 5, 10, 20, and 50 cents.

Most major banks have ATMs for bank cards and international credit cards, with instructions in a number of languages. Cash and traveler's checks can be exchanged in the larger banks and currency booths at railroad stations and airports.

OPENING TIMES

Banks 8 a.m–4 p.m. (around 5:30 p.m. on Thursdays); some in small towns close for lunch between 1 p.m. and 2 p.m. All banks are closed Saturdays and Sundays. **Museums** Generally 9 a.m.–6 p.m. Many museums are closed on Mondays but some in large cities will have extended opening hours on one night a week. **Pharmacies** Open during normal shop hours. In cities a few outlets (usually one per district) stay open all night and weekends for urgent cases. **Post Offices** Mostly 8 a.m.–6 p.m. weekdays and until noon on Saturday. **Stores** Weekdays 8:30 a.m.–6:30 p.m. (till 8 p.m. for many department stores and on Thursdays). On Saturdays, hours are 8:30 a.m.–8 p.m., although many smaller shops close noon–2 p.m. With a few exceptions, stores are closed on Sundays.

PETS

Bringing a pet has to be organized well in advance. Contact your local veterinarian about vaccinations and other requirements. Visitors from the U.S. and Canada must bring documentation with them in order to enter Germany; a certificate of permission will be issued by customs at the airport/port of entry.

REST ROOMS

Self-cleaning toilet cabins are usually located near the big

railroad and bus stations. Large department stores have public rest rooms, but charge a small fee (like €0.20). You can also slip into a bar or café, keeping an eye out for the doors marked Herren (men) and Damen (women).

TIME DIFFERENCES

Germany runs on CET (Central European Time), one hour ahead of Greenwich Mean Time and six hours ahead of Eastern Standard Time. Noon in Germany is 6 a.m. in New York. Remember that Germany uses the 24-hour clock, so that 8 p.m. becomes "20 Uhr" in German.

TIPPING

By law, sales tax and a service charge are included in your restaurant bill. It is customary, though, to include a small tip of an extra 5 to 10 percent if you are happy with the service. Tips in taxis vary widely—some people round up, while others pay 5 to 10 percent. Bellhops typically get €1 per bag in the top-end hotels.

TOURIST OFFICES

The German National Tourist Office (www.cometogermany.com and www.germany-tourism.co.uk) has branches with helpful staff in North America and the U.K.

UNITED STATES
New York
112 East 42nd St., 52nd floor
New York, NY 10168
Tel 212/661-7200
Fax 212/661-7174

Los Angeles
1334 Parkview Avenue, Suite 300
Manhattan Beach, CA 90266
Tel 313/545-1350
Fax 313/545-1371

Chicago
P.O. Box 59594
Chicago IL 60659-9594
Tel 773/539-6303
Fax 773/539-6378

PRACTICAL ADVICE/EMERGENCIES/FURTHER READING

CANADA
Toronto
480 University Ave., Suite 1410
Toronto, Ontario M5G 1V2
Tel 416/968-1685
Fax 416/968-0562

GREAT BRITAIN
London
P.O. Box 2695
London W1A 3TN
Tel 020 7317 0908
Fax 020 7317 0917

TRAVELERS WITH DISABILITIES

Germany is fairly well equipped for the needs of disabled travelers, especially the wheelchair-bound. There are access ramps and lifts in many public buildings, including restrooms, train stations, museums, theaters and cinemas. On public transportation, some buses, trams and commuter trains have special wheelchair ramps, but it varies. The national association for the disabled will send you details free of charge.
Bundesverband Evangelischer
   Behindertenhilfe
Postfach 33 02 20
tel 030-83 00 12 70
fax 030-83 00 12 75
14172 Berlin
www.beb-ev.de

EMERGENCIES

EMBASSIES

U.S. Embassy
Neustädtische Kirchstrasse 4–5,
10117 Berlin
Tel 030 238 51 74
Fax 030 238 62 90

U.S. Consulate
Clayallee 170,
14195 Berlin
Tel 030 832 92 33
Fax 030 83 05 12 15

Canadian Embassy
Leipziger Platz 17,
10117 Berlin
Tel 030 20 31 20
Fax 030 20 31 25 90

British Embassy
Wilhelmstrasse 70-71,
10117 Berlin
Tel 030 20 45 70
Fax 030 20 45 75 94

EMERGENCY PHONE NUMBERS

Fire department & ambulance
(*Feuerwehr*) 112
Police (*Polizeinotruf*) 110

WHAT TO DO IN A CAR ACCIDENT

You must switch on the hazard warning lights. All cars driven in Germany must carry a red warning triangle, to be placed on the road to warn approaching traffic of a stationary vehicle or accident. Position the warning triangle on an autobahn about 164 yards (150m) behind the vehicle. Next, exchange names, addresses, telephone numbers and registration details and ask to see the other party's driver's license to confirm. You should also make a note of the events leading to the accident, with drawings which you may need for your insurance claim. The police must always be called, regardless of whether injuries have occurred or not.

LOST PROPERTY

Your travel insurance should cover the loss or theft of your property if you are not already covered by your home insurance. Theft must be reported to the police so you can obtain a certificate saying that the crime was reported. For lost property, ask at the lost property office (*Fundbüro*) in any German city. The national railway DB and urban transportation systems have their own offices, if you forget something on a train.

HEALTH

In the case of minor health problems, the qualified staff of any pharmacy can offer expert advice. Doctors' hours are normally 9 a.m.–noon and 3–5 p.m., except weekends. For urgent attention outside office hours, simply go to the nearest hospital (*Kranken-haus*). German medical treatment and facilities are generally excellent. In Berlin the best-known of several hospitals with a 24-hour emergency ward is the Charité (Schumann Strasse 20–21, tel 030 450 50).

FURTHER READING

Fiction
Elective Affinities by Johann Wolfgang von Goethe. Classic 19th-century novel about the emotional turmoil of two couples and the weighty issue of free will.
The Buddenbrooks by Thomas Mann. Charts the decline of a North German mercantile family over four generations.
The Lost Honor of Katharina Blum by Heinrich Böll. A young woman's association with a hunted man leads her into a web of sensationalism and character assassination.
The Danzig Trilogy (The Tin Drum, Cat and Mouse, Dog Years) by Günther Grass. The three novels by the Nobel Prize winner are an inventive mix of fantasy and reality, set in the Nazi era.
The Reader by Bernhard Schlink. Love and secrets, compassion and horror in post-war Germany.

Non-fiction
The Harz Journey by Heinrich Heine. These travel vignettes are a poetic and ironic critique of man and society.
Steppenwolf by Hermann Hesse. An autobiographical work that blends Eastern mysticism with Western culture.
Bayreuth: A History of the Wagner Festival by Frederic Spotts. A fascinating look at how a composer's excesses spawned Germany's most famous operatic event.
A Concise History of Germany by Mary Fulbrook. A crisply-written account starting with medieval Germany and ending with unification in 1990.

HOTELS & RESTAURANTS

Germany offers a variety of accommodations from traditional grand hotels to palaces and other historic buildings that have been converted into hotels. You'll find no shortage of the more moderately priced hotel chains such as Holiday Inn, Best Western, or Mercure. Small, privately owned, and often charming hotels are more easily found in small towns. There are two visible trends in German hotels: streamlined, ultra-modern design hotels that enjoy great popularity, and a growing number of hotels that offer health and beauty treatments. Some of the newest hotels are in the east of the country and, after generations of Communism, they are working hard to match the standards of the rest of Germany, but there is still a discrepancy in quality and finesse.

In large cities and tourist resorts it may be harder to find an affordable bed. Enter the tourist offices, who supply lists of accommodations and can book rooms (sometimes for a small fee). Quite logically the facilities are reflected in the price, and cheaper hotels may not have private baths. As everywhere, prices vary depending on the seasons, scheduling of commercial fairs or special events. Taxes are included, but car parking and telephone often cost extra.

PRICES

HOTELS
An indication of the cost of a double room without breakfast is given by $ signs.

$$$$$	Over $270
$$$$	$200–$270
$$$	$120–$200
$$	$80–$120
$	Under $80

RESTAURANTS
An indication of the cost of a three-course dinner without drinks is given by $ signs.

$$$$$	Over $80
$$$$	$50–$80
$$$	$35–$50
$$	$20–$35
$	Under $20

HOTELS

Hotels are graded by the German hospitality association with one to four stars, a system designed to give an informed picture to the prospective guest. In reality, the stars say little about the overall quality of an establishment, which is why we omit them here.

Many hotels have their own restaurants, and in the country-side the "bed-and-breakfast" formula is a common feature. Half-board, or *Halbpension*, includes breakfast and dinner while *Vollpension* throws in lunch as well. If a hotel is a *Garni*, this means there is no restaurant but breakfast is (probably) served. A B&B place is called a *Pension* or *Privatquartier* and their addresses are best obtained from local tourist offices. They are inexpensive and bring you in contact with locals, but do not expect facilities like private bathrooms.

The following is a selection of good quality hotels throughout the country listed by price, then in alphabetical order. The choice is meant to be individual and typical of the area, perhaps with strong links to local culture or history. For that special occasion, *Gast Im Schloss* (www.gast-im-schloss.com) has information about hotels in former monasteries, palaces, castles, and mansions.

Please note that, unless otherwise stated:
• Breakfast is not included in the price.
• The hotel has a restaurant. Notable hotel restaurants are given an icon or a reference to a separate entry.
• All rooms have a telephone and television.
• Room price categories are no more than a rough guide and do not take into account seasonal variations. Local taxes (such as *Kurtaxe*, which is commonly levied in health resorts) may be added to the bill. Prices are per double room.
• In high season, always try to book in advance and confirm your reservation by fax or e-mail. You may be asked for a deposit or credit card number.

Credit & debit cards
Many hotels accept all major cards, but smaller ones may only accept those shown in their entry. Abbreviations used are: AE American Express, DC Diners Club, MC Mastercard, V Visa.

Hotel chains & groups
U.S. contact numbers are:
Hilton, tel 800/445 6667
Leading Hotels of the World, tel 800/745 8883

Relais & Chateaux, tel 800/735 2478
Steigenberger (in Germany), tel 49 (0) 696 65 64 01
Dorint, tel 866/576-2459

All the following hotel chains can be telephoned from the U.S. and Canada under the same standard reservation number, tel 1-877 678 9330, and sites such as europe-hotel-reservation.info: Best Western, Comfort Inns, Crowne Plaza, Design Hotels, Hyatt Hotels, Marriott Hotels, Novotel, Quality Inns, Ramada Ritz Carlton, Radisson, Sorat.

RESTAURANTS

Germany has a bewildering variety of restaurants, ranging from the humble Gasthof with everyday fare to vaunted temples of gourmet cuisine. In most *Kneipen* or *Bierstuben* (drinking pubs) you can enjoy simple dishes over a foaming mug of beer. A *Weinstube* is a wine bar, usually serving local specialities. And in many towns you will find an atmospheric *Ratskeller* in the basement of the town hall, a reliable bet for a tasty meal. Traditionally, the main meal of the day in Germany was lunch, but changing habits have shifted the balance towards the

---

⬛ Nonsmoking 🅰 Air-conditioning 🅰 Indoor/🅰 Outdoor swimming pool 🅰 Health club ⬛ Credit cards   **KEY**

HOTELS & RESTAURANTS

evening. The lunch menu (*Mittagstisch*) tends to be the best deal of the day.

German food is not as heavy as its reputation, although most dishes are anchored by a large helping of meat. Pork roast with crackling is a stereotype of Bavaria. Classic dishes from the Black Forest include ham, venison, trout, and black cherry gateau.

Many regions have their own favorite sausage; in Munich the specialty is *Weisswurst*, a bulging veal sausage flecked with parsley, while Nuremberg and Regensburg are renowned for their little grilled links. Tasty Mettwurst (soft smoked sausages) are popular in Westphalia. More than 500 years old, the Frankfurter lays a plausible claim to being the original hot dog.

The cultivation of asparagus is taken very seriously, and in season the 'king of vegetables' turns up in dishes all over Germany. Sole, plaice, and shrimp come from the North Sea coasts. Oysters are very good on the island of Sylt, and Helgoland is famous for its lobster soup. The Baltic Sea smokehouses supply tender *Kieler Sprotten* (smoked sprats).

In the Lower Rhine area, mussels come fresh from the coast and are cooked in white wine. An old-fashioned but still popular dish is *Biersuppe* (soup made of milk, beer, cinnamon, raisins, and egg whites).

The proximity to the Adriatic means there is a great selection of Italian cuisine in Germany. It is also easy to find choice pickings from a grab bag of nations including Greek, Turkish, Thai, Chinese, and Indian.

This selection (listed by price, then in alphabetical order) focuses on regional eateries offering local dishes as well as some of the great stars of German cuisine.

L = lunch   D = dinner

Eating in Germany

Breakfasts are substantial enough to see you through till dinner time. A full breakfast can consist of various types of bread, accompanied by marmalade, eggs, cold cuts and cheese, and perhaps a bowl of fruit-filled *quark* (white yogurt). Lunch usually starts around midday and continues until 2 p.m. Dinner starts at 7 p.m. to 8 p.m., while in smaller places or in the countryside you may be too late after 9 p.m. Dinner tends to start earlier in the north of the country, and later as you go south. In high season, or anytime if you have a particular place in mind, be sure to make a reservation.

Restaurants often have tables for alfresco dining. Such facilities are mentioned here only where the view, or perhaps the garden, is of particular note. Menus are displayed outside any place serving food, so you can size up the offerings before going inside. Most restaurants offer a fixed-price menu for lunch and dinner.

In Germany salad is usually eaten with the main course rather than as an appetizer. Tap water (*Leitungswasser*) is safe to drink.

Local wines tend to dominate wine lists. An increasing number of restaurants have a non-smoking (*Nichtraucher*) section, even if it's just a few token tables.

Cafés

Cafés are a German institution for morning coffee with a newspaper, leisurely drinks, a light lunch, and definitely for *Kaffee und Kuchen* (coffee and cake) in the afternoon. In small towns they are very much the center of local life.

Tipping

A service charge is always included in the bill, but it is customary to add 5 to 10 percent if the service has been particularly good. Give the server the tip upon payment, rather than leaving it on the table. If your bill is €14, you might hand the server a 20 and say "15."

BERLIN & BRANDENBURG

BERLIN

MITTE & POTSDAMER PLATZ

▥ ADLON KEMPINSKI
▯ $$$$$

UNTER DEN LINDEN 77
TEL 030 22 61 11 11
FAX 030 22 61 22 22
WWW.HOTEL-ADLON.DE

British club meets art deco at this portal of German history, where Marlene Dietrich was discovered and Joseph Göbbels chased his mistress down the corridor. The grand dame of Berlin hotels has been restored to its pre-WWII splendor, complete with grandstand views of the Brandenburg Gate and a first-class elegant restaurant.

ⓘ 256 + 80 suites   ▨ S1, S2
Unter den Linden   🅿   ⬍
🆂 🆂 🌊 📺 All major cards

▥ GRAND HYATT
▯ $$$$$

MARLENE-DIETRICH-PLATZ 2
TEL 030 25 53 12 34
FAX 030 25 53 12 35
WWW.HYATT.COM

A favorite haunt of movie stars, this temple of luxury on Potsdamer Platz has matte-black surfaces and fashioned hardwood that exude a Euro-Japanese elegance. Rooms have oodles of perks like heated bathroom floors and Bauhaus art, and on the rooftop you'll find a gym, pool and beauty center.

ⓘ 326 + 16 suites   ▨ S1, S2,
U2 Potsdamer Platz   🅿   ⬍
🆂 🌊 📺 All major cards

▥ HONIGMOND GARDEN
▯ $$$

INVALIDENSTRASSE 122
TEL 030 28 44 55 77
FAX 030 28 44 55 88
WWW.HONIGMOND.DE

This romantic, family-run hotel evokes late 19th-century

Berlin with original antiques, stucco ceilings and polished wood floors. The rear chambers and kitchen-equipped cottages face an idyllic, shady garden with a Japanese fishpond and century-old trees. Breakfast is included.

[i] 20 [m] U6 Oranienburger Tor [P] [S] [S] No credit cards

[h] ANDECHSER HOF
[r] $$$
ACKERSTRASSE 155
TEL 030 28 09 78 44
FAX 030 28 09 78 45
WWW.ANDECHSERHOF.DE
Not the trendiest part of town, but within staggering distance of Prenzlauer Berg's buzzing cafes. Rooms are large, quiet and furnished in a jumble of styles where comfort is writ large. The front wing has kitchenettes, and there are bikes for hire.

[i] 19 [m] U8 Bernauer Strasse [S] [S] [S] MC, V

SOMETHING SPECIAL

[r] VAU
Chef Kolja Kleeberg once aspired to acting, and his Michelin-starred restaurant in a courtyard near Gendarmen-markt is something of a movie set, with screaming orange walls, wooden floors, and halogen spots. You might start with a chestnut soup before moving on to breast of pigeon with blackroot and a lemon-grass-chili sherbet. Reserve ahead.

$$$$—$$$$$
JÄGERSTRASSE 54-55
TEL 030 202 97 30
[f] 115 [m] U6 Französische Strasse [C] Closed Sun.
[S] All major cards

[r] GANYMED
$$$
SCHIFFBAUER DAMM 5
TEL 030 28 59 90 46
This hair-down riverside brasserie exudes the spirit of la belle France on vacation.

The gutsy forté of chef Vincent Garcia is seafood—mussels from Brittany, shrimp, crabs, and oysters prepared in a bewildering number of ways. You can dine on the dreamy terrace or in the candlelit dining room with checkered tablecloths and Art Deco globes.

[f] 75 [m] S1, S2, S5, S9, U6 Friedrichstrass [S] All major cards

[r] WEINBAR RUTZ
$$$
CHAUSSEESTRASSE 8
TEL 030 24 62 87 60
A oenophile's dream, the Rutz has over 1,000 different wines and a terrific choice of contemporary cuisine. You can nibble on tapas in the bistro or go straight to the elegant upstairs restaurant. The show-stopper is the entrecote from milk-fed Kobe cattle served in a truffle gravy.

[f] 110 [m] U6 Oranienburger Tor
[C] Closed Sun. [S] All major cards

[r] METZKES DELI
$
BEHRENSTRASSE 72
TEL 030 206 28 80
Across the street from the Holocaust monument, this elegant deli sells Italian antipasti, bagel sandwiches, wraps and blueberry muffins. The inspiration is Harald Metzke, a Jewish painter whose "Poacher's Banquet" is on display. The shop stocks deli and kosher items as well as choice wines.

[f] 120 [m] S1, S2 [S] No credit cards

[r] MUTTER HOPPE
$
RATHAUSSTRASSE 21
TEL 030 24 72 06 03
This old-fashioned restaurant in the Nikolai quarter is named for a formidable cook who used to whip up mountains of food for her

family and friends. Tuck into a serving of Eisbein (pork knuckle) or oversized schnitzel while you savor hits from the '20s (live on weekends).

[f] 90 [m] U2, S3, S5, S9 Alexanderplatz [S] MC, V

CHARLOTTENBURG

[h] HOTEL Q!
[r] $$$/$$$$
KNESEBECKSTRASSE 67
TEL 030 810 06 60
FAX 030 810 066 666
WWW.LOOCK-HOTELS.COM
A cool grey facade signals your arrival at the Q, an ultra-chic retreat named for the nearby Ku'Damm. Hardwood floors curve up the walls, and you can literally slide from the tub into bed. The spa has its own self-contained "beach" with heated sand and aromatherapy.

[i] 77 [m] S5, S7, S9 Savignyplatz [P] [S] [h] [S] All major cards

[h] ASKANISCHER HOF
$$/$$$
KURFÜRSTENDAMM 53
10707
TEL 030 8 81 80 33
FAX 030 8 81 72 06
WWW.ASKANISCHER-HOF.DE
For a dose of Berlin history, stay at this delightfully intimate abode on the city's most famous shopping avenue. Furnished in roaring '20s style, rooms are individually designed with plenty of high-tech features. Rock star David Bowie was a regular guest here in the 1970s.

[i] 15 + 1 suite [m] S5, S7, S9 Savigny Platz [P] [h]
[S] All major cards

SOMETHING SPECIAL

[h] PROPELLER ISLAND CITY LODGE
Get ready for a surprise—nothing about this place is ordinary. This 19th-century apartment block has been rewired as an eccentric hotel where every room is an

inhabitable work of art. Most draw on fantasies: the Flying Bed hovers in the air, while the Two Lions features a pair of caged mattresses five feet above the ground. Every stick of furniture was crafted by the owner-artist himself.

$$/$$$
ALBRECHT-ACHILLES-STRASSE 58, 10709
TEL 030 891 90 16
FAX 030 892 87 21
WWW.PROPELLER-ISLAND.COM
🛏 42　🚇 U7 Adenauerplatz
💳 All major cards

🍴 BORRIQUITO
$$
WIELANDSTRASSE 6
TEL 030 312 99 29
After dark, things really get going in the 'little donkey' near trendy Savigny Platz. Night owls converge on this place for rioja and classic Spanish dishes like paella teeming with giant gambas. Someone's always singing or playing the guitar.
🪑 125　🚇 S5, S7, S9 Savignyplatz　🔴 Closed L
💳 No credit cards

🍴 CAFE IM LITERATURHAUS
$$
FASANENSTRASSE 23
TEL 030 882 5414
This café/restaurant in an old villa a hearbeat from the main Kurfürstendamm shopping artery provides a well-stocked bookshop in the basement, plus food from breakfast to supper in the first-floor salon. Supper dishes—perhaps roast lamb with rosemary or trout with new potatoes—are strictly seasonal. The regulars have a worldly sophistication that comes from a lifetime of intellectual debate over coffee.
🪑 100　🚇 U1 Uhlandstrasse
💳 No credit cards

PRENZLAUER BERG

🏨 HOTEL ADELE
🍴 **$$$**
GREIFSWALDER STRASSE 227, 10504
TEL 030 4432 4350
FAX 030 4432 4351
WWW.ADELE-HOTEL.DE
From the street this cool 'lounge hotel' is nearly invisible, fronted by separate coffee and wine shops as well as a fine Med-inspired restaurant. Rooms are straight out of Wallpaper magazine, with dark hardwoods and leathers set off by hand-picked colors.
🛏 14　🚇 U2 Senefelder Platz 🅿 🛗 🚫 💳 All major cards

🏨 HOTEL KASTANIENHOF
$$$
KASTANIENALLEE 65
TEL 030 443 050
FAX 030 4430 5111
WWW.KASTANIENHOF.BIZ
This guesthouse, one of east Berlin's first after reunification, has an enviable spot on Prenzlauer Berg's hippest strip. The furnishings are simple pinewood but have a genuine charm thanks to the historic photos which pepper the rooms and common areas.
🛏 35　🚇 U8 Rosenthaler Platz 🅿 🛗 🚫 💳 All major cards

🍴 MIRO
$$
RAUMER STRASSE 28-29
TEL 44 73 30 13
Miro means "hero" in Kurdish, but no courage is needed to enjoy the grilled meat and vegetarian dishes, all sated with Anatolian herbs and spices. The dining area is romantically lit, with fashionably bare brick walls and stripped wooden floor. An intimate rear chamber has traditional cushions and waterpipes.
🪑 100　🚇 S8, S41, S42 Prenzlauer Allee 💳 MC, V

🍴 WEINSTEIN
$$
LYCHENER STRASSE 33
TEL 030 441 18 42
Roy Metzger and his brother Marc serve up an eclectic mix of cuisines at this cozy winebar-restaurant. Mixed salad with Brandenburg veal, potato dumplings stuffed with goat's cheese or marinated tuna are typical of the changing fare.
🪑 65　🚇 U2 Eberswalder Strasse　🔴 Closed Sun lunch.
💳 MC, V

SCHÖNEBERG & KREUZBERG

🏨 HOTEL RIEHMERS HOFGARTEN
🍴 **$$$**
YORCKSTRASSE 83
TEL 030 78 09 88 00
FAX 030 78 09 88 08
WWW.RIEHMERS-HOFGARTEN.DE
This romantic small hotel near Viktoriapark was built by Wilhelm Riehmers, a renowned 19th-century architect. French double doors open into spacious rooms with high ceilings and tasteful contemporary décor. Its fine restaurant, ETA Hoffmann,

serves patrons in a cobblestone courtyard.

(i) 22 **U6, U7** Mehringdamm **P** ⇆ ⊘ All major cards

LE COCHON BOURGEOIS
$$$
FICHTESTRASSE 24
TEL 030 693 01 01
Chef-owner Hannes Behrmann puts his *je-ne-sais-quoi* into classy French game and seafood dishes, such as monkfish in bacon sauce on green lentils. Every night a pianist tickles the ivories in this former showroom of a colonial-goods dealer.
⊞ 5 5 ◎ U7 Südstern ⊕ Closed Mon. & Tues. No credit cards

DER GOLDENE HAHN
$$
PÜCKLERSTRASSE 20
TEL 030 618 80 98
This gem of a Tuscan restaurant has old farm implements and an apothecary's cabinet behind the bar. Stuffed pearl hen with anise sauce and pumpkin gnocchi in parma butter are a couple of highlights that the owner will pair with an excellent Italian wine.
⊞ 110 ◎ U1 Görlitzer Bahnhof ⊕ Closed L MC, V

ZUR HENNE
$
LEUSCHNERDAMM 25
TEL 030 614 77 30
Back in '63, President John F. Kennedy declined an invitation to visit this earthy bar-café just yards away from the Wall, and the president's signed letter now hangs framed over the bar. The menu is simple: delicious, corn-fed roast chicken, sauerkraut, and bouletten (meatballs). Reserve ahead.
⊞ 80 ◎ U1, U8 Kottbusser Tor ⊕ CLosed L & Mon. No credit cards

---

BRANDENBURG

POTSDAM

SOMETHING SPECIAL

▥ SCHLOSSHOTEL CECILIENHOF
Situated in a park on the shore of the Wannsee, this grand, half-timbered mansion was the setting for the Potsdam Conference, where Truman, Churchill and Stalin met in 1945 to discuss the fate of a defeated Germany. Furnished in classic Tudor style, the hotel is close to Potsdam but has a tranquil country atmosphere.
$$$
NEUER GARTEN
TEL 0331 3 70 50
FAX 0331 29 24 98
WWW.RELEXA-HOTEL.DE
(i) 35 + 6 suites ◎ S1, S7 Wannsee or Potsdam, then taxi **P** All major cards

ESPECKERS GASTSTÄTTE ZUR RATSWAAGE
$$$
AM NEUEN MARKT 10
TEL 0331 280 43 11
Enjoy country food such as hearty eel soup or roast rabbit filled with black pudding at this elegant restaurant in historic surroundings. Much of the produce is from local farmers. The old well in the romantic courtyard is much admired.
⊞ 70 ⊕ Closed Sun & Mon ◎ S7 to Potsdam AE

MECKLENBURG-WEST POMERANIA

KRAKOW

SOMETHING SPECIAL

▥ ICH WEISS EIN HAUS AM SEE
Five miles (8 km) outside Krakow, half hidden between a forest and a lake, this hotel offers an idyllic hideaway. Rooms are large, light, and furnished in country style; most

---

have a view of the park and lake. Under the auspices of owner/chef Michael Laumen, the modern European cuisine has earned Lower Pomerania its first Michelin star. Specials include bouillabaisse of local fish and wild herb risotto. Serious wines.
$$$
ALTES FORSTHAUS 2
18292 KRAKOW/SEEGRUBE
TEL 038457 232 73
FAX 038457 232 74
WWW.HAUSAMSEE.DE
(i) 10 **P** No credit cards

ROSTOCK

▥ HOTEL NEPTUN
$$$$
SEESTRASSE 19
ROSTOCK-WARNEMÜNDE
TEL 0381 777 800
FAX 0381 540 23
WWW.HOTEL-NEPTUN.DE
All rooms have balconies at this seaside hotel, the better to enjoy the magnificent ocean views.
(i) 318 + 5 suites + 8 apartments ⇆ ▦ ▥ All major cards

▥ HOTEL SONNE
$$$$
NEUER MARKT 2
TEL 0381 4 97 30
FAX 0381 4 97 33 51
WWW.ROSTOCK.STEIGENBERGER.DE
An efficient modern hotel in the new wing of the historic town hall. Well planned rooms (some for nonsmokers), health and beauty facilities, a good restaurant, a café with excellent cakes, and two bars make this a popular hotel.
(i) 102 + 9 suites **P** ⇆ ⊘ ▥ All major cards

ZUR GARTENLAUBE 1888
$$
ANASTASIASTRASSE 24,
ROSTOCK-WARNEMÜNDE
TEL/FAX 0381 526 61
In classy art deco surrounds, Chef Margrit Hass aims to

---

surprise diners with new gastronomic creations every day. Typical dishes are zucchini soup and wild boar fillet with cranberry sauce and chanterelles.

🛏 55   🕐 Closed Sun. 💳 MC, V

RÜGEN

🏨 PANORAMA HOTEL
🍴 LOHME
$$$

DORFSTRASSE 35
LOHME
TEL 038302 92 21
FAX 038302 92 34
WWW.LOHME.COM

High on the white cliffs of Rügen island, the Panorama Hotel has stunning views from its beautiful terrace and absolutely romantic rooms. Watch the sun set from the veranda while enjoying salmon marinated in fennel, or herring with a crunchy lentil-potato ragout.

🛏 41 + 6 suites   🅿 💳 No credit cards

🏨 VIER JAHRESZEITEN
🍴 $$$

ZEPPELINSTRASSE 8
BINZ
TEL 038393 5 00
FAX 038393 5 04 30
WWW.JAHRESZEITEN-HOTELS.DE

A classic example of seaside architecture, this renovated hotel has an up-to-date health and beauty center. In the Orangerie restaurant René Zühr, a revolutionary chef, improvises on variations of Pomeranian cuisine with appetizing results. Try the veal fillets or the fish sausages.

🛏 76 + 5 suites   🅿 💳 AE, MC, V

SCHWERIN

🏨 ARTE
$$/$$$

DORFSTRASSE 6
SCHWERIN-KREBSFÖRDERN
TEL 0385 6 34 50

FAX 0385 6 34 51 00
WWW.HOTEL-ARTE.DE

Just outside town, an exquisite country hotel in an extended old farmhouse with a fine on-site restaurant, the Fontane. In the German wellness vein there are a sauna, a solarium, and plenty of non-smoking rooms.

🛏 41   🅿   📺   💳 All major cards

🍴 SCHRÖTER'S
$$

SCHLIEMANNSTRASSE 2
TEL 0385 550 76 98

This intimate restaurant in the historic quarter has views of the Pfaffenteich Lake and offers regional cuisine with a French accent. A specialty is caramelized duck liver with asparagus. The Friesian beef is also notable.

🛏 40   🕐 Closed Sun. & L 💳 All major cards

STRALSUND

🏨 DORINT IM HANSE DOM
$$$

GRÜNHOFER BOGEN 18–20
TEL 03831 3 77 30
FAX 03831 3 77 31 00
WWW.DORINTRESORTS.COM/STRALSUND

Close to the beautiful Hanse Dom-Park, the hotel offers large rooms with pastel-colored walls, lots of polished wood, and wicker chairs.

🛏 109 + 5 suites   💳 All major cards

🍴 TAFELFREUDEN IM SOMMERHAUS
$$$

JUNGFERNSTIEG 5 ATEL
TEL 03831 29 92 60

Ambitious chef Axel Müller offers fusion cuisine at moderate prices in a pretty yellow summer house. Try the mussels, St. Pietro fish with polenta, and the avocado salad with a special vinaigrette.

🛏 50   🕐 Closed Mon.   🅿 💳 MC, V

TIMMENDORFER STRAND

🏨 LANDHAUS CARSTENS
🍴 $$$$$

STRANDALLEE 73
TEL 04503 60 80
FAX 04503 6 08 60
WWW.LANDHAUS
CARSTENS.DE

A country house hotel beside the sea. Local fish with a champagne sauce or pigeon with Madeira sauce will restore your strength after a beach walk.

🛏 30 + 3 suites   🅿 📺 📺 💳 All major cards

USEDOM

> **SOMETHING SPECIAL**

🍴 KÄPT'N NEMO

A quaint restaurant in a pavilion on the pier decorated with fishing nets and crabpots. Chef Mark Lübke serves the best fish on the island, also very good oyster or crabs fried in light batter.

$$$

STRANDPROMENADE 1
HERINGSDORF
TEL 038378 288 17

🛏 40   🕐 Closed L 💳 MC, V

> **HAMBURG SCHLESWIG-HOLSTEIN**

> **HAMBURG**

🏨 KEMPINSKI ATLANTIC
🍴 $$$$$

AN DER ALSTER 72–79
TEL 040 2 88 80
FAX 040 24 71 29
WWW.KEMPINSKI-ATLANTIC.DE

This Hamburg institution displays great elegance throughout. The best of the luxurious suites, of course, are those with Alster Lake views.

🛏 239 + 13 suites   🅿 📺 📺 💳 All major cards

⊞ VIER JAHRESZEITEN
🍴 $$$$$
NEUER JUNGFERNSTIEG 9–14
TEL 040 3 49 40
FAX 040 34 94 26 00
WWW.HVJ.DE
Hamburg's traditional grand
hotel presents rooms in classic
style. The restaurant Härlin
has exquisite Biedermeier
furniture. Favorites on the
menu include four variations
of goose liver, and juicy lamb
in a pecorino crust with
haricot beans and onion
confit. Excellent wines.
ⓘ 124 + 32 suites 🅿 ⮀
🐴 🐴 All major cards

⊞ DORINT AM ALTEN
🍴 WALL
$$$$
ALTER WALL 38–46
TEL 040 36 95 00
FAX 040 36 95 010 00
WWW.ACCORHOTELS.COM
Big rooms and an exciting mix
of materials—glass, felt, wooden
floors, stone—characterize
this central hotel. Eight studio
rooms have views of the canals.
ⓘ 241 + 18 suites 🅿 ⮀
🐴 🐴 All major cards

SOMETHING SPECIAL

⊞ HANSEATIC HOTEL
The quiet grace of this old
patrician villa in a residential
area close to the center is loved
by discerning individualists. Very
nice antiques, excellent breakfast.
$$$$$
SIERICHSTRASSE 150
TEL 040 48 57 72
FAX 040 48 57 73
WWW.HANSEATIC-
HAMBURG.DE
ⓘ 14 🅿 🐴 All major
cards

⊞ SIDE HOTEL HAMBURG
🍴 $$$$
DREHBAHN 49
TEL 040 30 99 90
FAX 040 30 99 93 99
WWW.SIDE-HAMBURG.DE
Hamburg's latest landmark is a
12-story glass tower designed
by the city's architect Jan

Störmer. Italian designer
Matteo Thun continues the
minimalist theme from the
reception area into the
bedrooms. Sushi is a big
feature in the restaurant.
ⓘ 168 + 10 suites 🅿 ⮀
🐴 🐴 All major cards

⊞ ELYSEE
$$$
ROTHENBAUMCHAUSSEE 10
TEL 040 41 41 20
FAX 040 41 41 27 33
WWW.ELYSEE.DE
A Hamburg favorite with light
comfortable rooms, a cheerful
lobby, two restaurants, a café,
and a bar.
ⓘ 299 + 6 suites 🅿 ⮀
🐴 🐴 All major cards

⊞ PREM
🍴 $$$
AN DER ALSTER 9
TEL 040 24 83 40 40
FAX 040 2 80 38 51
WWW.HOTEL-PREM.DE
Antiques furnish this beautiful
white house close to the
Alster Lake, though lakeside
rooms can be noisy. An
excellent formal restaurant
specializes in fish, and there's a
more relaxed bistro.
ⓘ 50 + 3 suites + 1
apartment 🅿 🐴 All
major cards

🍴 LE CANARD
$$$$
ELBCHAUSSEE 139
TEL 040 880 50 57
Chef Josef Viehauser presides
over the modern French
cooking at this award-winning
restaurant (one Michelin star).
Specialties include a sublime
fillet of North Sea turbot with
artichokes and juicy sautéed
venison.
🍴70 🕐 Closed Sun. 🅿
🐴 All major cards

🍴 LANDHAUS SCHERRER
$$$$
ELBCHAUSSEE 130
TEL 040 880 13 25
North German cuisine comes
with an exotic twist here:
bean soup with scallops,

North Sea fish with saffron,
caipirinhi-parfait with mangos.
One Michelin star and plenty
of return customers.
🍴95 🕐 Closed Sun. 🅿
🐴 All major cards

🍴 FISCHEREIHAFEN
RESTAURANT
$$
GROSSE ELBSTRASSE 243
TEL 040 38 18 16
A Hamburg tradition with a
classic fish menu (haddock
with mustard sauce, plaice
fried in bacon, broiled sole)
plus sushi. Usually crowded.
🍴150 🅿 🐴 All major
cards

SCHLESWIG-HOLSTEIN

KIEL

⊞ PARKHOTEL KIELER
KAUFMANN
$$$
NIEMANNSWEG 102
TEL 0431 881 10
FAX 881 11 35
WWW.KIELER-KAUFMANN.DE
Quietly located in a leafy park,
this picturesque villa dates
back to the turn of the last
century but also has a
modern annex. Rooms are
traditionally furnished.
ⓘ 43 + 1 suites 🅿 🐴
🐴 All major cards

🍴 ZUM HIRSCHEN
$$$
DÄNISCHE STRASSE 22 (IM
LÜNEBURG HAUS)
TEL 0431 98 26 00
Confident Mediterranean
cuisine served in a beautiful
early 20th-century house. Try
the turbot with a sorrel-
tomato ragout.
🍴65 🕐 Closed Sun.
🐴 All major cards

🍴 SEPTEMBER
$$
ALTE LÜBECKER CHAUSSEE 27
TEL 0431 68 06 10
The beautiful winter garden is
a feature of this second-floor
restaurant in the city center.

HOTELS & RESTAURANTS

Service can be slow, but the Holstein beef in red wine sauce is worth the wait. Huge wine list and 170 liqueurs.
🛏 70 🕒 Closed Sun. 🕒 🚫 No credit cards

LÜBECK

🏨 **KLASSIK ALTSTADT HOTEL**
$$
FISCHERGRUBE 52
TEL 0451 70 29 80
FAX 0451 7 37 78
WWW.KLASSIK-ALTSTADT-HOTEL.DE
You can explore picturesque Lübeck on foot from this traditionally decorated hotel.
🛏 19 + 2 suites + 1 apartment 🅿 🚫 All major cards

🍴 **WULLENWEVER**
$$$
BECKERGRUBE 71
TEL 0451 70 43 33
A splendid restaurant in a town-center patrician villa. Choose from dishes such as sautéed lobster with herb salad, perch with foie gras, pigeon carpaccio. The wine list has more than 600 entries.
🛏 79 🕒 Closed Sun. & Mon. 🚫 DC, V

SYLT

🍴 **SANSIBAR**
Watch the sunset from a beach chalet as evocative as its exotic name. It's quieter winter, but even then you should reserve in advance. Big portions of fried turbot and other fish, afternoon coffee and cakes.
$$
HÖRNUMER STRASSE 80
RANTUM
TEL 04651 96 46 46
FAX 04651 96 46 47
WWW.SANSIBAR.DE
🛏 95 🚫 AE, MC, V

🏨 **SÖL'RING HOF**
🍴 **$$$$**
AM SANDWALL 1
RANTUM
TEL 04651 83 62 00
FAX 04651 8 36 20 20
WWW.ACCORHOTELS.COM
A great location in the dunes for this vacation hotel with light, modern rooms, some with ocean views. The very popular restaurant has one Michelin star. Minibar and beach chair are included.
🛏 15 + 2 suites 🅿 🚗 🍴 🚫 All major cards

BREMEN

🏨 **PARK HOTEL**
🍴 **$$$**
IM BÜRGERPARK
TEL 0421 3 40 80
FAX 0421 3 40 86 02
WWW.PARK-HOTEL-BREMEN.DE
Bremen's premier hotel looks like a stately home with a domed central lobby. Room styles range from Japanese to Italian. Chef Christoph Otten proffers dishes such as marinated rabbit with rose petals or roast perch in almond sauce.
🛏 162 + 18 suites 🅿 🛗 🚗 🍴 🚫 All major cards

🍴 **L'ORCHIDEE IM BREMER RATSKELLER**
$$$$
AM MARKT 1
TEL 0421 334 79 11
The restaurant in the 600-year-old town hall cellar (Ratskeller) serves haute cuisine: roasted fish soup, veal filled with lobster, passion fruit tart with raspberries.
🛏 83 🕒 Closed Sun. & Mon. 🚫 DC, MC, V

🍴 **GRASSHOFF'S BISTRO**
$$
CONTRESCARPE 80
TEL 0421 147 40
Chef Rüdiger König has made this one-Michelin-star bistro into an institution. Haddock

with mustard sauce, caramel ice-cream with almonds—no disappointments.
🛏 55 🕒 Closed Sun. 🚫 DC, MC, V

🍴 **KAFFEEMÜHLE AM WALL**
$$
AM WALL
TEL 0421 144 66
Enjoy dishes such as herring with sour cream and fried potatoes in unique surrounds: a 19th-century windmill.
🛏 90 🚫 MC, V

BRAUNLAGE

🏨 **ZUR TANNE**
🍴
A well-preserved 18th-century inn, now a family-owned hotel. Rooms are furnished in cozy country style, in the main hotel and the modern annex. The restaurant specializes in Harz Mountain classics such as Harzer Bachforelle (local trout), followed by a plum or apple tart.
$$$
HERZOG-WILHELM-STRASSE 8
TEL 05520 931 20

FAX 05520 29 92
WWW.TANNE-BRAUNLAGE.DE
🚪 17 + 3 suites 🅿 🗹
🚳 All major cards

CELLE

🏨 FÜRSTENHOF
🍴 $$$
HANNOVERSCHE STRASSE
55–56
TEL 05141 20 10
FAX 05141 20 11 20
WWW.FUERSTENHOF.DE
Near the medieval town
center, a former palace (built
1670) with an annex, is
furnished with antiques and
oil paintings. The restaurant,
Endtenfang, features chicken
with truffles and lobster with
curry-cauliflower couscous.
Breakfast included.
🚪 73 + 5 suites 🅿 🚳
🗹 🚳 All major cards

GOSLAR

🏨 DER ACHTERMANN
🍴 $$$
ROSENTORSTRASSE 20
TEL 05321 7 00 00
FAX 05321 7 00 09 99
WWW.HOTEL-DER-
ACHTERMANN.DE
Part of this town-center hotel
dates back to 1501. The
annex is less atmospheric but
has a good fitness center. The
restaurant, Altdeutsche Stube,
specializes in local food.
🚪 152 🔁 🚳 🗹
🚳 All major cards

GÖTTINGEN

🏨 GEBHARDS HOTEL
$$$
GOETHEALLEE 22/23
TEL 0551 4 96 80
FAX 0551 4 96 81 10
WWW.GEBHARDSHOTEL.DE
This beautiful historic house
near the station is now a
splendid hotel, furnished with
antiques.
🚪 59 + 2 suites 🅿 🗹
🚳 All major cards

🍴 FREIZEIT IN
🍴 $$$
DRANSFELDER STRASSE 3
TEL 0551 9 00 10
FAX 0551 9 00 11 00
WWW.FREIZEIT-IN.DE
Up-to-date rooms make this a
popular business hotel. Best of
the three restaurants is the
bistro which serves regional
cuisine with a Mediterranean
slant: minestrone with pesto
to start, sole with spinach and
roast potatoes to follow.
Breakfast included.
🚪 211 🅿 🔁 🚳 🗹
🚳 All major cards

🍴 GAUSS
$$$
OBERE KARSPÜLE 22
TEL 0551 566 16
Owner Jacqueline Amirfallah, a
well-known cook on German
television, takes her inspirations
from France: sole with saffron
rice, poached chicken with
herb sauce, lamb in thyme jus.
You eat in a vaulted cellar or
outside in summer.
🚪 85 🕐 Closed Sun. &
Mon. 🚳 AE, MC, V

HANOVER

🏨 ARABELLA SHERATON
🍴 PELIKAN
$$$
PODBIELSKISTRASSE 145
TEL 0511 9 09 30
FAX 0511 9 09 35 55
WWW.SHERATON.DE/
HANNOVER
Converted from some
handsome early 20th-century
industrial buildings, this
business hotel has its best and
largest rooms on the second
and third floors where stylish
designer furniture says "cool."
The restaurant Grüner Pelikan
specializes in Euro-Asian
cuisine: Try roasted shark with
lemon grass and curry oil.
🚪 138 + 9 suites 🅿 🔁
🗹 🚳 All major cards

🏨 KASTENS HOTEL
🍴 LUISENHOF
$$$$
LUISENSTRASSE 1–3

TEL 0511 3 04 40
FAX 0511 3 04 48 07
WWW.KASTENS-LUISENHOF.DE
Between the main station and
the Opera House, Hanover's
grand hotel is furnished with
antiques. Enjoy pan-global
cuisine in the restaurant Luise:
Main courses include breast of
pigeon with caramelized apples
and veal in a curry-saffron sauce.
🚪 138 + 7 suites 🅿 🔁
🚳 All major cards

🍴 BIESLER
$$
SOPHIENSTRASSE 6
TEL 0511 1033
This basement restaurant
serves solid regional food,
such as lamb with a puree of
beans. Good wines.
🍽 75 🕐 Closed Sat. L, Sun
& Mon. 🚳 MC, V

🍴 PIER 51
$$
RUDOLF-VON-
BENNINGSEN-UFER 51
TEL 0511 807 1800
Here you can dine on the
terrace and look at the sunset
over the Maschsee. Unfussy
Mediterranean dishes such as
pasta with mushrooms in
cream sauce or salad with
scallops and scampi.
🍽 70 🅿 🚳 AE, MC, V

HILDESHEIM

🏨 LE MERIDIEN
$$$
MARKT 4
TEL 05121 3000
FAX 05121 300 444
WWW.MERIDIEN-
HILDESHEIM.COM
This modern hotel in the
medieval market square sits
right next to Germany's most
beautiful half-timbered house.
English-style interior and
modern conference facilities.
🚪 111 + 2 suites 🅿 🔁
🚳 🗹 🚳 All major cards

🍴 KUPFERSCHMIEDE
$$$
AM STEINBERG 6
TEL 05121 26 30 25

A delightful setting in a forest south of Hildesheim and 32 varieties of champagne at attractive prices are good reasons to come here. French cuisine of good quality.
🛏 90 🕐 Closed Mon. 🅿 🚗 MC, V

JUIST

🏨 ACHTERDIEK
$$$$
WILHELMSTRASSE 36
TEL 04935 80 40
FAX 04935 17 54
WWW.HOTEL-ACHTERDIEK.DE
Art and antiques in the entrance hall give a taste of grandeur to this hotel. If the wind blows too hard, retreat to the sauna or beauty spa.
🛏 49 + 4 suites 🕐 Closed Nov. 27–Dec. 22 🚊 🚗 No credit cards

LÜNEBURG

🏨 BARGENTURM
$$$
AM LAMBERTIPLATZ
TEL 04131 72 90
FAX 04131 72 94 99
WWW.HOTEL-BARGENTURM.DE
Pastel-colored rooms enhance this hotel in the historic center. Ask for directions as it's hard to find in Lüneburg's pedestrian-only zones.
🛏 40 🅿 🚗 All major cards

🍴 ZUM HEIDKRUG
$$
AM BERGE 5
TEL 04131 2 41 60
Lüneberg's top-rated restaurant is ambitious and often booked solid. The cuisine—for example, vegetable soup with black truffles or crepinette of venison—is modern international. Excellent desserts; don't miss the Black Forest cherry ice cream.
🛏 56 🕐 Closed Sun. & Mon. 🚗 MC V

NORDERNEY

🏨 VILLA NEY
🍴 $$$
GARTENSTRASSE 59
TEL 04932 91 70
FAX 04932 917 31
WWW.VILLA-NEY.DE
This whitewashed modern villa has good-sized bedrooms with comfy armchairs and marble bathrooms. Owner Peter Mackel inspires admiration for his imaginative treatment of fresh local fish.
🛏 4 + 10 suites 🕐 Closed 2 weeks Nov. & 2 weeks Jan. 🚗 All major cards

SCHNEVERDINGEN

SOMETHING SPECIAL

🏨 CAMP REINSEHLEN
An ecologist's dream on Germany's oldest nature reserve, only 40 minutes from Hamburg. Clean, modern design contrasts with rustic, traditional features. All rooms have terraces. Only organic ingredients are used in the restaurant.
$$$
REINSEHLEN
TEL 05198 98 30
FAX 05198 983 99
WWW.CAMPREINSEHLEN.DE
🛏 28 🅿 🚗 AE, MC, V

WOLFSBURG

SOMETHING SPECIAL

🏨 THE RITZ-CARLTON
🍴
Designed by renowned French interior guru Andrée Putman, the hotel is right in the middle of the six-acre Autostadt (Auto City)—a theme park northeast of the town. Only the best furnishings grace the rooms, from the finest Frette linens to the Eileen Gray sofas in the suites.
$$$$$
STADTBRÜCKE
TEL 05361 60 70 00
FAX 05361 60 80 00

WWW.RITZCARLTON.COM
🛏 153 + 21 suites 🅿 🚪 🚗 All major cards

WORPSWEDE

🏨 EICHENHOF
🍴 $$$
OSTENDORFER STRASSE 13
TEL 04792 26 76
FAX 04792 44 27
WWW.WORPSWEDE.DE/EICHENHOF
The fusion of rustic North German architecture with modern interiors works well at this country hotel in a quiet park. The restaurant, ARTisst, serves modern European dishes such as chervil soup with shreds of salmon, and roast beef with green pepper, spinach, and herb potatoes. Dinner only.
🛏 15 + 1 suite + 3 apts. 🚗 DC, MC, V

NORTH RHINE-WESTPHALIA

AACHEN

🏨 DORINTQUELLENHOF
$$$$$
MONHEIMSALLEE 52
TEL 0241 913 20
FAX 0241 913 21 00
WWW.SOFITEL.COM
Rooms in the premier hotel in Charlemagne's ancient capital are furnished in classical taste.
🛏 181 + 4 suites 🚗 All major cards

SOMETHING SPECIAL

🍴 CAFE VAN DEN DALE
A coffee house in a 17th-century building with beautifully preserved rooms. You can have breakfast, brunch, and afternoon coffee and cake. The specialties here are the *Reisfladen* (rice cake) and the famous *Printen* (ginger cakes).
$
BUCHEL 18
TEL 0241 357 24 0
🛏 95 🚗 MC, V

KEY 🏨 Hotel 🍴 Restaurant 🛏 No. of guest rooms 🚊 Public transportation 🅿 Parking 🕐 Closed 🚪 Elevator

☷ ST BENEDIKT
$$$
BENEDIKTUSPLATZ 12
KORNELIMUNSTER
TEL 02408 28 88
Aachen's best restaurant, and one of its coziest, is in a picturesque little town to the southeast. Owner/chef Gisela Kreus is celebrated for her top-notch cooking—just try her venison with morello cherry sauce. One Michelin star. Daytime bistro next door.
🍴 68 🕐 Closed Sun. & Mon L ⊗ No credit cards

BONN

☷ DORINT VENUSBERG
☷ **$$$**
AN DER CASSELSRUHE 1
TEL 0228 28 80
FAX 0228 28 82 88
WWW.ACCORHOTELS.COM
In a quiet and beautiful spot beside a forest with a view of the Siebengebirge (Seven Mountain Hills) and the Rhine. Ambitious restaurant.
🛏 85 + 7 suites 🅿 ⊗ ⊗ All major cards

COLOGNE

☷ DOM-HOTEL
$$$$
DOMKLOSTER 2A
TEL 0221 202 40
FAX 0221 202 44 44
WWW.LEMERIDIEN-DOMHOTEL.COM
Cologne's finest address, the Dom-Hotel has elegant rooms, some with views of the cathedral. The terrace is strictly for seeing and being seen.
🛏 124 ⊗ ⊗ AE, MC, V

☷ EXCELSIOR HOTEL ERNST
$$$$
DOMPLATZ
TEL 0221 27 01 FAX 0221 13 51 50
WWW.EXCELSIOR-HOTELERNST.DE
Directly opposite the cathedral and railroad station, the foyer and rooms of 140-

year-old hotel foyer are replete with antiques. Minibar use is included in the room price. The restaurant, Hanse Stube, offers creative French cuisine: sole with a citrus-fruit salad, tournedos of beef with marrow bones and cassis-chicory. The second restaurant, *taku*, serves Asian food. Try the Thai fish curry with bamboo sprouts, or perch with asparagus tempura.
🛏 121 + 31 suites ⊗ ⚕ ⊗ All major cards

☷ HOTEL IM ☷ WASSERTURM
A flamboyant hotel by French designer Andree Putman behind the walls of an old water tower. Chic rooms, some with African hardwoods, others in a yellow-and-blue color scheme, and even more elegant suites. The restaurant has city views from the 12th-floor roof terrace. Here, French cuisine comes with a twist: salmon paté with sturgeon mousse, loin of rabbit roulade, fillet of sea bass with tomato fondu and a beurre blanc sauce.
$$$$
KAYGASSE 2
TEL 0221 2 00 80
FAX 0221 200 88 88
WWW.HOTEL-IM-WASSERTURM.DE
🛏 54 + 34 suites ⊗ All major cards

☷ BIZIM
$$$
WEIDENGASSE 47-49
TEL 0221 13 15 81
Turkish tradition fused with modern European cuisine. The rabbit with aubergines and exotic spices is excellent.
🍴 65 🕐 Closed Sun. & Mon. ⊗ MC, V

☷ ALFREDO
$$$
TUNISSTRASSE 3
TEL 0221 257 73 80
An exclusive Italian eatery

next to the Opera House specializing in fish. Don't miss the langoustine with fennel.
🍴 58 🕐 Closed Sat. L & Sun. ⊗ M, AE

DÜSSELDORF

☷ STEIGENBERGER PARK
$$$$
KÖNIGSALLEE 1A
TEL 021 1138 10
FAX 021 1138 15 92
WWW.DUESSELDORF-STEIGENBERGER.DE
Classic grand hotel (the only one in Düsseldorf) with a convenient central location and time-honored service.
🛏 119 + 11 suites 🅿 ⊗ ⊗ All major cards

☷ HUMMER-STÜBCHEN
$$$$
BONIFATIUSSTRASSE 35
TEL 021 159 44 02
One of Düsseldorf's top restaurants, located in a small hotel. Specialties are sautéed lobster with marinated glass noodles, *ris de veau* with braised fennel and parsley sauce. Good wines.
🍴 49 🕐 Closed Sun. 🅿 ⊗ DC, MC, V

☷ MARUYASU
$
SCHADOWSTRASSE 11
TEL 021 113 21 57
Düsseldorf is well known for its good Japanese food. This chic sushi temple in the bowels of the Schadow shopping arcades prides itself on its 70 varieties of excellent sushi.
🍴 75 ⊗ No credit cards

☷ ROBERTS BISTRO
$
WUPPERSTRASSE 2
TEL 0211 30 48 21
A popular bistro with plain decor, pleasant food, and a trendy young clientele. Expect big portions of sausages, salads, and veal kidney in mustard sauce.
🕐 Closed Sun. & Mon. ⊗ No credit cards

HOTELS & RESTAURANTS

ESSEN

🏨 SCHLOSS HUGENPOET
$$$$
AUGUST-THYSSEN-STRASSE 51
TEL 02054 1 20 40
FAX 02054 1 2 04 50
WWW.HUGENPOET.DE
This baroque castle in the middle of a large park is stylish and restful. Antiques furnish the rooms.
🛏 20+5 suites 🅿 🖎 All major cards

🍽 KÖLNER HOF
$$
DUISBURGER STRASSE 20
ESSEN-FROHNHAUSEN
TEL 0201 76 34 30
Creative cooking inspired by the Mediterranean, with starched linens and personable service. Try the tender lamb with a pine nut crust, beef medallions in red wine sauce, and hazelnut nougat with caramelized apples.
🍴 48 🖎 No credit cards

KÖNIGSWINTER

🏨🍽 GÄSTEHAUS PETERSBERG

On a plateau high above Königswinter, a few miles south of the former capital of Bonn, this imposing early 20th-century building acted as a guesthouse for state visits to Chancellor Helmut Kohl's government. The timeless elegance of the hotel is matched by the restaurant's classic cuisine.
$$$$
PETERSBERG
TEL 02223 7 40
FAX 02223 7 44 43
WWW.GAESTEHAUS-PETERSBERG.COM
🛏 87 + 12 suites 🔁 🖼
📺 🖎 All major cards

🍽 REMISE
$$$$
STADTSTRASSE 14
TEL 02472 80 08 00

Modern European cuisine such as turbot with broad beans or lamb with gnocchi is the hallmark of this fine riverside restaurant, one of four eateries in this comely jumble of 16th- and 17th-century architecture.
🍴 130 🅿 🖎 MC,V

MÜNSTER

🏨 HOF ZUR LINDE
🍽 **$$$**
HANDORFER WERSEUFER 1
MÜNSTER-HANDORF
TEL 0251 327 50
FAX 0251 32 82 09
WWW.HOF-ZUR-LINDE.DE
A romantic old building on the banks of the River Werse with canopied beds, fireplaces and decoration veering from hunting lodge to French royal. The best rooms are in the adjacent *Spieker* house.
🛏 47 🅿 🖎 All major cards

🍽 DAVERT JAGDHAUS
$$
WIEMANNSTRASSE 4
MÜNSTER-AMELSBUREN
TEL 02501 580 58
The old Wirtshaus (pub) serves Westphalian *Himmel und Erde* (sautéed black pudding with potato puree), as well as the more refined cocotte of crabs and truffles.
🍴 52 🕐 Closed Mon. & Tues. 🅿 🖎 DC, V

TRIER

🏨 DORINT
$$$
PORTA-NIGRA-PLATZ 1
TEL 0651 270 1 0
FAX 0651 270 1 1 70
WWW.DORINT.COM
The view of the Roman Porta Negra is a major selling point for this business hotel just a few steps from the old town and its imposing cathedral. Fresh waffles for breakfast.
🛏 104 + 2 suites 🅿 🔁
🖼 🖎 All major cards

🍽 PFEFFERMÜHLE
$$
ZURLAUBENER UFER 76
TRIER-ZURLAUBEN
TEL 0651 261 33
Once home to fishermen, this 18th-century mill on the banks of the Moselle now houses a restaurant serving tempting dishes such as sautéed pike with broad beans or rabbit with port jelly. The dining terrace overlooks the river.
🍴 40 🕐 Closed Sun.
🖎 MC,V

🏨 BELLEVUE RHEINHOTEL
$$
RHEINALLEE 41-42
TEL 06742 10 20
FAX 06742 10 26 02
WWW.BELLEVUE-BOPPARD.DE
Stylish art nouveau house on the promenade overlooking the rushing waters of the Rhine River. The rooms come in different shapes and sizes, some with antiques and balconies.
🛏 93 + 1 suite 🅿 🔁
🖼 📺 🖎 All major cards

▥ GASTHAUS HIRSCH
$$
RHEINSTRASSE 17
56154 BOPPARD-HIRZENACH
TEL 06741 26 01
Family-owned restaurant
known for its very good game
and regional cooking. In
summer, eat in the courtyard.
✇ 56 🕒 Closed Mon., Tues
🅿 🅢 All major cards

KNITTELSHEIM

▥ STEVERDING'S ISENHOF
$$$
HAUPTSTRASSE 15A
TEL 06348 57 00
This restaurant is a rising star
on the culinary scene, run by
chef Peter Steverding in a
handsome timber-frame
house from the 15th century.
The sea bass with potato and
spinach tart is especially good.
✇ 60 🕒 Closed Mon., Sun.,
Sat L 🅢 No credit cards

KOBLENZ

▦ DIEHL'S HOTEL
$$
RHEINSTEIGUFER 1
KOBLENZ
TEL 0261 970 70
FAX 0261 970 72 13
WWW.DIEHLS-HOTEL.DE
Set beside the Rhine, the
hotel has views of Koblenz
and rooms in traditional style.
The restaurant puts a modern
spin on German cuisine.
Breakfast included.
🛈 53 + 4 suites 🅿 🗗
🕳 🕎 🅢 All major cards

NEUSTADT AN DER WEINSTRASSE

▥ BECKER'S GUT
$$$
WEINSTRASSE 507 67434
TEL 06321 21 95
Softly colored decor, powerful
regional cooking. Chef Harry
Becker makes excellent
Schupfnudeln (a Swabian
potato dish) and venison with
mushrooms.
✇ 60 🕒 Closed Mon. &

Tues. 🅿 🅢 All major
cards

SAARBRÜCKEN

▥ KUNTZE'S HANDELSHOF
$$$$
WILHELM-HEINRICH-STRASSE 17
TEL 0681 569 20
Good cooking in a region
renowned for it. Warm and
cold chicken dishes, veal
kidneys in champagne-
mustard sauce, and rustic
potato soup. Chandelier-lit
baroque rooms.
✇ 56 🕒 Closed Sat. L, Sun.
D, Mon. 🅢 All major cards

STROMBERG

SOMETHING SPECIAL

▦ STROMBURG
▥
A castle dating from the 11th
century set beside the River
Nahe is pure elegance, from the
grand lobby to guest rooms
furnished in different styles. Most
of the rooms have a view over the
romantic Soon Forest. Owner/
chef Johann Lafer runs the
restaurant, Le Val D'Or (closed
Mon.), and cooks classic French
haute cuisine. Try the fillet of
beef with foie gras, truffles, and
broad beans. One Michelin star.
$$$$
SCHLOSSBERG
TEL 06724 931 00
FAX 06724 93 10 90
WWW.JOHANNLAFER.DE
🛈 13 + 1 suite 🅿 🅢 All
major cards

ZWEIBRÜCKEN

▦ FASANERIE
▥ $$$
FASANERIE 1
TEL 06332 97 30
FAX 06332 97 31 11
WWW.LANDSCHLOSS-
FASANERIE.DE
Built in 1714 by Polish king
Stanislaus Lescynski, this
whitewashed villa sits in a
flower-filled park. Rooms are

in country style. French
cooking in the restaurant. Try
the venison, followed by pear-
vanilla ice cream. Breakfast
included.
🛈 37 + 13 apartments 🅿
🕳 🕎 🅢 AE,MC,V

HESSE

BAD HOMBURG

▦ STEIGENBERGER
$$$
KAISER-FRIEDRICH-
PROMENADE 69-75
TEL 06172 18 10
FAX 06172 18 16 30
WWW.BAD-HOMBURG
.STEIGENBERGER.DE
A gracious establishment
notable for its art deco
furnishings. This is where
assorted royalty stayed while
taking the rejuvenating spa
waters or spinning the wheel
in the nearby casino.
🛈 152 + 17 suites 🅿 🗗
🕳 🕎 🅢 All major cards

▥ ZUM WASSERWEIBCHEN
$
AM MÜHLBERG 57
TEL 06172 2 98 78
Popular for her hospitality and
good humor, Inge Kuper
serves traditional German
food made of the finest
ingredients. Many regulars
come especially for the
crunchy potato cake.
✇ 52 🕒 Closed Sat. 🅢 All
major cards

DARMSTADT

▦ JAGDSCHLOSS KRANICHSTEIN
$$$
KRANICHSTEINER STRASSE 261
TEL 06151 977 90
FAX 06151 97 79 20
WWW.JAGDSCHLOSS-
KRANICHSTEIN.DE
This enormous Renaissance-
era palace has been
converted to a traditional
hotel with two restaurants
and grand halls filled with

hunting trophies. Tours of the grounds and museum. Breakfast included.
🛈 11 + 4 suites 🅿 🚇 All major cards

🍴 EINSIEDEL
$$$
DIEBURGER STRASSE 263
DARMSTADT
TEL 06159 244
Another former hunting lodge, now a sprawling restaurant with art deco touches. Roast venison with *Spätzle* and rabbit with a tomato-basil sauce are popular local favorites.
🍽 110 🕐 Closed Tues. & Wed. 🅿 🚇 AE, MC

ELTVILLE

🏨 KRONEN-
🍴 SCHLOSSCHEN
$$$
RHEINALLEE
ELTVILLE-HATTENHEIM
TEL 06723 640
FAX 06723 76 63
WWW.KRONENSCHLOES
SCHEN.DE
A beautiful small castle with stylish rooms set in a leafy park. The French-inspired restaurant serves foie gras on a fig confit, sea bass with saffron paella, and chocolate soufflé.
🛈 8 + 10 suites 🅿 🚇 All major cards

> **SOMETHING SPECIAL**

🏨 GÄSTEHAUS KLOSTER EBERBACH
A dramatic mélange of Romanesque, Gothic, and baroque buildings on the grounds of a former monastery where Augustinian monks once cultivated their vines. Scenes from the medieval thriller *The Name of the Rose* were shot here. The restaurant offers venison and other regional dishes. Breakfast included.
$$$
TEL 06723 99 30
FAX 06723 99 31 00
WWW.KLOSTEREBERBACH
.COM
🛈 30 🅿 🚇 AE,MC,V

FRANKFURT AM MAIN

🏨 STEIGENBERGER
🍴 FRANKFURTER HOF
$$$$$
AM KAISERPLATZ 1
TEL 069 215 02
FAX 069 21 59 00
WWW.FRANKFURTER-HOF
.STEIGENBERGER.DE
The Frankfurter Hof dominates the city's main square. All the elegantly furnished rooms in this 125-year-old hotel are equipped with Internet connections and faxes—fitting for a city that plays a key role in international finance. The restaurant in French style, with chandeliers and tapestries, has equally French haute cuisine.
🛈 286 + 46 suites 🅿 ⬍
🛗 🔲 🚇 All major cards

🏨 HESSISCHER HOF
$$$$
FRIEDRICH-EBERT-ANLAGE 40
TEL 069 754 00
FAX 069 75 40 29 24
WWW.HESSISCHER-HOF.DE
Old-fashioned traditional hotel near the financial district and trade fair grounds. Its elegant rooms are furnished with plenty of fine art and antiques. Instead of a buffet, breakfast is served to you at your table.
🛈 107 + 10 suites 🅿 ⬍
🚇 All major cards

🏨 TURM HOTEL
$$$
ESCHERSHEIMER
LANDSTRASSE 20
TEL 069 15 40 50
FAX 069 55 35 78
WWW.TURMHOTEL-FRA.DE
Frescoes from Italian palazzos grace the rooms in this hotel near the banking district. Rooms have eclectic themes, from Mona Lisa to avant-garde to Oriental hip.
🛈 74 🅿 🚇 All major cards

🍴 ERNO'S BISTRO
$$$$$
LIEBIGSTRASSE 15
TEL 069 72 19 97

Specialties at this rustically decorated restaurant, one of Frankfurt's finest (and most expensive), include *tete de veau*; carpaccio with a caper-onion vinaigrette, and beef roulade. The copious wine list is an attraction in its own right.
🍽 80 🕐 Closed Sat. & Sun. 🚇 MC, V

🍴 HOLBEIN'S
$$
HOLBEINSTRASSE 1
TEL 069 66 05 66 66
Chic, modern, and conveniently located near the pubs and beer gardens in the suburb of Sachsenhausen, Holbein's serves its creative international dishes from a rear annex of the Städel Museum. Flagship dishes here include halibut and lobster.
🕐 Closed Mon. 🚇 All major cards

KASSEL

🏨 KURFÜRST WILHELM I
$$
WILHELMSHÖHER ALLEE 257
KASSEL-WILHELMSHÖHE
TEL 0561 318 70
FAX 0561 31 87 77
WWW.KURFUERST.BEST
WESTERN.DE
Modern facilities in a handsome late-19th-century building, located on a plateau high above Kassel. All quarters have 10-foot ceilings and state-of-the-art designer furnishings. Breakfast included.
🛈 42 + 1 suite 🅿 🚇 All major cards

🍴 ZUM STEINERNEN SCHWEINCHEN
$$
KONRAD-ADENAUERSTRASSE 117
TEL 0561 94 04 80
The "little stone pig" has a marvelous view that complements some of Kassel's best cuisine. Try the beef in Bordeaux sauce with braised onions.
🍽 55 🅿 🚇 All major cards

LIMBURG

🏨 ZIMMERMANN
🍴 $$
BLUMENRÖDERSTRASSE I
TEL 06431 46 11
FAX 06431 4 13 14
WWW.ROMANTIK-HOTEL-
ZIMMERMANN.DE
An intimate, atmospheric
hotel stuffed with precious
antiques and classy furniture.
Bathrooms have a separate
lavatory and fine Italian
marble, while some quarters
are in English country style.
The stylish restaurant serves
modern German cuisine.
🛏 16 + 4 suites 🅿 🚭
🔘 All major cards

WIESBADEN

🏨 NASSAUER HOF
$$$$
KAISER-FRIEDRICH-PLATZ 3-4
TEL 0611 13 30
FAX 0611 13 36 32
WWW.NASSAUER-HOF.DE
A grand hotel with elegant
rooms with what's reputed to
be Wiesbaden's best
restaurant. The Euro-Asian
cuisine of the Ente thrills:
perch with aubergines, roast
chicken with langustines.
🛏 139 + 30 suites 🅿 🔄
🏊 🔘 🔘 All major cards

EISENACH

**SOMETHING
SPECIAL**

🏨 AUF DER WARTBURG
🍴
A truly romantic hotel located
at the foot of the legendary
Wartburg castle. Enjoy the
country-house furniture, quiet
atmosphere, and views of the
courtyard or the Thuringian
forest. Local specialties are
served in the restaurant: venison
with Thuringian potato salad,
sauteed trout with tomato-bean
ragout. Breakfast included.
$$$$
AUF DER WARTBURG

TEL 03691 79 70
FAX 03691 79 71 00
WWW.WARTBURGHOTEL.DE
🛏 30 + 5 suites 🅿 🔘 All
major cards

🏨 HOTEL KAISERHOF
$$
WARTBURGALLEE 2
TEL 03691 21 35 13
FAX 03691 20 36 53
WWW.KAISERHOF-
EISENACH.DE
This nice, downtown hotel is
replete with English-style
furnishings. Chef Ivo Mamzed
combines regional traditions
with the latest trends in the
Turmschänke restaurant. Try
the excellent mussels, tasty
roast chicken breast with
spinach, and first-rate
cheeses.
🛏 96 🅿 🔘 All major
cards

ERFURT

🏨 DORINT
$$$
MEIENBERGSTRASSE 26-27
TEL 0361 594 90
FAX 0361 594 91 00
WWW.ACCOR.COM
The oldest part of this hotel
dates from 1450. Most
rooms, however, are located
in the 1995 annex and are
furnished with stylish
designer pieces. Breakfast
included.
🛏 141 + 2 suites 🅿 🔄
🔘 All major cards

🍴 CASTELL
$$
KLEINE ARCHE 4
TEL 0361 644 22 22
Features Mediterranean
cooking as well as local
specialties: creqinette of
pigeon and the suckling pig
with Thuringian potato
dumplings are famous.
🪑 60 🕐 Closed Sun. D &
Jan.-March L 🔘 No credit
cards

MAGDEBURG

🏨 HERRENKRUG
🍴 PARKHOTEL
$$$
HERRENKRUG 3
TEL 0391 850 80
FAX 0391 850 85 01
WWW.HERRENKRUG.DE
Historic house in a park
where large, well-furnished
rooms embrace art deco
furnishings and a wonderful
view of the park. The
restaurant, *Die Saison*, has a
winter garden and serves
ambitious European dishes.
🛏 126 + 21 suites 🅿 🔄
🏊 🔘 🔘 All major cards

WEIMAR

🏨 ARABELLA SHERATON
🍴 ELEPHANT
$$$$
MARKT 19
TEL 03643 80 20
FAX 03643 80 26 10
WWW.ARABELLA
SHERATON.COM
Weimar's oldest hotel (dating from
1696) and most renowned
hotel, with Bauhaus and art
deco touches. Artists and
poets were frequent guests
and work by painters like
George Baselitz and Rainer
Fetting is on display. For
Mediterranean fare visit the
restaurant, Anna Amalia,
where specialties include a
scallop millefeuille served with
salad and juicy roast venison
with two pepper sauces.
🛏 85 + 17 suites 🅿
🔘 All major cards

🏨 ALT WEIMAR
$$
PRELLERSTRASSE 2
TEL 03643 861 90
FAX 03643 86 19 10
WWW.ALT-WEIMAR.DE
This attractive 18th-century
building behind the theater
has quiet, airy rooms,
furnished with Bauhaus
designs. A small but exquisite
hotel.
🛏 17 🅿 🔘 All major
cards

🏨 DORINT AM GOETHEPARK
$$$
BEETHOVENPLATZ 1-2
TEL 03643 87 20
FAX 03643 87 21 00
WWW.DORINT.COM
Behind the Goethehaus, the hotel consists of two 18th-century villas and a contemporary building. The rooms, furnished in classic style of the era, are complemented by a restaurant and beer cellar.
🛏 143 + 6 suites + 3 apartments 🃏 All major cards

BAUTZEN

🏨 SPREE-HOTEL BAUTZEN
$$
AN DEN STEINBRÜCHEN 9
TEL 03591 213 00
FAX 03591 21 30 10
WWW.SPREE-HOTEL.DE
A lakeside hotel in this baroque town. Comfortable guest rooms and a restaurant with regional cooking. Breakfast.
🛏 69 + 12 suites 🅿 ⬆ 🃏 AE,MC,V

🏨 KEMPINSKI TASCHENBERGPALAIS
$$$$$
TASCHENBERG 3
TEL 0351 491 20
FAX 0351 491 28 12
WWW.KEMPINSKI-DRESDEN.DE
Dresden's number one hotel, between Zwinger and the palace, displays its old-fashioned luxury behind a baroque facade.
🛏 182 + 33 suites 🅿 ⬆ 🖼 🚇 🍽 🃏 All major cards

🏨 ART'OTEL DRESDEN 🍽
$$/$$$
OSTRAALLEE 33, 01067
TEL 0351 492 20
FAX 0351 492 27 77

WWW.ARTOTELS.DE
Situated a 10-minute walk from the Semper Opera House and the historic old town. Expect a voguish allure in these large, snazzy rooms where form scores highly over function. The stylish interior is the product of a Milan designer, and the in-house gallery features some challenging works by Dresden artist A.R. Penck. Staff speak good English.
🛏 164 + 19 suites 🅿 ⬆ 🖼 🚇 🍽 🃏 All major cards

🍽 FOUR RESTAURANTS & OPERNRESTAURANT
$$
THEATERPLATZ 2
TEL 0351 491 15 21
In a posh modern building behind the Semperoper, this sophisticated place offers varied cuisine from Italian to German, at stylish prices. Opera lovers flock here for refreshments before and after performances. Guests can enjoy the terrace in fine weather.
🍴 80 🕐 Closed Mon–Sat lunch 🃏 All major cards

🍽 KUPPEL RESTAURANT
$$
WEISSERITZSTRASSE 3
TEL 0351 490 59 90
Located in the former Yenidze cigarette factory, serving Middle Eastern and Saxon specialties under a terrific stained-glass dome. The building is styled after an oriental mosque with a smokestack disguised as a minaret. You can dine on the rooftop and admire the twinkling lights of Dresden.
🍴 130 🃏 MC, V

LEIPZIG

🏨 ARABELLA SHERATON FÜRSTENHOF 🍽
$$$
TRÖNDLINRING 8
TEL 0341 140 49 05
FAX 0341 140 37 00

WWW.STARWOODHOTELS.COM
Luxury in an old aristocratic palace that has been opulently renovated. Elegant restaurant with competent, if erratic, French cuisine. On the menu: soufleed fillet of turbot with fennel fondue, roast breast of pigeon with truffled bananas.
🛏 80 + 12 suites 🅿 ⬆ 🚇 🃏 All major cards

🏨 LEIPZIGER HOF
$$
HEDWIGSTRASSE 1-3
TEL 0341 697 40
FAX 0341 697 41 50
WWW.LEIPZIGER-HOF.DE
This 19th-century private residence has been transformed into a sleek hotel equipped with the latest technology. True to its sobriquet of "art hotel," there are paintings by local artists throughout. Breakfast included.
🛏 67 + 1 suite + 4 apts. 🅿 🚇 🍽 🃏 All major cards

🍽 AUERBACHS KELLER
$$
MÄDLER-PASSAGE, GRIMMÄISCHE STRASSE 2-4
TEL 0341 21 61 00
One of Germany's classic

restaurants founded in 1525, Auerbachs Keller has earned kudos for its contemporary European cuisine. The historical section depicts a scene from Goethe's Faust. Mephistopheles and Faust carouse with students before riding off on a barrel—a scene often re-enacted at night.
🛏 250 🕐 Closed Mon.
🔵 All major cards

🍴 BARTHELS HOF
$$
HAINSTRASSE 1
TEL 0341 141 31 13
This sprawling, historic eatery—Leipzig's oldest—has a bar, wine cellar and restaurant serving Saxon dishes such as *Heubraten* (marinated lamb roasted on hay). Waitresses wear traditional costume. The courtyard is nestled among Leipzig's oldest Renaissance buildings.
🛏 180 🔵 All major cards

MEISSEN

🏨 MERCURE GRAND HOTEL
$$
HAFENSTRASSE 27-31
TEL 03521 722 50
FAX 03521 72 29 04
WWW.MERCURE.COM
Once a rich industrialist's villa, this hotel close to the river and the historic center has art deco bedrooms in the old building, modern ones in the extension. Meissen porcelain decorates the restaurant.
🛈 92 + 5 suites 🔵 All major cards

ABENSBERG

🏨 STEIGENBERGER DREI MOHREN
$$$
MAXIMILIANSTRASSE 40
TEL 0821 503 60
FAX 0821 15 78 64
WWW.AUGSBURG

.STEIGENBERGER.DE
This venerable hotel in the center dates from 1723, although inside everything is a showcase of modern design. The large, contemporary rooms have Internet links. There are a bistro, a bar, and a formal restaurant serving Mediterranean dishes.
🛈 99 + 6 suites 🅿 🔵
🔵 All major cards

🍴 DIE ECKE
$$
ELIAS-HOLL-PLATZ 2
TEL 0821 51 06 00
Classic Swabian and Bavarian food, a relaxed bistro atmosphere, and modern art on the walls make Die Ecke immensely popular with the local student population. Try the game served with *Spätzle* (rolled noodles).
🛏 65 🔵 All major cards

BAMBERG

🏨 RESIDENZSCHLOSS
$$$$
UNTERE SANDSTRASSE 32
TEL 0951 609 10
FAX 0951 609 17 01
WWW.RESIDENZSCHLOSS.COM
A historic palace and former hospital on the banks of the River Regnitz, only a few minutes from the lovely medieval center of Bamberg. The classically styled bedrooms have WLAN and scads of amenities. Breakfast included.
🛈 180 + 4 suites 🅿 🔵
🏋 🔵 All major cards

🍴 BRAUEREI SPEZIAL
$
OBERE KONIGSTRASSE 10
96052
TEL 0951 243 04
Popular since 1536, this Franconian brewery inn serves the smoked beer that Bamberg is famous for. Mainstays of the menu include delicious sausages and crispy roast pork.
🛏 120 🕐 Closed Sat.
🔵 No credit cards

BAYREUTH

🏨 JAGDSCHLOSS 🍴 THIERGARTEN
A stylish hotel on the fringes of Bayreuth, set on the grounds of a former royal hunting lodge. The guest rooms have antique furniture and personal touches abound. The restaurant, Petit Chateau, is one of the finest in Bayreuth and serves Franconian fare with an Italian twist. Popular specials are fresh river fish with spinach canneloni and rabbit crepinette with bread dumplings. Breakfast is included.
$$$
OBERTHIERGÄRTNER STRASSE 36
TEL 09209 98 40
FAX 09209 984 29
WWW.SCHLOSSHOTEL-THIERGARTEN.DE
🛈 9 + 2 suites 🅿 🔵 MC,V

🍴 GOLDENER LÖWE
$
KULMBACHER STRASSE 30
TEL 0921 74 60 60
Enjoy homemade beer, sausages, or schnitzel in a restful country atmosphere. The restaurant is attached to a brewery.
🛏 75 🕐 Closed Sun.
🔵 AE, MC, V

HEROLDSBERG

🍴 FREIHARDT
$
HAUPTSTRASSE 81
TEL 0911 518 08 05
A country inn northeast of Nuremberg where owner Hans-Jürgen Freihardt whips up an excellent array of sausages, steaks, and pork fillets. As well as traditional recipes, he makes a good fish with green curry and other modern dishes.
🛏 68 🕐 Closed Mon.
🔵 All major cards

HOTELS & RESTAURANTS

NUREMBERG

🏨 LE MERIDIEN GRAND
🍴 $$$
BAHNHOFSTRASSE 1-3
TEL 0911 233 30
FAX 0911 232 24 44
WWW.GRAND-HOTEL.DE
Opposite the railroad station
on the edge of the old town,
this grandest of Nuremberg's
hotels has accommodated
plenty of celebrities over the
years such as Bob Dylan, The
Beatles and Robbie Williams.
The palatial rooms have tons
of marble and chandeliers as
well as art deco bedrooms.
🛏 178 + 4 suites 🅿 🚻
🗝 All major cards

🏨 ROTTNER
$$$
WINTERSTRASSE 17
NÜRNBERG
TEL 0911 65 84 80
FAX 0911 65 84 82 03
WWW.HOTEL-ROTTNER.DE
This traditional half-timbered
hotel with colorful rooms is
situated in a peaceful suburb
southwest of Nuremberg.
Savor excellent regional
cooking in the restaurant, with
favorites including sauteed
goat with buttered vegetables
and pigeon in aspic. There's a
good selection of Franconian
wines. Breakfast included.
🛏 33 + 4 suites 🅿 🗝 All
major cards

🍴 ESSIGBRÄTLEIN
$$$
WEINMARKT 3
TEL 0911 22 51 31
Nuremberg's premier
restaurant located in the
historic quarter. Andree Kothe
and Yved Ollech draw on
fresh local ingredients in
dishes such as lamb with
carrot jus, or breast of pigeon
served with nuts, arugula, and
figs. The restaurant has a
handful of tables that are
often booked solid.
🍽 30 🕐 Closed Sun. & Mon.
🗝 DC,MC,V

🍴 ALTE POST
$$
KRAFTSHOFER
HAUPTSTRASSE 164,
KRAFTSHOF
TEL 0911 30 58 63
Just north of Nuremberg, this
old village inn has a lively
atmosphere. Tables are
situated in cozy spots, around
a tiled stove or on a small
terrace. Regional cuisine is
offered, perhaps fish with
potato dumplings and Wesling
sauce, wild duck, or salads.
🍽 55 🗝 All major cards

SOMETHING
SPECIAL

🍴 HISTORISCHE BRATWURSTKÜCHE ZUM GULDEN STERN
A must for every visitor to
Nuremberg. This ancient
restaurant (founded in 1419) is
the oldest purveyor of sausages
in the world. The famous
Nürnberger Bratwürstchen
(small fried sausages) are roasted
over a beech fire and served on a
pewter plate with horseradish,
sauerkraut, and potato salad.
$
ZIRKELSCHMIEDSGASSE 26
90402
TEL 091 1 205 92 88
🍽 70 🕐 Closes 7 p.m.
🗝 No credit cards

PASSAU

🏨 SCHLOSS ORT
$$
IM ORT 11
TEL 0851 340 72 OR 73
FAX 0851 318 17
WWW.SCHLOSSHOTEL-
PASSAU.DE
This intimate palace hotel,
located in a quiet spot near
the confluence of the
Danube, Iltz and Inn, offers
large rooms in faux-rustic
styles. The pretty restaurant
with a terrace and river vistas
serves regional specialties
such as Passau fish soup and
suckling pig with a dark beer
sauce. Breakfast included.
🛏 18 🅿 🗝 MC,V

🏨 WILDER MANN
$$
AM RATHAUSPLATZ 1
TEL 0851 350 71
FAX 0851 317 12
WWW.WILDER-MANN.COM
Occupying four houses in the
historic quarter of Passau, this
ex-medieval court building
has storied rooms where
countless celebrities have
slumbered, including Austrian
Empress Elizabeth and Count
Zeppelin. It's attached to the
renowned glass museum next
door. Breakfast is included.
🛏 44 + 2 historical rooms
🗝 All major cards

🍴 PASSAUER WOLF
$
RINDERMARKT 6-8
TEL 0851 931 51 10
Owner Richard Kerscher, an
expert on fish and game, also
does a very popular Wiener
schnitzel. From the restaurant
windows you can watch the
River Danube.
🍽 55 🕐 Closed L,& Sun.
🗝 All major cards

REGENSBURG

🏨 HOTEL ORPHEE
🍴 $$$
WAHLENSTRASSE 1
TEL 0941 596 020
FAX 0941
WWW.HOTEL-ORPHEE.DE
A world of unparaled charms
in the historic center of
Regensburg, with an
uncommonly high standard at
reasonable prices. The careful
floor designs, wrought-iron
beds and exposed beams
convey a sense of easy luxury,
and some rooms have views
of the cathedral. Patrons come
from miles around to breakfast
in its renowned art deco café.
🛏 57 🅿 🚻 🗝 All
major cards

SOMETHING
SPECIAL

🍴 ROSENPALAIS
A beautiful, pint-sized
baroque castle built in 1730
by a banker and now owned by

Christian Graf von Walderdorff, whose ambitious cuisine has earned a Michelin star. The handsome restaurant on the second floor serves delicious lobster minestrone, venison with celeriac puree, and salad with marinated artichokes. The ground-floor bistro is more relaxed but equally good.
$$$
MINORITENWEG 20
TEL 0941 599 75 79
🛏 40 🕐 Closed Sun. & Mon. 🗝 MC, V

🍽 KNEITINGER
$
ARNULFSPLATZ 3
TEL 0941 524 55
This legendary 16th-century inn serves solid food such as Regensburg sausages, roast pork with potato dumplings, and a huge Brotzeit (selection of breads and hams), not to mention its own Kneitinger Pils. The brewery gives tours every Wednesday at 3 p.m.
🛏 140 🗝 No credit cards

ROTHENBURG OB DER TAUBER

🏨 EISENHUT
$$$
HERRNGASSE 3-5
TEL 09861 70 50
FAX 09861 705 45
WWW.EISENHUT.COM
This hotel in one of Germany's most romantic towns consists of several historic buildings (dating from the 15th and 16th centuries) on the market square. Rooms to the front have a grandstand view of the old town hall.
ⓘ 77 + 2 suites 🗝 All major cards

🏨 MITTERMEIER
🍽 **$$**
VORM WÜRZBURGER TOR 9
TEL 09861 945 40
FAX 09861 94 54 94
WWW.MITTERMEIER .ROTHENBURG.DE
The Mittermeier family has modernized two houses, one

dating from 1892, and turned them into a very friendly hotel. Cooking in the Michelin-starred restaurant is regional with fresh local produce from the market. Try the oxtail ragout with potatoes or venison with polenta and savoy cabbage.
ⓘ 14 + 13 suites 🗝 All major cards

🍽 DIE POST
$
ROTHENBURGER STRASSE, SCHILLINGSFÜRST
TEL 09868 95 00
An old inn southeast of Rothenburg with just a few dining rooms. After you have sampled the Schweinshaxe (leg of pork) in beer sauce, sample one of the schnapps from the house distillery.
🛏 40 🗝 DC,MC,V

WÜRZBURG

🏨 HOTEL REBSTOCK
🍽 **$$$**
NEUBAUSTRASSE 7
TEL 0931 309 30
FAX 0931 309 31 00
WWW.REBSTOCK.COM
This elegant hotel brings a touch of the Mediterranean to northern Bavaria. The restaurant is popular for its modern take on Franconian cooking; a favorite chef's special is the roast chicken stuffed with goose liver. Breakfast included.
ⓘ 69 + 3 suites 🅿 🗝 All major cards

🍽 ZUM STACHEL
$$
GRESSENGASSE I
TEL 0931 527 70
The specialty in this traditional wine restaurant is fresh fish, and in winter, the poached carp is a must. On summer evenings it's a delight to linger in the courtyard over a local vintage, poured from a distinctive *Bocksbeutel* flask.
🛏 63 🕐 Closed Sun . 🗝 MC,V

MUNICH & THE ALPS

MUNICH

🏨 KEMPINSKI VIER JAHRESZEITEN
$$$$$
MAXIMILIANSTRASSE 17
TEL 089 212 50
FAX 089 21 25 00 00
WWW.KEMPINSKI-VIERJAHRESZEITEN.COM
A grand hotel with all the amenities. The lobby bustles with international guests, the rooms are exquisitely decorated. Close to the best shopping in Munich. Three restaurants.
ⓘ 265 + 51 suites
🚇 Marienplatz 🅿 🛗 🚭 🧊 🚿 🛁 🗝 All major cards

🏨 ARABELLA SHERATON GRAND HOTEL
$$$$
ARABELLASTRASSE 5
TEL 089 926 40
FAX 089 92 64 86 99
WWW.ARABELLA SHERATON.COM
This modern luxury hotel close to the business district draws a large corporate clientele. Rooms have high-tech perks and decor from modern to traditional Bavarian.
ⓘ 468 + 31 suites
🚇 Arabella Park 🅿 🛗 🚭 🧊 🚿 🗝 All major cards

SOMETHING SPECIAL

🏨 BAYERISCHER HOF
This traditional grand hotel is the favorite of visiting celebrities, with a true Bavarian charm and the glamour of times past. Rooms vary from classic to modern, and the huge suites have fantastic views of the Alps. The basement jazz club is one of Munich's finest. Despite its size, it is still a family hotel. Breakfast included.
$$$$$
PROMENADEPLATZ 2-6
80333

HOTELS & RESTAURANTS

TEL 089 212 00
FAX 089 212 09 06
WWW.BAYERISCHERHOF.DE
🛏 337 + 58 suites 🚇 &
🚇 Marienplatz 🅿 ⬍
📷 💲 🏧 All major cards.

🏨 DAS PALACE
🍴 $$$$
TROGERSTRASSE 21
TEL 089 41 97 10
FAX 089 41 97 18 19
WWW.HOTEL-PALACE-
MUENCHEN.DE
A fine townhouse hotel
furnished in Louis XIV style
and decorated with charming
antiques. The garden is
peaceful oasis and a perfect
spot for breakfast (included).
🛏 66 + 6 suites
🚇 Prinzregentenplatz 🅿
🏧 All major cards

🏨 KÖNIGSHOF
🍴 $$$$
KARLSPLATZ 25
TEL 089 55 13 60
FAX 089 55 13 61 13
WWW.KOENIGSHOF-
MUENCHEN.DE
A family-owned treasure
overlooking the busy
Karlsplatz. Its modern facade
belies the traditional public
areas and interiors, a mélange
of modern and traditional
styles. The classy restaurant
serves up consistently great
Mediterranean cuisine. Try the
tuna tartare or sea bass with
arugula risotto.
🛏 84 + 13 suites
🚇 Karlsplatz 🏧 All major
cards

🏨 GÄSTEHAUS
ENGLISCHER GARTEN
$$
LIEBERGESELLSTRASSE 8
TEL 089 383 94 10
FAX 089 38 39 41 33
WWW.HOTELENGLISCHER
GARTEN.DE
A well run, small, simple hotel
in the trendy neighborhood of
Schwabing, famous for its
village atmosphere and café
life. The rooms are furnished
in an agreeable rustic style;

ones at the rear overlook the
English Garden. It's very
popular, so book ahead.
Breakfast included.
🛏 12 + 13 apartments
🚇 Münchner Freiheit 🅿
🏧 All major cards

🍴 TANTRIS
$$$$$
JOHANN-FICHTE-STRASSE 7
TEL 089 361 95 90
Among Munich's finest and
most creative chefs perform
their magic here, with prices
to match. Dishes include
terrine of beetroot, sauteed
sea bass with pepperoni and
spinach. The wine list and
service are expectedly first-
class. The zany '70s decor is
part of the allure.
🪑 90 🕐 Closed Sun. &
Mon. 🚇 Didlindenstrasse
🏧 All major cards

🍴 BÖTTNER'S
$$$
PFISTERSTRASSE 9
TEL 089 22 12 10
Opposite the famous
Hofbräuhaus (see p. 375)
Bottner's simple ambience
draws bigwigs from Munich's
business and media districts.
The menu is reliably trend-
free and hasn't changed for
years. Pumpkin risotto, parfait
of goose liver, pheasant with
sauerkraut, lobster tartare
with caviar and chive sauce
are among the favorite dishes.
🪑 60 🚇 Marienplatz
🕐 Closed Sun. 🏧 All major
cards

🍴 HIPPOCAMPUS
$$$
MÜHLBAURSTRASSE 5
TEL 089 47 58 55
FAX 089 47 02 71 87
Munich's many beautiful
people flock to this trendy
Italian restaurant in the
upscale Bogenhausen area. Try
the pumpkin risotto, squid
carpaccio with capers, and
delicious tiramisu. There are
minimalist decor and a little
garden discreetly surrounded
by a hedge for privacy.

<table>
<tr><td colspan="2">**PRICES**</td></tr>
<tr><td colspan="2">**HOTELS**
An indication of the cost
of a double room without
breakfast is given by $ signs.</td></tr>
<tr><td>$$$$$</td><td>Over $270</td></tr>
<tr><td>$$$$</td><td>$200–$270</td></tr>
<tr><td>$$$</td><td>$120–$200</td></tr>
<tr><td>$$</td><td>$80–$120</td></tr>
<tr><td>$</td><td>Under $80</td></tr>
<tr><td colspan="2">**RESTAURANTS**
An indication of the cost of a
three-course dinner without
drinks is given by $ signs.</td></tr>
<tr><td>$$$$$</td><td>Over $80</td></tr>
<tr><td>$$$$</td><td>$50–$80</td></tr>
<tr><td>$$$</td><td>$35–$50</td></tr>
<tr><td>$$</td><td>$20–$35</td></tr>
<tr><td>$</td><td>Under $20</td></tr>
</table>

🪑 75 🚇 Prinzregentenplatz
🕐 Closed Sat L 🏧 DC,
MC, V

🍴 KÄFER SCHÄNKE
$$$
PRINZREGENTENSTRASSE 73
TEL 089 416 82 47
A fabulous delicatessen plus a
series of dining rooms in
Bavarian style. Tasty dishes are
the vegetable lasagne,
mushroom risotto, and
venison with chanterelles in a
pear sauce. As much a part of
Munich as the Marienplatz
and always throbbing with life.
🪑 55 🕐 Closed Sun.
🚇 Prinzregentenplatz 🏧 All
major cards

🍴 ESSNEUN
$$
HANS-SACHS-STRASSE 9
TEL 089 23 23 09 35
The centerpiece of this swish
establishment is long narrow
dining room with buffed
wooden floors, white leather
banquettes and low lighting.
Modern European cuisine
rarely disappoints; try the
duck with Asian spices or one
of the excellent salads.
🪑 80 🚇 Fraunhofer Strasse
🕐 Closed L 🏧 AE,MC,V

☰ LENBACH

$$

OTTOSTRASSE 6

TEL 089 549 13 00

This gourmet temple was styled by British designer Sir Terence Conran. Lightweight and trendy meals (e.g., bean ravioli with calamari and spinach, or mango mousse with banana salad) for a cool, youthful crowd who dine here before hitting the nightclubs.
🛏 95 🍴 Karlsplatz
🕐 Closed Sun. 💳 DC, MC, V

☰ MESSAGE IN A BOTTLE

$$$

MAXIMILIANSTRASSE 35

TEL 089 24 21 77 78

Th is lively Italian restaurant has become a favorite haunt of Munich's smart set. Daily specialties such as pasta with tomatoes and zucchini, roast veal, or sauteed scallops are written on a blackboard.
🛏 60 🚇 Isartorplatz
🕐 Closed Sun. 💳 V

☰ ALTES HACKERHAUS

$$

SENDLINGER STRASSE 14

TEL 089 260 50 26

This rustic central inn with a beer garden and typical old-fashioned atmosphere is one of Munich's famous addresses. The traditional Bavarian menu features classics like suckling pig in dark beer sauce.
🛏 84 🍴 Marienplatz 💳 All major cards

☰ HOFBRÄUHAUS

$

AM PLATZL 9

TEL 089 22 16 76

World-famous beer hall where tourists let their hair down. Expect strong dark Weissbier and authentic *Schweinshax'n* and *Knödel* (knuckle of pork with potato dumplings), but don't expect any culinary highlights. Locals supposedly never eat *Weisswurst* (veal sausage, served with pretzels and sweet mustard) later than noon, to be sure it's still fresh.

🛏 250 🍴 Marienplatz
💳 MC, V

THE ALPS

ALTÖTTING

☰ WEISSBRAU GRAMING

$

GRAMING 79

TEL 08671 961 40

For distinctive Bavarian/Austrian cooking, this venerable country inn is just the ticket. The *Tafelspitz* (boiled rump of beef) is a local specialty, best washed down with the home-brewed Weissbier.
🛏 62 🕐 Closed Thurs.
💳 MC, V

ASCHAU

SOMETHING SPECIAL

☰ RESIDENZ HEINZ ☰ WINKLER

The owner, a celebrated chef, has won (and kept) three Michelin stars for his classic cuisine with an Italian accent. Whether you choose lasagne with scallops and white truffle sauce, roast lamb in a potato crust, or baked chocolate with coconut ice cream, the result is always magnificent. The beautiful guestrooms, located in a 1405 country manor between the Chiemsee and Chiemgau mountains, are a welcome blend of floral-filled antiques and modern comforts.
$$$$
TEL 08052 179 90
FAX 08052 17 99 66
WWW.RESIDENZ-HEINZ-WINKLER.DE
🛏 80 🚇 🍴 💳 ▲ II major cards

BAD FUSSING

☰ KURHOTEL HOLZAPFEL

$$$

THERMALBADSTRASSE 5

TEL 08531 95 70

FAX 0853 195 72 80

WWW.HOTEL-HOLZAPFEL.DE

In this modern health-resort hotel near Austria, beauty, health, and relaxation are taken seriously. Three restaurants, one serving Bavarian specialties. Breakfast included.
🛈 73 + 6 suites 🅿 ⬍
🚇 🍴 💳 No credit cards

☰ GASTHOF ZUR POST

$$

HAUPTSTRASSE 24

STUBENBERG

TEL 08571 60 00

Located a few miles south of Bad Füssing, this cozy wood-paneled restaurant prides itself on its fresher-than-fresh dishes—salads with organic herbal dressing, trout straight from the river, and juicy steaks from local farms. Don't miss the hazelnut ice cream. If you can't bear to travel after dinner, there are a few guestrooms upstairs.
🛏 85 🕐 Closed Mon. L
💳 No credit cards

BAD REICHENHALL

☰ STEIGENBERGER ☰ AXELMANNSTEIN

$$$

SALZBURGER STRASSE 2-6

TEL 08651 77 70

FAX 08651 59 32

WWW.BAD.REICHENHALL .STEIGENBERGER.DE

This famous health resort is situated in a beautiful park not far from both Salzburg and Berchtesgaden. Everything here is old school, from the Alpine-style rooms to the welcoming service in traditional Bavarian garb. Many patrons come for the excellent beauty treatments. Breakfast is included.
🛈 143 + 3 suites 🅿 ⬍
🚇 🚇 🍴 💳 All major cards

BAD TÖLZ

☰ JODQUELLENHOF-ALPAMARE

$$$

LUDWIGSTRASSE 13-15
TEL 08041 50 90
FAX 08401 50 95 55
WWW.JODQUELLENHOF.COM
In a picturesque spa town, this modern hotel offers a warm atmosphere. You'll be urged to enjoy the sports facilities, including the huge indoor pool.
🛏 90 🅿 🔀 🖼 🖤
🔀 All major cards

🍴 GASTHAUS BAIERNRAIN
$
LEHRER-VOGL-WEG 1
BAIERNRAIN
TEL 08027 91 93
A country idyll in a village northeast of Bad Tolz with fine Tirolean cooking at knock-down prices. The *Schweinsbraten* (roast pork) is succulent and tender, and there's locally-brewed beer on tap. What more could you possibly want?
🍴 60 🔀 MC,V

🏨 ALPENHOF
$$
RICHARD-VOSS-STRASSE 30
SCHÖNAU
TEL 08652 60 20
FAX 08652 6 43 99
WWW.ALPENHOF.DE
A short drive south of Berchtesgaden, this big hotel near the sparkling Königssee has tons of amenities with large rooms furnished in Alpine style. The indoor pool has panoramic views of the surrounding mountains. Breakfast included.
🛏 53 + 30 suites 🅿 🔀
🖼 🖤 🔀 All major cards

🏨 BERGHOTEL REHLEGG
$
HOLZENGASSE 16,
RAMSAU
TEL 08657 988 40
FAX 08657 988 44 44
WWW.REHLEGG.BEST WESTERN.DE
This amiable Swiss-style chateau is perched on a flowery slope above the pretty village of Ramsau, a few

miles southwest of Berchtesgaden. The décor is traditional hunting lodge, the atmosphere homey. Breakfast is included.
🛏 61 + 1 apartment 🅿
🖼 🖤 🔀 All major cards

FRAUENCHIEMSEE

SOMETHING SPECIAL

🍴 ZUR LINDE
After visiting King Ludwig's island castle on Herrenchiemsee, replenish your reserves on the smaller island, Frauenchiemsee. The informal eatery here dates from 1396, located next to a former Benedictine convent. Highlight of the menu is fish, freshly hooked in the Chiemsee and served with roast vegetables.
$
HAUS NR. 1
FRAUENCHIEMSEE
TEL 08054 903 66
🍴 70 🕐 Closed mid-Jan.–mid-March 🔀 MC

GARMISCH-PARTENKIRCHEN

🏨 REINDL'S
🍴 PARTENKIRCHNER HOF
$$
BAHNHOFSTRASSE 15
TEL 08821 94 38 70
FAX 08821 94 38 72 50
WWW.REINDLS.DE.
This venerable hotel is a prime stop for visiting royalty or sports celebrities. Expect lots of oil paintings with hunting motifs and exquisitely Bavarian-style carved bedsteads. Reindls Restaurant features a rotating menu of regional cuisine with the occasional nod to the French, e.g., hearty venison with red cabbage or more refined dishes such as scallops braised in Chablis. Breakfast is included.
🛏 25 + 30 suites + 7 apartments 🅿 🖼 🖤
🔀 All major cards

🏨 STAUDACHERHOF
$$
HÖLLENTALSTRASSE 48
TEL 08821 92 90
FAX 08821 92 93 33
WWW.STAUDACHERHOF.DE
This towering villa in the town center looks like something out of a Grimm's fairy tale. Expect large and cozy country-style rooms decked out in quality linens. It offers first-class views of the Alps. You'll leave its renowned beauty center feeling like a new (wo)man. Breakfast is included.
🛏 41 + 2 suites 🅿 🖼
🖤 🔀 MC,V

LANDSHUT

🏨 FÜRSTENHOF
🍴 $$$
STETHAIMER STRASSE 3
84034
TEL 0871 9 25 50
FAX 0871 92 55 44
WWW.FUERSTENHOF.LA
This rooms in this intimate hotel drip romance with a medieval flair. The breakfast buffet (homemade jams!) is one of the biggest we've seen. The Fürstenzimmer restaurant specializes in organic regional cuisine, such as hearty duck sausage with bread-dumpling carpaccio and honey-glazed suckling pig.
🛏 24 🅿 🔀 All major cards

🍴 BERNLOCHNER
$$$
LANDTORPLATZ 2-5
TEL 0871 899 90
Fine Bavarian and Austrian specialties are served here in a building dating from 1841. Recommended dishes include game, poultry and *Tafelspitz* (boiled rump of beef), and the *Mehlspeisen* (sweet pancakes with a variety of fillings) are irresistible.
🔀 No credit cards

MITTENWALD

🏨 HOTEL ALPENROSE
$
OBERMARKT 1
TEL 08823 92700
FAX 08823 3720
WWW.HOTEL-
ALPENROSEMITTENWALD.DE
This pretty baroque villa is decorated with Bavaria's famous *Lüftlmalerei*, or façade painting. Although supremely atmospheric, rooms tend to be on the snug side but the ones overlooking the square are more spacious. The wine cellar hosts live oompah bands, and the restaurant is a real museum-piece. Breakfast is included.
🛏 18 P 🍴 🔗 All major cards

SOMETHING SPECIAL

🍴 ARNSPITZE
On a clear day, this gourmet restaurant offers a wonderful view of the Karwendel range. Served in candlelit surrounds, the modern cuisine betrays an affinity with France and Italy, such as the lamb with a crust of grainy mustard or veal kidneys braised in red wine with a side dish of roasted sage.
$$$
INNSBRUCKER STRASSE 68
TEL 08823 24 25
🪑 55 🕐 Closed Tues. & Wed. 🔗 AE

MURNAU

🏨 ALPENHOF MURNAU
$$$
RAMSACHSTRASSE 8
TEL 08841 49 10
FAX 08841 49 11 00
WWW.ALPENHOFMURNAU
.COM
This Relais & Chateaux hotel northeast of Oberammergau has rooms in two sections: a Bavarian-style main building and a modern extension. Most rooms afford breathtaking views of the Alps. Breakfast is included.
🛏 60 + 6 suites + 11 apartments P 🔗 🔗
🔗 AE, MC, V

OBERAUDORF

SOMETHING SPECIAL

🍴 GASTHAUS WALLER
Set in the middle of a fruit orchard, this country inn takes you into a time warp with antlers on the walls, checked tablecloths and dirndl-clad staff. The restaurant serves excellent roast meats and dumplings, with drinks provided by what claims to be the smallest brewery in Bavaria. Also try the *Zwetschgenwasser* (plum schnapps) and the local *Weissbier*.
$-$$
URFAHNSTRASSE 10
TEL 08033 14 73
🪑 58 🔗 No credit cards

SCHWANGAU

🏨 RÜBEZAHL
🍴 $
AM EHBERG 31
TEL 08362 83 27
FAX 08362 8 17 01
WWW.HOTEL-RUEBEZAHL.DE
A typical family-run Alpine hotel, conveniently located in a busy little valley between two Bavarian royal palaces. Some of the modern quarters have a view of Schloss Neuschwanstein, the inspiration for Walt Disney's castle.
🛏 35 + 6 suites + 4 apartments 🔗 MC, V

BADEN-WÜRTTEMBERG

BADEN-BADEN

🏨 BRENNER'S PARKHOTEL & SPA
$$$$$
SCHILLERSTRASSE 4-6
TEL 07221 90 00
FAX 07221 3 87 72
WWW.BRENNERS.COM
Luxury is evident everywhere in this huge 19th-century building, from the enormous rooms furnished with exquisite antiques to the lavish spa area with every imaginable amenity. The swimming pool could rival anything Hollywood has to offer.
🛏 71 + 20 suites + 9 apartments P 🔗 🔗
🔗 🔗 All major cards

🏨 BELLE EPOQUE
$$$$
MARIA-VIKTORIA-STRASSE 2C
TEL 07221 30 06 60
FAX 07221 30 06 66
WWW.HOTEL-BELLE-
EPOQUE.DE
If you prefer a more intimate atmosphere, this graceful small hotel might be ideal. Rooms are in belle-epoque style.
🛏 6 + 10 suites P 🔗 All major cards

🏨 STEIGENBERGER
🍴 BADISCHER HOF
$$$
LANGE STRASSE 47
TEL 07221 93 40
FAX 07221 93 44 70
WWW.BADISCHER-HOF.DE
This luxury spa hotel occupies a former Capuchin convent. Guestrooms exude a historic elegance in the old section, while the modern extension has more amenities. The bathtubs dispense thermal spring water. Breakfast is included.
🛏 135 + 4 suites P 🔗
🔗 🔗 All major cards

🍴 ALDE GOTT
$$$
WEINSTRASSE 10
TEL 07223 5513
The imaginative food here includes dishes such as beans and cauliflower in a curry vinaigrette, and Charolais beef with savoy cabbage in a Burgundy sauce. It's just south of Baden-Baden.
🪑 60 D Closed Thurs. 🔗 MC, V

HOTELS & RESTAURANTS

BAIERSBRONN

SOMETHING SPECIAL

🏨 BAREISS
🍴

A sanctuary of peace in the deepest Black Forest, this is surely one of Germany's best-run hotels, with meticulous attention paid to all the important details. Flower-decked balconies grace the modern facade, and the stylish rooms are packed with perks like fluffy bathrobes and underfloor heating. You can dine in the restaurant with two Michelin stars or one of the pair of smart bistros. The main menu features blue-ribbon fare like warm lobster with a honey-thyme vinaigrette or millefeuille of goose liver with celery puree and truffle-glace. Breakfast is included.

$$$$
GARTENBÜHLWEG 14
BAIERSBRONN-MITTELTAL
TEL 07442 470
FAX 07442 473 20
WWW.BAREISS.COM
① 69 + 12 suites + 39
apartments 🅿 🚉 🛗
⊗ DC,MC,V

🏨 TRAUBE TONBACH
🍴 **$$$**
TONBACHSTRASSE 237
TEL 07442 49 20
FAX 07442 49 26 92
WWW.TRAUBE-TONBACH.DE
This traditional family-run hotel dates back to 1778, and some of the public areas positively ooze history. The four restaurants include the outstanding Schwarzwaldstube (see below) and the Köhlerstube, which serves international food such as crustaceans in Chablis aspic and river fish with gnocchi. Breakfast included.
① 175 + 12 suites + 55
apartments 🅿 🚉 🛗
⊗ DC,MC,V

SOMETHING SPECIAL

🍴 SCHWARZWALDSTUBE

This place shares a spot in the firmament of Germany's culinary elite, rating three whole Michelin stars for chef Harald Wohlfahrt's masterful creations. Restaurant critics come from far-flung corners to sample his goose liver in salt crust, the braised veal with truffle jus, and sauteed duck with rosemary and juniper berries. Superb wines, and faultless service round out an unforgettable experience.

$$$$
IM TRAUBE TONBACH
TONBACHSTRASSE 237
TEL 07442 49 20
🍴 40 🕐 Closed Mon. & Tues., & August
⊗ DC,MC,V

FELDBERG

🏨 ADLER
$$
FELDBERGSTRASSE 4
FELDBERG-BÄRENTAL
TEL 07655 12 42
FAX 07655 93 05 21
WWW.ADLER-FELDBERG.DE
This is a traditional Black Forest holiday hotel, located between the Feldberg and the pretty lakes Titisee and Schluchsee. The rooms are rustic but comfortable.
① 11 + 3 apartments 🅿
⊗ MC,V

🏨 COLOMBI HOTEL
🍴 **$$$$**
AM ROTTECKRING 16
TEL 0761 210 60
FAX 0761 314 10
WWW.COLOMBI.DE
This distinguished and welcoming hotel blends soft colors and well-chosen materials. The grand entrance hall looks like something out of a movie set, and you couldn't ask for a finer location in the heart of the old town. Excellent restaurant.
① 64 + 56 suites 🅿 🛗
🚉 🛗 ⊗ All major cards

PRICES

HOTELS
An indication of the cost of a double room without breakfast is given by $ signs.
$$$$$	Over $270
$$$$	$200–$270
$$$	$120–$200
$$	$80–$120
$	Under $80

RESTAURANTS
An indication of the cost of a three-course dinner without drinks is given by $ signs.
$$$$$	Over $80
$$$$	$50–$80
$$$	$35–$50
$$	$20–$35
$	Under $20

🍴 ZUM WEINBERG
$$
HAUPTSTRASSE 70
TEL 0761 3 54 90
It's rare to find a regional restaurant like this where the cooking is truly pretension-free, beguilingly simple but well prepared. Veal with hollandaise sauce and beef tongue with madeira sauce are special treats.
🍴 55 🕐 Closed Sun. & Mon. ⊗ No credit cards

HEIDELBERG

🏨 DER EUROPÄISCHE HOF
$$$$$
FRIEDRICH-EBERT-ANLAGE 1
TEL 06221 51 50
FAX 06221 51 55 06
WWW.EUROPAEISCHER HOF.COM
Originally built in 1865 but updated over time, the Europäischer Hof is a Heidelberg landmark. The handsome, thoughtfully-planned rooms are truly the lap of luxury, and there are an up-to-date fitness center and wood-paneled restaurant.
① 100 + 14 suites + 3 apts.
🅿 🛗 🚉 🛗 ⊗ All major cards

ZUM RITTER ST. GEORG
$$$$
HAUPTSTRASSE 178
TEL 06221 13 50
FAX 06221 13 52 30
WWW.RITTER-HEIDELBERG.DE
This 16th-century house in
the historic quarter is now a
traditional hotel with terrific
period rooms. Breakfast
included.
🛈 37 + 2 suites 🅿 🚭 All
major cards

SCHLOSSWEINSTUBE
$$$
SCHLOSSHOF
TEL 06221 979 70
This restaurant is comprised
of five dining rooms nestled
around a romantic castle
courtyard. Beautiful oil
paintings contrast with
tasteful modern elements.
Start with a warm potato
soup, followed by lamb in an
olive crust.
🍽 55 🕒 Closed Wed.
🚭 DC,MC,V

SIMPLICISSIMUS
$$$
INGRIMSTRASSE 16
TEL 06221 18 33 36
French cooking in the historic
quarter in a '70s interior,
somewhat dim but a
perennial favorite. The oft-
changing menu might include
marinated aubergines, sauteed
octopus with herbs, or fillet of
beef with wild mushrooms.
🍽 60 🕒 Closed Tues.
🚭 All major cards

INZLINGEN

INZLINGER WASSERSCHLOSS
$$$
RIEHENSTRASSE 5
TEL 07621 470 57
Situated in a delightful moated
castle, this restaurant offers
modern European cuisine
such as venison with
chanterelles and celeriac
puree, pigeon de Bresse with
risotto, and turbot with
artichokes.

🍽 75 🕒 Closed Tues. &
Wed. 🅿 🚭 MC,V

KARLSRUHE

SCHLOSSHOTEL
$$$
BAHNHOFSPLATZ 2
TEL 0721 3 83 20
FAX 0721 3 83 23 33
WWW.SCHLOSSHOTEL
KARLSRUHE.DE
Set conveniently between
the railroad station and city
park, this hotel has a broad
range of individually
decorated rooms, some in a
contemporary vein, others
more traditional. Breakfast
is included.
🛈 93 + 3 suites 🅿 🛗
🚹 🚭 All major cards

OBERLÄNDER WEINSTUBE
$$$$
AKADEMIESTRASSE 7
TEL 0721 250 66
This cozy little wine bar has a
charming courtyard for
drinking and dining. Solid
regional dishes include lamb
with chanterelles, pigeon with
fried potatoes, celeriac puree
and beans. Delicious sorbets.
🍽 45 🕒 Closed Sun. &
Mon. 🚭 DC, MC, V

NAGEL'S KRANZ
$$
NEUREUTER HAUPTSTRASSE
210
KARLSRUHE-NEUREUT
TEL 0721 70 57 42
This country restaurant just
outside Karlsruhe serves
local specialties such as turbot
with a potato crust, pork
braised in red wine, and sea
bass in Riesling.
🍽 70 🕒 Closed Sat L &
Sun. 🅿 🚭 No credit cards

KONSTANZ

GRAF ZEPPELIN
$$
AM STEPHANSPLATZ 15
TEL 07531 237 80
FAX 07531 172 26

WWW.ZEPPELIN.MDO.DE
This is a dyed-in-the-wool
German inn with an ornate
Gothic-style façade that dates
back to 1835. Most rooms are
modern and rather generic
but the restaurant gushes
atmosphere, and has a
respectable wine list. It's in a
nice spot near the Münster.
🛈 42 🅿 🚭 MC, V

LINDAU

SOMETHING SPECIAL

VILLINO
🍽

This enchanting house with a
Tuscan flavor towers at the
end of a steep lane overlooking
Lindau. It has pretty rooms, a
small health club, and a
wonderful rolling garden. The
restaurant, which has a Michelin
star, carefully marries the
regional with the international
in dishes such as tuna sashimi
with sesame spaghettini, or fresh
river fish stuffed with ricotta.
Breakfast included.
$$$
HOYERBERG 34
TEL 08382 934 50
FAX 08382 93 45 12
WWW.VILLINO.DE
🛈 11 + 5 apartments 🅿
🚹 🚭 MC, V

SINGEN

FLOHR'S
🍽 **$$**
BRUNNENSTRASSE 11
SINGEN-ÜBERLINGEN AM RIED
TEL 07731 932 30
FAX 07731 93 23 23
WWW.FLOHRS-
RESTAURANT.DE
A five-minute drive from Lake
Constance, this charming
village hotel has designer
furniture and a restaurant
known for its regional and
Mediterranean cooking. Chef
Georg Flohr's personal touch
shows in his mackerel and
potato terrine in apple
cucumber gelee, served with
tortellini, or sea bass with

HOTELS & RESTAURANTS

rosemary, parma ham, and a puree of white beans. Breakfast is included.

🛏9 🅿 🚫 AE,MC,V

STUTTGART

🏨 STEIGENBERGER 🍴 GRAF ZEPPELIN
$$$$
ARNULF-KLETT PLATZ 7
TEL 071 12 04 80
FAX 071 12 04 85 42
WWW.STUTTGART-STEIGENBERGER.DE
This distinguished hotel near the railroad station contains large rooms with either neoclassic or modern touches. Thomas Heilemann, chef of the Olivo restaurant, is an aficianado of all things Mediterranean, as suggested by dishes like pappardelle pasta with wild boar ragout or braised shoulder of lamb with artichokes.

🛏 174 + 15 suites 🅿 🛗 🚇 ♨ 🚫 All major cards

🏨 HOTEL AM 🍴 SCHLOSSGARTEN
Grand style and tradition are writ large at this venerable institution, located near the Opera House and the elegant boutiques along Königstrasse. Many rooms have a view of the Schlosspark, the sprawling municipal park. The atmosphere is warm and welcoming, more like someone's home than a hotel. There's a gourmet restaurant, the Zirbelstube.

$$$
SCHILLERSTRASSE 23
TEL 071 12 02 60
FAX 071 12 02 68 88
WWW.HOTELSCHLOSSGARTEN.COM
🛏 106 + 10 suites 🚫 All major cards

🍴 SPEISEMEISTEREI
$$$$
AM SCHLOSS HOHENHEIM
STUTTGART-HOHENHEIM
TEL 0711 456 00 37

If you feel like a well-deserved splurge, head over to the castle of Schloss Hohenheim and its legendary restaurant run by Chef Martin Oade. His two Michelin stars are evident in everything he serves, be it potato soup (from La-Ratte potatoes, served with imperial caviar), crepinette of chicken with poached goose liver, or roast goat with polenta. And the heated chocolate cake is to die for.

🍽 40 🕐 Closed Mon. & Tues., Wed.–Sat. 🅿 🚫 No credit cards

🍴 WIELANDSHÖHE
$$$$
ALTE WEINSTEIGE 71
STUTTGART-DEGERLOCH
TEL 0711 640 88 48
Owner-chef Vincent Klink excels in archetypical dishes such as *Maultaschen* (a kind of stuffed ravioli) as well as combinations of Asian and Mediterranean cuisine. The lunch menus offer tremendous value.

🍽 52 🕐 Closed Sun. & Mon. 🚫 All major cards

🍴 EMPORE
$/$$
DOROTHEENSTRASSE 4
TEL 0711 245 97 9
You'll find this Italian restaurant on the second floor of Stuttgart's art-deco market halls. Treat yourself to a cappuccino, glass of bubbly or a dish of pasta, then browse through the array of alluring produce stands and shops downstairs.

🍽 45 🕐 Closed Sun. 🚫 No credit cards

TÜBINGEN

🍴 WALDHORN
$$$
SCHÖNBUCHSTRASSE 49, TÜBINGEN-BABENHAUSEN
TEL 07071 612 70
About 3 miles (5 km) north of Tübingen, home to Goethe's old university, the Waldhorn has a rustic

---

PRICES

HOTELS
An indication of the cost of a double room without breakfast is given by $ signs.

$$$$$	Over $270
$$$$	$200–$270
$$$	$120–$200
$$	$80–$120
$	Under $80

RESTAURANTS
An indication of the cost of a three-course dinner without drinks is given by $ signs.

$$$$$	Over $80
$$$$	$50–$80
$$$	$35–$50
$$	$20–$35
$	Under $20

interior and authentic Swabian cooking. Few have dared to emulate its delectable *Hägenmarkeisbömble* (rose hip ice cream).

🍽 65 🕐 Closed Mon. & Tues. 🚫 No credit cards

🏨 KRONE
This tasteful and soigné hotel, owned by the same family since 1885, is typical of this delightful medieval town with a large student population. Look for Swabian specialties in the restaurant, Uhlandstube.

$$$
UHLANDSTRASSE 1
TEL 07071 133 10
FAX 07071 13 31 32
WWW.KRONE-TUEBINGEN.DE
🛏 45 + 2 suites 🚫 All major cards

SHOPPING

Germany excels at high-tech, upscale manufactured and designer goods—cars, all kinds of electrical goods from shavers to coffee grinders, furniture, and china. Well designed, elegantly produced items can be found in any major department store in a big city.

At the same time, age-old traditions of handicrafts and folk art are pursued with a vengeance. Whether it's cuckoo clocks in the Black Forest, porcelain from Meissen or Bavarian lederhosen, each region in Germany has a speciality. Markets are a good place to find a souvenir that can't be duplicated anywhere else.

Most towns have central pedestrian districts (*Fussgängerzonen*) filled with shops that are designed to invigorate urban commerce and counter the advance of shopping malls. Germans have the environmentally friendly habit of toting shopping bags for their purchases, although you can usually buy one at the checkout.

You'll quickly notice the mind-boggling variety of breads in *Bäckereien* (bakeries). The huge number of health food shops proves the Germans' pioneering obsession with organic products. Fans of yesteryear, meanwhile, are coddled by the numerous antique and second-hand markets, normally held on a Saturday.

Some leading *Einkaufsstrassen* (shopping streets), especially for designer fashion, are Kurfürstendamm and Friedrichstrasse in Berlin, Königsallee in Düsseldorf, Maximilianstrasse in Munich, and arcades around Jungfernstieg, Neuer Wall, and Mönckebergstrasse in Hamburg.

MARKETS
A weekly market, known as Wochenmarkt, is held in towns throughout Germany. In smaller communities the stalls are set up in the market square, while in larger towns and cities the market is held in specially designated squares. At these markets, you will find fresh fruit and vegetables, cheeses, a full range of sausages, cheeses, and regional specialties, as well as many useful everyday items. Every large town also has its Flohmarkt (flea market) where you might find something rare and unusual.

OPENING HOURS
Under German law, stores can open from 8:30 a.m. and close no later than 8 p.m. Many smaller ones start business at 10 or even 11 a.m. and close at 6.30 p.m. Newsagents and bakeries open as early as 6 a.m. On Sundays everything is closed with a few exceptions, such as bakeries and shops in train stations, airports, and service stations. Some cities have introduced an economy-boosting "shopping Sunday" once a month.

PAYMENT
Cash is still king in Germany. Department and luxury-goods stores will take credit cards and travelers' checks, but supermarkets and smaller shops usually do not; look at the door stickers. Most Germans either pay by cash or EC direct debit cards.

EXPORTS
Except for EU citizens, visitors to Germany are entitled to a refund on value-added (sales) tax for all non-edible goods bought in German stores. The usual minimum is €50 in a single store. Ask for a special form at stores displaying the tax-free sign. When you leave Germany, the form must be stamped by customs and you'll have to present goods in their original packaging. The tax can be refunded on the spot or sent on, which requires patience.

BERLIN & BRANDENBURG

BOOKS
Dussmann Friedrichstrasse 90, Mitte tel 030 20 25 24 40. This "cultural department store" has three spacious floors with padded armchairs inviting you to sit and read. Sections include a huge CD display and events stage.

Bücherstube Marga Schöller Knesebeckstrasse 33, Charlottenburg, tel 030 881 11 12. This venerable literary bookshop has been going for over 70 years and has an impressive English-language section.

DEPARTMENT STORES
Galeries Lafayette Französische Strasse 23, Mitte, tel 030-20 94 80. This upscale French department store chain is known for its funnel-shaped atrium made of translucent glass. Look for quality designer apparel, cosmetics and accessories.

KaDeWe Tauentzienstrasse 21–4, Schöneberg, tel 030 21 22 0. "If we don't have it, it probably doesn't exist" is the motto of the Germany's largest department store. The lavish sixth-floor food hall stocks delicacies from around the globe.

Wertheim Kurfürstendamm 231, Charlottenburg tel 030 88 00 30. Second only to the KaDeWe in size, this mainstream emporium is a good stop for souvenirs. You can enjoy views of the Gedächtniskirche from the rooftop café.

FASHION & ACCESSORIES
Bramigk Savignypassage Bogen 598, Charlottenburg tel 030 313 51 25. Form-fitting, timeless dresses, wraps, and trousers made of fine Italian fabrics, as well as hand-painted scarves and felt slippers.

Budapester Schuhe Kurfürstendamm, Charlottenburg 43 + 199, tel 030 88 62 42 06. Ladies' shoes from Prada, Miu Miu, Jimmy Choo. Gentlemen can choose from classic English brogues, handcrafted shoes from Budapest, or Gucci loafers.

Hut ab Oranienburger Strasse 32, Heckmann-Höfe, Mitte tel 030 28 38 61 05. Stylish hats, clothes, and accessories made from felt and combined with organza or chiffon.

Killerbeast Schlesische Strasse 31, Kreuzberg tel 030 99 26 03 19. Recyclable materials provide the fodder for the cool urban streetware rolled out anew almost every week.

Thatchers Hackesche Höfe, Rosenthaler Strasse 1, Mitte tel 030 27 58 22 10. Produces three trendy lines a year for both men and women, inspired by music, digital art, and architecture. It's playfully tongue-in-cheek—try on a translucent "heartache" blouse.

GIFTS
Ampelmann Galerie Shop Hackesche Höfe, Mitte tel 030 44 04 88 01. Ostalgie, the "crosswalk man," graces everything from T-shirts to beach thongs.

Erzgebirgische Volkskunst Dircksenstrasse 50, Mitte tel 030 28 38 80 10. Traditional wooden handicrafts from the Ore Mountains of eastern Germany—incense-puffing 'smoking men', Christmas pyramids and nutcrackers.

Meissener Porzellan Unter den Linden 39, Mitte tel 030 204 35 81. Fine plates, sculptures, and chandeliers from the famous Saxon porcelain maker, ranging from everyday crockery to elaborate works of art.

FOOD MARKETS
Turkish Market Maybachufer, Neukölln. Just across the canal from Kreuzberg, this lively, crowded market has delicious feta cheeses, teas, fresh breads and olives, perfect for stocking a picnic lunch. ⏲ Noon–6.30 p.m. Tues & Fri.

Winterfeldt Markt Winterfeldtplatz, Schöneberg. A beautiful array of premium cheeses, sausages, flowers and handmade designer clothes. Treat yourself to a coffee at one of the cafés lining the square. D8 a.m.—2 p.m. Wed & Sat.

BADEN-WÜRTTEMBERG

BLACK FOREST
Hubert Herr Hauptstrasse 8,

Triberg, tel 07722 42 68. In the town that claims the world's largest cuckoo clock, this workshop, now in its fifth generation of craftsmen, has carved out a formidable reputation. Orders can be shipped home.

BAVARIA

OBERAMMERGAU
Josef Albl Devrientweg, tel 08822 64 33. One of the premier carvers of religious icons, Herr Albl's thriving workshop is open for viewing. The craftsmen will chisel items to order at a reasonable price.

NUREMBERG
Christkindlmarkt (Christmas Market) Held from November 30 to December 24 in Germany's number one Christmas city. The highlight is the opening ceremony at 5:30 p.m. when the Christ Child speaks to the masses from the Frauenkirche (Church of Our Lady) gallery. Fragrances of cinnamon, roasted almonds, and mulled wine waft tantalizingly overhead.

Lebkuchen Schmidt Zollhausstrasse 30, tel 0911 896 60. Nuremberg's celebrated *Lebkuchen* (ginger spice cookies) are traditionally eaten at Christmas, but sold here year-round.

ROTHENBURG OB DER TAUBER
Käthe Wohlfahrt Weihnachtsdorf, Herrngasse 1, tel 09861 40 90. A eye-popping display of Yuletide decorations and ornaments at the year-round 'Christmas Village.' Charges a fee of Euro 1 in the jolly season.

MUNICH

BOOKS
Words' Worth Schellingstrasse 21a, tel 089 290 91 41. Situated near the university, this store has a large selection of English paperbacks.

Hugendubel tel Salvatorplatz 2, 01803-484 484. English-language outlet of the heavyweight Munich chain, with comfy couches for reading.

DELICATESSEN
Alois Dallmayr Dienerstrasse 14–15, tel 089 213 50. Founded in 1870, this exquisite delicatessen is famous for its large tea and coffee selection.

Käfers Prinzregentenstrasse 73, tel 089 416 82 47. The home emporium of this in-demand caterer has exotic foods from every corner of the earth.

DEPARTMENT STORES
Ludwig Beck Marienplatz 11, tel 089 236 910. A venerable haven of Munich style, occupying a tasteful niche between cutting-edge and mainstream.

Karstadt Neuhauser Strasse 18 80331, tel 089 290 230. Not the hippest merchandise but a reliable source for souvenirs like beer mugs, household goods and traditional fabrics.

FASHION & ACCESSORIES
Bogner Residenzstrasse 15, tel 089 290 70 40. Fabulous sports clothes for both men and women. Pioneer of the just-off-the-piste look.

Eduard Meier Residenzstrasse 22, tel 089 22 00 44. Its exquisitely made shoes, felt hats, hunting bags, and Bavarian-style suspenders are classics.

Escada Maximilianstrasse 27, tel 089 2423 9880. A German designer label with classic couture for every occasion, often mimicked without success.

Exatmo Franz-Joseph-Strasse 35, tel 089 33 57 61. Over-the-top versions of Bavarian style with plenty of humor. Handwoven linens and accessories (belts, handbags).

Loden Frey Maffeistrasse 7–9, tel 089 21 03 90. Wide choice of distinctive Bavarian folk costumes, not exactly cheap but made to last forever.

Schuh Seibel Reichenbachstrasse 8, tel 089

2601 7237. Topless footwear for more than just tree-huggers, Birkenstocks have a worldwide following who appreciate the home shipment of this resourceful vendor.
Trachtenmoden Guth Müllerstrasse 50, 80469, tel 089 26 69 69. More gems of Bavarian country fashion: lederhosen (leather shorts), dirndl (dresses), and loden (brushed wool).

PHOTOGRAPHIC
Foto-Video-Media-Sauter Sonnenstrasse 26, tel 551 5040. Great stock of leading manufacturers, and the place to look for steal-deals on new and used gear by Leica or Hasselblad.

GIFTS
Kunstgewerbeverein Pacellistrasse 6–8, tel 089 290 14 70. Handcrafted Bavarian pottery, jewelry, and carnival masks, next door to a church of the Carmelites.
Manufactum Kardinal-Fualhaber-Strasse 5, tel 089 55 50 40. Germany's premier vendor of prime-quality goods of nostalgia—produced, say, by secretive monasteries or top designers like Porsche—is inessential but easy to fall for.
Prantl Schreibwaren Von der Tann Strasse 12, tel 089 22 71 55. Exquisite writing tools and materials from silver cedarwood pens to the finest writing paper.
Obletter Spielwaren Karlsplatz 11, tel 089 55 08 95 10. A great selection of classic German toys such as the famous Steiff teddy bears, Märklin model trains and handpainted wooden playthings.

HERBS
Dehner Frauenstrasse 8, tel 089 24 23 99 89. For garden lovers: take a packet of Alpine flower seeds home, best with notes on the climate.
Kräuterparadies Blumenstrasse 15, tel 089 26 57 26. Germany's oldest herb specialist with more than 400 varieties including oils, teas,

organic medicines and beauty products.

MARKETS
Viktualienmarkt Munich's largest and most atmospheric food market, located near the central Marienplatz, is the source for Bavarian tidbits-Alpine herbs, mouth-watering Weisswurst (veal-parsley sausage) and Allgäu cheeses. Open Mon.–Sat.

PORCELAIN
Porzellan Manufaktur Nymphenburg Odeonsplatz 1, tel 089 28 24 28. Founded in 1747, the manufacturer became famous for its exclusive tableware created for the Bavarian royal court. The showroom displays the entire collection, from 18th-century traditional to modern.
Rosenthal Studio-Haus Dienerstrasse 17, tel 089 22 26 17. Contemporary designs in glass, china, and cutlery, from conservative classics to lines by designers like Versace.

HAMBURG

ART
Galerie Deichstrasse, Deichstrasse 28, 20459, tel 040 36 51 51. A thousand-plus paintings and drawings with Hamburg as their theme.

BOOKS
Sautter & Lackmann Admiralitätsstrasse 71–72, tel 040 37 31 96. Specialists in art, art history, photography, film, architecture. Many English-language titles.

FASHION & ACCESSORIES
Kaufrausch Isestrasse 88, tel 040 4802 728. Clothes, shoes, costume jewelry, and much more, all exquisite one-offs. Popular café.
Moneypenny & Schuhsalon Grabbe Marktstrasse 100, tel 040 43 25 04 84. Shoes by German designers such as Stefi

Talmann, Trippen and Ludwig Reiter. Also handbags, and home and fashion accessories.
0190 Bartelsstrasse 2, tel 040 43 25 36 65. Highly individual, exclusive creations for both men and women are the ticket at this intimate little shop.

GIFTS
Harry's Hafenbasar Erichstrasse 56, tel 040 31 24 82. This shop-cum-gallery exhibits over 300,000 curiosities brought back by sailors, from paintings to African masks. Many items are for sale, but there's an entrance fee of ?2.50. Closed Mon.

NAUTICAL ITEMS
Buddel-Bini Lokstedter Weg 68, 20251, tel 040 46 28 52. Maritime doo-dads and a mind-boggling selection of ships-in-bottles.
A.W. Niemeyer Rödlingsmarkt 25, 20459, tel 040 36 67 17. Serious outfitter with everything from sextants to foul-weather gear.

SCHLESWIG-HOLSTEIN

MARZIPAN
Fa Niederegger Holger Strait Breite Strasse 89, 23560 Lübeck, tel 0451 530 10. Their famous almond-filled confection comes in all shapes and colors.

DRESDEN
Elbe-Team Warenhandels-und Dienstleistungs, Spenerstrasse 35, tel 0351 43 35 20. A huge warehouse selling cult items from former East Germany—records, glassware, postcards, and other GDR nostalgia.
Weihnachtsland am Zwinger Kleine Brüdergasse 5, tel 0351 862 12 30. Traditional Christmas handicrafts, notably from the Ore Mountains of eastern Germany—incense-puffing 'smoking men', Christmas pyramids, nutcrackers, and more.

ENTERTAINMENT

Germany has a great tradition of drama, music and performing arts. The country boasts more than 120 opera houses, and in almost every town you'll find a choir and one or more orchestras giving regular recitals. Berlin enjoys world repute for its experimental theater and cabaret, a form with more than a whiff of 1920's decadence. Apart from its three big opera houses and world-class symphony orchestras, the German capital has a vibrant scene at its nightclubs and discotheques, many of which stay open till dawn. Berlin, Hamburg and Munich have the top jazz venues with performers from across the globe.

BALLET & OPERA

BAYREUTH
Bayreuth Wagner Festival
Opera lovers make a pilgrimage to the Richard Wagner Festival here in July and August, provided they can get tickets. The Festspielhaus (festival theater) was built in 1872–75 specifically for Wagner's operas, and the great acoustics offset the lack of air conditioning. For information tel 0921 78 780 or www.bayreuther-festspiele.de.

BERLIN
Deutsche Oper Berlin
Bismarckstrasse 35, Berlin-Charlottenburg, tel 030 343 102 49. The major opera house of the West during the Cold War, which fended off communism with a repertoire of grand 19th-century operas. Traditional ballet is still a forte.
Deutsche Staatsoper Unter den Linden 5–7, Berlin-Mitte, tel 030 2035 45 55. Built in 1742 at the time of Frederick the Great, this grand opera house stages great classics of ballet and opera, such as Tchaikovsky's Swan Lake.

COLOGNE
Oper der Stadt Köln
Offenbachplatz, tel 0221 282 56. Classical as well as modern performances, composed by both established and up-and-coming talent.

FRANKFURT
Oper Willy-Brandt-Platz, tel 069 21 23 79 99. Lavish and experimental productions, often with spectacular scenery and giddy budgets.

DRESDEN
Semperoper Sächsische Staatsoper, Theaterplatz 2, tel 0351 491 17 05. Badly damaged during World War II and recent floods, this classic opera house has been restored to its original splendor. Home to the renowned Staatskapelle Dresden.

HAMBURG
Hamburger Staatsoper
Dammtorstrasse 2, tel 040 403 56 80. The oldest opera house in Germany, giving it access to a pool of headline productions, concerts and Lieder recitals.

MUNICH
Bayerische Staatsoper Max-Joseph-Platz 2, tel 089 21 85 01. One of Germany's granddaddy opera houses, chief venue of the summer opera festival. Early booking essential.

CLASSICAL MUSIC & THEATER

Berlin Philharmonic Herbert-von-Karajan-Strasse 1, Mitte tel 030 25 48 80. The Philharmonic, conducted by Sir Simon Rattle, has a unique center podium with seating on all sides. Tickets can be booked at www.berliner-philharmoniker.de.
Staatsoper Unter den Linden 5-7, Mitte tel 030 20 35 45 55. The oldest of Berlin's three opera houses, the Staatsoper is conducted by Daniel Barenboim, who draws top talent to classy events like the annual Festival Days.
Schaubühne Leniner Platz, Kurfürstendamm 153, Charlottenburg tel 030 89 00

23. Berlin's (some would say Germany's) cutting edge of drama and choreography is honed here with the A-list of actors.
Konzerthaus
Gendarmenmarkt, Mitte tel 030 2030-92101. Home to the very capable Berlin Symphony Orchestra, the handsomely restored Konzerthaus is dripping in musical heritage, and holds more than 550 concerts every year.

CABARET

BERLIN
Bar jeder Vernunft
Spiegelzelt, Schaperstrasse 24, Berlin-Wilmersdorf, tel 030 883 15 82. Berlin's best known entertainers and artists perform in an atmosphere of '20s abandon in a huge mirrored tent.
Chamäleon Varieté
Rosenthaler Strasse 40–41, Berlin-Mitte, tel 030 282 71 18. A lovely old theater in the Hackesche Höfe where table seats treat you to a tour de force of singers, comedians, and acrobats.
Pomp, Duck & Circumstance Gleisdreieck/Möckernstrasse 26, Berlin-Kreuzberg, tel 030 26 94 92 00. A circus tent where you can enjoy a four-course-meal in which duck always features. The extravagant show is professional and great fun.
Wintergarten Varieté
Potsdamer Strasse 96, 10785 Berlin-Tiergarten, tel 030 250 0880. The Wintergarden Varieté shows feature magicians and acrobats in a pre-war style. Utterly charming.

CINEMA

BERLIN
Arsenal Potsdamer Strasse 2, Potsdamer Platz, Berlin-Tiergarten, tel 030 26 95 51 00. Art cinema at its finest, composed mainly of German, Russian and other European films, often with English subtitles.

Hosts the annual Berlin International Film Festival (Feb.).
Cinestar Sony Center Potsdamer Platz 4, Berlin-Tiergarten, 030 26 06 62 60. A plush multiplex shows movies in their original language without subtitles—a rarity in Berlin, where films are typically dubbed into German.
Sommerkino Museumsinsel Bodestrasse 1-3, Berlin-Mitte, tel 030 20 68 91 00. A big-screen outdoor cinema (open June to early Sept.). Cult, oldies, and independent movies shown on the courtyard of the Alte Nationalgalerie, with subtitles. Deck chairs are provided.

MUNICH
City & Atelier 1 + 2 Sonnenstrasse 12, 089 59 19 83. Subtitled and original American and European art films.
Atlantis Schwanthaler Strasse 2, 089 55 51 52. Arty films in the original language.
Cinema Nymphenburger Strasse 31, tel 089 55 52 55. The best pick for English-speakers, with salty popcorn, soundtracks in English and the occasional filmmaker's chat.

CONCERTS

BERLIN
Berliner Philharmonie Herbert-von-Karajan-Strasse 1, Mitte tel 030 25 48 80. The best place in Berlin to hear world-class classical performances, conducted by Sir Simon Rattle. The fine acoustics bounce to a center stage with seating on all sides. See www.berliner-philharmoniker.de for tickets.

COLOGNE
Philharmonie Bischofsgartenstrasse 1, tel 0221 20 40 82 22. This huge concert hall close to the cathedral does seminal classical, but also jazz and pop.

HAMBURG
Musikhalle Johannes-Brahms-Platz, 20355, tel 040 346 920. Built in 1908, this storied venue

hosts acts for jazz, blues and world music, as well as for classical concerts.

LEIPZIG
Neues Gewandhaus Augustusplatz, tel 0341 710 42 60. Europe's oldest orchestra performs here, with a tradition dating back to 1743 when Mendelssohn was a conductor. Classics and guest orchestras from around the world.

MUNICH
Philharmonie im Gasteig Rosenheimer Strasse 5, tel 089 480 980. Home to the city's celebrated Philharmonic Orchestra, conducted by James Levine and featuring a fine pedigree of world talent. The Bavarian Radio Symphy Orchestra performs every Sunday, boosted by the state's generous cultural budget.
Münchner Kammerorchester Wittelsbacherplatz 2, tel 089 636 359 70. A smaller hall with wonderful chamber music and formidable voices.

JAZZ

BERLIN
A-Trane Bleibtreustrasse 1, Charlottenburg tel 030 313 25 50. Blue-ribbon talent plays contemporary jazz on a regular basis in this cozy little club, one of western Berlin's most venerable. Special duo and Afro-Cuban nights are a regular feature. Book ahead.
Badenscher Hof Badensche Strasse 29, Berlin-Wilmersdorf, tel 030 861 00 80. An intimate club with a garden open in summer. Small African-American bands, modern jazz.
B Flat Rosenthaler Strasse 13, Mitte tel 030 283 31 23. Just north of Hackescher Markt, this is the best jazz club in Mitte with live concerts most nights. The program covers everything from blues and mainstream jazz to world crossover and even tango dance nights.
Quasimodo Kantstrasse 12A,

Berlin-Charlottenburg, tel 030 312 80 86. A favorite venue for visiting performers from the U.S.A. Smoky and crowded, but always of the highest caliber.

HAMBURG
Prinzenbar Kastanienallee 20, tel 040 3178 8311. Modern jazz in a small but tall room.

MUNICH
Café am Beethovenplatz Goethestrasse 51, tel 544 04 34. Old-style café-restaurant conveniently near the train station, with live music most nights and a piano brunch on Sunday.
Jazzclub Unterfahrt im Einstein, Einsteinstrasse 42, tel 089 41 90 29 54. One of the most important jazz clubs in all of Germany, with musicians from all over the world.
Jazzbar Vogler Rumfordstrasse 17, tel 294 662. Ex-journalist Vogler has built this little club into a top jazz venue without losing the intimate bar ambience.
Nightclub Hotel Bayerischer Hof, Promenadeplatz 2–6, tel 089 212 09 94. Top talent from Chick Corea to Kenny Barron stop off here, in the cellar of the grand Hotel Bayerischer Hof.

NIGHTLIFE

BERLIN
Adagio Marlene-Dietrich-Platz 1, Potsdamer Platz, Berlin-Mitte tel 030 25 92 95 50. If you've ever wanted to dance in a medieval banquet hall to Abba or INXS, then seek out this outlandish place underneath Potsdamer Platz.
Delicious Doughnuts Rosenthaler Strasse 9, Berlin-Mitte, tel 030 2809 9274. Startling décor of blood-red walls and black leather booths set the scene for dazzling waitresses and DJs. The brilliant cocktails are served till dawn.
Newton Bar Charlottenstrasse 57, Mitte tel 030 20 61 29 99. Named for Berlin-born photographer Helmut Newton

whose "big nudes" grace the walls of the downstairs bar. Upstairs are a well-stocked humidor and comfy lounge. **Sage Club** Köpenicker Strasse 76, Mitte tel 030 278 98 30. One of the trendiest clubs in Berlin, the Sage features house thumps over three dance floors with a high celeb quotient and outdoor swimming pool.

Spindler & Klatt Köpenicker Strasse 16/17, Kreuzberg tel 030 69 56 67 75. This sprawling waterfront club is on the A-list of Berlin's dinner-and-dance spots. Its beautiful guests pose on cool white dining futons for a tasty pan-Asian menu.

HAMBURG

Fabrik Barnerstrasse 36, tel 040 39 10 70. Catch jazz, reggae or Afro-funk from the galleries of this former factory, a listed monument in the suburb of Altona just south of the city center.

China Lounge Nobistor 14, tel 040 31 97 66 22. Four areas offering electro and house, hip-hop or R & B, attracting students on Thursday, and beautiful people Friday and Saturday.

Golden Pudel Club Fischmarkt 27, tel 040 319 53 36. A rickety fisherman's hut now plays host to this waterfront club that plays a mongrel program of indie and punk to a consciously grungy crowd.

MUNICH

Atomic Café Neuturmstrasse 1, tel 089 228 3052. American DJs play electro and acid-jazz, supplemented by top bands. Entrance in an anonymous back alley.

Babylon Kunstpark Ost, Grafingerstrasse 6, tel 089 49 00 27 30. The program varies from 70's disco and oldies, or house and trance. Patrons drift in from the 40-plus clubs in the adjoining party complex.

P1 Prinzregentenstrasse 1, tel 089 29 42 52. Trends come and go, but this remains disco for a fashionable crowd seeking

techno and hits from the recent past. Plan on picky doormen and expensive drinks.

Skyline Leopoldstrasse 82, tel 089 33 31 31. Fairly formal, with music produced by visiting DJs. There's a killer view of the chicest promenade in Munich.

STUTTGART
Perkins Park
Stresemannstrasse 39, tel 0711 256 00 62. This is a massive place with two dance floors, a restaurant, pool table and a personality that veers from rock 'n roll to funk to techno.

THEATER

BERLIN
Berliner Ensemble Theater am Schiffbauerdamm, Bertolt-Brecht-Platz 1. Berlin-Mitte, tel 030 28408155. On the banks of the Spree, this theater is renowned for its contemporary drama and connection with Bertolt Brecht. whose pieces are performed here.

Schaubühne Leniner Platz, Kurfürstendamm 153, Charlottenburg tel 030 89 00 23. Berlin's cutting edge of drama and choreography is honed here. Drawing on a deep well of material, productions feature some of the country's most accomplished actors (such as Bruno Ganz, who played the lead in the film "Hitler: the Downfall").

Volksbühne am Rosa-Luxemburg-Platz Rosa-Luxemburg-Platz, Berlin-Mitte, tel 030 6772 7694. Provocative, satirical political plays and cabarets held in a historic venue from the GDR era.

HAMBURG
Deutsches Schauspielhaus Kirchenallee 39, 20099, tel 040 248 713. Classic plays in a 100-year-old theater with deep pockets for stage design and the occasional radical outburst.

MUNICH
Münchner Kammerspiele Maximilianstrasse 26, 80539, tel

089 23 33 70 00. Once a private theater, now a show place for living writers and directors.
Residenztheater Max-Joseph-Platz 1, 80539, tel 089 21 85 19 40. A very important theater in the Bavarian art scene.

Theater am Gärtnerplatz Gärtnerplatz 3, 80469, tel 089 21 8519 60. This fashionable venue on the Gärtnerplatz specializes in light operetta, ballet, and musicals.

Münchner Kammerspiele Maximilianstrasse 26-28, tel 089 233 966 00. This theatre stages large-scale productions of serious drama by German playwrights or foreign playwrights whose works are translated into German.

Prinzregententheater Prinzregentenplatz 12, tel 089 2185 2899

OBERAMMERGAU
Oberammergau Passion Play Every 10 years, the Passion Play re-enacts a pious scenario thanking God for sparing the village from the plague back in the 17th century. Purchase tickets well in advance of the 2010 performance, as they sell out fast. Tel 08822 923 10.

STUTTGART
Staatstheater Stuttgart Oberer Schlossgarten 6, tel 0711 20 20 90. Since choreographers John Cranko and Marica Haydée made it world famous in the sixties, the dancing has been an almost greater draw than the drama.

WUPPERTAL
Tanztheater Alte Freiheit 26, Wuppertal, tel 0202 569 24 76. Coreographer Pina Bausch has found her unlikely niche here as a queen of expressionist dance. Her performances earn rave reviews.

ACTIVITIES

With its treasure-trove of natural riches, Germany has myriad choices for anyone seeking an active vacation. The mountains lure the masses for their climbing, hiking, or winter skiing, and the lake districts have near-perfect conditions for sailing and other water sports. Pleasure boaters are drawn to the North and Baltic Seas, as well as to the large freshwater lakes like the Chiemsee in Bavaria. Windsurfing and water skiing are also extremely popular. Idyllic areas for cycling with clearly-marked trails can be found just about everywhere. Detailed information such as maps, cycle guides, local sports options and activity holidays are available from the regional tourist offices.

CLIMBING

If you are keen on climbing—whether as a tenderfoot or as an expert—Germany has oodles of opportunities. Its Alpine mountaineering is world famous, but the rock formations found at lower altitudes provide challenges even for the skilled climber. Try to spend the night in one of the many rough hikers' cabins in the Alps, a wonderful experience.
Details and reservations: **Deutscher Alpenverein** Bayerstrasse 21, München, tel 089 551 70 70.

CYCLING

Germans are enthusiastic cyclists. Specially designated cycling routes are well signposted and maintained by the relevant local authority. For general information, contact the German Cycling Federation at tel 069-967 80 00 or www .rad-net.de.

BADEN-WURTTEMBERG

There are 17 routes to choose from—leisurely tours along flat riverbanks and on up to the challenging Central German Highlands Route. One of the most popular options is around Lake Constance, a trail which takes you through sections of Austria and Switzerland. For more details: **Freiburg Touristik**, Rotteckring 14, Freiburg tel 0761-388 18 80

BALTIC SEA ROUTE

Extending 529 miles (836 km) along almost the entire north German coast, from Flensburg to Usedom Island, the route is not particularly hilly but the winds can be strong. You pass through the city of Kiel and traditional fishing villages to reach Liibeck, only then to cross the Trave river on a ferry and pedal through the Baltic seaside resorts. The coast is in view nearly the whole trip. **Tourismusverband Mecklenburg-Vorpommern** Platz der Freundschaft 1, Rostock, tel 0381 403 05 00.

BERCHTESGADEN

This region has several cyclist 'service stations' that look after your bike and distribute maps and brochures listing bike-friendly hotels and inns. For details, contact the **Berchtesgadener Land tourist office**, Königsseer Strasse 1, Berchtesgaden tel 08652 96 70.

CHIEMGAU, BAVARIA

A relaxing tour through the picturesque villages of the south German plains with the splendid Chiemgau mountains as a backdrop. The local tourist office can organize tailor-made bicycle tours, while Urlaub auf dem Bauernhof (farm holidays) has a register of farmhouses for a charming overnight stay. For more information: **Tourismusverband Chiemgau** Ludwig-Thoma-Strasse 2, Traunstein, tel 0861 582 23.
Urlaub auf dem Bauernhof Kirchplatz 3, St. Georgen, tel 08669 40 01.

FRANCONIA

A romantic 150-mile (241 km) tour along the beautiful gorge of the River Altmühl, stretching from Rothenburg ob der Tauber to Kelheim. It's flat almost the whole way, perfect for families as the trails are easy with little road traffic. Contact: **Altmühl Valley Nature Reserve Information** Notre Dame 1, Eichsratt, tel 08421 98 76 0.
Romantic Franconia Tourist information, Am Kirchberg 4, Colmberg, tel 09803 941 41.

HESSE

Several cycling routes in Hesse take you through a variety of landscapes—secluded forests, villages with half-timbered buildings, the valleys of the Fulda, the rivers Werra, Eder, and Lahn, and mountain ranges. For information: **Hessen Touristik Service** Abraham-Lincoln-Strasse 38, Wiesbaden, tel 0611 774 80 91.

MECKLENBURG LAKES

For 373 miles (600 km) from Lüneburg to the town of Waren on Usedom Island, the route curls around the many glacier-formed lakes of the Mecklenburg plain. This is an great way to ease into some of the more challenging routes in our selection. For information: **Tourismusverband Mecklenburgische Seenplatte** Turmplatz 2, Robel/Müritz, tel 039931 53 80.
Tourismusverband Mecklenburgische Schweiz Am Bahnhof, 17139 Malchin, tel 03994 29 97 81.

NORTH SEA

This 560-mile (900 km) route along the North Sea coast starts in Leer and travels alongside the top of dykes, with views over endless mudflats and out across the sea. Remember to take into account the wind, which always seems to be in your face. See www.northsea-cycle.com for information resources.

ACTIVITIES

The North Sea-Seven Islands-One Coast
Postfach 2106, Schortens, tel 01805 20 20 96.

RHINE VALLEY
The route begins in Koblenz, taking you across the Moselle to Andernach and on to the vineyards around the mouth of the River Ahr. You follow the curves in the Rhine through the Siebengebirge (Seven Mountains) region, ending up at Bonn. For more details, contact the **Romantischer Rhein** via Koblenz Touristik, Bahnhofplatz, Koblenz, tel 0261 313 04.

GOLF
Germany's golf courses run the gamut of landscapes. Many are for members only, but for non-members there's a selection of clubs and specialized golf hotels. Contact the **Deutscher Golfverband (DGV)**, Viktoriastrasse 16, Wiesbaden, tel 0611 99 02 00.

HIKING
Every part of Germany has a network of well signposted and meticulously cared for paths ideal for hiking. The proximity to nature, the countryside and the local people make for an intimate encounter with Germany at its bucolic best. Along the routes you will find quite a few hotels and inns who specialize in accommodation for hikers. Many trip organizers offer comfy packages that send your luggage on to your next destination.

Popular routes include the **Hochsauerland-Path**, which weaves through the velvety valleys of Hesse and North Rhine-Westphalia; the nearby **Hoher Westerwald trail**, which traces the mountain ridges; and the **Northern Black Forest trail** through pristine forests. In Bavaria, the **Maximilian-Hiking Path** follows the spectacular footsteps of 19th-century nature buff King Maximilian, from the Allgäu region to Lake Königsee.

For more information, contact:
Verband Deutscher Gebirgs-und Wandervereine
Wilhelmshoher Allee 157-159, Kassel, tel 0561 938 730.
Deutscher Volkssportverband
Fabrikstrasse 8, Altötting, tel 08671 963 10. Naturfreunde Deutschlands Warschauer Strasse 58a, Berlin tel 030-29 77 32 60.
Deutscher Alpenverein
Bayerstrasse 21, München, tel 089 551 70 70.

HORSEBACK RIDING
Germans have a long association with horseback sport as its many medals in showjumping will suggest. Wherever you go, from the Baltic Sea to sticky moorlands to craggy Alpine trails, you will find an abundance of riding stables, farmhouses, and hotels who cater to riding enthusiasts. Staff are trained to look after a gamut of experience levels from beginners to the advanced. If you like Western riding with a German accent, try the **Clearwater Ranch**, tel 06697 91 96 81, in the wilds of the central state of Hesse.

www.reiten.de is an online portal offering a wealth of information on the world of riding, including details on national trade fairs, competitions, and hunting parties.

BOATING & SAILBOARDING

Germany's north coast is heaven for sailboating and sailboarding. The Baltic and North Seas provide delightful harbors, steady wind and plenty of thrilling whitecaps.

Order details on the Baltic Sea from:
Ostseebäderverband Schleswig-Holstein
Strandallee 75a, Timmendorfer Strand, tel 04503 888 50 or 01805 70 07 08.

Or for the North Sea from:

Nordsee-Tourismus-Service
Zingel 5, Husum, tel 04841 89 75 75 or 01805 06 60 77.

Water sport enthusiasts will be drawn to the larger lakes such as Lake Constance, the Starnberger See, and Chiemsee, all in southern Germany within a stone's throw of the snow-capped Alps.

Another popular options can be had in the rivers and canals. Berlin has 113 miles (182 km) of navigable rivers with the Wannsee at its spiritual hub. For a popular boat tour through the canals of central Berlin, try **Reederei Bruno Winkler**, Schlossbrücke, tel 030 349 95 95. In surrounding Brandenburg you can really spread out on 3,000 lakes and 18,640 miles (30,000 km) of rivers. Contact the sailing association **Berliner Segler-Verband**, Jesse-Owens-Allee 2, tel 030 30 83 99 08 for more details.

SKIING

In winter, Germany is a magical place of snowy landscapes with plenty of resorts to enjoy downhill and cross-country skiing, snowboarding and much more. The Bavarian Alps grab the headlines but some of the lesser-known ranges can be just as exciting. The gentle peaks of the Bavarian Forest have the most reliable snow conditions, and cross-country skiers here appreciate the diversity of the trails. Germany's northernmost winter sports area is in the Harz mountains, for Alpine-style or cross-country skiing as well as old-fashioned sleigh rides. You will find an extensive network of ski lifts, cable cars and pistes as well-groomed as anything in Bavaria. For details:
Deutscher Skiverband Hubertusstrasse 1, München-Plannegg, tel 089 85 79 00.
Harzer Verkehrsband Markttrasse 45, Goslar, tel 05321 340 40.

LANGUAGE GUIDE

USEFUL WORDS & PHRASES
Yes *Ja*
No *Nein*
Please *Bitte*
Thank you *Danke*
Excuse me *Entschuldigen Sie bitte*
Sorry *Entschuldigung*
Goodbye *Auf Wiedersehen*
Good-bye *Tschüs* (informal)
Good morning *Guten Morgen*
Good day *Guten Tag* (after noon)
Good evening *Guten Abend*
Good night *Guten Nacht*

here *hier*
there *dort*
today *heute*
yesterday *gestern*
tomorrow *morgen*
now *jetzt*
later *später*
right away *sofort*
this morning *heute morgen*
this afternoon *heute nachmittag*
this evening *heute abend*

large *gross*
small *klein*
hot *heiss*
cold *kalt*
good *gut*
bad *schlecht*
left *links*
right *rechts*
straight ahead *geradeaus*
Do you speak English? *Sprechen Sie Englisch?*
I am American *Ich bin Amerikaner (m)/Amerikanerin (f)*
I don't understand *Ich verstehe Sie nicht*
Please speak more slowly *Bitte sprechen Sie langsamer*
Where is/are...? *Wo ist/sind...?*
I don't know *Ich weiss nicht*
My name is... *Ich heisse...*
At what time? *Wann?*
What time is it? *Wieviel Uhr ist es?*

NUMBERS
one *eins*
two *zwei*
three *drei*
four *vier*
five *fünf*
six *sechs*
seven *sieben*
eight *acht*
nine *neun*
ten *zehn*
twenty *zwanzig*

DAYS OF THE WEEK
Monday *Montag*
Tuesday *Dienstag*
Wednesday *Mittwoch*
Thursday *Donnerstag*
Friday *Freitag*
Saturday *Samstag/Sonnabend*
Sunday *Sonntag*

MONTHS & SEASONS
January *Januar*
February *Februar*
March *März*
April *April*
May *Mai*
June *Juni*
July *Juli*
August *August*
September *September*
October *Oktober*
November *November*
December *Dezember*
spring *Frühling*
summer *Sommer*
fall *Herbst*
winter *Winter*

IN THE HOTEL
Do you have a vacancy? *Haben Sie noch ein Zimmer frei?*
a single room *ein Einzelzimmer*
a double room *ein Doppelzimmer*
with/without bathroom/shower *mit/ohne Bad/Dusche*
key *Schlüssel*
porter *Pförtner*

EMERGENCIES
Help *Hilfe*
I need a doctor/dentist *Bitte rufen Sie einen Arzt/Zahnarzt*
Can you help me? *Können Sie mir helfen?*
Where is the hospital?/police station?/telephone? *Wo finde ich das Krankenhaus?/die Polizeiwache?/das Telefon?*

SHOPPING
Do you have...? *Haben Sie...?*
How much is it? *Wieviel kostet es?*
Do you take credit cards ? *Akzeptieren Sie Kreditkarten?*
When do you open/close? *Wann machen Sie auf/zu?*
size (clothes) *Kleidergrösse*
size (shoes) *Schuhgrösse*
color *Farbe*
brown *braun*
black *schwarz*
red *rot*
blue *blau*
green *grün*
yellow *gelb*
cheap *billig*
expensive *teuer*
I'll take it *Ich nehme es*
enough *genug*
too much *zu viel*
check *Rechnung*

SHOPS
bakery *Bäckerei*
bookshop *Buchhandlung*
chemist *Drogerie*
delicatessen *Feinkostladen*
department store *Warenhaus*
fishmonger *Fischhändler*
grocery *Gemüseladen*
self-service shop *Selbstbedienungsladen*
antique shop *Antikladen*
junk shop *Trödelladen*
library *Bibliothek*
supermarket *Supermarkt*
market *Markt*
newspaper kiosk *Zeitungskiosk*
shoe shop *Schuhgeschäft*
clothes shop *Bekleidungsgeschäft*
special offer *Sonderangebot*
stationery *Schreibwaren*

SIGHTSEEING
visitor information *Touristen-Information*
exhibition *Ausstellung*
open *geöffnet*
closed *geschlossen*
daily *täglich*
all year *ganzjährig*
all day long *den ganzen Tag*
entry fee *Eintrittspreis*
free *frei/umsonst*
cathedral *Kathedrale*
church *Kirche*
abbey *Kloster*
castle *Schloss*
country house *Landhaus*
museum *Museum*
staircase *Treppe*
tower *Turm*
town *Stadt*
old town *Altstadt*
town hall *Rathaus*

MENU READER

I'd like to order *Ich möchte bestellen*
I am a vegetarian *Ich bin Vegetarier (m) Vegetarierin (f)*
The check, please. *Die Rechnung, bitte.*
Was it tasty? *Hat es geschmeckt?*
Cheers *Prost*
Enjoy your meal *Guten Appetit*
Was it tasty? *Hat es geschmeckt?*
lunch *Mittagessen*
dinner *Abendessen*
menu *Speisekarte*
snack *Imbiss*
knife/fork/spoon *Messer/Gabel/Löffel*
salt/pepper *Salz/Pfeffer*
mustard *Senf*
sugar *Zucker*
bread *Brot*
cheese *Käse*
wine list *Weinkarte*

DRINKS
Kaffee coffee
Tee tea
Apfelsaft apple juice
Orangensaft orange juice
Milch milk
Bier beer
rRotwein ed wine
Weisswein white wine
Sekt sparkling wine

FRÜHSTÜCK/BREAKFAST
Brötchen bread roll
Eier eggs
   hartgekochtes hard-boiled
   weichgekochtes soft-boiled
Rühreier scrambled eggs
Spiegelei fried egg
Schwarzbrot dark brown rye bread
Weissbrot white bread
Speck bacon

SUPPE/SOUP
Erbsensuppe pea soup
Gemüsesuppe vegetable soup
Hühnersuppe chicken soup
Linsensuppe lentil soup
Ochsenschwanzsuppe oxtail soup
Pilzsuppe mushroom soup
Spargelcremesuppe cream of asparagus soup

FLEISCH/MEAT
Blutwurst black pudding
Bockwurst large frankfurter

Brathuhn roast chicken
Bratwurst fried pork sausage
Currywurst curried sausage
Eintopf stew
Eisbein knuckle of pork
Ente duck
Fasan pheasant
gebratene Gans roast goose
Hackbraten meatloaf
Hühnerfrikassee chicken fricassee
Kalbsbrust breast of veal
Kalbshaxe roast knuckle of veal
Kassler Rippen smoked pork chops
Lammkeule roast lamb
Leberknödel liver dumplings
Leberwurst liver sausage
Rehkeule roast venison
Rinderbraten roast beef
Sauerbraten braised beef, marinated in spiced red wine
Schinken ham
Schlachtplatte mixed cold meat
Schweinebraten roast pork
Tafelspitz boiled rump of beef
Wiener Schnitzel veal escalope
Wildschweinkeule roast wild boar

FISCH/FISH
Aal eel
Austern oysters
Barbe mullet
Fischfrikadellen fish cakes
Flunder flounder
Forelle trout
Garnelen prawns
Heilbutt halibut
Hummer lobster
Jakobsmuscheln scallops
Kabeljau cod
Karpfen carp
Krabben shrimps
Lachs salmon
Makrele mackerel
Matjes pickled herring
Schellfisch haddock
Scholle plaice
Seebarsch sea bass
Seelachs pollack
Seezunge sole
Steinbutt turbot
Tintenfisch squid
Zander pike-perch

GEMÜSE/VEGETABLES
Aubergine eggplant
Blumenkohl cauliflower
Bohnen beans
Champignons/Pilze mushrooms

Erbsen peas
Feldsalat lamb's lettuce
Fenchel fennel
Gurke cucumber
Kapern capers
Kartoffeln potatoes
Kohl cabbage
Kürbis pumpkin
Lauch leek
Linsen lentils
Möhren carrots
Maiskolben sweetcorn
Pfifferlinge chanterelle mushrooms
Reis rice
Rosenkohl brussel sprouts
Rotkohl red cabbage
Sauerkraut pickled cabbage
Sellerie celery
Spargel asparagus
Spinat spinach
Tomaten tomatoes
Wirsing savoy cabbage
Zwiebeln onions

OBST/FRUIT
Ananas pineapple
Apfel apple
Apfelsine/Orange orange
Aprikose apricot
Backpflaumen prunes
Birne pear
Blaubeeren blueberries
Brombeeren blackberries
Erdbeeren strawberries
Himbeeren raspberries
Kirschen cherries
Pampelmuse grapefruit
Pfirsich peach
Rote Johannisbeeren redcurrants
Schwarze Johannisbeeren blackcurrants
Stachelbeeren gooseberries
Weintrauben grapes
Zitrone lemon

NACHSPEISEN/DESSERTS
Apfelkuchen apple cake
Bienenstich honey almond cake
Gebäck pastry
Kaiserschmarrn sweet pancake
Käsekuchen cheesecake
Kompott stewed fruit
Krapfen/Berliner doughnuts
Mandelkuchen almond cake
Obstkuchen fruit tart
Rote Grütze red fruit jelly
Sachertorte chocolate cake
Schlagsahne whipped cream
Schwarzwälder Kirschtorte Black Forest gateau

ILLUSTRATIONS CREDITS

Abbreviations for term appearing below: (t) top; (b) bottom; (l) left; (c) center (r) right.

Front Cover (l), AA Photo Library/S. McBride. (c), © David Noton Photography/Alamy. (r), AKG-London. Spine, © David Noton Photography/ Alamy

1, Hasenkopf/A1 Pix Ltd. 2/3, Gräfenhain/Bildarchiv Huber. 4, C. Tkaczyk/Tourist Office Munich. 9, Mecky Fogeling. 11, B. Ducke/A1 Pix Ltd. 12/13, Mecky Fogeling. 13, M. Strohfeldt/Deutsche Presse- Agentur (dpa Picture Alliance GmbH). 14, Kirsten Neumann/Reuters/ CORBIS. 14/15, H. Link/Deutsche Presse-Agentur (dpa Picture Alliance GmbH). 16, Action Press/Rex USA Ltd. 17, Th-Foto Werbung/Trip Photo Lib. 18/19, R. Schmid/Bildarchiv Huber. 20, K. Hart/ Robert Harding Picture Lib. Ltd. 21, Hasenkopf/A1 Pix Ltd. 22/23, F. Gaul/ Akg-images. 24, Erich Lessing/Art Resource, NY. 25, AKG - London. 26, Akg-images. 28, Schloss Friedrichsruhe, Germany/ Bridgeman Art Lib. 29, Akg-images. 30, Archive Photos/Hulton| Archive. 30/31, Akg-images. 32, Hulton|Archive. 33, G. Brelör/Deutsche Presse- Agentur (dpa Picture Alliance GmbH). 34, Erich Lessing/Art Resource, NY. 35, G. Gräfenhain/A1 Pix Ltd. 36, G. Gräfenhain/ A1 Pix Ltd. 37, N. Blythe/Robert Harding Picture Lib. Ltd. 38/39, Akg-images. 39, Hulton| Archive. 40, Alte Pinakothek, Munich, Germany/Lauros-Giraudon/ Bridgeman Art Lib. 42, Museum der Bildenden Kunste, Leipzig, Germany/ Bridgeman Art Lib. 43, Akg-images. 44l, The Cobbe Foundation, UK/Bridgeman Art Lib. 44r, Kunsthistorisches Museum, Vienna, Austria/Bridgeman Art Lib. 45l, Österreichische Nationalbibliothek, Vienna, Austria/Bridgeman Art Lib. 45r, Hulton| Archive. 46, Hulton|Archive. 47, Akg-images. 49, James Davis Worldwide. 50, Mecky Fogeling/travimage.com. 54/55, S. McBride/AA Photo Lib. 55, P. Pleul Zentralbild/Deutsche Presse- Agentur (dpa Picture Alliance GmbH). 57, P. Endig/ Deutsche Presse- Agentur (dpa Picture Alliance GmbH). 58/59, S. McBride/AA Photo Lib. 59, Aleksandar Hajdukovic/ Shutterstock. 62/63, Mecky Fogeling. Robert Harding Picture Lib. Ltd. 63, Pierre Adenis. 64, S. McBride/ AA Photo Lib. 64/65, T. Souter/AA Photo Lib. 66, Bildarchiv Preussischer Kulturbesitz/Art Resource, NY. 66/67, S. McBride/AA Photo Lib. 68, Mecky Fogeling. 69, S. McBride/AA Photo Lib. 71t, Bildagentur Schuster/ Robert Harding Picture Lib. 71b, Akg-images. 72, A. Baker/AA Photo Lib. 73, S. McBride/AA Photo Lib. 74, U. Welsch/ Photography. 75, Ludovic Maisant/CORBIS. 77, A. Cowin/Travel Ink. 78, S. McBride/AA Photo Lib. 79, S. McBride/ AA Photo Lib. 80, S. McBride/AA Photo Lib. 81, Gräfenhain/ Bildarchiv Huber. 82/83, S. McBride/AA Photo Lib. 83, S. McBride/AA Photo Lib. 85, Akg-images. 86, R. Schmid/Bildarchiv Huber. 87, Werner Otto. 88, Wolfgang Kähler Photog. 90, G. Gräfenhain/ A1 Pix Ltd. 91, Wolfgang Kähler Photog. 92, Rolf

Richardson/Alamy Ltd. 92/93, B. Wüstneck/ Deutsche Presse- Agentur (dpa Picture Alliance GmbH). 94, E. Bach/A1 Pix Ltd. 95, Hilbich/Akg-images. 96, G. Gräfenhain/A1 Pix Ltd. 97t, Brooks Kraft/CORBIS. 97b, Wolfgang Kähler Photog. 98, Wolfgang Kähler Photog. 99, Manfred Mehlig/ zefa/CORBIS. 100/101, G. Gräfenhain/A1 Pix Ltd. 101, B. Koch/ A1 Pix Ltd. 102, R. Schmid/Bildarchiv Huber. 103, K.-B. Kertscher/Punctum Photog. 104, M. Teller/ Akg-images. 105, R. Schmid/Bildarchiv Huber. 106, Erich Lessing/Art Resource, NY. 107, James Davis Worldwide. 109, James Davis Worldwide. 110, T. Freeman/Trip Photo Lib. 112, Mecky Fogeling. 113, Richard Klune/CORBIS. 114, B. Ducke/A1 Pix Ltd. 115, Akg-images. 116, B. Ducke/ A1 Pix Ltd. 118, C.L. Schmitt/ A1 Pix Ltd. 119, W. Pfeiffer/Deutsche Presse- Agentur (dpa Picture Alliance GmbH). 121t, A. Bartel/Trip Photo Lib. 121b, Akg-images. 122, G. Gräfenhain/A1 Pix Ltd. 123, Th-Foto Werbung/Trip Photo Lib. 124, Eckhardt/ A1 Pix Ltd. 125, D. Traverso/Robert Harding Picture Lib. Ltd. 127, M. Schreiner. 128, Ulrike Welsch Photog. 128/9, Robert W. Ahrens/Shutterstock. 130, Akg-images. 131, Werner Otto. 132, Gräfenhain/Bildarchiv Huber. 133, Gräfenhain/Bildarchiv Huber. 134, M. Schreiner. 135, Werner Otto. 137, P. Wright/Trip Photo Lib. 138, G. Gräfenhain/ A1 Pix Ltd. 139, Akg-images. 140, Akg-images. 140/141, Akg-images. 141l, Akg-images. 141r, H. Schmidbauer/ A1 Pix Ltd. 142/143, G. Gräfenhain/ A1 Pix Ltd. 145, Werner Otto. 147, G. Hartmann/ A1 Pix Ltd. 148, Wolfgang Kähler Photog. 149, Wolfgang Kähler Photog. 151, G. Gräfenhain/A1 Pix Ltd. 152, Akg-images. 153, Wolfgang Kähler Photog. 155, P. Robinson/Robert Harding Picture Lib. Ltd. 156, Oliver Berg/dpa/ CORBIS. 157, Akg-images. 158, A1 Pix Ltd. 159t, Mecky Fogeling. 159bl, Mecky Fogeling. 159br, Mecky Fogeling. 160, Bildarchiv Huber. 161, G. Gräfenhain - E. Bach/A1 Pix Ltd. 162, E. Bach/A1 Pix Ltd. 163, G. Gräfenhain/A1 Pix Ltd. 165, Mecky Fogeling. 166, F. Aberham/A1 Pix Ltd. 167, Werner Otto. 168, Ulrike Welsch Photog. 169, Erich Lessing/Art Resource, NY. 170, V. Vincke/Bochum Bergbaumuseum. 171, TH-Foto Werbung/Trip Photo Lib. 172, Werner Otto. 173, Klaes/Bildarchiv Huber. 175, Mecky Fogeling. 176, G. Gräfenhain/ A1 Pix Ltd. 178, Erich Lessing/Art Resource, NY. 179t, Action Press/Rex USA Ltd. 179b, Akg-images. 180/181, Gräfenhain/Bildarchiv Huber. 181, Mecky Fogeling. 183t, Klaes/ Bildarchiv Huber. 183t, M. Gottschalk/A1 Pix Ltd. 183b, D. Cumming/Eye Ubiquitous. 184/185, G Gräfenhain/A1 Pix Ltd. 185, Wolfgang Kähler Photog. 186, P. Ward/ National Geographic Society. 187, B. Ducke/A1 Pix Ltd. 188, A. Baker/ AA Photo Lib. 189, Werner Otto. 190, TH-Foto Werbung/Trip Photo Lib. 191, R. Schmid/ Bildarchiv Huber. 192, Werner Otto. 193tl, Werner Otto. 193tr, P. Grahammer/A1 Pix Ltd. 193c, R. Schmid/Bildarchiv Huber. 193b, Werner Otto. 194, R. Schmid/ Bildarchiv Huber. 195, Wolfgang Kähler Photog. 196, Mecky Fogeling. 198, Mecky Fogeling. 198/199, Mecky Fogeling. 200, A. Tovy Amsel/Eye Ubiquitous. 202, Akg-images. 203, B. Lucas/A1 Pix Ltd. 204/5, MICHAELA REHLE/Reuters/CORBIS. 205, H. Link/Deutsche Presse- Agentur (dpa Picture Alliance GmbH). 206, Erich

Lessing/Art Resource, NY. 207, G. Gräfenhain/A1 Pix Ltd. 208, S. Damm/ Bildarchiv Huber. 209, Werner Otto/BenU. 210, Wolfgang Kähler Photog. 211, Mecky Fogeling. 212, Szydzka/ Bildarchiv Huber. 214, B. Ducke/ A1 Pix Ltd. 215, Spectrum Colour Lib. 216, Mecky Fogeling. 217t, Krammisch/Bildarchiv Huber. 217c, Akg-images. 217b, Akg-images. 218, Gräfenhain/Bildarchiv Huber. 220, Schütze/Rodemann/Punctum Photog. 221, G. Gräfenhain/A1 Pix Ltd. 222, F. Damm/ Bildarchiv Huber. 223, Szyszke/ Bildarchiv Huber. 224, J. Korsch/ Deutsche Presse-Agentur (dpa Picture Alliance GmbH). 225t, J. Büttner/Deutsche Presse- Agentur (dpa Picture Alliance GmbH). 225b, J. Büttner/ Deutsche Presse- Agentur (dpa Picture Alliance GmbH). 227, B. Kober/Punctum Photog. 229, H.-Ch. Schink/Punctum Photog. 230/231, Kolley/Bildarchiv Huber. 233, Szyszka/ Bildarchiv Huber. 234, PUNCTUM/Bertram Kober. 235t, PUNCTUM/B. Blume. 235b, Wolfgang Kähler Photog. 236t, Peter Adams/ zefa/CORBIS. 236b, Matthias Heikel/dpa/ CORBIS. 238, Schmid/Bildarchiv Huber. 239, TH-Foto Werbung/Trip Photo Lib. 240, B. Ducke/ A1 Pix Ltd. 241t, Matthias Heikel/dpa/CORBIS. 241bl, Matthias Heikel/dpa/CORBIS. 241br, Patrick Pleul/dpa/CORBIS. 242, B. Ducke/A1 Pix Ltd. 243, P. Franke/ Punctum Photog. 245, P. Franke/ Punctum Photog. 246, B. Kober/ Punctum Photog. 247, Obermain Buch- und Bildverlag Bornschlegel. 248, Westend6/ Alamy Ltd. 250, B. Ducke/A1 Pix Ltd. 251, G. Gräfenhain/A1 Pix Ltd. 252, G. Gräfenhain/A1 Pix Ltd. 253, G. Mecky Fogeling. 254/255, Siebig/A1 Pix Ltd. 256, Werner Otto. 258, Gräfenhain/A1 Pix Ltd. 259, G. Gräfenhain/ A1 Pix Ltd. 260l, Bayreuther Festspiele GmbH/Jochen Quast. 260r, Adam Woolfitt/CORBIS. 261, Werner Otto. 262, Erich Lessing/Art Resource, NY. 263, E. Bach/ A1 Pix Ltd. 264/265, Wolfgang Kähler Photog. 265, Historisches Festspiel "Der Meistertrunk". 266, Image State. 267t, Patrick Hannon/Shutterstock. 267b, PanStock LLC/Imagestate. 268, R. Schmid/ Bildarchiv Huber. 269, T. Bognar/Trip Photo Lib. 271t, FAN travestock/Alamy Ltd. 271cl, Timmermann Foto-presse. 271cr, A. Baker/AA Photo Lib. 271b, Werner Otto. 272, R. Schmid/Bildarchiv Huber. 273, Ulrike Welsch Photog. 274/5, plainpicture GmbH & Co. KG/Alamy Ltd. 275t, R. Schmid/Bildarchiv Huber. 275b, Haga/ A1 Pix Ltd. 276, Ducke/Gräfenhain/ A1 Pix Ltd. 277, G. Gräfenhain/A1 Pix Ltd. 279, T. Souter/AA Photo Lib. 281, Steve Vidler/ Imagestate. 282, Mecky Fogeling. 284, Wolfgang Kähler Photog. 285, A. Tovy/Trip Photo Lib. 286, Ulrike Welsch Photog. 288, Alte Pinakothek, Munich, Germany/ Bridgeman Art Lib. 289, Alte Pinakothek, Munich, Germany/ Bridgeman Art Lib. 290, Bayerische Staatsgemäldesammlungen, Neue Pinakothek, Munich. 291, Robert Fishman/ dpa/CORBIS. 292, Städtische Galerie im Lenbachhaus, Munich, Germany/ Bridgeman Art Lib. 293, T. Souter/AA Photo Lib. 294, Wolfgang Kähler Photog. 295, Werner Dieterich/Alamy Ltd. 297, Mark Zanzig.www.zanzig.com. 298, B. Ducke/A1 Pix Ltd. 299, Wolfgang Kähler Photog. 300, E. Bach/A1 Pix Ltd. 300/301, Jamie Carstairs. 301, Mecky Fogeling. 302/3, altrendo travel/Getty Images. 303, Jamie Carstairs.

304, BMW AG. 305, Gräfenhain/Bildarchiv Huber. 306, A1 Pix Ltd. 307, G. Gräfenhain-E. Bach/A1 Pix Ltd. 308/309, R. Schmid/Bildarchiv Huber. 311t, G. Gräfenhain/A1 Pix Ltd. 311bl, T. Souter/AA Photo Lib. 311c, Bildarchiv Huber. 311cl, Simeone/Bildarchiv Huber. 311b, Ulrike Welsch Photog. 312/313, G. Gräfenhain/A1 Pix Ltd. 314/315, Bildarchiv Huber. 315, Lawrence Englesberg/Imagestate. 317, Mecky Fogeling. 318, Baden Baden. 320, Jamie Carstairs. 321, C. Martin/Robert Harding Picture Lib. Ltd. 322, Jamie Carstairs. 324/325, B. Radelt/Bildarchiv Huber. 325, Mecky Fogeling. 326, A. Cowin/Travel Ink. 327, E. Späth/Bildarchiv Huber. 328, Werner Otto. 329, B. Ducke/A1 Pix Ltd. 330, Werner Otto. 331, Steve Vidler/Imagestate. 332, Baden Baden. 333, Baden Baden. 334t, Mecky Fogeling. 334b, Mecky Fogeling. 335, James Davis Worldwide. 336, R. Schmid/Bildarchiv Huber. 337t, Pictures Colour Lib. 337b, P. Thompson/Eye Ubiquitous. 339, C.L. Schmitt/A1 Pix Ltd. 340, Mecky Fogeling. 340/341, R. Schmid/Bildarchiv Huber. 342, Zeppelin-Museum. 343, Mecky Fogeling. 344, J. Isachsen/Trip Photo Lib. 345, fl online/Alamy Ltd. 347, AKG – London.

Founded in 1888, the National Geographic Society is one of the largest nonprofit scientific and educational organizations in the world. It reaches more than 285 million people worldwide each month through its official journal, NATIONAL GEOGRAPHIC, and its four other magazines; the National Geographic Channel; television documentaries; radio programs; films; books; videos and DVDs; maps; and interactive media. National Geographic has funded more than 8,000 scientific research projects and supports an education program combating geographic illiteracy.

For more information, please call 1-800-NGS LINE (647-5463) or write to the following address: National Geographic Society, 1145 17th Street N.W., Washington, D.C. 20036-4688 U.S.A.

Visit us online at: www.national geographic.com/books

For information about special discounts for bulk purchases, please contact National Geographic Books Special Sales: ngspecsales@ngs.org

Published by the National Geographic Society

John M. Fahey, Jr., *President and Chief Executive Officer*

Gilbert M. Grosvenor, *Chairman of the Board*

Nina D. Hoffman, *Executive Vice President and President, Books Publishing Group*

Kevin Mulroy, *Senior Vice President and Publisher*

Marianne Koszorus, *Director of Design*

Leah Bendavid-Val, *Director of Photography Publishing and Illustrations*

Elizabeth L. Newhouse, *Director of Travel Publishing*

Carl Mehler, *Director of Maps*

Barbara A. Noe, *Series Editor*

Cinda Rose, *Art Director*

R. Gary Colbert, *Production Director*

Richard S. Wain, *Production Project Manager*

Lawrence M. Porges, *Project Editor, 2007 edition*

Steven D. Gardner, Kay Hankins, Lynsey Jacob, Amy Jicha, Val Mattingley, Jeff Peters, Carol Stroud, Ruth Thompson, Maura Walsh, Rob Waymouth, *Contributors to 2007 edition*

Edited and designed by AA Publishing (a trading name of Automobile Association Developments Limited, whose registered office is Millstream, Maidenhead Road, Windsor, Berkshire SL4 5GD, England. Registered number: 1878835).

Virginia Langer, *Project Manager*

David Austin, *Senior Art Editor*

Betty Sheldrick, *Editor*

Bob Johnson, *Designer*

Keith Brook, *Senior Cartographic Editor*

Cartography by AA Cartography Department

Richard Firth, *Production Director*, Sarah Reynolds, *Production Controller*

Liz Allen, *Picture Research Manager*, Picture Research by Zooid Pictures Ltd.

Drive maps drawn by Chris Orr Associates, Southampton, England

Cutaway illustrations (pp. 56–57, 64–65, 84–85, 152–153, 256–257, and p. 296) drawn by Maltings Partnership, Derby, England

National Geographic Traveler: Germany, Second Edition (2007)
ISBN-10: 1-4262-0028-5; ISBN-13: 978-1-4262-0028-1

Printed and bound by Cayfosa Quebecor, Barcelona, Spain. Color separations by Leo Reprographic Ltd., Hong Kong and Quad Graphics, Alexandria, VA. Cover separations by L.C. Repro, Aldermaston, U.K.

Printed in Spain

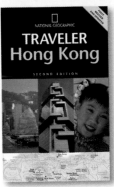